W9-CHX-246

The Laws of Change

The Laws of Change

I CHING AND THE PHILOSOPHY OF LIFE

Jack M. Balkin

Schocken Books, New York

 Published in the United States by Schocken Books, a division of Random House, Inc., New York, and simultaneously in Canada by Random House of Canada Limited, Toronto. Distributed by Pantheon Books, a division of Random House, Inc., New York.

Library of Congress Cataloging-in-Publication Data
Balkin, J. M.
The laws of change : I ching and the philosophy of life / Jack M. Balkin.
p. cm.
Includes bibliographical references and index.
ISBN 0-8052-4199-X
1. Yi jing. I. Title.

PL2464.Z7 B33 2002
299'.51282—dc21 2002021672

www.schocken.com

Book design by Soonyoung Kwon

Printed in the United States of America

First Edition

9 8 7 6 5 4 3 2 1
2 4 6 8 9 7 5 3 1

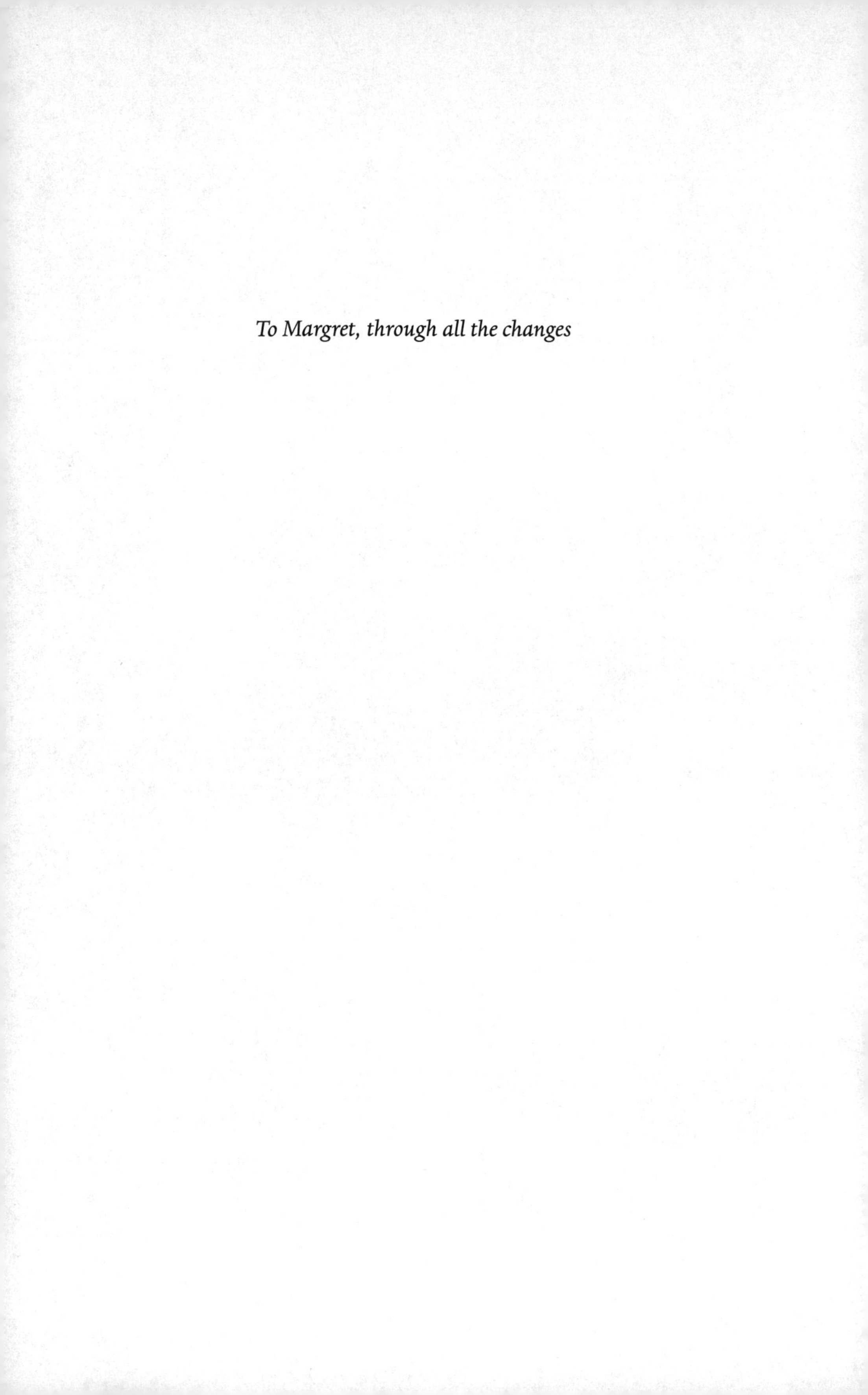

To Margret, through all the changes

Contents

Preface

The *Book of Changes* (or *I Ching*, as it is often known) is one of the treasures of world literature, and a central text in the history of Chinese civilization. Chinese medicine, geomancy (also known as *feng shui*), and countless other arts are based on its teachings. It has become increasingly popular in the United States as a fortune-telling device, and yet the underlying philosophy of the book is still not well understood.

The *Book of Changes* began three thousand years ago as a diviner's manual for Bronze Age kings. They wanted to know whether to sacrifice captives, go on royal hunts, make war, or form marriage alliances. Even when originally compiled, the laconic text of the *Book of Changes* was oracular and obscure, difficult to understand, and overflowing with complicated, multiple associations. Over time, the original meanings of many of the words in the book were lost or forgotten. Subsequent commentators created a new purpose for it—as a book of profound wisdom about how human beings can deal with the vicissitudes of change in human life and human fortune. It was infused with the philosophies of Confucianism and Daoism and eventually became recognized as one of the Confucian classics. Generations of philosophers and scholars added their ideas. The history of the *Book of Changes* is the history of the changing meanings of this great work.

The Chinese philosophers and scholars who commented on and reshaped the *Book of Changes* suffered greatly through many wars and conflicts. Kingdoms rose and fell, empires were created and destroyed. They witnessed all of this and they wondered: What are the laws of change that govern human fortunes, and how can human beings understand these laws and learn to live in harmony with the changing world around them? How should people comport themselves in the face of good fortune and bad, success and catastrophe? How can people maintain their principles and their integrity and lead happy lives when the world changes around them so quickly, in ways over which they may have little or no control? How can people cultivate themselves and structure their behavior so as to ensure the greatest chances of success and contentment in a complicated world?

These questions are still with us today. They are central questions about the human condition. And the lessons that the *Book of Changes* offers concerning them are as valid today as they were in ancient China.

These questions, and the answers to them, are the subject of this book.

In the West, and particularly the United States, the *Book of Changes* has become popular as a form of fortune-telling, like astrology or the reading of tarot cards. But for the Chinese, and for those countries influenced by Chinese civilization, this view is too narrow. The *Book of Changes* has always been understood as a book of wisdom. The practitioner of the book consults it through random divination—throwing coins or manipulating long stalks of dried plants (yarrow). But these practices of divination are designed to help the questioner confront the book's philosophy in practical, concrete contexts. It is this philosophy, learned through formulating specific questions and interpreting the answers received, that gives the work its value. And that philosophy is best encountered not through the memorization of abstract principles but through its application to specific issues in a person's life. One absorbs the wisdom of the *Book of Changes* through consulting it and allowing it to become, over time, a trusted friend and confidant.

The goal of the present work, *The Laws of Change,* is to bring the philosophy of the *Book of Changes* to a larger audience. I wish to reach intelligent readers from every walk of life who may have heard of the *Book of Changes* only as a fortune-telling device, and to explain to them, in simple and easy-to-understand terms, how they can benefit from its teachings and apply them to their everyday lives. I also wish to reach the millions of people who already use the book as a divination manual, and show them that behind their mystical practices lies a valuable philosophy of ancient lineage that will deepen and enrich their use of the book. In our age most serious philosophy is banished to the academy and is of no use to anyone. The *Book of Changes* stands as an important and necessary rejoinder to this predicament. Its concerns are among the most important questions in human life. Its philosophy should be made available and accessible to everyone.

I am grateful to many friends and colleagues for their assistance and advice in creating this book. My dear friend Thomas Seung, a scholar of deep learning in philosophies both ancient and modern, Eastern and Western, made many helpful suggestions about the underlying theory of the *Book of Changes* and its relationship to Chinese philosophy. Edward Shaughnessy graciously agreed to read Chapter Six and offered important corrections concerning the history of the *Book of Changes.* Phillip Bobbitt provided excellent advice about structuring the book for a general audience, as did my agent Glen Hartley. My colleagues at Yale Law School, who were no doubt a bit puzzled that I would take on a project so far removed from conventional legal scholarship, accepted my enthusiasms with grace and tolerance.

Finally, I would not have been able to start this book, much less bring it to completion, without the love and support of my wife, Margret Wolfe, who repeatedly encouraged me to follow my heart's calling. She exemplifies the virtues of modesty, sincerity, steadfastness, and generosity that the *Book of Changes* celebrates. In the words of the *Yijing* (Xian, Hexagram 31), to marry such a woman brings good fortune. Truly, she has been my blessing. This book is dedicated to her.

New Haven, Connecticut
March 2002

PART ONE

An Introduction to the Book of Changes *and Its Philosophy*

CHAPTER ONE

Introduction

䷟

The *Book of Changes* (*I Ching* or *Yijing*) is one of the world's oldest books. The earliest parts of the text date back three thousand years. To the Chinese the *Book of Changes* is as important as the Bible is to the West. It is probably one of the most commented on books in human history. Every Chinese thinker from antiquity forward has had something to say about it, and many have based their entire philosophies on the book. In modern times the *Book of Changes* has become influential in the West as a method of divination. That was its original purpose in the Bronze Age, and it remains a major use of the book throughout the world. But at least since Confucian times the book has also been regarded as a book of wisdom, containing the most profound lessons on how to live one's life in a changing and confusing world. That is because the subject of the *Book of Changes* is nothing less than the laws of change in the universe and how human beings can learn to live in harmony with them.

The Chinese name for the *Book of Changes* is *I Ching* in the older, Wade-Giles system of transliteration, and *Yijing* in the modern, Pinyin system. *Yi* means "change"; *jing* means "book," and later came to mean "classic." Hence another name for the book is the *Classic of Changes*.

At the heart of the *Book of Changes* is a set of sixty-four figures called hexagrams. (In Chinese they are called *gua*.) The hexagrams consist of six lines, which are either solid (———) or broken (— —).

For example, here is Hexagram 32, Enduring, which has three solid and three broken lines:

Hexagram 32
Heng (Enduring)

Because there are two types of lines and six positions, there are 2^6, or 64 different hexagrams. The broken and solid lines in the hexagrams are associated with the metaphysical symbolism of yin and yang. Broken lines (— —) are yin lines; solid lines (———) are yang lines. For example, in Hexagram 32, illustrated above, there are yin lines in positions one, five, and six, and yang lines in positions two, three, and four. The sixty-four hexagrams represent all of the possible combinations of yin and yang that can occur in six lines.

Yin and yang are central concepts in Chinese philosophy. Originally, they referred to the shady and sunny sides of a hill. Later they developed an elaborate series of metaphysical connotations. Yang is active, bright, male, hot, large, or superior, while yin is passive, dark, female, cold, small, or inferior. Everything in life and all change in the world is made up out of the alternations between yin and yang. Because the sixty-four hexagrams included every possible combination of yin and yang, the ancient Chinese thought, they included every possible situation under heaven and on earth.

Each hexagram has a name or title that corresponds to a different aspect of the human condition. These include emotions (Joy), actions (Biting Through), situations (Difficulty in the Beginning), strategies (Calculated Waiting), objects (The Well), persons (The Wanderer), characteristics (Modesty), and principles (Inner Truth). Together the sixty-four hexagrams attempt to describe the various phases of human life and human fortune.

Each hexagram is accompanied by a short divinatory statement, called a judgment. The hexagram judgments describe the situation symbolized by the hexagram and what people should do in that situation. As befits the origins of the book as a diviner's manual, the language of the judgments is often oracular and obscure. For example, the judgment for Hexagram 32, Heng (Enduring), reads:

Enduring. Success. No blame.
It is beneficial to persevere.
It it is beneficial to have somewhere to go.

The lines in each hexagram are numbered from one to six starting at the bottom and proceeding to the top. A short divinatory text is associated with each line. These texts are called the line judgments or line statements. Each line judgment describes a special case of the more general situation symbolized by the hexagram as a whole and offers more specific advice. Like the hexagram judgments, the line judgments are often obscure and feature striking metaphors or images. For example, the text for the fifth line of Hexagram 26, Da Xu (Great Accumulation), reads:

The tusks of a gelded boar.
Good fortune.

Just as you can identify parts of the Bible by chapter and verse (e.g., Genesis 1:1), you can identify sections of the *Book of Changes* by reference to hexagram number and line, separated by a period. The hexagram judgment is designated as line 0; 1 through 6 refer to the successive line statements. So the fifth line of Hexagram 26 is 26.5; the judgment for Hexagram 32 is 32.0.

People consult the *Book of Changes* by using a random method like tossing coins or manipulating yarrow stalks to generate the six lines of a hexagram. (These methods are described in more detail in Chapter Five.) The method chosen not only determines whether each line of the hexagram is yin (broken) or yang (solid), but also whether the line is moving (changing) or stable. The moving lines change into their opposites: Yin lines change to yang lines, and yang lines change to yin lines. This produces a second hexagram. The first hexagram represents the current situation, the second the situation into which things are changing, and the moving lines represent key aspects of this transformation. People then study the judgments for the two hexagrams and the line statements for the moving lines in order to stimulate creative thought about their current situation and to decide how they should adapt their actions to the needs of the time.

Although many people try to use the *Book of Changes* to tell the future, I believe this reflects a misunderstanding of the book's real value. The *Book of Changes* is best understood not as a fortune-telling device but as a book of wisdom that can help people think imaginatively and creatively about their lives. As I explain in Chapter Three, the processes by which hexagrams are generated are purely random. What is truly important is the underlying philosophy of the book. By formulating specific questions, contemplating the answers, and applying the book's principles and metaphors to their own situation, people who use the *Book of Changes* are gradually introduced to its characteristic philosophy of life in concrete contexts. Precisely because the book is structured not as a treatise but as an oracle, its philosophy is revealed not through memorizing a specific set of abstract doctrines, but through application and problem solving. In this way people assimilate over time an intuitive understanding of the book's approach and its distinctive take on the laws of change.

The earliest part of the *Book of Changes* consists of the hexagrams, the hexagram judgments, and the line judgments. This part of the book was complied sometime during the Zhou Dynasty in Bronze Age China, probably around 800 B.C. This core of the book is sometimes called the *Zhouyi,* or the Changes of the Zhou. Hundreds of years later a series of commentaries were added to the core text. They are divided into ten segments, known as Wings. The Ten Wings contain commentaries on each of the hexagram and line judgments, as well as a treatise on the philosophy and metaphysics behind the core text, sometimes called the Great Treatise. (The Great Treatise constitutes the Fifth and Sixth of the Ten Wings.) Together the Ten Wings and the *Zhouyi* constitute the *Classic of Changes,* or *Yijing*. In this book, when I want to refer only to the core text, I will speak of the *Zhouyi,* in order to distinguish it from the Ten Wings.

Tradition holds that much the text of the *Book of Changes* refers to the overthrow of the Bronze Age Shang Dynasty by the Zhou, a vassal state, and the subsequent founding of the great Zhou Dynasty. According to legend, the hexagram judgments were written by King Wen, the leader of the Zhou, while he was imprisoned by the tyrant Dixin, the last of the Shang kings; the line judgments, the story goes, were written by King Wen's son, the Duke of Zhou, one of the greatest statesmen in China's history. Finally, the Ten Wings were attributed to Confucius. As explained in Chapter Six, this traditional account is mere legend, part of the Chinese custom of attributing great works of antiquity to ancient sages. The core text was compiled and collated by Zhou diviners over many years, long after the time of King Wen and the Duke of Zhou, and there is no evidence that Confucius himself wrote the Ten Wings, although these commentaries contain many Confucian ideas. The mythological origins of the book nevertheless contributed greatly to the belief that those who wrote the *Book of Changes* were people of great wisdom who understood from their own experience the rise and fall of human fortunes.

Part One of this book introduces the history and philosophy of the *Book of Changes*. It describes the book's symbolism, the many changes the book has undergone in the course of its three-thousand-year history, and many of the most well-known methods of divination. Part Two—by far the larger portion of this book—is a translation of the core text (the *Zhouyi*) plus commentaries explaining how to apply its insights to everyday life.

I wrote these commentaries on the *Book of Changes* in order to explain its ethical teachings. By "ethics" I mean not simply questions of right and wrong but basic issues about how one should live and give purpose to one's life. The *Book of Changes,* whose primary concern is how human beings should deal with a changing universe, is ethical in this larger sense. There is much more to the book than this, of course. One could also study the *Changes* as a metaphysical or cosmological document, but that is not my goal.

Because of my objectives in writing the commentaries, I included the text of only one part of the Ten Wings—the Commentary on the Great Images *(Daxiang)*, which forms part of the Third and Fourth Wings. Other parts of the Ten Wings offer theories of metaphysics and cosmology, try to show why certain lines and hexagrams are auspicious or inauspicious, and suggest explanations for why one hexagram follows another in the received text. By contrast, the Commentary on the Great Images offers lessons about how to live one's life in each of the situations described by the sixty-four hexagrams. It is the most Confucian and for that reason the most explicitly ethical part of the Ten Wings. There is ample precedent for giving the Commentary on the Great Images special treatment. Richard Wilhelm's famous translation of the *Book of Changes* places the Commentary together with the text of the *Zhouyi,* leaving the rest of the Ten Wings to other parts of the book.

Many versions of the *I Ching* designed for popular audiences do not provide the text at all. Instead, they provide only summaries or paraphrases of the text. They offer interpretations of what the hexagrams and line judgments mean but eliminate much of the imagery that is so characteristic of the book. These interpretations are often quite good, but still something is lost in the process. It is not enough to encounter the *Book of Changes* as a series of abstract principles—one must grapple directly with its symbols, images, and metaphors if one is to understand its wisdom and its power. For this reason I undertook to provide my own working translation of the text. The term "working" is well advised. I do not regard the result as a serious academic translation—that would take much more skill than I possess. Instead, I aimed to provide a simple, easy-to-read version that would offer most of the imagery in the book and help make sense of the commentaries that follow.

The twentieth century has brought a revolution in *Yijing* studies. We now know much more about its Bronze Age origins. Several of the newest translations have tried to recover the meaning of the text when it was first compiled during the Zhou Dynasty. These translations dispense with the ethical and philosophical glosses on the book, which are the work of later centuries. The new scholarship corrects many errors and infelicities in previous translations, and I have learned much from it. Nevertheless, I am primarily interested in the *Book of Changes* as a book of wisdom. For this reason the version presented in this volume reflects the ethical interpretations of the Book that shaped its reception from the time of the Ten Wings onward.

To understand the philosophy of the *Book of Changes,* one must come to terms with two important facts. First, because the book is structured as an oracle, its philosophy is best encountered through asking the book questions and receiving answers, which the questioner then applies to specific problems and questions in his or her own life. Applying the book's insights to one's own situation is inevitably idiosyncratic and deeply personal. Offering a list of the book's basic principles necessarily fails to capture this process of interaction. Any description of the book's philosophy in propositional form must be general and abstract, far removed from the process of concrete problem solving that gives the book its practical value. In an important sense, the best way truly to understand the *Book of Changes* is to use it.

Second, there is not, strictly speaking, a single meaning to the text. Appropriately enough for a text whose basic theme is the inevitability of change, the *Book of Changes* has undergone many transformations in its three-thousand-year history. It has meant many different things to many different people over the ages. (Chapter Six, which chronicles the book's history, describes many of the most important of these changes.) The *Book of Changes* began as a Bronze Age manual of divination. The kings who consulted it wanted to know whether to make war, forge alliances, sacrifice human captives, or go on hunts. Later the book was almost completely transformed when philosophical and metaphysical meanings were grafted onto it in the series of commentaries known as the Ten Wings. Those meanings, in turn, were further glossed and supplemented by a series of commentaries stretching from antiquity to the present day. There are as many interpretations of the *Book of Changes,* one suspects, as there are people who have sought to understand this mysterious and marvelous text.

In the discussion that follows I will be primarily concerned with the philosophical glosses given to the *Book of Changes* by later commentators. None of this, or very little of it, can be found in the original Bronze Age diviner's manual. As explained in more detail in Chapter Six, by the time the Ten Wings were written, the original meanings of many of the words in the core text had been significantly transformed or completely forgotten. Nevertheless, convinced that the book contained deep and abiding truths from the ancient sages, generations of commentators constructed an elaborate set of philosophical and ethical meanings for the book. Key words and phrases in the text were reinterpreted in light of Confucian concepts such as sincerity, modesty, and perseverance. Moral and practical lessons on the proper conduct of life in a changing world were drawn from its oracular phrases and obscure metaphors. Through this process, the *Book of Changes* eventually became what its commentators assumed it always was—a noble and humane work of profound wisdom. Thus the *Book of Changes* is truly a work where the glosses are more important than the original understanding of the text. Over the centuries it has been customary to ascribe immeasurable and unfathomable discernment to the original text, and to regard subsequent commentaries as obscuring its insights. But the book has been made great by what later readers have made of it rather than by what it was originally.

CHAPTER TWO

The Philosophy of the *Book of Changes*

Elaborate metaphysical theories have grown up around the *Book of Changes* over the centuries, but for contemporary readers the most interesting feature of the book will probably be its philosophy of life. From the Han Dynasty (206 B.C.–220 A.D.) onward, the interpretation of the *Book of Changes* was strongly influenced by the Chinese philosophies of Confucianism and Daoism. The book's stress on the interdependence of opposites and the interrelatedness of all things, and its injunctions to behave simply and naturally and to move with the flow of events rather than against them, reflect Daoist teachings. The influence of Confucianism is, if anything, even more obvious, given the book's repeated emphasis on modesty, sincerity, devotion, cooperating with others, and self-cultivation.

The *Book of Changes* is pragmatic. Its focus is on this world, not the next. Its purpose is to help people live meaningful and fulfilling lives in a world full of changes over which they may have only limited control. Its ethical philosophy is rational, practical, humane, and nonfanatical. It is not concerned with the salvation of souls. It is very much concerned with redemption, but only in the sense that people always have the ability to turn their lives around and return to the Dao or Way that is appropriate for them. The book speaks of success and failure, and how to achieve good fortune and a happy life. But its focus is not purely instrumental, nor is its concern primarily with worldly success. It urges self-development, the cultivation of character, and the maintenance of emotional balance and personal integrity.

People in the modern world often distinguish instrumental or practical considerations from moral ones. They consider the question of what is likely to produce success to be separate from the question of what is moral or ethical. Even if pursuing success and deciding what is ethical do not necessarily conflict, they are two different forms of reasoning. The *Book of Changes* does not share this contemporary Western attitude. It does not distinguish practical or instrumental considerations from ethical ones in the way that moderns sometimes do. It emphasizes astute timing and wisely conserving one's resources until the moment is right to act. It also urges cultivation of perseverance and strength of character. It emphasizes the importance of forming alliances and gaining helpers. And it also urges generosity, sincerity, integrity, and benevolence. It does not treat these forms of advice as distinct. All of them conduce to a life that is in harmony with changing circumstances. Its concern is ethics in the larger sense of ethos—how a person should live and what kind of person one should become.

The book seeks to help people attain good fortune and avoid bad fortune, but, as the Great Treatise explains at one point, its real purpose is to allow human beings to be without blame; that is, to have done everything they can to live in concord with the world around them while maintaining their integrity. Hence in the *Book of Changes* success may not be power and esteem. It may be the success of the sage, who separates him or herself from worldly affairs and seeks enlightenment. It may be the success of the person who values family and friends and is rewarded with rich and satisfying relationships. Or it may simply be peace of mind. Success means finding one's proper path (Dao) and following it. It means becoming the right kind of person who can interact with a changing world in the right kind of way.

The Law of Change

As its name implies, the central premise of the *Book of Changes* is that the world is constantly changing. Neither being nor nonbeing is the most important concept in understanding the universe. Rather, the characteristic feature of existence is constant alteration. Things are born, grow, mature, age, and die. The fortunes of people, organizations, and countries rise and fall over time. Opposites grow more alike over time, and things that seem similar begin to diverge and become opposed.

The law of change is that all things eventually turn into their opposites and become something other than what they are now. What goes up will eventually come down, and what is reduced will eventually increase. This law of change is symbolized by the continual alternation of yin and yang.

Things that expand (yang) will eventually reach a limit and begin to decrease (yin). Similarly, what is diminished will eventually be renewed, reemerge, and grow once more. The same applies to human fortunes, which inevitably wax and wane over time. The constant alternation of good and bad in human life is symbolized by many of the paired hexagrams in the *Book of Changes,* including 1, Qian (The Dynamic), and 2, Kun (The Receptive); 11, Tai (Peace or Smoothly Flowing), and 12, Pi (Standstill or Stagnation); and 41 Sun (Decrease) and 42 Yi (Increase).

The law of change is both a warning and a cause for hope. It is a warning because it means that we cannot take our good fortune for granted. It will eventually diminish and disappear. When it is gone, we must take steps to prepare for its return. While it is here, we must make the most of it and ensure that it lasts as long as possible. The law of change is cause for hope because even though things may not be going our way at present, if we have patience and faith, things will eventually get better again. This attitude is summed up in 11.3:

There is no plain without a slope.
There is no going forth without a return.
One who perseveres in times of hardship
Is without blame.
Do not be worried about this truth.
Enjoy the blessings you possess.

Given the law of change, how should we behave? First, we must learn to understand the nature of the times and adjust our actions accordingly. Second, we must develop inner balance and inner strength so that we can ride out the bad times until they turn for the better. When things are not going our way, we must have patience, keep a low profile, preserve our integrity, maintain belief in ourselves, and trust that things will eventually get better. Hope, faith, and devotion are the central tools we have for persevering through times of adversity.

Third, we must be proactive rather than passive. Instead of simply accepting good or bad fortune when it comes, we should arrange things so that we can hasten the return of good fortune, prolong it, and make the most of it. In short, through wise planning and preparation we must lay the groundwork for our future success. The *Book of Changes* is anything but fatalistic. Although change is inevitable, there is much that we can do to shape our fortunes by understanding and responding to the flow of events. If there is one consistent piece of advice the *Book of Changes* offers, it is that good luck is the residue of good design.

Change often starts slowly and imperceptibly but will become powerful and pervasive if given enough time. This applies both to good and bad fortune. Therefore, the *Book of Changes* advises us to look for the first signs of decay in a situation and to nip problems in the bud when they are easier to manage and before they have a chance to grow large and difficult to handle. Thus 2.1 says:

The frost underfoot will soon become solid ice.

Conversely, the *Book of Changes* argues that if we make even small amounts of progress repeatedly and persistently, we will eventually have great influence over time. Thus, 46.5 states:

Perseverance brings good fortune.
One ascends step by step.

And the Commentary on the Great Images adds:

Thus the superior person, with adaptable character,
Accumulates the small,
In order to achieve the great.

Trust, Reciprocity, and Good Fortune

If the *Book of Changes* emphasizes the importance of faith in bad times, it also emphasizes the importance of generosity in good times. When things go well, we must remember to share the benefits of our good fortune with others. Generosity and magnanimity toward others encourage cooperation and reciprocity and this helps keeps the good times going.

This point is a special case of the book's more general theory about how good and bad fortune arise. Our fates, the book insists, are inevitably bound up with those of others. When people cooperate with each other and work together, good fortune naturally occurs. When people fail to cooperate and become selfish, things fall apart and bad fortune ensues. The ebb and flow of good and bad fortune in human life can be traced to the rise and fall of trust, cooperation, and humane social order among human beings. Disease and natural disasters surely shape human happiness. But they can be prevented or brought on, made better or made worse by what human beings do. The *Book of Changes* maintains that cooperation is the central means through which people can improve their lives. As long as people cooperate, they can do things that none of them could do individually. They can work together to improve everyone's quality of life. Indeed, their capacity for joint achievement is unbounded. Thus, 9.5 tells us:

Sincere and loyally attached,
Neighbors enrich each other.

Nevertheless, people will not cooperate unless they believe that their cooperation will produce benefits. Therefore, cooperation requires the development of bonds of trust and expectations of reciprocity. Trust and reciprocity are the cement of society. They are the harbingers of good fortune.

Those who benefit from cooperation must share their gains with others. Each person's contribution must be respected and rewarded appropriately, and everyone must believe that they have a stake in the joint activity and are important to it. That is why when things are going well, it is especially important to be generous and magnanimous. Showing others concern and respect renews bonds of trust and loyalty, and keeps things moving forward.

If generosity and cooperation are the keys to prosperity and success, selfishness and lack of cooperation are the source of much of human misery and suffering. When people try to keep everything for themselves, they destroy the delicate mechanisms of cooperation and reciprocity, and this brings about the end of good times. When people cut themselves off from others and try to take advantage of other people's generosity and trustworthiness, they destroy the conditions on which good fortune depends. They forget the ways that they are interconnected with others, and as a result they kill the goose that lays the golden eggs. They undermine social cooperation and eliminate the source of common benefit that would enrich them all. The text of 55.6 describes the end of a period of abundance brought on by a person who succumbs to selfishness and hoards his riches for himself:

Abundance in his house.
He screens off his family.
He peers through the door,
Lonely, abandoned.
For three years he sees no one.
Misfortune.

Similarly, 42.6 describes how a period of increase vanishes when people lack generosity and magnanimity toward others:

He increases no one.
Someone even strikes him.
He does not keep his heart and mind constant and steady.
Misfortune.

The *Book of Changes* teaches that generosity, magnanimity, and working for the common good is the proper path to a happy life, while selfishness, arrogance, and cupidity lead only to unhappiness and misery for everyone concerned. Yet the temptation to shortsightedness and selfish behavior is so great that the lesson is easily forgotten and must be learned over and over again. Thus 59.4 notes that "dissolv[ing] one's group"—that is, putting aside parochial concerns—and dispersing one's ego brings great rewards and leads to the highest achievements. Yet, no matter how often this occurs, the text says, it still seems like uncommon wisdom:

He dissolves his group.
Supreme good fortune.
Dispersion leads to the summit.
This is something that ordinary people do not think of.

Self-Cultivation and Our Relation to the World

True to its Confucian origins, the *Book of Changes* urges self-cultivation as a means of succeeding in the world. Once again, good fortune is the residue of good preparation. We can best adjust to changes in the world by working to improve our habits and attitudes. We cannot always control the world outside of us, but we do have some say about how we will interpret it and react to it. Our ability to cope with what life hands us is very much helped or harmed by our emotions and our ways of thinking. Defeatism and despair can be self-fullfiling prophecies, while hope, faith, and devotion can help us surmount whatever obstacles lie in our path. Inner conflict and unresolved tensions can hamper our efforts and make us our own worst enemy. Emotional balance and peace of mind put us at our best and help us succeed.

Many of the hexagrams in the *Book of Changes* have a dual meaning: they describe situations in the world and situations within our emotional life. For example, stagnation (Hexagram 12), oppression (Hexagram 47), and obstruction (Hexagram 39) can refer to external circumstances as well as to our attitudes and feelings. In fact, the two go together, for they are part of the same phenomenon. The *Book of Changes* does not treat individuals as inherently distinct from the world around them. We are a part of our world and our world is part of us. Our experience of stagnation or oppression is produced by our relation to the world. People who are at odds with their environment also face obstruction and oppression in their emotional life. People who learn how to maintain harmony with their world do so by achieving inner harmony. Without inner harmony, we may remove temporary oppressions and obstructions in the world, but new ones will simply take their place. Our attitudes toward the world and ourselves will continually bring us turmoil and conflict.

Thus the hexagrams not only describe situations in the outside world; they concern methods of self-cultivation to deal with analogous features of our inner life. To deal with the oppression that is without, we must master the oppression that is within. To remedy obstruction and stagnation in the outside world, we must throw off inner obstruction and stagnation, cultivate emotional balance and inner strength. In the same way, hexagrams with positive themes advise that to make the most of good times we should cultivate optimism, generosity, and magnanimity. In great times we should make ourselves great. Thus, transformation of the political order (in Hexagram 49, Ge, Revolution) requires a corresponding transformation of the self. And Hexagram 55 (Feng, Abundance) advises that during a time of zenith we too "should be like the sun at midday"—generous and optimistic, illuminating the world and making others feel warm and happy.

Modesty and Sincerity

The *Book of Changes* preaches the importance of faith in one's self, devotion to one's work, and courage to view the world with clarity. To this end it emphasizes the cultivation of two key virtues: modesty and sincerity.

Modesty is not the same as the Christian ideal of humility or meekness. Rather, it means doing what is necessary without fuss or ceremony. It means making commitments and living up to them, without ostentation or display. Modest people do not think they are more important than their work, their obligations, or their commitments. For this reason they are consistent and reliable, and other people can trust them and depend on them. Modest people do not regard any part of the work they must do as beneath them, and therefore they work steadily until they achieve success.

Modest people treat others with courtesy and respect. They pursue the "middle path" of moderation in all of their dealings. Thus in the *Book of Changes* modesty does not mean timidity or self-abnegation. It means inner balance and inner strength. Modest people put their egos at the service of their accomplishments and not the other way around. They are not distracted by hunger for the praise and approval of others. They do not allow pride and vanity, on the one hand, or self-doubt and despair, on the other, to get in the way of what needs to be done. That is why they succeed. Hence in Hexagram 15, Qian, which is devoted to the subject of modesty, the *Book of Changes* says:

Modesty. Success.
The superior person carries things through to the end.

In fact, all of the lines for this hexagram are favorable, symbolizing the *Book of Changes'* view that modesty will help a person no matter what befalls them.

A second important virtue in the *Book of Changes* is sincerity *(fu)*. Repeatedly, the *Book of Changes* advises the cultivation of sincerity, both as a trait of character and as a form of behavior. There is probably no other virtue that receives more extravagant praise. Thus 5.0 states that "sincerity and faithfulness bring shining success," while 17.5 says that "sincerity leads to excellence," and 42.5 tells us:

If you are sincere, and have kindness in your heart,
You need not ask.
Supreme good fortune.
When there is sincerity, kindness is your power.

Like modesty, sincerity is a complicated concept with multiple associations and interrelated meanings. At various points in the text the word *fu* is translated as "sincerity," "trustworthiness," "truth," and "confidence." Each of these meanings of *fu* is connected to or produces the others. Thus inner truth produces sincerity, which leads to trustworthiness, which in turn wins the confidence of others.

First of all, sincerity means candor and honesty in dealings with others. When people are openhearted and sincere, their honesty shines through in everything that they say and do, and people trust them. Openness toward others encourages others to be open and trusting in return. This leads to cooperation. Because the *Book of Changes* regards cooperation as the central ingredient to prosperity and success, it consistently argues for sincerity and trustworthiness in order to forge the social bonds that will bring people together, allow them to accomplish great things, and keep the good times flowing. For similar reasons, however, sincerity in the *Book of Changes* means more than subjective honesty. It also involves the ability to make commitments and follow through on them. A person who is sincere at the time he or she makes a promise but who frequently changes her mind later cannot be trusted. Therefore, sincerity demands not only good faith but devotion. It requires not only momentary honesty but commitment over time.

The *Book of Changes* argues that sincerity is the key to influence. Trustworthy people inspire confidence. People are more likely to be persuaded by those whom they trust and rely on. In addition, people who believe in what they say make the best advocates. Their honesty, commitment, and devotion call forth a natural response in others. This is the theme of Hexagram 61, Zhong Fu, which can be translated as either Inner Truth or Inner Sincerity. The force of inner sincerity is so great, the *Book of Changes* tells us, that it can influence even pigs and fishes.

Inner truth means conformity between what is on the inside and what is on the outside. Sincere people are what they appear to be. They do not put on airs or try to impress people. They are not pretentious or manipulative. These qualities also lead others to rely on them and have confidence in them.

In addition, inner truth means self-knowledge and self-awareness. The *Book of Changes* argues that you cannot be honest with others if you are not honest with yourself. You cannot make reliable and lasting commitments to others if you cannot make them to yourself. The ability to make commitments is premised on self-mastery and self-restraint. These in turn require self-understanding. Thus in the *Book of Changes* sincerity means more than good intentions. It also means being free of self-deception. Sincerity means that you are not engaged in wishful thinking and that you are not conflicted or divided against yourself.

In sum, sincerity—or inner truth—requires knowing who you are and what you want. It means having complete clarity about your values and your goals. Understood in this way, sincerity is a virtue that can serve a person in any situation. People who possess inner truth do not fool themselves and therefore do not engage in self-destructive behavior. That is why they succeed. Thus in Hexagram 29, Xi Kan (The Abyss), the *Book of Changes* insists that what a person needs most in times of danger is sincerity:

Repeated Abyss.
If you are truthful and sincere,
And follow your heart,
Then you will have success,
And your actions will bring esteem.

The lesson of this text is that, in times of peril, people who are divided and conflicted are their own worst enemy. People must be completely honest about themselves and their situation if they are to get through the danger unscathed

Not surprisingly, it follows that a sincere person has integrity. Thus sincerity is connected to modesty. Like modesty, sincerity is an essential ingredient for success. People who have clarity, integrity, and emotional balance are not only trustworthy and reliable. They are also best equipped to deal with life's changes.

Perseverance, Adaptability, and Integrity

The *Book of Changes* is supremely practical in its orientation. People should strive to understand the nature of the world with complete clarity and without any illusion or wishful thinking. They must accept the world for what it is and not as they would like it to be. And they must adapt to changing circumstances. The past is past, and we must continuously move on, in accord with the flux of events. Wise people try to understand the nature of the times and move in harmony with the world instead of vainly striving against circumstances. Nevertheless, adaptation is not the same thing as capitulation. All adaptation must be understood in light of the virtue of perseverance.

Perseverance *(zhen)* is one of the most important qualities in the Confucian reinterpretation of the *Book of Changes.* Like sincerity and modesty, it has multiple meanings. Sometimes it simply means continuing in the way one has been going without being deterred or discouraged. Simple perseverance can sometimes be a virtue, especially if the goals are worthy and one proceeds methodically, step by step. This is the theme of Hexagram 46 (Ascending). But perseverance can also be a vice. People who are stubborn and do not pay attention to changing circumstances or listen to good advice persevere in the wrong way—they are not trying to learn from or engage with the world, so if they are in harmony with circumstances it is only by accident. The law of change guarantees that they will soon be out of harmony if they persist. Normally, when the text says that "perseverance brings misfortune," the word "perseverance" has this simple meaning. The point is that one is on the wrong path and needs to change direction.

However, perseverance also has another interpretation, which has stronger ethical overtones. It means to be steadfast in one's principles and upright in one's behavior. In the *Book of Changes,* this sort of perseverance is almost always appropriate. Being steadfast and upright does not mean stubbornness. It means cultivating strength of character and learning how to adjust to changing events without betraying one's values or surrendering one's larger goals. It is principled pragmatism. When we encounter difficulties, we should not despair or give up but learn to be flexible and try to figure out how we might achieve our ends by other means. This sort of perseverance is not the opposite of adaptation. It is the appropriate form of adaptation.

Perseverance may require changing one's strategy but not one's ultimate objectives. Sometimes the best way to adapt is to lie low and engage in quiet preparation for later advance. This is the theme of several hexagrams, including 5 (Xu, Waiting), 26 (Da Xu, Great Accumulation), 33 (Dun, Retreat), 36 (Ming Yi, Darkening of the Light), and 53 (Jian, Developing Gradually). The *Book of Changes* warns against rash and premature action, and against wasting one's resources out of impatience and a desire to succeed at all costs. It continually preaches patience, rigorous preparation, gathering intelligence, and good timing. Acting when the moment is right often takes great courage. But just as often self-control is necessary to avoid advancing prematurely and to prevent ourselves from rushing forward out of frustration, anxiety, impatience, or fear of the unknown. One must cultivate self-restraint in order to be able to live with uncertainty and to await the unfolding of events. Patience does not mean refusing to take risks. Quite the contrary; often people act rashly because they want to avoid risk. When the situation is uncertain, people often forge ahead in order to get things settled, and as a result they settle for less. Or they try to force the issue and end up making things worse. Inner strength is necessary to wait until it is right to take the risk. Then one must by all means take it.

Adaptation means accepting the present situation for what it is and seeing what elements can be turned to our advantage. Successful action comes from recognizing both the limitations and the opportunities inherent in any situation. The two are often interrelated. What looks like a limitation may provide a hidden opportunity. This follows from the law of change itself, because all increase arises from and is prepared by previous conditions of decrease. Everything that is prolonged eventually changes back into its opposite. Enlightened people understand the play of opposites in changing circumstances. They are able to see how apparent restrictions and misfortunes can work to their ultimate advantage. That is why many of the hexagrams with negative titles, such as Standstill (12), Opposition (38), Obstruction (39), and Limitation (60), always hold out the hope of improvement. The point is to learn how to make the most of difficult times in order to pave the way for better times ahead.

Finally, adaptation does not mean surrendering to circumstances. In the *Book of Changes,* as in many other parts of Chinese philosophy, everything is determined and shaped by its opposite. Change is not a coherent concept without something that is held constant and against which change can be understood. All change, in other words, presupposes some degree of constancy. The *Book of Changes* draws an ethical analogy to this metaphysical point: Adaptability always means change against the background of a stable core of personality and an unswerving commitment to personal integrity. This is precisely what it means to persevere—to be steadfast and upright. Adaptation is pointless if it is not in the service of larger principles that remain constant in the face of adversity. If people abandon themselves to each passing fad or each change in power, they have nothing which is truly their own. Although the *Book of Changes* repeatedly advises flexibility, it insists that one adapts by preserving one's principles and one's integrity, not by surrendering them. Therefore, when one's views are out of favor, the right strategy is to keep a low profile and wait for the tide to turn rather than giving up or selling out. This is the great theme of Hexagrams 12 (Standstill), 47 (Oppression), and especially 36 (Darkening of the Light).

Conversely, the *Book of Changes* argues that what is constant in one's self can only become known through confronting the flux of experience. People learn who they are and what they believe by being faced with change, being presented with obstacles, and being forced to make decisions. Change confronts us and shapes our identities. It requires us to clarify our values. Thus, adaptation to change is not simply clever strategy. It is also a process of self-cultivation and self-education. Through dealing with change, one comes to understand who one is and what one truly believes in. Through encountering change, those parts of ourselves that remain stable and constant are discovered and refined.

Adaptation and perseverance are thus two sides of the same coin. Both require equanimity and inner strength. People who lack emotional balance will be swept into extremes of happiness and despair. They will be thrown about like driftwood in a storm at sea. That is because they lack a stable center. People who can maintain inner balance will roll with the tides and eventually come out on top. Inner balance is like a gyroscope that remains upright no matter how things move around it.

Sometimes, of course, determination and inner strength will not be enough. Life may be too hard, and we may be overwhelmed by circumstances beyond our control. But by developing habits of perseverance we have a better chance at surviving, creating a better environment for ourselves, and ultimately prevailing. The *Book of Changes* does not guarantee our fate—it only teaches the best way to go out and meet it.

Leadership, Politics, and Social Organization

In ancient China the family was believed to the appropriate model for the state and for all other social organizations. Thus the *Book of Changes* does not distinguish between different types of groups. Instead, it offers generalized advice about the proper conduct of organizations, and how leaders and followers should behave toward one another.

The political and organizational theory of the book is summed up by the Chinese proverb that to rule is to serve. Leaders must continually look out for the interests of their followers. That is their primary obligation and the source of their authority to lead. They must behave with rectitude and lead by example. Followers, in turn, must do their best to work for the good of the group or organization. By playing their part and giving of themselves, they will help things run smoothly and they will have influence on the organization and its direction. Thus the converse of the ancient maxim is that to serve is to rule. The *Book of Changes* argues that the best way to influence others is to be sincere and devoted toward them, and to work tirelessly on their behalf. People who become indispensable to their leaders often have greatest influence in the organization.

Hexagrams 41 (Sun, Decrease) and 42 (Yi, Increase) symbolize the maxim that the obligation of superiors is to benefit subordinates. The theme of Yi (Increase) is to decrease what is above in order to increase what is below. Doing this produces a net increase, because those above should serve those below. Conversely, the theme of Sun (Decrease) is to decrease what is below to serve what is above. This produces a net decrease, because those above should not enrich themselves at the expense of those below.

The *Book of Changes* presupposes an underlying reciprocal arrangement that justifies the power and authority of those who lead. Subordinates are expected to follow their leaders and work for the good of the group. In return, leaders are expected to work in the interests of their followers and for the greater good of the organization. In this way everyone benefits and good times are prolonged. The *Book of Changes* does not understand this arrangement as binding because of an explicit agreement or an implicit social compact. Rather, it holds that this is the appropriate nature of all social organization. It is what leaders and followers are simply supposed to do, whether they do it or not. After all, throughout Chinese history there were many greedy and power-hungry leaders who did not care about their followers.

If leaders fail to enrich and benefit those who work under them, they forfeit their right to rule. Then revolution is justified. This is the subject of Hexagram 49, Ge, or Revolution. However, given China's history, the influence of Confucianism, and the strongly hierarchical structure of ancient Chinese society, revolution is hardly encouraged in the *Book of Changes*. It is a device of last resort, when there is no other alternative. The purpose of revolution is not to seize power for its own sake but to restore the appropriate conditions of leadership, in which rulers serve the interests of the group and work for the welfare of those who follow them.

The *Book of Changes* teaches that good fortune comes from cooperation and that cooperation comes from the establishment of bonds of trust and reciprocity. The same principles apply to the conduct of organizations and the relationship between leaders and followers. Leaders must act loyally and honorably toward their followers if they want their followers to behave loyally and honorably toward them.

To be effective, leaders must gain the confidence and trust of others. They do this, first, by setting a good example for others. Both the ruler and the sage teach best by being role models. By doing what is best for the group rather than what benefits them personally, leaders encourage others to do the same. Second, leaders must demonstrate through their actions as well as their words that they are devoted to the larger goals of the enterprise rather than to their personal aggrandizement, and that they are concerned about the welfare of their followers. Third, leaders must instill and inspire their followers with enthusiasm, a sense of vision, and a common purpose. Thus, 16.4 says:

> *The very source of enthusiasm.*
> *Great things can be achieved.*
> *Have no doubts.*

Friends gather round you
As a hair clasp gathers the hair.

Fourth, leaders must display sincere and genuine commitment to the goals of the enterprise. No one will follow people who do not believe in their cause or who are unenthusiastic or cynical about what they are doing. The *Book of Changes* argues that great leaders influence others through the force of their character. Their sincerity and devotion to their cause shine through to others and therefore people look up to them and follow their example.

Fifth, in organizations everyone must know what their role is and what is expected of them. When everyone plays their assigned task in the organization, things run smoothly and the organization prospers. When assigned tasks and responsibilities are not clear, people interfere with each other and struggles for power increase.

Equally important, everyone should be respected for the work that they perform. No matter how lowly a part they play in the organization, people must be appreciated for the job that they do and rewarded and recognized when they do it well. Discipline is essential but must be seen to be consistent, fair, and evenhanded. When discipline is recognized as necessary, it will win the respect and obedience of others. Here again, it is important to lead by example. Leaders should not demand that others make sacrifices that they themselves are unwilling to make, and they should not hold their followers to standards that they themselves are unwilling to live up to.

Finally, leaders must encourage their subordinates and help them advance. When subordinates show talent and ambition, those who oversee them should respond and encourage their growth without feeling jealous or threatened. This is another way of putting the interests of the group ahead of one's own personal interests. Thus 19.2 says:

Finding response in overseeing.
Good fortune.
There is nothing that is not beneficial.

The same point applies to the king, who should not be afraid to surround himself with able ministers and advisors. Line 55.5 says:

Beauty and brilliance come forward.
Blessing and fame draw near.
Good fortune.

This refers to people of great talent who aid the ruler in governing the country. Although these people may become famous, the ruler should not be envious or feel threatened but should accept their contributions gladly because they will serve the common good. Wise leaders are not made insecure by others; they understand how to accept help and to subordinate their egos in order to make the organization stronger and get the job done.

In sum, the advice that the *Book of Changes* offers to leaders is the same that it offers to all mankind: Like everyone else, leaders must possess modesty and sincerity if they wish to succeed. Sincerity is necessary to inspire others and to forge bonds of trust and reciprocity. Modesty is necessary to follow things through to completion.

CHAPTER THREE

How the *Book of Changes* Works

People have consulted the *Book of Changes* for almost three thousand years. It may well be the oldest continuously used system of divination in human history. When a practice has been employed for so long, it is only natural to inquire why it has retained its popularity.

How, exactly, does the *Book of Changes* work? Early Chinese diviners in the Shang Dynasty believed that the spirits of their ancestors spoke to them. The Zhou diviners who compiled the *Book of Changes* may have believed that they were in contact with the impersonal forces of heaven. The Great Treatise (the Fifth and Sixth of the Ten Wings) argues that the *Changes* works because the figures and patterns in heaven and on earth are mirrored in the figures and patterns of the trigrams and hexagrams, so that the movements of one are mirrored in the movements of the other.

The most famous Western theory about how the *Changes* works is Carl Jung's; it bears interesting similarities to the account offered in the Great Treatise. In his preface to Richard Wilhelm's much beloved translation, Jung argued that the *Book of Changes* was an example of the principle of "synchronicity," a noncausal principle that connected disparate events in the universe. Jung held that events connected by synchronicity were not connected by mere chance, but by "a peculiar interdependence of objective events among themselves as well as with the subjective (psychic) states of the observer or observers."[1] In other words, although the hexagram received and

1. Carl Jung, Preface to *I Ching: The Book of Changes,* trans. Richard Wilhelm and Cary F. Baynes, p. xxiv.

the events it describes are not causally related, they are still connected, and the observer's understanding of this relationship is crucial to the connection's existence. Jung admitted that there could be no empirical testing of his hypothesis: "The only criterion of the validity of synchronicity," Jung explained, "is the observer's opinion that the text of the hexagram amounts to a true rendering of his psychic condition."

Jung's theory of synchronicity seems to beg more questions than it answers. Fortunately, there are much more straightforward explanations of how the *Book of Changes* works. In fact, this question is really two separate questions: The first is why the *Book of Changes* appears to speak to people directly and offer them relevant and often perceptive advice about their lives. The second question is whether the *Book of Changes* is a *useful* divinatory system. Many oracles seem to give intelligent advice, but surely the more important question is whether the advice is at all useful. Does divination with the *Book of Changes* give people genuine insights? Is consulting the *Book of Changes* any more helpful in making decisions than using the daily astrology column in a newspaper, or randomly flipping a coin? To answer these questions we need not assume any elaborate metaphysical assumptions about synchronicity or spiritual beings. Simple facts about human psychology answer the first question. The quality of the book's underlying philosophy answers the second.

Why Does the Book of Changes *Seem to Give Relevant Answers to Questions?*

The *Book of Changes* seems to offer relevant answers because of the way that the human mind interacts with three features of the book: its oracular language, its question-and-answer format, and its narrative structure. Any system of divination with these three features would also appear to give relevant answers. Nevertheless, not all such systems would be equally useful or insightful.

The oracular language of the *Book of Changes*. The *Book of Changes* works like any divinatory practice that produces ambiguous messages. Oracular language is equivocal and enticing. It creates a puzzle for the mind to solve. To do this, people naturally draw on their own knowledge and personal history. They try to make sense of the mysterious language in terms of their own life experience.

Oracles are most enticing when they balance substance with ambiguity. The oracle must be sufficiently substantive to seem relevant to people's lives, and sufficiently ambiguous to be consistent with a large number of possible outcomes. That way the oracle can appear to have been correct in hindsight no matter what actually happens. Astrology columns in daily newspapers are good examples: Consider the following representative entry—"Leo: A special someone wants to make amends. It's time to watch your finances. In the evening, have a ball." Obviously these three statements can apply to lots of things in different people's lives. And in hindsight it is not difficult to see them as relevant to something in almost everyone's experience. (Including, one might add, people who were not born under the sign of Leo.) Moreover, in judging the quality of oracles, people tend to remember those parts of a message that turned out "right," while disregarding or downplaying those parts that didn't fit subsequent experience.

Like many other oracles, the *Book of Changes* is vague and cryptic, and so it is not surprising that it produces similar results. Moreover, its language is not only ambiguous, but mysterious, enticing us to make sense of it. Hence we feel especially gratified when we find an appropriate and satisfying connection between its dreamlike metaphors and our mundane existence. As a result, we attribute even more wisdom and perspicacity to its oracular pronouncements. It seems to be a person who understands our lives intimately and knows all our secrets.

In fact, the book engages in no mental activity. As the Great Treatise says, "The *Changes* is without consciousness and is without deliberate action."[2] All of the mental activity is occurring in our own minds. We are bestowing meaning on the words and symbols of the *Changes* and forging connections with the events of our own lives as we understand them. All good oracles stimulate mental activity in a similar way. They induce us to abandon logical and linear thinking temporarily in order to focus our minds on other forms of mental calculation and judgment that we usually describe as intuition or inspiration.

Thus an oracle's ambiguity and mystery have two different effects. The first, and least important, is the most obvious—ambiguous oracles are easier to square with later events. No matter what happens, an ambiguous oracle appears to have been correct in hindsight. Second, and more important, an ambiguous oracle provokes people to connect its language to their personal experience. This produces the oracle's most important function—it incites thought, kindles the imagination, and stimulates self-reflection.

The *Book of Changes'* question-and-answer format. Generally speaking, oracles fall into one of two categories: oblative (offered up) and impetrative

2. The Great Treatise, I, x, 4 (Lynn trans., p. 63).

(obtained by entreaty). An oblative oracle presents itself without any prior request for information. Examples of oblative oracles are sudden events—like a person stumbling on a staircase or a clap of thunder; omens and portents—like a child born with a certain mark or an animal born with a particular disfigurement; dreams; the relative location of stars and planets at the time of a person's birth, or the configuration of lines on a person's hand. Oblative oracles simply happen naturally, and it is left to human beings to interpret their meaning.

By contrast, impetrative oracles are entreaties; they try to coax meaning out of nature. Casting lots, cracking tortoise shells, and reading tea leaves are impetrative oracles—the questioner deliberately attempts to produce portents and omens that can be read or interpreted. The *Book of Changes* is an impetrative oracle. More to the point, it is a questioning oracle, because not all impetrative oracles require the user to pose a specific question. For example, one can read tea leaves without formulating an prior inquiry. Divination with the *Book of Changes,* however, begins with the formulation of a specific question that casting a hexagram is supposed to answer.

The process of formulating a question and posing it to the oracle greatly enhances the psychological tendency to view the *Book of Changes* as a sentient intelligence. People ask the *Changes* a question as if it were a person, and they receive what appears to be an answer, also in the form of words, as if spoken by a human being. Hence it is not surprising that the mind tries to make sense of what it has received as an answer, imputing to the words a human (or superhuman) intelligence that is trying to communicate something relevant about the question that was asked.

To understand the words of an oracle as an answer, we must try to connect its advice coherently to the situation as we understand it. The mind tries to make what it regards as an answer coherent and intelligible to itself. This causes us to inquire into the situation more deeply and reflectively. Our minds draw on elements of our subconscious and unconscious, including our beliefs, memories, and desires. This produces the effect that the oracle knows us intimately and is aware of our most secret thoughts, including things we have not wanted to admit to ourselves. The effect is often overwhelming. But the person who speaks is not a disembodied oracle. The person who speaks to us is none other than ourselves.

The narrative structure of the *Book of Changes*. A third important feature of the *Changes*—shared by many other oracles—is that its texts and commentaries are implicit or explicit narratives. Many of the line texts are proverbs or miniature stories. Consider for example 10.3: "He treads on the tail of the tiger / With great caution and circumspection / In the end, good fortune." Another example is 60.3: "No limitation / Then lamentation." Proverbs, of course, are highly condensed narratives that offer a generalized story about human action and its likely consequences. Still other lines describe a situation one is in, a personal characteristic to embrace or avoid, or a course of action to forswear or follow. The texts of the *Book of Changes* offer hundreds of little stories about how things will turn out or are likely to turn out if people behave one way or another. Indeed, it is hard to find parts of the text that are not narratively structured.

Narrative structures have psychological power because narratives guide human behavior both descriptively and prescriptively. People understand what is happening to them and what they should do or not do in terms of background narrative structures and familiar stock narrative accounts. People draw on stories or experiences they are already familiar with to situate themselves and determine how to go on. The narratives in the *Book of Changes* mesh brilliantly with these psychological tendencies. They offer accounts of our situation in terms of highly condensed narratives. They also offer advice about what we should do in terms of these narratives. When people receive a text like 38.1—"If you lose a horse, do not run after it / It will return by itself"—they naturally connect the story of something lost that is restored if one does not chase after it to their own experience. Our minds effortlessly forge narrative connections between the story we draw from the *Changes* and the events of our own lives. Hence it appears that the *Book of Changes* understands our situation implicitly and counsels us accordingly. It seems to offer us relevant and often highly perceptive advice.

Yet these features of the *Book of Changes* apply with equal force to any system of divination that is structured in terms of proverbs, stock stories, or familiar narratives. Imagine, for example, a system of divination that was nothing more than a series of proverbs or familiar sayings:

1. Faint heart never won fair lady.
2. Look before you leap.
3. A stitch in time saves nine.
4. A fool and his money are soon parted.
5. He who hesitates is lost.
6. Forewarned is forearmed.
7. Marry in haste and repent in leisure.
8. Slow and steady wins the race.

When consulted by random divination, such a system would also appear to offer intelligent advice. The questioner's mind would immediately try to connect the proverb received to the questioner's situation. The proverbs are sufficiently open-ended that they could apply to lots of circumstances. It would probably not be difficult to forge connections between the question asked and the answer given. As noted previously, the *Book of Changes* contains many proverblike elements.

Next consider a system of divination based on famous historical events and personalities. Imagine a system with eight possible responses:

1. The Battle of Waterloo
2. Nixon in China
3. The Civil War
4. Washington at Valley Forge
5. Bill Clinton and Monica Lewinsky
6. The Winning of the West
7. Lincoln
8. Roosevelt

People could analogize their situation to the response they received. "The Battle of Waterloo" might symbolize hubris and bad strategy; "Nixon in China" might symbolize going against one's ordinary tendencies in order to secure a great achievement; and so on. In fact, such a system might be particularly rich because each of the terms has so many different associations. To some people "Roosevelt" might symbolize a great and adaptable leader; to others, it might symbolize a person who hid his disability from the public in order to be successful. "The Winning of the West" might symbolize a great victory or the terrible slaughter of Native Americans. The richer the set of associations, the more flexible the system would be, and the more often it would appear to offer relevant advice. In fact, the *Book of Changes* contains many historical references of this type. Several parts of the book refer to historical episodes in the history of the Shang and Zhou Dynasties that would have been well known to the compilers of the book but have since been forgotten.

What Makes the Book of Changes *Useful? Divination versus Fortune-Telling*

I have offered several reasons why the *Book of Changes* appears to give intelligent and perceptive answers when it is consulted. The same, however, is true of many forms of divination. I just gave examples of two systems—one based on familiar proverbs and one based on historical events and narratives—that would produce similar effects. This leads me to a more important question: Why is the *Book of Changes* a particularly useful or beneficial divinatory system? To answer this question we need to understand more about what divination is and what its objectives are.

We might begin by distinguishing divination from fortune-telling. Fortune-telling—at least in its most primitive forms—is an attempt to determine what will happen in the future. It is premised on the notion that people have destinies or that certain events are fated to occur. Divination, by contrast, does not presuppose the same degree of fixity to events. It is an aid to understanding one's situation and one's self. It tries to recognize tendencies in events as well as in one's own patterns of thought and behavior. The distinction between fated events and tendencies seems to have been perfectly clear to the ancient Chinese. Even during Zhou times the point of divination was not to inquire into what was preordained but to ask whether what the questioner was proposing was likely to succeed.

Second, unlike simple fortune-telling, divination, as its name implies, is an attempt to communicate with the divine. Some forms of divination—both ancient and modern—identify the divine with entities outside the self. They view divination as an attempt to communicate with gods or spirits. But the divine need not exist external to the self. It may refer to features of the soul or self that we have lost ordinary contact with and that must be regained through special methods. Under this second interpretation, divination is a method of introspection whose goals are self-cultivation and self-knowledge. What one divines is the nature of the situation, the nature of one's self, and the relation between the two. The word "divine" possesses each of these connotations: It means both godliness and ascertainment.

People can hold both of these views about divination simultaneously: They can believe that divination brings us closer to spiritual forces in the universe, and they can also believe that divination is a method of self-analysis and self-cultivation. To understand the value of the *Book of Changes*, however, one need only accept the second view about divination—that divination is a method of self-divination. Thus the *Book of Changes* does not presuppose a particular theology. People who use the *Book of Changes* can believe that they are communicating with gods and spirits, as the Shang did; they can believe in the impersonal forces of Heaven, like the Zhou; or they can be agnostics or atheists who merely seek self-awareness and self-understanding.

As noted above, the *Book of Changes* works by inducing or drawing out connections between the text and the interpreter's understanding of his or her situation. The questioner constructs an answer through interacting with the text and relevant commentaries. Interpreting the *Changes*' ambiguous and evocative text is a highly subjective process; it draws on the questioner's personal experiences, motivations, and unconscious desires. That is why the book appears to speak directly to the questioner. In fact, the book does not speak. Only the person who consults it speaks. People use the book to talk to themselves, to jostle their unconscious and stimulate their intuitions. The real oracle always lies within.

Such a hardheaded approach may seem deflationary to advocates of the *Book of Changes,* who may wish to believe that they are in contact with unseen spiritual forces, or to devoted Jungians who hold to the theory of synchronicity. But the point has long been understood. The Great Treatise, for example, states: "When the noble man would act in a certain way or would try to do something, he addresses his doubts to the *Changes* in terms of words. The charge that it receives comes back to him like an echo, with no distance or concealment to it."[3] An echo, of course, is nothing other than the reflection of one's own voice.

One might object that the oracle's efficacy depends on belief in its magical qualities. If people recognize that the oracle involves nothing more than random events, they will lose confidence in it. This seems implausible. The standard methods for consulting the *Book of Changes*—divination through manipulation of yarrow stalks or by tossing a set of coins—were designed to produce certain probabilities of yin and yang, fixed and moving lines. That design would make little sense if the outcomes were not randomly generated.

Nor is there anything special about the use of yarrow stalks or coins. Yarrow was probably chosen because of a belief in its magical properties. In fact, yarrow stalks have some medicinal value, but that is irrelevant to their ability to generate random numbers. Traditionally, yarrow stalks were consulted with elaborate ceremony and burning of incense. In like fashion, people who use the coin method are sometimes advised to use a special set of coins for divination, which are to be washed regularly and kept in a special place. But the point of these rituals is only to show respect for the process of divination and to focus the mind on the seriousness of the endeavor. The rituals themselves can have no magical power. Whether the rituals are per-

3. The Great Treatise, I, x, 2 (Lynn trans., p. 62).

formed or not, the yarrow and the coins will still produce random results. Indeed, many people today dispense with yarrow and coins entirely. They consult the *Changes* using computer programs.

In short, anyone who uses the oracle over a period of time must recognize that the generation of hexagrams is a purely random event. But this does not undermine the questioner's ability to gain insights from interacting with the book. The key to confidence in the oracle is not belief in supernatural entities but a sincere devotion to the cause of enlightenment and self-examination. Even a thoroughgoing atheist can use the book with profit.

If, as I have suggested, the proper goal of divination is self-examination and self-understanding, it is not difficult to see why some oracles might be more useful than others. An oracle is useful to the extent that it enables people to think creatively about themselves and their situation. It is useful to the extent that it serves as a helpful psychological aid to self-cultivation and self-knowledge. The *Book of Changes* has survived for centuries because it satisfies these criteria admirably.

Many of the features that make an oracle appear to come from an independent intelligence also make it useful for self-examination. Using the *Book of Changes* helps externalize ideas already within us and projects them outward onto the oracle's answers. Moreover, as noted above, ambiguity and mystery impel the mind to do cognitive work, stimulating intuitions and forging connections.

As we have seen, ambiguous oracles are easily adapted to many different types of situations and persons. But ambiguity is not enough. An answer such as "very soon, something important" is quite ambiguous. But it lacks substance. It offers little to arouse the imagination. To stimulate thought usefully, an oracle needs a language with rich associations and metaphorical connections. This the *Book of Changes* has in abundance, not only because of its condensed language and arcane imagery, but because of the hundreds of years of commentary that have grown up around the book. That is one reason why the *Book of Changes*—especially in its Confucian reinterpretation—is markedly superior to flipping a coin.

Similarly, to stimulate creative thinking, an oracle must be open-ended. An oracle that produces determinate yes and no answers offers resolution but does not give the mind much to create with. It cuts off the imagination instead of nourishing it. The hexagram judgments and line statements rarely tell us that something will or will not happen. Instead, they suggest tendencies, opportunities, and possible dangers if we pursue certain courses of action. They continually urge us to self-improvement and the cultivation of our character. They remind us of the subtle connections between the kinds of people that we allow ourselves to become and the kinds of experiences we are likely to have as a result.

Flipping a coin offers no philosophy. It gives no reasons for its decisions, only results. To stimulate self-examination, an oracle must suggest—even if indirectly—why a course of action is good or bad so that we can consider how its advice applies to our own situation. The *Book of Changes* offers an account of the sources of danger or opportunity, a narrative of how causes lead to effects, and a story about how a certain type of character leads to a certain type of destiny.

The Book of Changes as a Repository of Wisdom

Finally, an oracle is only as beneficial as its underlying philosophy. It is not enough to stimulate thought. One must do so in a positive way. It is not enough to offer narratives about how the world works. The narratives offered must emanate from a coherent and valuable philosophy of life. A system of divination that consistently offered messages of hopelessness and despair would not be very useful and would in all likelihood be a self-fulfilling prophecy. A system that offered a crabbed or limited view of human nature would inevitably bias our actions in unhelpful ways. A system that continually urged people to distrust others and attack them aggressively would eventually get people into considerable trouble, while a system that aroused unrealistic expectations would cause people to fail miserably. Finally, a system of divination that offered random and contradictory advice would not be of much help to people who were trying to achieve a coherent approach to their lives.

The *Book of Changes* has stood the test of time because it is not only a book of divination but also a book of wisdom. As it has been interpreted over the centuries, each of the hexagram judgments and line statements in the *Book of Changes* flows from an interconnected set of teachings, whose basic elements are summarized in Chapter Two. Therefore, no matter what hexagram or line statement one receives, the questioner receives an aspect of this philosophy. Obviously, it matters whether one receives a mantic text like "good fortune" or "misfortune." But what is more important is the reason why good fortune or misfortune accrues. In the ethical reinterpretation of the *Book of Changes,* good fortune and misfortune accrue because one acts wisely or foolishly. Through proper conduct and self-cultivation a person can secure a higher probability of success. By contrast, bad habits and improper behavior increase the chances of disaster, so that in the end one must blame one's self as well as outward circumstances.

The interpretations of the hexagram judgments and line statements all have this character. They hold out the hope of ultimate improvement while warning about the dangers of unwise decision. Thus no text in the *Book of Changes* is simply a prediction of good or bad fortune. It always carries an ethical lesson about the relationship between character and consequences, and about the best way to deal with life's vicissitudes. The *Book of Changes* is not simply a book of oracles, but a continuous sermon on how to negotiate the inevitable changes in human affairs and fortunes.

The authors of the Great Treatise understood the book in precisely this way. The *Changes*, they argued, was first produced when "the house of Yin [i.e., the Shang Dynasty] came to an end and the way of the house of Chou [Zhou] was rising," when "King Wen [the traditional founder of the Zhou Dynasty] and the tyrant [Dixin, the last Shang ruler] were pitted against each other." The Shang lost the mandate of heaven because they did not understand how to behave; the Zhou gained the mandate of heaven because they understood how to negotiate the dangers of the times. "That is why," the Great Treatise explains, "the book's judgements so frequently warn about dangers. He who is conscious of danger creates peace for himself; he who takes things lightly creates his own downfall." The goal of the *Changes,* the Great Treatise tells, is how to be "without blame," and therefore have the greatest chances of success in a changing and uncertain world. This, says the Great Treatise, is the basic principle [Dao] of the *Changes*.[4]

Although the *Book of Changes* is a book of wisdom, that wisdom is best understood through working through specific questions in the actual practice of divination. The proper way of understanding the book is the subject of an important dispute between two of its greatest commentators, Wang Bi in the third century and Zhu Xi in the twelfth. Wang Bi insisted that the principles behind the book were its most important feature. Zhu Xi insisted that interaction with its symbolism was the best way to get in touch with its wisdom.

In my view both of these thinkers are correct. Wang Bi understood that an oracle is only as good as the philosophy of life that emanates from it. It must do more than simply offer puzzling texts. It must also instruct. The *Book of Changes* may seem wise because it is ambiguous and obscure. It actually is wise because it offers the reader a subtle philosophy about the in-

4. The Great Treatise, II, xi, 1 (Wilhelm/Baynes trans., pp. 352–53).

evitability of change, the proper methods of adjusting to the flow of events, and the complicated ways that character leads to destiny.

Nevertheless, Zhu Xi was also correct in emphasizing that the best way to learn the philosophy of the *Book of Changes* is by doing. One grasps the book's lessons best through using it as a book of divination to solve particular questions in one's life. By themselves general principles are dry, difficult to put into practice, and easily forgotten. Psychological interaction with the book and application of its insights to one's daily life is the best way to assimilate its wisdom and learn its lessons. The *Book of Changes* teaches us by insisting that we must teach ourselves. For this reason, the choice between the *Book of Changes'* status as a tool of divination and as a book of wisdom is a false one. It operates as a book of wisdom in large part because it is structured as a book of divination. And it works as a book of divination because it is premised on a wise and humane philosophy of life.

The philosophy of change and human fortune that we find in the *Book of Changes* was not a matter of original design. The text that began as the Bronze Age diviner's manual *Zhouyi* has no philosophy in it. It is a hodgepodge of images, stories, and proverbs. Over time, however, people attributed important lessons to its oracular language, and through continuous reinterpretation and synthesis they infused the book with deeper meanings. The terrible wars and conflicts suffered by the Chinese during the Eastern Zhou Dynasty—and particularly the Warring States period—led to a great flowering of philosophical and moral inquiry in which people pondered the transitoriness of life and tried to give it meaning and moral purpose. The wisdom of the *Book of Changes* was forged out of a great crucible of human suffering, and the lessons of that period were characteristically ascribed to the ancient sages, who, according to legend, had themselves experienced many trials and tribulations. The Great Treatise explains that the *Book of Changes* "came into use in the period of middle antiquity," when the Shang persecuted King Wen of the Zhou. "Those who composed the Changes," it explains, "had great care and sorrow."[5]

By the time of the Ten Wings, the *Book of Changes* had been imbued with a relatively coherent philosophy, which was further elaborated in subsequent commentaries like those of Wang Bi and his successors. The philosophy generally ascribed to the book is a synthesis. It contains elements of both Daoism and Confucianism, and almost every philosophical trend that followed. It is sometimes said that the *Book of Changes* is the source of all

5. The Great Treatise, II, vii, 1 (Wilhelm/Baynes trans., p. 345).

Chinese philosophy. The opposite is more nearly the case: It has been invested with ideas from virtually every period in China's history. These speculations have accumulated over time and have been transmitted from generation to generation. The book is like a great caldron into which intellectual trends have been continuously added and cooked together. We might say that the *Book of Changes* is less a philosophical treatise than a *repository* of wisdom. It has been the opportunity and the provocation for generations of speculation about human character and human fate.

The book's gnostic qualities probably contributed to this result. Believing that the book contained the most profound wisdom, generations of Chinese thinkers poured their best efforts into trying to understand its puzzling language. Of course, the more the Chinese language mutated from the vocabulary found in the Bronze Age *Zhouyi*, the more mysterious the book became and the more the belief in its profundity grew. The Great Treatise, for example, repeatedly insists that everything that can be known is contained in the *Changes* if we only had enough wit to understand it. And the more efforts were made to explain the meaning of the hexagrams and accompanying judgments, the more scholars produced a rich body of philosophy about human nature and how people might deal with the incessant forces of change. All of this philosophy was naturally attributed to the book itself. The profundity of the *Book of Changes* is perhaps the best example of a self-fulfilling prophecy. Believing with unshakable certainty that this impenetrable book contained a philosophy of great depth and humanity, its commentators eventually constructed one for it.

In the twentieth century there has been a trend to strip away the elements of Confucianism in the text and return to the "original" meaning of the *Book of Changes*. This is not the first time such calls have been made. The same battle cry can be found, for example, in Zhu Xi's twelfth-century commentary, which ironically became part of the Confucian orthodoxy itself. For students of ancient Chinese civilization and history, trying to grasp the original meaning of the *Changes* makes perfect sense. The call for a return to original meaning is more puzzling coming from those who view the *Changes* as a spiritual guide. The great irony is that the book's wisdom inheres almost entirely in the glosses that grew up around it and not in the original Bronze Age divinatory text. When one strips away the layers of Confucian, Daoist, and Neo-Confucian interpretations, what one gets is not some profound and eternal vision of human life. What one gets is advice about whether the king should go on a hunt, what to do with captive soldiers, and the best way to perform human sacrifice.

The *Book of Changes* "works" because of the way that its language stimulates our intuitions, and because of the humaneness of its underlying philosophy. A final necessary ingredient, however, is devotion and seriousness of purpose on the part of the questioner. Because the book is only the echo of our beliefs and desires, people tend to get out of the book exactly what they put into it. Treat it as a party game and it will produce only random trivialities. But the more interested one is in self-examination, the more value the book will come to have over the years. As the Great Treatise says:

The Changes is a book
From which one may not hold aloof.
Its [d]ao is forever changing
. . . .
Without or within, [its lines] teach caution.
They also show care and sorrow and their causes.
Though you have no teacher,
Approach them as you would your parents.
First take up the words,
Ponder their meaning,
Then the fixed rules reveal themselves.
But if you are not the right [person],
The meaning will not manifest itself to you.[6]

6. The Great Treatise, II, viii, 1–4 (Wilhelm/Baynes trans., pp. 348–49).

CHAPTER FOUR

The Symbolism of the *Book of Changes*

Over the centuries an elaborate system of symbols has grown up around the *Book of Changes* to explain the meaning of the hexagrams and line statements. Some of this symbolism already appears in the Ten Wings, although much was added later on.

Much of the symbolism in the *Book of Changes* reflects its origins in a strongly traditional society. It was simply taken for granted in ancient China that society had a natural order that was strongly hierarchical and patriarchal. The state was modeled on the family, with the father as head of the household. The family, in turn, was a microcosm of the state and had to be kept in proper order, with all members playing their appropriate roles and showing each other appropriate deference and respect. To make the book relevant to our lives today, we must try to understand the book's imagery in the context of the society in which it was produced and transfer its insights to our own time. In the introduction to his translation of the *Yijing,* Richard Lynn notes that only if we understand the book's symbolism can we put its inegalitarian assumptions aside and let the work "address the primary issues with which it is concerned."[7] These include how character and destiny are interrelated, how "position defines the scope of action," how our position and our circumstances determine the right way to behave in any situation, how every person is tied to every other "in a web of interconnected causes and

7. Richard John Lynn, *The Classic of Changes: A New Translation of the I Ching as Interpreted by Wang Bi,* p. 9.

effects," how social organizations, power, and authority rise and fall, wax and wane, over time, and "how change itself is the great constant—and flexible response to it is the only key to happiness and success."[8] In the symbolism of the *Book of Changes*, we will find "a core of insights" about "the structure of human relationships and individual behavior that can . . . speak to this and any other age."[9]

Yin and Yang

The most basic symbolism in the *Book of Changes* is the association of broken and solid lines with yin and yang. The alternation of yin and yang represents the processes of change in the universe. Yin is constantly changing into yang and vice versa. Yang grows stronger until it reaches its maximum; then it turns into yin. The influence of yin grows until it can go no further, and then it turns into yang. The concepts of yin and yang represent the perpetual motion of things in the universe, and the continual flux of experience.

The original meanings of yang and yin were the bright and shady sides of a hill. Eventually, the two terms came to comprehend a great number of different oppositions:

Yin	Yang
feminine	masculine
negative	positive
yielding	firm
broken	solid
passive	active
acquiescent	dominating
receptive	dynamic
following	leading
subordinate	superordinate
small	large
petty	great
inferior	superior
dark	light
mundane	heavenly

8. Ibid.
9. Ibid.

rational	emotional
calm	excited
square	circle
heavy	light
body	soul

Associations of Yin and Yang

This list exemplifies the tendency of many cultures throughout the world to use sex differences as a master trope through which to categorize the world. The associations of yin and yang reflect the patriarchal nature of ancient Chinese society, although it is interesting to note that many of the associations with masculinity and femininity differ from those usually found in the West. The associations also reflect the strongly hierarchical nature of that society. Leaders were yang, followers were yin. Since everyone (except the emperor) was subordinate to someone, everyone was yin to someone else's yang. Thus, yin and yang are relational terms. Things are yin and yang in comparison to some other thing. The moon is yin in comparison to the sun, but the stars are yin in comparison to the moon.

Fixed and Changing Lines

Divination with the *Book of Changes* traditionally involves constructing a hexagram from some set of random events like throwing coins or collecting and dividing yarrow stalks. Chapter Five discusses many of the most popular methods of divination. At some point in the history of the book—we do not know precisely when—a distinction arose between fixed lines and changing lines. A changing (or moving) line changes into its opposite—solid (or yang) lines change to broken (or yin) lines, and vice versa. When the questioner receives a hexagram with changing lines, these lines turn into their opposites and a second hexagram is produced. In the following example, Hexagram 20, with two moving lines, changes into Hexagram 35:

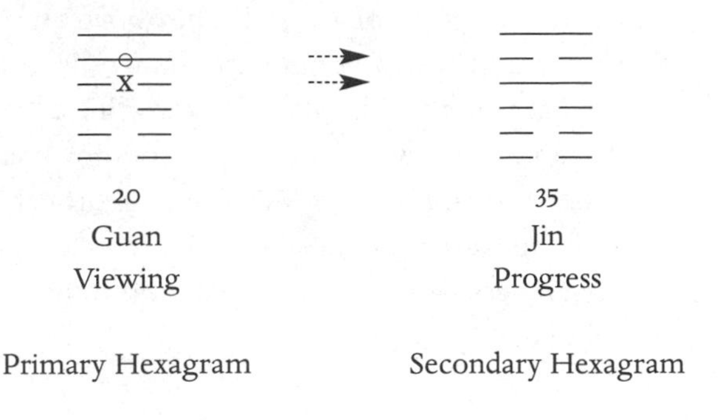

Moving or Changing Lines

In this case, the fourth and fifth lines are changing. As a shorthand, we can notate the transformation as follows:

20,4,5 ----➤ 35

The first hexagram is called the primary, or accomplished, hexagram and represents the present situation; the second one is called the secondary, or approached, hexagram and represents the future tendency or potential of the situation. The changing lines represent significant features of the old situation that produce this tendency.

In the above diagram the symbol —o— denotes a changing ("old") yang line; —x— denotes a changing ("old") yin line. The symbols ——— and — — represent fixed (or "young") yang and yin lines, respectively. By tradition, each type of line is assigned a number, called a *xiang* number. It is used primarily for purposes of divination, as described more fully in Chapter Five. Yin lines are even; yang lines are odd:

Type of line	Number
old (changing) yin	6
young (fixed) yang	7
young (fixed) yin	8
old (changing) yang	9

The texts of the primary hexagram, the changing lines, and the secondary hexagram are consulted to determine the meaning of the divination. Because line texts are ordinarily consulted only when they are changing (i.e., old yin or yang), the beginning of each line text reads "six" or "nine" depending on whether the line is yin or yang. In the above example involving Hexagram 20, the relevant line texts begin with the words "six in the fourth place" (a yin line) and "nine in the fifth place" (a yang line).

Because any line can, in theory, be a changing line, any hexagram can, in theory, change into any other hexagram. However, the probabilities of these changes vary. Some changes are more likely because the hexagrams differ by only one line; others are less likely because many or all of the lines would have to change simultaneously.

The Trigrams

Each hexagram can also be understood as composed of two constituent trigrams that consist of three lines. Because there are three lines and two different kinds of lines, there are 2^3 or eight possible trigrams. Because Chinese uses the same word *(gua)* to refer to both hexagrams and trigrams, the eight trigrams are sometimes called the *bagua* to distinguish them from the sixty-four hexagrams (*ba* means eight).

The eight trigrams are named after natural elements. They are Qian (Heaven), Kun (Earth), Zhen (Thunder), Kan (Water), Gen (Mountain), Xun (Wind or Wood), Li (Fire), and Dui (Lake).

Qian Heaven	Kun Earth	Zhen Thunder	Kan Water
Gen Mountain	Xun Wind, Wood	Li Fire	Dui Lake

The Eight Trigrams

Every hexagram can be constructed out of two trigrams. For example, Hexagram 32, Heng (Enduring), consists of Zhen (Thunder) on top of Xun (Wind or Wood), while Hexagram 26, Da Xu (Great Accumulation), consists of Gen (Mountain) on top of Qian (Heaven). The trigram on top is called the upper, or outer, trigram; the trigram on the bottom is called the lower, or inner, trigram. Together they are known as a hexagram's constituent trigrams.

Zhen (Thunder)	☳	(Upper) Outer trigram	☶	Gen (Mountain)
Xun (Wind, Wood)	☴	(Lower) Inner trigram	☰	Qian (Heaven)
Hexagram 32, Heng (Enduring)				Hexagram 26, Da Xu (Great Accumulation)

Inner and Outer Trigrams

Eight hexagrams are constructed out of a single trigram that is doubled. The Chinese names of the resulting hexagrams are the same as the trigrams, although the meanings are different. Thus, for example, Hexagram 30, Li (Radiance), consists of the trigram Li (Fire) doubled, and Hexagram 58, Dui (Joy), consists of the trigram Dui (Lake) doubled.

The Generation of the Trigrams and Hexagrams

According to the Great Treatise (the Fifth and Sixth of the Ten Wings), the trigrams and hexagrams are generated out of the alternation of yin and yang. In the beginning there is the Great Ultimate *(tai ji)*, an all-encompassing unity. The *tai ji* is usually symbolized by the familiar circle with two interlocking commas of black and white, representing yin and yang. The *tai ji* produces the two opposite tendencies of yin and yang, symbolized by a single broken or solid line.

Yin and yang can be subdivided into greater yang and lesser yang, lesser yin and greater yin. This is symbolized by adding a second line on top of the first line. Together, the two lines produce four possible images. By tradition, they are associated with the four seasons.

By adding a third line the four images produce the eight trigrams.[10] Each

10. The Great Treatise, I, xi, 5 (Lynn trans., pp. 65–66).

successive line doubles the number of possible combinations of yin and yang, so at each stage the possibilities increase by powers of two, from one to two, four, and then eight:

Tai Ji
(The Great Ultimate)

Yin				Yang			
Greater Yin (Winter)		Lesser Yang (Autumn)		Lesser Yin (Spring)		Greater Yang (Summer)	
Kun Earth	Gen Mountain	Kan Water	Xun Wind	Zhen Thunder	Li Fire	Dui Lake	Qian Heaven

Generation of the Trigrams

In fact, the structure of the trigrams and hexagrams can be represented in binary arithmetic. If we treat yin as 0 and yang as 1, then the eight trigrams are produced through binary counting from 000 to 111. The same is true of the hexagrams, which range from 000000 (representing Hexagram 2, Kun) to 111111 (representing Hexagram 1, Qian). (Further discussion of the connections between the *Book of Changes* and mathematics appears in the Appendix.)

The Meaning of the Trigrams

The interpretation of the sixty-four hexagrams has been strongly influenced by the meanings associated with their constituent trigrams. The authors of the Ten Wings were particularly fascinated by the trigrams, and the Eighth of the Ten Wings is devoted to a treatise about them. Over time, an entire body of thought sprang up concerning the meanings of the trigrams. Chinese scholars associated the eight trigrams with members of the family, times of year, animals, parts of the body, and so on. These associations, in turn, were used to create many other systems of thought, including systems of astrology, medicine, and geomancy (sometimes known as *feng shui*). Here is a partial list of the standard symbols and associations:

Note that the trigram representing the father has three yang lines and the trigram representing the mother has three yin lines. The trigrams for thc male children have two yin lines and one yang line, while the trigrams for the female children have two yang lines and one yin line. This is according to the symbolic idea that the one rules (or determines) the many. If we assign the number 3 to the yang lines and 2 to the yin lines, the sum of the lines for the mother is 6, for the male children 7, for the female children 8, and for the father 9. These correspond to the traditional *xiang* numbers used in divination: old yin (6), young yang (7), young yin (8), and old yang (9).

The Lines

The six lines of the hexagrams have also been given symbolic associations.

Generally speaking, the first line represents the beginning of a situation or endeavor, or the earliest stages of development. It may also represent someone who is still outside the situation and has not yet entered it. For the same reason, the first line also represents beginners. Socially, it refers to the lowest rank in an organization and the lowest rung of society. It is also associated with the feet, the big toe, or the tail.

Name	Element	Qualities	Family Member	Part of the Body	Animals	Season and Weather
Qian	Heaven	Creative, Dynamic, Strong	Father	Head, Mind	Horse	Early Winter, Cold, Ice
Kun	Earth	Receptive, Adaptive, Yielding	Mother	Belly, Womb	Cow	Early Autumn, Warm
Zhen	Thunder	Energetic, Arousing, Moving	Eldest Son	Foot	Dragon	Springtime, Earthquake
Kan	Water	Danger, Melancholy, Passion	Middle Son	Ear	Pig	Middle Winter, Cloudy
Gen	Mountain	Stillness, Tranquility, Stability	Youngest Son	Hand	Dog	Late Winter, Stillness
Xun	Wind, Wood	Gentle, Submissive, Persistent, Penetrating	Eldest Daughter	Thigh	Chicken	Early Summer, Mild Movement
Li	Fire	Clinging, Dependent, Brilliance, Clarity	Middle Daughter	Eye	Pheasant	Middle Summer, Lightning
Dui	Lake, Swamp	Joy, Pleasure, Satisfaction, Openness	Youngest Daughter	Mouth	Sheep	Late Autumn, Rain

Associations of the Eight Trigrams

The second line is the middle line in the lower trigram and is therefore usually considered auspicious. It represents the ordinary subject, slightly higher in the social hierarchy. As the central line in the lower trigram, it is considered the ruler of the lower trigram. Therefore, it often represents a government official or general who exercises authority far away from the capital city. Another frequent association is with women, wives, and the home.

The third line is the highest line of the lower trigram. It symbolizes the transition from the lower to the upper trigram. Socially, it represents someone who is trying to move from the rank of ordinary citizen into the higher ranks represented by the lines of the upper trigram. It therefore signifies unhappiness or discontent with one's situation. It also symbolizes the dangers and difficulties of trying to rise above one's station and making the perilous passage to the upper trigram. Generally speaking, the third line is not auspicious; often it refers to people who try to do something for which they are not adequately prepared or suited, or people who have difficulties dealing with change or with making a transition.

The fourth line is the lowest line of the upper trigram. Socially, it represents entry into government or a high position. Therefore, it is usually more auspicious than line three. It symbolizes the officer or minister who works closely with the ruler (symbolized by line five). Unlike line two, which is distant from the center of power (line five), the minister in line four directly supports the ruler. Thus it often symbolizes a person whose appropriate role is to subordinate his or her interests to those of the ruler.

The fifth line is the central line in the upper trigram. It is the place of the ruler. Usually, it is the most auspicious line in the hexagram. Often it states the hexagram's basic theme. It represents the culmination of an endeavor, or the moment of fruition. In families, it represents the head of the household, who was traditionally the husband.

The sixth line represents the time after culmination, when the situation described by the hexagram is ending, or when a person has gone beyond the situation or is outside it. Socially, it represents the sage or a person who has traveled beyond the ordinary conventions of society. It may also represent a person who has gone too far or reached too high, who has failed to recognize that times have changed, or who has failed to act when the moment was right. Because it comes at the end of a hexagram, the sixth line also sometimes represents a transition into the theme of the next hexagram. When the line represents the sage, or the end of an unfortunate situation, it is usually auspicious. When it represents a person who has gone too far or waited too long, or the end of a fortunate situation, it is usually inauspicious.

The six lines can represent the stages in a person's life:

Line six: Old age and death
Line five: Maturity and culmination
Line four: Middle age, career, and creation of a family
Line three: Adolescence and transition to adulthood
Line two: Childhood
Line one: Birth and infancy

They can also represent parts of the body of a human being or an animal:

Line six: The top of the head, the ears, or the horns of an animal
Line five: The head or the back of the neck, the nose or the mouth
Line four: The back or torso
Line three: The thigh, waist, or groin
Line two: The calves and ankles
Line one: The foot, the big toe, or an animal's tail

Still another set of associations holds that lines one and two represent earth, lines three and four represent humanity, and lines five and six represent heaven. Therefore, the lines symbolize a gradual ascent from mundane concerns to higher values:

Line six: Wisdom and egoless contemplation
Line five: Authority and rulership
Line four: Social consciousness and altruism
Line three: Ambition, striving, and individual endeavor
Line two: Rational self-interest
Line one: Instinct and emotion

Lines one and four, two and five, and three and six are *corresponding* lines. They are said to correspond because they have the same relative places in the upper and lower trigrams. In most cases, the lines in the center of a constituent trigram are the most auspicious and the lines in the upper trigram are usually more auspicious than the corresponding lines in the lower trigram. For this reason, the most auspicious line in a hexagram is usually line five, followed by lines two, four, one, six, and three, in that order. The third line is usually the least auspicious.

The relative placement of the lines can affect their auspiciousness. Generally speaking, a line tends to be more auspicious if it is central (i.e., in the second or fifth positions) and correctly placed (a yin line in an even-numbered position: two, four, or six; a yang line in an odd-numbered position: one, three, or five). A yin line in the fifth place is central but not correct; a yin line in the fourth place is correct but not central; and a yang line in the fifth place is both central and correct.

A line also tends to be more auspicious when its corresponding line is of the opposite kind; for example when a yang line in the fifth place corresponds to a yin lin in the second place. The traditional theories of why some hexagrams and some lines are more auspicious than others are discussed more fully in the historical materials in Chapter Six.

Ruling Lines

At least since Wang Bi's commentary in the third century A.D. (discussed in Chapter Six), each hexagram has been assigned one or more ruling lines. (The idea of ruling lines may date back even further to the time of the Ten Wings.) The ruling line states the hexagram's basic theme. The most common ruling line is the fifth line, but there are many exceptions. Generally speaking, if the hexagram has only one yin or yang line, that line is the ruler on the basis of the principle that the one rules the many. Thus the ruler of Hexagram 15, Qian (Modesty), is the third line.

There are two types of ruling lines, governing lines and constitutive lines. Governing lines are lines that state the hexagram's basic theme *and* are auspicious. These are ruling lines proper; when people speak of ruling lines without any further specification, they mean the governing line. In the commentaries in Part Two of this book, for example, governing lines are always referred to as ruling lines.

Constituting or constitutive lines occupy crucial positions that give the hexagram its basic theme; but they may or may not be auspicious. Hexagram 43, for example, features a single yin line that is being expelled by the five yang lines below it. The theme of the hexagram is resolution in the face of danger; so the top line is the constitutive line.

If the constitutive line is auspicious, it is also the governing line, and the hexagram has only one ruler. If the constitutive line is not auspicious (as in Hexagram 43), then the fifth line is usually designated as the governing ruler, and the hexagram has both a constitutive and a governing ruler. In a few cases there are two governing rulers, as in Hexagrams 19 or 31, or two constitutive rulers, as in Hexagram 33, and a few hexagrams have multiple constitutive rulers as well as multiple governing rulers. All of the governing and constitutive lines for each hexagram are identified in the commentaries in Part Two of this book.

CHAPTER FIVE

How to Consult the *Book of Changes*

Because the goal of consulting the *Book of Changes* is to open up a serious conversation with yourself, you should approach the task in the proper spirit. Imagine that you are having a conversation with a trusted advisor or friend. Be as courteous to the process as you would be to your friend. In general, the quality of the response you get from the *Book of Changes* depends on the quality of your purposes in consulting it.

Don't treat your consultation with the *Book of Changes* as a test of its predictive abilities. It does not predict the future. Rather, it stimulates you to think about the future (and about changes in your life) in creative ways. The *Book of Changes* offers the possibility of thinking outside the confines of your usual approach. It gives your unconscious mind an opportunity to say things out loud that you do not normally listen to or normally do not wish to hear.

Consulting the *Book of Changes* involves three basic steps:

- Formulating a question
- Choosing a hexagram (normally this is done at random)
- Interpreting the answer

Formulating a Question

Because the goal of divination is to stimulate creative thought, it is important to ask the right kind of question. Three very common kinds of questions are:

1. Whether to initiate or refrain from a proposed action (What to do)
2. How a certain situation will develop (What will happen)
3. How to judge a particular person or relationship (What someone is like)

Usually, the best questions are simple inquiries that are not either-or questions. Either-or questions presume that things are in one category or another, or that there are only two alternatives. The problem may be precisely that you have fallen into this way of characterizing the situation, and there is a third way you have not yet considered. Instead of asking, "Should I take the job in Montreal or stay in the bagel factory in Akron?" break the question into two parts and ask each separately. Remember that the goal is to stimulate your intuition and bring your unconscious understandings to the surface.

A question that uses the word "which," such as "Which car should I buy?" may look simple, but it already presupposes that you should buy a car. A better question would be "What is your advice about buying a car?"

A good way to frame the question is "What is your advice about X?"; "What will happen if X does Y?"; "I'd like to know about X"; or "I divine X." Here are some examples:

1. What will happen if I take the job in New York?
2. I'd like to know about my career prospects for the coming year.
3. Am I ready to get married?
4. I divine moving to Vermont.
5. What is your advice about opening a restaurant?
6. Should I apply to medical school?
7. What do you think of Mary?
8. What will happen if I change my major to biochemistry?
9. What is your view on my current difficulties with John?
10. Give me your advice on my relationship with my mother.

You can, of course, ask very open-ended questions such as "What should I do?" or "What lies ahead for my future?" However, asking a question this open-ended may not produce an answer that stimulates anything creative inside you. For that reason it is normally better to try to frame a more specific question. Nevertheless, if you are completely stuck, an open-ended question may sometimes help get your creative juices going and suggest a further question.

Some people cast a hexagram at the beginning of each day. If the point of this is to meditate on the meaning of the book through random selection, it seems perfectly reasonable. However, if it is an attempt to predict the day's events, it will probably be unhelpful. In retrospect, whatever hexagram you receive will probably conform to something that happened that day. A more enlightening approach is to choose a hexagram to think about during the day, like a daily Bible verse.

Choosing a Hexagram

There are many different ways to choose a hexagram. This chapter describes several of them. They produce different kinds of results. For example, some methods produce one, and only one, changing line; others can produce any number from zero to six. The probabilities of receiving a particular type of line can also differ. The two most well known methods—the yarrow-stalk and three-coin methods—produce different probabilities for changing lines. The very fact that so many different methods for choosing a hexagram exist, and that the different methods feature different probabilities and produce different numbers of changing lines, is perhaps the strongest argument that the real point of the *Book of Changes* is not prediction of the future but self-understanding and the stimulation of creative thought. If the *Book of Changes* were really about predicting the future, it would be important for every method to feature identical probabilities and produce identical results. But if the goal of the book is self-examination and self-cultivation, almost any randomized method for consulting the oracle will do.

In this section I describe one of the simplest methods: the six-coin method. The advantage of the six-coin method is that it produces one and only one moving line each time, and therefore it is easier to interpret than many other methods.

The Six-Coin Method

1. Take six coins. Five should be the same type, one should be of a different type. For example, you might use five pennies and a dime, or five nickels and a quarter.

2. Shake the coins in your hands as you think about your question.

3. Throw the coins on a flat surface in front of you.

4. Arrange the coins into a vertical column, with the coins that fell closest to you at the bottom and the coins that fell farthest away at the top. (If

two coins are equidistant from you, you may treat the coin on the left as beneath the coin on the right.)

5. Draw a hexagram corresponding to the position of the coins. The bottom coin is line one; the top coin is line six.

Heads are yang, or solid lines (———). Tails are yin lines, or broken lines (— —). The coin that is different from the others is the moving, or changing, line. If it is heads, it is a moving yang line (—o—). If it is tails, it is a moving yin line (—x—). For example, if the coins landed in the following order (the bottom coin is the one closest to you), you would draw the following hexagram:

Penny (Heads)	———
Penny (Heads)	———
Penny (Tails)	— —
Penny (Tails)	— —
Penny (Tails)	— —
Dime (Heads)	—o—

Drawing the Hexagram

6. Now identify the hexagram using the chart on page 58. (The chart can also be found at the back of this book.) Divide the hexagram into its upper and lower trigrams. (For the moment, you shouldn't worry about whether lines are fixed or changing. The key issue is whether the lines are yin or yang.)

The upper three lines are	——— ——— — —	or Xun (Wind, Wood)
and the lower three lines are	— — — — ———	or Zhen (Thunder).

The trigrams at the top of the chart list the possibilities for the upper trigram. Find the column that corresponds to the upper trigram. The trigrams on the left-hand side of the chart list the possibilities for the lower trigram. Find the row that corresponds to the lower trigram. The place where the row and column intersect is the hexagram number. Using the chart, you can see that the hexagram is Number 42, which is Yi, or Increase.

7. Next, look at the moving or changing line. In this case, the hexagram's first line is a moving line. When a hexagram has a moving line, it changes into its opposite. Yin becomes yang and yang becomes yin. Draw a second hexagram that takes into account the changing line.

Constructing the Second Hexagram

8. As before, look up the hexagram in the hexagram chart. The upper trigram is Xun (Wind, Wood). The lower trigram is Kun (Earth). The result is Hexagram 20, Guan (Viewing). Note that the second hexagram has no moving lines.

You can write the results as: 42,1 ----➤ 20.

Hexagram Chart

Trigrams upper ➤ lower ⮟	☰ Qian Heaven	☳ Zhen Thunder	☵ Kan Water	☶ Gen Mountain	☷ Kun Earth	☴ Xun Wind	☲ Li Fire	☱ Dui Lake
☰ Qian Heaven	1	34	5	26	11	9	14	43
☳ Zhen Thunder	25	51	3	27	24	42	21	17
☵ Kan Water	6	40	29	4	7	59	64	47
☶ Gen Mountain	33	62	39	52	15	53	56	31
☷ Kun Earth	12	16	8	23	2	20	35	45
☴ Xun Wind	44	32	48	18	46	57	50	28
☲ Li Fire	13	55	63	22	36	37	30	49
☱ Dui Lake	10	54	60	41	19	61	38	58

Interpreting the Answer

The six-coin method always yields an initial hexagram, a single changing line, and a second hexagram. To interpret the answer, read the hexagram judgment for the initial hexagram, and its associated commentaries. (In this book this includes the text called "The Image"—so called because it is taken from the Commentary on the Great Images, which forms part of the Third and Fourth of the Ten Wings.) The initial hexagram represents the basic elements of the present situation.

Next, read the text and commentary for the moving line. This represents the changes that are at work in the situation. (You should not consult the texts for any of the other lines, although you can read them if you are interested.)

Finally, read the hexagram judgment and associated commentaries for the second hexagram. (Do not read the line texts.) The second hexagram represents the future potential of the situation. Alternatively, it represents a deeper, background aspect of the situation that you should also keep in mind in interpreting the results.

Read the text and commentaries thoroughly and let the answers soak in. Try to apply them to your own situation and your own life experience. The commentaries explain the imagery of the text in relatively straightforward terms. However, the images and metaphors in the text—which are often vivid and unusual—may mean something different to you than the commentary suggests. If so, feel free to brainstorm with these ideas and associations. The Neo-Confucian philosopher Zhu Xi argued that the strange and oracular images in the text were more important than the principles derived from them because they stimulated thinking based on the questioner's personal history and experiences.

Try to approach the results with an open mind. You are trying to discover truths about yourself, not please yourself. Think of the *Book of Changes* as an advisor who has your best interests at heart. If you don't like the answer you receive, don't reject it out of hand. The answer may often be annoying or even infuriating, but the reason is often some conflict or hidden idea in yourself that the book is bringing out into the open. People who use the *Book of Changes* over time often report that they experience the book as if it were a wise and trusted friend who seems to know everything about them and will tell them the truth even if they don't particularly want to hear it. What is really going on, of course, is that you are tapping into your own understandings of the situation, including your unconscious. The goal of interpretation is to open a conversation with yourself about how best to understand your situation and how best to deal with changing circumstances in your life.

Sometimes the answer you receive will not seem germane to the question you have asked. If so, spend some time thinking about it. It may be relevant to some other issue that has been in the back of your mind. People often experience this as if the *Book of Changes* were saying, "You are asking me about X, but what you really want to know about is Y."

Generally speaking, it is not a good idea to ask the same question repeatedly within a short period of time. This will only produce a confusing array of answers. It is better to put the book aside and ask the question later. Obviously, you can keep throwing coins over and over again until you get the answer that you like, but you will learn nothing about yourself in this way (other than the fact that you don't like criticism or bad news).

A good way to pace yourself is to write down the question and the answers that you receive in a workbook. This will create a sort of journal or diary of the problems you have posed to yourself. You will probably discover that as you write out the answers, other ideas will naturally come to you. Write them down as well. Over time, you may come to discover a lot about yourself simply by recording your reactions to what the *Book of Changes* tells you.

All tools of divination can be misused. The *Book of Changes* is no exception. It is not a substitute for your own judgment. It is an aid to self-examination and self-cultivation. You should not question the *Book of Changes* repeatedly and obsessively—hoping that it will tell you what to do—instead of dealing with your emotional anxieties and confronting the situation realistically. It is not supposed to give ready answers to all the problems in your life. It is designed to stimulate you to think about them imaginatively and help you come to your own conclusions. If you find that you are consulting the *Book of Changes* too often, or for the wrong reasons, you should put the book away for a time. It is not designed to be a blueprint for your life or a cure-all for life's uncertainties. It is a tool for creative thinking, and should not become a crutch. If you become too dependent on it, or if you use it as a substitute for careful thought and rational judgment, you have missed the whole point of using it.

Other Methods of Consulting the Book of Changes

The remainder of this chapter lists a number of alternative ways of consulting the *Book of Changes*, beginning with the traditional method of consulting yarrow stalks. However, yarrow-stalk divination is quite complicated and elaborate, and readers who are not interested in the details should simply skip forward to the discussion of the more popular three-coin method.

Yarrow-Stalk Divination

The traditional method of consulting the *Book of Changes* was through manipulation of yarrow stalks. Yarrow can grow very tall, perhaps up to three feet high. However, for ease of use the stalks should be cut to about a foot in length. In fact, you can use any set of thin sticks to perform the divination, even drinking straws or toothpicks.

The Great Treatise gives a brief (and incomplete) description of divination with yarrow stalks in a chapter called *Dayan*. Since that time, many different people have offered theories about how the divination was actually performed. In the twelfth century A.D. the Neo-Confucian philosopher Zhu Xi wrote his own account of what the proper method should be. We have no way of knowing whether it was the actual method used during the time that the *Zhouyi* (or the Ten Wings) was written, but it has become the traditional and standard method of yarrow-stalk manipulation to this day.

Zhu Xi's Method

Casting a hexagram using Zhu Xi's method is a laborious process that can take up to a half an hour to complete. Each line requires three separate rounds of counting.

The divination begins with 50 stalks. One of the 50 stalks is purely ceremonial, and it is immediately set aside, leaving 49. (When stalks are set aside, you may place them in a basket or canister to keep them from being mixed in with the remaining stalks in the process.)

First Round of Counting

1. Divide the 49 stalks randomly into two bunches, placing them on the table in front of you.

2. Take one stalk from the right-hand bunch and place it between the ring finger and little finger of your left hand.

3. Take the left-hand bunch in your left hand. Use your right hand to take away stalks in groups of 4 until 4 or fewer stalks remain. Place the remainder

from the left-hand bunch between the ring finger and middle finger of your left hand.

4. Take the right-hand bunch in your left hand. Once again, use your right hand to take away stalks in groups of 4 until 4 or fewer stalks remain. Place the remainder from the right-hand bunch between the middle finger and index finger of your left hand.

5. You should now have stalks between all of the fingers of your left hand. Count them. There are four possibilities:

1+4+4

1+3+1

1+2+2

1+1+3

These add up to either 9 or 5. You may disregard the single stalk between the ring and little fingers. The numbers now add up to 8 or 4.

6. If the number is 8, write down 2. If the number is 4, write down 3. (Note that if you have correctly counted the first, or left hand bunch, the counting of the second, or right-hand bunch, should be unnecessary. If the remainder for the first bunch is 4, the remainder for the right-hand bunch must also be 4, and the number you must write down is 2. If the remainder for the first bunch is 1, 2, or 3, then the remainder for the right-hand bunch will be 3, 2, or 1, and the number you must write down is 3.)

Now take all the stalks from your left hand and put them aside.

Second Round of Counting

7. Now take up the remaining stalks that you counted out in groups of 4. You should now have either 44 or 40 stalks left. Divide them randomly into two bunches.

Take one stalk from the right-hand bunch and place it between the ring finger and the little finger of your left hand.

8. Take the left-hand bunch in your left hand. Use your right hand to take away stalks in groups of 4 until 4 or fewer stalks remain. Place the remainder from the left-hand bunch between the ring finger and the middle finger of your left hand.

9. Take the right-hand bunch in your left hand. Once again, use your right hand to take away stalks in groups of 4 until 4 or fewer stalks remain. Place the remainder from the right-hand bunch between the middle finger and index finger of your left hand.

10. You should now have stalks between all of the fingers of your left hand. Count them. There are four possibilities:

1+4+3

1+3+4

1+1+2

1+2+1

These add up to either 8 or 4.

11. If the number is 8, write down 2. If the number is 4, write down 3. (Note once again that if you have correctly counted the left-hand bunch, the counting of the right-hand bunch should be unnecessary. If the remainder is 4 or 3, the remainder for the right-hand bunch must be 3 or 4, and the number you must write down is 2. If the remainder is 1 or 2, then the remainder for the right-hand bunch will be 2, or 1, and the number you must write down is 3.)

Now put all the stalks in your left hand aside.

Third Round of Counting

12. Now take up the remaining stalks that you counted out in groups of 4. You should now have either 40, 36, or 32 stalks left. Divide them randomly into two bunches.

Take one stalk from the right-hand bunch, and place it between the ring finger and the little finger of your left hand.

13. Take the left-hand bunch in your left hand. Use your right hand to take away stalks in groups of 4 until 4 or fewer stalks remain. Place the remainder from the left-hand bunch between the ring finger and the middle finger of your left hand.

14. Take the right-hand bunch in your left hand. Once again, use your right hand to take away stalks in groups of 4 until 4 or fewer stalks remain. Place the remainder from the right-hand bunch between the middle finger and the index finger of your left hand.

15. You should now have stalks between all of the fingers of your left hand. Count them. There are four possibilities:

1+4+3

1+3+4

1+1+2

1+2+1

These add up to either 8 or 4.

16. If the number is 8, write down 2. If the number is 4, write down 3. (As before, if you have correctly counted the left-hand bunch, the counting of the right-hand bunch should be unnecessary. If the remainder is 4 or 3, the remainder for the right-hand bunch must be 3 or 4, and the number you must write down is 2. If the remainder is 1 or 2, then the remainder for the right-hand bunch will be 2, or 1, and the number you must write down is 3.)

17. Add the three numbers you have written down. The result will tell you what kind of line you have:

Number	Type of Line	Symbol	Probability
6	old yin	—x—	1/16
7	young yang	——	5/16
8	young yin	— —	7/16
9	old yang	—o—	3/16

This is line one of the hexagram. Repeat the process to produce the other lines.

A Modern Version of Yarrow-Stalk Divination

The complexity of Zhu Xi's method readily demonstrates why the coin method became so popular. Some scholars have offered a different and streamlined version of the yarrow-stalk method,[11] which focuses on the groups of 4 counted rather than the remainders, and uses only the result of the third count:

1. Begin with 49 yarrow stalks.
2. Divide the yarrow into two piles at random.
3. Take one from the left pile and set it aside.
4. Take the left pile and remove 4 stalks at a time until the result is 4 or less. Set aside this remainder. Repeat the process for the right-hand pile and set aside the remainder.
5. Gather up all the stalks counted in groups of 4, but do not include the remainders from the left- and right-hand piles. You should now have either 44 or 40 stalks. Three-fourths of the time you will have 44, and ¼ of the time you will have 40.

11. See Kerson Huang and Rosemary Huang, I Ching, pp. 67–68.

6. Repeat Steps 2 through 4, setting aside the remainders. Gather up all the stalks counted in groups of 4, but do not include the remainders. This will leave you with either 40, 36, or 32 stalks. Three-eighths of the time you will have 40, 4/8 of the time you will have 36, and 1/8 of the time you will have 32.

7. Repeat Steps 2 through 4, again setting aside the remainders. Gather up all the stalks counted in groups of 4, but do not include the remainders. This will leave you with either 36, 32, 28, or 24 stalks. Three-sixteenths of the time you will have 36, 7/16 of the time you will have 32, 5/16 of the time you will have 28, and 1/16 of the time you will have 24.

8. Divide the number of stalks by 4. This will tell you what kind of line you have:

Number	Type of Line	Symbol	Probability
6	old yin	—x—	1/16
7	young yang	——	5/16
8	young yin	— —	7/16
9	old yang	—o—	3/16

This is line one. Repeat the process to produce lines two through six.

The Three-Coin Method

The three-coin method developed as a substitute for yarrow-stalk divination, which was time-consuming and laborious. It was probably first used in the Tang and Song Dynasties sometime between 600 and 1200 A.D. It is probably the most popular method for consulting the *Book of Changes* today.

1. Take three coins. You can use traditional Chinese coins, which have a square hole in the center; the blank side is heads and the inscribed side is tails. However, you can also use ordinary coins of any size.

2. Shake the coins in your hand as you meditate on your question.

3. Throw the coins onto a flat surface.

4. Heads count as 3; tails count as 2. The sum total will be a number between 6 and 9. This tells you the nature of line one of the hexagram:

Number	Type of Line	Symbol	Probability[12]
6 (three tails)	old yin	—x—	1/8
7 (two tails, one head)	young yang	———	3/8
8 (two heads, one tail)	young yin	— —	3/8
9 (three heads)	old yang	—o—	1/8

Repeat the process to construct the remaining lines of the hexagram moving upward from line two to line six.

Note that the three-coin method, like the yarrow-stalk method, can produce one or many moving lines or none at all.

The traditional yarrow-stalk method produces different probabilities than the three-coin method. In the yarrow-stalk method the probability of receiving an old (or changing) yin line is 1/16, and the probability of young (fixed) yin is 7/16. The probability of receiving an old yang is 3/16 and the probability of young yang is 5/16. For this reason many people prefer to use methods that produce the same probabilities as the yarrow-stalk method.

Many people think that the coin method is somehow defective or inauthentic because its probabilities differ from the yarrow-stalk method. This is incorrect. Divination with yarrow stalks is probably older than divination with coins. However, there is no reason to think that the particular form of the yarrow-stalk method that has come down to us is authentic to the period in which the *Zhouyi* was written. (For example, the use of the numbers six and nine to represent moving yin and yang lines is probably a later innovation.) We do not even know whether the traditional method is authentic to the period in which the Ten Wings were written, although by that point the numbers six through nine had probably become associated with the different forms of yin and yang lines.

Similarly there is no reason to think that the probabilities produced by the traditional yarrow-stalk method are more "correct" or authentic to that era. Many scholars believe that the techniques of yarrow-stalk divination discussed in the Zuo Commentary (which dates from the Warring States pe-

12. The probability of either heads and tails is ½, so the probabilities are:
$P(6)= P(2+2+2) = \frac{1}{2} \times \frac{1}{2} \times \frac{1}{2} = \frac{1}{8}$
$P(7)= P(2+2+3) + P(2+3+2) + P(3+2+2) = \frac{3}{8}$
$P(8)= P(3+3+2) + P(3+2+3) + P(2+3+3) = \frac{3}{8}$
$P(9)= P(3+3+3) = \frac{1}{2} \times \frac{1}{2} \times \frac{1}{2} = \frac{1}{8}$

riod) were importantly different from what we now call the "traditional" yarrow-stalk approach.[13] It is likely that the traditional method we have is about as old as the coin method, so neither set of probabilities can be said to be more authentic.

The Two-Coin Method

The two-coin method produces probabilities identical to the traditional yarrow-stalk method but has the extra advantage of being extremely simple to use. It also can yield any number of changing lines.[14]

1. Toss two coins on the table. If both coins are tails, the result is 2. Otherwise the result is 3.

2. Throw the two coins again. Heads are 3; tails are 2. If you received two heads, the result is 6. If you received a head and a tail, the result is 5. If you received two tails, the result is 4.

3. Add the results of the first and second throws. The total will be 6, 7, 8 or 9. This tells you what kind of line you have:

Number	Type of Line	Symbol	Probability[15]
6	old yin	—x—	1/16
7	young yang	——	5/16
8	young yin	— —	7/16
9	old yang	—o—	3/16

Repeat the process to produce the other lines of the hexagram.

13. For a discussion, see Richard Rutt, *The Book of Changes (Zhouyi)*, pp. 160, 170–75; Gregory Whincup, *Rediscovering the I Ching*, pp. 228–29.
14. The method described here is adapted from the clarityonline Web site (http://www.onlineclarity.co.uk/).
15. The probability of 2 in the first throw is ¼; the probability of getting a 3 is ¾. The probability of getting a 4 in the second throw is ¼; the probability of getting a 5 is ½; and the probability of getting a 6 is ¼. Therefore the probabilities of the sum totals are:
$P(6)= P(2+4) = \frac{1}{4} \times \frac{1}{4} = \frac{1}{16}$
$P(7)= P(2+5) + P(3+4) = (\frac{1}{4} \times \frac{1}{2}) + (\frac{3}{4} \times \frac{1}{4}) = \frac{2}{16} + \frac{3}{16} = \frac{5}{16}$
$P(8)= P(2+6) + P(3+5) = (\frac{1}{4} \times \frac{1}{4}) + (\frac{3}{4} \times \frac{1}{2}) = \frac{1}{16} + \frac{3}{8} = \frac{1}{16} + \frac{6}{16}= \frac{7}{16}$
$P(9)= P(3+6) = \frac{3}{4} \times \frac{1}{4} = \frac{3}{16}$

The Method of Sixteen

This method also duplicates the yarrow-stalk probabilities.[16] It involves 16 objects of similar size but different colors: They can be marbles, shells, or pebbles. Choose 7 objects of color A, 5 of color B, 3 of color C, and 1 of color D. Each color will represent a different kind of line: Color A is young yin, color B is young yang, color C is old yang, and color D is old yin.

Place the 16 objects in a cloth bag. Shake the bag while thinking about your question. Randomly draw out one object, record the line it corresponds to, and place it back in the bag. This is line one of the hexagram. Repeat the process to construct the remaining lines.

Divination with Playing Cards

You can reproduce the same probabilities as the yarrow-stalk method using an ordinary deck of playing cards. One advantage of using playing cards rather than coins is that one can meditate on the question while shuffling the deck. Here is what to do:

1. Take an ordinary deck of playing cards. Remove any jokers and extra cards.

2. Shuffle the cards thoroughly.

3. Take a card at random from the deck. It the card is a club, the result is 2. Otherwise the result is 3. Return the card to the deck and once again shuffle the deck thoroughly.

4. Take a card at random from the deck.

If the card is red (a heart or a diamond), the result is 5.

If the card is a club, the result is 4.

If the card is a spade, the result is 6.

Add the two results together to get the number 6, 7, 8, or 9, which corresponds to old yin, young yang, young yin, and old yang, respectively. This is line one. Return the card to the deck.

5. Repeat steps 2 through 4 to construct the remaining lines of the hexagram.

A second method allows you to draw a single card to determine each line. It uses only 48 cards.

16. The method described here is taken from Larry Schoenholtz, *New Directions in the I Ching,* pp. 81–85. It is also described in Gregory Whincup, *Rediscovering the I Ching,* pp. 227–28.

1. Take an ordinary deck of playing cards. Remove any jokers and extra cards. Then remove all four kings. This will reduce the size of the deck to 48 cards.

2. Shuffle the deck thoroughly. Spread the cards out on the table and pick one at random.

3. If the card is red, it is a yang line.

If the card is a heart, or the 10, jack, or queen of diamonds, it is a young yang line (7).

If the card is the ace–9 of diamonds, it is an old yang line (9).

If the card is black, it is a yin line.

If the card is a spade, or the ace–9 of clubs, it is a young yin line (8).

If the card is the 10, jack, or queen of clubs, it is an old yin line (6).

4. Replace the card in the deck. (This is very important in order to ensure the correct probabilities.)

5. Repeat steps 2 through 4 until you have constructed a complete six-line hexagram.

Here is a simple version that duplicates the probabilities in the three-coin method:

1. As before, remove any jokers and extra cards, and all four kings, to reduce the size of the deck to 48 cards.

2. Shuffle the deck thoroughly. Spread the cards out on the table and pick one at random.

3. If the card is red, it is a yang line.

If the card has the value of 10 (i.e., it is a 10, jack, or queen), it is an old yang line (9).

Otherwise it is a young yang line (7).

If the card is black, it is a yin line.

If the card has the value of 10 (i.e., it is a 10, jack, or queen), it is an old yin line (6).

Otherwise it is a young yin line (8).

4. Replace the card in the deck.

5. Repeat steps 2 through 4 until you have constructed a complete six-line hexagram.

Finally, here is a version that produces a single moving line:

1. As before, remove jokers, extra cards, and all four kings.

2. Shuffle the deck thoroughly. Spread the cards out on the table and pick one at random.

3. If the card is red, it is a yang line.
If the card is black, it is a yin line.

4. Replace the card in the deck.

5. Repeat steps 2 through 4 until you have constructed a complete six-line hexagram from the bottom to the top.

6. Now shuffle the cards one more time and pick a card at random. If the card is

ace or 2, the first line is moving;
3 or 4, the second line is moving;
5 or 6, the third line is moving;
7 or 8, the fourth line is moving;
9 or 10, the fifth line is moving;
jack or queen, the sixth line is moving.

How to Interpret the Results When There Is More Than One Moving Line

The six-coin method always produces one and only one moving line. With other methods of divination, the number of moving lines varies so the method of interpretation is slightly more complicated.

The Standard Approach

1. When there are no moving lines, read the hexagram judgment but not any of the moving lines. If you need additional insights, you may also read the hexagram's ruling line, which usually states its basic theme.

2. When your divination produces one or more moving lines, read the hexagram judgment and all of the changing-line statements. Finally, read the hexagram judgment for the secondary hexagram that results from changing all the lines.

Normally, the primary hexagram represents the present situation and the secondary hexagram represents future tendencies. However, the two hexagrams can be related in other ways as well. For example, the secondary hexagram can refer to a deeper or more basic feature of the situation, the background context of the situation, or the way that the questioner relates to the situation.

Nuclear Hexagrams

In addition, some people like to consult the nuclear hexagram, which is formed from the four middle lines of any hexagram received in a divination. The nuclear hexagram is composed of the lower nuclear trigram, consisting of lines two, three, and four of the original hexagram, and the upper nuclear trigram, consisting of lines three, four, and five. Putting the two together yields a new hexagram, which offers additional insights into the situation.

For example, the nuclear trigrams of Hexagram 32 form Hexagram 43:

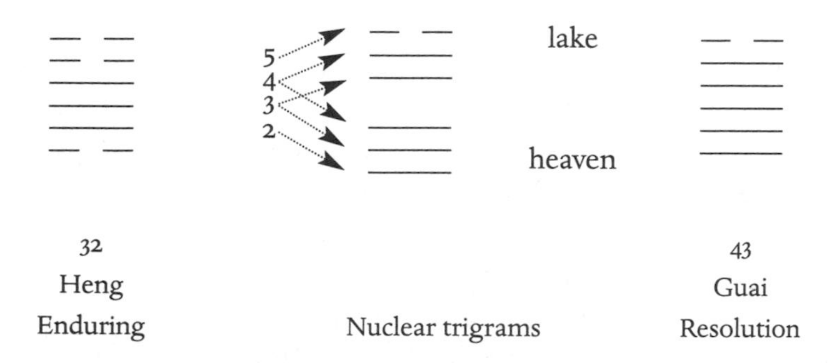

Forming a Nuclear Hexagram

Simplifying the Process

When there are several moving lines, the standard approach can be very confusing because the different line statements can point in opposite directions. There are several solutions to this problem. One solution is to interpret the line statements as describing successive situations that occur one after the other, from bottom to top. These lead ultimately to the result in the secondary hexagram.

Another popular solution is to adopt a convention for choosing which line to read. Here is a set of procedures offered by Alfred Huang:[17]

1. If there are two moving lines, one yin and one yang, consult the yin line.
2. If both moving lines are yin or yang, consult the lower one.
3. If there are three moving lines, consult the middle one.
4. If there are four moving lines, consult the upper of the two nonmoving lines.

17. Alfred Huang, *The Complete I Ching*, p. 17.

5. If there are five moving lines, consult the nonmoving line.

6. If there are six moving lines (and you are not dealing with Hexagrams 1 or 2), consult the hexagram created from changing all of them.

7. In the case of Hexagrams 1 or 2, consult the special seventh line for when all lines are changing.[18]

Other Techniques of Divination with the Book of Changes

Although most types of divination use some form of random selection, there are other ways to consult the *Book of Changes*. For example, the Plum Blossom method tries to read omens from naturally occurring events and associates them with trigrams in order to construct hexagrams. This system is described in detail in *The Tao of I Ching: Way to Divination* (1984), by Jou Tsung Hwa. There are also several systems of Chinese astrology associated with the *Book of Changes*. One of them is described in *The Astrology of I Ching* (1976), by W. A. Sherrill and W. K. Chu. These alternative systems of divination are well beyond the scope of this book.

Thomas Cleary offers a greatly simplified version of the Plum Blossom method. He suggests that one should choose hexagrams based on the traditional associations of their constituent trigrams.[19] From the list below, select two qualities that symbolize the situation you are facing—either the dominant forces at work, the nature of the environment or circumstances, or the personality and characteristics of the people involved. Then combine the two trigrams that are associated with those qualities to form a hexagram. Normally, this method will produce two hexagrams, because each of the

18. In *An Anthology of I Ching* (London: Routledge & Kegan Paul, 1977), pp. 27–28, W. K. Chu and W. A. Sherrill offer the following system:

1. When two lines are moving, consult both lines but take the upper line as more important.
2. When three lines are moving, consult all three lines but take the middle line as most important.
3. When four lines are moving, consult all the moving lines but give the greatest weight to the two unmoving lines in the secondary or approached hexagram—the hexagram that results from changing the moving lines. As between those two lines, the lower one is the more important.
4. When five lines are moving, consult all the moving lines but give the greatest weight to the single unmoving line in the secondary or approached hexagram.
5. When all six lines are moving, consult all the moving lines but make the evaluation based on the judgment for the secondary or approached hexagram.

19. This method is described by Thomas Cleary in the introduction to his translation, *I Ching: The Book of Change* (Boston and London: Shambhala, 1992), pp. xiv–xv.

Trigram Name	Symbol	Qualities
Qian (Heaven)	☰	Father, strength, creativity, dynamism
Zhen (Thunder)	☳	Oldest son, initiative, shock, action, arousal
Kan (Water)	☵	Middle son, passion, danger
Gen (Mountain)	☶	Youngest son, stillness, stopping
Kun (Earth)	☷	Mother, receptiveness, docility, nurturance
Xun (Wind, Wood)	☴	Oldest daughter, gentleness, penetration, submission
Li (Fire)	☲	Middle daughter, clarity, interdependence, enlightenment
Dui (Lake)	☱	Youngest daughter, joy, communication

Trigram Characteristics

two trigrams can serve as either the upper or lower trigram of a hexagram. However, if only one trigram adequately describes the situation, the resulting hexagram will simply be that trigram doubled.

For example, suppose you believed that the present situation involved danger and the need for clarity. Then you should read Hexagrams 63 (Water over Fire) and 64 (Fire over Water). If the situation involves a conflict that arises out of failure of communication and lack of patience, you might read Hexagrams 31 (Lake over Mountain) and 41 (Mountain over Lake). This trigram method involves a certain element of chance, because when you combine the two trigrams, the pair of hexagrams produced may take you quite far from your original problem. For this reason, the trigram method is probably best understood as yet another form of random consultation.

Consulting the Book of Changes *Without Randomly Selecting a Hexagram*

It is also possible to consult the *Book of Changes* purely as a book of wisdom without using random selection or other divinatory techniques. For example, you might decide to read and meditate on one hexagram a day. In a little over two months' time you will have gone through the cycle and can start again if you like.

If you already know what sort of situation you are facing, you can simply consult the hexagram judgment that is closest to that situation. The *Book of Changes* is designed to give relevant advice based on the situation you choose. If you are in a position of enormous power and do not know how to proceed, you should read Hexagram 34 (Great Power); if you feel oppressed, read Hexagram 47 (Oppression). When you do so, you might also wish to read the text for the ruling line, which ordinarily states the hexagram's basic theme. Used in this way, the *Book of Changes* can be a useful (and quotable) way to analyze everyday problems.

It is always possible that more than one hexagram seems relevant to your circumstances. If so, consult each of them to see which you think offers the most appropriate advice. But if too many hexagrams seem equally relevant, you probably should choose a hexagram using one of the traditional methods of divination.

If you believe that you already know what sort of situation you are currently facing, and would like advice about how to change it into a situation you would prefer, you can read both the hexagram judgment that describes your present situation and the judgments for each of the lines that would have to change in order to convert the hexagram into a new hexagram of your choice. For example, suppose you wanted to move from a situation of Oppression (Hexagram 47) to one of Peace (Hexagram 11). Then you would read the hexagram judgment for Hexagram 47 as well as lines one, three, four, and five:

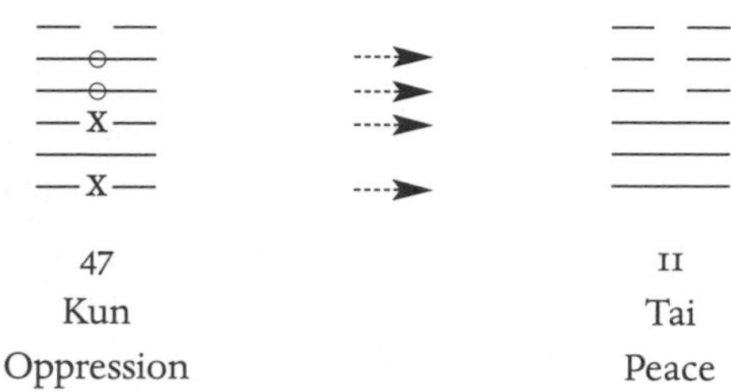

Choosing Lines Necessary to Produce a Second Hexagram

Although the *Book of Changes* can be usefully consulted without random selection, divination has always been a more popular practice. There are three reasons for this. First, the book began as a divinatory text and it has traditionally been understood as one. Second, many people prefer a more mystical approach in which the book appears to speak directly to them. The third reason, however, is the most important. Life is often simply very complicated, and it is often quite difficult to know how to characterize events. The best reason to choose a hexagram at random is that you do not know what sort of situation you are facing. Moreover, a great advantage of random consultation is that it opens you up to possibilities and perspectives on the situation that you may not have thought of. The *Book of Changes* teaches that one must adjust one's self to the nature of the time. Rest assured that if you already know enough about the nature of the time to pick the most relevant hexagram, you are already well ahead of the game.

CHAPTER SIX

A Short History of the *Book of Changes*

The history of the *Book of Changes* is, in many ways, the history of China itself. Until the twentieth century there was a widely accepted story about the origins of the book. Archeological findings in the last century have caused us to revise this story considerably. However, to understand what the book meant to its interpreters throughout most of its history, we must understand this myth.

The Mythological History of the Book of Changes

According to the standard story, the origins of the *Book of Changes* begin with the legendary emperor Fu Xi, who is said to have lived in the third millennium B.C. (Many other dates have been offered as well.) The Chinese traditionally explained the development of civilization by ascribing certain inventions and innovations to great and noble rulers of the distant past. Thus, Fu Xi is not only an emperor but also a culture hero: he is said to have invented writing, marriage, herding, netting, weaving, and the cooking of meat.

Most important for our purposes, Fu Xi is also credited with the invention of the trigrams. According to the Great Treatise that forms part of the Ten Wings, when Fu Xi ruled the world, he looked up and studied the heavens, then looked down and studied the forms of things on the earth. He observed the appearances of birds and beasts and how they lived in their habitats, and the nature of things within him and without him, both near and far. He then invented the eight trigrams in order to communicate with the spirits and classify and order the world.

Another part of the Great Treatise credits Fu Xi with inventing the hexagrams as well, and there is an elaborate but unconvincing account of how people got the idea for any number of useful inventions through copying the structure of the hexagrams. But in most versions of the legend the hexagrams were invented thousands of years later by King Wen, the founder of the Zhou Dynasty, which took power sometime in the eleventh century B.C. The Zhou were originally vassals of the previous Shang Dynasty (c. 1560 B.C.–c.1050 B.C. [trad. 1766 B.C.–1122 B.C.]), which had unified significant portions of what we now know as China and ruled for hundreds of years. King Wen, the leader of the Zhou, was an advisor to the last Shang king, the evil tyrant Dixin. Dixin became suspicious of King Wen, accused him of treason, and threw him in jail. According to the story, while languishing in prison King Wen hit upon the idea of doubling Fu Xi's trigrams to create sixty-four hexagrams. He then wrote the hexagram judgments to explain their meaning. Later, after the Zhou had overthrown the Shang, King Wen's son, the Duke of Zhou, one of the greatest statesmen in Chinese history, wrote the line statements. Finally, hundreds of years later, the great philosopher Confucius wrote the set of commentaries known as the Ten Wings. According to legend, Confucius was greatly enamored of the *Zhouyi* as a book of wisdom and wore out the leather binders of his copy three times from constant study.[20]

According to this legend, then, the *Book of Changes* was the product of four of the greatest figures in Chinese civilization: Fu Xi, King Wen, the Duke of Zhou, and Confucius. And according to the legend, the trigrams were invented first, then the hexagrams, then the hexagram judgments, and finally the line statements.

Almost everything in this story is probably incorrect. First, the earliest parts of the *Zhouyi* are probably the line statements, which seem to come from proverbs and familiar sayings that were attached to the hexagram lines in order to explain the results of divination. The hexagram names were probably invented after the hexagrams themselves as a sort of cataloging system. The *Zhouyi* says nothing about the trigrams, but we know that they became quite important in the Ten Wings. This suggests that the trigrams were among the last elements to develop in understanding the core text.

20. This is according to the statement of Sima Qian in the *Records of the Grand Historian (Shi Ji)*, chap. 47.

As for the authorship of the text, there is no reason to think that Fu Xi is anything other than a legend. King Wen and the Duke of Zhou were certainly real people, but it is more likely that the line statements and line judgments were collected over an extended period of time and put together long afterward, probably around 800 B.C. Finally, throughout much of its early history the *Zhouyi* was a diviner's manual for kings. Very few copies of the work existed, and the few copies that were available would probably have been quite expensive, and therefore unlikely to be in the hands of an itinerant philosopher like Confucius. So the story of Confucius wearing out three sets of bindings for the book is almost certainly fictional. We do not know how well Confucius knew the *Zhouyi* or even whether he knew it at all. There is a famous passage in the *Analects* in which Confucius seems to say that if a few more years were added to his life, he would devote them to the study of the *Changes*, and then he would be free from error. However, many commentators regard this to be either a misinterpretation of the passage or the result of an emendation by a later hand.[21] In any case, there is almost no evidence that Confucius wrote the Ten Wings, and the overwhelming evidence is that he did not. What does seem to be clear is that his followers took the work to heart, so that Confucian ideas appear in the Ten Wings and they permeate all of the interpretations that were subsequently made of the *Book of Changes*.

The Changes of the Zhou

Although the legends surrounding the origins of the *Book of Changes* are mostly fiction, the actual facts—as we now understand them—are if anything even more interesting. The core of the book—the *Zhouyi*—is a Bronze Age diviner's manual. Its primary concern is not ethics or the good life but offering advice to kings about whether to form alliances, conduct expedi-

21. *Analects* VII.17. This passage (numbered as VII.16) is translated by Wing-Tsit Chan as: "Give me a few more years so that I can devote fifty years to the study of Change. I may be free from great mistakes." *A Source Book in Chinese Philosophy*, trans. and ed. Wing-Tsit Chan, (Princeton: Princeton University Press, 1963), p. 32. D. C. Lau reads the word *yi* (change) as a particle *yi* meaning "and" and therefore translates the passage as "Grant me a few more years so that I may study at the age of fifty and I shall be free from major errors." Confucius, *The Analects*, trans. D. C. Lau (Harmondsworth, Middlesex, U.K.: Penguin Books, 1979), p. 88. In XIII.22, Confucius appears to refer to 32.3: "He who does not give duration to his character / May meet with disgrace." However, Confucius may have been quoting an old saying that also happens to appear in the *Zhouyi*. See the discussion in Richard Rutt, *The Book of Changes (Zhouyi)*, pp. 33–34.

tions, build cities, and begin wars. Chinese kings did not seek moral instruction from their diviners. They wanted to know about the weather, the quality of the harvest, the success of a hunting party, the meaning of a dream, the health of the royal family, the success or failure of their enemies, and the likelihood of receiving tribute.

The name *Zhouyi* means "Changes of the Zhou." It is named after the Zhou, the third of China's Bronze Age dynasties. The earliest was the Xia Dynasty, about whom little is known. They were succeeded by the Shang, whom the Zhou eventually overthrew. There is a tradition that *Zhouyi* is so named because there was also a changes of the Shang, called *Guicang* and a changes of the Xia, called *Lianshan*.[22] According to the story, the Xia oracle began with what is now Hexagram 52 (Gen, Keeping Still) and the Shang oracle began with what is now Hexagram 2 (Kun, The Receptive). This story is likely a legend designed to establish a symmetry between the three earliest dynasties. A third-century text of the *Guicang* was discovered in 1993, but we do not know whether this text really dates from Shang times. More likely, there were probably several different systems of divination using line figures during the Zhou Dynasty, many of which were spawned by the *Zhouyi* itself, and some of these may have been attributed to the earlier dynasties.

The earliest evidence we have of divination practices are oracle bones dating from the Shang Dynasty. These consisted of turtle shells and the shoulder bones of oxen. The Shang priests practiced pyromancy (fire divination). They would make knife cuts on a turtle shell or ox bone and then heat it with a red-hot poker until it cracked. They would then inspect the cracks to determine the augury, often writing the question asked, the prognostication, and the results on the shell or bone. Shang divinations were usually tied to sacrificial rites, in which human sacrifice often played a part. Large numbers of captives might be killed in a single sacrifice. The later Shang kings were particularly known for their cruelty and extravagance.

Among the Shang's vassals were the Zhou, a relatively backward nation centered in the western part of China on the fringes of the Shang territory. They prided themselves on their uprightness and simple virtue in contrast to the extravagant and worldly Shang. The Shang in turn depended on the Zhou to conduct their military expeditions. During the reign of the pen-

22. The report of the three systems of divination comes from the *Zhouli*, a history of the rites of the Zhou court, written during the Warring States period, and by the Later Han commentator Zheng Xuan (127–200), as quoted by the Tang commentator Kong Yingda (574–648). See Rutt, *The Book of Changes (Zhouyi)*, p. 27.

ultimate Shang emperor, King Diyi, the Zhou leader, a nobleman named Chang, became extremely influential and powerful. Today, Chang is known by his posthhumous title of King Wen. Apparently, Chang proved to be a particularly able general, and during King Diyi's reign he became the military commander of the Shang forces in the western part of the empire. Diyi even gave Chang one of his daughters to marry. This event is described at two places in the *Zhouyi*, at 11.5 and 54.5.

Diyi's successor, Dixin, the last emperor of the Shang Dynasty, was less enamored of Chang. He became suspicious of the Zhou nobleman and at one point imprisoned him for two years. Despite this (or perhaps because of it), the Zhou became increasingly independent from the Shang, and Chang (or King Wen) effectively became the ruler of the western half of the Shang Empire. The Zhou, however, did not break openly with the Shang until after Chang's death. Finally, Chang's son Fa declared war on the Shang and defeated Dixin's forces at the Battle of Muye around 1050 B.C. Fa declared himself King Wu (Warrior King) and posthumously gave his father the title of King Wen (Scholar King).

The Zhou justified their revolution by claiming that it was a continuation of the noble traditions of the Shang. They idolized the earlier Shang kings as great and beneficent rulers. However, they argued, the later Shang kings, and in particular Dixin, had become dissolute, cruel, and extravagant, and no longer served the people they ruled over. Therefore, the Zhou argued, the Shang had lost Heaven's mandate to rule. In order to punish the later Shang kings for their misbehavior, the mandate of Heaven had been passed to the Zhou.

King Wu died within two years after conquering the Shang. His son, King Cheng, was too young to rule, so King Wu's younger brother, Dan, who was known as the Duke of Zhou, served as regent. The Duke of Zhou is one of the most famous figures in Chinese political history and is considered one of the three founders of the Zhou Dynasty, along with King Wen and King Wu. Confucius regarded him as the ideal model of a statesman. The Duke of Zhou ruled wisely and moderately for many years and defended King Cheng's throne from usurpers. Then he stepped aside voluntarily when King Cheng was old enough to assume the throne.

The Zhou prided themselves on their simplicity and moral rectitude. They eliminated many of the extravagances of the Shang court and essentially did away with human sacrifice. They also engaged in pyromancy, but they also began to practice another form of divination that involved the manipulation of yarrow stalks. The yarrow is a milfoil plant. Its stalks are straight and can grow several feet high. When dried and cut into regular lengths, the yarrow becomes an elegant set of very thin, flexible stalks. A person engaged in yarrow-stalk divination would take a bundle of dried stalks and divide them into random piles. Through a series of elaborate manipulations the diviner would generate a single random number of stalks, which would represent either a solid or broken line of a hexagram. The process was repeated six times and the resulting hexagram would then be interpreted. (We do not know the exact details of the yarrow-stalk method used in Zhou times; the version that has come down to us—originating from a much later period—is described in Chapter Five.) Both turtle-shell and yarrow-stalk manipulation might be performed one after the other in order to answer a particular question. But the yarrow-stalk divination could also be performed on its own.

The Zhou probably did not invent yarrow-stalk manipulation—there is some evidence that it existed in Shang times as well—but it became an increasingly important form of divination. Yarrow-stalk manipulation was less costly than using tortoise shells. In addition, every tortoise-shell crack is different—although diviners could and did organize similar results into groups based on the cracks' size, shape, and position on the tortoise shell. By contrast, yarrow-stalk manipulation produces a finite number of discrete responses that can be precisely counted and categorized. Put in modern terms, if pyromancy was analog, yarrow-stalk manipulation was digital.

The original meaning of the word *Yi* in *Zhouyi* (as well as in *Yijing*) was probably "lizard," "salamander" or "chameleon" (a lizard that changes colors). Later, it came to mean "change" or "alter." However, the word *yi* can also mean "easy." (In ancient Chinese the same written character might be used to stand for several different homonyms, and readers determined the correct meaning through context.) Therefore, some people have argued that the *yi* in *Zhouyi* refers to the comparative ease of yarrow-stalk divination over pyromancy. In fact, the Shang also practiced milfoil divination, but there is nevertheless a grain of truth in the suggested wordplay. The increasing importance of yarrow-stalk manipulation in Zhou times probably spurred on the necessity for developing a diviner's manual to let rulers and priests know the meaning of a result based on previous divinations. As previously noted, yarrow-stalk manipulation produces discrete results, so the creation of a diviner's manual listing the meaning of each possible result would make perfect sense. The development of this diviner's manual eventually produced the *Zhouyi*.

Someone—and we do not quite know who—began to collect a series of omens, familiar proverbs, and descriptions of historical events; added mantic and divinatory comments like "good fortune," "ominous," "no troubles," and "beneficial determination"; and then associated the results with the lines of hexagrams. Possibly, generations of shamans and diviners gathered these texts, which were eventually collated and assigned to the individual lines.

Several of the line statements seem to be proverbs like "Red sky at morning, sailor take warning" or "Step on a crack and break your mother's back." Other lines seem to quote verses from popular songs. Finally, significant parts of the text refer to events in Shang and Zhou political history. We have already noted the two references in 11.5 and 54.5 to King Wen's wedding to the daughter of Diyi. Line 36.5 tells the story of the Shang minister Prince Ji, who remonstrated with his nephew, the tyrant Dixin, to mend his ways and eventually had to feign madness to escape punishment. Lines 63.3 and 64.4 refer to the conquest of the Gui (the so-called "Demon Territory" or "Devil's Country") in which the Zhou fought on behalf of the Shang. The hexagram judgment for 35.0 speaks of honors bestowed on the Marquis of Kang, who was the younger brother of King Wu. Many other hexagram judgments and line statements seem to be thinly disguised references to the plight of the Zhou leadership, their preparations for action, and their eventual overthrow of the Shang.

It is not clear why six lines were ultimately chosen as the repository for the line statements. Indeed, it has been speculated that the first figures were actually pentagrams consisting of five lines, and that a sixth line was added later to increase the number of possible permutations. This tends to explain why in fifteen hexagrams (1, 3, 4, 5, 7, 13, 15, 18, 27, 31, 33, 36, 56, 58, and 59) there are five lines with the same basic theme or metaphor and one that is different.[23]

How did the line statements get correlated with their respective lines? One theory is that diviners simply noted whether a particular result was good or bad or whether a particular omen occurred relatively contemporaneously following a particular yarrow-stalk divination. They passed these results along to subsequent generations. The compilers of the divination book that became the *Zhouyi* then assigned omen texts and prognostications on

23. See the discussions in Richard Rutt, *The Book of Changes (Zhouyi),* pp. 96–97; Iulian K. Shchutskii, *Researches on the I Ching,* trans. William L. McDonald and Tsuyoshi Hasegawa, with Hellmut Wilhelm (Princeton: Princeton University Press, 1979), pp. 145–47; Steve Moore, *The Trigrams of Han: Inner Structures of the I Ching* (Wellingborough, U.K: Aquarian Press, 1989), pp. 34–35.

the basis of these collected experiences. This theory might account for some of the text, but it seems incomplete for two reasons. First, there are 386 different line statements (64 x 6, plus two special lines for the first two hexagrams, Qian and Kun). If the divination process was truly random, it would have taken a great deal of time to produce observations for each one. Moreover, if multiple observations were obtained, there is no reason to think that the results were always identical. Second, many of the line statements within a single hexagram have repeated themes or phrases, which suggests conscious organization according to a common theme, rather than an inductive or experimental approach.[24]

The names of the hexagrams originally appear to have been a sort of cataloging system.[25] Today we know the hexagrams by their numbers. Qian is Hexagram 1, Kun is Hexagram 2, and so on. Those numbers, in turn, come from the received order of the hexagrams—sometimes called the King Wen, or later heaven, sequence. This sequence of hexagrams is divided into two parts: the Upper Canon, consisting of Hexagrams 1 through 30, and the Lower Canon, consisting of hexagrams 31 through 64. However, this sequence and the division into two canons were probably not fixed until the composition of the Ten Wings. In the original text of the *Zhouyi* the hexagrams were not numbered. Therefore, it was necessary to have a system for remembering them. This explains the development of easy-to-remember hexagram names, which are often (but not always) drawn from a word or phrase appearing in one or more of the line statements.

Today the individual lines of the hexagrams are numbered. The text of the line statements begins with expressions like "six in the second place" or "nine in the fifth place." (Six means that the line is yin; nine means that the line is yang.) However, the original *Zhouyi* text did not contain any numbering. In order to specify a line in a given hexagram, it was customary to refer to the hexagram that changing that line would produce. For example, changing the first line of Yi (Hexagram 42), produces Guan (Hexagram 20). There-

24. Competing theories are offered in Richard Alan Kunst, "The Original *'Yijing'*: A Text, Phonetic Transcription, Translation and Indexes, with Sample Glosses (Ph.D dissertation, 1985) (Ann Arbor: University Microfilms International, 1985); and Edward Shaughnessy, "The Composition of the *Zhouyi*" (Ph.D. dissertation, 1983) (Ann Arbor: University Microfilms International, 1983). Kunst emphasizes a more inductive method, which produced a sort of anthology of proverbs, prognostications, and omen texts (see Kunst, p. 1), while Shaughnessy argues that the *Zhouyi* "represents the conscious composition of an editor or editors" (Shaughnessy, p. 175).
25. See Rutt, *The Book of Changes (Zhouyi)*, pp. 118–22.

fore, the first line of Yi would be called *Yi zhi Guan*, that is, "Yi's Guan," or "the line in Yi that when changed produces Guan."[26]

The numbering system we know today was added years later, possibly as late as the fourth century B.C.[27] In the text of the *Yijing* found at Mawangdui, which dates from 168 B.C., the lines are numbered; in addition, yin lines are called sixes and yang line are called nines. However, the order of the hexagrams is different from the received order, and many of the hexagram names are different as well. This suggests that although the numbering of lines had occurred by the second century B.C., the received (King Wen) order of the hexagrams had not become canonical by this point. The use of different hexagram names in the Mawangdui manuscript tends to support the hypothesis that the hexagram names were a cataloging system rather than a symbol of the theme of the hexagram as a whole. The idea that the hexagram name states the basic theme of the hexagram and its line statements is a later interpretive innovation which is usually identified with Wang Bi's commentary from the third century A.D.

The Zhou dynasty that produced the *Yijing* lasted until 256 B.C. However, it reached the height of its power during its first three centuries, which are known as the Western Zhou. The Western Zhou period lasted until 771 B.C., when the capital was moved eastward from Hao to Luoyi as a result of an invasion precipitated by a struggle over succession to the Zhou throne. The period from 771 B.C. to 256 B.C. is called the Eastern Zhou. The move to the east meant that the Zhou kings lost their control over much of their holdings in western China. The Zhou king was still respected as a religious and ceremonial figure but lost most of his power and wealth. He was, politically speaking, a mere figurehead. The real power lay increasingly with the nobles who controlled the various states that comprised the Zhou Empire.

The political situation during Eastern Zhou gradually disintegrated. The first part is called the Spring and Autumn period (771–481 B.C.), named after a history of the period called the Spring and Autumn Annals *(Chunqiu)*. The second half of the Eastern Zhou (plus an interregnum after the death of the last Zhou king) is called the Warring States period (481–221 B.C.), named

26. Shaughnessy, "The Composition of the *Zhouyi*"; Rutt, *The Book of Changes (Zhouyi)*, pp. 118–22. This is how moving lines appear to be described in the Zuo Commentary, which probably dates from the fourth century B.C., as described more fully infra.

27. Edward Shaughnessy, *I Ching*, in *Early Chinese Texts: A Bibliographical Guide*, ed. Michael Loewe (Society for the Study of Early China, 1993), p. 218. The earliest known copy of the *Zhouyi* manuscript with the numbering system is currently housed in the Shanghai Museum and dates from the fourth century B.C.

after a chronicle called the Bamboo Records of the Warring States (*Zhan'guoce*). Political and social disintegration accelerated during these years, as rulers attacked each other, trying to seize each other's lands. The development of iron tools and weapons during this period only made the struggles more bloody. The confusion and chaos of the Warring States period caused people to try to make sense of the bloodshed and political upheaval, and thus led to a great flowering of Chinese philosophy. For example, Confucius (c. 551–479 B.C.) lived during the end of the Spring and Autumn period and the beginning of the Warring States period. During the Warring States period many of the major schools of Chinese philosophy were first developed, and the great works of Mencius, Zhuangzi, Laozi, and others were written.

The *Zhouyi* appears to be the work of the Western Zhou period. The earliest date for the text is fixed by its references to events in Shang and Zhou political history. For example, in 35.0, the text speaks of the award of horses to the Marquis of Kang, who was Feng, the younger brother of King Wu. Feng was only known by this title for a few years, however, because he subsequently was awarded the more important fief at Wei and became known in all of the histories as the Marquis of Wei. This suggests that the text of 35.0 was written shortly after the Zhou came to power around 1045 B.C.

Other features of the text refer to customs characteristic of the Western Zhou period, including the feigned abduction of a bride as part of the marriage ritual (see 22.4, 38.6), the marriage of several sisters or cousins to a single ruler (Hexagrams 11 and 54), the development of a royal feudal system (3.0, 7.6), and the use of cowrie shells as currency (41.5, 42.2). Line 14.3 speaks of princes offering tribute to (or preparing banquets for) the "Son of Heaven." That term for the Zhou king appears in bronze inscriptions from the latter part of the Western Zhou; and the relationship between nobles and the king implied by this line ended with the Western Zhou.[28] Finally, the military vocabulary in Hexagrams 30 and 7 is consistent with bronze inscriptions made during the reign of King Xuan (827–787 B.C.). All of this suggests that the compilation of the text occurred during the last years of the Western Zhou, perhaps around 800 B.C. Some of the material in the book, however, dates back several centuries prior to that; it was probably handed down by generations of diviners until it was finally collated into a working text.

The date of 800 B.C. is only a guess. In fact, the earliest mention of the

28. Rutt, *The Book of Changes (Zhouyi)*, pp. 32–33; Shaughnessy, "The Composition of the *Zhouyi*," pp. 33–49.

Zhouyi appears in the Zuo Commentary *(Zuozhuan)*. The Zuo Commentary is a description of political events between 722 and 464 B.C. Probably written in the late fourth century B.C., it came to be regarded as an expansion of the Spring and Autumn Annals *(Chunqiu)* and was printed together with it. The Zuo Commentary contains many examples of rulers and nobility consulting the *Zhouyi*. In most cases the quoted text is the same as the received text we have today. In other cases the Zuo Commentary quotes passages that have no correlation to the received text. This might suggest that multiple versions of the text existed even in the fourth century B.C.

In the Zuo Commentary diviners routinely talk about the constituent trigrams. That indicates that at least by the fourth century B.C. trigrams had become central to interpreting the meaning of the text. There is as yet no discussion of yin and yang in the Zuo Commentaries. Although the diviners had a notion of changing lines, it was different from today's understanding. Some lines that would today be considered changing (because they were assigned the numbers six or nine) would not be allowed to change. In addition, regardless of the number of changing lines, the diviners would sometimes look to the old hexagram and its constituent trigrams, sometimes the text of a single line, and sometimes the new hexagram and its constituent trigrams. Indeed, the actual procedures that were used in this period to perform a yarrow-stalk divination are still debated among scholars. The central point is that the "traditional" method of divination, which involves consulting the text of the old hexagram, the changing lines, and then the new hexagram, is not authentic to the *Zhouyi*. It may date from the time of the Ten Wings or much later.

Perhaps most important, during the period described by the Zuo Commentary, the meaning of the *Zhouyi* subtly began to change. It is still clearly a book of divination consulted almost exclusively by kings and nobles who inquire about matters of worldly success. There is still no deep philosophy of change or profound ethical system associated with the book. Nevertheless—if the Zuo Commentary is to be believed—by the beginning of the sixth century B.C. it begins to be treated as a book of wisdom. People start to quote it rhetorically as one might quote the Bible or Shakespeare rather than merely in the context of a particular divination. The earliest example of this in the Zuo Commentary comes from 603 B.C. A young man confided in Prince Boliao about his ambition to become a minister of state. The prince later remarked that a worthless character with high ambitions appears in the *Zhouyi* in the top line of Feng (Hexagram 55, Abundance). This line, which concerns a selfish person who tries to hog everything for himself, reads: "He peers through the door, / Lonely, abandoned. / For three years he sees no one. / Misfortune." The young man, the prince suggested, would live no longer than the *Zhouyi* says, and sure enough, the Zuo Commentary reports, he was killed a year later.[29] Here a prediction is made without consulting the yarrow—rather the *Zhouyi* is offered as a source of wisdom about human character and its likely consequences.

In one sense this development is hardly surprising. The *Zhouyi* is eminently quotable, especially given that parts of the line statements probably originally came from proverbs and songs. However, the fact that it was quoted in this way also suggests that the text of the book was becoming more widely known outside of a small circle of diviners and shamans. It was changing from a specialized book of divination practices into a canonical work of literature.

The Transformation of the Zhouyi *into the* Book of Changes

The chaos and strife of the Warring States period ended in 221 B.C. when the western state of Qin conquered most of the other states and united them into a single empire. The Qin Dynasty was totalitarian and ruthless. It lasted only fifteen years—from 221 B.C. to 207 B.C.—but accomplished a considerable amount during that time. The Qin simplified the writing system, standardized weights and measures, built roads, and combined the defensive walls of various former kingdoms to form the Great Wall of China. The first Qin emperor, Qin Shihuang, was not interested in tolerating any political opposition whatsoever. So in 213 B.C. he ordered the burning of most ancient books—including particularly Confucian books—and had a number of Confucian scholars buried alive to emphasize the point. Only useful books dealing with subjects like medicine, agriculture, and divination were spared. The *Zhouyi* was spared for two reasons. First, it was regarded as a divination manual for kings and therefore was considered to be a practical work. Second, and more interestingly, it was not at that point in history strongly identified with Confucianism.

The second Qin emperor was not as successful as the first and was soon toppled by Liu Bang, who became the first emperor of the Han Dynasty in 206 B.C. The Han Dynasty is usually divided into two periods, the Earlier (Western) Han (206 B.C.–9 A.D.) and the Later (Eastern) Han (25–220 A.D.),

29. As quoted in Rutt, *The Book of Changes (Zhouyi)*, p. 184; Kidder Smith, Jr. et al., *Sung Dynasty Uses of I Ching* (Princeton: Princeton University Press), p. 13.

separated by a brief interregnum, the Xin Dynasty. After the brutal repression of the Qin, the Han Dynasty witnessed a great flourishing of learning. The ban on books was officially lifted in 191 B.C. Confucianism was restored and eventually made the official philosophy of the state in 136 B.C.

The Qin had not succeeded in destroying all copies of the previously banned works. Many of the ancient texts were copied or were rewritten from memory in the new script introduced during the Qin Dynasty. Later other scholars claimed to have discovered copies of the texts written in the old-fashioned pre-Qin script that had survived the burning of the books because they were hidden in the countryside or had been buried in the walls of Confucius's house. Some of these "discovered" texts were probably forgeries. Multiple versions of the ancient texts now circulated, leading to a dispute between two schools of thought about scholarship, known as the new-text *(jinwen)* and old-text *(guwen)* schools. The two schools not only fought over which texts were authentic and which were spurious or altered, but also over how to interpret the texts.

The *Yijing* had been spared from destruction during the burning of the books, so there was little reason to think that the discovered copies should be very different from the ones written in new script. In fact, the real disagreement between the new-text and old-text schools concerned doctrine and approach. The new-text scholars focused on metaphysics and the supernatural, which were not traditional concerns of Confucianism. They revered Confucius as a superhuman being.[30] The old-text scholars arose as a reaction to these tendencies. The rejected the metaphysics of the new-text scholars and emphasized the rational and ethical features of Confucian philosophy. They regarded Confucius not as a deity but as a great man and a sage. The new-text school dominated throughout most of the Earlier Han Dynasty, and its members received official support. However, gradually the old-text school gained influence, and by the end of the Han Dynasty it became the dominant approach.

The new-text scholars were particularly interested in cosmology. They assimilated many previously non-Confucian elements, like Daoist metaphysics and yin-yang philosophy. They also adopted the five-element theory—which explained the processes of change through constant cycles of transformation and destruction of the five elements of earth, water, wood, fire, and metal. By bringing these diverse sources of philosophy together, the Con-

30. On the controversy between the old-text and new-text schools, see Feng Yu-Lan, *A Short History of Chinese Philosophy* (New York: Free Press, 1948), pp. 207–9; Moore, *The Trigrams of Han*, pp. 38–43.

fucian scholars of the new-text school contributed to the development of a Han Confucianism that was as interested in metaphysics and cosmology as in the traditional Confucian concerns of morals and statecraft. The eclecticism of Han Confucians helps explain how the *Yijing* became understood as a Confucian text. Indeed, in 136 B.C., the *Yijing*—which now contained most of the commentaries called the Ten Wings—was officially declared one of the Confucian Classics, along with the Book of Documents *(Shujing),* the Book of Odes *(Shijing),* the Book of Rites *(Liji),* and the Spring and Autumn Annals *(Chunqiu).*

All of this was in some sense ironic. In its original form the *Zhouyi* was not a book of moral instruction—it was a divination manual for kings. At most it was a manual of strategy designed to allow the nobility to pursue worldly success. Conversely, in its original form Confucianism was primarily concerned not with fortune-telling but with ethics and proper conduct. The early Confucians were uninterested in divination if not outright hostile to it, and they tended to shy away from discussions of spirits. A well-known passage from the *Analects* says that "Confucius never discussed strange phenomena, physical exploits, disorder and spiritual beings."[31] Finally, neither the original *Zhouyi* nor early Confucianism was particularly concerned with grand theories of metaphysics or change. However, none of that mattered to the Han Confucians, who happily transformed the *Zhouyi* into a book of wisdom, the *Yijing*, or *Classic of Changes*.

The very qualities that made the *Zhouyi* an effective tool of divination—its vivid yet ambiguous imagery and its terse oracular style—also made it possible to reinterpret it in Confucian terms. Perhaps equally important, the *Zhouyi* was written in a language five hundred years older than the Ten Wings. In significant respects it was as alien to the Han scholars as Chaucer is to us today. Many of the words in the text had changed their meanings in the interim. The social and philosophical milieu had also been transformed. By the time the Ten Wings were composed, no one living understood the context in which these oracular pronouncements were first made. Instead, people read the language in light of the philosophical and ethical concerns of their own age. They brought the philosophies of Confucianism and Daoism, and the theories of yin-yang and the five elements—none of which existed when the *Zhouyi* was originally written—to bear on the text. The result was a very significant transformation.

31. *Analects* VII:20/21, as translated in *A Source Book in Chinese Philosophy,* trans. and ed. Wing-Tsit Chan (Princeton: Princeton University Press, 1963), p. 32.

Consider as an example the opening words of the *Zhouyi*: *Yuan heng li zhen*. *Yuan* originally meant "head" or "prime," *heng* meant "sacrifice" or "offering," *li* meant "favorable" or "beneficial," and *zhen* meant "divination" or "determination." Thus the original meaning was probably something like "prime sacrifice; a favorable determination," or perhaps "the first offering has been received; it is beneficial to make a [further] determination."

By the time of the Han Dynasty, most of these words had changed their meanings. *Yuan* now meant "supreme" or "sublime." *Heng*, which originally meant "sacrifice," also meant "an offering favorably received by the spirits." Hence it came to mean "auspicious," and hence "success." *Li* still meant "beneficial" or "advantageous." But the meaning of *zhen* had mutated. Originally, it meant "divination" or "determination"; then it changed from determination in the sense of fixing or determining something to determination in the sense of perseverance. Thus the opening phrase of the *Zhouyi* came to mean: "Supreme success. It is beneficial to persevere." In addition, the four words *yuan heng li zhen* came to represent the four cardinal qualities or virtues of a superior person: sublimity, accomplishment, beneficence, and perseverance.

In this way, the rather amoral vocabulary of the Bronze Age diviner's manual was reinterpreted in decidedly moral terms. For example, the word *jiu*, which originally meant "misfortune," was reinterpreted to mean "blame." The expression *jun zi*, which originally mean "son (or descendant) of a ruler," i.e., a nobleman, later came to mean "gentleman," and eventually a "superior person," that is, one who is enlightened and follows proper modes of conduct. Hence the original meaning of a text such as 20.5, "Observing our victims, no misfortune for nobles," was transformed into the more high-minded "Viewing my life. The superior person is without blame." The word *hui*, which originally meant "trouble," was reinterpreted to mean "remorse" or "regret," suggesting not simply bad luck but unhappiness caused by improper attitudes or past behavior. In like fashion the ubiquitous expression *hui wang*, which originally meant "troubles go away" now became "regrets vanish" or "remorse disappears."

The transformation of the word *zhen* from "divination" to "perseverance" was particularly crucial. It was further glossed by Confucian scholars to mean something more than mere persistence; perseverance meant being steadfast and morally upright. This produced many significant changes in the interpretation of the text. Thus in 17.3 the words *li ju zhen*, which probably originally meant "a favorable determination about a dwelling" became "it is beneficial to dwell in perseverance."

Finally, there is the transformation of the word *fu*, which plays an important role in the Confucian interpretations of the text. As we have learned from twentieth-century archeological studies, the original meaning of *fu* was "captive." It mutated to "submissive," then "reliable," and then to "trustworthy" and "true." From there it took on the additional meanings of trust, sincerity, and confidence. The earliest meaning of *fu* was long forgotten by the time of the Ten Wings. Trust, sincerity and behaving so as to inspire confidence in others became central elements of the moral interpretation of the *Book of Changes*. However, it is fairly certain that the *Zhouyi* of the Bronze Age was concerned with something quite different: the procurement and use of captives, particularly enemy soldiers who might subsequently be bound up and offered as sacrifices. According to the standard interpretation of *fu*, line 46.2 says, "If one is sincere, / It is beneficial to bring even a small offering. / No blame." However, the original meaning of the text was probably somewhat less morally uplifting: "If the captives are taken / It will be beneficial to use them in the summer sacrifice. / No misfortune."

The Ten Wings

An important intellectual achievement of the Han period was the creation and redaction of the set of commentaries on the *Zhouyi* known as the Ten Wings. The earliest parts of the Ten Wings may well have been written during the Warring States period, but the collation and canonization of the texts probably occurred later; and it is possible that the very last components were completed as late as the first or second centuries A.D. The composition of these texts thus overlapped with the ascendance of cosmological and ethical strands of Confucianism during the Han Dynasty. Through the glosses provided by the Ten Wings the *Zhouyi* was reinterpreted and transformed from a Bronze Age diviner's manual into a manual of humane moral instruction and from a collection of omens into a book of profound metaphysical importance. In its own way this is as ingenious an accomplishment as the creation and organization of the original diviner's manual in the first place.

The Ten Wings actually consist of seven different texts, but three of them are divided into two parts, making ten in all. The division reflects the fact that the sixty-four hexagrams are traditionally divided into two sections, the Upper Canon (Hexagrams 1–30), and the Lower Canon (Hexagrams 31–64).[32]

The first two wings are the Commentary on the Judgments *(Tuan-*

32. The traditional explanation for this division is that the Upper Canon is concerned with metaphysics of heaven and earth, while the Lower Canon is concerned with human affairs. In

zhuan). The First Wing offers commentaries on the hexagram judgments 1.0 through 30.0, and the Second Wing offers commentaries for the hexagram judgments 31.0 through 64.0. For the most part, these commentaries are explanations of why the hexagrams are auspicious or inauspicious as determined by looking at the relative placement of yin and yang lines and the interrelation of the constituent trigrams. They have only a moderate amount of ethical content. The Third and Fourth Wings are the Commentary on the Images *(Xiangzhuan).* Again, this commentary is divided between the Upper and Lower Canons. The Third Wing features commentaries on Hexagrams 1–30 while the Fourth Wing has commentaries on Hexagrams 31–64.

The Commentary on the Images is actually an amalgam of two separate texts written at different times. The first of these texts is called the Commentary on the Great Images *(Daxiang).* The "great" images are the hexagrams themselves, or rather the hexagrams as understood in terms of their constituent trigrams. The Commentary on the Great Images explains the theme of each hexagram in terms of the interaction of the elements (heaven, earth, etc.) that are symbolized by its constituent trigrams. Then it draws a moral lesson about how a person should behave appropriate to the time and the conditions represented by the hexagram. Here, for example, is the text of the Commentary on the Great Image for Hexagram 28, Greatness in Excess. It is notated as 28.GI (GI stands for Great Image). The lower trigram is Xun (Wind or Wood), the upper trigram is Dui (Lake):

The lake rises over the trees:
This is the image of Greatness in Excess.
Thus the superior person, when he stands alone, is unafraid,
And if he has to renounce the world, he is undaunted.

The Commentary on the Great Images is the most overtly Confucian part of the Ten Wings. Its language is often quite beautiful. Its insights are also among the most profound. Richard Wilhelm thought so highly of the Commentary on the Great Images that in his famous translation of the *Book of Changes,* he placed it together with the *Zhouyi* itself in the first part of the

---

fact the hexagrams in the two halves do not divide up in this way but range over a wide array of subjects. Moreover, the two canons are not symmetrical: One has only thirty hexagrams while the other has thirty-four. It is possible that at some point two hexagrams were moved from their places in the traditional order, creating the asymmetry. The Mawangdui manuscript of 168 B.C. uses a completely different order, and it includes none of the Ten Wings that depend on the traditional order.

book. He put the rest of the Ten Wings in separate sections. For similar reasons the Commentary on the Great Images is the only part of the text of the Ten Wings that I have included in the commentaries in this book.

The other text in the Third and Fourth Wings is the Commentary on the Small Images *(Xiaoxiang).* These are very brief commentaries on the line statements. They usually repeat parts of each line statement and add a few more words. They are mostly explanations of why the lines are auspicious or inauspicious given their placement and interrelation with the other lines. Although they form part of the Third and Fourth Wings, they have more in common with the Commentary on the Judgments (the First and Second Wings) than they do with the Commentary on the Great Images.

The Fifth and Sixth Wings are the two halves of the Great Treatise *(Dazhuan).* The Great Treatise appears to be a collection of different texts written at different times, but most of it was found in the Mawangdui manuscript.[33] Like the Commentary on the Judgments and the Commentary on the Images, the Great Treatise was probably written near the end of the Warring States period in the third century B.C.[34]

If the Commentary on the Great Images is the most ethical part of the Ten Wings, the Great Treatise is the most metaphysical. It offers a theory of change in the universe, and argues that changes in heaven and earth can be understood through understanding the changes in the hexagrams. The trigrams and the theory of yin and yang are mentioned, but not the theory of the five elements. At the end of each wing are a series of comments on hexagram and line statements that are considerably more detailed than those appearing in the Commentary on the Small Images and express ethical concerns. Because of these comments, the Great Treatise is also known by another name, the Commentary on the Appended Statements *(Xici* or *Xicizhuan).* There is also a section on divination with yarrow stalks *(Dayan)* and a section that tries to show how the early development of Chinese civilization was produced from imitating the structure of the hexagrams *(Guzhe).* But the most important features of the Great Treatise for later generations were its metaphysical theories about change.[35] The Great Treatise became the central text of *Yijing* philosophy, more important in some ways than

33. These portions are translated in Edward Shaughnessy, *I Ching: The Classic of Changes.*
34. The dates offered for the various parts of the Ten Wings are taken from Rutt, *The Book of Changes (Zhouyi),* pp. 365, 372, 433–34, 439–40, 453.
35. An important essay on the Great Treatise's theory of change is Willard J. Peterson, "Making Connections: Commentary on the Attached Verbalizations of the *Book of Changes,*" *Harvard Journal of Asiatic Studies* 42, no. 1 (June 1982), pp. 67–116.

the *Zhouyi* itself. It influenced Chinese philosophy from the Han Dynasty to the present.

The Seventh Wing is the Commentary on the Words of the Text (*Wenyan*). It is the beginning of what might have been a larger treatise on all the hexagrams and line statements, but contains only commentaries on the first two, Qian (The Dynamic) and Kun (The Receptive). It was probably written in the second or first century B.C.

The Eighth Wing is the Treatise on the Trigrams *(Shuogua)*. The first three paragraphs are a brief discussion of the origin of the hexagrams, which were probably written much earlier than the rest of the treatise. In the Mawangdui manuscript a very similar discussion was found embedded in the text of the Great Treatise. This suggests that it was written about the same time—the late third century or early second century B.C. The remainder of the Eighth Wing concerns the trigrams; it was written much later, possibly as late as the first century A.D. It describes the properties of each of the trigrams and their associations with forces of nature, parts of the body, members of the family, directions of the compass, and miscellaneous items. It is the least Confucian part of the Ten Wings but was among the most important to philosophers interested in cosmology.

The Ninth Wing is the Sequence of the Hexagrams *(Xugua)*. It recites a series of explanations of how one hexagram leads to another in the traditional ordering. The explanations are not always very convincing, and the document is probably a mnemonic device for remembering the traditional order, because, as pointed out earlier, in the traditional text the hexagrams are not numbered. The text of the *Xugua* is probably a late composition, possibly as late as the early second century A.D.

The Tenth Wing is called Miscellaneous Notes on the Hexagrams *(Zagua)* and offers glosses on many but not all of the hexagrams arranged in rhymed couplets. There seems to be no particular order to the pairs except as a way of remembering the contents of the hexagrams. This text is probably the latest part of the Ten Wings, and may even date from the second century A.D.

Here is a summary of the different parts of the Ten Wings:

Wing	Name	Chinese Name	Contents	Date of composition
First	Commentary on the Judgments, Part I	*Tuanzhuan*	Explanation of why Hexagrams 1-30 are auspicious or inauspicious	Late third century B.C.
Second	Commentary on the Judgments, Part II	*Tuanzhuan*	Same as First Wing,but for Hexagrams 31-64	Late third century B.C.
Third	Commentary on the Images, Part I	*Xiangzhuan*	Ethical meanings of Hexagrams 1-30 (Commentary on the Great Images, or *Daxiang*); explanation of why line statements for Hexagrams 1-30 are auspicious or inauspicious (Commentary on the Small Images, or *Xiaoxiang*)	Late third century B.C.
Fourth	Commentary on the Images, Part II	*Xiangzhuan*	Same as Third Wing, but for Hexagrams 31-64	Late third century B.C.

Fifth	The Great Treatise, Part I (Commentary on the Appended Statements)	*Dazhuan* (*Xici* or *Xicizhuan*)	Metaphysical theories of change; ethical import of various line statements.	Late third century B.C.
Sixth	The Great Treatise, Part II (Commentary on the Appended Statements)	*Dazhuan* (*Xici* or *Xicizhuan*)	Same as Fifth Wing	Late third century B.C.
Seventh	Commentary on the Words of the Text	*Wenyan*	Commentaries on Hexagrams 1 (Qian) and 2 (Kun)	Late second century or early first century B.C.
Eighth	Treatise on the Trigrams	*Shuogua*	Brief account of origin of hexagrams; longer treatise on meaning and associations of the trigrams	On hexagrams, late third century or early second century B.C.; on trigrams, as late as first century A.D.
Ninth	Sequence of the Hexagrams	*Xugua*	Mnemonics for the traditional order of hexagrams	As late as early second century A.D.
Tenth	Miscellaneous Notes on the Hexagrams	*Zagua*	Mnemonics for characteristics of hexagrams	As late as early second century A.D.

Two traditions have grown up about how the Ten Wings should be published together with the *Zhouyi*. The dominant tradition was begun by the old-text scholars Fei Zhi (c. 50 B.C.–10 A.D.) and Zheng Xuan (127–200). It divides up the first four wings by hexagram and places the relevant commentaries following the text of each hexagram judgment and line statement. After each hexagram judgment comes the associated Commentary on the Judgment, then the Commentary on the Great Image, then each line statement, followed by the corresponding Commentary on the Small Image. Then, in the cases of Hexagrams 1 and 2, the *Wenyan* commentary follows. The remaining five wings are placed afterward. In some versions, the Ninth and Tenth Wings are also divided up and placed either at the beginning or the end of each hexagram chapter.

This arrangement suited the purposes of the old-text scholars, who wanted to offer rational and ethical interpretations of the core text. It guaranteed that the reader always confronted the text in light of the commentaries for each line. Nevertheless, the original arrangement was quite different: The Ten Wings followed the core text, and each Wing was presented as an integral whole. It is also the arrangement preferred by the Song Dynasty philosopher and commentator Zhu Xi (1130–1200).

The Xiangshu and Yili Schools

During the Han Dynasty, two major schools of thought developed about how to interpret the *Book of Changes*. The *xiangshu* ("image and number") school tried to discover knowledge from the linear composition of the trigrams and hexagrams. The *yili* ("meaning and principle") school tried to glean ethical principles from a careful study of the text.[36]

The "image" in "image and number" refers to the symbolic associations of the trigrams, which are listed in the Eighth Wing, the *Shogua*. Each trigram had a wealth of different associations ranging from colors to substances to family members to animals to compass directions to parts of the body. The trigram Kun (three yin lines), for example, is associated with earth, with the mother, with the mare, with the southwest, and so on. The "number" in "image and number" refers to the mathematical structure of the hexagrams and trigrams and how they can be transformed from one to another through mathematical operations. In short, the *xiangshu* school

36. On the differences between the two schools, see Smith, et. al., *Sung Dynasty Uses of the I Ching*, pp. 18–19, 21–24.

tried to explain the hexagrams and line statements in terms of the symbolic associations of the trigrams. It also tried to understand the deeper meanings of hexagrams by studying how they could be transformed into other hexagrams through mathematical procedures. For example, if one takes Hexagram 32, Heng (Enduring), and replaces each line by its opposite (yin for yang, yang for yin), one obtains Hexagram 42, Yi (Increase). Therefore, a *xiangshu* scholar might conclude that the meaning of Heng is secretly related to its complement, Yi.

32	42
Heng	Yi
Enduring	Increase

Complementary Hexagrams

Alternatively, one might study a hexagram in terms of its so-called "nuclear" trigrams. Nuclear trigrams are constructed from lines two through five of the hexagram. The lower nuclear trigram consists of lines two, three, and four; the upper nuclear trigram consists of lines three, four, and five. The idea is that lines two through five form the "heart" or nucleus of a hexagram, because line one represents what precedes the situation described in the hexagram and line six represents what comes after it. The nuclear trigrams for Heng are Qian (Heaven) and Dui (Lake). Together they form hexagram 43, Guai (Resolution), which is the nuclear hexagram for Heng. Therefore, a *xiangshu* scholar might conclude, Guai (Resolution) lies at the heart of Heng (Enduring). Obviously, because all hexagrams can be transformed into each other by changing a certain number of lines, the *xiangshu* scholars could demonstrate that all of the hexagrams were related to each other with varying degrees of intimacy.

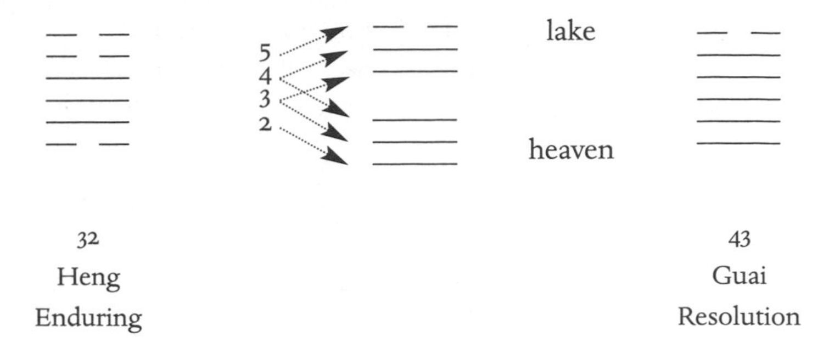

Nuclear trigrams

In similar fashion one could study the meaning of hexagram lines through the study of hexagram transformations. According to the *xiangshu* scholars, the metaphors and oracular pronouncements in the line statements were a sort of secret code book, which explained what would happen if one changed a line from yin to yang, moved a line from one place to another, and so on. A very simple example is the text of line six of Hexagram 12, Pi (Standstill): "The standstill is overthrown. / First standstill, then great joy." If one overturns Hexagram 12, one obtains Hexagram 11 Tai (Peace). Here is a more complicated example: Line six of Hexagram 24, Fu (Return), says, "Blunder and disaster. / If one sends armies marching, / In the end one will suffer a great defeat." A *xiangshu* scholar might point out that "sending armies marching" refers to Hexagram 7, Shi (The Army), which is obtained by moving the third line of the Hexagram Fu down to the bottom and pushing up the first two lines. When that transformation is performed, the upper trigram becomes Kun (Earth), which symbolizes burial, and the lower trigram is Kan (Water), which symbolizes danger.[37] If this seems rather complicated and far-fetched, that is because it probably is. The *xiangshu* approach saw the text of the *Zhouyi* as an elaborate code that could be cracked by clever mathematical manipulation. The goal of this process was to reveal secret relationships of order in a universe that was predictable, knowable, and operated with mathematical precision. In this sense, it is not too different from a contemporary scientist's belief that the structure of the universe is a set of mathematical laws that require us to crack the code of surface appearances.

Members of the *xiangshu* school also developed elaborate correspon-

37. This example is taken from Smith et al., *Sung Dynasty Uses of the I Ching,* pp. 18–19.

dences between the hexagrams and the calendar. For example, each month was correlated with a hexagram, beginning with 24, Fu (Return), and adding yang lines successively, until 1, Qian (The Dynamic), is produced. Then yin lines enter from the bottom until 2, Kun (The Receptive), is reached:

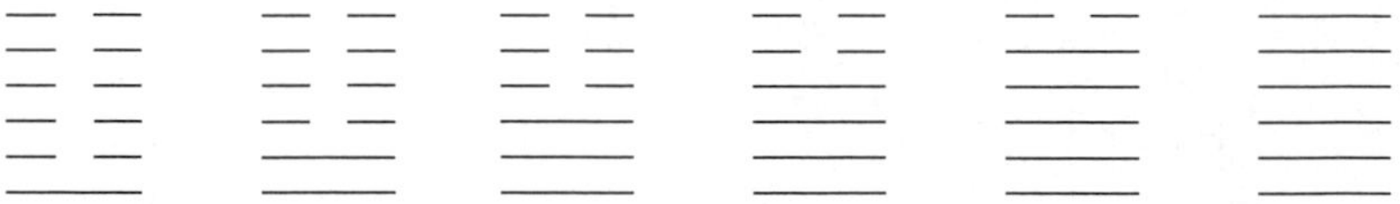

24 19 11 34 43 1

44 33 12 20 23 2

Months of the Calendar as Symbolized by Hexagrams

Using the hexagrams this way essentially dispenses with the hexagram judgments and line statements. It views the hexagrams purely as mathematical structures whose importance lies in their ability to be transformed one into the other. In some ways this defines the *xiangshu* approach in its purest form.

By contrast, the *yili* ("meaning and principle") scholars looked for very different things in the *Book of Changes*. The *yili* school focused on the ethical meanings of the hexagrams and line statements. *Yili* scholars believed that through careful study the opaque language of the hexagram judgments and line statements could be shown to contain profound moral truths. One could better understand those truths by paying attention to constituent trigrams and line positions—in this respect the *yili* and *xiangshu* schools were not completely at odds. But according to the *yili* school, the goal of *Yijing* interpretation was not to explain the hidden laws of the universe but to grasp the ethical teachings of the book. Whereas the *xiangshu* school relied heavily on the trigram associations listed in the Eighth Wing, the *Shogua*, the *yili* approach made the first seven Wings particularly important, because they offered textual commentaries about the meaning of the individual hexagram judgments and line statements.

The most famous member of the *yili* school revolutionized the study of the *Book of Changes*, changing its subsequent interpretation and reception forever. His name was Wang Bi.

Wang Bi's Commentary

The first great commentary on the *Book of Changes* following the Ten Wings was produced by a brilliant young scholar, Wang Bi (226–249), who had been trained in the old-text tradition. Wang Bi is a remarkable figure in Chinese letters. In addition to his commentary on the *Book of Changes*, he also wrote an influential commentary on Laozi's *Dao De Jing*. Yet he died at the age of twenty-three. His influence on the *Yijing* powerfully shaped the way we think about the book today, so much so that many of his innovations now seem obvious or even invisible.[38]

Wang Bi offered his theories in his Commentary on the Changes of the Zhou *(Zhouyi Zhu)*. His commentary discussed all 64 hexagrams and 386 line statements of the *Zhouyi* as well as most of the Ten Wings. It also included a series of introductory essays called the *Zhouyi Lueli* (Basic Principles of the Book of Change) in which he offered a sort of manifesto of his views about the *Yijing*.

Wang Bi argued that the symbols or images traditionally associated with the trigrams and hexagrams are symbols of abstract ideas or principles. The symbols are analogies designed to invoke these principles, and the words of the hexagram and line judgments help to articulate these principles. For example, the early Han commentators pointed out that the symbol of Hexagram 1, Qian (The Dynamic), is a horse and the symbol of Hexagram 2, Kun (The Receptive), is a cow. In their correlative cosmology, whatever applied to Qian applied to horses and vice versa. By contrast, Wang Bi argued that this symbolism is just a way to indicate that the theme of Qian is strength and dynamism and the theme of Kun is docility and receptivity. Qian is not really a horse any more than Kun is a cow. Once we understand the underlying principles, we can forget about the horse and the cow. Instead, we should focus on the ethical principles and abstract ideas they symbolize. In essence, Wang Bi rejected the basic assumptions of the image-and-number school and its correlative cosmology. Wang Bi's approach deemphasized the study of intri-

38. Wang Bi's commentary has been translated by Richard John Lynn in *The Classic of Changes: A New Translation of the I Ching as Interpreted by Wang Bi* (New York: Columbia University Press, 1994). It includes a helpful introduction to Wang Bi's life and thought written by Lynn. Another good discussion appears in Smith et al., *Sung Dynasty Uses of the I Ching*, pp. 21–25.

cate mathematical relationships between the hexagrams and the elaborate metaphysical associations between the hexagrams and the calendar. Instead, Wang Bi and the commentators that followed him interpreted the *Zhouyi* and the Ten Wings as a rich repository of literary symbols pointing to important ethical, political, and philosophical ideas.

Next, Wang Bi argued that each hexagram has a single theme or principle, which is stated by its name and is further developed by the hexagram judgment. Moreover, the central theme of the hexagram can usually be found in one of the hexagram's line statements, which Wang Bi called the "ruling" line. This line is ruling because its meaning is sovereign over all of the other lines. Different hexagrams have different ruling lines, but the most usual ruler is the fifth line, which ordinarily represents the leader or sovereign. There are exceptions to this rule. When five of the lines are of one type (yin or yang) and one line is of the opposite type, then the single line is the ruler and states the theme of the hexagram, because the one rules the many. This is so even if the ruling line is yin. Finally, Wang Bi argued, sometimes the meaning of the hexagram does not correspond with any particular line, but must be derived from the interrelation of the two constituent trigrams.

Wang Bi also offered a systematic account of why hexagrams and line statements were considered auspicious or inauspicious. He built on explanations given in the Ten Wings, particularly the Commentary on the Judgments and the Commentary on the Small Images, and combined them with his own theory of change.

Wang Bi argued that change occurs because of harmonies or clashes between the innate tendencies of things. Harmony produces change for the better; clashes produce change for the worse. Therefore, one can tell whether hexagrams and individual lines are auspicious or inauspicious by studying the relationships of harmony or discord between the hexagram lines. If we understand whether the innate tendencies of things are producing harmony or dissonance, we can understand whether things are going well or badly. Then we can make adjustments in our own conduct in order to achieve success.

Wang Bi's theories of harmony and discord draw upon the traditional associations of yin with soft, weak, and yielding, and yang with hard, strong, and firm. Thus yin (broken) lines are weak, yang (solid) lines are firm. Traditionally, yin was also associated with even numbers and yang with odd numbers. Hence yin and yang can describe positions in a hexagram as well as solid and broken lines. The positions in a hexagram are numbered from one to six, starting from the bottom and moving to the top. Odd-numbered positions—one, three, and five—are yang, or strong, positions. Even-numbered positions—two, four, and six—are yin, or weak, positions.

Based on his reading of the Ten Wings, Wang Bi argued that harmony or resonance comes from the appropriate placement of lines in positions that are similar to their natures. All other things being equal, yang lines are more harmonious in the first, third, and fifth positions; yin lines are more harmonious in the second, fourth and sixth positions. These lines are said to be "correctly" positioned. (The idea of "correct" position already appears in the Ten Wings.) Conversely, when a yin line is in a yang position or a yang line is in a yin position, it is incorrectly positioned; this is a source of disharmony or discord. Correct positioning is most important for lines two through five. It is least important for lines one and six, because these signify the beginning and end of the situation described in the hexagram. They look back to the previous situation or forward to the next situation. As a result, they do not have a stable nature.

Second, harmony or resonance comes from the mutual attraction of opposite lines. Disharmony and discord come from the mutual repulsion of similar lines. Opposites attract; similar lines repel. Yin lines resonate with yang lines and vice versa, but two yin or two yang lines are discordant.

Positions as well as lines resonate. In a six-line hexagram, the first three positions in the lower trigram resonate with the second three positions in the upper trigram. The first (yang) position resonates with the fourth (yin) position; the second (yin) position resonates with the fifth (yang) position; and the third (yang) position resonates with the sixth (yin) position. These are also called corresponding positions.

If the lines occupying these corresponding positions are opposites (one yin and one yang), they are said to resonate or correspond. This increases harmony, particularly if the correspondence is between the "central" lines in each trigram—the second and fifth positions. The situation is even more harmonious if the lines are correctly placed—yang lines in yang positions and yin lines in yin positions. For example, Hexagram 11, Tai (Peace), is very harmonious—all of the lines correspond to each other, and four of the six lines are correctly placed. (The only exceptions are the second and fifth lines, which are central and correspond but are not correct.) In theory, the most harmonious hexagram should be hexagram 63, Ji Ji (After Completion), because every yin line is in a yin place, every yang line is in a yang place, and all the lines in corresponding positions resonate with each other. However, ironically, because the situation is so perfect, any change will make things worse, so Ji Ji is only moderately auspicious:

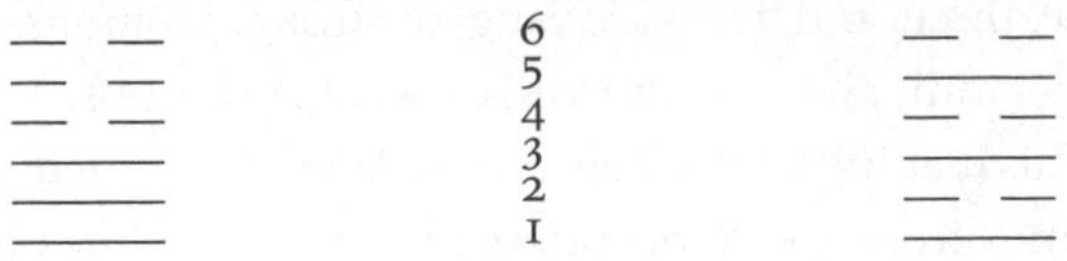

— —	6	— —
— —	5	———
— —	4	— —
———	3	———
———	2	— —
———	1	———
11		63
Tai		Ji Ji
Peace		After Completion

Harmony and Resonance

Another source of harmony and discord is the relationship between adjoining lines. All other things being equal, it is more harmonious when a line in the yang position is yang and the line immediately below in the yin position is yin, because a superior should be above a subordinate. This is called "yang riding atop yin" or "yin carrying yang." Conversely, when yin rides yang or yang carries yin, this is inappropriate and leads to disharmony. Again, this is more important for lines two through five than for lines one and six.

Finally, lines are more likely to be auspicious if they are "central," an idea that appears in the Commentary on the Judgments and the Commentary on the Small Images. The central line in the lower trigram is the second; the central line in the upper trigram is the fifth. Central lines symbolize "balanced" or proper behavior and adherence to the Confucian notion of the Mean, or the central path. Hence they are auspicious. If a line is both central and "correct"—a yin line in the second place or a yang line in the fifth place—it is especially auspicious.

Note that these criteria of harmony and disharmony often point in different directions. In almost every hexagram one can find elements that are both harmonious and inharmonious. This gives the commentator enormous leeway to "explain" the auspiciousness or inauspiciousness of each line or hexagram in order to draw an ethical lesson. Although the rules about harmony and discord are often stated with the certainty of a science, they are perhaps better understood as rhetorical devices alternatively employed and omitted that enrich the resources available to commentators.

It is important to recognize how far Wang Bi has taken us from the original *Zhouyi*. The notion of yin and yang positions, or correct or incorrect placement of lines, appears nowhere in the original text, nor do Wang Bi's notions of corresponding lines or riding or carrying lines. His view that the hexagrams have a central theme that is stated by the ruling line has little basis in the original understanding of *Zhouyi*. Originally, the hexagram names were probably little more than tags used to catalog the hexagrams, and as we have seen, in several cases the Mawangdui manuscript of 168 B.C. has different tags than the received text. The original collators of the *Zhouyi* probably did try to produce some degree of thematic unity in many of the hexagrams, but many hexagrams lack thematic unity. And there is no indication that they assigned a single ruling line to state the basic theme for each hexagram. The naturalness of these assumptions today reflects the ingenuity of the commentators who came afterward, including, of course, Wang Bi himself.

Some of Wang Bi's innovations concerning line placements have their beginnings in casual or isolated remarks appearing in the Ten Wings. But Wang Bi turned them into a systematic way of understanding and interpreting the *Book of Changes*. He created a theory and a language that could harmonize and explain the apparently chaotic judgments that some hexagrams and line statements were auspicious or inauspicious. Perhaps more importantly, he deemphasized the previous emphasis on mathematical calculation and mystical association. By focusing attention on the abstract themes represented by the hexagrams, he made it easier to see the connections between the obscure language of the hexagram judgments and line statements on the one hand and ethical and philosophical principles on the other. Finally, by reconstituting the *Book of Changes* as a literary text with rich symbolism, he made it possible for later generations to use it for many different purposes—from philosophy and politics to relationships and personal growth.

The Book of Changes in the Song Dynasty

Wang Bi's magnum opus, the *Zhouyi Zhu*, became established as the official commentary on the *Book of Changes* from the Tang Dynasty (618–907) through the Song Dynasty (960–1279). It also contained the received text of the *Book of Changes*, based on old text sources. So central was Wang Bi's contribution that Kong Yingda (574–648) even wrote a commentary on his commentary called the *Zhouyi Zhengyi* (Correct Meaning of the *Zhouyi*). The next great interpretations of the *Book of Changes* came with the flowering of Neo-Confucian philosophy in the Song Dynasty. To these scholars the metaphysical theories of the Great Treatise became the most important part of the *Book of Changes*.

Shao Yong (1011–1077) revived the *xiangshu* (image-and-number) approach. He created elaborate mathematical diagrams of the hexagrams and, in the process, demonstrated that the sixty-four hexagrams could be produced through a binary system of counting from zero to sixty-three. This astonished the German philosopher Wilhelm Leibniz when he first learned of it centuries later. Ouyang Xiu (1007–1072) anticipated twentieth-century criticism by taking the radical view that the *Zhouyi* had changed its meaning from the time of Confucius to the Han Dynasty and that Confucius could not have written all of the Ten Wings. However, his views were largely disregarded. Cheng Yi (1033–1107) wrote a famous Commentary on the *Changes (Yichuan Yizhuan)* in the *yili* (meaning-and-principle) tradition of Wang Bi.

A century later the Neo-Confucian philosopher Zhu Xi produced the next great commentary on the *Changes*. Zhu Xi's work was called *The Original Meaning of* the Zhouyi *(Zhouyi Benyi)*. Zhu Xi's great theme was that it was necessary to return to the original meaning and original intention behind the *Book of Changes*. He argued that the original meaning of the *Changes* was the oracular language of the basic text, and the numerological features and symbolic associations of the hexagrams, trigrams, and individual lines. The original intention of the *Changes*, he insisted, was as a book of divination prepared by the sages. They created the work so that ordinary people could connect to their wisdom through the practice of divination.[39]

By trying to draw abstract moral principles from the *Book of Changes*, Wang Bi and the members of the *yili* school had forgotten that knowledge and practice are interdependent. People cannot understand the *Book of Changes* by reading it passively. Rather they must engage with it actively and apply it to their own circumstances. This is only possible through the act of divination. By formulating a question, dividing the yarrow, consulting the hexagrams and oracular pronouncements, and applying the answers to their own lives, Zhu Xi thought, people could connect themselves to the wisdom of the sages. The point is not to recover that wisdom through learning a sterile set of maxims or doctrines but to create something new through interacting with the hexagrams and the plain language of the text. Every person will react differently to these concrete elements because everyone's situation and circumstances are different. Through consultation with yarrow stalks, the book will resonate with each individual's unique thought patterns and experiences. When we regard the *Book of Changes* properly as a book of divination, Zhu Xi argued, it becomes much more than a philosophical text accessible only to the learned. People from all walks of life can use it.

39. An excellent discussion of Zhu Xi's thought appears in Smith et al., *Sung Dynasty Uses of the I Ching*, pp. 169–205.

Thus, Zhu Xi disagreed with Wang Bi's notion that once people understood the principles behind the hexagrams and line statements they could dispense with the imagery. To the contrary, Zhu Xi insisted, it was necessary to encounter the actual language of the text and the actual meanings that were intended by the authors. Then the striking imagery of the text and the wealth of symbolic associations would spur the individual's imagination given his or her peculiar circumstances and life history. The *xiangshu* (image-and-number) commentators of the Earlier Han Dynasty recognized this, Zhu Xi thought, but they failed to apply it to human life and instead wasted their time on sterile discussions about mathematical transformations and the calendar. Wang Bi and the members of the *yili* school rightly focused on the centrality of the problems of the human condition, but they thought they could dispense with the concrete imagery of the book and speak instead only about abstract principles.

According to Zhu Xi, the sages understood the deep connection between knowing and doing and between morality and divination. They created the hexagrams in order to encourage people to engage in divination. In this way people would understand how to act appropriately in particular circumstances in accordance with the time. The goal of the *Changes* was oracular and not philosophical; the book was to be used to determine how to behave correctly in concrete situations but not to articulate a set of universal moral principles. Zhu Xi explained that King Wen and the Duke of Zhou added the hexagram judgments and line statements to assist people in divination, but not to offer moral instruction. Similarly, Confucius added the Ten Wings in order to explain why lines were auspicious and inauspicious but not to explicate moral theories. In effect, Zhu Xi argued, divination was a special kind of moral instruction, much more effective than the study of universal principles. Milfoil divination assisted people in self-cultivation. And because it was available to everyone, everyone from the nobility to the common people could use it to improve their morals and help order the state. To this end Zhu Xi wrote several essays and a book on the correct methods of divination.

There is profound wisdom and profound irony in Zhu Xi's theories about the *Book of Changes*. He saw that the most moving elements of the book lay in its concrete imagery. He also correctly emphasized that for most people the wisdom contained in the book could best be grasped through doing—discovering ethical truths through asking the oracle specific questions and applying the principles of the *Book of Changes* to concrete situations in one's own life. Finally, he insisted that the *Changes* was a book for everyone, available to all and interpretable by all. This anticipates many modern and more egalitarian ideals about the politics of interpretation, although Zhu Xi himself was no egalitarian in the contemporary sense. He lived in a very hierarchical society. Nevertheless, there is something decidedly "protestant" about his focus on individual encounters with the hexagrams and text. It is no accident that people who take what we might call "protestant" approaches to canonical works emphasize a return to the "original meaning" that can be found in the plain words of the text. Focusing on the plain meaning of the text allows the ordinary individual to participate in the interpretation of the sacred work without the intervention or supervision of a body of learning created by specialists.

On the other hand, Zhu Xi's insistence on a return to the original meanings and intentions of the sages is particularly ironic. His version of "original meaning" is surely not the original meaning of the Bronze Age diviners who created the *Zhouyi*. As we have seen, the meaning of many important words changed in the two thousand years that separates Zhu Xi from the Western Zhou Dynasty. Given what we know about the book's Bronze Age origins, his theory of the original intention of the sages is also fictional. The original purpose of the *Zhouyi* was decidedly not for ordinary people to gain wisdom through divination. The book was a diviner's manual for kings, not common folk, and they were interested not in wisdom but in victory, tribute money, good hunts, and successful alliances through marriage.

Of course, this sort of discrepancy is often the case when people claim to be returning to the original intention or original meaning behind an ongoing practice. Usually, they are inventing and imagining the very traditions that they would like to return to. They are projecting the cultural anxieties and aspirations of their own time onto the past; hence they see worthy values in the past whether or not these values actually existed in the way they now imagine them. In Zhu Xi's case, his focus on divination as a method of self-cultivation seems to reflect, if anything, the political milieu of the Song Dynasty in which he lived. Over the years, institutional and political reforms had been tried and had failed; hence Zhu Xi came to believe that only cultivation of individual character would save China from its problems. His approach to the *Book of Changes* reflects this.

Perhaps the greatest irony in Zhu Xi's work on the *Changes* is how it was later received. Zhu Xi argued that the *Changes* should not be reduced to a set of abstract scholastic principles, and that it must be interpreted by each individual based on his or her personal interaction with the hexagrams and text. Nevertheless, his work—like that of the other Song literati—became part of the Confucian orthodoxy of succeeding generations. In particular, both his interpretation and that of Cheng Yi became the orthodox interpretations of the *Book of Changes,* and together the two commentaries cemented the idea that the *Book of Changes* was a book of ageless wisdom that could not be improved upon. Both were included in the great compilation of the official text and commentaries of the *Book of Changes* ordered by the emperor and published in 1715.

Modern Interpretations

During the course of the twentieth century our understanding of the *Book of Changes* has changed drastically. Three separate phenomena have contributed to this reappraisal.

The first was the discovery of oracle bones, which gave the first indications of the divination practices in ancient China. The first oracle bones were discovered in 1899, and over the years thousands more have been uncovered.

The second important development was the application of modern methods of historical and textual criticism to the *Book of Changes*. Until the 1920s most scholars held to the mythological origins of the classic. However, during that decade Chinese scholars began to apply philological techniques to recover the original meaning of the *Zhouyi*. In 1929, Gu Jiegang published an important essay discussing the historical background of several of the different hexagram statements and line judgments. Two years later an issue of the journal *Gushi Bian* (Debates on Ancient History) reprinted this essay along with several others on the *Book of Changes*. Arthur Waley wrote a famous essay in 1933 discussing the new findings from China and pointing out the similarities between the line texts in the *Book of Changes* and what other cultures and civilizations regarded as omens and portents. During the 1930s, Iulian Shchutskii produced pioneering studies of the *Changes* in Russian, which were not translated into English until the 1970s. In 1947, following years of work, Gao Heng published an entire critical commentary on the text, *Zhouyi Gujing Jinzhu* (Modern Annotations to the Ancient Classic, *Zhouyi*).

The critical study of the text was propelled forward by the discovery of a manuscript of the *Changes* at Mawangdui in 1973. Since that time there has been a blossoming of *Yijing* studies, including important work on the origins of the *Zhouyi* by Richard Kunst and by Edward Shaughnessy (who also translated the Mawangdui manuscripts into English). These scholars have taken up Zhu Xi's injunction to present the original meaning of the book, although not in the way that Zhu Xi himself would have imagined or intended. What they have revealed is not Zhu Xi's book of timeless wisdom from the sages but a practical manual of divination for nobles and kings.

The third important development is the gradual reception of the *Book of Changes* into the West. Although the first translation into Latin took place in 1687, the book was not widely known in the West until the twentieth century. Thomas McClatchie produced the first English version in 1876, but the first truly great translation was James Legge's in 1882. Then, in 1924, Richard Wilhelm produced a magnificent translation into German, which quickly became recognized as a classic. Wilhelm's German translation was itself translated into English by Cary Fink Baynes in 1950, and became the standard translation in English. Its mystical and quasi-biblical style appealed greatly to readers with a spiritual bent in the English-speaking world. It achieved cult status beginning in the 1960s and has been the favorite of the New Age movement. John Blofeld produced a more homespun version of the *Changes* in 1965. Dozens of versions of the *I Ching* have been produced in the last half of the twentieth century. Most of these are not fresh translations but paraphrases of the text and commentaries cribbed from Legge and from Wilhelm / Baynes.

Legge's, Wilhelm's, and Blofeld's translations and commentaries reflect the tradition of the Song commentators as it was handed down by scholars in China's last dynasty, the Qing. For the same reason, they also reflect the traditional accounts of the book's origins. As a result, a very large number of popular accounts of the *Book of Changes*—most of which are based on the Wilhelm / Baynes translation—have incorporated none of the critical and archeological discoveries of the past century, and simply perpetuate the old myths. That began to change in the last years of the twentieth century, as new translations based on context criticism emerged. Richard Kunst reconstructed an English version of the Bronze Age *Zhouyi* in 1985, followed by Gregory Whincup in 1986 and Richard Rutt in 1996. That same year Edward Shaughnessy produced a translation of the Mawangdui manuscripts from the second century B.C. In 1994, Richard John Lynn produced the first English translation of Wang Bi's commentary, giving us a sense of the book's interpretation in the third century A.D.

At the beginning of the twenty-first century it has become clear that there is not one *Book of Changes* but many. The *Book*'s great strength has been its ability to be adapted and reinterpreted to suit the needs of successive cultures and generations over the course of three thousand years. Like all great classics, the *Book of Changes* speaks to different times in different ways. It is entirely fitting that a book about the inevitability of change should itself have undergone so many changes in its interpretation and reception from its origins in the Bronze Age to the present day. There is no doubt that a century from now—or even a millennium—it will appear different still.

PART TWO

The *Book of Changes* with Commentaries

A Note on the Text and the Commentaries

In the commentaries that follow, a separate section is devoted to each hexagram. Each section begins with the hexagram name, followed by a series of keywords. The keywords describe the hexagram's basic themes in a few short words and phrases and list other common English names for the hexagram. Following the keywords, I note the hexagram's constituent trigrams and offer a brief commentary about the structure of the hexagram. Next comes the text of the hexagram judgment, followed by the Commentary on the Great Image, and the line judgments, with commentary on each portion. All of the text from the *Book of Changes* is in italics. The commentary that follows is in roman type.

At the end of each section I have provided a few translator's notes, with occasional quotes from the Wilhelm/Baynes and other well-known translations for comparison so that the reader has some sense of the interpretive choices I have made.

A full discussion of the sources used in preparing the translation and the commentaries appears in the Bibliographical Essay at the end of the book.

The Upper Canon

HEXAGRAMS 1–30

ONE

Qian • The Dynamic

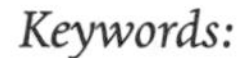

Keywords:

Activity
Creativity
Dynamic force
Assertion
Strength
Decisiveness
Strong action
Going forward
Moving upward
Undertaking something
Constant and ceaseless exertion

Above: Qian • Heaven
Below: Qian • Heaven

The hexagram for Qian consists of six yang lines. It represents the yang principle in its purest form. It is the natural complement of Kun, the Receptive, which is pure yin. Together Qian and Kun symbolize the basic principles of alternation and change in the universe.

THE JUDGMENT

The Dynamic.
Supreme success.
It is beneficial to persevere.

The *Book of Changes* begins with the dynamic principle, which has four basic attributes. It is (1) fundamental (sublime, originating, and supreme), (2) successful (bestowing power), (3) beneficial (advantageous, and morally appropriate), and (4) persevering (determined, steadfast, and upright). These are the four virtues of the *Book of Changes*. The four Chinese words for these attributes *(yuan heng li zhen)* are often used to represent the four seasons, or virtually anything that can be divided into four.

The four virtues are usually paired: fundamental with successful, and beneficial with persevering. Thus, the text says that dynamic action will help you achieve supreme success; and it is beneficial to persevere—that is, to keep moving forward. To conduct yourself in accordance with the nature of the times, you should make the four virtues your own: attend to what is basic and fundamental, and persevere in what is beneficial and morally upright. The text enjoins you to use your creative power for good—to bring order out of chaos, beauty out of squalor, peace out of tumult, and justice out of injustice.

Qian signifies that you are in a very favorable situation if you take the right approach. This is not a time to hold back. Rather, you must take strong, decisive action. Seize the initiative. Go out into the world and make a difference. Be creative. Look for fresh and original ways to solve your problems. It is time to try something new and bold. If you move forward now with confidence, others will have confidence in you. If you are willing to act on your beliefs and stand up for what you believe is right, people will look up to you and follow you. Your energy and enthusiasm will inspire them and this will help you achieve your goals. Have faith in yourself and maintain a positive attitude. You have every reason to be optimistic. And the more optimistic and enthusiastic you are about your project, the more you will help to ensure your ultimate success.

No matter how dynamic and forceful you may be, however, strong action will amount to nothing if it is not for the right purposes. If you want to harness the right kind of creative power, you must be convinced that what you are doing is correct and you must steadfastly maintain your integrity and uprightness. Go back to basics. Return to your most fundamental principles. People who know that their cause is just are the most powerful of all. Their heart, mind, and spirit all aim at the same end. They embody the dynamic principle perfectly; hence they are like a force of nature. Because they harbor no doubts or inner conflicts, their energy and initiative are put to their highest use, and that is why they succeed. In the same way, if you want to make the most of this propitious hour, you must devote yourself to something that is truly worthy. You must employ your energies for honorable goals. Do not waste your time on things that are base, trivial, or beneath you. The moment for creative action will not last forever, so do not squander it.

Strong action also will not succeed if it is not carefully thought through and carried forward. Do not confuse dynamism with recklessness or creativity with carelessness. Plan ahead. Try to gauge the consequences of what you are about to do. Marshal your resources carefully, and when the time is right, do not be afraid to move forward boldly and decisively. Moreover, once you have begun, you must finish what you start. Behind creativity there must be commitment or your plans will amount to nothing. You must keep moving forward steadily and determinedly until you succeed. Hence the text says that it is beneficial to persevere.

THE IMAGE

Heaven moves constantly.
Thus the superior person strengthens himself without pause.

"Heaven moves constantly" refers to the doubling of the trigram Qian (Heaven), symbolizing the movement of heaven from one day to the next. Just as time moves forward ceaselessly at a constant pace, and the sky moves without slackening or pausing as the earth spins on its axis, you should make progress continuously.

This is a time of great opportunity and abundant energy. You can make the best use of it by following a few simple principles. First, employ your energy wisely. Decide what your priorities are and don't waste your resources by aimlessly chasing after too many different things. Second, your energy is only as valuable as the goals you pursue. If you devote yourself to positive ends, you will have considerable influence. Other people will look up to you and follow you. On the other hand, if you use your energy for selfish or improper purposes, you will merely spread chaos and conflict. Third, do not be arrogant or throw your weight around because things are going well. Listen to other people. Be kind, tolerant, and willing to cooperate. If other people are on your side, your opportunities for progress will increase. Fourth, work on developing your talents and acquiring endurance. This will help you take advantage of the good times while they last and help prolong them into the future. Fifth, work steadily and continuously until you achieve your goals. The text compares how you should behave to the movement of the heavens around the earth. This motion is completely natural, ceaseless, and unforced, yet nothing is more powerful and enduring.

THE LINES

The lines tell the story of the rise of the dragon, who symbolizes dynamic and creative force. The dragon is a good omen in Chinese thought. In line one the dragon has not yet appeared; in line six it has gone too far. In this hexagram and Kun (The Receptive), the text gives a special indication for when all lines are moving. This is possible only for some systems of divination that allow for more than one changing line, like the yarrow-stalk and three-coin methods.

Initial Nine

The dragon is submerged. Do not act.

The dragon symbolizes a dynamic creative force. The fact that it is submerged (or hidden) means that the time is not yet right for action. The situation is not yet clear. Your strength and abilities are not yet recognized by others. Therefore, it is best to be patient. Wait for the right moment to act decisively. Don't waste your energies on a premature display of power.

You shouldn't become discouraged because your efforts have not yet been recognized. Nor should you fear that if you delay the outcome will go against you. Instead, have faith that the ultimate result will be successful. In time, matters will become clear and the time for action will arrive.

Nevertheless, there are still things you can do in the meantime. The submerged dragon is still a creative force, but it does not make a show of its creativity. In the same way, you should be like the hidden dragon and keep a low profile. Prepare for action quietly, behind the scenes. Gather intelligence and try to clarify the situation until it is time for you to emerge on the scene.

Nine in the Second Place

The dragon appears in the field.
It is beneficial to see a great person.

"The dragon appears in the field" means that it is now possible to exercise your creative abilities to accomplish great things. You have begun to make your presence felt, but you are not yet in a dominant position or in a position of leadership. Hence it is beneficial to "see a great person," i.e., to seek advice from or to cooperate with a person of influence and experience who has interests similar to your own or is in the same field of endeavor. Great people are not merely those with power and influence; they also set an example through greatness of spirit and proper conduct. They are role models for others. Seek out such a person to emulate or work with. Try to find these sagelike qualities within yourself. In fact, the lines in this hexagram can be seen as the stages in the development of your own creative powers.

Nine in the Third Place

All day the superior person is active,
At night he remains alert.
There is danger,
But no blame.

Your creative powers are increasing, and with them come new influence and new opportunities. You feel full of energy; there is so much to do. In such times temptations inevitably arise. You see so much you want to accomplish and you find it hard to concentrate on the right things.

People make new demands on you, and others try to take advantage of your influence and your resources. It is important not to become sidetracked and dissipate your growing energies. Do not let your ambitions or your desires to please and impress others lead you astray. Rather, you must decide what your priorities truly are. You must find your own voice and your own vision and maintain your integrity at all costs. Hence the text tells us "danger, [b]ut no blame." If you act with integrity and clarity of vision, you can avoid the dangers of temptation in a time of growing creative power and influence.

Nine in the Fourth Place

Wavering over the depths.
No blame.

In the fourth line, the dragon is pictured as wavering over the ocean, not sure whether to ascend higher or remain below.

As your creative powers emerge, you are presented with a choice. Creativity can be expressed either in the outer world through service to others or within the self in the quest for enlightenment and self-development. You can soar high in the public world of fame and fortune or withdraw into seclusion. You can take a higher profile in the situation at hand or retreat and pursue other goals. Faced with such a choice, you must exercise your own free will and discover what is right for you. Decide which course of action best suits your temperament and who you really are. The text tells us, "no blame." This means that if you act with integrity and are true to yourself, you will not make a mistake. Trust your intuitions. Either path is correct for you.

Nine in the Fifth Place (Ruling Line)

The dragon flies high in the sky.
It is beneficial to see a great person.

A dragon flying high in the sky is not only powerful and awesome but can be seen by many as it soars across the heavens. In the same way, your creative power and influence are at their height. Others look up to you for inspiration. You are a role model for others and should act accordingly. Like the dragon, you should fly in the heavens and shun any base designs or actions.

This is a favorable time of great clarity and it offers enormous possibilities for achievement. Your actions and creative powers are completely in accord with the time. If you set your mind to it, you can accomplish virtually anything you want. You have abundant influence and resources, so use them well. Be like the dragon: Aim high and try to achieve something truly worthy and noble.

Nine at the Top

An arrogant dragon will have cause to regret.

In this line the dragon has flown so high that it leaves the world altogether. As in the Greek myth of Icarus, whose wings melted when he flew too close to the sun, the dragon overreaches and suffers a catastrophic fall. The text symbolizes people whose ambitions exceed their creative power. Just as the dragon separates itself from the earth (the symbol of receptivity and interdependence), these people forget that their success depends on the support of others. Wrongly assuming that they are sufficient unto themselves and have no need of anyone else, they treat others with disrespect and ultimately undermine their position.

If your pride becomes too great and your ambitions too unrealistic, you will become arrogant and selfish. This will inevitably lead to failure. If you try to fly too high, you will become isolated from others and lose touch with reality. Do not let previous successes go to your head. Restrain your unrealistic ambitions and reestablish links with people in your community. Do not overreach and do not go to extremes. Be modest and humble and understand the limits of your power. Recognize how your influence depends on the cooperation and goodwill of others. If you do not ground yourself now, you will fall to earth later on.

All Lines Moving

A flock of dragons appears without heads.
Good fortune.

When all lines are changing, the hexagram is transformed into Hexagram 2, Kun, The Receptive. This symbolizes a perfect balance between yin and yang, the receptive and the dynamic, and connotes exceptional good fortune. Strength coupled with mildness, power and ability coupled with open-mindedness and adaptability, ensure a favorable result, for the universe itself reflects the alternation of yin and yang. And if one is in accord with the way of the universe, how can one go wrong?

NOTES

N.B.: In these notes the individual lines are identified as .1, .2, .3, etc. The text of the hexagram judgment is identified as .0. The text of the Commentary on the Great Image (or "The Image") from the Third and Fourth Wings is identified as .GI. Thus, 35.5 refers to the fifth line of Hexagram 35; and 42.GI refers to the commentary on the Great Image for Hexagram 42.

1.0 "Dynamic." Or "Creative" (Wilhelm/Baynes). "Dynamic" better captures the notion of strong action moving ceaselessly upward. Moreover, in the Western tradition the word "creative" suggests creation. The temptation to read Qian in this way may be compounded by the fact that Qian is the first hexagram in the sequence. However, Qian is not the beginning of all things like the creation ex nihilo described in the book of Genesis. Rather, it is only the beginning of a new cycle of upward movement. The Chinese vision of history is cyclical rather than unidirectional. Yin and yang alternate ceaselessly and endlessly. Hence "dynamic" is a better translation. Alfred Huang translates Qian as "Initiating," Gregory Whincup translates it as "Strong Action," and Richard John Lynn translates it as "Pure Yang."

1.0 "The Dynamic," etc. This judgment lists the four basic properties of Qian. This formula *(yuan heng li zhen)* appears in a number of other hexagrams as well. Cf. 2.0, 3.0, 17.0, 19.0, 45.0. An alternative rendering is "The Dynamic is fundamental (originating, sublime), successful, beneficial, and persevering," or "Creative action offers supreme success; it is beneficial to keep going." The original meaning of *yuan heng li zhen* in the Bronze Age had little to do with the moral concepts later attributed to these words. At the time the *Book of Changes* was first compiled, the words probably meant "Great reception [of sacrifice]; the divination is beneficial," or possibly "The primary [sacrifice] has been received; it is beneficial to divine [again]," i.e., advising a second divination.

1.GI "Heaven moves constantly." The text of the Commentary on the Great Image usually lists the hexagram's constituent trigrams, repeats the name of the hexagram, and then offers an ethical comment on what a superior person would do in the situation governed by the hexagram. In the case of the hexagrams Qian and Kun, however, the Commentary on the Great Image does not state the hexagram name.

1.GI "The superior person." *jun zi*. Originally, "prince's son," or "nobleman"; in Confucian parlance "the superior person." It means someone who follows appropriate conduct and lives according to the Dao, or Way. One might also translate it as "the enlightened person." The subject of the Commentary on the Great Image is the appropriate behavior of the superior person during the time indicated by the hexagram.

1.GI "strengthens himself without pause." *yi zi qian bu shi:* uses origin strength no pause. Or, "develops his vitality ceaselessly," "develops himself so that his work endures," "never ceases to strengthen himself" (Lynn), "makes himself strong and untiring" (Wilhelm/Baynes).

1.1. "submerged." *qian*: immersed in water. Hence, "hidden," "secret," "reserved."

1.2 "A great person." *da ren*: literally, "big man," a noble or powerful lord; the expression later takes on the additional meanings of a person of importance, a wise person, a sage. (Cf. Wilhem/Baynes, "see the great man.") Another interpretation is to consult the sage within yourself.

1.4 "wavering." *huo*: some, maybe, hesitating; *yue*: leap, play. Another possible translation is "Someone leaps (or hesitates over leaping) into the depths."

1.5 "high in the sky." *zai tian*: in the heavens.

1.6 "arrogant." *kang*: overreaching.

1.6 "regret." Or, "repent."

TWO

Kun • The Receptive

䷁

Keywords:

Receptivity
Docility
Acceptance
Acquiescence
Adjustment
Nurturing

Above: Kun • Earth
Below: Kun • Earth

The hexagram for Kun consists of six yin lines. It represents pure yin, the natural complement to Qian, which is pure yang. Kun symbolizes the dark as opposed to the light, the yielding as opposed to the forceful, the female as opposed to the male, the maternal as opposed to the paternal, the receptive as opposed to the dynamic, following as opposed to leading, submission as opposed to domination, the acceptance of the world as opposed to the imposition of will. Each element in these dualities depends on the other for its coherence; hence there is no question of one being more important or more essential to life. In proper balance Kun promises success every bit as great as Qian. Only when yin struggles against yang and attempts to lead or dominate does it produce evil, just as misplaced yang energy equally results in wickedness and corruption.

THE JUDGMENT

The Receptive. Supreme success.
It is beneficial to be constant like a mare.
If the superior person sets out to do something, he will go astray,
But if he follows, he will find guidance.
It is beneficial to find friends in the southwest and to forego friends in the northeast.
Serene perseverance brings good fortune.

The four fundamental attributes *yuan heng li zhen* (fundamental, successful, beneficial, and persevering) describe Kun as they do Qian. However, the "perseverance of a mare" in Kun contrasts with Qian's injunction to steadfast endurance. Whereas Qian advises us to pursue our ends constantly, doggedly, and incessantly like the ceaseless movement of the heavens, Kun advises us to accept and endure change, adjusting to and even welcoming what occurs. In place of untiring striving we should adopt the gentle and devoted perseverance of the mare. The mare follows the lead of others and is by nature accommodating and accepting—qualities which are appropriate to the situation. The mare also contrasts with the dragon featured in the line statements of Qian. The dragon flies in the heavens and so symbolizes heaven; the mare roams freely throughout the full extent of the earth and hence symbolizes earth. The southwest is also traditionally associated with the earth; hence to find friends in the southwest means to seek assistance from others employing the virtues associated with earth—humility, devotion, cooperation, and responsiveness. In this context the northeast represents the opposite qualities. Therefore, in seeking friends one should avoid arrogance, lack of commitment, selfishness, and indifference. Serene perseverance brings good fortune because we adapt ourselves to the situation and accept it for what it is. Hence we are able to do what the situation demands of us naturally and are able to make progress in exactly the right way.

The situation you face requires responsiveness to circumstances and devotion to doing the right thing given the specific context in which you find yourself. Responsiveness does not mean lassitude or passivity—it means action that is in accord with the demands of the situation, action that flows naturally with events rather than trying to resist or confront them directly. This is not the time to try to seize control of things or take the initiative. Nor should you move ahead without consulting other people. If you do so, you will only create chaos and confusion. Rather, you should do your best to understand what circumstances require and how you can best adapt and respond to them. To do this you must put aside your preconceptions and your ego. Keep an open mind. Listen to other people and try to learn from them. Act with generosity and kindness. Put your talents and abilities in the service of others. Seek out friends and helpers to work with. Through devotion, adaptability, and careful attention to detail, you can achieve very great things. For the text tells us that the receptive, like the dynamic, offers the possibility of supreme success.

Receptivity to circumstances is not inertia. It is not the opposite of dynamic action but rather its natural complement. Receptive people follow and adjust to the course of events in the world. They do not try to mold the world to their will or pretend that matters are what they are not. They accept the world as it is and respond to it naturally. They follow the lead of others and consider how best to make a contribution. They assist those who need assistance; they are generous where generosity is required. They put themselves at the disposal of the situation so that they can improve it. Although receptive people do not try to lead or enforce their will, through their resilience and dedication they nevertheless succeed in having the most powerful influence on events.

Implicit in receptiveness is realism—adapting to things as they are rather than the way we would like them to be. (English has a similar metaphor that identifies earth with realism. We say that a realistic person does not have his head in the clouds but is down to earth.) This realism is the very opposite of surrender or capitulation. Indeed, it is the necessary prerequisite to effective action, and to doing what the situation truly demands. As the text says, if we set forth blindly, we will soon go astray, but if we follow, we will find guidance from the situation itself. In this way the situation begins to adapt itself to us even as we adapt ourselves to it. If we do not try to impose willful preconceptions on the world, it will perpetually surprise us with all manner of possibilities. An attitude of receptivity thus produces a fertility of imagination, which is able to behold a similar fertility in the world itself.

Finally, receptiveness does not mean conforming to the world resignedly. It means that one acts so as to nourish it. Kun teaches that through acceptance and adaptability we can redeem what is base and ignoble and make what is good in the world even better. In this way we can bring something to the situation and add peace and prosperity to the world. Instead of trying to dominate or impose our will on those around us, we act as a midwife or assistant, helping others achieve their ends and in this way exerting our influence indirectly, gently, and persistently. Kun teaches us that one does not have to take the lead in order to have influence, one does not have to be dynamic in order to exercise power, one does not have to be arrogant in order to impress others, and one does not have to be first in everything in order to prevail in the end.

THE IMAGE

The basic disposition of Earth is Receptive.
Thus the superior person supports all things with his generous virtue.

The doubling of the trigram symbolizes the vast expanse of the earth, which is able to carry and support everything upon it, no matter how great or small, good or bad, significant or inconsequential. The support that earth offers to all things is a metaphor for broad-mindedness, generosity, devotion, endurance, and receptiveness. Enlightened people develop these qualities in themselves so that like the earth they can accept and bear with everything they encounter. Open your mind and your heart. Rely on your instincts and your intuition. Abandon artifice and cunning. Instead of trying to control things, allow the situation to guide you. Then without any special effort on your part, you will naturally take the proper path.

THE LINES

Lines two through five of the hexagram describe different forms of receptivity. The first line explains what happens if one does not respond to changing circumstances and takes no precautions; the sixth line tells the story of one who fails to be receptive to others and winds up in a power struggle with harmful consequences. As with Qian (The Dynamic), there is a special text for when all lines are changing.

Initial Six

The frost underfoot will soon become solid ice.

The hoarfrost symbolizes the onset of winter, and hence, metaphorically, the beginning of decay, deterioration, and death. If events proceed in their natural course, what begins as the mere hoarfrost of autumn eventually becomes the cold and snow of darkest winter.

The meaning is that you should be on the lookout for the first signs of things going wrong in a situation. It is best to deal with problems when they are small, before they have had a chance to grow large and become more difficult to manage. The law of change is inexorable, but with alertness and patience, one can head off decay and difficulty before they become too great.

Six in the Second Place (Ruling Line)

Straight, square, and great.
He does nothing, yet nothing fails to be beneficial.

Square, straight, and great are characteristics of the earth. Square means solid and grounded; straight means dependable and unprepossessing; and great means abundant and tolerant. These are all qualities associated with the Receptive. The Receptive accommodates and furthers the initiatives of others, hence it "does nothing," that is, it acts naturally without calling attention to its efforts or imposing its own will.

The text suggests that you imitate the good qualities of the earth. Be tolerant and accepting of others. Act without artifice or pretension. Behave naturally, simply, and straightforwardly without any machinations or hidden motivation. Rely on your intuition instead of trying to overthink things. Be generous and tolerant of others. Accept people for what they are and try to be accommodating.

When you imitate the earth, you do exactly what is necessary in any situation, no more and no less. Hence you "do nothing"; that is, you do not put on a show or draw attention to your work. Because you do not make a fuss, your progress appears effortless. At the same time, "nothing fails to be beneficial" because everything that needs to be done is done.

Six in the Third Place

One who effaces his brilliance will be able to persevere.
If he works for his lord,
He should take no credit for success,
But bring about a successful conclusion.

To "efface one's brilliance" means that you should not actively pursue fame. Resist vanity and give up the constant need to be recognized. Leave grandstanding and showy display to others. Rather, just do the best job you can. By devoting yourself to the work at hand and by not drawing attention to yourself, you can develop your talents naturally and without interference. If you focus on cultivating yourself and perfecting your abilities, your efforts will eventually pay off. People will recognize your contributions in the long run, so don't try to take credit for them or boast about your talents and accomplishments. Instead of pursuing your own interests selfishly, work for the good of all. Pave the way for others, and they will be grateful for your help.

Six in the Fourth Place

A tied-up sack.
No blame, no praise.

"A tied-up sack" means keeping your own counsel. This line describes a difficult time when it is important to be reserved and reticent. Maintain a low profile. Do not provoke a confrontation. Drawing attention to yourself now will lead to jealousy or antagonism from others, or burdensome obligations and responsibilities. Whether you withdraw into solitude or remain in society you must learn how to act with reserve and keep your thoughts and feelings to yourself during periods of danger.

Six in the Fifth Place

A yellow skirt brings supreme good fortune.

Yellow is the color of the earth. It symbolizes the mean, the middle way, and the path of moderation. It also symbolizes sincerity, genuineness, and reliability. These are all qualities you should cultivate. A skirt is a lower garment worn below the waist. It symbolizes discretion and reserve.

Behave with modesty and tact. A low-key approach will bring about good results. Be discreet and respectful of others, and everything will turn out for the best. Avoid confrontation or braggadocio. Do not make a show of your virtues or try to impress others with your accomplishments. Be sincere and genuine, and your good qualities will reveal themselves in everything that you do and say.

Six at the Top

Dragons fight in the meadow.
Their blood is black and yellow.

Here heaven (symbolized by black, or midnight blue) is at war with earth (symbolized by yellow). Heaven and earth should not be in conflict but should work together harmoniously, with earth taking its proper place below heaven. The text describes a battle in which a person tries to overthrow someone with greater authority. He fails, and both parties are injured in the attempt.

Do not engage in power struggles. Arrogance, overreaching, and competitiveness will only backfire and make everyone worse off, including yourself. Be accommodating, cooperative, and flexible. Do not try to usurp others or demand more than you are entitled to, or you will someday regret it.

All Lines Moving

It is beneficial to be perpetually persevering.

When all lines are moving, Kun, The Receptive, is transformed into Qian, The Dynamic. The text explains that if you persevere in correct conduct you will eventually win. Do not lose heart but be committed to what is right and see things through to the end. In so doing you will become the sort of person whose steadfast nature is the deep and powerful source of his or her success. Thus, the virtues of earth (steadfastness, commitment, sincerity) are miraculously transformed into the characteristics of heaven (power, ascendancy, success). Learning to persevere through life's vicissitudes will develop and strengthen your character and give you the inner resolve that will help you in any situation.

NOTES

2.0 "The Receptive. Supreme success." Or, "The Receptive offers supreme success," "The receptive is fundamental, successful." *yuan heng:* fundamental success. Cf. 1.0. Like 1.0, this text also lists the four fundamental attributes. However, in this case, the text separates the first two attributes from the second two, *li* and *zhen*.

2 Kun • The Receptive

2.0 “southwest . . . northeast.” Or, “the south and the west . . . the north and the east.” Cf. 39.0. By tradition the trigram Kun (Earth) is associated with the southwest.

2.2 “does nothing.” *bu xi:* literally, “not repeating,” or “not practicing.” Cf. 29.GI (carrying on), 58.GI (practicing). Cf. Wilhelm/Baynes, “Without purpose.” The idea is that one does not make a fuss but rather acts naturally and responsively.

2.6 “meadow.” *ye:* countryside, open fields. Cf. 13.0.

THREE

Zhun • Difficulty in the Beginning

Keywords:

Pushing up out of the ground
Growing pains
Birth throes
Birth pangs
Initial difficulties
Time to gather helpers

Above: Kan • Water
Below: Zhen • Thunder

The ancient Chinese ideograph for Zhun features a blade of grass that tries to push against the soil as it sprouts up from the earth. The lower trigram of the hexagram is Zhen (Thunder), which symbolizes the arousing and upward motion. The upper trigram is Kan (Water), which symbolizes danger and downward motion. The combination of thunder and water represents the initial chaos and formlessness of the beginnings of a new situation. After the initial confusion, rain eventually falls and tensions are relieved. The symbol of the blade of grass pushing up into darkness counsels patience during a difficult time. One must conserve one's energies and gain strength. Yet the very conditions of chaos—the rain that falls from the storm—will nourish the plant and help it grow upward. Thus there is the promise of ultimate success when the grass reaches the light of day.

THE JUDGMENT

Difficulty in the Beginning. Supreme success.
It is beneficial to persevere.
Do not use this as an opportunity to undertake anything.
It is beneficial to establish feudal lords.

"To undertake something" means to engage in something ambitious. In ancient China, rulers granted lands and titles to feudatories in exchange for their promise of help and support, and in particular promises of military assistance when the ruler was attacked. Hence "to establish feudal lords" means to seek help from others during a difficult time.

You face a situation akin to growing pains. A new era is beginning. Things are struggling to take form. Chaos is slowly and painfully being converted into the first semblance of a new order. This confusion may reside in your projects and undertakings, in your own thoughts and desires, or even in your relationships with others. You may find that what you once thought was settled and clear has now become unsettled and uncertain. You may be questioning old assumptions and beliefs, although you are not yet quite sure what to replace them with. You are leaving the confines of the safe and familiar and moving to a new frontier of indeterminate scope and abundant possibilities. Indeed, there are so many possibilities now that you may find yourself adrift and confused. But the current lack of form brings the promise of ultimate success, for there is much potential here. Nevertheless, precisely because things are still so unsettled, you must not act prematurely or attempt any great undertakings. This is not the time to be overly ambitious. Rather, you must move slowly and carefully, feeling your way about and beginning to consolidate your position. You could benefit greatly from the help and advice of other people during this difficult time. Do not be too proud to ask for assistance. Look to people more experienced than yourself to advise you. They will help you sort out your thoughts and establish new priorities. Then you will be able to decide the path that you must follow.

THE IMAGE

Clouds and thunder:
This is the image of Difficulty in the Beginning.
Thus the superior person regulates and brings order.

Clouds and thunder represent the beginning of a storm, but after the storm is over, tension is released and peace and order are restored. A storm may seem to be the very embodiment of disorder, but it brings rain to the earth and the promise of new growth. In the same way, the current chaos you are experiencing already contains the seeds of future possibility. An enlightened person strives to recognize the beginnings of new order in the current confusion and helps them develop naturally. The text analogizes this process to weaving—this is the literal meaning of "regulates and brings order." First one must untangle the threads and separate them. Then one must slowly and carefully weave them into a new order. Neither the untangling nor the weaving can be done quickly. Each requires patience and care so that the threads are not broken and the weaving is done properly.

The greatest virtue you can have right now is patience. Especially when matters are complicated and confused, you may be tempted to push forward recklessly, or to seize the first opportunity that presents itself. This would be a mistake. You do not yet know all of the parameters of the situation or how things will gradually emerge. Instead, you must remain calm and take the longer view of things. You must gather your resources and slowly but surely clarify your thoughts and organize your plans. The way forward is not yet clear, but it soon will be. Have faith that things will ultimately work out for the best.

THE LINES

The lines describe different strategies for dealing with initial difficulties. Lines one and two counsel patience; lines four and five counsel perseverance. These attitudes produce favorable results in the long run. By contrast, in line three, one pushes ahead recklessly, and in line six, one gives in to despair. These attitudes meet with misfortune.

Initial Nine (Ruling Line)

Back and forth; making no headway.
It is beneficial to remain persevering.
It is beneficial to establish feudal lords.

At the beginning of a new enterprise, you meet with obstacles and hindrances. Do not force matters. Stop and think about the situation. Just because you have met with resistance does not mean you should give up. On the contrary, now is the time to be steadfast. Persevere and do not lose confidence in yourself. Keep sight of your ultimate goal. But the difficulties you face suggest that you may need help from others; hence the reference to establishing feudal lords. In ancient China a king would award fiefs and appoint lords. In return for land and noble titles, the lords promised to assist him in times of trouble.

Do not be afraid to ask for help. A vain and stubborn person insists on doing everything himself because he does not trust others or seeks all the glory. For different reasons the same is true of people who lack the courage to persevere. Afraid to seek help, they simply flounder, become paralyzed with self-doubt, and eventually give up. A wise person knows when the path to success requires the assistance of others. Be humble and open-minded and you will attract the support you need.

Six in the Second Place

Difficulties create an impasse,
Like a team of yoked horses pulling against each other.
He does not seek to plunder;
He seeks to marry.
The maiden practices constancy,
She does not pledge herself.
After ten years—then she pledges herself.

This story of the betrothed woman is a metaphor for dealing with difficulties. Sometimes, nothing seems to be going right in our efforts to advance. Things seem to be at cross purposes. Hence, the text tells us, it is as the horses of our carriage were pulling in opposite directions. Suddenly, someone offers an unexpected solution, a quick and easy escape, or a clever end run around the situation. This solution may be offered with the best of motives. Nevertheless, we must not be tempted to take the easy way out. This solution is not right for us. Like an offer of marriage, it has serious consequences, and it imposes new and undesirable obligations and responsibilities. It will keep us from making the right choice later on. Instead, we should bide our time until things become clearer. Hence the text says to wait "ten years," the length of a fulfilled cycle of time. If we are patient and have faith, we will get the help we need from the right people at the right time.

Six in the Third Place

Hunting deer without the forester
Only gets one lost in the forest.
The superior person understands that it is better to desist.
Going forth leads to humiliation.

A forest is a strange place with many unforeseen difficulties and dangers. A person who plunges into such a forest without an experienced guide often meets with disaster. In the same way, when an unfamiliar situation produces difficulties, you should recognize that you lack experience in dealing with the situation. If you go ahead without advice or help, you will lose your way in the forest. If you aggressively push forward out of stubbornness, vanity, and egotism, you will meet with humiliation. A wise person understands when the time is not right to achieve something and when a desired adventure would be premature and insufficiently prepared. This is not the right time for the hunt; you should pick another goal.

Six in the Fourth Place

Like a team of yoked horses pulling against each other.
Nevertheless one strives for union.
To go on brings good fortune.
There is nothing for which this is not beneficial.

The lesson of this line is that you must never be too proud or too afraid to accept help or join with others if it will allow you to achieve your goals. Recognizing that you cannot succeed alone and having the humility to ask for assistance is not a sign of weakness or disgrace but evidence of wisdom and clarity of thought. You must take the first step to find the right people and ask for their aid and advice. Trust that if you do, everything will go well. As the text says, "[t]here is nothing for which this is not beneficial."

Nine in the Fifth Place (Ruling Line)

Difficulty in achieving abundance.
A little perseverance brings good fortune.
Too much perseverance brings misfortune.

In this situation, you know what must be done to succeed but you cannot yet achieve your goals. Some people misinterpret your meaning and intentions; others actively interfere with your progress. Thus, you must act with great caution and discretion. Do not make a show of your efforts or try to force matters. Take things one step at a time. Act with patience and sensitivity to others around you. If you are to prevail, you will need to get others to trust you and have confidence in your abilities. In the meantime, have faith, and work conscientiously behind the scenes. Start small; don't try to take on too much. Eventually, the difficulties will resolve themselves and you will succeed.

Six at the Top

Like a team of yoked horses pulling against each other.
One weeps tears of blood.

Faced with difficulties, some people despair and become trapped in cycles of failure and recrimination. They convince themselves that the struggle is too great and it becomes too great; they tell themselves that it is all too much for them and so it becomes too much; they see themselves as failures and so inevitably they fail. You are in danger of falling into such a cycle of resignation and remorse. You have lost your perspective, and hence lost your way in the situation. You cannot see the difficulties you face for what they are—they are real but not limitless—and hence you cannot find your way past them. If you do not take a more realistic attitude, things will never improve. The obstacles to your success are now located not in the outside world but within yourself.

Take a fresh look at the situation. Recognize that you do have the ability to succeed, and that the problems you face are not insurmountable ones.

Have faith that you can overcome your current frustrations. Leave the past behind and learn to move on to better things before it is too late.

NOTES

3.0 "Difficulty in the Beginning. Supreme success." Or, "Difficulty in the Beginning can yet produce supreme success." Here again, the four virtues of the *Book of Changes* are listed, so one could render the line as follows: "Difficulty in the Beginning is fundamental, successful, beneficial, and persevering."

3.0 "establish feudal lords." *hou:* skilled archers, also, a leader, a head, or a feudal lord. The idea is to appoint skilled people who can render assistance. Hence "appoint helpers" (Wilhelm/Baynes).

3.GI "Regulates and brings order." *jing lun:* brings order and weaves things together, i.e., weaves the fabric of government.

3.1 "to establish feudal lords." Or, "to appoint helpers," "to establish a leader (chief)." Cf. 3.0.

3.2 "like a team of yoked horses pulling against each other." *cheng ma ban ru:* riding (driving) horses arrayed thus. The line can be translated many different ways—e.g., "as yoked horses pulling apart" (Lynn); "Mounting on horses, still not going forward" (Alfred Huang); "Horse and wagon part" (Wilhelm/Baynes). The present translation, like Lynn's, tries to convey the source of the difficulties.

3.2 "does not seek to plunder, etc." Cf. 22.4, 38.6.

FOUR

Meng • Youthful Inexperience

䷃

Keywords:

Innocence
Ignorance
Immaturity
Youthful folly
Wisdom not yet revealed
The young shoot
Beginner's luck

Above: Gen • Mountain
Below: Kan • Water

Meng originally referred to a twining plant called the dodder, which like ivy grows everywhere and spreads easily. The ideograph for Meng shows the plant covering and spreading over the roof of a house. Eventually, it came to stand for children (the young shoot) and for the covering or concealment of wisdom that is inherent in children. Hence the idea of "youthful folly" carries the dual meanings of inexperience and of the wisdom that lies beneath the surface and can be brought out through education and proper training. To educate and instruct means to uncover the wisdom that is already within the heart of a child. The trigram Kan (Water) gushes forth without direction from beneath Gen (The Mountain), symbolizing the enthusiasm of youth that needs to be channeled and guided in order to realize potential and achieve success.

Both this hexagram and the preceding one, Zhun, describe the problems of beginners. In Zhun one sets out to achieve something and immediately encounters difficulty because the situation is still unformed. In Meng one already has the rudiments of experience but does not know what to do. The neophyte often experiences "beginner's luck" in dealing with a new problem, but this intuitive ability must be disciplined and trained if it is to become a lasting form of skill.

THE JUDGMENT

Youthful Inexperience. Success.
It is not I who seek the ignorant youth;
The ignorant youth seeks me.
The first time he performs the divination, I answer him;
The second or third time it is insulting.
Because it is insulting, I tell him nothing.
It is beneficial to persevere.

Meng describes a situation in which you have limited experience and do not know how to deal with the situation before you. Whether you realize it or not, you need to seek help. But instruction is useless unless the pupil understands the need for instruction and is genuinely willing to learn. That is why the text says that the teacher does not seek the youth; the youth must seek the teacher. (Conversely, if you have been approached for help, remember that you cannot teach a person who is not yet ready to listen and learn.)

Do not be ashamed to admit that the complications in the situation are beyond your ken and that you do not know all the answers. Rather, try to see this as an opportunity to expand your vision and your experience. Open your mind and put aside preconceptions and prejudices. Remember that your goal is to learn, not to show off what you already know. Combine eagerness to learn with modesty and humility. In this way you will maximize the benefits of your education. If you express a desire to learn and seek out people you trust and respect, the results will be positive. Once you have begun the course of instruction, neither you nor your teacher should give up until you have thoroughly mastered the information you need. Successful education requires not only the initial assimilation of material but also the development of good habits and consistency of effort. Hence the text says, "It is beneficial to persevere."

Another traditional interpretation of Meng is that you already know what you must do in the current situation but you do not like the answer. Such unwillingness to face reality is a form of close-mindedness and hence in its own way an inability to learn from experience. Knowing what is the case and pretending that it is otherwise, or recognizing what has to be done and refusing to accept it is truly a manifestation of folly. If you know the answer to your question, there is no point in asking the *Book of Changes* for a different answer.

Many commentators read the text literally: They suggest that you will eventually receive the hexagram Meng if you ask the *Book of Changes* the same question repeatedly after getting an answer you do not like. Receiving Meng (youthful folly) is the book's way of rebuking you for pestering it when it has already given you an answer. This standard interpretation is fanciful but dubious, since there is no evidence that Meng is more likely to appear through random selection than is any other hexagram. A better interpretation of the text is more consistent with the hexagram's general theme: Meng teaches that one cannot learn the truth until one is ready to receive the truth. Hence if you actively seek enlightenment, you should not then ignore or dismiss it if the truths it reveals are unpleasant. To make progress in life is to grow up, to put aside youthful folly and replace illusion with clarity. You cannot live your life through wishful thinking.

THE IMAGE

A spring emerges from beneath the mountain:
This is the image of Youthful Inexperience.
The superior person acts with resolution and so cultivates his character.

A mountain spring continues to flow forward and replenish itself. By contrast, a motionless body of water soon becomes stagnant. You must be like the mountain spring—you must continue to move forward with the process of your enlightenment. Nevertheless, education involves more than reading books and memorizing information. It also requires developing habits of mind and consistency of effort that will stand you in good stead over the long haul. The greatest folly often arises not from incorrect ideas but from the inability to make commitments and carry good ideas through to conclusion. The wise person develops himself; the fool only wishes that he had. Thus, whatever else you learn, you must also learn thoroughness, patience, and consistency. And you must not only be willing to open your mind to new ideas but also to put them into practice in your own life. By cultivating your character in the proper way, you ensure your future success.

THE LINES

The lines tell the story of how one deals with youthful inexperience. To educate, discipline is important—but not too much.

Initial Six

At the beginning of inexperience
It is beneficial to use discipline,
But remove shackles and fetters.
Going on this way brings humiliation.

Nothing important can be accomplished without discipline. If you flit from project to project, or play at life, you will achieve only trivial things. Lack of discipline will hamper your growth as a human being. So when one is at the beginning of an enterprise, it is important to develop the seriousness and inner commitment that will see you successfully through. If you are in charge of others, you must help them learn the lessons of self-discipline. Nevertheless, the text also warns that we should "remove shackles and fetters." Discipline properly exercised helps people enjoy life more by structuring their activities, giving them articulable and achievable goals, and helping them develop skills and talents that they can take pride and pleasure in. But discipline applied rigidly and for its own sake takes the joy out of life. Do not subject others—or yourself—to a heartless or mean-spirited discipline. This is humiliating and debilitates human potential every bit as much as lack of discipline.

Nine in the Second Place (Ruling Line)

To treat the inexperienced with kindliness and magnanimity brings good fortune.
Taking a wife brings good fortune.
The son is capable of taking charge of the household.

The lesson of this line is that to appreciate humanity we must be tolerant of human shortcomings. Each of us engages in his own folly at some point, and each of us has been young and inexperienced. We all make mistakes. It is often very hard to do the right thing when life is so complicated. If we recognize the ubiquity of human folly, we will not be so judgmental and we can approach others with love. Hence the text says, "taking a wife brings good fortune." A wise person cultivates traits of kindliness, compassion, and understanding. He is able to put himself in the other person's place and show mercy. In the same way, we should not treat ourselves mercilessly. We should not continually punish ourselves for our own past folly and our own previous shortcomings but rather forgive ourselves and try to do better in the future.

One who is inwardly strong and outwardly reserved and nonjudgmental in this way is well equipped to lead others. Looking past the rough edges, such a person is able to see the potential for good in others and is able to inspire them to do better. These acts of toleration and compassion pay off in the end, because others respond naturally and willingly to the leader's guidance. Hence the text informs us, "The son is capable of taking charge of the household"; that is, he is able to grow out of his former inexperience and assume important responsibilities.

Six in the Third Place

Do not marry a maiden who, when she sees a man of bronze,
Loses possession of herself.
There is nothing for which this is beneficial.

Out of inexperience or weakness, you may be tempted to throw yourself at something or someone you ardently desire. Or you may be taking the easy way out by trying to imitate or attach yourself to someone you think has high status or power. In this way you hope to elevate yourself in the eyes of others. Do not act this way. Maintain your dignity. Develop some strength of character and do not surrender your integrity or your individuality.

Do not try to get rich quick or achieve everything in one fell swoop. This will simply lead you to one reckless attempt after another. You will accomplish nothing of importance, and you will lose your self-respect in the process. You need to ground yourself, develop steadfastness and inner equilibrium, and proceed one step at a time in pursuit of your goals.

In the same way, you should not ally yourself with people who have not learned this lesson about controlling their desires and committing themselves for the long run. People of such weak character cannot be relied on when the chips are down. Thus, the text warns us, do not take such a person as a "wife"; i.e., as an ally. For people like this will surely abandon you as soon as they see something better coming down the road.

Six in the Fourth Place

Trapped in foolishness and ignorance. This brings humiliation.

It is important to face reality and deal with things as they are. You must not allow yourself to be overtaken by your fantasies, or confused and tormented by your obsessions and fears. The more you cling stubbornly to what is not real, the greater the danger that you will meet with humiliation.

In dealing with people who are entangled in their own folly, we should try our best to reason with them. Yet we must also recognize that when people are so consumed by fantasy or obsession that they will not listen to reason, it is sometimes best to leave them to fend for themselves. They will only be saved by experiencing the humiliation of recalcitrant experience.

Six in the Fifth Place (Ruling Line)

Childlike innocence brings good fortune.

The innocence of a child is accepting and sincere. If you are humble and unassuming and seek help and advice from others, you will succeed. Be open-minded and willing to learn, and all will be well.

Nine at the Top

In disciplining youthful inexperience,
It is not beneficial to act like a criminal.
It is beneficial to prevent crimes.

Generally speaking, it is better to instruct than to punish. But sometimes, in the case of an inexperienced or foolish person who will not learn, punishment is appropriate. Nevertheless, you should not punish out of anger or revenge; rather use punishment to instill proper values, encourage appropriate behavior, and restore harmony and order. Keep things in perspective.

Excessive punishment, or punishment in the heat of anger, breeds resentment and rebellion and may lead to a cycle of violence or repeated misbehavior. Even though you think you are controlling others when you punish them, you must first and foremost control yourself, for uncontrolled violence unwittingly duplicates the very thing it is supposed to prevent. No matter how exasperated you may feel by foolish conduct, do not overdo things. Recognize that you are teaching a lesson, not evening the score.

NOTES

4.0 "Youthful Inexperience. Success." Or, "Youthful Inexperience can bring success."

4.0 "It is beneficial to persevere." *zhen:* perseverance. This might also be translated as "It is beneficial to be constant"; i.e., that the beginner needs to develop consistency.

4.GI "resolution." *guo:* fruit, bring to fruition: The idea is that one is not easily dispirited or distracted but sees things through to their conclusion. Cf. 15.0.

4.GI "cultivates." *yu:* raise, foster. Cf. 53.3. Another reading is "fosters his character / By thoroughness in all that he does" (Wilhelm/Baynes).

4.3 "When she sees, etc." A less delicate reading is "When she sees a rich man, loses her chastity."

4.3 "a man of bronze." Or, "a man of gold," "a rich man." *jin:* metal, bronze, gold. *fu*: husband, married man, responsible adult.

4.4 "trapped in foolishness and ignorance." *kun*: oppressed, exhausted, limited. This is the name of Hexagram 47. Another reading is "entangled folly" (Wilhelm/Baynes).

4.5 "Childlike innocence." *meng:* youthful innocence, the name of the hexagram. The emphasis here is on innocence rather than inexperience. Cf. 25.0.

4.6 "It is not beneficial," etc. Another reading would be "It is not beneficial to harass. / It is beneficial to guard against harassment."

FIVE

Xu • Waiting

Keywords:

Calculated waiting
Biding your time
Waiting for rain
Nourishment
Replenishment

Above: Kan • Water
Below: Qian • Heaven

The ideograph for Xu has two interpretations. Under one account it shows a picture of rain falling from clouds in the heavens. The rain nourishes and replenishes the earth by soaking it. Hence Xu may have originally meant "getting wet." Another interpretation is that Xu shows a picture of a person praying and waiting for rain to come. Under this view Xu is about waiting and needing. Hence the hexagram symbolizes taking appropriate preparations for future action. If we recognize that nourishment is itself a method of preparation, the two interpretations merge into one.

5 Xu • Waiting

THE JUDGMENT

Waiting. Sincerity and faithfulness bring shining success.
Perseverance brings good fortune.
It is beneficial to cross the great river.

Because of circumstances beyond your control, you must wait patiently. You cannot take direct action at present. Nevertheless, you must have faith that things will work out for the best eventually. Just as we cannot force the rain to fall, we cannot force the propitious circumstances for action. Instead, we must let them come to us, just as the rain will eventually come and replenish and nourish the earth.

There are two kinds of waiting: the apprehensive waiting of the weak and the calculated waiting of the strong. The weak person waits out of fear and despair, becomes increasingly filled with anxiety and agitation and so finally plunges ahead at the wrong time with disastrous results. In contrast, the strong person waits because waiting is the best way to maximize the chances for eventual success. Such calculated waiting is a sign of strength, not weakness; of assurance, not resignation; of competence, not deficiency. While the weak person waits ever fearful that matters will spin out of control, the strong person waits knowing that success is inevitable, and that all the elements for success will appear when the time is right.

Calculated waiting is not merely a matter of hope for better days. It is a matter of faith—faith in the ultimate success of your endeavors, and, equally important, faith in yourself. You must believe that you are going to succeed and that you deserve to. You must visualize success in your mind's eye. You must imagine the path you will travel to achieve your goal. You must believe in the narrative of your eventual triumph. Then your faith will unconsciously adapt your actions to maximize your chances. Hence the text says, "Sincerity and faithfulness bring shining success." The power that faith provides allows a person to persevere in even the most difficult endeavors, symbolized by crossing the great river.

Just because you are waiting does not mean that there is nothing to do. First and foremost, you must try to understand the situation objectively. Your faith must be nourished by realism. You will prevail only if you can develop the necessary inner strength and self-confidence to meet the conditions that actually exist, and to do this you must be uncompromisingly honest with yourself. Only when you face the situation as it is without self-deception or illusion will you be able to see what holds you back and what you must do to prevail. At this point the way forward will slowly emerge; the light of your inner truth will gradually illuminate the path to success. Make all the necessary preparations. Do not cut corners and do not take half measures. When and only when the time is right, you must go forward with tenacity. Along the way you will inevitably experience doubts about whether you have what it takes to succeed. Put them aside. Keep your ultimate goal ever before you. When the time has come to act, you must be resolute and persevering. Go out to meet your fate with determination, with faith and with courage. Then you will get what you seek.

THE IMAGE

Clouds rise up to heaven:
This is the image of Waiting.
Thus the superior person eats and drinks
In joy and repose.

Because you can take no direct action at present, it is easy to become anxious and insecure. Resist the temptation. Do not worry. If you try to force matters now, you will only spoil things for yourself. You may squander your resources and lose all that you have gained. You may even snatch defeat out of the jaws of victory. Instead, recognize that you must bide your time. The text analogizes your situation to seeing clouds forming in the sky. Clouds are a sign of rain. But there is no guarantee when the rain will fall. Hence you must wait. When matters are still in the womb of time, you must allow them to develop naturally. You should not needlessly interfere with circumstances beyond your control, nor should you needlessly agitate yourself emotionally. Neither inner distress nor outer turmoil will serve your interests now. Instead, make the best of this time by preparing for the coming endeavors ahead. Cultivate a positive attitude. Take good care of yourself, grow strong, and gather resources. Pay attention to your physical and your emotional well-being. Engage in healthy habits and occupations. Enjoy life as best you can, and take pleasure and delight in what life gives you to enjoy. Maintain a cheerful outlook and a quiet confidence. Fate will bring events forward according to its own schedule. When it does, you will be rested and refreshed, and thus as ready to meet it as you will ever be.

THE LINES

The first four lines describe preparation for a calamity or danger that comes progressively nearer, so that by line four one must calmly and decisively withdraw from the situation. The fifth line is the ruler of the hexagram and states its basic theme—preparation for future action through nourishment. In the sixth line, the time for waiting is past, and one must embrace the unexpected.

Initial Nine

Waiting in the countryside.
It is beneficial to rely on what is enduring.
No blame.

You may be anxious about impending difficulties, but your problems are still a long way off. It is best to live each day as it comes. Continue in the regular rhythms of your life. Do not engage in extraordinary exertions out of fear or apprehension. Do not waste your time or your strength worrying about what might lie ahead. In this way you will conserve your energies for the future.

Nine in the Second Place

Waiting on the sand.
Although there may be a little criticism,
In the end there is good fortune.

In the *Book of Changes*, water is a symbol of danger, and sand is close to water. Sand is also less stable than the earth, and can easily shift toward the water. The text suggests that you are coming closer to dangerous events. You may be embarked on a course of action that will make your life more difficult and subject you to criticism. When danger and difficulty approach, people often lose heart. They quarrel among themselves and blame each other. In such a time, it is especially important to remain calm and centered. Focus on what you need to do. Don't let yourself be drawn into arguments. If you become the victim of gossip, let the matter pass. Responding to slanders will only give weight to the accusations and make matters worse. Have faith that matters will improve and that you will ultimately succeed.

Nine in the Third Place

Waiting in the mud
Will bring about the arrival of robbers.

Mud is earth mixed with water; hence it symbolizes that one has already gotten into danger. The line describes a person who does not properly prepare for an advance, whether out of foolishness, anxiety, or bravado, but rushes forward without fully considering the consequences. Trying to cross a muddy stream gets one bogged down in the mud and hence one finds one's self "waiting" in the mud. People stuck in the mud can be easily ambushed, and others will no doubt take advantage of their weakened and exposed condition.

In the same way, your premature actions have made you vulnerable to attack or manipulation by others. But do not give up hope. You may still be able to extricate yourself. However, you must remain calm and exercise the utmost caution. You did not wait for the right moment for action or prepare yourself adequately before. It is essential that you do so now.

Six in the Fourth Place

Waiting in blood.
Get out of the pit.

You are now squarely in the middle of a very dangerous and difficult situation. Blood symbolizes the closeness of the danger, the high emotions that the situation arouses, and the gravity of what is at stake. The pit symbolizes that you are deep in troubles that keep you from going forward or backward. Now more than ever you must remain calm and composed. Do not make things worse by a violent confrontation with the situation, for this will only drag you deeper into difficulties. Instead, exercise patience and discretion. Maintain your self-control. You must extricate yourself from the situation quietly and unobtrusively. And you must free yourself from emotional anxieties and entanglements that draw you into cycles of greater involvement and prolong the danger. Distance yourself from the situation emotionally and withdraw without making a show of force. In this way you will "get out of the pit."

Nine in the Fifth Place (Ruling Line)

Waiting at the banquet.
Perseverance brings good fortune.

The banquet symbolizes a time of peace and relaxation in which you can nourish and renew yourself. Your difficulties are held in abeyance for the time being. Take advantage of the opportunity to strengthen and nourish yourself for the struggles that lie ahead. Such moments of rest and recreation are important to a balanced life; they give people the ability to persevere until they have achieved their ambitions. Enjoy this time, but do not be self-indulgent. Recognize that there is still much work to be done. You should be like a person at a banquet who is free to sample many delicacies and can take genuine pleasure in them but also knows when to leave the table refreshed instead of overfed and bloated. If you keep your ultimate goals in mind, you can rejuvenate yourself now with a serene and cheerful confidence that all will turn out well in the end.

Six at the Top

One enters the pit.
Three uninvited guests arrive.
Treat them with respect, and in the end there will be good fortune.

Difficulties are upon you now. It is as if you are trapped in a pit: You cannot go forward or backward. There seems to be no way out. Yet when all seems lost, something unexpected happens. Help is at hand, if you know how to take advantage of it. Although an offer of assistance may come from an unanticipated direction or in an unusual form, do not be afraid to accept it. Good fortune often comes in the strangest of disguises.

The lesson of this line is that when you are in the midst of difficulties you must not lose heart or withdraw into despair and resignation. A negative attitude will only ensure your defeat. You must allow yourself to remain flexible in thought and try to reimagine the situation. Consider how an unforeseen change in circumstances may create the possibility of a new strategy or alliance that will work to your advantage. Events continually change in ways that no one can fully anticipate, and in this central fact of life lies the source of your salvation. Be open and accepting in heart and mind. Embrace the new and unexpected as you might welcome the uninvited guests described in the line. In this way you may be able to escape your difficulties and all will turn out well.

NOTES

5.GI "In joy and repose." Or, "With joy and peace of mind."

5.1 "rely on what is enduring." Or, "make use of what endures," "remain for a long time."

5.2 "criticism," *yan:* words; hence talk, gossip. Cf. 6.1, 36.1, 51.6, 53.1.

5.3 "Will bring about the arrival of robbers." Cf. 40.3.

SIX

Song • Conflict

Keywords:

Contention
Arbitration
Demanding justice
Speaking out

Above: Qian • Heaven
Below: Kan • Water

This hexagram is the inverse of the previous one, Xu. Xu waits patiently for the right moment for action and grows strong, while Song voices grievances and fights for what is right. The ideograph of Song symbolizes a person speaking out in public and asking for justice. The two constituent trigrams symbolize opposition: The upper trigram, Qian (Heaven), flows upward, while the lower trigram, Kan (Water, Abyss), flows downward. Heaven connotes strength and firmness, while Water represents danger and emotion. Taken together, the two trigrams symbolize conflict and contention, for a person who is both stubborn and emotional will surely get involved in many struggles and disputes. However, the theme of the hexagram is not to encourage struggle but to understand its causes and the importance of settling disputes through compromise and fair arbitration. Like every topic in the *Book of Changes*, contention is only appropriate some of the time. The wise person knows when it is proper to fight for what is right and when it is better to desist.

THE JUDGMENT

In conflict, be sincere. Be prudent in dealing with obstruction.
To halt halfway brings good fortune.
To carry things through to the end brings misfortune.
It is beneficial to see a great person.
It is not beneficial to cross the great river.

Conflicts arise when two people believe that they are right and their interests become opposed. This may be because the parties have not been communicating with each other effectively or because they no longer trust each other. And if the parties are strangers, then they have never had the chance to communicate or develop trust. Thus if you wish to understand conflict, you must understand its beginnings.

If you do not believe that you are in the right, you should not become involved in conflict. This is true both as a moral and a practical matter. If you do not believe in yourself and in the justness of your cause, you will not win a fight with a determined opponent. Indeed, you should never go into combat without a sincere commitment to success and without understanding your goals in advance. Conflict is a matter of values, not a matter of force. If you do not fight to vindicate values that you believe in, there is no point in going forward. Even if you have superior strength, dominating another when you know that you are wrong does not mean that you have won. It only means that you have debased yourself through the use of violence or trickery.

"Be prudent in dealing with obstruction" means that you should not rush into conflicts thoughtlessly. Because a struggle destroys the resources of both parties, it is always better to explore how direct confrontation can be avoided. Try to adjust matters and reach a settlement before conflicts grow and get out of hand. Open up lines of communication and try to establish trust and reciprocity. Attempting to reach accommodation keeps each side from wasting valuable capital and may even produce unexpected synergies. Nevertheless, some things are simply worth fighting for, and if there is no other choice, conflict becomes a necessity. Indeed, conflict and a show of strength is sometimes necessary as a prerequisite to later agreement.

If you find yourself in a conflict, remain calm and collected. A conflict is a potentially dangerous situation. It can easily spin out of control if you do not pay careful attention. Having entered into it, you now must find a way out of it. The most aggressive approach is not always the best one. You should first decide exactly what you want to achieve and what you will accept as a satisfactory ending to the conflict. Unless you know what your goals are, you will not be able to plan an effective strategy. By prolonging conflict without a clear plan or direction, you may destroy something very valuable in the process—not only what belongs to your adversary but what belongs to yourself.

Once you have begun a conflict with another, you must have the inner strength and confidence to settle your dispute and meet your opponent halfway. Often this requires courage every bit as great as the courage to fight on. The secret of success in conflict is not the ability to prevail. It is the ability to compromise. If you cannot compromise, every conflict must become either an ignominious defeat or a fight to the death. But if you have the ability to compromise, you can turn a deadly conflict into a potential source of growth and improvement.

Nevertheless, you will be able to reach an effective compromise only when you know what your own values and goals truly are and what you will be willing to give up in order to get them. If you are confused about what you want, you will find it difficult to end a conflict without great loss. That is why the text says that in conflict you must be sincere. You must be honest with yourself at each stage of the process—in getting into the conflict, in carrying the conflict forward, and in getting out of it.

Compromise becomes possible precisely because conflicts are conflicts of value as well as conflicts of interest and resources. By learning to respect and understand your opponent's values, you can find your way to a solution. The most successful compromises are those in which each side feels that it has gained something important or that some elements of its cause have been recognized and vindicated.

Even if you are convinced that you are in the right, you must know when to stop halfway. Even if compromise is not possible, you will have to let go at some point. If you fight to the bitter end, you will not only use up your resources but you will also create lasting enmity. Words once spoken and blows once struck cannot be taken back. It is easier to forgive a minor skirmish than a bloodbath. And if you fight to the bitter end, you may so weaken yourself that the victory you gain is not worth the cost.

Because conflict can be so destructive to all sides, it is important to put your disputes before a neutral arbiter that both parties can trust. Hence the text says that one should "see a great person," not merely for advice but to help end the conflict. The legitimacy and authority of an arbiter—whether a person or an institution—allows the parties to settle the dispute and save face. Quite literally, it allows them to have their day in court—to state fully and publicly the nature of their grievance and have it considered fully and fairly by a neutral third party, even if they do not ultimately win the day. The ability of both parties to be heard and heard equally is an important feature of a just legal system.

Finally, the text advises that when you are engaged in conflict, you should not "cross the great river"; that is, you should not attempt significant new undertakings, start new projects, or make major life changes until the conflict is satisfactorily resolved. Conflict drains both physical and emotional resources. If your attention is divided on several fronts, you weaken yourself and make it more difficult to prevail in any aspect of your life. Similarly, to win a conflict in the outside world you must not be conflicted on the inside. If you and your allies are at odds, or if you are divided within yourself, you lessen the chances of successful compromise or ultimate victory.

THE IMAGE

Heaven and water go their opposite ways:
This is the image of Conflict.
Thus in all his affairs the superior person carefully considers how things begin.

To understand why conflicts arise, and how to prevent them, you must understand their origins. Lack of trust, communication, and consultation are the most frequent causes. The best way to avoid conflict is to bring people together from the start, to create institutions that promote trust and reciprocity, and to provide people with clear expectations about their duties, rights, and responsibilities to each other. If you make your position clear from the beginning and act in a trustworthy and reliable fashion, you can often prevent conflicts from arising or from spiraling out of control.

The next-best approach is to exercise caution and circumspection before you embark on a path that will lead you to conflict. Don't let yourself be drawn to a point of no return. Consider carefully how conflicts might arise beforehand and take steps to prevent them from multiplying and getting out of hand.

Finally, even in the midst of conflict, you must pay attention to its origins and be objective about yourself and about what you are trying to achieve. Be willing to swallow your pride and end the struggle if it becomes counterproductive. If you are stubborn, things will only get worse and you may end up destroying something very valuable and precious. Do not give up your principles, but try to listen to other people's point of view and understand their position and their grievances. By trying to comprehend how you and your opponents have come to this point, you may be able to forge a creative solution that makes something good and healthy out of an emotionally difficult situation. Although conflict is often painful, it can also spur growth and innovation. Resolving the conflict may open up a new world to you. If you approach conflict in this way, it becomes more than a challenge; it becomes an opportunity.

THE LINES

The lines tell the story of how to deal with conflict. In lines one through four, one avoids conflict at different stages. In the ruling line, line five, one is victorious not through the use of force but by setting the matter before a just arbiter. In line six, one overreaches, with unfortunate results.

Initial Six

If one does not perpetuate the affair,
Although there may be a little criticism,
In the end there is good fortune.

Conflicts quickly spin out of control when people egg each other on and when they answer small aggressions with larger ones. If a conflict has just arisen, end it quickly, without bringing matters to a head or forcing a decision, even if this means dropping the issue entirely. This approach is especially appropriate when your adversary is stronger or has greater resources. If you do not exacerbate conflict when it first appears, things will calm down and the conflict will end without too much bad feeling on all sides. You may feel taken advantage of, or you may fear that you will be disparaged for being cowardly, but do not let these criticisms faze you. Discretion is the better part of valor. Pick your battles carefully. Things will turn out well in the end.

Nine in the Second Place

Unable to contend,
One escapes the situation and returns home.
The people of one's town,
Three hundred households,
Remain free of calamity.

When you face an adversary who is stronger and has superior resources, discretion is no dishonor and retreat is no disgrace. Pride, an exaggerated sense of honor, and the desire to establish one's self all tempt people into conflicts with others. So too, ironically, does a sense of insecurity that makes a person lash out at others. Do not allow yourself to be drawn into open conflict when the odds are stacked against you, and do not rush off to fight battles that you are unlikely to win. People who meet defeat at the hands of a stronger power are often not the only ones who suffer. The loss also has unfortunate consequences for their friends, family, and those around them. Thus, if you withdraw from conflict at the right time, you can avoid disaster for yourself and those close to you. Wise conciliation and diplomacy spare a person's community from harm, and keep allies, associates, and loved ones from being drawn into a potentially ruinous conflict.

Six in the Third Place

Nourish yourself on ancient virtue,
Persevere in the face of danger,
And in the end good fortune comes.
If one works for a lord,
One should take no credit for success.

To "nourish yourself on ancient virtue" means that one should rely on traditional virtues of hard work and take quiet pride in the quality of one's accomplishments. What you have achieved through your own merits and your own hard work is yours. Even if others try to take credit or contest the value of your accomplishments, the knowledge that you have done good work cannot be taken from you. Material goods and status are enjoyable things, but they can be snatched away in a moment through the vicissitudes of fortune. Your inner worth, however, belongs to yourself alone. What a person has achieved because of the strength of his or her own character can never be lost.

For this reason the text advises that people who are devoted to doing the best job that they can for its own sake should keep a low profile. Do not try to gain prestige or recognition by boasting about your accomplishments, for this will only create conflicts with others. This advice is even more appropriate when one works for someone else or in a group. Be willing to let others take credit and bask in the sunlight. Do not work simply to achieve status and recognition, for the thirst for status is unquenchable and never-ending and cannot nourish you. The important thing is that you accomplish good work that you can be proud of.

Nine in the Fourth Place

Unable to contend,
One turns back and submits to fate,
Changes one's attitude,
And finds peace.
Perseverance brings good fortune.

Like line two, this line advises against prolonging conflict. In this case, however, you are the stronger party. You see an opportunity to gain an advantage through conflict with a weaker party or someone who is vulnerable. You may well be able to have your way or inflict considerable damage. But in your heart you know this is not the right thing to do; you will not be able to square such behavior with your conscience. You should turn back and accept your fate. In this way, you will find peace of mind and, ultimately, good fortune.

Nine in the Fifth Place (Ruling Line)

Contending.
Supreme good fortune.

The advice in this line is as old as civilization itself. Conflicts can be resolved through appeal to a person or institution that both sides regard as worthy and just, and who possesses the power and authority to enforce what is right. Confidence in such a person or institution is essential to end the cycle of conflict and bring peace to society.

If you have a dispute with another, and feel that you are in the right, bring your dispute before a worthy arbiter whose judgment you trust. If your cause is a just one, good fortune will result.

Nine at the Top

Even if one is awarded a leather belt,
By morning's end
It will have been stripped away three times.

The leather belt symbolizes a prize awarded the victor in a contest. The metaphor means that if you carry your conflict to the bitter end, you may prevail, but at an unacceptable cost. Others will lose respect for you and resent you. They may gather strength and challenge you again and again. You may find yourself in an unending cycle of conflict and reprisal. This is not a real victory.

NOTES

6.GI "go their opposite ways." Or, "move (act) in contradiction (contradictory ways)."

6.3. "One should take no credit for success." Another rendering is "one can achieve nothing," or "one cannot bring things to completion." The present translation makes more sense in context. A similar but not identical formulation appears in 2.3.

6.5 "Contending." Or, "they contend before him," i.e., before an arbiter.

SEVEN

Shi • The Army

䷆

Keywords:

Military virtues
Discipline
Self-discipline
Honor
Loyalty
Integrity
Massing of force
The multitude

Above: Kun • Earth
Below: Kan • Water

The hexagram Shi consists of five yin lines with one yang line in the second place, the place of a government official who is far away from the capital, in this case the commander of an army. According to the principle that one rules many, the five yin lines obey the general in the second place. The ancient ideograph for Shi features the symbol for a multitude and the symbol for a circle or pivot. It depicts the masses gathering around a center or pivot, which is a leader or teacher. The constituent trigrams represent water (Kan) that flows hidden below the earth (Kun). Like water beneath the ground, great power lies stored up within the mass of the people, but it needs the guidance of an exceptional military leader to bring it forth and give it direction.

THE JUDGMENT

The Army needs perseverance and a strong leader.
Good fortune. No blame.

A mass of people is not an army, but it can become one if it is trained, organized, and led by a great general. Discipline is crucial. It converts a disorganized mob into an effective fighting force. But discipline is not achieved through threats or violence. Rather, it requires leadership. Good generals know how to inspire their troops and create a sense of esprit de corps. They know how and when to exercise authority and punish disobedience, to encourage resourcefulness and reward ambition. They train their troops so thoroughly that discipline and obedience become second nature, and then organize and arrange them so that their force and effect is amplified and maximized. Great generals always show care and concern for the welfare of their soldiers. They understand the destructiveness of war and therefore risk the lives of their soldiers only when it is necessary to do so. They are bold when the situation requires it but hold back when it is prudent. They use force sparingly and with precision. And because they are loyal and honorable to those who serve beneath them, their troops willingly follow them into battle. Just as troops are loyal to good generals, good generals are loyal and trustworthy to their king and country. Hence rulers have complete confidence in their military leaders and give them the responsibility to conduct the war to its conclusion.

The same considerations apply to all effective leadership. Any organization needs a strong leader who knows how to gain the trust of others and inspire them with a sense of vision and common purpose. You must be able to convey your sense of enthusiasm and commitment to others, and you must recognize the importance of planning, organization, and discipline. Exert your authority fairly and consistently and you will win the respect and obedience of others. Act loyally and honorably to others if you want them to act loyally and honorably to you.

The army is also a metaphor for the conduct of your life. You are both the potential army and the general who must train it and transform it from a disorganized mass of peasantry into a disciplined and motivated force. Like the general, you are entrusted with great possibilities. But like the undifferentiated mass, your ambitions will amount to nothing if you do not establish priorities and organize and structure your life. If you want to succeed, you must have clear-cut goals and you must be enthusiastic about them. Otherwise you will not have the courage to persevere when you meet opposition. Discipline yourself and your desires so that healthy and effective habits become second nature. Marshal your forces and abilities and put them to the best possible use.

In the same way, apply the basic elements of good military strategy to your life. Once you have settled on your goals, decide what course of action will be most likely to achieve them, and pursue it with steadfast determination. Be resourceful and open to new solutions. Make no rash assaults but instead move forward only when you have carefully planned everything in advance and fully considered the consequences of your actions. Seek all available intelligence and information and carefully consider the correct terrain in which to act. Put yourself in the right place so as to maximize your effectiveness. In dealing with others, adopt the military virtues of honor, loyalty, and integrity. Finally, treat yourself and your resources with the same degree of care that a wise general would treat his own troops. Do not enlist in reckless sallies and do not engage in self-destructive behavior. Respect yourself and behave toward yourself as someone who is worthy of loyalty and honor. Have courage and maintain faith in yourself and your aspirations. Follow the principles of a great general and you will help ensure your victory in the long run.

THE IMAGE

In the middle of the earth is water:
This is the image of the Army.
Thus the superior person marshals his forces through generosity to the common people.

Earth shelters water beneath the ground, protecting it, directing it, and giving it force. When a general turns a mass of civilians into a trained and orderly army, he protects them as well as disciplining them, because their discipline makes it possible for them to survive in battle and win. In the same way, you must learn to let your resources work for you rather than against you. This includes, above all, your emotions. Do not allow your feelings to be like an uncontrolled mob that creates havoc in your life. If you cannot discipline your emotions, you will suffer greatly and you may engage in wasteful and self-destructive behavior. But if you can direct your emotions to useful ends, they will empower you, just as water that flows beneath the ground can have great hydraulic force.

A great general never goes into battle unprepared. He gathers whatever his troops need and takes the time to put everything in order. He prepares his soldiers for battle by inspiring them with his vision; and he wins their trust by acting with firmness and magnanimity. In the same way, for any great undertaking you must marshal your resources carefully and patiently. Short-term sacrifice will lead to long-term benefits. Along with self-discipline you must show care and concern for others. Generosity is essential if you want other people to work with you. Do not impose on them any burdens that you would not take on yourself. By demonstrating that you have their interests at heart as well as your own, you will win their confidence and their cooperation.

THE LINES

The lines tell the story of the proper conduct of an army and its leader. The army must be disciplined (line one); it must await the arrival of proper leadership (line two); it must know when to retreat and when to attack (lines three, four, and five); and after the battle is won, the spoils must be divided and a new political system founded (line six).

Initial Six

The army must go forth disciplined by regulations.
If discipline is not good, misfortune.

This line compares the beginning of any enterprise to that of a military mission. The cause must be worthy and just, or one will not be able to sustain it. The plan of action must be clear, or the soldiers will not know what to do in a time of crisis. The troops must be disciplined and organized; otherwise they will be routed in battle. In the same way, make sure that what you are planning to do is worthwhile, articulate your objectives, and organize your resources before you act. If you rush forward unprepared or without clear goals, the result will be chaos and defeat. Exercise self-discipline if you want to succeed.

Nine in the Second Place (Ruling Line)

In the middle of the army.
Good fortune. No blame.
Three times the king bestows a decoration.

This line compares your situation to that of a general among his troops. A good general remains with his troops, eats with them and sleeps with them. This allows him to stay in touch with his forces, and because he shares both the good and bad with those who serve under him, they respect him and trust him. Hence when the king honors him, the whole army feels honored. A successful general also maintains a good relationship with his superior; without political support the army will not prevail. But he achieves this good reputation through his connection with and care for his soldiers, for a good commander with loyal troops is an asset that brings accolades and praise from his superiors.

Emulate these characteristics in your own life. Take care of your own resources, and take care of those who work for you, as a general takes care of his troops. Establish good lines of communication with others, both those whom you command, and those whom you report to. Be flexible and diplomatic, and you will succeed and gain recognition from others.

Six in the Third Place

There is uncertainty.
The army carries corpses in the wagon.
Misfortune.

An army cannot prevail in battle unless it has clear goals and wise leadership with foresight and vision. The text advises that these qualities are lacking now. Perhaps you are uncertain about the right course, or you lack genuine commitment. If you do not plan ahead and consider the consequences of your actions, or if you are not clear about what you want to do, you will not succeed. Vacillation is permissible during a time of deliberation but not during a time of action. An army whose leaders vacillate when lives are at stake will meet with disaster. They will carry the corpses of their young soldiers home in wagons.

Six in the Fourth Place

The army retreats. No blame.

This line describes an army that makes a strategic retreat or takes a defensive position. Such a strategy is followed by the most able commanders and indicates no lack of courage and certainly no dishonor. A wise retreat saves the army and its resources from disaster and allows them to fight another day.

When you face insurmountable obstacles, a superior adversary, or overwhelming odds, it is useless to fight. You will only harm yourself and others around you in the process. Make an orderly retreat. Hold back and gather your strength for a more opportune time.

Six in the Fifth Place (Ruling Line)

There is game in the field.
It is beneficial to catch it.
No blame.
The eldest son should command the army.
If the youngest, they will cart corpses,
And perseverance will bring misfortune.

"Game in the field" refers to forest animals that are now boldly eating the crops. The analogy is to an enemy invasion. You face a problem that must be dealt with efficiently and promptly. Hence the text says "catch it." But it is not enough to act with determination and force. Proper leadership is essential, symbolized by the eldest son. The situation calls for a wise, experienced hand. Take the time to consult with other people whom you respect, and gather all the necessary information and advice. Open your mind to new possibilities and be willing to learn from others. Be moderate and balanced in your judgments. If you learn how to control yourself and your resources, you will succeed. But if you act rashly and enthusiastically, hoping to punish or obliterate your adversary in a wild display of force, you will be like the youngest son, who does not know how to lead the troops. Then you will meet with disaster.

Six at the Top

The great ruler issues commands,
Establishes states, bestows feudal houses.
Inferior people should not be employed.

In ancient China a king would bestow feudal estates and honors among his victorious forces. He gave them lands and authority over those lands in return for feudal service. In this way he rewarded those who had faithfully served him; and by giving them a role as subrulers in his kingdom, he bound them ever closer to him, ensuring their future loyalty. However, a wise king would not elevate untrustworthy or malicious people to such newly created fiefs, for they might abuse their power and turn on him someday. They were given money, not titles and land.

The same considerations apply to you. Now that the battles are won and you have achieved your goals, you need to think carefully about what to do next. Do not be complacent, for there is still work to be done. You now face the task of building on your victories and creating a new and rewarding situation. Be grateful to those who have helped you and acknowledge their assistance. Reward them for their loyalty. Delegate authority, but be realistic about what people are capable of. Give real power only to trustworthy people whose values you respect. If someone lacks ability or judgment, recognize their contributions appropriately but do not promote them out of a misplaced sense of loyalty. Do not permit inferior ideas or influences to infiltrate the new situation or you will undermine everything you have accomplished.

NOTES

7.3 "uncertainty." *huo:* "some, perhaps." I.e., "maybe the army carries corpses in the wagon." A better reading in context is "uncertainty" or "hesitation," traits that would lead to defeat.

7.4 "retreats." *zuo ci*: "to the left camps (moves, settles)." One keeps the high ground to the right and to one's back; hence to pitch camp to the left is to take a defensive position.

7.5 "game in the field." Cf. 32.4: "no game in the field."

7.6 "Inferior people should not be employed." Cf. 63.3.

EIGHT

Bi • Union

Keywords:

Joining with others
Joining in
Rallying around a leader

Above: Kan • Water
Below: Kun • Earth

Five yin lines surround a single yang line in the fifth place, which is the position of the ruler. Thus the hexagram symbolizes union around a strong and wise person who gives the group direction and purpose. The ideograph for Bi features two persons standing close together. It thus symbolizes not only the relationship of a king to an entire nation, but also a smaller, closer, and more intimate association of people.

THE JUDGMENT

Union. Good fortune.
Look deep inside yourself and divine
Whether you have greatness, perseverance, and constancy,
For then there will be no blame.
Those who lack peace gradually come from all sides.
Those who arrive too late meet with misfortune.

The theme of Bi is unity with other people, and one's relationships to individuals and groups. Successful unions can help all of their members grow as individuals and prosper. But they also require that people be willing to cooperate and work for each other's good rather than for their own selfish interests. People must also believe that they have something in common if the union is to succeed. You should not join a group if you do not feel connected and committed to others and do not share their values and beliefs. Joining in because you can think of nothing better to do or because other people are doing so is a recipe for eventual estrangement, disillusionment, and unhappiness. But if the relationship is right, joining in will be good for your own growth and self-development. Your contributions to the group will be recognized, and all of the members will mutually support each other.

Unity is more than coming together; it also requires holding people together over the long run, and dealing with the stresses and strains, the difficulties and disagreements that inevitably arise in any group. Holding people together requires leadership—a central person or figure whom others depend on and around whom they can unite. Being the center of a group carries great responsibilities. It requires that you have magnanimity, vision, inner strength, perseverance, and constancy. If you are called upon to take up the responsibility of forming a group or keeping it together, the text advises that you look deep inside yourself to see whether you have these important qualities. If you take up a leadership role without a genuine sense of commitment or without a sense of being truly called to the task, you may only create confusion and chaos and you will stand in the way of others who could forge a successful union.

When a group forms around a common project, ideal, or value, it naturally attracts others who want to share in the vitality and happiness of a successful union. As the text says, people who are at first hesitant to make a commitment gradually take heart and join in from all sides. The power of a healthy union is that it can inspire others and give them something to believe in when they are full of confusion or self-doubt. If you are contemplating joining a group that you think is right for you, do not wait too long. People form strong bonds and alliances through their shared experiences in a group. If you join in too late, those connections will already be in place and you will have missed being a part of the formative influences that give a group its identity. You may feel like an outsider, and you may find it difficult or even impossible to fully integrate into the group and feel fully a part of it.

THE IMAGE

On the earth, water:
This is the image of Union.
Thus the kings of old established myriad feudal states
To foster close relations with the feudal lords.

Water can dissolve earth, but water joined with earth in the right way holds earth together—it produces bricks and mortar that can create something large and great. In ancient China kings created a commonality of interest with their feudal lords by giving them lands and titles in exchange for promises of loyalty and support. When a union is constructed out of a commonality of interest and mutual benefit and esteem, it holds people together just as earth mixed with water holds together. Each person recognizes that his interest is served by uniting and cooperating with others for a common good. Each works with and respects the others, and as a result all are made happier.

The same principles apply to the effective leadership of any group. If you wish to bring people together, you need to inspire them with a common goal or purpose. You must establish that you are stable, trustworthy, and reliable. No one will follow a person who lacks staying power or commitment. Show the proper regard and esteem for those who work with you. Respect the dignity of everyone in the group and honor their contributions appropriately. Do not play favorites and do not foster cliques or internal divisions. It is important for the success of the group that its members trust you and believe that you will treat them fairly and honorably. And you must do your best to encourage the same attitudes of fairness and reciprocity in others. Trust and mutual respect are the cement that will keep the group together during periods of difficulty and crisis. Above all, demonstrate both through your words and your deeds that you genuinely wish to work for the common good of the group and not for personal aggrandizement. If you are devoted to those who follow you, they will be devoted to you, and all will benefit.

THE LINES

The lines describe different kinds of union, culminating in line five, the ruler of the hexagram. In line six, union comes too late, or was defective from the start; there is no proper leadership.

Initial Six

When there is inner truth and sincerity, union is without blame.
Fill the earthen bowl with truth and sincerity,
And in the end from others good fortune comes.

Relationships work best when people are trustworthy and sincere. The text speaks of "inner truth," an expression that appears often in the *Book of Changes*. It means conformity between one's thoughts and one's actions, so that a person is on the inside what he or she appears to be on the outside. The virtues of sincerity, trustworthiness, and inner truth are symbolized by an earthen bowl. Such a bowl is plain and simple, yet it is able to hold much of value, which it displays without drawing attention to itself. Mere form is unimportant; the contents inside the bowl are what count. In the same way, you should be honest and unaffected, without pretension or secret designs. What matters in forming long-lasting relationships is not how pretty your words are but the quality of your character: not how much you can impress people but who you really are inside. If you possess sincerity and inner truth, you will attract the right people to you. And when you attract the right people through your honesty and strength of character, the rewards of your relationships with others grow over time, bringing good fortune in many different guises and in unexpected ways.

Six in the Second Place

Joining with others on the inside.
Perseverance brings good fortune.

Joining with people "inside" has two separate meanings. First, it means that you should be loyal to those in your existing circle, including your friends and relatives and those closest to you. Sometimes people treat their enemies better than their friends. This is a sign of their insecurity. They want everyone to like them so much that they bend over backward to win over those who show displeasure with them, while forgetting those who have stuck by them through thick and thin. In a similar fashion some people forget their friends because they are seducers who continually need new conquests. But such seductions are not true union. Lasting relationships require that we continue to look out for those who have looked out for us. They require continuous reciprocity and effort over sustained periods of time. Such relationships bring rich rewards. Hence the text tells us, "Perseverance brings good fortune."

The second meaning of joining "inside" is that you should join with people "inwardly," that is, out of sincere conviction in your heart. The *Book of Changes* teaches that successful relationships with others depend on a particular kind of relation within yourself. This is "inner truth," being true to yourself.

Inner truth means first that you must accept yourself for who you are: Do not punish yourself in destructive self-loathing or delude yourself with visions of grandeur. Ironically, both the extremes of too much and too little love for ourselves lead us to seek the approval of others in the wrong way and ultimately hamper our relationships. Second, being true to yourself means that you should respond naturally and sincerely in your dealings with others. Do not be pretentious in order to impress, do not be obsequious in order to curry favor, and do not bemoan your fate in order to gain sympathy. Third, inner truth means that you should act out of conviction and always maintain your integrity in your relationships with others. If you want others to respect you, you should behave like a person who deserves respect.

If you are true to yourself, you will be true to others. You will attract good people who will esteem you for who you are rather than what use they can make of you. Conversely, if you lack integrity and inner balance, you will waste your time seeking the approval of others, attempting to fill a perpetual hunger that cannot be satisfied, and you will lose your dignity and self-respect in the process.

Six in the Third Place

Joining with the wrong people.

This line suggests that you are chasing after the wrong people for alliance, intimacy, or union. This may be because you are engaged in self-destructive choices, because you are acting out of force of habit, or because you have settled for too narrow a circle of acquaintances. Civility and sociability with such people is certainly permissible, but true intimacy is a mistake. If you cling to people who are not right for you or who do not understand you, then, whether you do so out of ignorance or out of inertia, you will be unhappy. Worse yet, your behavior may keep you from developing richer and more rewarding relationships with others. And if the people you cling to are of bad character, your alliance with them will put you in an unfavorable light later on.

Six in the Fourth Place

Joining with others on the outside.
Perseverance brings good fortune.

Once again, this line has a dual meaning. Joining with others "outside" means looking beyond your ordinary circle of acquaintances. Consider joining with others who might have something to teach you. Open your mind to new people, to new thoughts, and to new experiences. Breaking out of old habits and meeting new people is hard. The familiar is comfortable, even if it is stifling. It is easier to stay in your shell, because venturing outward puts your self-esteem at risk. But the richest rewards come from courage and persistence. Hence the text advises, "Perseverance brings good fortune."

Another meaning of joining with others "outside" means to join "outwardly." To act with integrity means that you should be loyal and openly support others whom you know are right for you. If you find yourself in contact with the leader or the center of your group, or an influential person whom you admire or respect, do not be afraid to show your support publicly. At the same time, integrity also means that you must always remember your own principles and who you are. Do not let your allegiances, however worthy, take over your life or cloud your judgment. Do not act in a way that would compromise your self-respect.

Nine in the Fifth Place (Ruling Line)

An illustration of union:
In the hunt the king uses beaters three times
And spares the game that comes before him.
Thus the citizens need not fear him.
Good fortune.

The text compares how a great king brings his subjects together with the customs of the royal hunt. A true leader inspires by his example. He attracts others through his good qualities. He accepts all those who approach him voluntarily; those who are not attracted he lets go. He flatters no one, yet the strength of his character is such that people naturally flock to him of their own accord. They do not have to be coerced into obedience through fear of punishment. And because the leader accepts them as they are, their union with him becomes ever more secure. They feel able to express their views about what should be done freely and openly, and they naturally cooperate for the good of the whole.

The same idea applies to all cooperative enterprises. If you possess sincerity and strength of character, those qualities will shine through to others. You do not need to flatter or cajole others to follow you. Those whom you are meant to associate with will naturally be drawn to you. Bonds of trust and fellowship will grow naturally over time. Together you will achieve great things.

Six at the Top

No head for union.
Misfortune.

The opportunity for joining with others lasts only so long. If you miss your chance to cooperate with others, you may come to regret it. If you hesitate to make a commitment until it is too late, a lasting union will never form, or else it will form without you.

When unity does break down, it is often because something was wrong from the start. The seeds of failure in a joint enterprise are often sown in the beginning. You or your associates may have been unable to make a sincere or genuine commitment. Because you were not able to give yourself to the enterprise fully, bonds of trust and reciprocity did not form or did not grow strong enough to weather the stresses and strains that naturally occur in any relationship or joint undertaking. Perhaps one or more of the participants harbored secret misgivings or mistrust. Or perhaps you had genuine incompatibilities and conflicts that you papered over. Whatever the reasons, you need to examine the situation to determine why the union failed before you can begin again.

NOTES

8.0 "Look deep inside yourself and divine." *yuan shi:* literally, "repeat the yarrow-stalk divination," or "consult again." Thus many read the text as requesting the subject who receives the hexagram Bi to divine again and ask whether he or she possesses the qualities necessary for leadership. Lynn translates this as "plumb and divine," and I follow his basic notion: the hexagram is not asking for a second divination but for introspection.

8.0 "greatness." *yuan:* supreme, primary, originary, sublime. Or, "fundamentality" (Lynn). *Yuan* is the first of the four virtues of the *Book of Changes*. The idea is that a leader must be connected to what is sublime, noble, essential, and primary.

8.0 "lack peace." *bu ning:* are restless, troubled.

8.2 "inside." This means either "inside one's circle," or "inwardly," i.e., in one's heart.

8.4 "outside." This can mean joining with others "outside one's circle," or joining with people "outwardly," i.e., openly announcing or demonstrating one's ties to them through action.

8.5 "In the hunt," etc. Most read this as "In the hunt the king uses beaters on three sides and spares the game that runs away from him." That is, the servants blocked three sides of escape. If animals did not take the chance to flee through the open side but approached the king "voluntarily," they were hunted and killed. I follow Lynn's reading: The king chased the animals that fled—which was sporting—but spared the ones who approached. This reading also makes more sense in context. If the king killed the game that stayed, why would the citizens have no reason to fear if they approached him?

8.6 "No head for union." *bi zhi wu shou. Shou* means "head" or "beginning." One might translate this as "the union had no proper leadership," or "the union had no proper beginning." The translation tries to capture both meanings.

NINE

Xiao Xu • Small Accumulation

Keywords:

The taming power of the small
Restraint of the powerful by the weak
Small farming
Taking care of the little things
Accumulation of small advantages
Using gentleness and friendly persuasion
Temporarily held back, but the rain will come

Above: Xun • Wind (Wood)
Below: Qian • Heaven

The hexagram Xiao Xu features five yang lines that are held in check by the weak yin line in the fourth place, the place of the minister. The hexagram has two interrelated themes. The first theme is the potential of the strong that is temporarily held in check or impeded by the weak. Such restraint can eventually be overcome, not through force but through gentle persuasion. The ideograph for Xiao Xu combines the image of the small *(xiao)* with the image of a field on which two piles of grass are stacked, one on top of the other, with a cover on the top. This image symbolizes accumulation, farming, or caretaking. It suggests the hexagram's second theme: the small accumulation of advantages through meticulous care that eventually leads to success. Taken together, these two themes counsel that when one's potential is restrained by what is small, the best strategy is to imitate the nature of the time and engage in small measures.

THE JUDGMENT

Small Accumulation. Success.
Dense clouds, no rain from the outskirts of our western region.

Rain symbolizes nourishment, release of tension, and success. Dense clouds offer the promise of eventual rain. However, the rain has not yet fallen; hence there is nothing to do but wait for events to play themselves out.

The situation is not unfavorable. There is the promise of success in the long run. But circumstances currently prevent you from doing much to bring your plans to fruition. Your advance is blocked by factors that you are not yet fully aware of. Although this may be frustrating, you should maintain a realistic attitude. Even though the barriers to progress seem minor and frustratingly trivial, do not underestimate them. Exercise caution. There is considerable potential in the situation, but your position is not yet secure. Do not try to force the issue. Instead, do all that you can do now to prepare in small ways for the eventual breakthrough. Pay careful attention to everyday questions. Be meticulous and painstaking in your efforts. Plan ahead for the future. Gather information and discuss the situation with others. Accumulate whatever small advantages you can.

Do not threaten or coerce others or order them around to get your way. Instead, try to influence people through gentle persuasion and friendly behavior. In this way you can act as a partial restraint on their behavior if they are contemplating something unwise. The key is to be firm and determined on the inside and adaptable and gentle on the outside. Have faith that eventually the obstacles that are holding you back will give way, and the rain will fall.

THE IMAGE

The wind blows across the sky:
This is the image of Small Accumulation.
Thus the superior person
Cultivates his graceful virtues.

Wind can move clouds together but cannot force them to rain. In the same way, you can have only limited effects at present. Nevertheless, this does not mean that there is nothing to be done. First and foremost, you can work on improving yourself for the times that lie ahead. Develop patience and self-control. Practice tolerance and gentleness, even with those who are uninformed or thoughtless. Learn to deal with people using poise, tact, and diplomacy. By maintaining inner strength and outer friendliness, you will gradually influence others and win their confidence. Cultivating habits of self-discipline, discretion, and adaptability will pay abundant dividends in the long run.

THE LINES

The lines describe how virtuous behavior and cooperation with others bring good fortune; in line three a breakdown of social graces produces the opposite result. In line six, the rain finally comes: one has achieved success and must desist from further action.

Initial Nine

Returning to the Way.
How could there be blame in this?
Good fortune.

To return to the Way means to recognize the true nature of the situation rather than trying to force matters through an exercise of will. As you try to move forward boldly, you encounter obstacles and obstructions. When this happens, hold back and return to a position that gives you maximum flexibility to advance or retreat as the situation warrants. Be patient and do not try to force matters. Events are not fully in your control. Concentrate on dealing with day-to-day affairs. Once you have retreated to a secure position and ascertained the real nature of the situation, you may take action with confidence. This will bring you good fortune.

Nine in the Second Place

Drawn into returning.
Good fortune.

You probably would like to take action now, but if you study the situation carefully, and particularly how others have fared in similar circumstances, you will see that the time is not right, for obstacles block your path. When you consider what others have done in your situation, you will recognize that you need to hold back and work in cooperation with people who can help you reach your goals. Pushing forward now may provoke unnecessary conflicts. Hence the text says "drawn into returning," for the experience of others pulls you away from a perilous situation that might lead to defeat. Retreating in these circumstances saves you from error and brings good fortune.

Nine in the Third Place

Cart and axle separate.
Husband and wife roll their eyes at each other.

You want to press forward, because you believe that the obstacles are not too great. This makes you overconfident. If you look more closely, you will see that events are not fully in your control. Seemingly minor difficulties will loom larger than you expect. Thus the text says, "Cart and axle separate," suggesting the possibility of accidents and unforeseen vulnerabilities in your position. What looked like an easy victory is actually much more complicated. Your opponent, who seems weaker, is actually more powerful in this situation, and you, who seem stronger, will find yourself unable to make events conform to your will. Petty annoyances and minor impediments will hinder you and sap your strength. Hence the text tells us, "Husband and wife roll their eyes at each other." If you force matters now, you risk a very unpleasant rebuff—for which you will be criticized—and loss of dignity.

Six in the Fourth Place (Constitutive Line)

If one is sincere, blood vanishes and fear departs.
No blame.

Be honest and sincere in your dealings with others, and you need not have anxieties. The situation may appear fraught with dangers. People expect your advice, and you may feel burdened with responsibilities. You worry that others will do the wrong thing and that the situation will descend into chaos and bloodshed. But if you speak truthfully and from the heart, you will give the right counsel and inspire confidence in others. Your beneficial influence will lead others to respect you and cooperate with you, and this will allow you to escape the difficulties.

Nine in the Fifth Place (Ruling Line)

Sincere and loyally attached,
Neighbors enrich each other.

When people cooperate and support each other, everyone benefits. Loyalty and a desire to work for the common good multiply the resources that each party brings to the table. Individual strengths can complement each other; individual skills can produce synergies. Not only are the chances of success increased, but each party gains additional satisfaction from working together on a common goal. And instead of selfishly hoarding their wealth, people who cooperate sincerely take pleasure in sharing the good fortune that results with people they have come to care about in the process. If you cooperate with others in a spirit of loyalty and goodwill, you can achieve success that will enrich all concerned.

Nine at the Top

The rain comes, there is rest.
The virtues one carries are esteemed.
Yet even the perseverance of a woman brings danger, for
The moon is nearly full.
If the superior person goes forth and acts,
Misfortune comes.

In the *Book of Changes*, the appearance of rain often symbolizes a release of tension, or things coming to fruition. Thus the hexagram judgment tells us "Dense clouds, [but] no rain." In the final line, the rain comes, meaning that the patient accumulation of small advantages over time—the theme of the hexagram as a whole—has ultimately paid off.

Through persistence and unremitting effort, you have achieved success. Your efforts are rewarded and your contributions are recognized. Now is the time to rest and regroup. Do not become greedy or tempt fate. Do not seek a greater victory. Be content with what you have. As the text advises, "the moon is nearly full." This means that things have expanded as far as they can without waning. A time of adversity and decline is coming; new and unforseen obstacles await. Therefore, it is time to consolidate and secure your achievement. A bold or audacious attempt to push ahead in the hopes of winning everything may jeopardize all you have worked for.

NOTES

9.0 "outskirts." *jiao:* "suburbs," contrasts with city, countryside, and forests. Cf. 13.0.

9.2 "Drawn." *qian:* to be hauled along or led like an animal on a rope. Cf. 43.4.

9.3 "roll their eyes." *fan mu:* literally, "reverse eyes," hence, look away from each other, glare at each other.

9.5 "Sincere and loyally attached," etc. Wilhelm/Baynes translates this as "If you are sincere and loyally attached / You are rich in your neighbor." This beautifully conveys the idea of mutual enrichment between people who trust each other and work for the common good.

9.6 "The moon is nearly full." Cf. 54.5, 61.4.

TEN

Lü • Treading

Keywords:

Conduct
Circumspection
Daring
Treading carefully
Stepping on the tiger's tail

Above: Qian • Heaven
Below: Dui • Lake

In this hexagram, five yang lines are surrounded by a single weak yin line in the third place. The third line usually connotes difficulty or a painful transition, so the hexagram suggests the possibility of danger if proprieties are not observed. The original meaning of Lü was probably "shoes," and the ideograph is a picture of a person walking in shoes. This was eventually extended to the idea of walking cautiously, and hence to proper conduct and fulfilling one's duties in the right way.

"Treading," however, has a second meaning: It indicates not only stepping carefully but also treading on something, and hence the notion of taking a risk, symbolized by stepping on the tail of a tiger. Here the weak and the lowly tread on the strong and the mighty; yet no harm is done because the strong take it with good humor. The trigrams tell a similar story: The upper trigram is Qian (Heaven), symbolizing the father; the lower trigram is Dui (Lake), symbolizing the youngest daughter. The proud father views the precocious energy of his youngest child with tolerance and affection, and hence all goes well.

THE JUDGMENT

Treading on the tail of the tiger.
It does not bite.
Success.

The theme of Lü is the need for care and circumspection in conduct and social interaction. You find yourself in a difficult situation. It is like treading on the tail of a tiger. If you make a wrong move, you may bring strong forces down upon you. Therefore, it is important to behave with the utmost delicacy and decorum. Plan your moves in advance. Think carefully what you want to do before you act. Move toward your goal steadily and avoid rash behavior. This is not the time to engage in reckless adventures or radical approaches. Stick to traditional, tested and proven methods.

In personal relations, be pleasant and tactful, particularly to difficult people who might have reason to harm you. Don't allow their irritability and bad temper to throw you or cause you to respond sarcastically or in anger. Maintain your poise and composure. Even though your position is perilous, you can still make progress if you behave with the utmost tact and consideration during this difficult time. Don't forget your sense of humor or your manners. They will help you avoid potential problems and smooth over misunderstandings. Above all, do not lose your cool. Doing the right thing now requires that you keep your wits about you. Imagine yourself walking along a balance beam. If you keep your balance emotionally as well as physically and move forward with grace and dexterity, you will get to the other side unharmed.

THE IMAGE

Heaven above, the lake below:
This is the image of Treading.
Thus the superior person distinguishes between the high and the low,
Improving the hearts and minds of ordinary people.

The constituent trigrams of Lü are Qian (Heaven) and Dui (Lake or Swamp). The high heavens are very far from a lowly swamp. But each has a place in the order of the universe, and that place should be recognized and valued on its own terms.

An important part of tact and decorum is treating people with the respect that they deserve appropriate to their place and situation. This does not mean treating people who are poor or lowly with disdain or condescension. It means respecting each person for who they are and not treating them with disrespect or discourtesy because they do not meet your standards or because they are not who you want them to be. All human beings have inherent dignity and deserve to be treated with such, no matter how young or old they are, or how high or low they find themselves in society. A central theme of the hexagram Lü is that just as all things in the universe alternate, people will inevitably rise and fall in social standing. What endures is their common humanity. To "distinguish between the high and the low" thus does not mean that you should discriminate among people or against them, but that you should meet people on their own terms. In this way you show proper regard for them, for to approach what we have in common with others we must first recognize our differences from them and how those differences cause us to see the world differently. Once people understand that you respect them for who they are, you will put them at ease and you can work together even if you have great differences in experience and background.

The point of good manners is not to put people in their place or to make people uncomfortable. Quite the contrary: decorum is designed to smooth social situations, to bring harmony to personal interactions, and to allow people to navigate difficult and potentially unpleasant circumstances with dignity and self-respect. In your dealings, try to recognize in others your own feelings and experiences. Be patient with others and listen carefully to them. Be sensitive to what they do as well as what they say. Behind a gruff exterior may lie insecurity and hurt; beneath a placid demeanor may lurk vulnerability and resentment. Respond to anger with equanimity and to belligerence with good humor. Strive to generate harmony in the situation without surrendering your own dignity. If you feel threatened or insecure, do not lash out. Do not put on airs or pretend to be something that you are not. You have nothing to prove. Just as Lü counsels that you should accept and respect others for who they are, you should also accept and respect yourself for who you are. This is the lesson of courtesy applied to the self.

THE LINES

The lines offer advice on how to conduct oneself in a dangerous and difficult situation. In line one we are just beginning, and we should act simply and honestly, without drawing undue attention to ourselves. Lines two, four, and five preach the virtues of moderation, caution, circumspection, preparation, and resoluteness, while line three warns that without these virtues a person will meet with disaster. In line six, the work is completed, and we can measure our conduct by the good or bad effects it has had.

Initial Nine

Simple conduct. One proceeds without blame.

When you are in a lowly position, you can still make progress. First, keep matters simple. Focus on the matters that are immediately before you. Take things one day at a time. Be content to move step by step. Second, don't make unnecessary demands on others. Then you will not become overly dependent upon others or unduly obligated to them. Because you are free from unnecessary entanglements, you will be able to proceed at your own pace and make steady progress. Finally, do not try to use other people as a means to an end. They are not mere instruments for your personal aggrandizement.

People who are too eager to make progress cannot abide their modest position. They try to advance not as a consequence of doing something worthwhile but simply to gain praise and esteem in the eyes of others. This leads to envy, jealousy, and bitterness if they do not succeed, and arrogance and corruption if they do. By contrast, simple conduct means adhering to the most basic principles of behavior: doing the best you can given your circumstances, taking pride in your work, behaving honorably and honestly, and treating others with respect. These are appropriate values for a person in any position, but especially so for a person at the beginning of an enterprise. Strive to do something of value in this world and treat others with integrity and compassion. In this way you will be without blame.

Nine in the Second Place

Walking a smooth, level path.
The perseverance of a recluse
Brings good fortune.

To walk a smooth and level path means behaving with moderation and modesty. Keep a low profile. Do not engage in reckless enthusiasms or get carried away in unrealistic desires. Don't be demanding or engage in self-pity. Instead, focus on what needs to be done without show or ceremony. Move forward quietly and you will succeed.

The text compares this way of behaving to that of a recluse. A hermit does not get entangled in the affairs of others and is content with his lot. He does not allow himself to get caught up in the hustle and bustle of the world. He does not chase after the ever-shifting criteria of fame and renown. He does not measure his worth through the eyes of others and he does not feel the pangs of worldly striving. Because he maintains his independence and his integrity, and because his needs and desires are few, he gains true freedom. Because he struggles with no one, no one struggles with him.

Six in the Third Place (**Constitutive Line**)

A one-eyed man is able to see,
A lame man is able to walk.
He treads on the tail of the tiger.
The tiger bites him.
Misfortune.
Like a warrior acting on behalf of his great prince.

Although a one-eyed man can see, he does not see very well. Although a lame man can walk, he is not very agile. The text suggests that you are not as well prepared for what you want to do as you think you are. Like the one-eyed man, you do not see the situation completely or clearly. Like the lame man, your abilities are not necessarily up to the task. Beware of overconfidence. Don't bite off more than you can chew. If you plunge ahead recklessly, you will meet with disaster. Nevertheless, sometimes you have to take calculated risks with insufficient knowledge or untested abilities, because of your duty or loyalty to others, or because there simply is no other alternative. Hence the text advises that you should only take such risks when you are in the position of "a warrior acting on behalf of his great prince."

Nine in the Fourth Place

He treads on the tail of the tiger
With great caution and circumspection.
In the end, good fortune.

When you are faced with a dangerous task, it is still possible to succeed. However, you must proceed with great caution. Use your common sense. Try to get all the intelligence you can about the situation you face. Maximize your resources. Plan ahead and leave nothing to chance. With the right preparation, you can tread on the tail of the tiger and escape unscathed.

Nine in the Fifth Place (Ruling Line)

Resolute conduct.
Be constant in the face of danger.

When you face a difficult or dangerous situation, remember two things. First, get all the information you can. Be aware of exactly what the dangers are. Learn from others who have tried something similar, and be open to new approaches and methods. Second, be resolute. Don't lose heart just because the goal is difficult. Make a sincere commitment to see things through to the end. If you can't do this, you should definitely rethink your goals. Half measures and halfhearted attempts will mean failure. But if you know what you are facing and you are determined to overcome it, you will succeed in the end.

Nine at the Top

Examine your conduct and consider whether its effects are favorable.
When everything is fulfilled, supreme good fortune.

Be pragmatic and proactive in pursuit of your goals. Regularly take stock of what you have accomplished and how you have handled things. The past results of your strategy are usually the best evidence of its future success. Spend some time analyzing what worked well and what did not and, equally important, why things went as they did. If the consequences are good, maintain your chosen path. If not, don't be proud or defensive; make the necessary adjustments and don't be afraid to try something new. As you move forward, continually reassessing and readjusting your tactics, you will learn more and more about what it takes to succeed. Eventually, your hard work will pay off, and your efforts will bear fruit.

NOTES

10.2 "a recluse." *you:* dark, retired, lonely, solitary, subtle. Cf. 54.2.

10.3 "A lame man is able to walk." Cf. 54.1, where the result is happier.

10.3 "Like a warrior," etc. I.e., this is the sort of risk that only a loyal soldier would take. Another reading is "The one-eyed man thinks he can see. / The lame man thinks he can walk. / He treads on the tail of the tiger. / The tiger bites him. / This is what happens to a soldier who tries to play the part of a great prince." I.e., the subject was too ambitious (like the one-eyed man or the lame man) and is punished for his arrogance and audacity.

10.6 "are favorable." That is, whether the effects are good or bad, whether one's conduct has produced good or bad results.

10.6. "When everything is fulfilled." I.e., when the cycle is completed, when all the results are in.

ELEVEN

Tai • Peace

䷊

Keywords:

Harmony
Smoothly flowing
Prosperity
Union of high and low
Harmonious interaction
Things go well
Advance

Above: Kun • Earth
Below: Qian • Heaven

In Tai three yang lines are at the bottom, moving upward and displacing the three yin lines, symbolizing the arrival of the great and the departure of the small. An alternative interpretation is that the three yin lines, which symbolize earth, move downward. They meet the three yang lines, which symbolize heaven and are moving upward. Thus the two influences meet, symbolizing harmony. When yin and yang, heaven and earth, work together in perfect concord, all things prosper. Under either interpretation, Tai connotes a particularly auspicious time.

This hexagram and the next, Pi (Standstill), are among the most important pairs of opposites in the *Book of Changes*. In their own way they are as important as the first two hexagrams, Qian and Kun. Just as Qian and Kun alternate in the processes of change, Tai and Pi represent the alternation in human fortunes and social life. Good times do not last forever: Prosperity and cooperation eventually give way to stagnation and alienation. However, just when hindrances and obstacles are at their greatest, harmony and prosperity emerge once again. Enlightened people, understanding this, try to nourish harmony and cooperation in order to keep the good times going as long as they can, and to begin the process of renewal in times of difficulty.

THE JUDGMENT

Peace. The petty depart,
The great arrive.
Good fortune. Success.

Tai represents a time of great prosperity and concord. Heaven and earth operate together happily and effortlessly. The high act in harmony with the low, the strong with the weak, the great with the small. Progressive forces make great strides; worthy elements advance without obstacle. People of talent, ability, and wisdom obtain the respect due them, and others work with them freely and happily without envy or rancor. Those who join in are honored and respected in turn for their contributions. Peace descends on the world, and everything flows smoothly and easily. It seems indeed as if heaven were on earth.

During this period your relationships with others become more congenial. Old problems will be resolved; new intimacies will develop. Cooperation and coordination become easier, almost effortless. You can begin new projects with confidence, and the ones you are currently pursuing will blossom. If you make the effort and devote yourself to achieving your goals now, you will flourish and prosper.

The propitiousness of the time is an opportunity, not a guarantee. Even though things are proceeding smoothly, there is still work to be done. Make the most of the favorable conditions. Forge new alliances. Work with others on common goals. Share your ideas with others. If you are contemplating a relationship, let others know how you feel. This is a time when the possibilities of communication are enhanced. Make new contacts and take advantage of opportunities when they arise. Plan new projects and enterprises. Lay the groundwork for your future success. Do all the little things that are necessary to prevail in the long run. Although this is a time of peace, peace does not mean lassitude or inactivity. It means that things are flowing forward at an easy, fortunate pace. It is up to you to take advantage of that momentum.

THE IMAGE

Heaven and earth unite:
This is the image of Peace.
Thus the great prince acts to fulfil the Dao of heaven and earth,
Supports their harmonious interaction,
And so aids the people.

Times of harmony and prosperity do not last forever. You must do your best to keep things flowing smoothly. Hence the text speaks of "fulfil[ling] the Dao of heaven and earth" by "[s]upport[ing] their harmonious interaction." Wise people understand that the seeds of inertia and decay are present when things are flourishing, just as the seeds of future renewal and success are present during a time of stagnation. Concord is a precious resource that must ever be renewed.

You can prolong the good times in the world around you by acting synergistically with others and encouraging people to cooperate with each other. Working together will make everyone better off. It is important to understand that harmony does not mean giving in. It means establishing conditions of mutual respect that make cooperation possible. In the long run harmony is only possible if everyone feels that they are respected and honored for who they are and for the contributions that they make. If you take advantage of other people, or they take advantage of you, the situation will not be stable, and as people withdraw their cooperation, the time of prosperity will eventually come to an end.

Similar advice applies to yourself. The best way to ensure that things continue to flow smoothly in your own life is to seek harmony in your relations with others and to promote harmony within yourself. Make peace with others. Forgive old injuries. Put aside long-standing resentments. Free yourself from all hatred, envy, and bitterness. Let go of whatever has held you back in the past. Let this be a time of spiritual renewal. Imagine your life as if it were spring; a time to discard what is stagnant and outmoded and to embrace what is healthy and new. Let yourself grow and blossom like a flower in spring. Broaden your horizons and try something new and adventurous. Treat your fellow man with generosity and respect. Cultivate your own inner harmony and you will be better able to experience the harmony in the world outside you.

THE LINES

The lines tell the story of the rise of peaceful, smooth, and prosperous conditions, culminating in line five, which is the ruler of the hexagram. In line six, the time of peace is drawing to a close; a time of disorder and stagnation is just beginning.

Initial Nine

When reeds of grass are pulled up,
Other roots of the same kind come with them.
To set forth brings good fortune.

The roots of the rush plant are intertwined, so that when one strand is pulled up, others come with it. The metaphor means that in times of peace and prosperity an able person who goes out into the world to accomplish something naturally draws others along, to the benefit of all. When prosperous and peaceful conditions are just beginning, it is particularly important for people to cooperate with each other. Working together for the common good propels the good times forward and helps make them last.

It is time to make a difference. Decide on a worthy goal and go out into the world to accomplish it. As the text says, "to set forth brings good fortune." Your efforts will attract people with similar aims and values. If you work to benefit others in addition to yourself, you will meet with success.

Nine in the Second Place (Ruling Line)

Embrace the uncouth and the common.
Ford the stream.
Do not abandon those far away.
Then cliques dissolve.
One obtains honor by walking the central path.

Especially when things are going well, you must cultivate worthy habits to keep things running smoothly. First, do not become arrogant or treat people with condescension. Just because you are prospering does not make you better than everyone else. Be tolerant and open-minded. Now is the time to undertake important and difficult tasks. Everyone, no matter how lowly or ordinary, may have something valuable to contribute. Try to see the good in people and you will encourage them to grow and live up to your positive expectations.

Second, try to take the longer view of things. Do not neglect important questions even if they seem distant from current concerns. Small problems turn into large ones because we are too busy to take care of them early on.

Third, avoid playing favorites and do not fall prey to factionalism. Do not engage in divisive practices that corrode trust and cooperation. Many a prosperous time has been ruined because people became greedy, or clannish. Work for the common good rather than for a selfish or special interest.

Finally, practice moderation and avoid going to extremes. Avoid self-indulgence. If you can follow these principles in your life, you can prolong the good times and help ward off the onset of bad ones.

Nine in the Third Place

There is no plain without a slope.
There is no going forth without a return.
One who perseveres in times of hardship
Is without blame.
Do not be worried about this truth.
Enjoy the blessings you possess.

The basic lesson of the *Book of Changes* is that everything changes. Good times turn to bad, and bad times eventually improve. Even during the most peaceful and prosperous conditions, difficulties, decay, and evil are merely held in check and are never completely eliminated. But one should not dwell on this obsessively. Negative thinking keeps you from enjoying the present. It may actually contribute to the hastening of decay, for if you think that things will go wrong, they probably will. Rather, the right attitude is to be realistic and to accept the law of change. First, because good times will not last forever, you should not waste them but make the most of them. Learn to live in the here and now. Take advantage of opportunities to grow while resources are available to you. Second, recognize that you cannot rely on external circumstances or the approval of others to make you happy, for these things inevitably fluctuate over time. If you are overly dependent on them, you will suffer greatly when fortune changes. The best way to deal with change is to develop your own inner resources. Strength of character and independence of spirit help you enjoy the good times and persevere through the bad times. Inner resolve and faith in your own abilities bring you good fortune in the long run no matter what happens in the short run.

Six in the Fourth Place

Fluttering down,
He does not use his affluence on his neighbors.
Without admonition, there is sincerity.

"Fluttering down" refers to the wings of a bird; it symbolizes a light touch. The line tells the story of a person who is rich and powerful but does not force himself on others through threats or try to sway them through a tawdry display of wealth. Instead, he acts simply and shows respect and concern for his neighbors, and they willingly come to his assistance.

When people trust one another, they do not need to impress, cajole, or threaten in order to gain cooperation. Rather, cooperation flows naturally from their mutual interaction. Whether you are in the position of a superior or a subordinate, be sincere and keep lines of communication open, and people will be more receptive to you. Work with other people in a spirit of openness and generosity if you want them to cooperate with you.

Six in the Fifth Place (Ruling Line)

The sovereign Yi
Gives his daughter in marriage.
This brings blessings
And supreme good fortune.

"Giv[ing] his daughter in marriage" meant that the emperor united his family through marriage with the families of his subordinates. The cooperative union of the higher and lower, the stronger and the weaker, is like the cooperation of heaven and earth. It brings happiness and blessings to all.

Emulate this union of heaven and earth. You can achieve great success and good fortune through modesty and humility in your dealings with others, particularly the people you lead or work with. Eschew arrogance. Listen closely to what other people are saying. Reach out to them in a spirit of co-operation. If you are willing to be of service to others, you will win their support.

Six at the Top

The city walls fall back into the moat.
Use no army now.
Issue commands only within your own city.
Perseverance brings humiliation.

The meaning of the metaphor of city walls falling into the moat is that what was built up out of the earth eventually falls back into it. The time of peace and harmony symbolized by the hexagram is nearing an end. A period of decline has begun. This is a natural fact of life and you cannot prevent it. Fighting against the law of change only results in humiliation and wasted resources. When you notice that such a period of decay is at hand, violent opposition is the wrong strategy. Instead, you need to cultivate your character to withstand the period of stagnation that lies ahead. Live up to your responsibilities and exercise self-control. Strengthen your ties with those in your inner circle and look after those closest to you. The coming dark times will eventually give way, leading to a new period of prosperity and harmony.

NOTES

11.0 "Supports their harmonious interaction." Or, "their proper mutual interaction," "their harmonious mutual assistance."

11.1 "When reeds of grass," etc. *Mao:* cogongrass, or rush plant, was used to make thatched roofs. Its roots are intertwined so that when one is pulled up, sod and other roots come out too.

11.1 "To set forth." *Zheng,* which appears throughout the *Book of Changes,* means to attack or to chastise. More generally, it means to set out, to go forward, or to undertake, i.e., to engage in purposeful activity.

11.3 "In times of hardship." *jian:* drudgery, repetitive hard work, hence distressing and sorrowful. Alternatively, "in the face of difficulty," or "in the face of adversity."

11.3. "This truth." *qi fu*: "its truth." Or, "Grieve not over your sincerity and truthfulness" (Alfred Huang). However, as Edward Shaughnessy points out in his translation of the Mawangdui manuscript, *fu* (truth) may be a phonetic loan for *fu*, meaning "return," which is used earlier in the same line. If so, this would translate as "Don't worry about its (or one's) return [to the way things were before]." Thus one might translate the line, "Don't worry about your restoration."

11.3 "Blessings," *fu*. Or, "Enjoy the good things you [still] possess." It is possible that this *fu* is also a loan for *fu*, "return."

11.4 "Fluttering down." The fourth line, the first of the three yin lines, is described as "fluttering down" to the three yang lines, which represent its neighbors.

11.4 "He does not use his affluence on his neighbors." Cf. 15.5.

11.5 "The sovereign Yi gives his daughter in marriage." Cf. 54.5.

TWELVE

Pi • Standstill

䷋

Keywords:

Stagnation
Blockage
Misfortune
Disharmony
Hindrance

Above: Qian • Heaven
Below: Kun • Earth

Pi is the natural opposite of Tai. Three yin lines enter from the bottom, driving the three yang lines at the top away, symbolizing the arrival of the petty and the departure of the great. Alternatively, the three yang lines, which represent heaven, are moving upward; while the three yin lines, which symbolize earth, are moving downward. Hence, the two great powers of heaven and earth are moving away from each other. They do not cooperate and stagnation is the result.

The alternation of Tai and Pi—progress and standstill, prosperity and impoverishment, opportunity and hindrance, success and failure—is an inevitable feature of human life. The two hexagrams taken together are as profound in their implications as Qian and Kun. Pi, however, is not cause for pessimism or despair. The law of change is always in operation: Through hardship and adversity new possibilities for renewal are formed. The seeds of future success are sown in times of greatest difficulty. The Chinese have a saying: "Out of the depths of misfortune happiness arrives."

THE JUDGMENT

Standstill. Inferior people do not further
The perseverance of the superior person.
The great depart; the petty arrive.

Pi describes a time when heaven and earth are estranged and communication is difficult if not impossible. People in different areas of life have lost touch with each other, social relations have broken down, and disorder proliferates. The time is truly out of joint. Because people cannot cooperate, they cannot make progress. Because people pursue only their narrow self-interest and regard everyone else as rivals and enemies, harmony and reciprocity wither away. In a time of standstill, petty and inferior people are on the rise. Their bad habits, small-mindedness, selfishness, and meanness poison the atmosphere of social life. People of goodwill and enlightenment must persevere through this difficult time, keeping a low profile. They should not count on the assistance of intolerant, shallow, and fawning people, for the latter seek only to maximize their own glory and power. Indeed, during the time of Pi, the petty make sport of people of integrity and hinder their progress at every turn. Enlightened people should not contribute to the disharmony and mean-spiritedness of the time, and they should not be tempted to surrender their principles in order to advance. In these circumstances they cannot exert much influence; therefore, they should remain faithful to their values and wait until better days arrive.

In personal terms, Pi signifies that you face a standstill in your life. Matters have stagnated. Obstacles block your progress. Your efforts meet with failure and rejection at every turn. You may well feel that life has dealt you a bad hand and that your luck has run out. Relationships with others have become more complicated and troublesome. You have difficulty getting people to understand you and consider your point of view. Misunderstandings proliferate. You may feel estrangement, alienation, and despair.

During this period you should not expect help from people who do not share your values or have your best interests at heart. They have their own agendas and they will not much care what happens to you. Do not rest your hopes on shallow, vain, or selfish individuals. They cannot save themselves;

they will certainly not be able to save you. You may be tempted to go against your better judgment and abandon your principles in order to fit in or to gain the acceptance of such people. Resist the temptation. It is not worth throwing yourself away on something that is unseemly and wrong for you.

Instead, the proper strategy is to withdraw from the situation. Preserve your integrity and maintain your faith in yourself. Do not try to force things to improve. They will improve in their own time. Until then, the way to combat the stagnation outside you is to combat the stagnation within. You must hold yourself together and draw on the best parts of yourself. Remember that no matter what happens now and whatever mistakes you may have made in the past, there is good within you. Foster and nurture those most valuable facets of yourself and let them lead you through this difficult period. Keep hope. Have patience. Better times are coming.

THE IMAGE

Heaven and earth do not unite:
This is the image of Standstill.
Thus the superior person restrains himself and preserves his inner virtue
In order to escape difficulties and hardships.
He does not allow himself to be honored with rank or salary.

Standstill and stagnation tempt you to take the easy way out. Don't give in and don't lower your standards. Your self-worth is the most precious commodity you have. If you sacrifice it in order to please others now, you will have to keep sacrificing it repeatedly as more and more compromises are expected of you in order to maintain your position. You must learn to be self-reliant and deal with the pain and heartache of the situation in your own way and on your own terms. The text says that you must preserve your inner virtue in order to escape the difficulties and hardships in your life. Do not betray your values, because they are the means by which you will ultimately prevail. Withdraw from the situation and hold on tight to what is most important. Your ability to persevere now will give you great strength in the future.

THE LINES

The lines tell the story of the eventual overthrow of stagnation and standstill. The superior person is advised to persevere (lines one, two, and three) through the darkest days and make himself ready for the work of the upper trigram. In line four, the superior person commits himself to the will of heaven and benefits not only himself but others; in line five, the great person with caution and circumspection finds the strength to bring about a change in conditions. Finally, in line six, the standstill is ended and there is great rejoicing.

Initial Six

When reeds of grass are pulled up,
Other roots of the same kind come with them.
Perseverance brings good fortune and success.

In the first line of Hexagram 11, Tai, the theme is drawing like-minded people out into the world. In Hexagram 12, Pi, the theme is how to deal with stagnation. Here the text advises you to persevere rather than to undertake something. In times of standstill you must draw on your inner reserves and maintain your character and help others do so as well.

If you discover that you cannot change or influence the situation without compromising your integrity, you should withdraw from it entirely rather than betray your principles. This is not a defeat but is actually a form of success, for you have preserved your own sense of self-worth and the integrity of those around you. In the long run, this will bring you good fortune.

Six in the Second Place (Constitutive Line)

They bear and endure.
Good fortune for the petty.
The great person accepts the standstill to achieve success.

During times of stagnation petty people often rise through backstabbing and flattery. The world seems contaminated by vanity, dishonesty, and self-promotion. Those who are honest and upright seem like naïve fools, while the shallow and corrupt only seem to grow richer and more powerful with each passing day. Resist the temptation to follow the path of the latter. If you try to play this game, you will become desperately unhappy and will compromise your principles in the process. Do not be drawn into a form of striving that is beneath you. It is perfectly acceptable to be tolerant of others who live in this world, but do not get involved out of a hope of influencing petty people and elevating yourself in their eyes. Under these conditions it is best to retain a low profile. Accept the standstill for what it is. Maintain your independence and your integrity and you will succeed in the long run.

Six in the Third Place

They bear shame.

The third line of a hexagram often describes a person who tries to press forward with unfortunate results. In a time of stagnation we are often tempted to try to break through the standstill by whatever means we can. Do not try to do something that you know is beyond your abilities, or you will meet with an ignominious defeat.

The emotional suffering felt during a time of stagnation also tempts people to cut corners and engage in unethical or illicit practices as a way of making progress. Questionable methods and tactics may bring success in the short run, but only humiliation in the long run. Do not use them, for they will backfire and bring you shame and sorrow. If you have acted in an underhanded or dishonest fashion in the past, then recognizing this fact, accepting responsibility, and engaging in sincere repentance can be the beginning of a real improvement in your life. Return to the best part of your nature and you will eventually succeed.

Nine in the Fourth Place

He who follows the will of heaven
Is without blame.
His comrades share in the blessing.

The law of change is in operation now. The time of stagnation and standstill is drawing to an end and beginning to change into its opposite. Take heart. New opportunities now open up to you. You can be instrumental in bringing about a renewal if you act from the right motives. Hence the text speaks of one "who obeys the will of heaven"—that is, one whose motives are upright and who acts in accordance with the situation. Put aside all selfishness. Think about what the occasion demands as opposed to what benefits you personally. If you use this opportunity simply to promote yourself, you will not succeed. But if you feel sincerely called to the task of bringing order and harmony, your endeavors will be favored by the time—you will be acting in accordance with "the will of heaven"—and both you and those who associate with you will benefit.

Nine in the Fifth Place (Ruling Line)

The standstill is giving way.
Good fortune for the great person.
It might be lost, it might be lost.
So he ties it to a bushy, flourishing mulberry tree.

The bad times are ending and the good times are coming. But they will not come of themselves. You need to play your part. If you are up to the task, you can bring about a radical change for the better. There is much to do. During this crucial period you must avoid falling into temptation, laziness, or despair. Do not let matters slide or take things for granted. Pay careful attention to what might go wrong. Fix what needs to be fixed. Just because things are starting to go well, do not forget that elements of chaos still lurk in the beginnings of a newly created order, and dangers still remain in a time of growing security. The text says that good fortune will come to "the great person." You will obtain good fortune now if you rise to the challenge. Act like a great-souled person and you will become one. In order to eliminate the standstill in the outside world, you must first eliminate the standstill within yourself.

Ending a long period of stagnation is no easy matter. It takes all of your effort and your faith. You may feel the forces of stagnation within you trying to maintain themselves. But do not let them. Now is the time to hold yourself together. Hence the text says, "he ties it to a bushy, flourishing mulberry tree." The mulberry symbolizes something that is resilient, for tradition states that when a mulberry's branches are cut off, it sends out shoots that are even sturdier than before. The chips are down; it is time for you to show what you are made of. If you can ride through the time of stagnation, you will achieve great success.

Nine at the Top

The standstill is overthrown.
First standstill, then great joy.

Turning the hexagram Pi (Standstill) upside down produces the hexagram Tai (Peace). Hence by overthrowing the standstill, one puts in place the conditions for happiness and success.

The time of stagnation is almost at an end. But you have an important role to play in establishing the new conditions. Purposeful activity and steadfast commitment to restoring the good times are essential. The more effort that you put into eliminating stagnation, the greater your success will be. That is why the text says that standstill is "overthrown" rather than that it just fades away. There is a fundamental asymmetry between order and chaos. If one does not work at preserving peace and prosperity, they naturally decay into chaos and disorder. But chaos does not decay back into order of its own accord; people must make concerted efforts to restore harmony and prosperity. Ending a period of stagnation requires creativity and commitment. But the effort is worthwhile. When you see the opportunity to make things better, join in. You will have reason to celebrate, as the text tells us: before there was standstill, afterward there will be great joy.

NOTES

12.0 "further." *li:* benefit. This is one instance where the Wilhelm/Baynes translation of *li* as "to further" makes particular sense. In a time of standstill, inferior people are on the rise; enlightened people must persevere, but they should not count on assistance from petty and fawning people who seek only to maximize their own glory and influence.

12.GI "restrains himself and preserves his inner virtue." *jian te:* literally, "parsimonious (stingy) virtue (action)." The translation tries to capture both meanings of limiting action and conserving integrity.

12.1 "When reeds of grass," etc. Cf. 11.1.

12.2 "bear and endure," *bao cheng:* enwrap and receive. Or, "bear and accept."

12.4 "Follows the will of heaven," *you ming:* literally, "has orders." However, *ming* also means "fate" or "destiny," i.e., the mandate of heaven.

12.4 "His comrades." For *chou* (field division, plowed field), most translators read *chou,* multitude, or *chou,* comrades. The last reading seems to make the most sense in context. Cf. Wilhelm/Baynes: "Those of like mind partake of the blessing." Another possibility is "who," as in "Who will share in the blessing?"

12.4 "Share in," *li:* radiance, clinging, fasten on, dependent on, hence partake in.

12.5 "It might be lost, it might be lost." *qi wang qi wang:* "its destruction, its destruction." The words are doubled for emphasis. Cf. Wilhelm/Baynes: "What if it should fail, what if it should fail?"

One possible rendering of the line is that the great person thinks to himself, "The moment for overcoming standstill might be lost." Hence he takes extra precautions and tries to keep himself together. This is symbolized by tying "it" (himself, the situation) to a bushy, flourishing mulberry tree. Another reading is that "its destruction" refers to the time of standstill. The great person keeps the goal of ending standstill always in mind and so fortifies himself. To be tied to the mulberry tree would be to keep grounded, or to avoid temptation, like Ulysses being tied to the mast.

THIRTEEN

Tong Ren • Fellowship with People

䷌

Keywords

Joining with others
Fellowship
Concord
Community
Keeping the group together

Above: Qian • Heaven
Below: Li • Fire

Tong Ren is the complement of Shi, Hexagram 7. It features five yang lines surrounding a single yin line in the second place. In Shih a single strong personality holds people together. In Tong Ren strong personalities are held together by a single yin line, symbolizing humility, flexibility, and the ability to compromise. These are the virtues necessary for a successful fellowship. When a group of people is held together by common goals and a spirit of charity and mutual affection, its cumulative power is greatly enhanced.

Another interpretation of the hexagram is based on its constituent trigrams. The outer trigram of Tong Ren is Qian (Heaven), which stands for strength and endurance; the inner trigram is Li (Fire), which stands for clarity and enlightenment. In the same way, a successful fellowship requires strength and endurance against the outside world and clarity and enlightenment among its members.

THE JUDGMENT

Fellowship with people, even in the open fields.
Success.
It is beneficial to cross the great river.
It is beneficial for the superior person to persevere.

The best way to realize your goals now is through participation in a group. You can achieve great influence and success through a collective endeavor. The group may be your friends, or it may be a political group, a social club, a religious organization, or the people you work with every day. If you are willing to join in with like-minded people, you can accomplish much more than you ever could on your own.

For a group to succeed, people need to feel that they have a common purpose and that the members are committed to each other. Trust and reciprocity are essential ingredients to success. The text speaks of fellowship "even in the open fields." Fields are a metaphor for what is far and wide, broad and distant. Thus, fellowship "even in the open fields" means fellowship that is maintained through thick and thin, and that can extend to all sorts of people who possess common values and goals. A sense of commitment and shared devotion make it possible for a group to achieve important and ambitious tasks, symbolized by being able to cross the great river. If you find a group with whom you can identify and whose values you admire, give your support without reservation. If others see that you are earnest and sincere, they will be willing to join in as well.

Over time, groups are subjected to many stresses and strains. The important thing is to let everyone in the group feel that they are needed and that their contributions are valued. If you take advantage of people or treat them with condescension, they will not be willing to give their all for the group, and they will be more likely to abandon the enterprise in times of hardship. Whatever your position in the fellowship or organization, be open-minded and willing to listen to others. Keeping lines of communication open not only preserves harmony and stability over time, but it also helps the group achieve its goals more effectively. The collective intelligence of many people working on a single project is often more powerful and thorough than that of any single individual, no matter how talented. Individual efforts and skills become greater than the sum of their parts when they are brought together in a common endeavor.

THE IMAGE

Heaven and fire combine:
This is the image of Fellowship with People.
Thus the superior person organizes the clans
And makes distinctions among things.

Successful groups require organization and distribution of functions, especially as they get larger and more complicated. The leader of the group must make thoughtful judgments about which people are best suited for which tasks. The group needs a chain of command, lines of appropriate authority, and expectations about proper roles. Without these distinctions, the group will be an undifferentiated mass, and it will not function properly. Yet although distinctions and differentiations may be necessary to the group's efficiency, in the long run it is what members have in common—the group's common purpose—that gives the fellowship its power. What unites the group is much more important than its divisions. Therefore, it is important not to allow cliques and inside groups to form. Nip the causes of dissension and separatism in the bud before alienation and resentments have a chance to grow. Encourage openness and mutual respect. Give everyone something meaningful to do and make sure that they are recognized for their successes and held responsible for their failures. If people feel that they are making a valued contribution, they will be more loyal and willing to work together for the common good.

THE LINES

The lines describe the gradual development of fellowship, symbolized by different locations (the gate, the city wall, the countryside, and so on). Line one represents the moment when true fellowship is emerging out of common interest. In line two, factions and cliques have begun to develop. In lines three and four, mistrust and internal disputes grow stronger and the fellowship is tested by conflicts. These are resolved in line five, the ruler of the hexagram; after great trials the members of the fellowship find each other again. Line six describes a mere modus vivendi, or fellowship without deep connection.

Initial Nine

Fellowship with people at the gate.
No blame.

This line describes the sort of fellowship that begins when people have similar needs; they unite because they have similar ends. This is a fellowship of mutual advantage that does not yet have firm ties other than commitment to a goal that all happen to share. For this reason everything will go well until people's interests start to diverge and come into conflict. More work will be necessary to transform this sort of fellowship into a true union of hearts and minds. Trust, respect, and a sense of mutual responsibility must be developed over time. In such a rudimentary fellowship it is important that there are no hidden agendas. Secret agreements and designs among parts of the group will damage developing bonds of trust and loyalty and bring misfortune to everyone concerned. But as long as the goals of fellowship are open and its basic terms equally understood by all, there is no blame.

Six in the Second Place (Ruling Line)

Fellowship with members of the clan.
Humiliation.

By "clan" the text means a faction, a clique, or a special interest. If a group becomes divided into factions, its unity is weakened. Factions enhance regrettable tendencies toward elitism, exclusivity, or clannishness. Members of one faction begin to think less well of others in the group; competition, misunderstanding, and distrust begin to grow. Baser motives replace the joint aims that originally brought the group together, and the group's energies are wasted in internal politicking and countless internal disputes. If nothing is done to stop these trends, there will be constant infighting, undermining the group's ability to achieve its goals, and leading ultimately to defeat and humiliation. Wise leaders do their best to head off factionalism before it occurs by continually reminding all of the parties why they originally joined the fellowship in the first place, instilling a common sense of purpose and urging the participants to put aside petty disputes for the good of the whole.

Nine in the Third Place

Hiding armed troops in the thicket,
He climbs the high hill.
Yet for three years he does not rise up.

In the third line the group's unity has been compromised by mistrust. The participants have developed divergent interests and goals. Cooperation has given way to competition. Each person has his own secret ambitions and seeks to dominate the others. Hence the text says, "Hiding armed troops in the thicket." Moreover, knowing his or her own mental reservations, each person suspects the others of having similar designs, for when people are no longer trustworthy, they no longer trust anyone else. Each person begins to spy on the others, hoping to catch them in their duplicity. And all of the remarks and actions of others, however innocent, can be interpreted as signs of impending betrayal or ambush. Cycles of mutual distrust and alienation grow. As a result, the group can make no progress.

You must break the cycle of mistrust before it becomes too pronounced. Reexamine your goals and your hopes for the group. Secrecy must give way to open discussion. A new agreement on the goals and aims of the fellowship must be forged in light of changed circumstances so that trust can be reestablished and bonds of loyalty renewed. If the participants can recognize that they are indeed working on a joint enterprise, they will be able to live with disagreements about how to proceed.

Nine in the Fourth Place

He climbs onto the city wall, but cannot attack.
Good fortune.

Selfishness and misunderstandings have isolated you. Feelings of distrust have impaired your relations with other people. You see yourself in confrontation with others and begin to feel defensive. Hence the text says, "He climbs onto the city wall." If you try to go your own way, you will become increasingly lonely and disconnected. And you will soon discover that it is much more difficult to go it alone than you anticipated.

Luckily, these feelings of alienation and emptiness will bring you to your senses, helping you recognize the true costs of a break in your relations and the price you would pay for open warfare. Hence the text says, "He cannot attack." Once you realize that you and the other party need each other and that fighting will get you nowhere, tensions will start to ease. And as you come to see the situation more realistically, you will be able to begin the process of making necessary compromises and reestablishing trust, which will ultimately lead to good fortune.

Nine in the Fifth Place (Ruling Line)

People in fellowship at first cry out and weep,
But afterward they laugh.
After great struggle they manage to find each other.

You find yourself continually separated from people you want to be with or a group that you belong to. Difficulties, obstacles, and misunderstandings keep you apart, and this causes you great unhappiness. Do not despair. The text advises that you express your feelings and your desire for union publicly. Make your sense of commitment clear. You will find that other people feel the same way. The ties between you are strong, and if you remain devoted to each other, ultimately nothing will keep you apart. Working together, you can conquer the problems that divide you, and your sadness will turn to joy.

Nine at the Top

Fellowship with people on the outskirts of town.
No remorse.

The time for deep unity and fellowship is past. Because of circumstances, only a mutually convenient alliance is possible. You join together with others for limited purposes, and even then you join not with the whole community but only with those close by, "on the outskirts of town." It is not a true joinder of hearts and minds, but more of a relationship of convenience. Nevertheless, such an arrangement is valuable if you recognize it for what it is.

NOTES

13.0 "Fellowship with people, even in the open fields. / Success." Or, "Fellowship with people, even in the open fields, brings success."

13.0 "the open fields." *ye:* countryside, distinguished from *jiao:* outskirts or suburbs, which are closer to the city. Cf. 9.0, 13.6.

13.0 "to persevere." *zhen*. Here the familiar gloss "to practice constancy and steadfast faithfulness" is particularly appropriate.

13.3 "He climbs the high hill." Or, "He climbs the high hill to observe."

13.4 "city wall." *yong:* wall, also ramparts, battlements.

13.4 "but cannot attack." *fu ke gong*. Cf. 6.2, 6.4, "unable to contend." *bu ke sung*.

13.5 "After great struggle." *da shi:* literally, "great army." Hence another reading would be "The great armies can meet each other," i.e, they are no longer at war, or they have joined forces.

FOURTEEN

Da You • Great Possession

䷍

Keywords:

Possession in great measure
Sovereignty

Above: Li • Fire
Below: Qian • Heaven

This hexagram consists of five yang lines surrounding by a single yin line in the fifth position, the place of the ruler. It represents a leader whose modesty and receptivity allows him to gather the most talented people around him. As a result, he prospers greatly. The lower trigram, Qian (Heaven), symbolizes inner strength; the upper trigram, Li (Fire), symbolizes clarity and enlightenment directed toward the outside world. This combination of strength and clarity, determination and enlightenment, results in a graceful and adept use of power that produces supreme success.

THE JUDGMENT

Great Possession.
Supreme success.

Da You represents a time of exceptional achievement and good fortune. Vast possibilities are now available to you. Opportunities abound. Whatever you undertake now has the greatest chance of success. Your relationships with others will blossom and thrive. Your resources multiply. Because you have so much going your way, you are effectively in command of the situation. Therefore, the time of great possession is also a time of sovereignty and control over your life. You are now able to take charge of the situation and move your life in the direction in which it should go.

Nevertheless, the lesson of this hexagram is that when you are in such a commanding position you must remain modest and unassuming. Then your success will not arouse envy or resentment, and your good fortune will not alarm or threaten others. Hence people will be willing to gather around you and cooperate with you. Put another way, in the time of great possession, one needs great self-possession. If you are magnanimous, generous, and humble, you can make great progress, gather increased support, and draw even more resources to your side. This is the meaning of the weak line in the fifth place that is able to attract the other five yang lines and lead them: Through unselfishness, receptivity, and generosity, you attract valuable people to your cause. By expressing your influence and your authority in subtle, controlled, and graceful ways, you help ensure continued success and prosperity not only for yourself but for those who ally themselves with you.

A time of great possession should also be a time of great clarity and enlightenment. When you have so much going for you, it is important to remain true to your principles. Use this time to pursue something truly worthy. You now have the chance to change your life for the better, so make sure to use the opportunity to move in the right direction. If you cannot live your life according to your highest aspirations and values when things are going well, when else will you be able to do so?

Finally, a time of great possession should be a time of great generosity. People are given much so that they can share it with others. Remember those who have helped you in the past, and support other people along the way. By acting with magnanimity and kindness now, you lay the groundwork for many good deeds in the future.

THE IMAGE

Fire above the heavens:
This is the image of Great Possession.
Thus the superior person curbs evil

And promotes good,
Obeying the beneficent will of heaven.

Fire in the heavens is sunlight. It shines on the earth, bringing clarity and illumination. In like fashion you have been given the opportunity to shine. Put another way, you are in the spotlight and all eyes are upon you. It is precisely at this time that you must devote yourself to promoting what is good in you and ridding yourself of what is bad. That is because great power magnifies both your good features and your less desirable ones. When you are blessed by material success and social advancement, it is all too easy to succumb to pride, excess, greed, and laziness. All of these vices will weaken you and ultimately eat away at your good fortune. Don't let the good times go to your head. Keep your ego firmly in check. Avoid any tendencies toward narcissism or arrogance, conceit or hubris. Don't throw your weight around or try to impress or dominate other people. By remaining modest and generous, you will win the admiration and respect of other people in a much healthier way. Give thanks for the blessings you have received, and share your good fortune with others. Through humility, cooperativeness, and benevolence, you can truly make these the best of times, not just for yourself but for everyone.

THE LINES

The lines describe how to behave in a time of great possession. The basic lesson is that when people have much, they should give much to others. The hexagram culminates in line six, in which one has transcended earthly possessions, and now enjoys the blessings of heaven.

Initial Nine

There is no relationship with harmful things,
So of course there is no blame.
If one recognizes the causes of difficulty,
One remains without blame.

Things are going smoothly. You have abundant resources and much to offer. But do not become complacent. You have not yet faced a major challenge. Nothing serious has had a chance to go wrong yet. The situation is still in its infancy, and many obstacles may lie ahead. The path will not always be smooth, so don't be overconfident and don't waste your resources needlessly. Instead, use this opportunity to secure your position. Forewarned is forearmed. If you prepare for difficulties in advance, you will succeed.

Nine in the Second Place

A great wagon to carry things.
One may set forth.
No blame.

The wagon symbolizes your ability to coordinate your assets and put them to good use. It also stands for people who can help you achieve your goals; they can shoulder the responsibilities that you place upon them just as a great wagon can bear a heavy burden.

The key to great possession is the ability to put your resources into action. Your assets mean little if you lack the ability to do anything with them. You are fortunate because you have abundant talents and means at your disposal and, equally important, the capacity to employ them to great advantage. Because you have ingenuity and the assistance of able helpers, you can undertake the most ambitious of goals. Be confident. It is time to make plans, organize your resources, and put together a winning team. Go forward now and you will succeed.

Nine in the Third Place

A prince offers tribute to the Son of Heaven.
A petty person cannot do this.

In ancient China princes would stage elaborate banquets to honor their kings. These expenditures demonstrated that the prince was a generous and loyal subject who would willingly share his resources for the common good, and in this way the prince earned the favor of the king.

Adopt the virtues of magnanimity and generosity in your own life. Your possessions, gifts, and abilities do not exist solely for your benefit. They must be placed in the service of others as well. This is the point of great possession—the greater your resources, the more you should be willing to put them at the disposal of others. When you allow others to benefit from your bounty, you are rewarded in countless ways, for you win the support and trust of others.

Small-minded people cannot see this. They are incapable of such generosity. They worry that they only have so much, and so they try to hoard everything for themselves. As a result, people regard them with jealousy and resentment. Because they do not understand the moral duties of great possession, small-minded people find that they must continually expend resources to protect themselves from others and gain their cooperation. By contrast, the magnanimous person, who offers his resources generously and for the benefit of all, finds that people are naturally drawn to him out of loyalty and gratitude; they seek to help and protect him of their own accord.

Nine in the Fourth Place

In no way arrogant.
No blame.

The secret of maintaining great possession is to enjoy it in ways that lead neither to envy or to self-aggrandizement. If you are blessed with talents or material goods, do not be boastful or conceited about your good fortune, and do not engage in ostentatious display. This will only make others envious and resentful, and then they will try to better you or to topple you from your exalted position. Arrogance inevitably generates rivalry and contention that will cause you trouble in the long run.

Just as you should not invite the envy of others, you should not be envious yourself if others have more than you. Do not be tempted to compete with others in order to cut them down to size or to establish your superiority. These desires are destructive. They will only make you unhappy and undermine your ability to enjoy the genuine blessings you already possess. Be modest and cooperative. Instead of trying to lord your accomplishments over others, focus instead on doing the best job that you can. In this way you will remain free of blame.

Six in the Fifth Place (Ruling Line)

One's truth and sincerity shine through to others,
In this way one earns respect.
Good fortune.

Your sincerity and trustworthiness naturally draw others to you. This is truly a fortunate time. If you act from the best motives, people will be attracted to you because of who you are rather than what you have, and you will reap great rewards. But you must be both accessible and dignified. Do not let people take advantage of your good nature, or let your openness lead people to treat you with disrespect. Exercise discretion and judgment in choosing your intimates and confidants. Do not compromise your principles or do anything that is beneath you. Maintain your integrity and your dignity, and all will go well.

Nine at the Top

Blessed by heaven.
Good fortune.
There is nothing that is not beneficial.

Line six often signifies one who has transcended the situation. Here it suggests the blessings of heaven that go beyond mere material possession. People who are unassuming and dedicated to the good, and who abide in truth and sincerity, place themselves under heaven's influence, and therefore receive heaven's blessing. Their benevolence shines through to everyone and they receive the assistance of others as if by magic.

You have the potential for great influence and achievement if you can maintain balance in your life and humility in your dealings with others. If you are devoted in your endeavors but do not seek recognition for your efforts, if you are modest in your manner and appreciative of others' contributions, you will be blessed by heaven. People will look up to you and help you and you will enjoy good fortune and supreme success.

NOTES

14.GI "promotes." Or "promulgates."

14.GI. "Obeying the beneficent will of heaven." *shun tian xiu ming:* literally, "obey heaven rest (relinquish, blessing, prosperity) fate (will, command, decree)." Alternative readings include: "And thereby obeys the benevolent will of heaven" (Wilhelm/Baynes); "Obeying Heaven's beneficent decrees" (Rutt); "He obeys the will of Heaven and so brings out the beauty inherent in life" (Lynn).

14.1 "causes," *ze:* model, sources, patterns.

14.5 "One's truth," etc. Willhelm/Baynes translates this, "He whose truth is accessible, yet dignified / Has good fortune."

14.5 "One's truth and sincerity," etc. Or, "Sincere and truthful communication/Makes dignity shine through" (Alfred Huang); "Trust in him makes him attractive, makes him awesome" (Lynn).

FIFTEEN

Qian • Modesty

Keywords:

Humility
Humbleness
Moderation
Temperance
Maintaining a balanced attitude
Fulfilling one's duties
Carrying things through to completion

Above: Kun • Earth
Below: Gen • Mountain

Qian consists of five yin lines surrounding a single yang line in the third place. In most cases the third position is unfortunate because it symbolizes one who strives to move upward (into the upper trigram) but is unable to do so. Here the symbolism is reversed: The ruler of the hexagram is a sage who is strong and powerful but who nevertheless stays in the lower trigram, thus symbolizing modesty.

The constituent trigrams are Kun (Earth) over Gen (Mountain). Mountains usually soar over the earth, but here the great and powerful mountain remains below, in a modest position. In the same way, one should always act with courtesy and respect toward others even if one is mighty and influential. Conversely, earth is lowly, but here it is raised over the mountains, symbolizing that one who adopts a gentle and humble attitude will eventually be exalted and achieve success.

THE JUDGMENT

> *Modesty. Success.*
> *The superior person carries things through to the end.*

According to the *Book of Changes*, modesty is one of the most important virtues. It is not innate but rather is the product of long, continuous, and conscious self-development and self-cultivation. It differs from the Christian ideal of meekness in important respects. Modesty does not mean submissiveness or passivity. A modest person may be quite active in the world; working steadily and unobtrusively, making commitments and living up to them. The text says that the modest person carries things through to their conclusion. Why is this attitude modest? It is because modest people do not think that they are more important than the work that they perform or the commitments that they have made to others. Therefore, they are consistent and reliable. Modest people do not regard anything that they must do as beneath them. Therefore, their pride does not get in the way of their success. They put their work, their obligations, and their commitments before their egos. That is why they are able to prevail in the long run.

Thus, modesty does not imply inaction. Rather, it means acting positively, cooperatively, and harmoniously. It means respecting other people and treating them as equals. By contrast, proud people think that they are better than everyone else or act as if they were. Often their pride hides a deeper insecurity. But truly modest people know who they are and therefore do not need to engage in pretension in order to impress others. Conversely, they do not think of others as beneath them; they treat other people with the inherent dignity that all people deserve. Thus modesty means being tolerant and accepting rather than haughty or judgmental.

The virtue of modesty is connected to the principles of yin and yang underlying the philosophy of the *Book of Changes*. Whatever is extended too far will eventually be contracted and diminished; conversely, whatever is modest will eventually be expanded and increased. People envy and fear what is too great and too powerful and seek to undermine it; but they do not feel threatened by what is lowly and humble and so they treat it with kindness and affection. By adopting the virtues of humility and modesty you make it easier for people to accept you and cooperate with you to your mutual advantage. And by not pushing things too far you avoid pride and overreaching that might bring about a fall.

THE IMAGE

In the middle of the earth, there is a mountain:
This is the image of Modesty.
Thus the superior person lessens what is too much
And increases what is too little.
He weighs things and makes their distribution equal.

Over very long stretches of time mountains wear down and become level with the earth, while the lowly places are raised up. Thus balance is restored. In the same way, modest people avoid excess and embrace the mean in their personal life and in their dealings with others. They restore equanimity to their emotions and bring harmony to society. They work to eliminate unjust inequalities and the extremes of thought and action that produce jealousy in private relations and discord in society as a whole.

Modesty does not require self-abnegation but rather a realistic and balanced attitude toward life. This means, first of all, that you should have a balanced and realistic attitude toward yourself. Recognize your assets as well as your limitations, your strengths as well as your weaknesses. You should not be conceited, but neither should you be overly self-deprecating. Excessive self-love and self-loathing are equally self-destructive. A person who nourishes a negative self-image may come to as much harm as one who is arrogant and overconfident. In like fashion you should not boast of your achievements or engage in empty display, but you should also not engage in false displays of humility, for excessive humility can often mask another form of pride. If you have something to contribute, there is no need to hide your light under a bushel. Just go about your business naturally, and do your best without making a show of your efforts.

Second, take a balanced attitude to the ebb and flow of events. Keep your feet planted firmly on the ground and do not engage in wishful thinking. Do not be overly dramatic when things go badly. Do not engage in self-pity, and do not try to coax others into feeling sorry for you. Keep your sense of humor and accept the world for what it is. The world does not care whether you win or lose. It keeps going regardless of your concerns and your wishes. It is your job to maintain your balance within the changing flux of events. Things will not always go your way, but if you maintain emotional stability and keep your wits about you, you will have your share of victories.

Third, take a balanced attitude to your relationships with others. You should be neither patronizing nor obsequious, neither overbearing nor fawning. Rather, be natural and unpretentious in your dealings. Do not take people for granted and do not try to take advantage of them. Remember that modesty is a form of balance, and in this context balance means reciprocity and mutual respect. Be generous and accepting, temperate and mild, and you will attract the right kind of support.

THE LINES

The lines describe different aspects of the virtue of modesty, or humility. This hexagram is unique in that all of the lines are favorable. That is, being modest can help one through any situation. This shows how greatly the ancient Chinese revered the value of modesty.

Although the third line in most hexagrams usually indicates conflict and potential misfortune, here it is the ruler of the hexagram, and states its central theme: the superior person, being humble, does not regard himself as too important for hard work or for fulfilling his obligations to others. Thus he lives up to all of his commitments and finishes what he starts.

Initial Six

The superior person is especially modest;
That is why he may cross the great river.
Good fortune.

Modesty means not calling undue attention to yourself but devoting yourself to the matter at hand. Be unassuming and determined and you will make steady progress. Carry out your business quietly, efficiently, and thoroughly, and you will succeed at even the most difficult tasks. The secret of the modest person is that he makes no demands or ultimatums. He does not try to impress others with his abilities. He engages in no dramatic gestures. He simply gets the job done. Because his attitude is disciplined and his demeanor unassuming, he invites no challenges and creates no resistance, and things flow more smoothly.

One can call attention to one's self either through self-promotion or through conspicuous self-abnegation and self-deprecation. The latter are also forms of pride, though they pass themselves off as modesty. The truly modest person does not engage in false displays of modesty, feign helplessness, or complain loudly about how difficult things are. Self-deprecation and emotional martyrdom are just other ways of asserting one's ego. Therefore, the modest person is modest even about his own modesty. He understands that completing the work is more important than his ego.

Six in the Second Place

Modesty expresses itself.
Perseverance brings good fortune.

If you are truly modest, your modesty will shine forth in your words and deeds. Other people will recognize your inner worth and respond naturally to you. Even though you do not try to draw attention to yourself, your actions will nevertheless have influence. People will respect your quiet confidence and entrust you with important responsibilities. Live up to your commitments and go about your work in a thorough yet unassuming manner, and you will enjoy good fortune.

Nine in the Third Place (Ruling Line)

Working at modesty.
The superior person
Carries things through to their conclusion.
Good fortune.

The secret of the modest person is that he devotes himself to his work and finishes what he starts. He does not labor so that people will think that he is great and worthy, but he becomes great and worthy because of his labors. He regards nothing in the task as beneath him, for he treats the work as more important than he is. He subordinates his ego to achievement and therefore does whatever is necessary to carry things through to a successful conclusion. Modesty is not self-deprecation but a productive denial of self-assertion. It is not a weakness of will but a strength of character. The modest person is not egoless; rather, he puts the power of his ego in the service of something higher than himself, and that is why he succeeds.

By contrast, the weak-willed person continually pauses in his efforts. He despairs when things get too difficult. He constantly looks around to see if others are watching how much he labors and how great a sacrifice he is making. He seeks to show off his efforts before they are finished because he regularly needs the approval of others. He cannot subordinate his ego to a project, not because his ego is too strong but because it is too weak. Therefore he cannot commit himself to anything great and lasting. He is good at starting things but not at finishing them. He is destined to a life of cut corners and half measures, and he comes to despise himself for it.

Apply these lessons to your own life. If you are committed to hard work and to seeing things through, you will achieve your share of honor and renown. But you should not allow this success to go to your head. Remain constant and steadfast. The promise of greater recognition must not divert you from the habits of character that allowed you to succeed in the first place. Do not compromise your integrity in the quest for approval, and do not regard any part of the work as beneath you now just because you have succeeded in the past. If you maintain a modest attitude, you will continue to gain the support of others, and you can bring your work to a successful conclusion.

Six in the Fourth Place

There is nothing that is not beneficial.
He displays his modesty everywhere.

Modesty requires continuous cultivation; it requires a balanced attitude toward life, in which nothing is done to excess. To "display modesty everywhere" means that you nourish a steady, even-tempered perspective and cultivate a sense of responsibility to others in society. It means that you make the continuous development of your character part of your everyday life.

If you work for someone else, do not simply go through the motions thinking that someone else will pick up the slack. Make a sincere effort to do the best job you can. You will gain the recognition you deserve. Conversely, if others work for you, give recognition to those who loyally support you. Set an example for others through your own commitment to the enterprise. Then you will gain the support you need.

Six in the Fifth Place

No need to use wealth to influence one's neighbors.
It is advantageous to attack the rebellious with force.
There is nothing that is not beneficial.

Modesty is not weakness or lassitude. It means doing what has to be done without fanfare or unnecessary display. It means acting in a reasoned and objective manner rather than through emotional outbursts or excessive force. Often it is necessary to take action to move things forward. Strong measures may be necessary to correct serious problems. It is perfectly all right to be assertive and to take the lead in such circumstances. The point is to avoid being boastful or flaunting one's power. This will only alienate people and may actually undermine your authority. Instead, you should assess the situation calmly and objectively and then act firmly and decisively. When they see that you are resolute but fair, people will have increased respect for you and confidence in your abilities, and they will be more willing to support and cooperate with you.

Six at the Top

Modesty expresses itself.
It is beneficial to set armies in motion
To chastise the capital city.

Metaphorically, the capital city is at a country's center rather than at its borders, where attacks on other countries usually begin. Hence in the *Book of Changes* to "chastise the capital city" means to engage in self-discipline. When things do not go as you would like, do not place the blame on others. Instead, take responsibility for your own life. Exercise some self-control. Consider whether your own negative attitudes are keeping you from success. Modesty is not an excuse to be weak-willed or self-pitying. If anything, it requires constant disciplining of the ego so that one does not despair when faced with setbacks but rather does whatever is necessary to bring things to completion. The lesson of this line is that in order to successfully marshal your forces against the outside world, you must first learn to marshal them against yourself. Once you put your destiny in your own hands, you will succeed brilliantly.

This line announces a transition to the next hexagram, Yu, which advises us to stir up the masses and set armies marching. In the final line of Qian, which concerns self-discipline, we stir up not others but ourselves.

NOTES

15.0 "carries things through to the end." Or, "brings things to conclusion," "maintain[s] his position to the end" (Lynn).

15.1 "especially modest." *qian qian:* literally, "modest, modest." Doubling the word signifies emphasis and intensification. Another rendering is "modest about his modesty," i.e., appropriately modest, suggesting the importance of avoiding excessive self-deprecation or excessive displays of modesty. As the Chinese saying goes, "Too modest is half proud."

15.2 "expresses itself." *ming:* to call out or sing out like the call of a bird or a wild animal. The metaphor conveys the notion that modesty emerges from one's true nature. Thus alternative readings would be "modesty sings out," or "modesty shines through." Cf. 15.6, 16.1.

15.3 "Working at modesty." Or, "Diligent about his modesty" (Lynn).

15.4 "displays." Or, demonstrates, signals, as one would wave a flag. "[H]e flies the banner of Modesty everywhere" (Lynn).

15.5 "No need to use wealth to influence one's neighbors." *bu fu yi qi lin.* Cf. 11.4. The opposite formula, *fu yi qi lin,* appears in 9.5, but there it means that neighbors enrich each other.

SIXTEEN

Yu • Enthusiasm

䷏

Keywords:

Stirring up
Inspiring
Broadcasting
Undertaking
Preparing for
Providing for
Planning ahead
Enjoyment
Delight

Above: Zhen • Thunder
Below: Kun • Earth

Yu features five yin lines surrounding a single yang line in the fourth place, the place of the minister or official, who makes the necessary preparations on the ruler's behalf. The upper trigram is Zhen (The Arousing); the lower trigram is Kun (The Receptive). The hexagram thus symbolizes inspiring leadership that rouses the masses to follow. In the previous hexagram, Qian, (Modesty), one humbly plays one's part and carries things through to the end. By contrast, in Yu (Enthusiasm), one stirs up others to action and begins new undertakings and adventures.

The ideograph for Yu originally may have depicted a child riding on an elephant. This symbolizes two important features: The first is importance of preparation—for the elephant must be trained so that it is safe for the child to ride it. The second is the enjoyment or delight of the child that is made possible by making appropriate preparations in advance. Hence the two interrelated themes of the hexagram: preparing in advance in order to generate spontaneous enthusiasm and create spontaneous delight.

THE JUDGMENT

Enthusiasm.
It is beneficial to establish feudal lords
And set armies in motion.

This hexagram has two meanings. On the one hand, it means to make preparations for future action. On the other hand, it means to stir up enthusiasm and delight in one's self and in other people. Taken together, the message is that if you make proper arrangements early on and provide for things in advance, you can feel free to relax and enjoy the fruits of your labors later without concern or guilt. You may justifiably take delight in what you have put in place and set in motion. Conversely, if you are trapped in inertia, indolence, or deluded satisfaction, you cannot make plans for the future. To take precautions and to work for the future, a person needs to be stimulated and motivated. That is why preparation is the flip side of enthusiasm.

The words of the hexagram judgment reflect this duality: Establishing feudal lords is a matter of prior preparation. One creates feudatories because one will need their support someday. On the other hand, to set armies in motion is a matter of inspiring the troops to action after one has made the proper preparations. In like fashion, you should anticipate your needs and gather people around you who can help you achieve your aims.

The traditional metaphor of enthusiasm in the *Book of Changes* is music. The metaphor of music simultaneously captures the notions of delight, harmony, inspiration, and sympathy between people. The vibration of one string brings sympathetic vibrations from others. Sounds resonate with other sounds, harmonies blend, fundamentals produce overtones. Moreover, music exemplifies how to stir people up and get them to act as one. Music is the great unifier. Catchy melodies and vigorous drumbeats cause people to sing and move their bodies in unison. Music joins the spirits of many individuals into one great spirit; rhythms transport bodies and souls toward a single goal.

If you want to inspire others, you must first have sympathy with them. You must be like a string on a musical instrument that resonates with other strings. To motivate people you must adjust and adapt yourself so that you are in harmony with their needs and their values. Great leaders and teachers inspire because they understand and are in harmony with the tenor of their times. They are able to lead people because they follow the people's spirit and act in accord with it. Nothing significant and lasting can be accomplished—and no laws can be effectively enforced—unless it is in accord with popular sentiment.

Second, you can inspire no one if you are not yourself inspired. If you have confidence and enthusiasm, you can do a great deal; without them you can do very little. To bring people together for a common purpose, you must feel roused and motivated to something important. Following the calling of your heart will create a natural and spontaneous response in others. Do not be afraid to be passionate about what is truly important to you. Your inspiration will draw able helpers to your side. This is how great masses of people are unified and how they achieve victory.

Third, you must combine your passion with preparation and hard work. Thomas Edison once said that genius is 1 percent inspiration and 99 percent perspiration. The same is true of stirring people up to something great. It is not enough simply to arouse passions momentarily. The groundwork for inspiration must be carefully laid. That is why music is so apt a symbol of this hexagram. Great musicians inspire and ennoble us, but their ability to do so is the result of years of hard work and practice at their craft. Music is the perfect example of the preparation that results in a seemingly spontaneous inspiration and connection with a higher power. As it is in music, so it is in life: creativity and improvisation are made possible by prior development; instinct is the child of practice; spontaneity is the residue of design.

THE IMAGE

Thunder rises out of the earth:
This is the image of Enthusiasm.
Thus the kings of old made music
To rouse the spirits
And inspire virtue.
They offered it in splendor to worship the Supreme Deity,
So that they might be worthy of their illustrious ancestors.

Thunder rising out of the earth symbolizes both enjoyment and inspiration. The flash of lightning represents a release of tensions and a clearing of the air. The peal of thunder echoing over the earth signifies the great power that comes from the unification and release of potential energy.

Music has the miraculous ability to join people together and release cares and anxieties. Like rhetoric, music has this power because it taps into our emotions. It produces a resonance in our souls that moves and motivates us. But music, like rhetoric, can do this for good or for ill. Good music can uplift and ennoble us; bad music can make us cynical, pessimistic, and despairing. If you want to influence others properly, you must have genuine sympathy with them. Manipulation is not true sympathy; it is merely the appearance of concern. Equally important, if you want to influence people in the right way, you must try to resonate with the best parts of them. Enthusiasm should always be directed for positive ends, to release what is great and good in people's hearts, to bring out the nobility and decency that is all too often submerged in the struggle and routine of everyday life, to allow people to become better than they were before. You can certainly stir people up by appealing to their worst instincts. But that will only unleash destructive energies. The healthiest form of influence brings out the best that people have to offer. Fuel people's confidence rather than their fear, stoke their courage, not their paranoia. In short, give people something to believe in. In this way, you can achieve great things, and they can realize goals that they only dreamed of.

THE LINES

Although this hexagram is concerned both with inspiration and preparation, the lines primarily focus on various aspects of stirring things up. (This is the opposite of the last hexagram, Qian (Modesty), which involved carrying things through to their conclusion.) The ruler is line four, in which enthusiasm draws people together and inspires them to beneficial collective action. By line six, the time for stirring things up is past, but reform is still possible.

Initial Six

Enthusiasm expresses itself.
Misfortune.

Even if you have important connections, you should not boast about them. Do not flaunt your advantages or your achievements. You will simply alienate others and invite opposition. Enthusiasm is a strong emotion. It should not be used for self-aggrandizement or self-promotion. Enthusiasm is a virtue when it inspires people to beneficial collective action. It should always be used to unite people rather than to divide them.

Six in the Second Place

Making one's armor solid as a rock.
One does not let a whole day pass.
Perseverance brings good fortune.

It is a great virtue to be able to see the seeds of change in any situation and to respond to them without delay. To achieve this you must possess great clarity of mind. Do not be swept up by other people's fads and enthusiasms. Maintain your integrity and rely on your own judgment. The text advises that you must make your "armor solid as a rock." This means that you are solid and reliable. You stick to your principles and do not allow yourself to be misled by the illusions that inevitably accompany the latest crazes and fashions. You neither flatter those above you nor disdain those beneath you.

When the first signs of change appear, take appropriate action immediately, regardless of what others may think or what the conventional wisdom says. When it is time to go forward, go forward; when it is time to withdraw, withdraw. As the text says, "do [ ] not let a whole day pass." If you persevere in this approach, you will enjoy abundant good fortune.

Six in the Third Place

Looking upward wide-eyed with enthusiasm brings remorse.
Hesitation brings remorse.

You cannot rely on others to provide for your needs or inspire you to take action. You must learn to motivate yourself. Become more self-reliant. Perhaps you are waiting for someone to tell you what to do, perhaps you hesitate because you are afraid, or perhaps you delay out of simple inertia or idle enjoyment. Whatever the reasons, if you do not act soon, you will lose your independence and your self-respect. Do not wait around expecting others to provide for you or save you. It is up to you to take care of yourself.

Nine in the Fourth Place (Ruling Line)

The very source of enthusiasm.
Great things can be achieved.
Have no doubts.
Friends gather round you
As a hair clasp gathers the hair.

If you have prepared properly for action, it is time to act. Have no doubts about the future. Express your ideas with confidence. Your optimism and sincerity will inspire others. Seeing that you have no doubts or hesitations about the right course of action, they will join in enthusiastically and cooperate with you. Together you can accomplish great things. In the same way that a "hair clasp gathers the hair," a great leader brings people together through the power of his inner conviction; his enthusiasm gives them the faith that sustains them in any enterprise.

Six in the Fifth Place

Persevere.
Ill for a long time, but does not die.

"Ill for a long time" means that you are subjected to constant afflictions and difficulties. Do not lose hope. It is easy to be enthusiastic when everything is going well. But your faith means the most when you must struggle to succeed. Persevere. The opposition you face will make you stronger in the long run.

Six at the Top

Deluded enthusiasm.
But if after it is over
One changes one's ways,
There is no blame.

The sixth line usually represents going beyond the situation. Here it means that the time for enthusiasm is past and we need to adapt to the changed conditions.

Do not let yourself become deluded by your enthusiasm. Things may have been going quite well in the recent past, but now you are in danger of becoming carried away in self-indulgence. Take a realistic look at the situation. If you can achieve clarity and reform yourself, you will grow and benefit greatly from the experience.

NOTES

16.GI "made music to rouse the spirits and inspire virtue." Literally, "arousing delight (harmony, music) honor virtue." Cf. Wilhelm/Baynes: "Made music in order to honor merit." The present translation tries to capture the notion that music both inspired and ennobled.

16.1 "expresses itself." *ming:* calls out, sings out, shines through. Cf. 15.2, 15.6.

16.3 "Looking upward wide-eyed with enthusiasm." Or, "for enthusiasm," i.e., depending on others for nourishment. Cf. 27.2, which expresses a similar warning. The idea is that one must motivate one's self and provide for one's self and one must not rely solely on others for inspiration.

SEVENTEEN

Sui • Following

䷐

Keywords:

Following
Allegiance
Loyalty
Hunting
Pursuits
Adaptability
Being adaptable

Above: Dui • Lake
Below: Zhen • Thunder

The word *sui* originally meant "hunt." It carries the dual meanings of pursuing something and following it.

In the hexagram Sui the strong learn the lesson that in order to lead they must first learn to follow. The strong ruling lines in the first and fifth places follow weak lines in the second and sixth. The lower trigram Zhen (Thunder) follows the upper trigram Dui (Joy, The Lake). By being adaptable and following in the right way, one learns valuable lessons about how to deal with people and eventually earns the right to be followed.

17 Sui • Following

THE JUDGMENT

Following. Supreme success.
It is beneficial to be constant and steadfastly faithful.
No blame.

Sui concerns the obligations of followers and leaders—how to get others to follow you and when and how to follow others.

If you want others to follow you, you must know how to adjust yourself to them. In the words of the old Chinese proverb, to rule is to serve. No one can be a true leader who does not have sympathy for those in one's charge. You must adapt yourself to the demands of the time and the needs of your supporters. Then you will gain the respect and trust of others so that they will follow you with joy and gladness. If you try to gain mastery over other people through force and fraud, or through conspiracy and connivance, you will poison social relations and breed resentment and resistance. At most you will gain control only of a faction that must suppress its opponents. If you win power through injuring others, you will have to keep injuring them to maintain your base. The injuries you do to others will not fade away; they will haunt you later on. On the other hand, if you gain power through winning the trust and affection of others, they will give you the benefit of the doubt when you must make tough decisions that you feel are in the interest of all. When your leadership is established on trust rather than fear, you maintain your base of support by continuing to work on behalf of those who follow you. They in turn will support your endeavors, and in this way everyone will benefit.

Conversely, if you are in the position of following others, you must make sure that you are doing so for the right reasons. Hence the text warns you to be constant and steadfastly faithful. One can only be faithful in this way to principles that last for a long time rather than to fads and fashions that come and go. If you follow a group because it is currently powerful and influential, you are not really following anything but your own ambition and your own need for approval. But if you follow a group or leader because of the quality of its beliefs and goals, and not merely to advance your own selfish interests, you will be without blame.

Sui has a dual meaning. It means both to follow something and to pursue it. Thus, Sui also concerns the deeper question of what you should pursue in life. The answer to this question is deceptively simple to state but often difficult to put into practice: First of all, you must follow your conscience.

Second, you must follow what gives you happiness. In the hexagram Sui, Zhen—the symbol of the Arousing—follows Dui (Joy). So should you. Life is too short to squander on things that are unrewarding. Devote yourself to things that will enrich you and give meaning to your life. Aim high. If you settle for less than the best, you will almost certainly get it.

Just because you pursue something valuable does not mean that you will attain it immediately and without effort. Nothing worth having is attained so easily. You must cultivate the virtues of patience and flexibility. Sui teaches that you can achieve great success if you know how to adapt your efforts to the demands of the time. Indeed, this is a central theme of the *Book of Changes*. Be open-minded and willing to learn. Instead of exhausting your energies in vain struggles against the world, try to see how you can make progress by moving in different directions. Be willing to experiment. Take a fresh view of the situation. Overcome old prejudices and try new ways of doing things. Flexibility without and persistence within will bring you to your goal.

THE IMAGE

Thunder in the middle of the lake:
This is the image of Following.
Thus the superior person
Goes indoors at night for rest and recuperation.

Thunder in the middle of the lake symbolizes the renewal of energy, like the charging of a battery. Adaptability requires time for rest and recuperation in two respects. First, prolonging struggles that you cannot win and engaging in needless resistance to circumstances will exhaust you. Knowing when to forbear and when to change your approach conserves energy in the short run and produces great success in the long run. Second, adapting to ever-changing circumstances while preserving your basic goals and principles requires persistence, stamina, and careful attention to detail. If you do not allow yourself some quiet time, you will make mistakes and undermine your position. Action requires rest in order to be truly successful.

THE LINES

The lines describe different aspects of following. Line one advises developing community with others. The text of the lines plays on the fact that the word *sui* ("follow") also means "hunt" or "pursue." Thus in line four, following the Way is good, but chasing after momentary fame and popularity is not. In lines two and three, following the path of maturity is sound, but forsaking that path to chase after immature desires or to take the easy way out is not. Line five, the ruler of the hexagram, teaches that finding and following the truth within one's heart leads to success. In line six, one attempts to leave worldly pursuits behind but is now called upon to advise and lead others.

Initial Nine (Ruling Line)

One's situation is changing.
Perseverance brings good fortune.
Leaving one's gate and communing with others
Produces achievements.

You cannot pursue something effectively if you do not respond to changes in the environment around you, nor can you lead others effectively. This does not mean that you should vacillate or alter your goals with every change in fashion. Change is meaningless if it does not serve something deeper that remains constant. The point is that to realize your deepest values you must adapt to changing circumstances.

"Leaving one's gate and communing with others" means that you need to take a wider view of things. Consult with others and listen to their views. Do not take advice only from people who already agree with you, but expand your circle of acquaintances. Open your mind to the possibility of learning something new. Often you can learn as much from your adversaries and those who disagree with you as you can from your friends. Then use your best judgment to decide how to alter your plans and adapt to the changes around you. Here again, successful change relies on constancy of virtue.

Six in the Second Place

One clings to the small boy and loses the strong man.

Make sure that you are not taking the easy way out of a situation. Reexamine your goals and methods. If your standards are too low, and your effort is halfhearted or weak, you will not develop yourself to your full potential. Then, as the line says, you are "cling[ing] to the small boy" inside yourself. Lacking courage and faith in your own abilities, you shy away from challenges that would develop your character and bring you success. Lacking maturity, you crave immediate gratification and therefore fail to expose yourself to good influences. As a result, you do not realize your promise. You never grow up.

The same is true with the company you keep. If you waste your time on unworthy connections or associates, you will lose touch with good people and beneficent influences that can help you grow and realize your goals. Treat yourself with more respect and you will prosper as you should.

Six in the Third Place

One clings to the strong man and loses the small boy.
Through following,
One gets what one seeks.
It is beneficial to remain constant and steadfastly faithful.

To succeed and to grow as a person, you must put aside inferior influences and superficial pleasures. You must let go of relationships and behaviors that you cling to out of familiarity but that are no longer right for you. Only in this way can you open yourself to new relationships with worthy people and to newer, healthier ways of living. The lesson of this line is that getting something better means giving up something worse.

It is hard to give up old habits and forge new relationships, but you must have the courage to see things through. Be determined to put aside old self-destructive ways and follow a better path. If you can remain firm, you will get what you are seeking and you will develop strength of character that will help you in the long run.

Nine in the Fourth Place

If one pursues, there will be a catch,
But perseverance brings misfortune.
Living sincerely in the Way brings clarity.
How could there be blame in this?

Often people whom you think you are influencing attach themselves to you for selfish reasons and ulterior motives. Don't be taken in by their insincere flattery. Conversely, don't think that you can extend your influence through sweet-talking others. If you rely too much on such people, they will let you down, because they are not really devoted to you. The relationships that you can trust when the chips are down are based on sincerity and mutuality rather than flattery, subservience, or the desire to curry favor. Remember what your principles are and do not stray from your original goals. Maintain your integrity and you will be able to see through people who have wormed their way into your circle for selfish reasons.

Nine in the Fifth Place (Ruling Line)

Sincerity leads to excellence. Good fortune.

The theme of the hexagram as a whole is following and pursuing. Everyone needs to follow or pursue something in life. Each of us has goals and aspirations whose pursuit gives our life richness and meaning. The *Book of Changes* teaches that the quality of the pursuer and the value of one's pursuits depends on the quality of what is pursued. If we seek only mediocre and base things, that is all that we will achieve. And our choice of goals reflects on us, for only a base and mediocre person seeks base and mediocre things. But if we set our sights on something noble and good, we become better persons. And if we devote ourselves to worthy pursuits, we increase the chances that we will get them.

If you are going to pursue something, make it the very best thing you can imagine. Set your sights on something truly worthy. Do not settle for second best. Pursue your goal with sincerity, persistence, and devotion and you will be richly rewarded.

Six at the Top

Seized and bound,
Tied up, they follow.
The king makes an offering in the Western Mountains.

The king's sacrifice at the Western Mountains symbolizes his piety and the extension of his sovereignty over a new region. His power is increased by the assistance of noble sages whom he calls on to act as counselors. Although they would rather remain in seclusion, they feel compelled to follow him and offer their services out of a sense of loyalty to what is right.

The point of the metaphor is that even people who devote themselves to inner development and self-cultivation may have obligations to the world if other people who value and look up to them call upon them for help. You should not put yourself in the service of base and ignoble causes. But when you are approached by people who truly understand your gifts, you should not be ungenerous.

The same point applies at a personal as well as a political level. Line six often describes a sage or someone who is beyond the situation. You would like to free yourself from worldly pursuits. However, in this case, you are still bound by obligations to others. You have expertise and wisdom as a result of your past experiences. People look up to you for guidance. Assist them. You will be rewarded for your unselfish commitment to the general good.

NOTES

17.0 "constant and steadfastly faithful." *zhen:* persevere. Once again, this standard gloss on *zhen* seems particularly apt.

17.1 "situation." *guan:* house, office. I.e., one's place of allegiance, one's social group.

17.1 "communing." *jiao:* literally, "cross" or "mingle"; hence, "joining in" or "joining together."

17.2 "clings to." *xi:* binds, holds on to.

17.2 "the strong man." *zhang fu*. Alternatively, "the mature adult."

17.3 "Through following." I.e., through following this advice.

17.3 "Beneficial to remain constant and steadfastly faithful." *li ju zhen:* beneficial [to] dwell [in] perseverance. Cf. 17.0, 49.6.

17.6 "Seized and bound / Tied up, they follow." Or, "tied up, made to follow," "seized and bound, thereupon making them follow."

17.6 "The king makes an offering in the Western Mountains." *heng:* offering, sacrifice, success. Another reading is, "The king uses this to extend his sway (power, prevevalence) to the Western Mountains." Cf. 46.4.

In the earliest versions of the *Book of Changes* this line probably referred to exactly what it describes, i.e., the taking of captives, who are tied up and forced to follow the king's army. In the Confucian reinterpretation the binding is treated metaphorically. His subjects and his ministers follow him as if tied up and bound. Their ties to him are metaphorical ties of allegiance, which allow him to extend his dominion and to make an offering in the Western Mountains.

EIGHTEEN

Gu • Remedying

䷑

Keywords:

Working on what has been spoiled
Decay
Repair
Restoration

Above: Gen • Mountain
Below: Xun • Wind (Wood)

The ideograph for Gu is a bowl with breeding maggots, symbolizing decay. This decay requires a remedy. The previous hexagram, Sui, concerned pursuing the right path; Gu is concerned with repairing a situation that has gone astray.

THE JUDGMENT

Remedying what has been spoiled.
Supreme success.
It is beneficial to cross the great river.
Before starting, three days.
After starting, three days.

Although the theme of Gu is decay, the hexagram also symbolizes the possibility of hope. Gu is concerned not so much with the natural forces of decay, as with the decay that comes through bad habits and unwise choices. Such decay results from inertia, carelessness, muddled thinking, selfishness, and lack of discipline. In order to remedy this decay you must adopt the opposite traits: energetic activity, careful preparation, thoughtful deliberation, determination, and commitment. What has gone wrong through mistake, lassitude, or inaction can be repaired through self-discipline, commitment, energy, and enterprise. Gu thus symbolizes both the inevitable weaknesses and shortcomings of human will that cause conditions to decline and the abundant potential of human freedom that can bring about renewal and recovery. This is a message of hope; the text tells us that working to repair what has become stagnant promises supreme success. That is why it is worth "cross[ing] the great river," that is, undertaking something difficult and arduous.

Something is going wrong in your life. It may be your environment or it may be your own habits and attitudes. The problem is the legacy of previous bad choices. It has existed for some time, although you may not have realized it. Its origins lie in past action or inaction, mistakes of judgment and missed opportunities. Even so, you now have the ability to do something about it. You can make things better. You can start anew. But you must make the effort to do so. Inertia is a big reason why things have come to this state. If you let things slide, the problem will not go away. Indeed, the situation will only get worse.

Success in remedying what has been spoiled requires, first of all, that you ascertain what has gone wrong and why. You must ask yourself how things got this way. In order to do this you will have to face the situation honestly. You may have to confront unpleasant and unresolved issues in your life or your environment, and you may have to acknowledge features of the situation that you previously neglected, denied, or hid from yourself. The task calls for deliberation and self-examination. This may be emotionally difficult, but gaining insight is essential to success. Hence the text says, "Before starting, three days," meaning that before you act you must take the time to understand the source of the problem so that you can devise an appropriate remedy. You should not be afraid to act for fear of doing the wrong thing; but you should exercise caution and restraint at the beginning. Seek advice from people you trust. Do not be too proud to ask for help. Once you have started working to repair the situation, spend some time evaluating what you have done. Ask yourself: Is the new strategy working? Does it need to be readjusted? That is why the text says, "After starting, three days." After you begin reforms, your actions must be guided by continuous investigation and deliberation. In this way you will avoid falling back into bad old habits. Above all, have courage. Maintain faith in yourself no matter how difficult making the necessary changes may be at the beginning. If you persevere and remain determined to see things through, your efforts will be rewarded.

THE IMAGE

Below the mountain, the wind blows:
This is the image of Remedying what has been spoiled.
Thus the superior person stirs up the people
And nourishes their virtue.

When air is trapped in a valley below the mountains, it becomes stagnant. Temperature inversions keep polluted air from escaping upward. In the same way lassitude, inertia, and lack of imagination keep people locked in worn-out conventions and bad habits that have outlived their usefulness. Bereft of direction or purpose, people waste their time in idle pursuits. They cling mindlessly to outmoded rituals and conventions, or they chase after fads and short-term pleasures to give their lives meaning. Both approaches corrupt and debilitate people's spirits and eventually bring them unhappiness.

To reform stagnant conditions, a leader must rouse people from their lethargy and upset their unthinking acceptance of the status quo. The leader must not only show what is wrong with current conditions, but also give people renewed hope that things can actually improve. That is because the standard objections to reform are that change is futile or will only make things worse. A leader must combat such negative attitudes by giving people a sense of purpose and grounds for hope.

Similarly, if you wish to remedy stagnation in yourself, you must shake yourself loose from bad habits, recognize your previous errors, and have faith that you can open a new chapter in your life. The constituent trigrams exemplify the proper approach. The wind symbolizes the stirring of the spirit, the engagement of public opinion, and continuous deliberation over the right methods; the mountain symbolizes strength, patience, endurance, and the commitment to see things through to the end.

Repairing decay in your environment or in yourself may take considerable time and effort. Things did not go wrong in a single day, and they will not be put right in a single night. Therefore, you must be patient but determined. Steady, step-by-step progress will eventually produce the desired results. Resolve to identify and eliminate the bad habits and unhealthy attitudes that have blocked your progress. Do not be angry or vindictive, either toward yourself or toward others. The goal is not to exact retribution but to free yourself and others from the negative and destructive influences of the past. If you spend your time pointing fingers in blame or punishing yourself for your previous failures, you will remain entangled in the old situation. This will do nothing to improve present conditions. It will only undermine your self-respect and make it more difficult for you to move forward. Instead, take a positive, long-term approach. Forgive others for the past, and forgive yourself. Accept responsibility for the future instead.

THE LINES

The lines tell the story of a son who must return home to take care of the disorder in the family business due to a parent who has fallen ill. The real subject of the lines, however, is decay or corruption produced by past practices; hence the lines speak of ills "caused by the father" (instead of the father's illness). In remedying decay and disorder one must not be too harsh (line two) or too lax (line four). Using just the right amount of perseverance and gentleness wins praise (line five). In the sixth line the subject has gone beyond any concern with worldly affairs and devotes himself to the activities of a sage.

Initial Six

Remedying the ills caused by the father.
If there is a son,
No blame rests upon the departed father.
There is danger,
But in the end good fortune.

"Ills caused by the father" is a metaphor for old patterns of behavior that have outgrown their usefulness. Sticking to traditional ways of doing things has led to decay. The problem may be rigid, inflexible attitudes and structures or simply lack of energy and imagination. In any case, for too long you have clung to old habits and have simply carried on doing whatever was expected. As a result, you are in a rut. But when decay is at its beginning stages it is easier to remedy. Traditions and established ways of doing things are usually resistant to change, so do not overlook the dangers or take things too lightly. But if you exercise caution and circumspection, your reforms can succeed.

Nine in the Second Place

Remedying the ills caused by the mother.
It is not appropriate to be steadfast.

"Ills caused by the mother" refer to patterns of behavior that are best handled through attributes traditionally associated with femininity—sensitivity, receptivity, gentleness, and concern for the feelings of others. One must be flexible and find a middle path between laxity and rigidity.

Harsh and aggressive measures are not always the best way to reform past mistakes. Sometimes a gentle and sensitive approach is the best way. This is especially so because you must take into consideration how your reforms will affect other people. It would be a good idea to consult with others and get some advice before doing anything drastic. Making major changes may harm people close to you or unnecessarily hurt their feelings, so proceed with care.

Nine in the Third Place

Remedying the ills caused by the father.
There is slight regret, but no great blame.

This line describes the converse situation from the second. You are eager to start over and reform past errors. You want to move forward energetically, perhaps a little too energetically. This may produce minor misunderstandings and disputes. People may think that you are too aggressive and not considerate enough. But when problems are entrenched and the need for reform is great, it is better to have too much energy than too little. Although you may have some regret over the annoyance and disharmony your forceful approach causes, in the end you will do no great harm.

Six in the Fourth Place

Dealing leniently with the ills caused by the father.
Proceeding in this way one experiences humiliation.

When you face serious and long-standing forces of decay, responding with indecision, lassitude, and irresolution will not help matters. Such behavior will only let things degenerate further. Weak responses will only weaken you. You may think that by doing nothing you are merely being tolerant and forgiving of yourself or others. But tolerance and forgiveness must be accompanied by a genuine desire for reform if they are to mean anything. Do not be indecisive, and do not settle for second best. If you do not act soon to remedy the situation, you will meet with humiliation.

Six in the Fifth Place (Ruling Line)

Remedying the ills caused by the father.
One obtains praise.

Reforms have been needed for a long time to correct problems caused in the past. You can change things for the better now. Take responsibility and move forward. Do not be afraid to ask for help from others. If you take the lead in putting things right, others will be happy to support you, and your efforts will meet with praise.

Nine at the Top

He does not serve kings and princes.
He seeks higher goals.

Line six often refers to a person who has gone past the situation. In this case, it refers to a sage who does not bother with worldly affairs in the hope of reforming them but works on his or her spiritual development. Although a concern with higher things may not produce concrete reforms in the short run, it benefits others in the long run if the wisdom gained from the quest inspires and educates others.

Sometimes the best way to deal with the evils of the world is to transcend them. When you do, you will find that your attention is drawn to spiritual questions rather than material advancement or worldly ambition. You no longer need to focus on mundane matters or the demands of public life but instead may concern yourself with universal goals and higher values. You should not confuse this path with a license to laziness or insensitivity to others. And your withdrawal must not become an excuse for sour grapes or secret despair. Above all, you should not allow yourself to become cynical, condescending, or uncaring. But if you sincerely devote yourself to spiritual self-development and enlightenment you will benefit not only yourself but others as well. By setting yourself higher goals, you will become an example to others and help reduce, even if only to a small degree, the selfishness and meanness of the world.

NOTES

18.GI "And nourishes their virtue." Or, "strengthens their spirit" (Wilhelm/Baynes).

18.3 "slight regret." *shao you hui:* there is a little remorse.

18.4 "Dealing leniently with." *yu:* enrich, mild, lenient, hence tolerating, condoning.

18.6 "He seeks higher goals." *gao shang qi shi:* high esteem one's affairs. Or, "He is concerned with higher matters." Cf. Wilhelm/Baynes: "Sets himself higher goals."

NINETEEN

Lin • Overseeing

☷
☱

Keywords:

Approach
Oversight
Cooperation

Above: Kun • Earth
Below: Dui • Lake

Lin features two yang lines in the first and second positions. These correspond appropriately to the yin lines in the fourth and fifth places, the positions of the minister and the ruler. This symbolizes a happy working relationship between people of talent and energy in lower positions and their magnanimous superiors. The superiors oversee their subordinates' activities with generosity and goodwill, recognize their subordinates' talents, and encourage them to advance upward. For this reason Lin has the dual meaning of "overseeing" and "approach," signifying both the beneficent oversight of superiors and the fortuitous ascent of their subordinates. When leaders and subordinates work together and recognize each other's value, a happy outcome is assured.

THE JUDGMENT

Overseeing. Supreme success.
It is beneficial to persevere.
When the eighth month comes,
There will be misfortune.

By tradition, Lin is a symbol of springtime. More generally, it symbolizes happy, joyous times of natural progress and advancement, like the first stirrings of spring. The low advance upward to the high, who happily accept them. Matters move forward naturally. Relationships thrive. Success blossoms like the flowers of spring.

However, just like growth during springtime, everything must take its natural course. Do not try to hurry things; let matters develop in a normal and healthy fashion. Full growth is not achieved in the spring but in the summertime. Thus, you should not become impatient: success will come eventually if you lay strong foundations now and if you nurture things appropriately. Energy and initiative are important during this time. Make the most of opportunities for growth when they present themselves. This is an especially fertile period, so be on the lookout for ways to improve your situation and your relationships with others. When things are going well for you, remember to share your good fortune. Consider how your actions will affect others. Encourage people who work under you and help them advance. Think of them like young plants in springtime that need to be tended and helped so that they will grow upward and become healthy, beautiful, and strong.

Finally, remember that spring does not last forever. The good times will eventually evaporate, so it is important to make the most of them while they last. Hence the text says, in "the eighth month" (September in the Chinese calendar), "there will be misfortune," because summer is fading away and autumn is approaching. For this reason it is important to nip problems in the bud before they have a chance to grow large. Keep your eyes open for early signs of difficulty or deterioration. If you make the effort now, you will be in a much stronger position when you face obstacles in the future. Take advantage of this favorable time to establish the groundwork for future success.

19 Lin • Overseeing

THE IMAGE

The Earth is above the Lake:
This is the image of Overseeing.
Thus, the superior person
Teaches and shows concern without exhaustion,
Tolerating and protecting the people without limit.

The earth is nourished by the lake and shelters it from above. This symbolizes the symbiotic relationship of leaders and subordinates. The earth is broad and receptive; it supports and cares for everything that is on it; the lake waters the earth and sustains its fertility.

If you have responsibility for others or have authority over them, be caring and magnanimous. Be loyal to your subordinates and they will be loyal to you. Work unselfishly for their good and they will work unselfishly for yours. Your influence is magnified now, so make the most of it. Share your expertise and wisdom freely. Recognize people's talents. Listen to what they have to say and encourage their growth. Delegate authority where you feel that it is appropriate. If you act with generosity and benevolence, the people under your care will flourish and prosper, and the results will be fortunate for everyone.

THE LINES

The lines describe different forms of oversight. The two yang lines at the bottom are the ruling lines. They call out to the yin lines above them. Hence an alternative name for the hexagram is Approach.

Initial Nine (Ruling Line)

Finding response in overseeing.
Perseverance brings good fortune.

This line describes a period of new growth and new possibilities. When you begin a new enterprise, cooperate with other people who have similar aims. Working together can benefit everyone involved. But remember that the point of cooperation is to achieve something of value. Don't follow the crowd if it makes you stray from your values. That is why the text advises that "perseverance brings good fortune." Stick to your principles and continue in what you know is right and you will enjoy good fortune.

Nine in the Second Place (Ruling Line)

Finding response in overseeing.
Good fortune.
There is nothing that is not beneficial.

Your star is on the rise. Your efforts begin to win recognition from high places. Keep going. You will get the support that you need. Because you are on the right track, you can overcome any difficulties as they arise.

The lesson of this line is that when you have good ideas, and the strength of character and consistency of mind to push them forward, you will eventually meet with a welcoming response. And when that response comes, you should not have fears about the future. Such is human nature that when after long struggle we finally gain acceptance and meet with success, we begin to have doubts and worries. Difficulties will surely arise at some point, but don't be concerned. Simply continue to make progress in the determined spirit in which you began.

Six in the Third Place

Overseeing with flattery.
There is nothing beneficial in this.
But if one has come to grieve over it,
There will be no blame.

"Overseeing with flattery" refers to a person who makes early progress and lets the praise for it go to his head. To "grieve over it" means to repent one's mistakes and reform.

When things are going especially well, you may be tempted to relax and lose concentration. As you gain influence, people may flatter you and you may tend to believe them. This will lead to overconfidence and careless behavior. Enjoy your easy progress now, but keep your goals in mind. Every increase in fortune brings new obligations as well as new opportunities, so you will need to pay attention to the new responsibilities that come with your higher position. Exercise foresight and caution. Don't waste the resources that you have accumulated. Return to the habits of hard work and determination that helped you succeed in the past, and you will continue to make steady progress.

Six in the Fourth Place

Complete overseeing.
No blame.

Your approach to the situation is completely appropriate. You are moving in the right direction. Even if you encounter difficulties along the way, your behavior is correct and therefore you will be able to enjoy continued success.

The fourth and fifth lines in this hexagram represent overseers who respond to the subordinates in the first and second lines. The lesson of this line is that as you progress upward, you must ensure that your relations with those below you are helpful and appropriate. Remember that you too were once a newcomer or a subordinate, hoping that someone would recognize your talents and give you a chance to prove yourself. (You are probably still in that relationship to someone else.) Therefore, as you gain influence, be sure to help others along the way. Recognize the talented people who work with you and look up to you. Reward promise and merit without prejudice. Be a good mentor and try to set an example for others to follow. Bestow your influence on able people and draw them into your circle. In this way both you and they will benefit.

Six in the Fifth Place

Wise overseeing.
Appropriate for a great sovereign.
Good fortune.

You are now in a position of leadership and responsibility. You need to learn how to make use of subordinates to inform you about the situation and help you carry out your plans. A wise leader is good both at finding the right people and delegating the necessary authority to them. The more able your helpers, the more appropriate it is to let them shine by showing what they can do. And giving people the room to excel in turn attracts other people of talent in the future. Pick people whom you trust and whose aims and values are similar to your own, and you will not have to micromanage them. Guide them but do not interfere unnecessarily in their work. In this way you will gain in authority and they will bring you great success.

Six at the Top

Magnanimous overseeing.
Good fortune. No blame.

Line six is the position of the sage who has accumulated wisdom and is beyond personal ambition. He is magnanimous and helpful, and shares his knowledge with others. His benevolence and devotion bring riches to everyone.

If you have wisdom and experience, be generous and share it unselfishly with others. Do not lord your knowledge over others but offer it humbly out of a sincere desire to be of assistance. Your cooperation will benefit everyone concerned. To be able to do this happily and without reserve bespeaks a true greatness of spirit.

NOTES

19.GI "Teaches and shows concern without exhaustion." *jiao si wu qiong:* teach, contemplate (ponder, care about) without exhaustion. Or, "willing to teach inexhaustibly" (Alfred Huang); "teaches and cares without end" (Rutt); "inexhaustible in his powers to edify others and feel concern for them" (Lynn).

19.1 "Finding response." *xian:* joined together, influencing each other. The response is between lines one (yang) and four (yin).

19.2 "Finding response." Cf. 19.1. In this case, the response is between lines two (yang) and five (yin).

19.3 "flattery." *gan:* literally, "sweetness." Hence sweet phrases and expressions, blandishments, flattery. Cf. 60.5.

19.3 "come to grieve over it." *ji you:* already grieve. That is, if one becomes sorry about it, has learned to regret it, repents of it.

19.4 "complete." Or, "perfect."

19.5 "Appropriate for." Or, "characteristic of."

19.5 "sovereign." *jun:* ruler, one who gives orders, prince.

19.6 "Magnanimous." *dun:* honest, generous, important, sincere. Cf. 24.5, 52.6. Wilhelm/Baynes translates it variously as "greathearted" and "noblehearted."

TWENTY

Guan • Viewing

Keywords:

Observation
Contemplation
Serving as an example
Taking an overview
Understanding
Self-examination
Spiritual connection
Inner clarity leads to successful action in the world

Above: Xun • Wind (Wood)
Below: Kun • Earth

The hexagram Guan features two yang lines over four yin lines. It resembles the sort of observation tower used in ancient China. A person can see a great distance from such a tower, but at the same time, because the tower is high, it serves as a landmark that can be seen from a great distance. Hence, Guan means both "to look" and "to be seen." More broadly, it means both contemplation (i.e., taking the larger view) and serving as an example to others (because one is in the public eye).

The previous hexagram, Lin, concerned superiors overseeing their charges; Guan concerns people looking up to their leaders as an example and contemplating their own lives and conduct. In Lin the leader looks downward. In Guan the leader looks up to heaven for guidance and contemplates the mores of the people, the methods of good governance, and the course of human life. In Lin the ruler energetically oversees and governs the people. In Guan the ruler contemplates and surveys the scene before action, and the people pause and look up to the ruler for edification and instruction.

THE JUDGMENT

Viewing. The ablution has been made,
But not yet the offering.
Filled with trust and sincerity, they are reverent and dignified.

The text describes a religious ceremony in ancient China in which the leader first pours out a ritual libation and then makes a sacrifice in front of the people. The text focuses on the magical moment between these two acts, when all attention is focused on the leader; religious reverence and spiritual contemplation are at their height.

In the *Book of Changes,* Guan (Viewing) is a metaphor for contemplation. Contemplation does not mean turning away from the world. Rather it means taking the time to understand the workings of the universe, one's own nature, and one's place in a world of continuity and change. Contemplation is more than the accumulation of bits of knowledge, more than the assimilation and memorization of true factual propositions. It is a profoundly spiritual practice. Through opening one's self to hidden realities and to the possibilities latent in the world, the self is transformed. People who are able to contemplate themselves and the world with utter clarity are thereby imbued with the power to change themselves and the world. Their understanding gives them an uncanny spiritual force that naturally emanates from them and influences others. Sensing the power of their thought, others look up to them and follow them. This is the connection between looking and being looked up to, between contemplation and serving as an example for others. It is the connection between inner truth and outward effect.

The challenge you face now is to take a new look at the situation. Put aside older ways of imagining things and take a broader view. Be open-minded and do not allow your emotions to cloud your judgment. Try to face reality as it is and not as you might want it to be. Stop thinking about things from the standpoint of how they affect you personally and try to see the larger picture. Consider the origins of things and how matters arrived at their present state. This is a time to learn and to expand possibilities. If you can approach the situation with complete clarity and dispassion, you will be able to see the direction in which events are moving. And if you are willing to embrace the truth, whatever it may be, you will gain enormous power and influence in the long run. Do not be too concerned if people do not listen to you at first. As people recognize your commitment to the truth and the clarity of your thought, they will come around.

Knowledge is not simply a collection of true statements. It is a social practice and a terrain of power. The force of conformity is very strong. Many people compromise their beliefs and alter their understandings in order to fit in. And many others use their knowledge not for the good of mankind but to seize power and manipulate others in the short run. Do not follow this path. The right kind of influence will accrue to you only if you maintain your integrity.

THE IMAGE

The wind blows over the earth:
This is the image of Viewing.
Thus the kings of old inspected the four corners of the earth,
Observed the people,
And gave them instruction.

The earth is a broad expanse, and when the wind blows over the earth, it travels far and wide. Wind is invisible yet its power is great. Few things are more powerful than hurricanes and tornadoes and yet they are only made of wind. Over time wind can shape and move everything on earth, from the oceans and rivers to the fields and the mountains. In the same way, people who understand the world with complete clarity can transform it even though their influence is not obvious at first. The force of their commitment to the truth eventually impresses their fellow human beings so deeply that the latter are moved like blades of grass in a powerful wind.

Like the wind, ancient kings visited the four corners of the world. Before they could influence the world, they had to learn about it. In the same way, the search for truth must come first, but truth means little if it is not converted into practice. The new understandings that you gain from contemplation must become part of your life. If the wind is not active, it is not wind at all.

When the ancient kings inspected the world, they discovered customs that were strange and unusual. But they could not influence others unless they put away their preconceptions about how things should be done and tried to see things from the other person's point of view. They could not instruct others until they understood what others understood, so that they could teach in the context of that understanding. In the same way, you must learn to contemplate the world with tolerance, openness, and curiosity. Do not be dismissive of what you encounter. Try to understand how it came about and what purpose or function it serves. Only then can you recognize what is good and what is bad about it, what needs to be changed and what should be preserved and built upon. Above all, you must not take things personally. Do not view the world defensively, or regard everything that happens as a personal slight. If you can free yourself from the emotional demands of your ego, you will be able to see things more clearly. You will be able to understand how you fit into the larger picture. You will be able to discover what is most important to you and the true nature of your calling.

THE LINES

The lines tell the story of different ways of seeing things, which also represent different ways of understanding the world and our own lives. The hexagram Guan is shaped like an observation tower, and the lines of the hexagram are like the levels of the tower from which one gains a progressively better view. In the first line, which is closest to the ground, understanding is very limited, but as one climbs higher and higher, the perspective broadens and one sees more and more. In the second line one's perspective is still largely circumscribed and one understands only what is close by. In the third line one analyzes one's life and the lives of other individuals. In the fourth line one comes to understand the ways of politics and the fates of nations. In the fifth line one has the vision of a great and noble leader. In the sixth line one has traveled beyond worldly ambition and gains the highest viewpoint, that of the sage.

Initial Six

A childlike view.
For the inferior person, no blame.
For a superior person, humiliation.

"A childlike view" means that you have a very limited understanding of the situation, like that of a child. You see things only in terms of how they relate to you, and only in the most superficial way. You do not yet have a grasp of the wider picture. This is perhaps permissible in a child, but it is inappropriate for an adult. You need to become more open-minded. Take a broader perspective. Try to understand the situation as part of a larger and interconnected whole. Then you will discover that your initial judgments are quite misleading. As you gain a greater understanding, you will come to see not only how events touch your interests but what part you play in the larger scheme of things.

Six in the Second Place

Viewing furtively, from behind the door.
This is beneficial for the perseverance of a woman.

A person who sees through a crack in the door necessarily has a very limited view of matters. The line suggests that you are judging things from a very narrow perspective, largely in terms of how things affect you personally or threaten your emotional tranquility. If you travel only in narrow circles and do not concern yourself with the larger world, this may be excusable. Hence the text says "beneficial for the perseverance of a woman," because in the patriarchal society of ancient China women were deliberately restricted to the home and were prohibited from engaging in political affairs. Keeping women in relative ignorance may have been comforting to the male ego. Today, however, in a world in which men and women alike play important roles in public life, such a limited perspective is a vice, not a virtue.

If your goals and your dreams extend beyond the confines of your own little world, you will need to develop a broader viewpoint. Try to become more conversant with other people's values and ways of living. Try to imagine how things look from the other person's perspective. Learn to be more tolerant and open-minded. Unless you do this, you will not be able to understand people and their motives. Perhaps most important, you will not be able to grow as a person if you insist on judging everything by your own experiences and values, of if you care about things only insofar as they affect your interests. If you want to fully realize your potential, you must expand your sphere of concern.

Six in the Third Place

Viewing my life.
Deciding whether to advance or retreat.

In order to determine who you are and what you should do next, you need to examine yourself objectively. You need to think about things not merely in terms of your own private emotional life but in terms of the practical impact your actions have on others. Self-critique is appropriate here but self-absorption is not. The worth of a person is judged not by his private dreams but by his public actions. You make a difference in this world because of the good you produce that is felt by others.

You can also begin to understand the path you should follow by recognizing how the consequences of your actions return to affect you. Every choice you make affects the world around you, and every action you take in the world has a reaction in your own life. What kind of feedback are you getting from your environment when you act in a certain way? If your habits work to make you feel healthier, happier, and more confident about yourself, you are probably headed in the right direction. But if your patterns of behavior repeatedly leave you feeling unhappy, lonely, empty, and despairing, something is amiss. Use your moments of self-examination to uncover self-destructive behavior and correct it. That is why the text says, "Viewing my life" determines "whether to advance or retreat."

Six in the Fourth Place

Viewing the brilliance of the state.
It is beneficial to be a guest of the king.

"Viewing the brilliance of the state" means to understand the larger forces of politics and economics that shape the public world. Your experiences give you new opportunities to expand your influence and your horizons. Develop a sense of social awareness. Take a larger view of the social world. Your broadened outlook will benefit not only yourself but many others as well.

The text says, "It is beneficial to be a guest of the king." In Confucian times kings sought out wise people to serve as advisors. Confucius himself was one such example. Because these philosophers were independent agents who were asked to stay at the royal court, they were called "guests" of the king. In like fashion, think about society as a whole and decide what cause, organization, or leader you should support. At the same time, make sure that you retain a necessary independence of mind. By turning your focus from your own life to that of society, you can grow as an individual and exert a beneficial influence.

Nine in the Fifth Place (**Ruling Line**)

Viewing my life.
The superior person is without blame.

If you are a leader or are in an influential position, you have important responsibilities and obligations to others. By considering the effects that your actions have on other people, you can tell whether you are succeeding. Are you setting a good example for others to follow? Are you influencing others to do the right thing? Are your decisions and your policies making people better off or worse off? If you are producing positive results, you are without blame.

Nine at the Top (**Ruling Line**)

Viewing his life.
The superior person is without blame.

"Viewing his life" (as opposed to "viewing my life"—the text of line five) means to examine yourself liberated from your ego and from your desire for personal gratification. The sixth line represents the sage who is able to escape the emotional distress that inevitably accompanies personal ambition and constant striving for personal success. Freed from these burdens, he concentrates only on doing what is right and becoming free of mistakes.

The lesson of this line is that you can gain freedom through pursuing the ideal of egoless contemplation. This does not mean that we think without a perspective or that we rid ourselves of our embodied experience as persons with values, thoughts, and feelings. It means that we should try to see past the ambitions, strivings, and emotional hurts that consume our daily lives and try to contemplate what is good and worthy whether or not we gain fame and fortune from it.

You have the power to transcend the situation and contemplate your life without the blinders of emotional involvement. Liberated from self-interest and ambition, you will discover a new kind of freedom. The anxieties and fears that drive you ceaselessly to gratification have less of a hold on you. You feel liberated to do what is right whether or not it benefits you personally. And without any special effort on your part, you will influence others in a beneficial way.

NOTES

20.0 "they are reverent and dignified." *yong ruo:* literally, "big-headed-like." Hence, reverent, respectful, dignified, noble, admirable, solemn. Cf. Wilhelm/Baynes: "Full of trust, they look up to him."

20.GI "inspected." Or, "made inspections throughout," conveying the idea that they made regular tours of inspection to learn and gather information.

20.GI "Observed the people, and gave them instruction." Or, "established their teachings in conformity with their Viewing of the people" (Lynn).

20.2 "Viewing furtively, from behind the door." Or, "Peering through a crack in the door."

20.2. "the perseverance of a woman." In ancient China, women were largely confined to the home. Hence the reference to "the perseverance of a woman" means someone who is (fairly or not) confined to a limited set of experiences.

20.3 "Deciding whether to advance or retreat." *jin tui:* advance, withdraw. Cf. 57.1. The extra words are added for clarity. Or, "To advance or to retreat?" (Alfred Huang); "Decides the choice / Between advance and retreat" (Wilhelm/Baynes).

20.4 "the brilliance of the state." *guo zhi guang:* the city's shining. Alternatively, "the glory of the kingdom."

TWENTY-ONE

Shih He • Biting Through

Keywords:

Reform
Acting decisively
Administering punishments
Doing justice

Above: Li • Fire
Below: Zhen • Thunder

Shih He features an open mouth with lips in the first and sixth positions and teeth biting through an obstruction in the fourth line. The obstruction represents an obstacle to harmony or unity and a corresponding need for justice or reform. The upper trigram is Li (Fire), symbolizing clarity and enlightenment; the lower trigram is Zhen (Thunder), symbolizing energy and vigor. Faced with obstruction, we must proceed with energy (Zhen) and clarity (Li) to remedy the problem immediately.

THE JUDGMENT

Biting Through. Success.
It is beneficial to do justice.

This hexagram traditionally represented criminal penalties, or recourse to law in order to enforce justice. More generally, Shih He concerns the need for energetic reform. The basic metaphor of the hexagram is a person who bites through an obstruction. When there is danger of significant deterioration or lasting injury, vigorous action is necessary to do justice and restore proper conditions.

Something has gone wrong. It may be a transgression or an injustice. Someone may be taking advantage of you. Or you may have fallen prey to bad habits. Whatever the cause of the situation, reform is imperative. You must take a firm stand now. Things must change. Half measures will not do. You must cut through to the heart of the situation and approach it with complete clarity. Then when you understand what needs to be done, you must act. This is no time to be meek and pliant. Attack the problem with energy and determination. If you do not act quickly and decisively, the problem will not go away, and it may only become worse. Nevertheless, this does not mean that you should be reckless. Prompt and efficient action is necessary, but your action should be based on clear thinking rather than emotion. And it should be the result of careful planning rather than blind instinct. The best approach now is one that is firm but reasonable, fair but resolute.

THE IMAGE

Thunder and lightning:
This is the image of Biting Through.
Thus the ancient kings enforced the laws
Through clearly defined penalties.

Thunder symbolizes action; lightning symbolizes clarity. In setting things right, the need for action is obvious. But both energy and enlightenment are necessary to achieve justice and sensible reform. Clarity means, first of all, that you must consider whether a great penalty or a small one is required to set things right, and where and when reforms must take place. Justice is not served by disproportionate penalties, either those that are too severe or those that are too mild. Heavy-handed and arbitrary action only creates new injustices. It breeds resentment and a continuing cycle of pathology. Moreover, reforms that are not adapted to real problems can make things worse. Conversely, if people believe that your actions are just and your prescriptions are appropriate, you will gain support and cooperation in your efforts. People will respect you for your energy and your integrity.

Second, clarity means that you should be honest with yourself about whether you are the one who has done something wrong or has fallen from the right path. If so, you must make amends and reform yourself with the same energy and zeal that you would use to rebuke others.

Third, clarity means that when you enforce rules and regulations they should be rational, understandable, and promulgated in advance of the actions you wish to regulate. If people do not know where they stand and what is expected of them, your punishments will seem arbitrary and unjust.

Just as lightning is followed by thunder, clarity must be followed by energy and active commitment. If something has gone wrong, find out what it is as soon as possible. If reforms are necessary, put them in place as soon as practicable. If you need to change your life, don't procrastinate. You will only prolong the source of your unhappiness. Do not be afraid of confrontation if it is necessary to set things right. Have courage. Doing the right thing may be unpleasant for a short time, but not doing the right thing will be much worse for a much longer time. Once you have identified the problem, determine the best way of remedying it, and then put your plan into action. Do not shirk the problem or hope that others will take care of it for you. If you want to ensure that justice is done, you must take responsibility. It is up to you to put things in order.

THE LINES

The lines describe different ways in which one might engage in reform. In lines two through five the metaphor of reform is biting through flesh and bone; in lines one and six it is receiving punishment in the stocks. Note that, consistent with the metaphors of the *Book of Changes,* line one involves the feet, while line six involves the head.

When the transgression is small, only mild penalties are needed (line one). Matters become increasingly difficult and urgent as the lines progress upward. Line six describes an incorrigible situation or person, beyond reform. Note that all of the lines are favorable (or not too unfavorable) except line six. This symbolizes the *Book of Changes'* view that sincere willingness to reform one's self and adapt to the times almost always meets with a favorable outcome. Only the person who is willfully deaf to the need to reform meets with an untoward fate.

Initial Nine

His shoes are fastened in the stocks,
So that his feet disappear.
No blame.

This describes a person who has committed an offense for the first time. The appropriate punishment is swift and certain, but mild. It is corrective punishment—just strong enough to remedy the situation and prevent the person from straying again. Hence symbolically, the feet are put in stocks to keep a person from moving in the wrong direction. By checking stubbornness, anger, aggression, and hatred as soon as they appear, a person becomes free of blame.

In the same way, you should always try to deal with destructive or wrongful tendencies early on, before they have a chance to get out of hand. If you make your corrections quickly, you need only take relatively limited measures.

Six in the Second Place

He bites through the tender meat,
So that his nose disappears.
No blame.

Biting through is a metaphor for reform. Often reform is difficult because every course of action has its pros and cons and one must be fair to conflicting values and viewpoints. Tender meat, however, is easy to bite through, symbolizing that in this case there is a clear choice between what is right and wrong. To bite so hard that one's nose disappears means to be so energetic that one goes a little too far. But where the choice is clear and the misconduct is serious, it is better to err on the side of being too energetic. Hence, the text advises, there is no blame.

Whether you or someone else is behaving inappropriately, you must have the courage to make reforms. Look inside your heart and decide what is right and what is wrong. Then stand up for what you think is just. Take appropriate and decisive measures to set things right. You may worry that your remedies are overly severe, but they will help you achieve needed changes and deter future misbehavior. There is no blame in this.

Six in the Third Place

He bites through dried meat
And encounters something poisonous.
Slight humiliation. No blame.

"Dried meat" symbolizes a problem of long standing. So to bite through dried meat means to tackle something that has long needed fixing. To encounter something poisonous means to confront not only adversity from the outside world but also anger and hatred within ourselves. Nevertheless, what we are doing is just and so there is no mistake.

You face a problem that has existed for some time. You may lack complete power or authority to eradicate it. When you act, your efforts will probably meet with resentment and resistance. No doubt you will find yourself becoming angry and humiliated at your ineffectiveness. But reform is necessary. Get past your negative emotions. Be willing to do the right thing. In this way you will be free of blame.

Nine in the Fourth Place

He bites through dried meat bones
And finds a metal arrow.
It is beneficial to persevere through difficulties.
Good fortune.

You face great obstacles in your efforts at reform. They are like dried meat bones that are difficult to bite through. Yet a metal arrow can pierce even through armor because it is hard and straight. These are the qualities that you must emulate if you are to succeed in your efforts. Act with determination and do not deviate from the correct path. Recognize the difficulty of the task before you but do not be discouraged. Persevere. Think of yourself as chewing through something very tough. Proceed one step at a time and do not give up. Through continuous and persistent effort you will succeed.

Six in the Fifth Place (Ruling Line)

He bites through dried meat
And finds yellow gold.

Persevere. There will be danger.
But no blame.

To bite through dried meat and find yellow gold means that when we face a difficult decision we should find certain qualities within ourselves. Gold symbolizes purity of motivation. Yellow is the color of the mean, symbolizing impartiality and a balanced attitude.

You know that reform is necessary and that a decision must be made. It is clear what the situation requires. Still, you find it difficult to take action. You would like to be lenient. However, you must weigh your personal predilections against your responsibility to do what is right in the situation. You must strive to be impartial and objective. Approach the matter with firm resolution and carry through. Commit yourself to doing what needs to be done. If you remain aware of the dangers, there will be a successful outcome.

Nine at the Top

His neck is fastened in the stocks,
So that his ears disappear.
Misfortune.

In line six, the time for reform has come and gone without being heeded. Thus the text offers a warning. The *Book of Changes* teaches that redemption is always possible if we are willing to recognize our errors, mend our ways, and return to proper principles. But a person who refuses to recognize that what he is doing is wrong will continue to stray more and more from the correct path. Such a person does not read the signs of recalcitrant experience or heed the warnings of those who are concerned for his welfare. "His ears disappear," meaning that he cannot or will not listen to reason. When a person invites trouble in this way and obstinately refuses to reform himself, misfortune is the inevitable result.

NOTES

21.0 "do justice." *yong yu*: literally, "take advantage of legal proceedings"; hence, administer the law.

21.2 "meat." *fu*: flesh, skin. Cf. 38.5.

21.4 "through difficulties." Or, "in times of hardship," "through adversity." Cf. 11.3.

TWENTY-TWO

Bi • Adornment

Keywords:

Grace
Beauty
Persuasion
Ornamentation
Simplicity
Inner beauty

Above: Gen • Mountain
Below: Li • Fire

Bi is the converse of Shih He. While Biting Through demands that we ignore surfaces and get down to essentials, Bi recognizes that adornment and grace are also necessary to life. Civilization cannot survive without persuasion and civility. Manners ease tensions, diffuse conflict, and make social life smoother and more bearable. Beauty and style rescue everyday life from drabness and despair. The message of Bi is that we must recognize the limited but important role that grace and adornment play in society and in personal well-being.

The structure of the hexagram reflects this: The lower trigram, Li (Fire), illuminates and beautifies the upper trigram, Gen (Mountain). The fire lends grace to the mountain, but does not fundamentally alter its nature. Rather, it shows what is already there in its best light. In the same way, adornment properly employed can help reveal the beauty of life that lies beneath the surface.

THE JUDGMENT

Adornment. Success.
In small matters it is beneficial to undertake something.

Adornment brings success as a small thing. It smooths the path of life and makes it more bearable. When adornment becomes the central thing, it can easily become perverted because it is placed above other human values and human needs.

Nevertheless, the study of beauty helps us understand the profundity of the world. Through the contemplation of beauty and form, we discover both the demands of a particular time and the power of the unchanging. And through attention to how beauty is produced, we apprehend the connections between outer form and inner nature. The beauty of fire or of a mountain range is the natural product of the processes that give rise to these things.

It is the same in human life. The *Book of Changes* teaches that outer beauty should emerge as the natural product of inner beauty. Then adornment does not simply cover or disguise a person's nature but becomes its organic expression.

In practical terms, Bi signifies that you cannot exert great influence on the situation. But you can have a a positive effect in small ways. Behave with tact and consideration to others. For the time being, you must accept aspects of the situation that you do not like, but you can make progress at the periphery if you act with charm and grace. Work on polishing your appearance and your powers of persuasion. Brush up your talents. Smooth out the rough edges in your life and in your relationships with others. This is a good time to improve your habits of communication and self-expression. Consider making minor changes to your surroundings so that they better express and reflect who you are.

All of these activities should be understood as means of improving the presentation of your inner self and your real values. They are not ends in themselves. Bi reminds you that as you focus on self-presentation you should not take yourself too seriously. Do not allow yourself to become conceited or self-indulgent, and do not waste your time on trivial things. The outer persona must serve the inner person, and not the other way around. The best way to achieve outer beauty is to let the beauty within shine forth in your words and deeds. If inner beauty is lacking, outward display will not compensate for it in the long run, for without the nourishment of what is within, outer beauty will soon fade. Therefore, the best long-term strategy for the maintenance of grace and beauty is the development of a graceful and beautiful soul.

Thus any focus on adornment must inevitably lead back to the care and cultivation of the soul. Charm and attractiveness are genuine assets in life; gracefulness and poise are talents that can be mastered and fostered with good effect. But your first priority must always be self-development. If you pay too much attention to how you appear to other people, your life will become meaningless and superficial. A beautiful face does not compensate for selfishness and shallowness; beautiful possessions cannot compensate for lack of healthy human relationships; beautiful form does not excuse ugly behavior.

If the *Book of Changes* has a preferred aesthetic, it is one of simplicity and sincerity that naturally expresses the healthiness and soundness of one's character. You should not expect that public dress and deportment can remedy a private lack, or that external possessions can substitute for internal self-possession. Outer worth flows from inner worth and cannot replace it. No amount of fancy clothes or material goods will give you peace, emotional balance, and self-esteem. If you want others to value you, you must first value yourself as you are.

THE IMAGE

Fire at the foot of the mountain:
This is the image of Adornment.
Thus the superior person regulates the masses through enlightenment,
But he does not dare decide legal controversies and enforce criminal punishments.

One should work to eradicate evil and celebrate and adorn the good. Hence in Hexagram 21, Shih He, one decides criminal cases and inflicts the necessary punishments. But not all matters of governance require the threat of force, and not all regulation is criminal regulation. If people are enlightened, they will cooperate naturally. If they have been instilled with proper values, they will not think of doing wrong. Hence during the time of adornment, it is best to channel behavior through rhetorical appeals and through the development of healthy cultural norms. One persuades rather than enforces; one educates rather than threatens. Wise people understand the different ways of governing a situation. They recognize that different times call for different approaches and different measures. One cannot reduce everything to threats of force, or all human behavior to prices and penalties.

Nevertheless, charm and persuasion have their limits in human governance. The most serious matters cannot be resolved through smiles and pleasantries. They require us to face hard choices and take determined action that will not please everyone. Then we must understand beautiful words and charming expressions as auxiliary to the real issues at stake.

THE LINES

The lines describe different varieties of adornment. In almost every case the lines offer the same message: Simplicity is preferable to ostentation; sincerity is more important than pretentious display. In line six one discovers that the most elegant form of adornment is utter simplicity that is beyond adornment.

Initial Nine

He adorns his feet.
He discards the carriage and walks.

To adorn one's feet means to recognize that you are at the beginning of a new endeavor and therefore in a comparatively lowly position. In such a situation you need to learn how to develop your talents. "Discard[ing] the carriage" and walking on foot means that you refuse to take the easy way out and instead prefer to rely on your own resources.

This advice is valuable for anyone who is at the start of a new enterprise. Learn to make the most of your abilities. Do not cut corners. It is certainly all right to ask for help from others, but ultimately there is no substitute for hard work and commitment. Do not engage in ostentatious display or pretend to be something that you are not. It is far better to make progress slowly and step by step through your own efforts than to try to gain quick results through flattery, trickery, or leaning on others. You will have greater satisfaction in your achievements when you know that you have obtained them through your own labors, and you will gain confidence and self-assurance that will benefit you greatly in the long run.

Six in the Second Place (Ruling Line)

He adorns his beard.

The beard is a decoration of something else. The right way to adorn it is to recognize this fact. Form is important because of its content; decoration is valuable because it lends grace to what it decorates. Outward appearance should serve inner beauty; outer grace should reflect inner worth. Focus on what is truly valuable now. In this way you will recognize beauty's proper role and avoid shallowness and vanity.

Nine in the Third Place

Adorned and glistening.
Continual perseverance brings good fortune.

When things go well, one should enjoy the beauty of the time. But do not allow yourself to become lazy. Moments of perfect grace are the culmination of sustained effort and devotion. Remember your responsibilities and do not desert your principles. If you persevere in what is right, you will continue to enjoy good fortune and you will be able to enjoy many other moments of happiness in the future.

Six in the Fourth Place

Adorned with simplicity.
A white horse, soaring on the wing.
He is not a robber,
He seeks marriage.

You are at a crossroads. You can choose the path of adornment and the pursuit of external brilliance or you can choose the path of modest simplicity and the cultivation of inner worth. To ask the question is to answer it, for your doubts about the first path have led you to the second, which is symbolized by the white horse. In the *Book of Changes*, white is the color of simplicity and honesty; wings symbolize transcendence of worldly things.

You may regret this choice because you fear that you are giving up the prestige of a glittering life. But you have no assurance that the path of adornment will bring you happiness or peace of mind. The relentless pursuit of honors and prizes is never-ending, and it never fills up the sense of lack inside you. But the path of honesty and simplicity brings rich rewards: true friendship, trustworthy associates, and meaningful relationships with others. This brings contentment and peace of mind. Hence what appears to be loss is actually gain, as the text says: "He is not a robber, he seeks marriage."

Six in the Fifth Place

Adorning the hills and gardens.
The roll of unbleached silk is paltry and small.
Humiliation, but in the end good fortune.

The text offers an allegory: A person is called upon to decorate a great house and its gardens, but has only a small roll of plain silk. Although he seems inadequate to the task, in the end all turns out well.

The lesson of the line is that sincerity is more important than display of material resources. You may seek connection with other people but worry that you have little to offer. Do not be concerned. What you have on the outside is less important than who you are on the inside. Sincerity of feeling and generosity of spirit will attract others to you. People will recognize your inner worth and you will enjoy good fortune.

Nine at the Top (**Ruling Line**)

Adorned in white.
No blame.

In line six the time for mere adornment is past. White is the color of simplicity and plainness, so to be adorned in white is not to be adorned at all. Perfect grace and beauty occur where content and form have become one; then form and adornment have no independent existence but naturally express the substance of things.

It is time to discard all pretense in your dealings with others. Do not try to impress. Give up attempts at display. You have nothing to hide and no need to pretend that you are something that you are not. Ornament and ostentation are completely unnecessary now. Just be sincere and true to yourself. The quality of your inner nature will then shine through to others. By behaving simply and straightforwardly you will avoid mistakes and everything will go as it should.

NOTES

22.0 "Success," etc. Or, "Success in small matters. In such matters it is favorable to undertake something."

22.GI "regulates the masses through enlightenment," etc. Or, "curbs others through enlightenment produced by culture." An alternative reading of the whole phrase is "clearly understands the different forms of governance, and does not try to reduce everything to criminal penalties."

22.2 "his beard." *xu*. This can also mean "patience, waiting." Cf. 54.3. Hence the line could also read, "He cultivates his patience."

22.3 "glistening." *ru:* damp, moist; hence, glossy, sleek, or lustrous.

22.4 "white." *po:* hoary, the white hair of the aged; hence, white; hence, plain and simple.

22.5 "paltry." *jian jian:* meager, small, narrow, insignificant, petty. The word is doubled for emphasis.

22.6 "white." *bai:* literally "white adornment." White is the color of purity and simplicity. Hence, "plain adornment."

TWENTY-THREE

Bo • Splitting Apart

Keywords:

Deterioration
Stripping away
Collapse
Falling apart

Above: Gen • Mountain
Below: Kun • Earth

Bo features five yin lines ascending upward, with only a single yang line left at the top. The yang lines that were below have been stripped away one by one, and the last one is about to be displaced by the rising yin lines. The hexagram Bo symbolizes the approaching victory of the forces of disintegration and disorder. Inferior elements undermine what is valuable through gradual deterioration, so that in the end, the old order falls apart.

Another way to understand the top yang line is as the roof of a house. The house gradually falls into disrepair, and its foundations are gradually eaten away. In the end, the roof disintegrates and the house collapses. By tradition, the hexagram is identified with the ninth month (October–November), when the days grow appreciably shorter and darkness is about to reach its peak.

23 Bo • Splitting Apart

THE JUDGMENT

Splitting Apart.
It is not beneficial to have somewhere to go.

Things are falling apart. The situation around you is deteriorating. Inferior people are on the rise and they are displacing people of value and merit. Relationships that once could be taken for granted have frayed and dissolved. Old ways of doing things are disintegrating and nothing has yet taken their place. Because the time is not propitious, there is no advantage in trying to undertake anything now.

The deterioration that you face may result from changes in outer conditions over which you have no control. In that case, you should not blame yourself for the fact that everything changes.

Alternatively, the problem may be that elements of your life now seem to have outlived their usefulness. Old habits no longer serve your interests. Old assumptions no longer make sense. Things that you once took for granted no longer seem solid and dependable. This means that you too are undergoing change. You are experiencing the end of an old cycle without the comforting assurance of what is yet to come.

In either case, it is useless to struggle against the time. Your position has been weakened by the changes around you. You are vulnerable, either due to your position, your emotions, or both. For this reason avoid confrontation. You will only make things worse.

The structure of the hexagram Bo suggests the proper course of conduct at this time. The lower trigram, Kun (Earth), symbolizes devotion and acceptance. The upper trigram, Gen (Mountain), symbolizes stillness and patience. These are the virtues to adopt now. You must endure this period of deterioration and wait for better times to emerge. According to the law of change, they inevitably will. In the meantime, acquiesce in the new conditions without surrendering your principles. Keep quiet and maintain a low profile. Try to remain detached and untroubled to the extent that circumstances allow. Emotional reactions will only drain you and cause you to do foolish things. But if you can stay calm, collected, and above the fray, you can safeguard your position during this difficult time and you will be less vulnerable to manipulation.

Change is coming both to your outer world and to your inner experience. This change may be painful and upsetting. But you must let it run its course. It is a law of nature. Whatever becomes great will eventually be lessened, and whatever becomes full will eventually be emptied. You cannot alter this general trend. Therefore, the wisest course is to withdraw and wait for the time of renewal.

THE IMAGE

The mountain rests on the earth:
This is the image of Splitting Apart.
In the same way, those above make their foundations secure
By generosity to those below.

The stability of a mountain stems from the fact that it is broad and expansive, its mass dispersed widely over the earth that supports it. By contrast, a narrow and steep precipice with loose stones is likely to precipitate an avalanche.

If you want to survive a period of deterioration, you must be like the broad expansive mountain, which abides in serenity and stillness. First, you must have firm and stable foundations. Because you cannot move forward at present, it is best to renew and replenish yourself. You must begin slowly but surely to amass resources and build secure foundations for the new time that will eventually emerge from the chaos of the old. Do not lose heart. The past is gone and will not return. Start preparing for the future now, in a spirit of tranquility and hope. Have faith that things will ultimately work out in the right way when the time is right.

Second, like the mountain, you must keep a low center of gravity. This means that you should avoid pride and aggressive display, which will only make you a target. Avoid power struggles or attempts to dominate the situation. Have patience and do not try to force matters. Your time will come again. Until then you must keep a low profile.

Third, just as the mountain rests on the earth that sustains it, you must rely on those beneath who are the real source of your support. When the chips are down, you will discover who your true friends are. During the time of deterioration, it is important to be generous and benevolent, not to the famous and the influential, but to those people who support you and who ultimately count most in your life. If you behave with kindness and magnanimity even when everything is falling apart, you will make your position as secure and stable as a broad expanse of mountains.

THE LINES

The lines tell the story of increasing deterioration and decay. The first four lines use the metaphor of various parts of a bed that are stripped away or fall apart. Line five teaches that only through reestablishing cooperation and trust can people end the difficult times. In line six, deterioration has proceeded as far as it can. The stage is set for renewal, signified by the succeeding hexagram Fu, or Return.

Initial Six

The legs of the bed are split apart.
Those who persevere are destroyed.
Misfortune.

The legs of the bed are destroyed. The metaphor means that someone or something is undermining your position from beneath. People with ulterior motives have entered your environment and are setting in motion the forces of deterioration. Because it is not yet clear what elements are at work, you need to act with circumspection and caution. If you insist on going ahead without taking these facts into account, you will meet with misfortune. Right now there is little to do but wait until events become clearer.

Six in the Second Place

The frame of the bed splits apart.
Those who persevere are destroyed.
Misfortune.

The source of the danger has become clearer. You are in a very difficult position now. You lack allies to help you. Hence you must be extremely cautious. This is no time to be stubborn or self-righteous. You must adapt to unfavorable conditions as best as you can. Quietly move to avoid the danger. Distance yourself from people who are not supporting you. It is time to retreat. If you try to make a stand now, you could be seriously hurt.

Six in the Third Place

He splits with them.
No blame.

You find yourself in a negative situation from which you cannot easily escape. This may be an inferior environment, untrustworthy people, or a combination of the two. Do not compromise your integrity. If others choose to act badly, that is their choice. Let them go their own way. Separate yourself from them as best you can, even if this leads them to misunderstand you and criticize you. If you do not fall in with them, you can maintain your own principles during this dark time. Conversely, try to foster connections with good influences and align yourself with decent people whom you can trust. This will give you the strength you need to ride out your current difficulties.

Six in the Fourth Place

The skin of the bed splits apart.
Misfortune.

Disaster has struck. Misfortune is imminent and you cannot avoid it. Deterioration has reached its lowest point. You must gather your strength together to survive this dark time.

Six in the Fifth Place

Like a string of fish
The court ladies form a line.
One is favored.
There is nothing that is not beneficial.

The "string of fish" refers to the five yin lines, of which the last is at the fifth position. It draws the others upward like a string of fish toward the yang line in the sixth place, the ruler of the hexagram. (The reference to "court ladies" compares this to a princess who approaches her prince with her four maids-in-waiting following after her in a line.) Led by the fifth line, the lower elements now place themselves under the beneficent influence of the higher. Instead of trying to eradicate the leader—as in the text of the lower four lines—they now cooperate.

The basic lesson is that disorder in society is caused by a deterioration in trust. Without trust, society degenerates into the war of all against all and all good things are destroyed. Conversely, chaos ends when people learn to trust each other again. Only when mutual confidence is reestablished does beneficial collective action become possible.

The line indicates that the time of deterioration is drawing to an end. Things are changing for the better. People who were at odds before now learn to cooperate for their mutual benefit. Trust is restored. As a result, success is now possible. Do your best to nurture these positive conditions. Work with others and help things move forward. You will be richly rewarded; as the text says, "there is nothing that is not beneficial" in this.

Nine at the Top (Ruling Line)

The largest fruit remains uneaten.
The superior person receives a carriage.
The house of the inferior person is split apart.

The forces of chaos have reached their peak and are on the wane. A period of decay and collapse has begun to dissipate. Better days are coming. According to the philosophy of the *Book of Changes*, the law of change affects not only the order of society but also the forces of evil and social disorder. Those forces thrive off social order and consume all that is good. But when they have reached their peak, they too start to disintegrate, and evil then begins to feed on itself. People eventually tire of chaos and they hunger for a return to peace and harmony. Herein lies the promise of hope even in the darkest hour. It is symbolized by the fruit that remains uneaten. When the last fruit falls to the ground, it spreads the seeds of new growth. As the time of deterioration comes to an end, good people begin to gain power and influence once again. Others trust them and support them as if they were lifted up in a carriage. Conversely, untrustworthy people destroy themselves, because others know that they cannot be relied on.

Now that the bad times are ending, a new period of hope and opportunity opens up for you. You have been tested by the difficult time that is drawing to a close, but if you have maintained your integrity, you will have grown stronger and more resilient, and better able to handle the challenges ahead. When people see that you have been tested by adversity and still remained true to your values, they will look up to you and support you. Thus, by developing strength of character in dark times, you help to guarantee your future success.

NOTES

23.3 "He splits with them." Or, "He breaks away," "He splits it."

23.6 "The house of the inferior person is split apart." Or, "The house of the petty person is destroyed," "The inferior person lets the shelter split apart." The "largest fruit" refers to the sixth yang line, which acts like a roof over the others. In the hands of a wise and virtuous person, it can carry and support others; in the hands of incompetent or venal persons, it is destroyed and thus offers no shelter to those below.

TWENTY-FOUR

Fu • Return

Keywords:

Renewal
Turning back
Repentance
Reform
Restoration
Renovation
Rejuvenation
The turning point

Above: Kun • Earth
Below: Zhen • Thunder

While the previous hexagram, Bo, represents deterioration and the end of a cycle, Fu represents a turning point—the reemergence of order and the first glimmerings of new life.

The hexagram Fu features a single yang line in the bottom position. Above it are five yin lines. This represents the beginning of a new cycle, for just when the forces of darkness have pushed all of the yang lines out of the hexagram, a new yang line enters from below. The forces of disorder and disintegration have reached their zenith and a new era dawns. Yang energy, which was all but extinguished, has finally appeared again and is now on the rise. By tradition this hexagram is associated with the eleventh month (December–January). This is also the first month following the winter solstice, when the days begin to grow longer again.

THE JUDGMENT

Return. Success.
Going out and coming in without harm.
Friends come.
No blame.
Turning around and returning to the Way.
On the seventh day return comes.
It is beneficial to have somewhere to go.

Fu represents the beginning of a new cycle of growth. The text offers the metaphor of seven days as the length that a cycle must take before it renews itself. If one begins with Qian (pure yang) and, starting from bottom to top, replaces each line with its opposite, in six transformations the yin lines will have fully displaced the yang lines, and Qian (pure yang) will become Kun (pure yin). The seventh transformation then begins a new sequence, with a yang line moving up from the bottom.

You have reached a turning point, and the beginning of a new cycle. The law of change is in operation, and after a period of decline, confusion, and stagnation, there are new possibilities for renewal, clarity, and improvement. The old order is passing away and a new one is dawning. As things begin to change imperceptibly in your favor, new alliances and relationships can form, and old ones that had grown stale and frayed can become renewed and strengthened; hence the text says "friends come."

Nevertheless, you should not expect that everything will get better overnight. Rather, this hexagram describes the moment at which the tide begins to shift in your favor. The days start to become longer at the winter solstice, but spring is still many months off. For this reason it would not be wise to try to force matters. Things are still in their earliest stages, and it would be best to let them develop naturally, in their own time. Your position is not yet strong enough to take aggressive action, and in any case you cannot make everything better all at once. Instead, you should conserve your energies, secure in the faith that things are bound to improve if you give them time. What is most important is that you make a sincere and honest commitment to take the first steps in what will be a long and steady process of improvement.

The hexagram Fu also represents an opportunity handed you to begin again. If you have made mistakes in the past, or have strayed from the proper path, you must take this opportunity to correct yourself, repent, and ask forgiveness as necessary. Hence the text speaks of "[t]urning around and returning to the Way."

The *Book of Changes* is both optimistic and pragmatic about the possibilities of self-renewal. Every period of darkness is followed by new light. The *Book of Changes* thus holds out the hope that redemption is still possible if you devote yourself to it wholeheartedly. But you must act at the proper time. That is why the text says, "It is beneficial to have somewhere to go." The possibilities for return and renewal are not endless. If you lack resolve and commitment, or if you wait too long to change your ways, the path of redemption will be closed and you will have to wait through a new cycle. Fortunately, you are now in a propitious time when change is possible. A door has been opened for you. It is up to you to pass through it. Nothing can be forced. Everything must unfold in its natural time. But even if you cannot change everything immediately, before you begin your journey, you must first turn yourself around so that you can move in the right direction.

THE IMAGE

Thunder within the earth:
This is the image of Return.
Thus the ancient kings closed the borders
At the time of the solstice.
Merchants and travelers did not move about,
And princes did not go forth to inspect the provinces.

The lower trigram, Zhen, is thunder, representing aroused action; the upper trigram, Kun (Earth), represents patience and devotion. The presence of thunder beneath the earth symbolizes the new energies that are just beginning to stir beneath the surface, like the initial growth of plants that have yet to push through the surface of the soil. Thunder under the earth means that it is not yet time for strong and decisive action. During a time of renewal your energies must be channeled and conserved appropriately so that they will not be dissipated by being used up prematurely. In this way your enthusiasm will not wane when it meets with recalcitrant experience. You must be patient and devoted to making things better again slowly and methodically.

The basic principle is that when energy is being renewed, one must give it time to grow strong and replenish itself. In the same way, a person recovering from a long illness requires rest, and two people who attempt to reconcile after estrangement must take time to restore trust and confidence in each other. Plants just beginning to develop beneath the surface of the earth will blossom if they are tended carefully. But premature growth can be disastrous if the weather turns cold again and the plants are not hardy enough to survive a frost.

The text compares the situation to the behavior of the ancient kings during the winter solstice. They closed the city gates and proclaimed a day of rest so that people could have time to reflect on the year that had just passed. Similar considerations apply to you. You are poised between the end of an old era and the beginning of a new one. You must use this time to recharge your batteries and replenish your energies for the times ahead. But recuperation is not the only goal. When things are about to change for the better, it is worth taking stock of yourself and your situation. Reflect on the old cycle that is just passing away and consider what went wrong. Perhaps you strayed from the proper path because you were not true to yourself, because you weakened yourself by harboring the wrong attitudes, or because you allowed negative thoughts and emotions to overwhelm you and lead you into the wrong choices. Whatever the causes, it is important to be honest with yourself, for self-understanding is necessary if you are to begin again. Nevertheless, do not wound yourself with recriminations or allow self-criticism to discourage you. What is past is past. The future lies ahead. Have faith in yourself and in your capacity for renewal.

THE LINES

The lines describe different forms of return or repentance. All of the lines, except for line six, are favorable (or not unfavorable). This exemplifies the *Book of Changes'* view that a sincere return to righteous behavior always brings improvement. As the *Book of Changes* says in Hexagram 9 (Xiao Xu), line one: "Returning to the Way. / How could there be blame in this?" In line six, by contrast, one has missed one's chance to return, and disaster occurs.

Initial Nine (Ruling Line)

Returning before going too far.
Only a little regret.
Supreme good fortune.

If you are contemplating something that is contrary to your principles, or even if you have only strayed a little, go no further. Stop immediately while very little damage has been done, for it will be much harder to turn back later on. Now is the time to listen to your conscience, when the problems are still relatively small and bad influences have not taken hold very strongly. You may experience a little regret for going astray, but if you act from good motives now, ultimately everything will turn out for the best. Moreover, by learning to nip problems in the bud, you will strengthen your character.

Six in the Second Place

Stopping, letting go, and returning.
Good fortune.

Turning back to the right path can be difficult. It is often easier to make the right choices when you are in good company, or when you have good role models to look up to. Listen to people whom you trust and respect, and follow their example. Ask yourself what people whom you admire would do. This will improve your judgment and help bring you success.

Six in the Third Place

Repeated return.
Danger. No blame.

A person repeatedly returns because he repeatedly strays. You may find that you constantly vacillate because you imagine that the grass is greener elsewhere. This is unwise. Flirting with temptation increases the danger that you will abandon the right path. Remember what your values are. Teach yourself to persevere. Then all will go well.

Six in the Fourth Place

Walking in the middle,
One returns alone.

To walk in the middle and return alone has a dual meaning. First, it may mean that your environment or milieu is no longer suitable for you. (I.e., you "walk in the middle" of those around you.) You may have outgrown the people you deal with or your current situation may be holding you back. In either case, you need to move on without worrying about what other people will think. It is better to go your own way now than to force yourself to fit in. Be true to yourself and stand up for what you believe in even if this means that for a time you will stand alone. Eventually, you will find a new environment and new people who will respect your ideas, and this will bring its own rewards.

Second, to walk in the middle means to adopt "the middle way," that is, the path of moderation. This involves, among other things, practicing modesty and humility and not taking things to excess. Others may lose themselves in fads and enthusiasms. Do not follow them. Return to proper principles, even if this means returning alone.

Six in the Fifth Place

Magnanimous return.
No remorse.

The great lesson of the *Book of Changes* is that a person must adapt to the times consistent with principles that do not change. It is time to make a new beginning. Have the courage to make the necessary adjustments and reforms. Look deep within yourself and decide what needs to be done. Do not be distracted by either nostalgia or regret. Don't make excuses. If you have done something wrong, admit it. Be honest with yourself and resolve to correct your faults. But the important thing is to move on. Then you will be without blame.

Six at the Top

Returning in confusion.
Misfortune.

There is blunder and disaster.
If one sends armies marching,
In the end one will suffer a great defeat,
With misfortune for the country's ruler.
For ten years
It will not be possible to start out again.

"Returning in confusion" means missing the right time for return. The confusion is internal; it stems from a misunderstanding of the outside world. Obstinacy and bad judgment lead a person to mischaracterize the situation and hence to miss opportunities for reform. Thus the text says "blunder and disaster," meaning both misfortune from external causes and from one's ignorance or mistake in dealing with the situation. The text analogizes the situation to warfare. In conducting a campaign, timing is essential. If one delays attacking when one should move forward, or attacks at the wrong time, the result is certain defeat. The ruler wastes lives and resources and must wait "ten years"—metaphorically the length of a complete cycle—for circumstances to improve.

Either through stubbornness or neglect, you have refused to see that change was necessary. As a result, you have missed the opportunity to make a turn for the better. If you try to strike out boldly now, you will simply make things worse. Instead, you must be patient and wait until a new opportunity presents itself.

NOTES

24.0 "harm." Or, "affliction." *ji:* illness, disease, affliction.

24.0 "to have somewhere to go." I.e., to have a goal or purpose.

24.GI "go forth to inspect." Or, "travel through."

24.GI "provinces." Or, "far reaches of the kingdom," "domains of the kingdom."

24.1 "Only a little regret." *wu zhi hui:* literally, "without here regret." This might also be rendered as "without great regret." A textual variant is *wu qi hui*: without much regret.

24.2 "Stopping, letting go." *xiu:* stop, end, beautiful, joyful, or jubilant. Hence "returning with delight," or "beautiful return." Wilhelm/Baynes translates this as "quiet return."

24.4 "Walking in the middle." Or, "Walking in the midst of others" (Wilhelm/Baynes). The fourth line is a yin line between two other yin lines, hence the phrase is probably a play on words, meaning both "to walk in the middle way" and "to walk amidst others."

24.5 "Magnanimous." *dun:* simple honesty. Hence, sincere or "noblehearted" (Wilhelm/Baynes). Cf. 19.6, 52.6.

24.6 "Returning in confusion." Or, "Missing the return."

24.6 "blunder and disaster." *zai sheng:* harm from natural causes and from one's own ignorance. Or, "Calamity and disaster from without and within," "Misfortune from within and without" (Wilhelm/Baynes). Cf. 62.6.

24.6 "start out again." Or, "launch out again," "attack again."

TWENTY-FIVE

Wu Wang • Innocence

䷘

Keywords:

Without expectations
Without guile
Acting naturally
Being spontaneous
The unexpected

Above: Qian • Heaven
Below: Zhen • Thunder

With three yang lines at the top, Wu Wang appears superficially similar to Pi (Standstill). But just as the three yang lines are about to depart upward away from the yin lines, another yang line suddenly appears at the bottom. It symbolizes the unexpected and unpredictable that resides in any situation. In Wu Wang the lower trigram is not Kun (Earth), which naturally gravitates downward, but Zhen (Thunder), symbolizing arousal, energy, and upward movement. Thunder is primitive and spontaneous, a force of nature that propels itself upward toward heaven (Qian). Natural movement is unconscious and without guile; and one who naturally follows the path of heaven is innocent. This provides the hexagram with its second theme.

THE JUDGMENT

Innocence. Supreme success.
It is beneficial to persevere.
If one is not what he should be,
He meets with calamity,
And it is not beneficial for him
To undertake anything.

In the *Book of Changes*, innocence does not carry the Christian connotation of being without sin. Rather to be innocent means to be genuine, sincere, and unaffected, without guile or deceit. For similar reasons, innocence does not mean being naïve or unaware of one's surroundings. A wild animal acts naturally and instinctively, but its senses are often finely attuned to its environment.

To act innocently means to act spontaneously and naturally, without ulterior motives. However, human innocence means more than this, because aggressive, selfish, and depraved behavior can also be spontaneous. Innocence has a necessary moral dimension. It means doing the right thing for its own sake without thought of reward. An innocent person is naturally drawn to what is good and right and moves in this direction instinctively and without ceremony or calculation, without manipulation or deception. The text says that innocent behavior offers the possibility of supreme success, whereas impulsive, unreflecting behavior that lacks moral qualities will only bring unhappiness and misfortune.

Innocent action is the best way to deal with the unexpected events that life inevitably hands us. You cannot always prepare for every contingency and you cannot run your life according to a script, no matter how intricate and well thought out. You must be willing to improvise and respond naturally to the situation.

This hexagram suggests that the best path for you to follow now is one of simplicity, honesty, and naturalness. Try to do the right thing because it is the right thing to do. Your reward will come in due course. Don't overthink things and stop trying to turn every situation to your personal advantage. Getting lost in intricate machinations and devious plottings will only cause anxiety and confusion. Above all, don't try to manipulate people or take advantage of them. Your scheming will backfire. A sincere and uncomplicated approach has a much greater chance of success. Act simply and spontaneously and you need not worry about the result. You will do the right thing in exactly the right way.

Innocence means accepting your own nature and allowing the best parts of yourself to emerge naturally and spontaneously. You don't need to be something that you are not and you shouldn't try. Stop comparing yourself to other people, and don't worry whether you are sufficiently popular or influential. That way of thinking is simply a recipe for unhappiness. Be content to be yourself. Let your inner qualities shine through in your dealings with others, and they will respond. Conformity is a great pressure in social life. But there is no need to conform just for conformity's sake. Don't be tempted to do something that is beneath you just to fit in. Refuse to be drawn into anything deceptive or base. Instead, trust your instincts. You have the resources within you to judge the situation. Let your heart be your guide.

THE IMAGE

Thunder rolling under heaven:
All things behave with natural innocence.
Thus the ancient kings,
Rich in virtue,
And in harmony with the seasons,
Nourished the ten thousand things.

Thunder rolling under heaven is an apt symbol of the sublime powers of nature. The lesson is that if you want to deal successfully with the forces in the world outside yourself, you must respond to them with what is natural within yourself. You must behave toward them as the world behaves toward you, with natural innocence. A spontaneous, unforced response will allow you to handle whatever comes your way. Let go of your fears and worries and trust that things will work out naturally in their own time in the right way.

Wu Wang means "without guile"; but it also means "without expectations." Do not try to force things to behave according to a preset plan. The world is much too interesting for that. You cannot plan everything out in advance, so do not try. Instead, be open to what the world has to offer. No doubt you will experience both ups and downs, and some of life's surprises will be unpleasant. But try to maintain your balance, and learn to accept the ebb and flow of events philosophically. You will learn a great deal in the process. And a welcoming attitude toward life will bring many rich and unexpected opportunities your way.

The text speaks of ancient kings who were able to nourish all things in the world by accepting them for what they were and treating them appropriately according to the time. In the same way, you will succeed if you are willing to receive the world on its own terms. Accept people for who and what they are and do not try to force them to conform to your expectations. Treat them with respect and consideration, and they may surprise you.

THE LINES

The lines describe the consequences of innocent, spontaneous behavior. The basic theme is stated in line one: Innocent, natural action generally brings one good fortune. One who perseveres in this approach eventually wins praise (line four). Innocence does not act for the purpose of gain, but makes gains anyway (line two). Although the innocent suffer calamities like anyone else (line three), they often find that problems take care of themselves (line five). Nevertheless, in extreme situations the time for innocent action has passed, and in these cases one should simply do nothing (line six).

Initial Nine (Ruling Line)

Innocence. Going forward brings good fortune.

Innocence means responding to the inherent goodness within your nature. Follow your heart. If you are truly sincere and act with integrity, whatever move you make will be correct.

Six in the Second Place

If one does not count on the harvest while plowing,
Or on the use of the land while tilling,
It is beneficial to undertake something.

Do the work for its own sake and not for the success and esteem it will bring you. Although a person always should labor for a good result, that result can only be obtained through pride in the work itself. Devote your attention to the task at hand. Don't continually stop to admire your progress. If you spend your time dreaming about your future success, you will not finish the job before you. But if you are committed to making steady progress and to doing the best job that you can, all will go well.

Six in the Third Place

Innocence meets with disaster.
Someone's tethered cow, taken by a passerby,
Is the wanderer's gain,
The villager's loss.

Sometimes bad things happen even though you have done nothing wrong, and sometimes other people reap the benefits of your hard work. The *Book of Changes* teaches that shifts of fortune are inevitable, for the law of change is always at work. When unexpected misfortunes occur, don't despair or become bitter. Recognize that life has its ups and downs. Accommodate and adjust yourself to the demands of the time. Although living your life with integrity and natural innocence does not always prevent bad luck, it can help you deal with setbacks when they occur. A blade of grass bends with a strong wind because it is flexible, while a dried-up branch snaps because it is not. If you respond with flexibility and spontaneity, you can sometimes avoid misfortune or lessen its impact. And natural optimism and an adaptive attitude help prepare the way for the return of good times.

Nine in the Fourth Place

One who is able to persevere is without blame.

Be true to yourself and to your values. Do not allow yourself to be swayed by people with base designs or inferior standards. You must maintain your integrity at all costs. Look inside your heart and you will instinctively know what is right.

Innocence and integrity are deeply connected. Being true to yourself means acting from your nature. But a person's nature should be formed through self-cultivation and commitment to the right values. Therefore, if you maintain your integrity, you will respond naturally to new situations from the goodness of your heart and thus you will spontaneously conduct yourself in the right way.

Nine in the Fifth Place (Ruling Line)

Innocence falls ill.
Use no medicine. There will be rejoicing.

An unexpected difficulty arises. Before rushing off to take active measures to solve it, consider whether external remedies are really necessary. It may be that the best strategy is to exercise patience. Let nature take its course. Things will get better on their own without your intervention. If you are confused about what to do, stop worrying about the problem for a while. The solution will occur to you in due course, when you are ready to receive it.

The more general lesson is that, faced with unexpected misfortune from without, one should imitate nature. Nature is infinitely patient and yet infinitely resourceful. It adjusts to change and responds to it naturally and simply. It accepts everything and eventually transforms it. In the same way, one should adapt spontaneously to the unexpected. Maintain an open attitude toward the world and have faith that things will better themselves.

Nine at the Top

Innocent action brings troubles.
Nothing is beneficial.

When the time for action has passed, do not persist in trying to impose order and direction on events. This is so even if your motives are pure. A wise person understands that the secret of progress is knowing when not to push forward. At such a time even innocent and spontaneous action will cause troubles. There is no more that you can do at present. Instead, you must wait patiently for conditions to change on their own.

NOTES

25.0 "is not what he should be." Or, "correct," "righteous." *fei zheng:* not be correct.

25.0 "To undertake anything." Or, "To have somewhere to go."

25.GI "All things." Or, "beings," "creatures."

25.GI "behave." Or, "consort," "combine."

25.GI "seasons." Or, "times."

25.GI "the ten thousand things." Or, "the myriad things." Ten thousand signifies a multitude, or an indeterminately large number. Cf. Wilhelm/Baynes: "all beings."

25.5 "There will be rejoicing." Recovery from a serious illness was an occasion for celebration. Cf. Wilhelm/Baynes "Use no medicine / In an illness / Incurred through no fault of your own. / It will pass of itself."

25.6 "brings troubles." Or, "leads to mistakes (blunders)."

25.6 "Nothing is beneficial." *wu you li:* there is nothing for which this is favorable. I.e., there is no action that is beneficial under the circumstances. Do not attempt to impose a direction on events.

TWENTY-SIX

Da Xu • Great Accumulation

Keywords:

The taming power of the great
Great amassing
Accumulation
Great restraint
Great caretaking
Storing up
Preparation
Gathering knowledge
Cultivating your abilities
Improving yourself
Waiting for the right moment

Above: Gen • Mountain
Below: Qian • Heaven

Da Xu is the inverse of the previous hexagram Wu Wang. While Wu Wang preaches the importance of openness and spontaneity, Da Xu counsels restraint and accumulation of resources in expectation of the right moment for advance.

With three yang lines at the bottom, the hexagram bears a superficial resemblance to Hexagram 11, Tai (Peace). However, instead of a broken yin line at the top there is a solid yang line. The hexagram looks like a bottle with a lid on top that stores the creative power and prevents its dissipation or its escape. The yang line at the top is the position of the sage, whose wise counsel restrains the other lines until the time is right for action. The same theme appears in the constituent trigrams: The upper trigram, Ken (Mountain, Keeping Still) restrains the lower trigram, Qian (Dynamic Force). Hence a second meaning of Da Xu is "great restraint" or "the restraining power of the great."

Structurally, Da Xu also resembles Hexagram 9, Xiao Xu, which can be translated either as "small accumulation" or "the restraining power of the small." In Xiao Xu one yin line in the fourth place must restrain five strong yang lines. In Da Xu, the fourth line of the minister is joined by the fifth line, representing the ruler, who is strong and mighty; hence the restraining power of "the great."

A third and final meaning of Da Xu is "great care" or "great domestication." This is also represented by the sixth line, the position of the sage. The sage cares for and nurtures everyone and everything, holding back creative energies until they can mature to their fullest extent and emerge in their greatest power.

THE JUDGMENT

Great Accumulation.
It is beneficial to persevere.
Not eating at home brings good fortune.
It is beneficial to cross the great river.

The theme of Da Xu is storing up and developing energy and resources for future use. Hence "[i]t is beneficial to persevere" in marshaling your resources and developing your abilities. Cultivating a determined and steadfast character is essential, because if you wish to remain at the height of your powers you will need to hone your skills continually and renew yourself daily. "Not eating at home" refers to persons of great ability and talent who advised rulers in ancient China and lived with them as their honored guests. (Cf. Hexagram 20, Guan, Viewing, line four.) Here it means that good fortune will come from working for the public good rather than for private advantage. Devote yourself to the perfection of your talents and to the achievement of something beyond your narrow self-interest, and you will have both the power and the vision to achieve great things, symbolized by crossing the great river.

This hexagram offers advice both about how to achieve future success and how to make yourself into the sort of person who naturally succeeds. Whatever your goals in life, you can achieve them if you go about things in the right way.

First, size up the resources that you currently have available. These include not only your financial resources but also your social resources—your friends, relationships, and connections. Take stock of your talents and abilities, including any special knowledge and expertise you may have.

Second, decide what needs to be improved or accumulated in order to reach your goal. Perhaps you need to make new connections or raise funds. Or perhaps you need to brush up on your talents or your social skills. Whatever it is, make a plan and stick to it. Gather the necessary knowledge and information. Enlist friends and helpers. To prevail you will need commitment and dedication over the long haul. The key is not to be impatient. You will succeed because you have wisely gathered the right resources and then controlled and wielded them properly.

Third, work on yourself. Your character is the most important resource that you have. Develop good habits. Plan your actions in advance. Instead of rushing forward impetuously, stop to consider the consequences. Stay focused and don't let yourself become distracted from your long-term goals. Organize your life so that you can make progress step by step rather than in a single valiant effort. Keep on top of things and don't slack off. Be industrious. Challenge yourself. If you make the effort, you can do more than you ever thought yourself capable of. Giving your best each and every day will bolster your confidence and make you feel better about yourself. Developing and stretching yourself will contribute to your overall happiness and well-being as well as making it easier for you to succeed.

Fourth, work for something larger than yourself. Don't confuse determination with isolation from others. This is a time for new possibilities, new situations, and even new relationships. Let go of your fears and inhibitions. It is time to go out into the world and make a difference. Dedicating yourself to others will redound to your benefit in the long run.

THE IMAGE

Heaven dwells in the center of the mountain:
This is the image of Great Accumulation.
Thus the superior person gathers knowledge of
The words and deeds of the past,
In order to strengthen his character
And accumulate his virtue.

Heaven within a mountain symbolizes the accumulation of creative energy. It also symbolizes the development of one's character through resolution and restraint. In preparing for the future, the most important strength is strength of character, and the most important things to accumulate are knowledge and virtue. One "gathers knowledge of [t]he words and deeds of the past" in order to be inspired by their example and instructed by their failings. The past is not merely an archive of disconnected facts to be memorized but a treasure of stories and lessons that we can identify with and put to use in our own time. Think about what other people have done in your situation. Find role models that you can look up to and emulate. Identify where people have gone wrong before and resolve not to make the same mistakes. It is much easier to find the right path when you know how others have traveled before you.

THE LINES

The lines describe the process of accumulation in preparation for action. The earliest stage is line one. Lines two through five describe different forms of accumulation and restraint. (The name of the hexagram means both "gathering" and "holding back.") Line six describes the fruition of the entire process: great success because one has acted in accordance with the way of heaven.

Initial Nine

There is danger. It is beneficial to desist.

When you begin a new enterprise, it is only natural to wish to push forward. However, the time is not right. There are obstacles in your path. Energetic action now would waste your resources. Instead, you should compose yourself and desist. Gather your strength and accumulate your resources. Wait until the right opportunity presents itself. When a proper outlet for your energies emerges, you will be much stronger and more likely to succeed.

Nine in the Second Place

The cart is separated from the axle strap.

You cannot advance now. Forces beyond your control hold you back. It is as if someone had removed the axles from your cart. This is a blessing in disguise, for if you had been able to set forth recklessly, you probably would have been rebuffed. Since you cannot move forward, stay where you are. Be content and turn the situation to your advantage. Keeping your goals firmly in mind, use this time to accumulate your resources. By exercising self-restraint now, your potential will continue to develop and make you stronger than ever. In this way you can make a virtue out of necessity.

Nine in the Third Place

A fine horse that follows others.
It is beneficial to persevere in the face of difficulties.
Practice chariot driving and armed defense daily.
It is beneficial to have somewhere to go.

An opportunity for action presents itself now. You want to rush forward in concert with other people, like "a fine horse that follows others." But your advance must be more circumspect. Dangers lurk ahead. You need to prepare yourself better so that you can move forward effectively, and you need to guard yourself against attacks from others. Remember what your ultimate goals are and proceed cautiously, one step at a time. Prepare and persevere. That is the way to success in dangerous times.

Six in the Fourth Place

A horn guard for the young bull.
Supreme good fortune.

A "horn guard" is a headboard that is attached to a young bull's forehead, so that when his horns grow out they cannot harm others. The line contains three lessons. First, the best way to deal with problems is to prevent them from happening in the first place. Think ahead. Anticipate difficulties. Take action now to prevent troubles from occurring, or if they have already begun, deal with them when they are still small and easy to manage. Second, restrain and guide the aspirations and the abilities of those in your charge and curb any bad tendencies so that people can make the most of their talents. Third, make a virtue of necessity. Instead of squandering your resources on premature adventures, hold back and develop your potential, and you will be stronger later on. Circumstances that seem to restrain you from action may often, like the horn guard of a young bull, actually aid in your growth.

This same advice applies to your own inner development. Deal with faults in yourself when they are still minor ones and easier to remedy. Put yourself in situations where you can foster healthy behaviors and constructive habits. Build up your strength to deal with obstacles ahead. Cultivate your character continuously and you will not have to make superhuman efforts to succeed. Success will come naturally from your everyday activities.

Six in the Fifth Place (Ruling Line)

The tusks of a gelded boar.
Good fortune.

A wild boar is dangerous and uses its tusks to harm others, but if the boar is gelded, it becomes docile and less likely to do damage because it no longer desires to. In the same way, one should "geld" evils and difficulties to eradicate them or restrain them so that they do no harm, instead of trying to combat them directly.

When you find yourself faced with a wild and impulsive force, do not attack it directly, for this will merely exacerbate the problem. Avoid overt confrontation. Instead, look for the underlying causes of the difficulty. Consider how you might cut off the source of the problem at its roots, so that you can restrain and rechannel its energies. An indirect approach may prove more effective than a frontal assault, and will bring you success and good fortune.

Nine at the Top (Ruling Line)

Hence one attains the highway of heaven.
Success.

By steadily accumulating resources and preparing yourself for action, you have put yourself in an excellent position. Now obstacles give way and you can achieve great things. Nothing holds you back now from realizing your full potential. Stick to your principles and maintain your integrity—or as the text puts it, follow "the highway of heaven"—and you will have supreme success.

NOTES

26.GI "Heaven dwells." Or, "resides," "is stored."

26.1 "desist." *yi:* cease, culminate, stop.

26.2. "The cart," etc. Or, "The cart is freed from the axle"; "The axle strap comes off the wagon." Cf. 9.3.

26.3 "A fine horse that follows others." *zhu:* follow. It has the dual meaning of following on the one hand, and chasing or pursuing on the other.

26.3 "It is beneficial to persevere in the face of difficulties." Or, "in the face of adversity," "in times of hardship." Cf. 11.3, 21.4.

26.3 "Practice chariot driving and armed defense daily." *yue zhan yu wei:* literally, say enclose (train, restrain) cart (carriage) guard. Thus another rendering would be : "This is called 'enclosing the cart and guarding it' "; i.e., a metaphor for perseverance in the face of difficulties, somewhat akin to the Western phrase "circling the wagons." Cf. Shaughnessy: "It is called a barrier-cart." However, many commentators read *yue* as *ri* (day, daily), hence the injunction to practice daily."

26.5 "The tusks of a gelded boar." Or, "The boar's tusks are removed." *fen:* remove, geld.

26.6 "Hence one attains the highway of heaven." I.e., because of all that one has done before to accumulate knowledge and power, one naturally travels the correct path. *he tian zhi qu:* literally, "what (or wherefore) heaven's highway." Possibly, "highway of heaven" means the Way (Dao) of heaven, hence one might translate the line "one obtains the way of heaven" (Wilhelm/Baynes). Still another version is "one receives heaven's blessing."

TWENTY-SEVEN

Yi • Nourishment

Keywords:

Jaws
Bulging cheeks
Nourishing others
Being nourished
You are what you eat

Above: Gen • Mountain
Below: Zhen • Thunder

The hexagram Yi resembles an open mouth, with the yang lines at the top and the bottom representing the lips. Alternatively, the hexagram can be viewed from the side, so that the outer lines form jaws and the broken lines represent rows of teeth. The theme of the hexagram is nourishment of all types, including not only the food that we take into our mouths but also our spiritual nourishment. The hexagram thus concerns the proper care of both mind and body, heart and soul. The lower three lines focus on the nourishment of the self; the top three lines emphasize the nourishment of others. Both are concerns of the hexagram as a whole.

The lower trigram is Zhen (Thunder); the upper is Gen (Mountain). The primal energy of thunder buried beneath the mountain symbolizes restraint and the careful cultivation of a person's spiritual development. In the previous hexagram, Da Xu, the creative energy of Qian (Heaven) was hidden beneath the mountain. Thus, both the previous hexagram and this one share a special concern with proper development of human character and faculties.

THE JUDGMENT

Nourishment.
Perseverance brings good fortune.
Observe carefully
How a person provides nourishment to others,
And what he seeks to fill his own mouth with.

This hexagram has a double theme: the nourishment of the self and the nourishment of others. Both are important to a happy life.

Nourishment of the self means care and cultivation of the self. The *Book of Changes* is concerned with much more than the nutrition that comes from eating good food. Nourishment means proper care of the different aspects of the self, including the body, the mind, and the spirit. Just as the health of your body is affected by the quality of the food that you take into your mouth, the health of your life is determined by the quality of the activities that you engage in and the ways that you take care of yourself. Thus, the lesson of Yi is that you truly are what you eat when it comes to bodily nutrition and to forms of intellectual and spiritual nourishment.

If you nourish yourself in the right way, you will be healthier, happier, and better able to deal with the blows and misfortunes of life when they inevitably occur. If you do not attend to your mental, physical, and spiritual health, you will weaken and debilitate yourself. We might make an analogy to junk food: Junk food fills you up in the short run but makes you unhealthy in the long run. There is also spiritual junk food. It is attractive and seductive but ultimately leaves you feeling empty and craving more.

It is up to you to decide what nourishment you will take into your body, what ideas you will take into your mind, and what people you will take into your company. If you neglect exercise and sound diet, you will ruin your body. If you allow negative emotions in and focus your thoughts on what is unimportant or unworthy of you, those thoughts and emotions will frustrate and distract you. If you associate with people who use you and mistreat you, you will harm yourself in the long run. Thus, if you find that you lack peace, it may be because you have brought the causes of disturbance within yourself.

A plant that is regularly watered and attended to grows and flourishes. In the same way, whatever you nourish and attend to will grow and become more important in your life. If you nourish the best parts of yourself, you will become a better, happier, and more well adjusted person. You will be better able to handle whatever life throws at you. And you will help realize the full potential of what your life can be. But if you attend to and nourish what is inferior in yourself, those aspects of your life will eventually come to dominate and you will suffer the consequences. Pander to the worst parts of your character and appetites, and you will debase and devalue yourself and make yourself needlessly unhappy. You will waste your life's potential on what is meaningless and trivial. And you will weaken your body, mind, and spirit so that life can more easily overwhelm you and defeat you. The care of your body and your soul is a question of self-respect. A person who has proper respect for himself takes care of himself; a person who does not respect himself harms himself.

The *Book of Changes* does not insist that human beings are either essentially good or essentially bad. Rather, like everything else in the universe, human beings have inherent tendencies and potentials for change. You can realize the best part of your potential through wise activity and cultivation; you will foster the worst part by taking a contrary path. For this reason one can tell the quality of people by what they cultivate and what they fail to cultivate, what elements of their character they nourish and what they leave untouched, what they lavish their attention on and what they neglect.

It is not enough to nourish yourself. You must also nourish and care for others. One can judge the quality of people not only by how they take care of themselves but also by how they take care of others and on whom they bestow their concern. This hexagram suggests that you should think carefully about who you nourish and who you have failed to nourish properly. To nourish others is a way of nourishing the best parts in your self.

Just as you should exercise judgment in nourishing yourself, you should exercise judgment in nourishing others. Do not waste your time on people who abuse you or manipulate you. There is no point casting your pearls before swine. You should take care of those who cannot take care of themselves, for that is the mark of a superior and generous person. But you should not lavish your attention on those who can but who will not properly take care of themselves. If people do not learn to nourish themselves but repeatedly rely on you to help them out of their problems, you are offering them the wrong sort of nourishment. You must help them learn to help themselves.

THE IMAGE

At the foot of the mountain, thunder:
This is the image of Nourishment.
Thus the superior person is careful in his choice of words,
And temperate in his eating and drinking.

Thunder symbolizes energy and optimism; the mountain symbolizes stillness and tranquility. Taken together the two forces produce balance and symmetry. In the same way you must maintain balance and symmetry in your life.

The activities that you engage in and the food that you eat affect your emotional and physical well-being. So too do the thoughts that you take into your mind. If you eat excessively, or eat unhealthy food, you should not be surprised at the result. In the same way, if you nourish yourself on negative attitudes, negative expectations, self-loathing, and self-abuse, you will not only make yourself miserable but you will help produce a self-fulfilling prophecy. If you expect things to go badly, they are more likely to. If you see every encounter as evidence of your own inadequacy, you will make yourself inadequate. If you view even the good things that happen to you as tinged with bitterness and defeat, bitterness and defeat will come all the more frequently.

Conversely, if you eat good food and are temperate in your diet, you will feel healthier and more energized. In the same way, you nourish your spirit by maintaining emotional balance and tranquility. If you remain faithful and optimistic, and cultivate a positive and hopeful outlook, you are surely not guaranteed to succeed in everything. But your life will be happier. You will find it much easier to adjust to the inevitable changes that life brings, and you will greatly increase the chances that you will find a way out of any difficulties you currently face. You cannot control the world, but you can exercise self-control. You cannot choose how events external to you will play out, but you can choose how you will respond to them.

You also have a say about how you treat other people. That is how you nourish others. Hence the text says that a superior person "is careful in his choice of words." Words spoken foolishly or in anger cannot be taken back. They may cause harm that reverberates long after they are spoken. If you treat others badly, you should not be surprised if they return the favor some day. On the other hand, if you treat people with respect and consideration, you will reap rewards in the long run. Here again bad nourishment leads to bad results; good nourishment leads to good results.

The text argues that there is a deep connection between your "choice of words"—one's behavior toward others—and your temperance "in eating and drinking"—the maintenance of emotional balance and tranquility within the self. Turmoil within yourself leads to turmoil in your dealings with others; conversely, you are more likely to act in a balanced fashion toward others when you yourself are balanced. To nourish others properly, you must nourish yourself properly and vice versa. To make peace, put yourself at peace.

THE LINES

The lines describe various aspects of nourishment and the spiritual ascendance of the subject from the one who seeks nourishment to the one who provides it to others. The first three lines concern nourishing one's self. The last three lines concern nourishing others. The first three lines depict improper nourishment and are generally inauspicious; the last three concern proper nourishment and are generally auspicious.

In line one, the subject is greedy and envious. In line two, he does not recognize that he must learn to nourish himself. In line three he nourishes himself on the wrong things. In lines four and five, the subject begins the process that culminates in line six: He takes on the heavy responsibility of being the source of nourishment to others.

Initial Nine

You let your sacred tortoise go,
And look at me with open mouth.
Misfortune.

The shell of the sacred or magic tortoise was used for divination. To let go of one's magic tortoise means to give up one's independence, control, and self-reliance. One neglects one's spiritual nourishment and instead looks at others enviously "with open mouth."

Do not become consumed with concern for what other people have. Envying others does you no good. It fills your heart and mind with negative emotions and destroys your self-respect. If you spend your time comparing yourself to others and feeling deprived and slighted because they have things that you do not, you will lose control of your destiny. You will neglect your spiritual nourishment and fill yourself with bitterness, resentment, and despair. Your own situation and accomplishments will seem petty and base and you will live your life in thrall to your imagined vision of others. This can only lead to disaster.

Try to appreciate the good things that you have in life. Don't act out of a desire to even the score or to get what others have. Pursue your own goals. Forge your own destiny. In this way you will gain peace of mind.

Six in the Second Place

Overturning,
Seeking nourishment.
Rejecting the standard way.
Moving toward the hill for nourishment.
Continuing in this way brings misfortune.

You need to learn how to nourish yourself properly. You must take care of your own needs and not turn to others to do what you can do for yourself. If you shirk your responsibilities, and inappropriately lean on others as a crutch, you will weaken yourself in the long run. Learn to be more self-reliant.

Six in the Third Place

Rejecting nourishment.
Perseverance brings misfortune.
Do not act like this for ten years.
There is nothing for which this is beneficial.

"To reject nourishment" means to seek nourishment from the wrong places. You are what you eat both physically and spiritually. A person who rejects healthy things and gorges on junk food fails to give himself proper nutrition and in the long run injures his health. A person who abandons things that strengthen his character and who absorbs the spiritual equivalent of junk food also fails to nourish himself properly. Thus, the text advises, "Do not act like this for ten years," ten years being a complete cycle of time.

Because you are looking for the wrong things to nourish you, you feel unhappy and incomplete. You are caught in an endless cycle of desire and gratification that never fills you up. This analysis may apply to what you eat, how you behave, or the company you keep. As a result, you coarsen your character, deplete your energies, and turn away from people who might be good for you. Unless you change your ways, misfortune will result.

Six in the Fourth Place

Overturning,
Seeking nourishment.
Good fortune.
The tiger fixes its gaze, glaring, staring.
Its desire reaches far.
No blame.

A tiger is an animal full of desire. However, if your desires are upright, there is no harm in going after them with the single-mindedness of a tiger. In particular, seeking to nourish others is an especially worthy endeavor and you may pursue it zealously. You have the necessary talents to support and benefit others, but because you cannot do this alone, you should look for the right people to help you. There is no blame in doing this, because you are working for the good of others and not simply for yourself.

Six in the Fifth Place (Ruling Line)

Rejecting the standard way.
Remaining constant and steadfastly faithful brings good fortune.
It is not appropriate to cross the great river.

"Rejecting the standard way" means turning from ordinary activities and achieving things through indirection. You would like to nourish and help other people, but you find that you are unable to do so by yourself, because you lack the ability or the resources. Hence you should not try to attempt such a great undertaking by yourself. Seek out people with the knowledge and the ability to do the job and work under their guidance and direction.

Nine at the Top (Ruling Line)

The source of nourishment.
Danger, but good fortune.
It is beneficial to cross the great river.

You are in an excellent position to educate, influence, and nourish others. But taking on such a task carries heavy responsibilities. If you are aware of the seriousness of the endeavor, you can do much good and you will bring much happiness to others.

NOTES

27.0 "Observe carefully." Or, "Pay attention to."

27.GI "careful in his choice of words." Or, "watches his words carefully."

27.1 "sacred tortoise." *ling:* numinous, sacred, magic. *gui:* tortoise, tortoise shell used for divination.

27.1 "And look at me with open mouth." This could be translated as either "And look at me with your mouth open (jaws hanging down, jaws dropped open)," or "And look at me with my mouth open." Either way, the line connotes envy of what another person has, to the neglect of one's own spiritual nourishment and development.

27.2 "Rejecting the standard way." Or, "Deviating from the standard," "Deviating from the path." *jing:* standard, normal, canonical, classic.

27.2 "toward the hill." *qiu:* hill, summit. Cf. 22.5, 59.4.

27.3 "Rejecting nourishment." Or, "Turning away from nourishment."

27.4 "The tiger fixes its gaze, glaring, staring. / Its desire reaches far." *hu shi dan dan qi yu zhu zhu:* This line is subject to many different translations, viz., "Such a one should stare down with the ferocious look of a tiger, and his will should be strong and persistent" (Lynn); "Spying about with sharp eyes / Like a tiger with insatiable craving" (Wilhelm/Baynes); "The tiger's gaze is steady, / but what it wants lies far away" (Whincup).

27.5 "constant and steadfastly faithful." *zhen:* persevering. Here again the familiar gloss seems appropriate.

27.5 "It is not appropriate." *bu ke:* it is not possible; one should not.

TWENTY-EIGHT

Da Guo • Greatness in Excess

䷛

Keywords:

Preponderance of the great
Too much
Overload
Critical mass
Taking a stand
Setting priorities
Making choices

Above: Dui • Lake
Below: Xun • Wind (Wood)

Da Guo consists of four yang lines situated between two broken lines at the top and bottom. Viewed from the side, the hexagram represents a supporting beam that is strong and thick in the middle and weak and thin on the ends. Thus it tends to sag in the middle. Because of the heavy weight that the beam bears, it cannot remain without support for long. Hence the hexagram symbolizes a condition that cannot last, or a phase that one must pass through. Something must be done; a choice must be made, or else misfortune is the likely result.

THE JUDGMENT

Greatness in Excess.
The ridgepole sags.
It is beneficial to have somewhere to go.
Success.

The ridgepole is a support beam on which the weight of the entire roof rests. The load that it bears is too great; therefore, it sags to the breaking point. The ridgepole is a metaphor for a situation in which stresses and strains have reached their maximum. Something will have to give.

Da Guo describes an exceptional time. Circumstances have reached a point of crisis. You face great pressures from all directions. Perhaps you have taken on too much, or perhaps obligations and expectations that were at one point bearable and reasonable have slowly but surely increased to the point that they have become too great. Whatever the case, something needs to be done, and quickly. You must make a transition to a new situation without delay. Nevertheless, you cannot force matters. A sudden movement of the ridgepole under great stress will snap it, bringing the whole roof crashing down. In the same way, the stresses and strains of the situation cannot be relieved by rash action.

Instead, you must carefully consider the underlying causes of the crisis that you now find yourself in. There is "too much" in the situation, but you need to figure out what that "too much" is. Perhaps you have overestimated what you can do because you are too eager to get ahead, or because you lack the necessary skills and talents. You have not learned the value of patience and proper preparation. Perhaps you have become too aggressive or too obsessive, on the one hand, or too anxious and apprehensive on the other. Your fears and obsessions have cut you off from others, or have led you to engage in self-destructive habits. Perhaps the pressure comes from your relationships with others. You or another person may be engaged in obsessive or excessive behavior. Your judgment—or theirs—is impaired because emotions and insecurities are running high.

Whatever the problem, you must act now to restore balance in your life. It is up to you to restore a sense of reality and stability to the situation. Things cannot go on as they have been. You must reassess your priorities. You must make a change.

Once you have decided what the problem is, you must act quickly but with gentleness and composure. The time calls for extraordinary measures, but the transition to the new situation must be peaceful and nonviolent. The problem has been a growing imbalance. The solution will only come from restoring balance, not from exacerbating the problem. A time of greatness in excess calls for a corresponding greatness in your character. Not only must you recognize the need for change, but you must carry it out gently and swiftly, without fear or anxiety.

THE IMAGE

The lake rises over the trees:
This is the image of Greatness in Excess.
Thus the superior person, when he stands alone, is unafraid,
And if he has to renounce the world, he is undaunted.

When the lake floods and rises over the trees, it is time to take extraordinary measures. This is no time for panic or despair. You must simply put your priorities in order and do what is necessary. You must remain firm and undaunted in the face of difficulties. In a time of crisis you must give up some things to preserve others. People will not always approve of your choices. But you cannot let your life be determined by the approval of others. You must do what is best for you now, given the circumstances that you alone face.

It is not possible to meet all of the demands and expectations placed upon you. Some of those expectations have been created by other people; and some have been self-imposed through ambition, desire, anxiety, and fear. Take a close look at all of the demands on your time and resources. Some of these may have gone unnoticed, and they may be distracting you from things that are actually much more important to you.

It is time to stop and take the larger view. What are your values? Who and what is most important to you? What relationships are most central to your happiness? What is most worthy of your time and attention? These may be difficult questions. But you cannot hope to make the right choices unless you confront them. You should regard the current crisis as an opportunity to clarify your values, straighten out your priorities, and set yourself on the right path. Life is short. You cannot do everything. Your time and your abilities are finite. You must decide who you are and what you hope to be, what you seek to preserve and what you need to relinquish. In the end, your individuality is determined not only by what you decide to do but what you decide not to do, not only by what you cling to but by what you let go.

The quandary you now face may turn out to be a blessing in disguise, because it forces you to confront what has been happening in your life. You need to pare away what is inessential so that you can reorganize your thoughts and actions around what is most meaningful and important to you. To do this you may have to give up things. You may have to go it alone. But if you have courage and determination, you will succeed.

THE LINES

The lines use a variety of different metaphors to describe the theme of the hexagram. One metaphor is the withered willow tree (lines two and five), which concerns unusual alliances with people whose situation is beneath or subordinate to the subject. Support from those below is also implicit in a second metaphor—the ridgepole of a house (lines three and four), which buckles if it is not properly braced from below. The metaphor of the offering mat in line one describes a state of solemn preparation for the arduous task ahead, while in line six, one has no choice but to go forward. The striking metaphor of walking into water that is over one's head anticipates the theme of the next hexagram, 29, Xi Kan, which is variously translated as Water, Danger, or The Abyss.

Initial Six

Spreading white cogon grasses as an offering mat.
No blame.

One spreads white grasses in preparation for religious devotion. This is a metaphor for earnestness and circumspection at the beginning of any great enterprise. Although arranging white grasses to form an offering mat might seem to be a minor or merely symbolic detail, doing so helps achieve the right frame of mind.

When you begin an important endeavor, be cautious. Approach the task ahead with seriousness and devotion. Prepare carefully and plan meticulously. Do not regard any aspect of the work as beneath you. Difficult undertakings require great attention to detail at the beginning in order to achieve great success at their completion.

Nine in the Second Place (Ruling Line)

A withered willow sprouts new branches.
An old man takes a young wife.
There is nothing that is not beneficial.

It is unusual that a withered willow tree could sprout new branches; it is unorthodox for an old man to take a young wife. But both cases also symbolize hope and the possibility of renewal. In like fashion, consider how strange and unexpected elements might bring new life to the situation. Consider alliances with different people or unorthodox means of achieving your goals. People who are new to the situation may have a fresh approach. Join forces with beginners, with people in comparatively humble circumstances, and with those who have not yet made their way up the ladder of success. They will be grateful for your confidence. You in turn will gain much from their support, and you may learn something new and different from them.

Nine in the Third Place

The ridgepole buckles.
Misfortune.

When a ridgepole carries a heavy burden, it will buckle unless it receives support from below. When you find yourself overloaded or faced with serious obstacles, you should not become arrogant and stubborn. Do not try to push forward, for you cannot overcome the problem through brute force. No matter how determined you are to succeed, do not become a victim of tunnel vision. The most important thing now is not to shut yourself off from people. Listen to what others have to say, even if it is not what you want to hear. Consulting with others is important not merely because they may have a useful perspective but because if you do not listen you will isolate yourself. Cooperation and modesty are essential in a difficult situation. If you will not accept help and advice from others, or if you become overbearing and obstinate, people will not be there to help you when you need it. You will not have support from below to brace you, and hence the situation will fall apart or you will buckle under the pressure.

Nine in the Fourth Place (Ruling Line)

The ridgepole curves upward.
Good fortune.
If there is something else,
Humiliation.

This line is the converse of the third. A ridgepole that is braced can bear a heavy load. Similarly, if you reach out to others, especially people with less status than yourself, you can achieve important goals that will benefit everybody. But cooperation carries obligations of mutuality and respect. Do not use people instrumentally, or for ulterior motives. Do not misuse your connections to enrich yourself or attempt to enhance your power at the expense of others, or you will destroy the trust that now supports you. If you work for selfish aims instead of for the good of the group, you will meet with humiliation.

Nine in the Fifth Place

A withered willow puts forth flowers.
An old woman takes a young husband.
No blame. No praise.

In line two the metaphors offered the hope of renewal. The metaphors in line five symbolize an attempt at renewal that is fruitless. Flowers exhaust the energies of a withered willow and hasten its end; an older woman may marry a younger man, but she still will not be able to bear children. In both cases the renewal does not succeed because the foundations were not appropriate. The expression "No blame. No praise" means that the situation is simply laid bare, presented as it is.

You are faced with difficult and critical problems. You must assess them realistically rather than place your hopes on an uncertain adventure or a last-gasp effort. You need to get to the heart of the matter and look deeply into the foundations of the current situation. Find out what the real problems are and take action before things get out of hand. If you ignore the roots of the difficulty, your solutions will not last.

This line also offers advice about cooperation with others. In difficult times people are often tempted to forge alliances with people above and forsake those below. They try to curry favor with powerful or influential people and forget the people who they regard as less powerful or beneath them. Do not be a fair-weather friend. Your relations with people should not depend on whether they can help you in the current milieu. This is not a proper basis for trust or cooperation and ultimately will being instability and humiliation.

Six at the Top

Passing through the water.
It goes over one's head.
Misfortune. No blame.

The message of this line is simple: You are in over your head, but it is not your fault. You have courage and you wish to achieve your goals no matter what happens. If your goals are worthwhile, this is commendable. Nevertheless you are in great danger, and the sacrifices that it will take to go forward may be enormous. You are the only person who can decide whether the cost of success is worth it. Hence the text advises, "No blame." If you are truly called to do good, no one has the right to judge you. Some things are worth any sacrifice, including life itself.

NOTES

28.0 "The ridgepole sags." I.e., to the breaking point.

28.GI "when he stands alone, is unafraid." Or, "though he may have to stand alone, he does so without fear (is undaunted, unconcerned)."

28.GI "And if he has to renounce the world, he is undaunted." Or, "If he has to withdraw from the world (the age), he remains free from resentment (without melancholy)."

28.2 "willow." Or, "poplar."

28.2 "sprouts new branches." Or, "produces sprigs," "sprouts shoots."

28.3 "buckles." Or, "collapses," "sags to the breaking point" (Wilhelm/Baynes). *rao:* sags, buckles. The same word appears in the hexagram text at 28.0, but line three is usually a line of unfortunate circumstances, so the word "buckles," or "collapses," would be more appropriate.

28.4 "curves upward." Or, "bulges upward," "is braced" (Wilhelm/Baynes).

28.4 "If there is something else." *you ta:* "there is this." This can be translated in several ways. For example, *ta* might mean harm, so the line might be translated, "If there is harm," "If there is an accident (unanticipated harm)," or "If there is disaster." Another reading of *ta* is as "more," "something else," or "this in addition." Hence the line might be translated, "If one has more." Wilhelm/Baynes translates this as "If there are ulterior motives." Cf. 61.1, which Wilhelm/Baynes translates as "If there are secret designs."

28.5 "puts forth." Or, "produces."

TWENTY-NINE

Xi Kan • The Abyss

䷜

Keywords:

Water
Darkness
Danger
Despair
The abysmal
Courage and devotion
Maintaining faith
Pushing through the rapids
Getting through to the other side

Above: Kan • Water
Below: Kan • Water

Xi Kan is the trigram Kan (Water) doubled. (Xi means "repeated.") The trigram Kan features a yang line between two yin lines. The yin lines symbolize a deep and dark ravine; the yang line symbolizes the water that flows through it. Hence, Xi Kan means both danger and abyss. Water is a symbol of danger in the *Book of Changes*. When water rushes through a narrow passage, it is quite powerful and therefore dangerous. Similarly, to "cross the great river" means to attempt something difficult and therefore potentially hazardous. Water doubled means repeated danger, like a series of rapids that one must plunge into again and again.

However, water also symbolizes emotion and, more generally, a person's heart and soul. The connection between these two ideas—danger and the soul—suggests the hexagram's central theme: When faced with danger from without, one can escape unharmed if one maintains an attitude of devotion. To survive through a period of danger, one must preserve faith in one's self and in the possibility that one will get through. The *Book of Changes* teaches that even in the times of greatest distress one must never lose hope that one can still turn circumstances to one's advantage. One must have faith of ultimate success because it is only through having such faith that one can have a chance at ultimate success. To despair is to fall into the abyss. The abyss symbolized in the hexagram is thus both a physical danger and an emotional state. Thus, one must follow one's heart to ride out a time of danger. To lose heart during such a time means that one does not hold one's self together. This leads to disaster.

THE JUDGMENT

Repeated Abyss.
If you are truthful and sincere,
And follow your heart,
Then you will have success,
And your actions will bring esteem.

You face a difficult and dangerous situation. You cannot wish it away. You must rise to the challenge and handle the dangers in front of you. Water symbolizes danger, and water also symbolizes the proper way to behave during times of danger. Water is a part of nature and behaves naturally. No matter what happens, it is true to itself. It flows forward without pause. It fills up every place it travels, no matter how lowly. It does not hesitate to move downward in order to move forward. It does not refuse to travel through dangerous places or to take a plunge. It follows its own course, pressing ever onward through rocks and ravines until it reaches the calmness of the ocean. In like fashion, when confronted with difficulties, you must be like water: true to yourself, moving forward without hesitation, and not disdaining to do whatever is necessary to push through the dangerous conditions into safety.

The text emphasizes truth and sincerity. It says that you can proceed through danger successfully if you are sincere. To be sincere means first that you are not lying to yourself or deluding yourself. Do not engage in wishful thinking. Accept matters as they are and not as you would like them to be. Equally important, be true to yourself. Understand who you are, what you believe, and what you stand for.

Sincerity also means that you are connected to and making use of all of your emotional resources. You must summon up all your courage. If you can master yourself, you are in the best possible position to master the situation. And once you have gotten in touch with your heart, you will instinctively know what you have to do to survive. Being honest with yourself does not mean pessimism or despair. Quite the contrary: The lesson of the *Book of Changes* is that true courage comes from confronting yourself as you are, making use of what you have inside you, and not running away from your nature. People who engage in pessimism and self-abuse may be as out of touch with reality and with themselves as people who display an excess of pride. If you are sincere, and willing to accept yourself, you will discover that there is much more to you than you imagined.

Sincerity means, finally, that you must believe in yourself. Do not lose heart. Stand up for your beliefs and maintain your integrity. When the chips are down, it is less important what other people think than what you believe. Remain true to your deepest values. To face danger and to face the disapproval and misunderstanding of others takes courage. But if you are not true to yourself in time of danger, you will lose yourself in time of danger.

To succeed in a dangerous situation, you must be thorough and persistent, proceeding without hesitation, like water flowing through a deep ravine. You must do whatever it takes to move past your difficulties. To vacillate when there is work to be done will only increase the perils you face. Like a person traveling through rapids, you must propel yourself forward through the situation in order to reach safety. You must push through, no matter how bad it may seem, for safety lies not where you are but on the other side.

Danger is a part of life. It cannot be avoided. Like the rapids, we must move through it in order to get to safety. That is why courage is one of the most important values in life. To risk danger may sometimes require physical courage. But the most important asset you can have is emotional courage—the ability to face up to your situation and to who you really are. Emotional courage is a form of self-knowledge. That is why the *Book of Changes* emphasizes truth and sincerity in times of danger, for one succeeds in facing danger through self-knowledge. Danger can clarify your thinking. It can help you understand yourself, what you truly care about, and what you must do. Thus, paradoxically, danger protects as well as threatens: Facing danger makes you stronger if you do not allow yourself to be overwhelmed by it.

THE IMAGE

Water flows incessantly toward its goal:
This is the image of the Abyss repeated.
Thus the superior person walks in lasting virtue
And carries on the work of edification.

Water flows incessantly toward its goal. It never gives up. In the same way, you must be determined to see things through. No matter how severe the obstacles that you face, you must carry on. The world is testing you. You must maintain your patience and your devotion. Take things one day at a time. Just make sure that you keep going and do not lose heart.

The enemy you confront is more than a set of forces in the outside world. The enemy is pessimism and lack of faith in yourself. This is the abyss that is the subject of the hexagram. It is not a physical abyss but a spiritual one. To give up and give in now is the worst possible thing that you could do. It leaves you trapped in the abyss. To get out of the abyss you must free yourself from negative thinking. You must not allow yourself to become a prisoner of despair. To ride through the danger that is without, you must face up to and vanquish the danger that is within. Hence you must follow the example of water, which stops for nothing, which pushes through every crack and crevice, which never loses heart, but continually flows forward until it reaches its goal.

Your ability to withstand difficult times depends on your inner strength. Adversity breeds character, but character is necessary to survive adversity. Therefore, you should not wait for danger to arise to test your mettle. You should develop habits of persistence and devotion and make them part of your everyday life. If you carry on the work of edification each and every day, it will be easier to get through the rough times when they occur.

THE LINES

The lines describe what to do in a condition of extreme danger. The danger begins in line one. In lines two through five, the *Book of Changes* advises caution and circumspection. In line six, one has become trapped in danger, and must wait for better times.

Initial Six

The Abyss repeated.
Entering the abyss, one falls into a pit.
Misfortune.

You have allowed yourself to become accustomed to a dangerous and harmful situation. This may be due to ignorance, weakness of will, or simply a belief that bad things will never happen to you. Whatever the reason, you have "fall[en] into the pit." You have lost your way. What is worse, because you have become used to bad influences and decaying conditions, you fail to recognize their seriousness or understand how they might be harming you. If you keep going the way you have, misfortune is inevitable. You need to wake up, reassess the situation, and reform yourself.

Nine in the Second Place (Ruling Line)

The abyss is dangerous.
Try to achieve small things only.

Great dangers usually cannot be escaped in a single valiant effort. Often they have come about through a long sequence of events, and they can only be overcome through patience and persistence. Right now the best thing to do is to try to keep afloat while you gather intelligence and take stock of the dangers you face. Be patient and plan your comeback carefully. Try to progress steadily and cautiously, step by step. You must content yourself with small improvements now, because the situation is not entirely clear and you cannot achieve complete success overnight.

Six in the Third Place

Before and behind,
Abyss upon abyss.
Dangerous and deep as well.
If one enters the abyss, one falls into the pit.
Do not act.

You are surrounded by forces that you do not fully understand. If you try to act now, you will only make matters worse. You are in more trouble than you think. Do not dig yourself in deeper. Exercise self-control. Stop struggling in vain and try to regain some clarity of mind. You must wait patiently now until a solution to your difficulties becomes apparent.

Six in the Fourth Place

A jug of wine, along with a bowl.
Earthenware vessels,
Lowered by rope through the window.
In the end, no blame.

Earthenware vessels are a symbol of simplicity and sincerity. They signify that content is more important than form, and that what is inside is more important than the vessel that contains it. When the chips are down, people drop pretense and ceremony. What matters are the most basic virtues: sincerity, trustworthiness, integrity, and courage. People with such virtues modestly offer themselves to work with others in times of danger, and hence they are accepted gratefully, like a jug of wine and a bowl of food lowered through a window to a hungry captive.

To get through your present difficulties you must be like the earthenware vessels. Drop all pretense and return to basics. Clarify your thoughts and focus on substance rather than outward display. In your dealings with others, be straightforward and sincere and you will gain allies. If people trust you, everyone can work together to surmount the obstacles. You may worry that you are not good enough or that you have nothing special to offer, but if you demonstrate that you are genuinely willing to be of help, others will accept you.

Nine in the Fifth Place (Ruling Line)

The abyss does not overflow.
It is filled only to the rim.
No blame.

The metaphor of the water that fills to the rim but does not overflow describes both your present situation and how to respond to it. Water is a symbol of danger. Water that fills almost to the rim but does not overflow means that although you are in great difficulty, if you act correctly, you will escape from harm in the end.

The metaphor of water also suggests the proper approach. A person in a rushing stream should not fight the current. He should float or swim with the tide, pointing himself toward the bank so that the force of the water will carry him to land. In like fashion you should not try to force matters now, but rather follow the flow of events and take the path of least resistance to safety. Do not be too ambitious. Be content with getting out of danger, and leave great undertakings to another day. If you are patient, the situation will gradually improve itself.

Six at the Top

Bound with cords and ropes,
Placed in a thicket of thorns.
For three years one achieves nothing.
Misfortune.

The cords and ropes are ceremonial symbols of authority used in criminal sentencing. The thicket of thorns is one that surrounds a prison. The sentence of three years represents a cycle of time that must run its course before one can regain one's spiritual and physical freedom.

The text describes a person who has forsaken the correct path and has become entangled in wrongful conduct with no prospect of escape. By responding incorrectly to danger, one makes it all the more difficult to extricate one's self from it. The point of the metaphor is that there are really two kinds of confinement—the external prison of unhappy circumstances and the internal prison of one who cannot break free from self-destructive attitudes and behaviors. The second form of confinement leads inevitably to the first. Then all one can do is to bear one's situation patiently until the cycle has run its course.

You have been traveling in the wrong direction for some time, but obstinacy, pride or self-indulgence have kept you from seeing this. As a result, you are stuck in a very difficult situation that prevents you from making things better. Now you face a long period of disorder. Take stock of your life and prepare yourself to return to the proper path. Until you commit yourself to your spiritual redemption, matters will not improve. The sorrow of this final line prepares the way for the next hexagram, Li, symbolizing the emergence of clarity and enlightenment after a period of great darkness.

NOTES

29.0 "And follow your heart." Or, "rely on," "hold fast to." *wei*: link to, connect, hold together. *xin*: the heart, or heart and mind. Cf. 42.6. The point is both that you must stay connected to your feelings and that you must rely on your heart to hold yourself together during a time of crisis. Wilhelm/Baynes translates the entire passage as "If you are sincere, you have success in your heart, / And whatever you do succeeds."

29.GI "And carries on the work of edification." Or, "carries on the business of teaching" (Wilhelm/Baynes); "constantly engages in moral transformation" (Lynn).

29.3 "Before and behind." Or, "Coming and going," "Forward and backward."

29.3 "Do not act." Or, "Do not act this way."

29.4 "a bowl." Or, "a platter," "a bowl of rice."

29.4 "Lowered by," etc. Or, "Passed in by."

29.5 "does not overflow." I.e., it is not filled to overflowing.

29.6 "Bound with cords and ropes," etc. Because these are metaphors of imprisonment, the line could be translated, "Bound and sentenced to jail, he is imprisoned for three years."

THIRTY

Li • Radiance

䷝

Keywords:

The clinging
Interdependence
Synergy
Understanding connections and interdependencies
Fire
Brilliance
Clarity
Shedding light on things
Enlightenment

Above: Li • Fire
Below: Li • Fire

Li is the complement of the previous hexagram, Xi Kan. It consists of the trigram Li (Radiance, Fire) doubled. The trigram Li consists of two yang lines surrounding a single yin line. Thus, fire is symbolized by brightness without and an empty space within. Fire is radiant, shedding light on things and clarifying them. This is the first theme of the hexagram. However, fire is only radiant as long as it burns; and it burns only as long as it has fuel that it clings to. Thus the second theme of Li is interdependence and synergy.

THE JUDGMENT

Radiance.
It is beneficial to persevere.
Success.
Raising a cow brings good fortune.

The two great themes of Li are enlightenment and interdependence. Fire sheds light on everything as its radiance extends outward; but it burns brightly only as long has it has fuel to draw on. As long as the fuel lasts, the fire lasts. Whatever gives light, clarifies, and enlightens depends on something else to which it clings, something whose persistence and perseverance allows the light to shine. Hence the text says that in order to be radiant, it is beneficial to persevere. Our brilliance cannot continue long if we do not take care to preserve the things that allow us to shine.

Enlightenment means understanding the conditioned and interdependent nature of existence—how things depend on each other for their being and their continuation. What seems to be self-sustaining and independent actually clings to something else that is the source of its power and preservation. When what supports a thing changes, so too must the thing that depends on it. It is like the flame that clings to its fuel; when the fuel is exhausted, the fire will not last long. We cannot change one element in an interconnected system without changing the others as well, or remove one element without affecting the things that depend on it and on which it depends. If we fail to understand the multiple forms of interdependence in life, the network of interrelated causes and effects, and the existence of synergies and interconnections, we are not truly enlightened.

So it is with human life. The life of human beings is not free and independent. It is conditioned on circumstances and, in particular, on other human beings. If you wish to gain clarity in your life, you must understand who and what you depend on and who and what depends on you. You are never free of everything and everyone. You cling to something just as a fire clings to its fuel. But it is up to you to decide what to cling to. If you cling to what is beneficial and healthy, you will be secure and your life will be well ordered. If you cling to what is disordered and decaying, you will be thrown about as conditions change, and your position and your peace of mind will not last long. If you hold on to things that are bad for you, or have outlived their usefulness in your life, you are enslaved. But if you cling to what is good and ally yourself with what is beneficent and harmonious, you are free.

Human freedom emerges out of unfreedom, out of the spaces created by our conditioned existence and our dependence on others. To realize your freedom you must first understand those conditions and interdependencies. That is the sense in which enlightenment makes a person free. It is not because having understood your situation you are no longer conditioned or interdependent; it is because you come to understand its hidden possibilities—what can be changed and what cannot. This knowledge allows you to imagine how to capitalize on dependencies and create new synergies. In this way you can achieve success.

According to the text, "raising a cow" brings good fortune. The cow symbolizes docility; care of the cow symbolizes nurturance. Enlightenment means accepting the world for what it is, recognizing one's connection to others, and taking care of what needs to be taken care of. This is the path to clarity and to peace. Acceptance does not mean resignation. It means facing up to the facts. Only when we accept the world can we begin to work with it to improve it and our situation within it.

Do not cling to the past, for it is gone and it will not return. Accept change. Be open-minded and adaptable. Don't overreact with anger or despair and don't bury your head in the sand. Don't bemoan your fate. Consider how you can change things for the better, given the situation you now face. Nurture others and you will nurture yourself.

THE IMAGE

Brightness doubled generates radiance that spreads in all directions:
This is the image of Fire.
In the same way great people perpetuate their brilliance
To illuminate the four corners of the world.

To shed light on your situation you must gain some emotional detachment. Do not take things personally, and do not allow snubs and slights, whether real or perceived, to get to you. Do not let yourself become enslaved to anxiety, pessimism, or despair. If you allow emotions to cloud your thinking, you will be unable to respond to changing circumstances in the best way. Put aside any selfishness and self-centeredness. If you view matters only in terms of how they might benefit or harm you, you will either engage in wishful thinking or you will fail to see the larger picture, or both. Hence the text says that illumination within—clarity, unselfishness, and acceptance—brings illumination to the world around us.

Enlightenment is not for ourselves alone; it is for others as well. Through clarity about ourselves we can bring clarity to others. Fire is a symbol of synergy as well as of enlightenment: fire lets loose potential energies already contained in wood. In the same way, clarity of mind will help you release positive energies latent in the situation. It is up to you to rethink and reassess things. Consider how you can turn short-term disadvantage into long-term advantage. Consider how you and others can work together to achieve what none of you could do alone.

Fire is an apt symbol of enlightenment because the power of truth is increased when it spreads to other minds. One candle lights another, and the amount of illumination is doubled without anyone's light being diminished. For this reason, superior people do not hoard their knowledge or their wisdom but willingly share it with others who are willing to receive it. In this way enlightenment eventually can reach "to the four corners of the world."

THE LINES

The lines emphasize the two attributes of fire: dependence and illumination. Lines two, three, and four concern interdependence. Line two, the ruler of the hexagram, states its theme: Fire burns brightly as long as it can depend on something else to fuel it. Line three describes a person who clings too tenaciously to what is passing away. By contrast, in line four one pays no attention to dependence and therefore is a mere flash in the pan. Lines one, five, and six stress illumination and clarity. Clarity of mind dispels confusion (line one), allows us to recognize the transitoriness of all things (line five); and helps us distinguish the real sources of evil in any situation (line six).

Initial Nine

Confused footsteps.
If one has respect,
No blame.

People who wake from sleep are at first confused about their surroundings. In the same way, people who begin a new task face a confusing set of impressions and potential pathways. There is much to do, and it is not yet clear where to start or what direction to travel. Hence the text says, "Confused footsteps."

When you face a new situation, you must sort out the possibilities and gain some perspective before you can make any progress. Remain composed. Proceed carefully, paying close attention to detail. Decide what your goals are and keep them always in mind. In this way you will not be distracted and confused by the hustle and bustle of events. Remember that you are only at the beginning of this endeavor. Treat its complexities with seriousness and respect and you will make steady progress.

Six in the Second Place (Ruling Line)

Yellow light. Supreme good fortune.

Yellow is the color of the mean; hence "yellow light" means that you can achieve clarity and enlightenment through following the path of moderation. By taking a balanced attitude toward life, and by avoiding excess and extravagance, you will be able to see the world more clearly. Moderation allows you to be more open-minded and pragmatic than people who lack inner composure. You can respond to new ideas and situations without feeling unduly threatened or disoriented by them. Hence when confronted with change or novel ideas, you are not easily thrown. Because you possess a stable core, you don't get carried away by reckless enthusiasms or feel threatened and fall into harsh and aggressive reactions. Instead, you are able to adjust to changing circumstances, selecting the best elements from the new while preserving the most sensible features of the old. By following this path you will succeed brilliantly.

Nine in the Third Place

In the light of the setting sun,
They either beat the pot and sing
Or loudly bewail the approach of old age.
Misfortune.

The setting sun symbolizes that something that you have depended on in the past is about to end. Misfortune befalls people if they "beat the pot and sing"—pretending that circumstances have not altered—or if they "loudly bewail" the end of old conditions and refuse to acknowledge new ones. The lesson of this line is acceptance of changed conditions. What is past is past. It is gone and will not return. Living in the past and refusing to acknowledge the future are forms of servitude. Be adaptable. Do not make yourself unhappy with regrets. Look forward, not backward. Live in the here and now. Even though what you once took for granted or depended on has passed away, the future holds new and different opportunities if you learn to look for them. Wise people recognize the signs of transition and do not bemoan the inevitable. Such people have true clarity of mind.

Nine in the Fourth Place

It comes suddenly.
It burns up, dies out, and is thrown away.

Fire lasts only so long as it has fuel to burn. Clarity lasts only so long as a person maintains and nourishes his sources of enlightenment. Achievement depends on a constant source of energy and commitment.

You are in danger of becoming too enthusiastic without having the necessary follow-through. The text compares this to a meteor or a fire that burns very hot at the beginning but quickly flares out. Slow down. If you are excitable and restless, you will not be able to achieve anything of lasting value. If you expend too much energy in the initial stages, there will be none left later on. You will burn yourself out and your efforts will be a mere flash in the pan.

The text also describes people who seek quick and sudden prominence, fame or wealth, but are unwilling to make the necessary preparations or do the necessary work to make their accomplishments worthy and lasting. Without the right values and commitments, a meteoric rise often presages an equally rapid descent. Such people may enjoy favor for a time, but they usually leave nothing of value and the world quickly discards them. On the other hand, the sudden rise of a truly successful person is a mere illusion, for it is usually the result of commitment, sacrifice, and long efforts at perfecting one's craft that have gone unnoticed by the outside world.

Six in the Fifth Place (Ruling Line)

Tears fall like heavy rain.
Sighing and lamentation.
Good fortune.

With enlightenment comes an understanding of the transitoriness of life, the persistence of change, and the necessity of adapting to it. As you perceive your situation more clearly, you realize that you must give up certain things. You must come to terms with important matters in your life that you had previously downplayed or neglected. Your values and priorities become clearer, and you undergo a genuine change of heart. This experience inevitably brings a deep sense of sadness because you recognize all too clearly what you must leave behind. But these feelings will pass. True clarity of mind also brings acceptance of new realities. In time, your sadness will turn to joy. Because you better understand your situation, you know what changes you must make, and this will bring you good fortune in the end.

Nine at the Top

The king sends him out to attack.
It is praiseworthy to execute the leaders,
But only capture the followers.
No blame.

To execute the leaders but spare the followers means to get to the real source of a difficulty and leave untouched what is harmless or can be turned to advantage. As a matter of military strategy, it is always best to turn an adversary's resources into one's own rather than destroying them outright. Thus in putting down a rebellion one should eliminate only the ringleaders but spare those followers who can be turned to a better path. In this way one does not perpetuate social strife unnecessarily but instead moves toward reestablishing peace and harmony.

You need to get to the heart of the problems in your current environment and eliminate them forthwith. The cause may be bad behavior by particular individuals or bad habits and practices in a group or organization. Act decisively in holding the appropriate people responsible. But exercise moderation and restraint in dealing with people who may have been misled or misinformed. They can be valuable allies if you treat them with respect. Do only what is necessary to set things right.

Similar considerations apply if the problem that needs eradicating is personal—a bad habit or a weakness of character. Don't engage in wishful thinking. Accept reality. Start changing your behavior immediately. But don't be too hard on yourself or engage in dramatic acts of self-sacrifice or asceticism that will eventually prove counterproductive. You are trying to restore a proper balance to your life, not punish yourself needlessly. Just do what is necessary to turn to the right path, and then stick to it.

NOTES

30.0. "Raising a cow." Or, "Taking care of (keeping) cows."

30.1 "Confused footsteps." Or, "Footsteps follow in disorder." *cuo ran:* criss-cross, crosswise, suggesting confusion or disorder.

30.4 "thrown away." *qi:* abandoned, discarded.

30.5 "Tears fall like heavy rain." Or, "Tears in floods."

30.5 "Sighing and lamentation." Or, "Sadness and lamentation, "Sad enough to wail," "Sighing like lamentation."

30.6 "But only capture the followers." *chou:* enemy, friend, follower, ugly, sort (i.e., class or kind). Hence the line can be translated in many different ways; for example: "Take prisoner those who are not of the same ugly sort" (Lynn).

The Lower Canon

HEXAGRAMS 31–64

THIRTY-ONE

Xian • Mutual Influence

Keywords:

Influence
Reciprocity
Mutual attraction
Courtship
Wooing

Above: Dui • Lake
Below: Gen • Mountain

In the traditional (King Wen) sequence of the hexagrams, Xian (Mutual Influence) and Heng (Enduring) begin the second half of the *Book of Changes*, also known as the Lower Canon. Qian (The Dynamic) and Kun (The Receptive) begin the first half, which is known as the Upper Canon. According to tradition, the Upper Canon is predominantly concerned with the forces of change in the universe as a whole, and the Lower Canon is concerned primarily with change in the area of human relationships. Hence the Upper Canon begins with Qian and Kun, symbols of heaven and earth, while the Lower Canon begins with Xian and Heng, which symbolize courtship and marriage, and which are among the foundations of human relationships and hence human society. Xian is the story of courtship, or the beginnings of a relationship, while Heng is the story of marriage, a relationship that endures over a long period of time.

Xian features three yang lines that have risen almost to the top but are not yet past their peak—as is the case with Hexagram 12, Pi (Standstill). It symbolizes the heady joy of mutual attraction and infatuation that occurs in the first flush of love. The upper trigram is Dui (Lake, Joy), the lower trigram is Gen (Mountain, Keeping Still). By tradition Dui represents the youngest daughter; Gen represents the youngest son. The union of the two trigrams represents the mutual attraction of young love. The mountain and the lake seem to be opposites, yet each accepts and defers to the other, and together they find harmony and commonality.

More generally, Xian symbolizes human influence—the ability to attract others and sway them to your way of thinking. Good and appropriate influence should not be manipulation of one person by another but rather mutual influence—in which each person is open to the other and responds to the other. The manipulator seeks merely to change others and make them conform to the manipulator's will. But influence, like change itself, is never unidirectional; it spreads its effects in many different directions. Even the person who seeks merely to manipulate or compel others may be changed by the process of attempting to persuade or influence them. Given that mutual influence is inevitable in any case, the more important question to ask is whether you have behaved appropriately and with respect for the other and whether the mutual influence that results from your actions is healthy and beneficial.

THE JUDGMENT

Mutual influence.
Success.
It is beneficial to persevere.
To marry a woman brings good fortune.

The theme of Xian is attraction, influence, and the formation of relationships. The relationship in question may be a love affair, but it could also be a friendship, family relations, a professional relationship, a business connection, or a political alliance. Relationships need time to grow, so that the parties can gradually gain trust and a degree of comfort with each other. This is symbolized by the union of Dui (Joy, Acceptance) with Gen (Patience,

Keeping Still). Aggressiveness and impatience may damage the relationship in its initial stages. Do not try to force matters or achieve everything overnight. Mutual attraction has its own special ways that are not fully under the control of either party. It must develop naturally, on its own terms.

The theme of Xian is not simply influence but mutual influence. In forming relationships, do not try to manipulate or dominate, or force the other person to your own way of thinking. Influence must always be reciprocal, a matter of give and take. Only in this way can it be happy and long-lasting. There is an important difference between courtship and seduction. Courtship is a matter of mutual desire, mutual affection, and mutual respect. Although it seems heady and giddy at first, it actually involves rituals designed to create bonds of trust. It establishes the basis for a happy and prosperous relationship of mutuality that will endure. In this way it enriches both parties. Seduction is the result of momentary enthusiasm; it is a desire to manipulate and control in order to fill up the emptiness that lies within the heart of the seducer. That emptiness, however, can never be filled, and therefore it leads to ever new desires, ever new attempts at conquest and control, ever new struggles to force the production of love in another's heart. Because it is not founded on mutual trust and respect, it will inevitably end in betrayal and unhappiness.

If you desire to form a relationship with another, ask yourself whether you and the other person are engaged in courtship or seduction. Hence the text says, "It is beneficial to persevere," for perseverance marks the difference between short-term seduction and long-term commitment. Courtship should not be pursued for its own sake but for the commitment it produces. Influence should not be pursued for its own sake but for the good things that it helps bring into being. Through mutual attraction, people with complementary talents and affinities are brought together and create something great and lasting. Hence the text says, "To marry a woman brings good fortune." Just as one should not seek love merely in order to seduce but in order to produce relationships that last, one should not seek to be influential simply to become famous and powerful but in order to achieve something of purpose and value.

Finally, Xian teaches that the nature of a thing can be determined by what it attracts and what it is attracted to. What kind of company do you keep and what kind of people do you pursue? If your relationships are unhappy, perhaps it is because you are attracting (or pursuing) the wrong sort of people, or perhaps it is because of some unhealthy vision you have about yourself. Good relationships bring out the best in ourselves and in others. Consider what your relationships are bringing out in you and in the people you are connected to.

THE IMAGE

A lake on the mountain:
This is the image of Mutual Influence.
The superior person receives others because he is open to them.

Water collects on the top of a mountain because the top is recessed. The summit does not jut upward haughtily but instead forms an open space so that water can gather in it and create a lake. If the top of the mountain were a proud peak, water would simply run off it, and nothing would accumulate. In the same way, if you want people to accept you and stick with you, you should be open and receptive to them. If you are proud and overbearing, you may be very impressive, but few people will see the point of trying to cooperate with you or form lasting relationships with you. Be modest and accepting, and the quality of your character will shine through to others. This will naturally attract them to you.

The text says that a superior person "receives others because he is open to them." Influence requires mutuality and receptivity. If you want to influence people and situations, it is best to be yourself. Do not put on airs or try to create a false impression. Do not try to manipulate people. Instead, be cooperative and ready to learn from others. Put aside your prejudices and preconceptions. Listen. Open your heart to others if you want them to open their hearts to you. If you are anxious and too eager to impress, you will surely create the wrong impression. But if you act naturally, people will naturally respond to you.

The same principles apply if you seek to influence others as a leader. First, be open to learning from those whom you would seek to influence or to lead. It is entirely appropriate to conduct yourself with natural dignity but not with pretension, haughtiness, or snobbishness. Second, the greatest gift you have to influence others is your own sincerity and spontaneity. You cannot move or inspire others if you are not moved or inspired yourself. You cannot call others to a larger cause unless you yourself hear a calling. If people believe that you are genuine, you will touch their hearts and they will be drawn to you. In this way you will bring the people who have a real affinity with you to your cause.

THE LINES

The lines describe the various stages of courtship and mutual attraction. The stages are represented by different parts of the body, from the toes to the head.

Initial Six

Influence in the big toe.

Movement begins as a person wills his feet to move. The line symbolizes the very beginnings of a new influence. It may be an attraction, an enthusiasm, or a new idea. But you should not make too much of this, since its effects have not yet been felt. Much more has yet to be done if this potential influence is to become a reality.

Six in the Second Place

Influence in the calves of the legs.
Misfortune.
If one remains still, there is good fortune.

The calves of the legs go as the feet go. They cannot help following. Metaphorically, this describes a situation in which a person feels obligated to go forward without really being in control.

Although you may feel compelled to act now, you do not fully understand the situation and you are not in full control of events. Hold back until you get more information. Exercise patience and self-control and watch how things develop. You should only move forward when you have gathered your wits about you and know what you are facing. If you act prematurely, you may risk harming yourself.

Nine in the Third Place

Influence in the thighs.
Compelled to pursue.
To continue brings humiliation.

The thighs (or loins) symbolize desire, lust, and impulse, which drive people to take rash action.

You have not learned to control your emotions properly. You chase after every desire, acting on the spur of the moment. You force your ideas, emotions, and moods on others. This makes you capricious and unstable. Worse yet, because you lack balance, you are particularly susceptible to the seductions and enthusiasms of others. This undermines your judgment.

You need to get hold of yourself. If you allow everything to influence you, you will never be able to influence anyone else. If you indulge every whim, you will never achieve anything of value. Eventually, your rash actions will lead to humiliation. Don't sacrifice your dignity. Learn to exercise self-restraint. Cultivation of emotional balance and good habits is a central theme of the *Book of Changes*. The secret of autonomy is not license but limitation of the will. In order to control the outer world you must first learn to control your inner self. Self-discipline is essential to human freedom. If you chase after every desire and impulse, you will become little more than a slave to your passions. Hence, the text says, you become "[c]ompelled to pursue."

Nine in the Fourth Place (Ruling Line)

Perseverance brings good fortune.
Regrets vanish.
Restless, uncertain,
He paces back and forth.
Only his friends can follow his thoughts.

This line symbolizes the heart, the seat of emotion.

You would like to influence others, perhaps someone in particular. Do not try to manipulate them. If you become calculating and manipulative, you may well influence other people in the short run, but in the long run you will destroy the bonds of trust between you and them, for you will have to strive continually to maintain your control and subject their will to yours. You may lose respect for people whom you can so easily push around. You may come to doubt whether their affections for you are real or genuine. And you may come to doubt whether they value the real you, especially if their attachment is the result of continuous deception and manipulation on your part.

If you really want to influence others, be sincere and act naturally. Then you will attract people who are right for you. When you let your character shine through to others, and act from sincere conviction, those who genuinely value you will respond and help you achieve your goals.

Nine in the Fifth Place (Ruling Line)

Influence in the upper back.
No remorse.

The upper back is the stiffest part of the body, suggesting firmness and strength of conviction.

If you want others to believe in you, you must believe in yourself. If you want to influence others, you must act out of firm and deep conviction. No one will follow a person who vacillates or is guided by whims. And no one should trust a person who is too eager to please others and influence them. If you act from deeply held beliefs and a profound inner resolve, there is no need to pander in order to gain influence in the outer world. Your sincerity and integrity will naturally attract others with similar views, and through this influence you can accomplish a great deal.

Six at the Top

Influence in the jaws, cheeks, and tongue.

In line six the moment and the capacity for genuine influence have passed. Nothing significant can occur in these circumstances, hence there is no indication of good or bad fortune.

You cannot hope to influence people through mere words. Do not make empty promises or waste your time on pipe dreams. Talk is cheap unless it is backed up by something real and solid. Unless you are committed to executing your ideas, you will accomplish nothing.

NOTES

31.GI "The superior person," etc. Or, "The superior person encourages people to approach him / By his readiness to receive them" (Wilhelm/Baynes).

31.GI "Open to them." *xu:* literally, "emptiness." In other words, the enlightened person opens his heart and mind; he receives others with openness and accepts them without prejudice. That is why he attracts and influences others.

31.1 "the big toe." *mu:* thumb, big toe. Usually, the first line symbolizes the lowest part of the body (e.g., the foot), so "big toe"makes more sense in context. Cf. 40.4.

31.2 "calves." *fei:* calves, lower legs.

31.2 "remains still." *ju:* dwell, reside, stay; hence in this context, delay, tarry.

31.3 "Compelled to pursue." Or, "Insisting on following others."

31.4 "Restless, uncertain." *chong chong:* literally, "wavering, wavering," "hesitating, hesitating," or "unsettled, unsettled."

31.4 "He paces back and forth." *wang lai:* go, come. I.e., "He comes and goes." He "pace[s] back and forth in consternation" (Lynn).

31.5 "upper back." *mei:* neck, neck muscles, back of the neck.

31.6 "Influence in the jaws, cheeks, and tongue." The commentary on the small images (in the Fourth Wing) states, "The open mouth makes empty promises."

THIRTY-TWO

Heng • Enduring

Keywords:

Constancy
Long-lasting
Perseverance
Endurance
Duration

Above: Zhen • Thunder
Below: Xun • Wind (Wood)

This hexagram is the inverse of Xian. It features three yang lines rising from the second position. The lower trigram is Xun, traditionally identified with the eldest daughter; the upper trigram is Zhen, traditionally identified with the eldest son. Together the two represent maturity. Thus, while Xian represents the initial attractions of young love, Heng represents the institution of marriage, an enduring union between husband and wife. Just as Qian and Kun interact in the world, combining dynamism and receptivity, Xian and Heng interact in the world of human relationships, combining mutual influence (reciprocity) and endurance (commitment). A successful marriage is a relationship of long-lasting mutual influence between the partners.

In the Western tradition things endure because they are unchanging. The *Book of Changes* takes a different view. Things endure not because they do not change but because they do change: They grow, they evolve, they respond, and in this way they continue. The symbol of the eternal is not the unchanging but the cycle, which is a process of constant movement and alteration governed by principles of order. In a cycle every beginning results from a previous ending, and every end point is followed by a new beginning. What endures are not the momentary manifestations of physical reality but the basic principles that shape change and give it order and continuity. Analogous principles apply to the world of humanity. Change is inevitable: The secret to endurance is to make the changes in one's life intelligible through principles that endure; it is to learn to grow continuously with integrity.

THE JUDGMENT

Enduring. Success. No blame.
It is beneficial to persevere.
It is beneficial to have somewhere to go.

To endure means to keep going despite obstacles. Endurance is neither stagnation nor a state of rest. It progresses forward, unlike stagnation, and it keeps moving and growing, unlike rest. What endures renews itself and its effects through continuous activity. What endures does so through change, not in spite of change. Its effects are understood against the experience of change. We see this in the cycle of the seasons that continually renew themselves as the earth moves around the sun. The cycle of the seasons repeats perpetually because its underlying causes continue. Plants and animals grow and change as they endure over time. When they cease to grow, they die, and then they cease to endure.

So it is in life. All life is change. But in order to make change intelligible, there must be things that persist, against which change can be understood. To give your life meaning, you must have something that endures: your identity, your relationships with others, and your principles. If you surrender what is enduring within you, then you surrender to the flux of events and become indistinguishable from them. Then there is nothing left of you.

The lesson of Heng is that you must learn to be consistent and persevere in the face of a changing world. Circumstances around you are changing, but you must maintain your integrity. Be consistent. Do not allow yourself to be blown about by a momentary alteration in fortunes. Do not let concerns about what others might think or how well others are doing by comparison lead you to take drastic or reckless action. Instead, focus on what is and should be enduring in your life: your relationships, your character, and your principles.

The situation that you face now requires you to persevere even though you face adversity and obstacles. Choose a path and stick to it. Keep your long-term goals firmly in mind and progress slowly but surely toward them. Employ routines, practices, and cycles of activity that you can engage in over the long haul that will bring you closer and closer to your goal. Be content to make progress step by step through time-tested methods. Attend to the little things. If you neglect them, they will cause problems in the long run. But if you take care of everyday tasks, you will head off problems before they can become large.

The secret to endurance is character. Stick to your principles. Maintain your vision. This will see you through difficult times. You will inevitably have to adjust your strategy as events change, but do not give up its essential features. Don't be tempted to make radical alterations out of fear or anxiety. Slow and steady will win this particular race. When things go well, keep going and do not become lazy. When things go badly, keep going and do not become disheartened or afraid. But whether things go well or badly, you must keep going. Never give up. Through endurance and continuous practice, advantages will slowly but surely accumulate, and the situation will eventually move toward your desired goal.

THE IMAGE

Thunder and wind:
This is the image of what is Enduring.
Thus the superior person stands firm
And does not change his direction.

The Commentary on the Image presents a paradox: Thunder and wind would seem to be the most transitory of events. How can they represent the image of what is enduring? The answer is that although thunder and wind are transitory, the laws of nature that produce them are enduring. In the same way, you must maintain basic features of your character despite the vicissitudes of fortune. Your decisions about how to conduct yourself must flow from virtues that persist through the many changes and crises in your life, like the blowing of the winds or the howling of thunder. Although you must adapt yourself to the time, you cannot and should not surrender what is most characteristically yours. You must stand up for what you believe even as you adjust to circumstances.

This apparent paradox is the secret to dealing with change. Endurance requires flexibility, not rigidity. A blade of grass blows in the wind but is not uprooted because it is flexible, while a dried-up branch snaps and flies away because it is rigid. Even though the blade of grass bends, it remains in its place, while the pieces of the branch that could not bend are blown about. This is the deep connection between flexibility and endurance, between adaptability and consistency of character: Surface changes must always be accompanied by a deeper inner balance and stability.

The text says, "The superior person stands firm / And does not change his direction." If you face the question whether or not to make a commitment, you must make up your mind. Reach a decision and stick to it. If you have already begun something, you should see it through. Practice persistence so that it becomes an essential element of your nature; view obstacles in your life as challenges that will help you develop your character. Learn to be more tolerant and flexible so that you can ride out difficult times and stay true to your goals.

Finally, remember that Heng symbolizes both endurance and marriage. Among the most important commitments that we have are commitments we make to others. Change tests relationships, but it can also strengthen them. You can become closer to people if you are willing to work through problems together rather than trying to solve all your problems unilaterally.

THE LINES

Only the middle (second and fifth) lines in this hexagram are favorable, suggesting that balance and moderation must accompany perseverance.

Initial Six

Diving into duration.
Such perseverance brings misfortune.
There is nothing beneficial in this.

You are eager to get started. But Rome was not built in a day. Anything that is truly enduring requires commitment and continuous efforts extended over a long period of time. Stop and carefully reflect on exactly what you want to do. Plan ahead. Consider the consequences. Do not think that you can cut corners. If you try to get quick results, your efforts will amount to nothing.

A similar point applies to the cultivation of the self. Often when people see that they must make a change in their lives, they rush forward trying to become the person they want to be overnight. Hence the text speaks of "diving into duration." But you cannot change your habits and attitudes so quickly. They did not arise overnight; they too resulted from a long process of acclimation and adjustment. Reform requires perseverance and continuous commitment to replacing old habits with new ones. If you try to change your lifestyle too quickly without the necessary commitment, you will quickly tire of your efforts and succumb to temptation. This kind of reckless attempt at perseverance brings misfortune; hence the text says, "There is nothing beneficial in this."

Nine in the Second Place (Ruling Line)

Regrets vanish.

The meaning of this laconic text is that regrets vanish when the type and degree of perseverance you employ is appropriate to the situation. Here as elsewhere the principle of the mean applies. Maintain your equanimity and avoid going to extremes. Use just enough force to move the situation in the right direction. If you try too hard to make things happen, you may go too far and undermine yourself.

Perseverance is more than the strength to move forward in the face of external obstacles. It also demands an inner strength of character: discipline, self-control, and the ability to know when to hold back and when to push ahead. You must draw on that strength of character now if you are to manage your efforts wisely. Consider how far you should go at the present time. If you act with self-discipline and devotion, all cause for regret will disappear.

Nine in the Third Place

He who does not give duration to his character
May meet with disgrace.
Persistent humiliation.

Perseverance requires commitment and integrity as well as strength of will. Hence the text says that you must also give duration to your character. Preserve your emotional balance. Do not allow your moods to be swayed by the changing circumstances of the outside world or the approval or disapproval of others. If you let your state of mind become too dependent on the rise and fall of events in the world, you will never know peace, because that world is constantly changing. Your sense of self will rise and fall with each passing moment. You will alternate helplessly between hope and despair, bravery and fear. The only thing that will remain constant is your sense of unease and your inability to achieve your ever-shifting goals. Hence the text says, "Persistent humiliation."

When you do not give duration to your character, your efforts fail not because of changing circumstances in the outer world but because of inconsistency within yourself. Because you are easily led by others and emotionally unreliable, others will lose respect for you, and, eventually, you will lose respect for yourself. You cannot always control the outer world, which is perpetually in flux. What you can control is your reaction to that world. You can do this by developing inner balance so that sudden changes and enthusiasms do not knock you off your feet. Or, to vary the metaphor slightly, inner balance helps you navigate toward your goals despite the rough winds that blow from all directions. This is what is meant by "giving duration to one's character."

Nine in the Fourth Place

No game in the field.

You cannot be successful in a hunt if there is no game, no matter how much you persevere. Conversely, if you choose the right place to hunt, your persistence will eventually pay off. Dogged determination must be accompanied by planning, self-reflection, and common sense. If you are not achieving your goals, no matter how hard you try, you may be going about things in the wrong way, or you may have characterized your goal so that it is impossible to achieve. This leads you to chase after the wrong things. Be realistic. Clarify your values and reexamine your methods. Think about what you really want to accomplish and then consider the best way to achieve it. Then your perseverance will help you accomplish something of genuine value.

Six in the Fifth Place

Giving duration to one's character,
One perseveres.

Good fortune for one in the position of a wife,
Misfortune for the head of the household.

One must adapt one's methods of perseverance to one's circumstances. The text contrasts "the position of the wife" to that of "the head of the household." In ancient China many different forms of social organization—including the state itself—were modeled on the patriarchal family. "The position of the wife" is that of a loyal adherent or follower. The position of "the head of the household" is that of a leader. Different social roles require different virtues and different forms of perseverance. Followers must be devoted and carry out the tasks assigned to them; leaders must be flexible, enterprising, and adaptable so that they can work for the benefit of those in their care.

Giving duration to one's character means having constancy, determination, integrity, and inner balance. These virtues will help you no matter what you seek to achieve. But duration of character is not the same thing as constancy of strategy or constancy of approach. And commitment to values does not always mean commitment to a particular person or organization. You need to reflect on what sort of situation you find yourself in. Sometimes the best policy is to follow the lead of others and merge your goals into those of a larger group. In other cases the best way to be true to your goals is to strike out on your own, using your own best judgment and adapting to new circumstances as they arise. In both cases steadfastness and emotional maturity are necessary, but the paths are different. Reflect on which approach is right for you now. Adapt your strategy to the demands of the time while preserving your underlying values.

Six at the Top

Persistently agitated and restless.
Misfortune.

This line describes a person who perseveres in behavior that continually causes anxiety and distress. Misfortune results because lessons about the proper cultivation of character—the true source of perseverance—have not been learned.

You cannot live in a constant state of anxiety, always moving from one crisis to the next. If you do not change your ways, agitation will exhaust your energies and will prevent you from thinking clearly and seeing what is in your best interests. This will make it more difficult to achieve your real goals.

If you find that you lead your life in a perpetual hurry, or in a state of perpetual upheaval, the cause may lie in yourself. Although you may feel that circumstances leave you no choice, your sense of anxiety may be due in part to your lack of inner resolution. People often take on too many things because they do not know what they want and everything seems inviting, because they cannot establish priorities and because they seek to keep too many options open. You have not been able to make the hard choices necessary to end the crushing cycle of events and bring yourself peace of mind. The world seems out of control because you have not learned to control yourself. Calm down. You must regain your balance before it is too late.

You will also achieve little of value if you are continually restless and dissatisfied, always looking for the next big thing that will solve your problems. Your sense of unease stems from lack of clarity and emotional commitment. Restlessness will lead you to inconsistent, halfhearted efforts, which will only make you more unhappy with your life. You need to center yourself and adopt a more realistic frame of mind. Otherwise, perpetual agitation will eventually bring you grief.

NOTES

32.1 "Diving into duration. / Such perseverance brings misfortune." Or, "Diving into perseverance; such perseverance brings misfortune." The first kind of perseverance is *heng,* duration. The second is *zhen,* perseverance or steadfast constancy.

32.3 "meet with disgrace." *cheng:* meet with, suffer, endure. *xiu:* shame. Cf. 12.3.

32.3 "Persistent humiliation." *zhen lin:* normally this would be translated as "perseverance brings misfortune," but in this context "persistent humiliation" is a better translation. Another version would be "persevering [with a bad or changeable character] brings humiliation."

32.4 "No game in the field." Cf. 7.5: "There is game in the field."

32.5 "One perseveres." Another reading is "Giving duration to one's character through perseverance," or "Giving duration to one's character through being steadfast and upright."

32.5 "Good fortune for one in the position of a wife," etc. Literally, "Good fortune for wife people; misfortune for husband, son." Once again, we must understand this line in the context of the patriarchy and hierarchy characteristic of ancient China. "Wife people" would include not only women but all who were subordinate to a leader. They were *yin* (feminine, subordinate) to someone else's *yang* (masculine, superordinate). The husband was the head (or leader) of the household; and the metaphor of family was applied routinely to all social organizations. Thus the state was a great family, whose head or father was the king or emperor; the general was the father of his troops; and so on.

32.6 "Persistently agitated and restless," etc. Wilhelm / Baynes translates this, "Restlessness as an enduring condition brings misfortune."

THIRTY-THREE

Dun • Retreat

Keywords:

The piglet
Strategic withdrawal
Live to fight another day

Above: Qian • Heaven
Below: Gen • Mountain

Dun features four yang lines ascending away from the yin lines that are encroaching upon it. The original meaning of Dun was a piglet, who is advised to retreat from danger in order to grow fat and strong. Thus the theme of Dun is strategic retreat in order to avoid harm and renew one's energies.

THE JUDGMENT

Retreat. Success.
In small things, it is beneficial to persevere.

You face hostile conditions and therefore should make a strategic retreat. This is entirely appropriate under the circumstances and should not be confused with cowardice or resignation. You should withdraw when you are in the strongest position to do so, preserving your resources in order to fight another day. An army that retreats only after it is defeated in battle has waited too long. As a result, it often suffers heavy casualties as it flees and must leave its arms and provisions on the field. In this case, by timing your withdrawal appropriately, you avoid losses and conserve your power. In this way you can actually strengthen yourself and begin preparations for effective countermeasures.

Indeed, by retreating in the right way, you can actually make things more difficult for your opponent by limiting his options and means of attack. You can retreat to a position of strength with full power and resources still at your disposal. By making yourself less vulnerable to your adversary, you make your adversary less powerful and less able to harm you.

Applied outside of the battlefield, the lesson of Dun is that properly timed retreat from a situation that is not serving your best interests can be constructive and liberating. It can enhance your power rather than detracting from it. By withdrawing from the situation you can free yourself from entanglements that sap your energies and from negative personalities who drag you down. This gives you the chance to take a broader view and rethink your priorities.

Knowing when and how to retreat properly requires shrewdness, careful planning, and complete coolheadedness. Good timing is essential. But when your exit is properly prepared and performed, the results are entirely favorable. Hence the text predicts "success."

Similar considerations apply if your question concerns your own lifestyle. You need to reassess the choices you have made and the habits that you have fallen into. If your behavior is not making you happy and fulfilled, there is something wrong. Perhaps you are acting in a way that is contrary to your best interests. The adversity you face may lie within yourself and your own self-destructive tendencies. If so, it may be time to withdraw and start over. Move away from what is harmful and take the time to replenish yourself.

THE IMAGE

Mountain under heaven:
This is the image of Retreat.
Thus the superior person keeps petty people at a distance,
Not with anger but with reserve.

A mountain can reach only so high. Heaven rises higher, and therefore always remains outside its grasp. In the same way you can escape the influence of harmful people by retreating to what is good within yourself. There is no point in struggling with difficulties that cannot be resolved, or with people who are negative and hostile. Some people simply want to fight; others want to rile you up emotionally or manipulate you. Do not let them. Sidestep head-on confrontations and withdraw from the situation with complete equanimity. Do not allow yourself to become angry or vindictive. Anger and hatred merely bind you all the more closely to the negative situation you are trying to escape. If you have anger and hatred in your heart, you become enslaved to the object of your emotions. Then you may well torment yourself as effectively as anyone could torment you. Instead, simply let go of the confrontation and retreat to a better place. This strategy is reflected in the constituent trigrams. Heaven symbolizes transcendence; mountain symbolizes standstill. By transcending the situation with dignity and with reserve, you can bring the people and things that oppress you to a standstill, leaving them far behind you.

It may be especially difficult to withdraw when people goad you, lie about you, or attack you personally. But do not let your pride or your desire for vindication ensnare you in counterproductive behavior. Lashing out or fighting back will only keep you involved and entangled. It will only exacerbate the violence and the negativity inherent in the situation. This is not a battle worth fighting. Maintain your composure and keep your emotions in check. By retreating with dignity you will win a greater victory. When you refuse to be involved in a struggle, you make it more difficult for others to struggle with you and injure you.

THE LINES

The lines describe different situations of retreat. In the lower three lines, retreat is not yet possible (line one), or there are obstacles (lines two and three). In the upper three lines retreat becomes genuinely feasible and the results are quite favorable. Indeed, the only unfavorable line is the first because it is the closest to danger.

Initial Six (Constitutive Line)

At the tail of a retreat.
Danger.
Do not try to undertake anything.

The bottom line of the hexagram represents the tail of a retreating army, while the top line represents the head that has retreated the farthest. Because the tail of a retreating army is, in effect, the front lines, the enemy is still nearby and so it is the most precarious position from which to retreat.

You are in the middle of a dangerous situation. You are in immediate contact with your adversaries. Difficulties surround you. If you had retreated earlier, you would be in a much better position, but it is too late to do anything now. Be patient and wait for the situation to clarify itself. If you act precipitously, you will only make things worse.

Six in the Second Place (Constitutive Line)

Holding fast with yellow oxhide.
No one can tear him loose.

To hold fast means to join with another loyally. Yellow is the color of the mean, and hence signifies inner balance and righteous conduct. The hide of an ox is particularly strong and difficult to tear; it symbolizes perseverance and inner determination.

You would like to withdraw but find that you cannot do it alone. You need help. Ally yourself with, or seek advice from, a respected superior or someone whom you trust. Turn to good people and ask for their guidance and assistance. If your motives are just and if you are determined to do the right thing, you will succeed.

Nine in the Third Place

One retreats, attached.
Affliction and adversity.
Keeping manservants and handmaidens
Brings good fortune.

You find it difficult to leave a situation that is bad for you because of emotional baggage. You are fearful and anxious about what the future will bring. Take courage. Stand up for your own interests and do not let yourself be held back by negative emotions. You cannot rely on other people to do your fighting for you. It is time to move on.

As you try to extricate yourself from your present difficulties, others may cling to you and make it more difficult for you to go. But you cannot let their negativity drain your strength. It is altogether admirable to show concern and care for those who are dependent on you, and you should live up to your genuine responsibilities to them. But these people are not the answer to your problems. You must move forward regardless.

Nine in the Fourth Place

Graceful retreat.
Good fortune for the superior person,
And downfall for the inferior person.

A wise person knows how to make a retreat gracefully. When it is time to withdraw, do so of your own accord, willingly and voluntarily. Be courteous to all involved. And when you detach yourself from the situation, let yourself become detached emotionally as well. Don't concern yourself with what others will say or do as you leave the scene. Resist the temptation to take parting shots. Above all, don't get drawn back into a struggle. If you let yourself become consumed with bitterness, spite, regret, or a desire for revenge, you will suffer emotionally and you will make it more difficult to adjust to your new situation. On the other hand, if you withdraw firmly and with grace, you will make a smooth transition to a better life. The only ones who will suffer are the petty persons that you leave behind.

Nine in the Fifth Place (**Ruling Line**)

Praiseworthy retreat.
Perseverance brings good fortune.

A praiseworthy retreat is one that is performed at the correct moment, in a dignified and courteous manner and without vacillation or indecision. If you withdraw from the situation at the right time, you can leave with friendliness and without rancor. Be polite but firm. Don't get drawn into irrelevant considerations or bogged down in discussions. When the time to depart has arrived, don't look back. Make your decision and stick to it. As the text says, "Perseverance brings good fortune."

Nine at the Top

Cheerful retreat.
There is nothing for which this is not beneficial.

The happiest retreat comes when you have emotionally prepared yourself for it. You have become sufficiently removed from the situation that you can judge matters objectively. Because you know that the time has come to leave, you can go your way happily. The word translated as "cheerful" in the text also means "with abundant resources." Those resources are not just material. They are also emotional. When you have made peace with yourself and your decision, you are well prepared for whatever lies ahead. If you do not allow yourself to be hampered by bitterness, regret, or self-doubt, you will travel smoothly from the old situation to a new one, instinctively following the correct path. Such clarity of mind inevitably brings good fortune and success in whatever you do.

NOTES

33.GI "reserve." I.e., dignity. Another interpretation is "aloofness"—that which causes awe or intimidation in others.

33.1 "Do not try to undertake anything." Or, "Do not use this (view this) as an opportunity to go somewhere," "One should not wish to undertake anything."

33.2 "Holding fast," etc. This might also be translated as "Holding him (it) fast."

33.2 "No one can tear him loose." *sheng tuo:* literally, "conquer [and] take off." Or, "no one can loosen it," "nothing can break free." The line could mean either that the person who wants to remain binds himself to the other, or that the one who wants to retreat cannot break free.

33.3 "attached." Or, "halted." That is, one has responsibilities. One cannot leave one's problems behind.

33.3 "Affliction and adversity." *ji li*. Or, "illness and danger," "nerve-wracking and dangerous" (Wilhelm/Baynes).

33.3 "Keeping." Or, "Retaining," "Caring for," "Feeding."

33.3 "manservants and handmaidens." *chen qie:* male and female bondservants.

33.4 "Graceful." *hao:* good, love, fond of, fine, excellent; hence, graceful. One might translate this, "Retreating from what he is fond of," or "A fine retreat." Wilhelm / Baynes translates it as "Voluntary retreat."

33.5 "Praiseworthy." *jia:* admirable, commendable, excellent, appropriate, fine. Wilhelm / Baynes translates this as "Friendly."

33.6. "Cheerful." *Fei* literally means "fat" or "rich." It is translated here as "cheerful" or "happy," as in "fat and happy," i.e., wealthy and therefore content. One retreats in control of the situation, with abundant resources. Hence another translation is "Resourceful retreat."

THIRTY-FOUR

Da Zhuang • Great Power

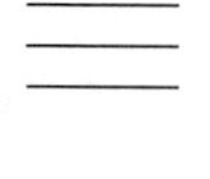

Keywords:

The power of the great
Dominance
Great strength
Using your power wisely
Uniting strength with justice

Above: Zhen • Thunder
Below: Qian • Heaven

Da Zhuang features four yang lines ascending from the bottom. In contrast to Hexagram 11 (Tai), which perfectly balances three yin and three yang lines, a fourth line enters the upper trigram, suggesting the possibility of imbalance and an excess of force. The proper use of great force is a central theme of the hexagram. The lower trigram Qian (Heaven, the Dynamic, Strength) joins with the upper trigram Zhen (Thunder, Shock, The Arousing, Movement), suggesting enormous drive and energy and the ability to move forward through obstacles. However, precisely because this power can be so destructive, it is crucial to understand the right time to push forward and the right time to desist. This is the hexagram's second theme. Finally, because Qian is heaven and Zhen is thunder (activity), a third theme of the hexagram is that truly great power must always unite strength with justice and righteousness. This is the way of heaven.

THE JUDGMENT

Great Power.
It is beneficial to persevere.

You have enormous power and influence on the situation now. But the secret to great power is knowing when and how to use it. And the moral responsibility of great power is to use it only for good purposes and not simply to attain selfish ends.

The situation has great potential. You can achieve a great deal now. But do not become reckless or overconfident. Perhaps you think you hold all the cards, or that you can bully your way forward to get what you want. But if you become aggressive and try to impose your will on others, you will simply create resistance and opposition. You should carefully consider how other people will be affected by your actions and what would be in the best interests of everyone before you go ahead. Exercise caution and circumspection. The proper use of great power is a matter of timing. Patience and care amplify your strength and influence; recklessness and carelessness dissipate them. Wait for the right moment to act. If you rush ahead and try to force matters, you may well make everything worse. Even if you do prevail ultimately, acting aggressively at the wrong time may make your ultimate victory much more difficult to achieve or much less happy and fulfilling when it arrives.

Great power is truly great not when it is vast or mighty but when it is used in the pursuit of something good and just. Great power that is exercised selfishly degenerates into tyranny; great power exercised thoughtlessly degenerates into chaos. If you find yourself in a position of strength and influence, let your conscience be your guide. Don't allow yourself to be moved by greed, self-indulgence, or vanity. Do not act on impulse, and do not lord your power over others. Rather, simply decide what is right and do it without arrogance and without letting yourself be distracted by irrelevant or petty considerations. Unite strength with justice, influence with integrity, and power with principle, and you will achieve something that is truly great.

THE IMAGE

Thunder in heaven above:
This is the image of Great Power.
Thus the superior person does not act in any way contrary
To codes of proper courtesy and decorum.

Precisely because you have great power, it is important not to brandish it recklessly. Thunder peals in heaven at an appropriate distance from earth in order to display its grandeur. If it were to force its way onto the ground, it would cause needless damage and the earth would deaden its sound. However, because thunder moves in accordance with heaven, it echos powerfully in the sky and its reverberations are amplified. In the same way, the greatness of a person's achievements depends on their consistency with what is right.

When you wield power, you should do so sparingly and with the utmost grace and tact. People who are truly powerful are so well situated that they never even have to threaten force overtly; everyone understands their power and immediately complies. Thus in *The Art of War,* Sunzi says that the greatest general—and the most powerful army—is one that never has to fight.

Conversely, people who succeed only through the use of force do not have great power, for if they were truly strong, they would not have to expend such energy; moreover, they exhaust their resources in the process. The general who manages to squeeze out a victory only after a great loss of life is neither as powerful nor as skillful as the general who wastes no resources and loses no men in securing the desired goal. And a general who wins without shedding the blood of his enemy is the most powerful of all. No one even dares attack his army; as a result, no one on either side is injured.

In like fashion, people who get their way only through showing off or bullying others are not powerful. They are insecure. They need to demonstrate their value to themselves by imposing their will on others. The truly strong know their strength. Therefore, they do not waste it on shallow display. Those with real power do not have to wield it. Therefore, they remain modest and courteous to all.

When you are in a strong position, tact and discretion can enhance your power. Consider the feelings of others before you act and you will avoid unnecessary opposition. Move with the flow of events rather than against them and your influence will be magnified. Play by the rules and the rules will in turn support the authority of what you do. Exercise power in the interests of what is just and right, and those with good in their hearts will be happy to support you. Petty individuals will be too ashamed or afraid to criticize your noble efforts, and they will withdraw of their own accord. On the other hand, if you abuse your authority and act arrogantly or self-righteously, more people will be tempted to oppose you. If you break the rules or act discourteously, you place yourself against the order of things and lose support for this reason alone.

Do not try to force your way to a solution, or manipulate or bully people. Whatever you do out of arrogance and insecurity will eventually come back to haunt you. Control your temper. Rash or thoughtless action will diminish your resources. Modesty and circumspection will strengthen them and ensure that your power is employed in the right way.

THE LINES

The lines offer advice about how to behave in a position of great power. The lesson in each case is that those who have great power must use it with restraint and decorum and should not try to resolve matters by brute force. The key metaphor in lines three through six is the ram, who butts his head against the hedge and is ensnared.

Initial Nine

Power in the toes.
To go forward brings misfortune.
Be confident of this.

The toe represents what is lowly and base as well as the beginning of any step forward. Hence power in the toes symbolizes power that is put to inferior ends. In the symbolism of the *Book of Changes* attribution of power to the toes or feet also usually suggests impatience and an ill-prepared or premature advance.

It is not enough simply to have great power. You must also understand how to use it wisely. Although you feel confident of your abilities, the time is not yet right for you to advance. If you push ahead recklessly, you will do great damage to yourself and others and you will lose face. That does not mean that there is nothing to be done. You may use this time to gather intelligence, plan ahead, and prepare for later action. However, don't waste your resources on an impetuous adventure now. Guard against overenthusiasm and exercise prudence.

Nine in the Second Place

Perseverance brings good fortune.

"Perseverance brings good fortune" because one acts moderately in pursuing one's goals. Moderation means both care in the deployment of one's resources and modesty in one's attitude.

Obstacles begin to fall away, opposition disappears, and you are able to make real progress. This is exciting, but now is the time to maintain humility and inner balance. Don't become cocky, overconfident, or careless because you now experience smooth sailing. Manage your resources wisely and don't engage in reckless or excessive displays of power. If you persevere in maintaining balance inwardly as well as outwardly, you will have great success.

Nine in the Third Place

The petty person uses power.
The superior person does not.
Perseverance is dangerous.
A ram butts against a hedge
And gets its horns entangled.

A ram caught in a hedge weakens itself in a futile burst of energy as it tries to escape. Its horns—the symbol of its power—become entangled in matters beyond its control. The secret of power lies in the character of the person who possesses it. Petty people cannot wait to display their power and wield it over others. As a result, they attract hostility and fall into an endless series of disputes. They end up like the ram who ensnares its horns in the hedge. By contrast, wise people never flaunt their power. They reveal it only when it is appropriate, and they use it only when necessary. They are always aware of the danger of becoming ensnared in other people's disputes, and hence conserve their forces for when they are truly needed.

If you boast about your power and throw your weight around, you will soon find yourself in countless contests and entanglements. This will sap your strength and deplete your resources. Instead, act with modesty and circumspection and do not engage in meaningless displays of force. Truly powerful people rarely have to use power, because others naturally respond to them. Their character signals that they are truly a force to be reckoned with.

Nine in the Fourth Place (Ruling Line)

Perseverance brings good fortune.
Regrets vanish.
The hedge opens; there is no entanglement.
Power from the axle of a big cart.

The axle symbolizes the inner force of a person's character that motivates commitment and determination. An axle is small in diameter compared to the rim of a wheel. Yet it is the real source of its power to push forward. Located at the center, the axle seems hardly to move at all, and yet it drives the outer rim quickly around it. In the same way, the source of a person's true power lies deep within.

If you persevere quietly in your efforts and proceed one step at a time, you will eventually reach your goal. You will make progress steadily and persistently, without any excessive show of power. Yet over time the effect of your efforts will be great. It takes genuine strength of character to have such persistence and patience. But proceeding in this way pays real dividends over time, and it further fortifies your personality in the process. Great character is the source of great power.

Six in the Fifth Place

Loses the ram in the field.
No remorse.

The ram symbolizes stubbornness and impulsive use of energy. To "lose[ ] the ram in the field" means to let go of these qualities in yourself and thereby progress without hindrance. It also means that one accepts changes in fortune with equanimity.

A stubborn and belligerent attitude within generates hostility and resistance from the outside world and produces a self-fulfilling prophecy. This is not the proper way to use one's power. It is time to move past such immature behavior. A changing situation offers new opportunities if you know how to look for them. There is no need to be obstinate or aggressive. If you can let go of these negative attitudes, you will not regret it. And the change in your inner nature will be reflected in the outer world: Matters will progress with ease, and you can resolve the situation harmoniously, responding naturally without a display of force.

Six at the Top

A ram butts against a hedge.
It cannot withdraw. It cannot push through.
Nothing is beneficial.
If one can endure the difficulty, there will be good fortune.

Like the ram caught in the hedge, you find yourself at an impasse. You cannot make any more progress. The more force you employ, the more your problems mount. Everything you try to do just makes things more difficult and more complicated. The answer is clear: Hold back and stop trying to force your way out. Recognize that you have done all that you can in this direction. It is time to pause and rethink your approach. Compose yourself and try to get a sense of perspective. If you can stop struggling against your predicament, you can take the time to understand it. Then the right course of action will present itself.

NOTES

34.0 "persevere." Given the theme of the hexagram—the need to unite strength with justice and righteousness—the familiar gloss "to be steadfast and upright" is particularly appropriate.

34.GI "to codes of proper courtesy and decorum." *li:* rites, rituals, manners, proper conduct; hence, decorum.

34.1 "Be confident of this." Or, "This is true." *you fu:* possessing sincerity (truth).

34.1 "Power in the toes." Cf 43.1., "Powerful in his forward toes," also suggesting impatience and an ill-prepared or premature advance.

34.3 "And gets its horns entangled." Another translation is "weakens (damages) its horns," which conveys the idea that the ram saps its strength in a futile burst of energy. *lei:* weaken, damage, entangle. However, the gloss employed in the text is more consistent with line six—a ram entangled in the hedge cannot advance or retreat.

34.4 "there is no entanglement" *(bu lei)* might also be translated "there is no damage."

34.5 "Loses the ram in the field." The word *yi* usually means "ease" or "change." Cf. Wilhelm/Baynes: "Loses the goat with ease." But the line may be employing an older use of *yi,* meaning a field or a place to dry grain. Cf. the discussion in the notes to 56.6. The line probably refers to the story of Wang Hai, a legendary ancestor of the Shang, who lost his cattle at Youyi, or Yi. Wang Hai is a culture hero, credited with inventing the practice of breeding cattle.

34.6 "It cannot withdraw. It cannot push through." *bu neng tui bu neng sui*. Or, "It cannot retreat. It cannot advance."

34.6 "endure the difficulty." Cf. Wilhelm/Baynes, "notes the difficulty," suggesting that the real problem is one of self-realization and enlightenment.

THIRTY-FIVE

Jin • Progress

☲☷

Keywords:

Advance
Recognition
Proceeding forward

Above: Li • Fire
Below: Kun • Earth

Because it features two yang lines in the upper trigram, and three yin lines below, Jin might seem to resemble Hexagram 12, Pi (Standstill). But its meaning is quite the opposite. In Jin the upper trigram Qian (Heaven) is replaced by Li (Fire, Enlightenment). Instead of heaven separating from earth—which symbolizes stagnation—Jin symbolizes the sun rising over the earth at dawn. The theme of the hexagram is a natural, unforced progress that brings light and clarity, just as the light of the sun expands upward and outward as it rises in the sky.

THE JUDGMENT

Progress.
The Marquis of Kang
Is honored with horses in great numbers.
In a single day he is granted audience three times.

The time is propitious. You can now make smooth and rapid progress toward your goals. The text compares the situation to a powerful feudal lord who is granted an audience by his king and rewarded for his service to the country. The feudal lord does not act independently of the king. Rather his progress results from serving the king and becoming part of something greater than himself. In like fashion the feudal lord rallies others around him, and they willingly cooperate because he does not act merely to further his own ambitions but to serve a higher cause. The king is not jealous of the lord's power and success; he recognizes his servant's contributions and showers him with praise and rewards. The relationship between the two is symbolized by the two constituent trigrams: The lord is like earth—reliable, modest, and dependable, supporting the king with his strength. The sovereign is like fire—clear-headed and enlightened, understanding how his power ultimately depends on others. Out of such a relationship progress naturally flows.

The hexagram Jin teaches that progress comes from cooperation and mutual recognition. Those who work for others help them achieve important goals; those in charge recognize the contribution of the people who serve them, reward them appropriately, and show appreciation for their efforts. Jealousy and self-centeredness destroy progress. Respecting the dignity of others and rallying around a common cause produce progress. It is important not to confuse selfishness—which hinders progress—with ambition—which furthers it. The feudal lord is ambitious, but there is nothing wrong with ambition when it is combined with loyalty and uprightness. Ambition leads to progress when it serves a higher cause.

Because you have devoted yourself to something larger than your own self-interest, you can now make easy, sustained progress. People will recognize your abilities and acknowledge your contributions. Like the sun rising over the earth, it is your time to shine. But don't let success go to your head; remember not to become self-centered and narrow-minded. Cooperate with people and help them achieve their goals. Be generous. The more valuable you make yourself to others, the more influence and esteem you will have. Share your insights. You have good ideas; don't hide your light under a bushel. This is a time of uncommon clarity. If you are willing to communicate what you know, and work for the common good, you can have a beneficial influence on the situation. In turn, this will cause people to have increased confidence in you. They will support you and help you achieve your goals.

THE IMAGE

Brightness rising above the earth:
This is the image of Progress.
Thus the superior person illuminates himself
With his bright virtue.

Progress comes from combining the virtues of earth (dependability) with fire (clarity). An enlightened person understands that progress comes out of cooperation and personal relationships. Just as fire depends on fuel to burn, your progress depends on working together with others. Just as earth supports and nourishes everything without complaint, your progress depends on finding something that you can nourish and support.

The sun rising over the earth brings light—and hence clarity—to a larger and larger expanse. In the same way, the text says that a superior person "illuminates himself with his bright virtue." Enlightenment means understanding how your progress is linked to that of others. But it also means being true to yourself. Your progress in life is hindered when you are not clear about who you are and what your values are. If you don't know where you are going, how can you expect to make progress? If you become too worried about what people think and too concerned about winning praise and esteem in the eyes of others, you will forget your own values and lose track of what is important in life. In this way your vision becomes clouded over and your life grows increasingly out of sync with what matters most to you. And if your life is not in harmony with your deepest values, it is no wonder that you feel unhappy and unfulfilled. Indeed, the more you chase after success, the more it will elude you.

To make progress, then, you must "illuminate yourself"—shed light on your values and clarify what is most central to you. Equally important, you must begin to live by those values. You must make your lifestyle compatible with who you are rather than with what you imagine others want you to be. Doing this may take considerable courage. But it is worth it. For it is the path to real progress.

THE LINES

The lines tell the story of an individual's rise from a lowly position. In line one the time for recognition has not yet arrived; we should be patient and prepare ourselves. In line two progress is difficult. In line three we progress because others trust us. In line four we progress through stealth and invite danger and humiliation. Line five is the ruling line of the hexagram and states its theme: In a time of recognition and progress, we should not worry about gain or loss but have faith in the ultimate success of our endeavors. In line six the time of progress has passed; we must turn our attention inward, cultivating our strength and virtue and preparing for the darker times ahead.

Initial Six

Progressing, but driven back.
Perseverance brings good fortune.
If there is an absence of confidence and trust,
Be generous and improve yourself.
No blame.

You want to make progress, but you feel held back because others do not recognize your abilities and lack confidence in you. Don't become discouraged. The most important thing is to have faith in yourself and keep doing what you feel is right. You may be worried that people will not like you or respect you. But you cannot make your self-worth turn on the approval of others. Don't try to force matters or curry favor. And don't become bitter or angry at your current lack of progress. Instead be generous—both to others and to yourself—and work diligently on improving your abilities. If you keep faith and devote your efforts to doing good work, you will succeed admirably and will eventually get the recognition you deserve.

Six in the Second Place

Progressing, but in grief and apprehension.
Perseverance brings good fortune.
One receives great blessings from one's departed grandmother.

Your progress is blocked because you are unable to connect with people who could help you. But do not be discouraged. This is only a temporary setback. Persevere in your efforts and maintain your integrity and your principles. Good fortune often comes in the most unexpected ways. The text speaks of blessings from "one's departed grandmother" or ancestress—

symbolizing maternal care, unselfishness, and gentleness of approach. Put these virtues to work in your own life and you will get the help you need.

Six in the Third Place

Everyone trusts him.
Regrets vanish.

A great leader succeeds because people have confidence in him. A businessman prospers because people trust him. A pioneer makes discoveries because people support his adventures. You may want to be totally independent, but your progress depends on cooperation and collaboration. Do not be too proud to join in. Accept help when it is offered. You can make great strides now with the support and encouragement of others. Take the opportunity and you will succeed. Work with others toward a common goal and they will put their trust in you. The happiness you will derive from your connection to them will eliminate any cause for regret.

Nine in the Fourth Place

Progressing like a rodent.
Perseverance brings danger.

The rodent spoken of in the text has many abilities, but each is limited in some way so that it lacks the ability to make progress. The rodent also symbolizes underhanded methods and devious, fearful, and skulking people.

Whether out of timidity, lack of ability, or circumstance, you lack the wherewithal to make progress through upright methods. Now an opportunity for advance presents itself, but it involves questionable methods, secret designs, or unethical activities. Don't compromise your integrity. If you try to make progress this way, you will put yourself at enormous risk and are likely to be found out. Your self-respect is worth much more than this. Be content with what you can do in a worthy and reputable fashion.

Six in the Fifth Place (Ruling Line)

Regrets vanish.
Do not worry about gains or losses.
Undertakings bring good fortune.
There is nothing that is not beneficial.

You are now in a fortunate position and can make great progress toward your goals. Maintain modesty and gentleness even though events now swing your way. You may worry whether you have taken advantage of every opportunity during these good times. Don't be concerned. Momentary gains or losses will not affect the final outcome. The fact that you did not rush to capitalize on every possible alternative available to you will not matter much in the long run. Minor setbacks are inevitable even in the best of times, and do not matter if you do not obsess about them. The most important thing is to maintain the principles that got you to this point and to make progress steadily. Stick to the path of moderation and proper conduct. When fortune smiles on you, don't worry about keeping your options open or accumulating as much as possible, for those concerns will only distract you. Instead, use this golden opportunity to do your best. Then you will enjoy good fortune, and all regrets will disappear.

Nine at the Top

He progresses with his horns.
Holding fast, he uses them to subdue the city.
Danger, but good fortune.
No blame.
But perseverance brings humiliation.

The sixth line represents the period after a situation has ended. "To make progress with horns" means to take the offensive. "Holding fast" means to be steadfast and upright. The city represents the self or those closest to the self. The point of the text is that assertive behavior is now only justified for purposes of self-improvement. When it is no longer possible to make progress in the outside world, one must try to make progress in the cultivation of the self.

The time of rapid and easy advancement is now coming to an end. If you try to force matters any further, you will meet with humiliation. The best strategy now is to exercise self-control and self-discipline. This will keep you from making mistakes and will ensure your future success when the good times return again. Even here you must not become overzealous in your efforts at self-correction. In any case, an aggressive attempt to discipline others, however well intentioned, is the wrong strategy now. It will only alienate people.

NOTES

35.0 "The Marquis of Kang." Or, "The powerful prince." *kang hou:* literally, "lord Kang,"or "the Marquis of Kang." The Marquis of Kang was Feng, the younger brother of King Wu; he was known primarily by his later title, the Marquis of Wei. However, *kang* also means "vigorous," "easy," "healthy," "at peace"; *hou* is a feudatory, feudal lord, or prince. Cf. 3.0, 3.1, 8.GI, 16.0, 18.6. Hence "the powerful prince."

35.0 "in great numbers." *fan shu:* "increase [the] multitudes."

35.1 "driven back." *cui:* stopped, arrested, turned back.

35.1 "If there is an absence of confidence and trust." *wu fu:* without trust. *Fu* also means "truth" or "sincerity"; here it means the confidence or trust that others repose in one.

35.1 "Be generous and improve yourself." *yu:* lenient, mild, rich, abundant, generous; here meaning to have generosity of spirit and to amass one's resources.

35.2 "in grief and apprehension." *chou:* sorrow.

35.2 "one's departed grandmother." Or, "ancestress."

35.3 "Everyone trusts him." *zhong yun:* crowds [have] confidence. Or, "All trust."

35.4 "a rodent." *shi shu:* big rat; hence, mean, thieving people; timid or skulking people. Lynn translates *shi shu* as "flying squirrel," an animal that does not have the wherewithal for success. It has many skills (another name for *shi shu* is the "five-skills rodent"), but each of its abilities is limited in some way. Thus its skills are not sufficiently great that it can keep safe, protect itself, and thereby gain success.

35.5 "Undertakings bring good fortune." Or, "To set forth brings good fortune."

35.6 "He progresses with his horns." *jue,* "southwest," is usually read as *jiao,* "horns"; hence the line reads, "Progressing with horns; using them to attack the town (city)." Lynn, following Wang Bi, reads *jue* as "southwest," i.e., the farthest reaches of ancient China, because it is the last place in northern China where one would see the sun travel as it sets. Hence the line might read that he has "advanced as far as he can go, so now all he can do is attack the city" (Lynn). This interpretation also assumes that because this is line six, the time of progress is coming to an end.

THIRTY-SIX

Ming Yi • Darkening of the Light

䷣

Keywords:

The crying pheasant
Eclipse
Hiding one's light
Brilliance injured
Censorship
Keeping a low profile
Hiding your feelings

Above: Kun • Earth
Below: Li • Fire

Ming Yi features two yang lines surrounding a single yin line in the lower trigram, situated below three yin lines. Although it superficially resembles Hexagram 11, Tai (Peace), it has a very different meaning. Instead of Qian (Heaven), the lower trigram is Li (Fire). The hexagram thus symbolizes the sun sinking beneath the earth, and hence the darkening of the light. Ming Yi is sometimes translated as "the wounding of the bright" or "brilliance injured."

Ming Yi is the opposite of Hexagram 35, Jin. While in Jin a wise king accepts and rewards his talented subordinates and together they make progress, in Ming Yi an inferior person is in control and oppresses the able and wise people who work under him, leading to a dark and gloomy time. The original name of the hexagram was probably "crying pheasant" but later was reinterpreted to mean "brightness hidden" or "brightness wounded." The pheasant, with its brilliant plumage, may have been viewed as a metaphor for an upright minister who must keep in the background and hide his brilliance during a time of darkness and adversity.

THE JUDGMENT

Darkening of the Light.
In adversity
It is beneficial to persevere.

You face unfavorable circumstances. You encounter criticism and opposition, your projects fail to prosper, or those who have control over your life lack confidence in you. Whatever the problem, there is little that you can do about it for the time being. You must wait out the bad times until things take a turn for the better.

Because you are currently trapped in a hostile environment, the best strategy right now is to keep a low profile. You must hide your light. If you try to assert yourself, the people who surround you will not be sympathetic and will rebuff you. If you object to your treatment, people will not understand, and you may make things even worse for yourself. Instead of protesting, it is better to allow those in your environment to believe that you accept the situation. Someone may be jealous of you or resent you. You should not give them an opportunity to harm you. Do not be aggressive and do not call attention to yourself. This is no time to pick a fight. Conditions are not in your favor right now, and you do not have the resources to prevail.

Nevertheless, during this difficult time you must continue to have faith in yourself. Do not give up just because things are not going well. As the text says, in times of adversity, it is beneficial to remain steadfast and to persevere. It is a test of your will and your endurance. You must preserve your inner light—the still, small voice within. Do not let the darkness on the outside extinguish the light on the inside, for then there will be nothing left of you when times improve.

People and events will surely provoke you. But you must maintain your composure and your emotional compass. Do not let what others say and do cause you to lose heart. You cannot let their ignorance or their bad judgment undermine your self-confidence. They see only a small part of the picture. Their values are not your values. And even though things seem rough right now, time has a way of turning present disadvantages into the seeds of later advantage. You will not be down forever.

Hostile circumstances require you to accept the situation outwardly for the time being. You must allow people to think that you acquiesce and are going along. But you must never surrender. Maintain your resistance on the inside. Hold fast to your enduring values and to your ultimate goals. Remember who you are and what you stand for. Even though there is little that you can do at present, you must preserve your integrity during these dark times. Keep your heart and soul steadfast and ever fixed on what is most important. Eventually, things will change for the better, and you will prevail.

THE IMAGE

The light has descended into the center of the earth:
This is the image of the Darkening of the Light.
Thus the superior person oversees the masses.
He hides his light, yet it still shines.

When the sun descends below the horizon, it does not disappear forever. It merely goes into hiding for a time. Anyone who thinks that the sun will never rise again has lost touch with reality. The same is true in your situation. Things will eventually improve. In the meantime, you must not let conditions defeat you. The enemy you face is not simply the darkness without. It is the darkness within—despair and discouragement, the temptation to surrender totally to evil and adversity. You must maintain your principles and keep hope and faith alive. Thus the text says, "He hides his light, yet it still shines." For as long as you maintain your inner light, you are not defeated.

Because circumstances are adverse, it is wise to avoid confrontations. Keep your feelings to yourself. If you lash out against others or reproach them, you will not make any friends and you will probably make life much worse for yourself. During this period you will no doubt experience many things that offend and oppress you, but let them pass. Although it is best not to crusade against inappropriate behavior at this time, neither should you approve of it or fall in with it. Instead, bide your time. Be courteous and friendly to the extent that you can without compromising yourself. If you cannot be friendly, at least be unobtrusive. If interaction with others is too painful or difficult, simply withdraw. If you need to, spend time alone, in prayer or meditation. Take care of yourself and wait for things to improve. In time, they most certainly will.

THE LINES

The lines describe how one behaves during a time when one is eclipsed. The situation is just beginning in line one; it becomes increasingly dire as the lines progress. In line six, evil has reached its zenith, and now suffers a fall.

Initial Nine

Darkening of the light during flight.
He lowers his wings.
The superior person does not eat for three days on his travels.
There is somewhere to go.
The host gossips.

You face great obstacles now. You cannot surmount the current difficulties; and any attempt to do so will only meet with hostility and opposition. Hence, as the text tells us, you must "fold your wings." You need to withdraw from the current situation and move on. While you wait for matters to improve, it is important not to compromise your principles. You may suffer disadvantage for doing so, and people may misunderstand your motives and criticize you. As the text says, "[t]he superior person does not eat for three days" and "[t]he host gossips" against him. Nevertheless, you must maintain faith in your ultimate goals. You have a mission—"somewhere to go"—and you must not surrender your values simply because things are not going well at present.

Six in the Second Place (**Ruling Line**)

Darkening of the light.
Injured in the left thigh.
Saved by a strong horse.
Good fortune.

"A strong horse" symbolizes spirit. The lesson of the line is that an indomitable spirit that works for the good can turn a temporary loss to advantage.

You have suffered a setback that seems crippling at first. But do not be discouraged. Rouse your spirits. Let this state of affairs spur you on to do something genuinely worthy that serves the interests of everybody concerned. By focusing on others rather than pitying yourself, you will gain strength and purpose. Remain calm and balanced now, and you can turn apparent defeat into victory.

Nine in the Third Place

Darkening of the light.
Hunting in the south,
The great chief is captured.
Do not be hasty.
Persevere.

You come face-to-face with the source of your difficulties and you now understand what has been holding you back. Gather your wits about you. The time has come to act with determination. You must take control and reform the situation. Nevertheless, you must also proceed carefully. It is dangerous to try to remedy everything at once, especially when you are fighting against ingrained patterns of behavior. The problems you face—whether due to negative thinking, bad habits, or outmoded practices—have not arisen overnight, and they will take a long time to rectify. Hence the text advises: "Do not be hasty," but "[p]ersevere."

Six in the Fourth Place

He penetrates the left side of the belly.
He gets at the very heart of the darkening of the light,
And leaves the gate and courtyard.

You see the situation now with perfect clarity. All illusions are stripped away. You understand the sources of the difficulty and you recognize that things will not improve. Therefore, the best strategy is to withdraw while you can still protect your interests.

Six in the Fifth Place (Ruling Line)

The darkening of the light of Prince Ji.
It is beneficial to persevere.

Prince Ji was the uncle of Dixin, the last Shang king, who was an evil tyrant. Prince Ji remonstrated with his nephew to stop his cruelty and dissolution. When the king refused to listen, Prince Ji wanted to resign as minister, but he could not leave the court because of his family connection. Instead, he feigned madness so that he could avoid doing evil. Although he was treated like a slave, he did not allow his misery and deprivation to divert him from his principles. After Dixin was overthrown by the Zhou, Prince Ji was rehabilitated and was asked to instruct the new Zhou rulers about the wise polices of the Shang kings of old. The lesson of Prince Ji is that when a person cannot escape dark times he should hide his light and persevere rather than compromise his integrity. During a time of corruption one must hold one's self apart from the powers that be rather than join them and let one's self become corrupted.

Your environment is inhospitable to you now, and you find that you must endure difficulties and hardships. Your powers of perseverance are being severely tested. Recognize the extent to which your problems are due to events beyond your control. It is not wise to struggle against circumstances right now. You must adapt to the situation, but there is a right way and a wrong way to do so. The wrong way is to compromise your principles and abandon your values so that you can fit in. The right way is to keep your true thoughts and feelings to yourself and maintain a low profile. You must acquiesce to the current situation for the time being, but do not let yourself be taken over by it. Be cautious and exercise self-control. Ultimately matters will improve and your perseverance will be rewarded.

Six at the Top (Constituitive Line)

Not bright, but dark.
First he ascended to heaven,
Then he fell into the earth.

The darkening of the light has gone as far as it can. The law of change is in operation, for as soon as the forces of darkness reach their zenith, they begin a precipitous decline. Evil feeds off good. When the good is fully extinguished, evil has no means of sustenance and inevitably must decline. When disorder has consumed all order, it begins to consume itself.

The bad times are coming to an end. Power and resources have been misused in the past, but these regrettable practices have now begun to decay and will eventually disintegrate, opening the way for new possibilities and better days to come. Recognize the seeds of change now emerging in the situation and take heart. There is hope for the future.

NOTES

36.0 "Darkening of the Light." *Yi* means "darken," a similar ideograph means "injure." Hence another name for the hexagram is Injuring of the Light, or Brilliance Injured.

36.GI "oversees." *li:* overlook, manage, supervise. Or, "lives with" (Wilhelm/Baynes); "remains in harmony with" (Alfred Huang).

36.3 "hasty." *ji:* affliction, or illness; also means "rash" or "hasty."

36.4 "gets at." *huo:* catches.

36.4 "leaves." *chu:* goes out.

THIRTY-SEVEN

Jia Ren • The Family

䷤

Keywords:

The household
The family
The clan
Close-knit groups
House people
Playing your part
Establishing expectations
Serving as an example
Creating mutuality and trust

Above: Xun • Wind (Wood)
Below: Li • Fire

Jia Ren literally means "house people." It refers to all the members of a household. The constituent trigrams are Li (Fire) and Xun (Wind, Wood). Fire burning under wood represents the hearth, a traditional symbol of house, home, and family.

The basic theme of the hexagram is that when all of the members of the family have their appropriate relationships to one another, the family is well ordered and will be at peace. The structure of the hexagram is thought to model these ideal relationships. Thus all the yin lines are in the even-numbered places, representing the women in the family, and (with one exception) the yang lines are in the odd-numbered places, representing the men in the family. Each of the yin lines corresponds to a yang line—the second to the fifth and the fourth to the first. In addition, the second and fifth lines are both correctly placed and central. They represent the wife and the husband, respectively.

In this sense the Hexagram resembles Hexagram 63, Ji Ji (After Completion) in which all of the lines are in their "appropriate" positions—yang lines in odd-numbered positions, yin lines in even-numbered positions. The only difference from Ji Ji is that the sixth, or top, line is yang. This reflects the strongly patriarchal vision of ancient Chinese society. The top line represents the head of the family, and is therefore expected to be a man. Hence the line is yang. This wrecks the perfect symmetry of the lines, for the yang line in the sixth line does not properly correspond to the yang line in the third place. Thus, it appears that to the creators of the *Book of Changes,* patriarchy was more important to proper social ordering than symmetry.

THE JUDGMENT

The Family.
The perseverance of a woman is beneficial.

Although the hexagram Jia Ren concerns the family, in ancient China the family was a metaphor and model for virtually all other forms of social organization. Hence the hexagram is also about the ideal forms of social life and social relations. Each of the members of the family—father, mother, son, daughter, elder sibling, younger sibling—had specific duties and relationships. When each of them fulfilled their proper obligations to the others, each of them played their respective role (as father, mother, son, daughter, etc.) appropriately, and the family was well ordered. The Chinese believed that if the family was well ordered, then all of society would be well ordered.

In ancient Chinese society, men were expected to be the heads of households; women were expected to be subordinate to them. The relationship between superior and subordinate was analogized to that between a man and a woman in a family. Hence a subordinate is always yin to the superior's yang. Because, in China, everyone was subordinate to someone else, everyone—including all men—were yin to somebody else's yang. Thus when the text says "the perseverance of a woman is beneficial," it refers to the steadfast uprightness of a person who is in a yin (subordinate) position.

In today's more egalitarian society, we cannot accept the *Book of Changes'* assumptions about the respective roles of the sexes, or its acceptance of natural hierarchies among people based on the model of the family. Nevertheless, the more general advice that the *Book of Changes* offers is still valid. It applies to any social relationship, and especially to close-knit organizations. If you want the relationship or the organization to run smoothly, you must be committed to it. Play your appropriate and assigned role and work for the greater good of everyone involved. If everyone in the organization does this, it will be well ordered and peace will reign.

Duties and responsibilities should be laid out clearly in advance so that everyone knows their role and feels that they will be valued for their contribution, whether they are a leader, a follower, a specialist, or one among equals. The group should be well ordered so that people know what they can expect from others and know what is expected of them. They must be able to take pride in their contribution to the greater good and they must be honored and recognized for what they do. Then they will not feel abused or put upon and social bonds will be strengthened over time.

It is not enough to assign people roles and expect them to fill them. Trust, consideration, and mutual affection are also necessary for relationships to thrive and prosper. Mechanically enforcing order misses the informal elements of mutuality, reciprocity, and affection that are necessary to any successful long-term alliance. If the relationship is too rigid, it will not stand the stresses that everyday life puts on it, much less the strains caused by a genuine crisis. Mutuality and benevolence bind the group together and give it the flexibility to improvise and change to meet changing times.

If you have not been paying enough attention to your relationships, now is a good time to mend fences, renew lines of communication, and show people that you care about and respect them. Remember that the social cement of courtesy and reciprocity binds close-knit groups together. All too often we treat the people we live with every day with less respect and give them less attention than we do perfect strangers or mere acquaintances that we are trying to impress. Intimacy should not mean taking people for granted. Rather, it should mean valuing those close to you especially. Showing a little consideration every now and then will help keep the relationship together through adversity.

If the problem is lack of discipline, you should immediately take steps to restore order. It may be necessary to get tough for a while until appropriate expectations are reestablished. But the point of discipline is not to wield power or to inflict punishment for its own sake. It is to let everyone know where they stand and show them how others rely on them. Good discipline and clear expectations within the family can actually support the mutual trust and affection of its members, just as trust and affection can help keep relationships well ordered and running smoothly.

THE IMAGE

Wind emerges from the fire:
This is the image of the Family.
Thus the superior person ensures
That his words have substance
And his deeds constancy.

Wind emerges from fire because fire contains energy that propels the air around it outward. In the same way, the outward effects you have on others depend on the qualities that are deep inside you. The key to your influence lies in your character.

If you want your family or close-knit group to function well, you must be cooperative and prepared to do your part. Do not be arrogant or assertive. Listen to other people's point of view and try to see things from their perspective. Look out for their interests as well as your own. Consider what you can do to nurture and benefit them.

Keeping a relationship going requires sensitivity and tact. It also requires influencing and guiding people. If you want to influence people in the right way, you must be honest and sincere. Don't engage in double talk or try to manipulate people. If you do, people will either try to manipulate you in return or they will grow to resent you. Don't speak in abstract generalities. Let people know where they stand and what you expect them to do. Give people encouragement and instruction when they need it; don't leave them to fend for themselves.

If you want to have a positive effect on others, you must lead by example. Trust and reciprocity must be established by your actions as well as your words. What you say to others will have influence only if people know that you will back it up with your deeds. If people see that they can rely on you to act unselfishly in the interests of the group, they will listen to you and follow your example. But if you simply exhort them to behave, order them around, and don't follow through on what you say, they will lose respect for you and their efforts will be halfhearted. "Do as I say, not as I do" is the wrong strategy if you want people to take you seriously. You must practice what you preach. Don't ask people to do anything that you yourself would be unwilling to do if you were in their position. If you willingly take on burdens for yourself and happily contribute to the well-being of others, people will believe in you and they will be willing to play their appropriate roles. Then the group will run smoothly.

The same principles hold in imposing discipline on the group. The rules you apply to others must apply to yourself as well. Treat others with the same respect that you would want for yourself. If people think that you are being arbitrary, they will resist you. But if they see that you are trying to be fair and consistent, they will respond positively to your guidance.

THE LINES

The lines describe different duties and responsibilities of persons in a family or close-knit social group. In each case, the lines are, on the whole, positive, suggesting how highly the ancient Chinese regarded the values of mutual respect and cooperation within the family and in society as a whole. Line one advises that at the outset we determine who belongs to the group and what each person's responsibilities are. Line two counsels us to subordinate our ambitions for the good of the group. Line three emphasizes the need for discipline to maintain harmony. In lines four and five the dual virtues of cooperation and leadership are duly rewarded. In this hexagram, line six represents the ultimate outcome of following the advice of the other lines: Our efforts earn respect and bestow good fortune.

Initial Nine

Enclosing and guarding the family.
Regrets vanish.

To "enclos[e] and guard the family" means to define the family (thus separating it from the outside) and to maintain its integrity (thus preventing it from dissolution).

In a close-knit group it is essential that everyone feel equally accepted and committed to the enterprise. Acceptance leads to trust, trust leads to loyalty, and loyalty leads to a desire to work for the greater good. For this reason you must decide who is part of the group and who is not, for if the boundaries are unclear, then people will feel anxious and uncertain about their status in the group and how and whether they fit in. You cannot expect people to be committed to you if you are not committed to them.

In addition, each member of the group must understand his or her role and responsibilities, and how he or she fits into the larger picture. If you let people know where they stand, they will be more willing to trust each other and work together. Establish basic ground rules for cooperation, and exercise discipline so that people can expect that things will run smoothly. When lines of command and responsibilities are clear and respected at the outset, things can grow naturally and organically. Moreover, the group will be able to bear the disagreements, stresses, and strains that inevitably come when people must work closely together. On the other hand, if you do not set ground rules at the beginning, you will cause trouble for yourself later on.

Six in the Second Place (Ruling Line)

Not chasing after whim or desire.
Remain in the center and prepare the food.
Perseverance brings good fortune.

To "remain in the center" means to cultivate the virtues of modesty and moderation in your actions and desires. To "prepare the food" means performing everyday labors, living up to your duties, and taking care of others.

Attend to your immediate responsibilities and quietly carry out your obligations to the best of your abilities. Do not act impulsively. Do not make yourself unhappy by pining after things you do not have. This is not a time to put yourself forward or to try to achieve things through force. Rather you should progress step by step and labor unselfishly. Stick to the business at hand and consider how you may be of help to others. If you act to nourish others and if you work steadily without fuss or show, others will respect your unselfish devotion. You will become an indispensible member of the group; indeed, you will be positioned at its very center. Hence the text says, "Perseverance brings good fortune."

Nine in the Third Place

Family members are scolded and rebuked.
Repenting this severity
Brings good fortune.
Yet if women and children giggle foolishly,
There will be humiliation in the end.

A close-knit group needs discipline, but you should not be too strict or too severe. You must not try to force your will on others or lose your temper and lash out at people. Words spoken in anger cannot be taken back. Treating people badly or denying them respect destroys trust and can produce lasting damage. Rather, it is best to set basic ground rules so that everyone knows their responsibilities and obligations to others, and then let people exercise their best judgment within these boundaries.

Here as elsewhere a moderate approach is best. But it is better to err on the side of discipline. If you do not give people clear expectations about what is permissible and what is not, things will become increasingly disordered. If you are overindulgent, people will take advantage of your laxity, cut corners, and fail to show proper respect for others. This will weaken the group's bonds and lessen the commitment of its members. The result will be chaos and humiliation.

Setting boundaries and asking people to live up to high standards can be healthy if it is done from the right motives and if you lead by example and hold yourself to the same standards that you expect of others. Discipline that is enforced not out of a selfish desire for power but out of genuine respect for the group and its members promotes the group's spirit and improves the quality of its performance.

Six in the Fourth Place

Enriching the household.
Great good fortune.

"Enriching the household" means working for others rather than merely for yourself.

Consider how you can contribute to the economy of your group. Others depend on you for sustenance, whether material or spiritual. Do not let them down. If you are willing to be of service, you will enjoy great good fortune. Your modesty and benevolence will make you invaluable to others, and your good deeds will enrich you as well as them.

Nine in the Fifth Place (Ruling Line)

The king approaches his family.
Do not worry.
Good fortune.

This describes a relationship of trust and mutual affection between the leader of a group and its members. The leader is magnanimous; he looks after the interests of others rather than trying to control them, aggrandize himself, or maximize his power. Hence, they have no reason to fear his authority. The leader exercises a beneficial influence through his character and through the example he sets for others. Because there is love and mutual respect, people can be open with each other. The result is happiness and success.

Apply these principles to your own life. Treat those under your authority and care with kindness and magnanimity. Behave with dignity and integrity, as a great king would, and set a proper example for others to follow. Then all your efforts will meet with good fortune.

Nine at the Top

He inspires trust and commands respect.
In the end, good fortune comes.

The success of a group depends on the quality of its leaders. This applies both to those who are in official positions of authority and those who lead by their example. Examine yourself and hold fast to your ideals. If you are true to yourself, you will influence others in exactly the right way. You will not need to exert authority; rather the strength of your character and your benevolence naturally will draw others to follow your lead. Carry out your responsibilities faithfully and you will win people's confidence. In the end, you will gain the recognition you deserve and you will be respected for your ideas and for your good works.

NOTES

37.0 "The perseverance of a woman is beneficial." Or, "It is beneficial to persevere like a woman."

37.GI "And his deeds constancy." *heng:* duration, endurance, constancy. Or, "And his deeds endure," "And his deeds (actions) are consistent."

37.1 "Enclosing and guarding the family." This translation tries to combine the meaning of two different interpretations of this line, "Firm seclusion within the family" (Wilhelm/Baynes), and "strict control" over the family (Lynn).

37.2 The hexagram has two rulers, one yin and one yang, which symbolize woman and man, respectively. Because this is a yin line, it is often translated as "She does not follow her whims (is without ambition), but stays inside and prepares the food." However, *xiong* is often translated as "the middle," e.g., 24.4 ("Walking in the middle, / One returns alone"). The present translation not only has the advantage of being less sexist; it also makes a better connection to the theme of being centered and walking in the middle way.

37.3 "scolded and rebuked." *he he:* sound of sighing, literally, "moan, moan."

37.3 "Repenting this severity." *hui li:* literally, "regret danger (harshness or adversity)"; hence "If one regrets such harshness."

37.3 "giggle foolishly." *xi xi:* sound of giggling.

37.3 "There will be humiliation in the end." *xiong lin:* end distress (abashment). Or, "This results in humiliation."

37.4 "Enriching the household." *fu jia.* Because this is a yin line, it is sometimes translated "She is the treasure of the house."

37.5 "The king approaches," etc. Or, "Like a king he approaches his family," suggesting that success will come from kingly (magnanimous, noble, generous) behavior.

37.5 "Approaches." *Jia* is also translated "imagines," or "influences," but "approaches" seems more correct in context. Cf. Hexagrams 45 and 59. Wilhelm / Baynes writes of this line: "A king is the symbol of a fatherly man who is richly endowed in mind."

37.6 "He inspires trust and commands respect." *you fu:* possessing trust. *wei ru*: awelike, dignified, garnering respect. Wilhem / Baynes translates this, "His work commands respect," that is, his efforts are rewarded in the end. "Being sincere and upright, / With dignity, / Ends in good fortune" (Alfred Huang).

37.6 "He inspires trust and commands respect." The commentaries add "he relies on self-examination."

THIRTY-EIGHT

Kui • Opposition

䷥

Keywords:

Estrangement
Misunderstanding
Different points of view
Polarity
Diversity
Creative tension
Finding commonality within difference

Above: Li • Fire
Below: Dui • Lake

Kui means "estrangement" or "misunderstanding." Its original meaning was "eyes that do not look at each other" or "eyes out of alignment." It is the reverse of Jia Ren. In Jia Ren, the family is well ordered and everyone is in their place; in Kui things are disordered and everything is out of place. This is reflected in the structure of the hexagram lines. In Jia Ren, all of the lines of the hexagram (except the sixth) are appropriately positioned—yang lines in odd-numbered places and yin lines in even-numbered. In Kui all the lines (except the first) are inappropriately positioned—yin in odd-numbered places and yang in even-numbered. In this respect the hexagram resembles Number 64, Wei Ji (Before Completion); the only difference is that the first yang line (which represents beginnings) is properly positioned. This symbolizes one of the hexagram's main themes—that even in opposition the possibilities of realignment and reconciliation are still present. Thus, Kui does not necessarily signify permanent estrangement. It concerns temporary misunderstandings that will persist if nothing is done but that nevertheless can be overcome with the proper effort and sensitivity. It is therefore a hexagram of hope rather than despair. In addition, although all of the lines are wrongly placed, the second and fifth lines correspond, as do the third and sixth. This symbolizes that opposition, even if unpleasant, often has important synergies. Creative tension can sometimes be beneficial. This is the hexagram's second major theme.

The upper trigram is Li (Fire); the lower is Dui (Lake). Fire and water are opposites that do not blend well together. Fire boils (and hence dissipates) water; water extinguishes fire. Fire burns upward; the water in the lake seeps downward. The upper trigram represents the middle sister in the family, while the lower trigram represents the younger sister. Sisters often quarrel and are jealous of each other, but each is part of the same family. Their differences flow out of what they have in common. The recognition of commonality within opposition is the hexagram's third theme.

THE JUDGMENT

Opposition. In small matters there is good fortune.

Opposition and estrangement have entered the situation. Misunderstandings have arisen, and so people mistrust and doubt each other. For this reason they are not cooperating and cannot make any progress. In these circumstances it is important to proceed slowly and carefully. Mistrust has to be dissipated gradually, in small steps. Hence the text says that good fortune comes from small things.

Even in marked opposition there is usually some kind of commonality. In order to relax the tensions, it is best to remind people of what they have in common and turn their attention to values that all share.

If you find yourself estranged from other people, try to see things from their point of view. Consider that they are probably as mistrustful of you as you are of them. Viewing other people not as enemies but as fellow human beings trying to make their way in the world is the first step to resolving the conflict.

Be tolerant and gracious. Be willing to make the first move in order to meet other people halfway. Doing this will begin to dissipate the atmosphere of confrontation and mutual suspicion. By altering the tone of your interactions and making signs that you seek understanding and reconciliation, you can begin breaking down barriers of mistrust and soften attitudes that have hardened over time. But it is important to proceed with great sensitivity and caution. Do not think that you can make everything better overnight. Trust takes time to be reestablished, especially when opposition has been severe or longstanding. Do not rush things. Give people—including yourself—time to move closer together and find a method of reconciliation.

In a time of opposition, making the first move takes courage. Don't allow your pride or your fear of being thought weak keep you from reaching out to others and resolving misunderstandings. People cling to opposition not because they are strong but because they are weak: The situation makes them feel insecure and they are afraid of what will happen if they expose themselves. As a result, they allow resentments to build and misunderstandings to fester. By contrast, people who know their own worth are the ones who can afford to be tolerant and generous. They understand that people can improve their lives if they are willing to risk a little emotional pain and uncertainty. They do not confuse tolerance with deficiency or magnanimity with weakness.

THE IMAGE

Fire is above, Lake below:
This is the image of Opposition.
The superior person seeks common ground,
While recognizing differences.

Fire and water are opposites, but their opposition is part of a larger whole. In the same way, what appear to be opposites may have hidden elements of commonality in a greater scheme. Indeed, opposition is an essential part of life and propels it forward. According to the *Book of Changes,* everything comes from the interaction of opposites, yin and yang. Opposition gives life creative tension. It is a source of change, growth, and renewal.

Opposition often seems like a misfortune or a hindrance, but it can also stimulate you. It can shake you out of old ways of thinking and present you with new possibilities. On the other hand, opposition can also exhaust you and make you unhappy. It is up to you to decide how to handle it. Try to maintain a positive attitude in the face of uncertainty. When faced with opposition or disagreement, consider how it may actually be useful. You and the other person may each have something to learn from the situation. If you can resolve your differences, each side may grow in the process.

Nevertheless, resolution of opposition is not the same thing as surrender. Each side must respect the other and recognize that there are genuine differences. Listen to the other person's point of view, but do not give up your own sense of what is right and wrong. Hence the text says that you must seek common ground while understanding that differences still remain. In fact, it is only through maintaining your own integrity and your own moral compass that you can begin to understand other people and give them their due. Thus your perspective is not simply what separates you from others; it is what allows you to understand their perspective and respect them as human beings. Through differences common ground can be recognized; through commonalities difference can be accepted and respected.

THE LINES

The lines describe various stages of misunderstanding that arise among people, and how they are overcome. The first line concerns only a minor misunderstanding; the sixth line is most serious. Yet in almost every case, the estrangement is overcome, and there is a good ending. The *Book of Changes* views difference between people as creative rather than merely destructive. It holds out the hope of eventual harmony for all of humanity.

Initial Nine

Regrets vanish.
If you lose a horse, do not run after it;
It will return by itself.
If you see evil people,
There will be no blame.

Every now and then minor disagreements and misunderstandings flare up between people who naturally belong together. Do not worry when this happens. The estrangement is upsetting, but it is only temporary. Things will eventually return to normal if you do not try to force a reconciliation immediately. Instead, let matters sort themselves out at their own pace. If people truly belong with you, they will eventually return to patch things up because the relationship is as important to them as it is to you. Nevertheless, it is important to take a gentle and patient approach because pride and self-esteem are often at stake in such misunderstandings. Let tempers cool and give people a chance to save face.

What is true of relationships is also true of situations. If elements that belong together are momentarily estranged, you should not try to bring them back together by force. Let things return to normal naturally. Have faith that things that are together are together for a reason and that momentary disturbances in equilibrium will usually be self-correcting. The text compares this principle to a horse that knows and trusts its rider; if let go it will come back of its own accord.

On the other hand, sometimes misunderstandings lead people whom we should not deal with to approach us. Treating them harshly will only anger them and produce unnecessary hostility and conflict. Be diplomatic, but keep them at a distance, and they will eventually get the message. Similarly, if something base or inferior is being forced upon you, do not react violently. Simply refuse it politely but firmly.

Nine in the Second Place (Ruling Line)

One meets his lord in a narrow lane.
No blame.

The line tells the story of a vassal who comes across his lord in a narrow passage or alleyway. There are two different interpretations of the tale. In the first version the vassal is momentarily estranged from his superior, but the chance encounter clears the air and the misunderstanding is resolved. Metaphorically, one's "lord" refers not merely to a superior but to a soul mate or a person with whom one has an important affinity. Hence the meaning is that when misunderstandings have estranged you from others that you belong with, you may be able to reconcile if you meet them under informal circumstances, where expectations are low and there is no pressure.

In the second version of the story the vassal encounters the lord for the first time in the narrow lane. He would not dare approach him otherwise, but the accidental encounter makes the meeting possible. Each recognizes a kindred spirit in the other, and the result is a happy union. The meaning here is that you should be open to chance encounters or an unexpected turn of events. Out in the world there are many people and many situations that we might have natural affinities with, and if we open ourselves to the possibilities of such encounters, we may benefit greatly. Never underestimate the ability of destiny to bring you in contact with others. Chance often provides opportunities that you could never have pursued directly.

Six in the Third Place

One sees the cart dragged back,
One's ox halted,
One's forehead tattooed,
And one's nose cut off.
Not a good beginning, but there will be a good end.

The text describes the apprehension and punishment of a criminal. His forehead is tattooed and his nose is cut off. The meaning is that estrangement makes one feel like a criminal in the eyes of others, but that if one persists in proper conduct this feeling will pass and the situation will improve.

Everything seems to be going wrong. Your best efforts are blocked. People misunderstand you and treat you with disrespect. Do not give up hope. Although things have not begun the way you wanted, have faith that matters can still work out for the best. Stick to your principles and stand up for what you know is right. Turn to good and able people that you can trust to help you. In the end, things will turn out well.

Nine in the Fourth Place

Isolated through opposition,
He meets a person of fundamental maturity.
They can trust each other.
Thus, despite danger,
There is no blame.

You feel isolated and estranged. But things will improve. You will find someone of like mind whom you can trust and with whom you share a deep affinity. Your feelings of estrangement will dissolve. Together you can overcome your difficulties and achieve much.

Six in the Fifth Place (Ruling Line)

Regrets vanish.
Members of his clan bite through the tender meat.
If one goes forward,
What blame could there be?

Because of mistrust and estrangement, you may fail to recognize that another person sincerely wants to help you or genuinely seeks reconciliation. Despite your initial misgivings, you should accept the offer. Working together now will bring good fortune for all. The text compares your difficulties to tender meat, which is easy to bite through; in other words, the difficulty is illusory. The other party has made the first step and has "bit[ten] through the tender meat"; the problem can easily be resolved if you open your eyes and allow yourself to make the right decision. When people display genuine sincerity, even in a time of abundant mistrust and opposition, it is not a mistake to cooperate with them. Hence the text says, "If one goes forward, / What blame could there be?"

Nine at the Top

Isolated through opposition,
One sees the other as a pig covered in mud,
As a wagon full of demons.
At first one draws the bow,
Then one lays it aside.
He does not seek to plunder; he seeks to marry.
Going forward, one meets with rain.
Then good fortune comes.

Here estrangement arises from inner turmoil that leads to illusions and unrealistic fears. Hence you "see[ ] the other as a pig covered in mud," or as "a wagon full of demons." Your emotions and fears have eaten away at the trust you have for others and have caused you to lose all perspective on the situation. You now question the motives of your true friends and other people who in fact mean you well. As a result, you become defensive and aggressive. But eventually you will realize that you are mistaken, and the tensions in the situation will begin to dissipate and ebb. As opposition reaches its height, it begins to change into its opposite, and trust is restored. When you try to see the other person's point of view, you will recognize that those you are angry with are not the evil people you imagined but in fact mean you no harm. When you stop imagining slights and injuries where there are none, your attitude toward others will become more realistic and your relationships will be strengthened and renewed. Meeting people halfway clears the air like the period following a rainfall. The time of opposition comes to an end, and the way is now prepared for union with others that brings good fortune to all.

NOTES

38.1 "If you lose a horse, do not run after it; / It will return by itself." Cf. 51.2, 63.2.

38.1 "There will be no blame." *wu jiu:* no blame. "Guard yourself against mistakes" (Wilhelm / Baynes).

38.3 "forehead tattooed and . . . nose cut off." A punishment administered to criminals.

38.3 "Not a good beginning, but there will be a good end." *wu chu you zhong:* literally, "without a beginning, there is an end."

38.4 "fundamental maturity." *yuan fu:* literally, "prime husband." *yuan:* initiating, primary, source, originary, supreme. In 17.2 and 17.4, *fu* means "adult," hence "mature." Another translation is "prime stalwart" (Lynn).

38.4 "They can trust each other." Or, "whom he can trust." *jiao fu:* literally, "cross-sincerity."

38.5 "bite through the tender meat." Cf. 21.2.

38.6 "sees the other as." Or, "sees him as." The reference is to the person or persons from whom one (the subject of the line) is estranged.

38.6 "lays it aside." Or, "loosens it," "unstrings it."

THIRTY-NINE

Jian • Obstruction

䷦

Keywords:

Limping
Stumbling
Adversity
Impediment
Trouble
Difficulty
Hardship
Hindrance
Looking inward
Self-reflection
Surmounting the obstacles within

Above: Kan • Water
Below: Gen • Mountain

Jian originally meant "limping" or "stumbling"; here it means obstacles more generally. The constituent trigrams feature a dangerous abyss (or water) on one side and a steep mountain on the other side. One is between the proverbial rock and a hard place. Water symbolizes heart; mountain symbolizes patience and keeping still. Hence the hexagram's theme: When faced with obstacles, we should not lose courage but remain calm, redirect our attention to our spiritual development, and wait for conditions to improve.

THE JUDGMENT

Obstruction.
The southwest is beneficial.
The northeast is not.
It is beneficial to see a great person.
Perseverance brings good fortune.

The southwest represents receptivity and patience; the northeast represents assertion and advance. Hence the text says that instead of pressing ahead urgently one should hold back and accept the situation for what it is.

You are faced with obstacles that you cannot overcome. The more you struggle with your problems, the larger they seem to loom. It is time to take a break from your efforts and pause. Stop trying to make everything work. Stop trying to make the world conform to your wishes. Your current strategies clearly have not been successful. You need time to reassess things. For a while, at least, you need to let go of your emotional involvement with the situation, step back, and take a broader view. Admit to yourself that you simply do not know what to do. Instead, open your heart and your mind and patiently rethink your situation. Stop trying to enforce your will. Instead, look at things with detachment, humility, and acceptance. Be willing to learn.

The point of detaching yourself from your current struggles is not to give up hope of eventual success. Quite the contrary: You must be absolutely determined to prevail in the long run. Rather, the point is to restore your emotional balance and clear your head. Before you can regroup, you must free yourself from the emotional entanglements of past approaches that have proven counterproductive. You need a fresh start and a fresh attitude. This is the meaning of the statement that the "southwest" is beneficial. In the *Book of Changes*, the southwest is the direction associated with the earth. By adopting the virtues associated with earth—acceptance, humility, devotion, and patience—you will regain your composure and recharge your batteries.

The text says, "It is beneficial to see a great person." After you have taken the time to reassess the situation, you need to join forces with others. Ask for advice from people you respect and trust, and who understand you and your goals. They may have fresh perspectives. Don't be too stubborn to admit that you need help or too proud to accept it from others. Work together with people to tackle the problem rather than trying to go it alone.

Finally, do not give up hope. Persevere. Even though you may have to wait, or make a strategic retreat, if you maintain an enduring devotion to achieving your goal, you will eventually prevail. The test of great character is the ability to let go and walk away temporarily from a goal while being utterly devoted to achieving it in the long run. The obstructions that you face today will help develop your character so that you can better meet the challenges of the future. When obstruction leads to reassessment and self-improvement, it can even be a blessing in disguise.

THE IMAGE

Beyond the mountain, there is water:
This is the image of Obstruction.
Thus the superior person reflects on himself
And cultivates his character.

A mountain is difficult to cross, but so is water. This suggests that you face repeated obstacles and hindrances. Water represents emotions and inner being; the mountain symbolizes patience. When water is calm, it reflects an undistorted image of the mountain beyond it. Hence in times of adversity wise people calm themselves so that they can better reflect on their situation.

The secret to dealing with obstruction is to recognize that the problems you face are both external to you and inside you. To deal with the obstructions without, you must focus on the obstructions within. Emotional baggage, unrealistic expectations, and narrow, limited ways of thinking can hinder you every bit as much as physical obstacles. You must free yourself from these internal impediments if you want to have any chance at freeing yourself from impediments in the outside world.

Stop blaming other people for your troubles. Stop viewing yourself as a victim of circumstances. Look deep inside and consider how to improve yourself. The problem may be negative thinking, lack of vision, pride, obstinacy, inflexibility, or simple selfishness and immaturity. Perhaps you have your priorities misaligned. Perhaps you have unrealistic expectations of other people or hold yourself to too high a standard. Whatever the problem, now is the time for reassessment and reflection. You need to give up illusions and gain some much-needed perspective on the situation.

Use the obstacles that you face in the outside world as the occasion for your introspection. So much of this world is out of your hands, and there is little that you can do about it. But how you deal with life's changes and challenges is very much within your control. Obstacles and hindrances throw you back on your own devices. They are the true test of your character. Instead of wallowing in self-pity, make the most of this opportunity for self-development.

THE LINES

In most of the lines the proper strategy for dealing with obstruction is "coming back"—not forcing the issue but maintaining the right attitude toward the situation and dealing with the impediments and obstructions within one's self. All of the lines in this hexagram are favorable or not unfavorable, for the *Book of Changes* teaches that no matter how great the obstacles, there is always hope for one who returns to the Way.

Initial Six

Going forward means obstruction;
Coming back means praise.

Do not try to overcome the obstacle you face immediately or attempt to move past it by force. Hold back and consider the best way to deal with it. Make a strategic retreat for the time being and wait for the right moment to act.

Six in the Second Place

The king's servant suffers obstruction upon obstruction,
But it is not on his own account.

You come face-to-face with obstacles. You would like to take the path of least resistance and avoid them. But this is not possible because of your duties and obligations to others. Hence you must meet the problem head-on. This would not be advisable if your interests alone were at stake. But when you have important responsibilities to others, or when you act in the service of a higher cause, it is the honorable way and there will be no blame.

Nine in the Third Place

Going forward means obstruction;
So he comes back.

This line is the converse of the last one. The second line counsels that you should encounter danger when your responsibilities to others require it. In this case you must not jeopardize your security because other people depend on you. If you go forward recklessly, you may not only injure yourself but also expose others close to you to danger; by compromising your own position you may leave those you care about without a source of support. On the other hand, if you desist and return to your circle, you will meet with approval and make no mistakes.

Six in the Fourth Place

Going forward means obstruction;
Coming back means connection.

You cannot deal with the obstacles you currently face by yourself. You lack the necessary strength, resources, and degree of preparation. If you try to take on your problems singlehandedly, you will be defeated. Instead, gather reliable allies. Reestablish your connections. Pool your resources and skills with others. Accept help and advice from people you know and trust. This is the right way to overcome your problems.

Nine in the Fifth Place (Ruling Line)

In the midst of great obstruction
Friends come.

A friend in need is a friend indeed. If people you care about are facing difficulties, do not hesitate to pitch in. Give whatever help and support you can and together you will overcome the obstacles. Do for them what you would want them to do for you.

Conversely, you may facing serious obstacles yourself. Do not give up hope. Gather your wits about you and resolve to confront your problems and overcome them. People will be attracted by your perseverance and strength of character. Your indomitable spirit will inspire others to come to your side. When they see that you do not buckle under when faced with adversity, they will be more willing to cooperate with you and help you prevail. The results of this alliance will benefit everyone.

Six at the Top

Going forward means obstruction,
Coming back means great achievement.
Good fortune.
It is beneficial to see a great person.

You may think that you are beyond the situation now. You would like to stick to your own business and let other people deal with the turmoil around you. But your hope rests on an illusion. Your fate is connected to the fates of others. You have duties and responsibilities even if you do not yet recognize them. You will inevitably be drawn back into this struggle. Therefore, you must decide what the right course of conduct is and join in. Ask for advice and assistance from people you trust. You have something important to contribute. If you work with others now you can achieve something truly great.

NOTES

39.0 "southwest. . . . northeast." Or, "the south and the west. . . . the north and the east." Cf. 2.0, 40.0.

39.GI "Beyond." *shang:* literally, above. The idea is that, having crossed the mountains, one must still cross the water, implying hardship upon hardship.

39.GI "reflects on himself." *fan shen:* reverse (turn around) individuality (psyche, body, self). Or, "turns attention to himself," "introspects," "is introspective."

39.GI "cultivates his character." *xiu de:* renovate virtue. Or, "molds his character" (Wilhelm/Baynes); "cultivates his virtue."

39.2 "suffers obstruction upon obstruction." *jian jian:* obstruction, obstruction. Or, "is beset by obstruction upon obstruction."

39.2 "But it is not on his own account." *fei gong zhi gu:* literally, "not body its cause." This might also be rendered as "But he is in no way the cause," or "But it is in no way his fault."

39.4 "means connection." *lian:* cart; i.e., "comes back in a cart." Or, "leads to involvement," "brings union."

39.5 "In the midst of great obstruction." etc. Or, "To one facing great obstruction," "To one in great Adversity friends will come" (Lynn).

39.6 "means great achievement." *shuo:* ripe, mature, full-grown; hence, great, eminent. Or, "ripens into something great," "brings eminence."

FORTY

Jie • Deliverance

䷧

Keywords:

Release
Relief
Separation
Removal
Loosening the knot
Untying
End of obstruction
End of hardships
Redemption
Forgiveness
Letting go of the past

Above: Zhen • Thunder
Below: Kan • Water

Jie originally meant to cut away, or to untie or loosen a knot. Later it came to mean to release; and eventually, to release or relieve a person from difficulty or suffering. Still later, it took on the moral connotations of redemption. It is the natural successor to Hexagram 39, Jian, Obstruction; it represents the moment when obstacles begin to be removed and deliverance is at hand. The trigrams Zhen and Kan symbolize a thunderstorm—thunder and rain—

that clears the air and washes away past grievances. The connection between deliverance and forgiveness is a central theme of the hexagram. One cannot break free of the past and experience redemption until one forgives others as well as one's self.

THE JUDGMENT

Deliverance. The southwest is beneficial.
If there is no longer somewhere to go,
Return brings good fortune.
If there is still somewhere to go,
An early start brings good fortune.

Things have been frustrating for a long time. You have been unable to make progress, or your relationships have been full of conflict and misunderstanding. Now things start to get better. Tensions begin to be eased. Difficulties begin to resolve themselves. It is as if a storm has broken and the air has suddenly cleared. You feel liberated from what had been a seemingly endless cycle of failure and frustration. There is new hope.

When conditions start to improve after a long period of stagnation, it is perfectly all right to celebrate and feel joy. A heavy burden has been lifted from your shoulders; it is no wonder that you feel stimulated. But the most important thing is to regain your balance. Hence the text speaks of the "southwest"—the direction traditionally associated with the earth. It is time to put yourself on solid ground and restore conditions of normalcy. Return to a healthy pattern of living and restore the natural rhythms of your life.

Now that tensions have begun to be relieved, you don't need to make any bold or audacious gestures. Things are already moving in the right direction. Instead, simply accept the changes and give thanks for your deliverance. Ask yourself whether there are any remaining matters that need to be taken care of to restore things to their regular and proper order. If there are, take care of them immediately. Do just what is necessary, promptly and unobtrusively, without making a fuss.

Spend some time thinking about why things went wrong. Did something in your behavior and your attitudes hold you back? Did you unwittingly keep the cycle of frustration going through your thoughts and actions? When the moment of deliverance comes, you have the opportunity to make things right and to let go of the mistakes of the past. There is no better time for this than the present. As the text says, "An early start brings good fortune."

THE IMAGE

Thunder and rain invigorate:
This is the image of Deliverance.
Thus the superior person forgives misdeeds
And pardons mistakes.

A thunderstorm clears the air. During the time of deliverance, you should endeavor to do the same. Conflict, stagnation, and unhappiness come from human failings and limitations—both the failings and limitations of others and those that are our own. Difficult times lead to difficult emotions, and difficult emotions lead to further difficulties. You may have regrets or anger about the past, or long-standing grievances. Now you must confront the unresolved issues in your life and deal with them. You must clear the air just as the rain does.

Don't dwell on past slights and injuries, or fixate on other people's faults and mistakes. This will not make you happy. Dwelling on the past means dwelling in the past. If you hold on to hatred and resentments, they will hold on to you and you will never be free of them. If you insist on taking your anger out on others—or on yourself—you will simply reenter the frustrating cycle that you have just left behind. Deliverance requires a fresh start—acceptance and forgiveness both of yourself and others—because that is the only way to restore normalcy and return to the natural rhythms of life. This is the meaning of the symbol of the rainstorm. Thunder disturbs old patterns; water washes everything clean.

Redemption is not merely freedom from outside forces. It is an inner freedom—the joy that comes from breaking the chains of an inner servitude that has crippled the soul. To attain peace of mind, let go of old scores and upsets. To deliver yourself from the past, deliver yourself from the emotions that chain you to the past. Doing this will free you and enable you to live in the here and now. You cannot always redeem others, but you can redeem yourself. Take a more positive attitude. Get rid of the hate in your heart. Be generous and forgiving. Then you will feel less like a victim and more in control of your life.

Don't bottle up your resentments, but bring your concerns out into the open. When you do, remember that the point is not to vent your anger or wreak vengeance; it is to resolve tensions and restore peace. Be willing to meet others halfway and talk over your problems in a spirit of goodwill.

Reconcile with those you can reconcile with. As for the others, simply let go of your hatred and move on.

THE LINES

The lines describe the various stages through which a person travels to attain deliverance. When obstacles first begin to be removed, one should simply recuperate and gain strength (line one). Later one should work on ridding one's self of bad influences and inner faults (lines two and four); become aware of one's limitations and understand who one really is (line three); and develop the inner resolve to succeed (line five). In line six careful planning and preparation pay off and one obtains a great victory.

Initial Six

Without blame.

When deliverance comes, it is time to recuperate. Be calm and at peace with yourself. You have surmounted your difficulties, and now you can progress naturally. But first it is important to consolidate your position, rest and recharge your batteries before going forward. Doing so is without blame.

Nine in the Second Place (**Ruling Line**)

One catches three foxes in the field
And receives a yellow arrow.
Perseverance brings good fortune.

The "three foxes" represent greed, ignorance, and fear—they hinder and obstruct your progress by filling you with negative emotions and incorrect assessments of the world around you. Yellow is the color of the mean. It represents the virtues of modesty and moderation—the ability to maintain emotional balance in the face of changing circumstances and to carry things through to completion. A straight arrow symbolizes taking the straight and upright course of action. Thus, to slay three foxes with a yellow (or golden) arrow means to overcome those negative emotions that create troubles in your life—to deliver yourself from the internal impediments that make external obstacles seem to loom so large. One slays these three foxes with a golden arrow—through cultivating virtues of modesty, steadfastness, and uprightness. This is the path of redemption. For even if we have failed ourselves in the past, and have undermined our own lives through inner turmoil and confusion, there is still hope. The golden arrow has yet another meaning. By tradition a golden arrow was awarded to a person who had achieved something great and honorable. Thus the text suggests that people who can internalize the virtues of modesty and moderation and commit themselves to a straight path deliver themselves from internal servitude and therefore can achieve great things.

Another interpretation of the text is that the three foxes are external to the self. They are cunning persons who bring disorder and hinder your progress; they represent destructive influences that work against you. You must act to protect your interests when people try to undermine you. But it is wrong to engage in unscrupulous methods to deal with unscrupulous behavior. Rather, one should slay these foxes with "a golden arrow." Be straightforward, upright, and honest in your dealings. That is the proper path to deliverance. Devote yourself wholeheartedly to redemption and you will gain the inner strength and confidence that will help you vanquish all that is base and low in your environment.

Six in the Third Place

Carrying a burden on one's back
While riding in a carriage
Brings about the arrival of robbers.
Perseverance brings humiliation.

Here an ordinary person who carries a heavy burden on his back rides in the carriage of an aristocrat. He pretends to be something he is not and takes on the trappings of a power he is not ready for. He burdens himself with baggage even though he could have stowed it with the rest of the luggage. As a result, he causes problems for himself, symbolized by the robbers who attack him on the road.

If you pretend to be something that you are not, you will invite envy from other people, who will try to make life difficult for you and even try to usurp you. Moreover, your own sense of insecurity may cause you to be pretentious, haughty, insolent, and aggressive. This will make others resent you all the more and try to bring you down. On the other hand, if you are modest and true to yourself, people will cooperate with you and respect you for who you really are. They will value you because you are what you appear to be.

A similar difficulty arises if you find yourself in a position of power that you do not know how to control. If you insist on doing something for which you are inadequately prepared or are not really suited, you will only bring trouble on yourself. In both cases you take on heavy baggage that you cannot carry, and you bring with you baggage of another sort—emotional baggage. You may harbor a secret sense of inadequacy and a fear that others will find you out. These emotions are self-destructive—they are a form of inner servitude that will only bring you grief. Take a more realistic attitude about yourself. Recognize both your limitations and your strengths. Acknowledge what is not really for you and what you are truly called to do. People with all the trappings of power and wealth will nevertheless remain unhappy, weak, and vulnerable if their situation does not match who they feel they really are. Being true to yourself is the best protection against such unhappiness and vulnerability.

Nine in the Fourth Place

Deliver yourself from your big toe.
Then a friend comes
Whom you can trust.

The "big toe" represents both inferior influences and something we come to depend on, just as we depend on the big toe in order to walk.

You have become accustomed to living with bad habits or inferior influences in your life. People who do not have your best interests at heart have attached themselves to you for selfish reasons. You may be in a parasitic or unhealthy relationship, which you have come to depend on emotionally. You need to free yourself from bad influences and behaviors and let go of relationships that are not healthy for you. These entanglements keep you from forming new and beneficial relationships with other people, and they repel valuable and trustworthy allies who could help you achieve your goals.

Six in the Fifth Place (Ruling Line)

If the superior person can deliver himself,
It brings good fortune.
He inspires trust even in petty people.

It is time to eliminate bad habits and behaviors and free yourself from relationships and situations that drag you down. Deliverance requires inner resolution and perseverance. You alone can save yourself. No one else can do it for you. But if you stay the course, people who undermine your self-worth or have an unhealthy influence in your life will see that you cannot be taken advantage of and they will withdraw of their own accord.

"Delivering yourself" means treating yourself with respect and developing a positive attitude toward who you are and what you do. Deliverance requires a narrative of redemption. It means believing in a vision of yourself and in a story of your life in which things can get better. If you hold fast to this vision and make this story your story, your life will indeed improve. By believing in yourself and becoming committed to your deliverance, you will no longer attract harmful people, and you will no longer get yourself entangled in unhealthy behaviors and difficult circumstances that you could have avoided.

Six at the Top

The duke shoots at a hawk atop a high wall.
He hits it.
There is nothing that is not beneficial.

The hawk on the high wall symbolizes inferior elements that have achieved a high position and are hindering your progress. It may refer to an actual adversary or to a bad habit or situation that holds you back. In any case, this obstacle is powerful and it stands between you and deliverance. Therefore, you must take forceful steps to eliminate it. The secret to success is clever timing and adequate preparation. Plan your response with care. Bide your time and make sure that your aim is true, like a marksman trying to hit a target perched on a high wall. Then, when the moment is right, take appropriate action. If you have planned correctly, you will hit the mark and your difficulties will fall away. Then nothing will stand in the way of your progress.

NOTES

40.0 "southwest." Or, "south and west." Cf. 2.0, 39.0.

40.0 "An early start." *su:* literally, "daybreak"; hence, hastening, with no delay.

40.GI "invigorate." *zuo:* arouse, stimulate, project, generate, appear, arise. Or, "set in" (Wilhelm/Baynes); "perform their roles" (Lynn).

40.2 "One catches three foxes in the field." *tian huo san hu*. Or, "One kills three foxes in the hunt." Cf. 40.6.

40.2 "And receives a yellow arrow." *de huang shi*. Or, "And obtains a golden arrow."

40.3 "Carrying a burden on one's back," etc. The traditional interpretation of this line began with the assumption that it was wrong for a common person—symbolized by the burden he carried—to ride in the carriage of an aristocrat. Because he failed to stay in his lowly position, he was punished by circumstances. A better interpretation is that one who pretends to be something he is not asks for trouble. A still better interpretation begins by asking the simple question why a person who rides in a carriage would carry a burden on his back rather than stow it as luggage. He does so because the burden is emotional—he carries it with him everywhere, even when he rides in a fancy carriage. This interpretation is more consistent with the spirit of the hexagram as a whole—deliverance from internal burdens is necessary for our redemption. A person who cannot get rid of his emotional baggage cannot succeed even if he rides in the carriage of a rich person—i.e., even if he has all the trappings of power and success.

40.3 "Brings about the arrival of robbers." I.e., he tempts robbers to attack him. Cf. 5.3.

40.4 "big toe." *mu:* thumb, big toe, great toe. Cf. 31.1.

40.5 "He inspires trust even in petty people." An alternative rendering is "He is sincere and truthful to the common people."

40.6 "duke." *gong*. Or, "prince." Cf. 14.3, 42.3, 42.4, 50.4, 62.5.

40.6 "He hits it." *huo:* catch, kill. Cf. 40.2.

FORTY-ONE

Sun • Decrease

䷨

Keywords:

Diminution
Loss
Reduction
Scaling back
Avoiding excess
Less is more

Above: Gen • Mountain
Below: Dui • Lake

Sun (Decrease) and Yi (Increase) are an important conceptual pair in the *Book of Changes,* like Qian and Kun (Hexagrams 1 and 2) or Tai and Pi (Hexagrams 11 and 12). When things have increased as much as they can, they begin to decrease, and vice versa. The *Book of Changes* argues that increase relies on decrease. Every increase either involves a decrease somewhere else or eventually produces decrease. Conversely, decrease relies on increase: Every decrease either involves a corresponding increase, or eventually leads to an increase.

The hexagram for Sun symbolizes this relationship. It is a transformation of Hexagram 11, Tai (Peace), which features three yang lines below and three yin lines above. In Sun, the third line—originally yang—has moved to the top, and the top line—originally yin—has moved to the third position. As what is below is decreased, what is above is increased. However, decreasing what is below to serve what is above is regarded as a net decrease. That is because those above should serve the interests of those below. When rulers impoverish their people in order to enrich themselves, the country as a whole is made worse off. Decrease is only proper when the interests of all are taken into account. Similarly, when the foundation of a building is weakened so that the roof can be made strong, the building is made weaker as a whole, not stronger. Nevertheless, when decrease is used properly, it strengthens the whole. This is the basic theme of the hexagram.

THE JUDGMENT

Decrease with sincerity
Brings supreme good fortune.
No blame.
One is able to persevere.
It is beneficial to have somewhere to go.
What should be used?
One may use two small bowls to make the offering.

Decrease is not necessarily a bad thing. Increase and decrease are basic features of life. They are part of a natural cycle and succeed each other inevitably. Everything that expands too far will eventually contract. Everything that is made great will eventually be made small. A wise person tries to understand the nature of the time, in order to discern when decrease is appropriate. When things have proceeded too far, or when practices have become excessive, it is time for decrease. When aspects of your life have become too confusing or too complicated, it is time to step back and simplify.

Decrease means understanding that you must give up some things to get other things. In the long run, your happiness and success depend on learning to recognize what you must surrender as well as what you wish to obtain. The task before you now is to put your priorities in order. What is most important to you? What must be given up? Face facts. There is no shame in decrease if it is appropriate to the time, and it is appropriate to the time if it helps you clarify your values, achieve your goals, or get you through a difficult period in your life.

The same principles apply to your conduct and demeanor. Because you want too much too badly, you fill your life with complications and entanglements. Simplify. Get rid of excess and affectation. Return to basic principles and straightforwardness in your dealings with others. Perhaps your ego has gotten a bit inflated or your expectations have gotten out of hand. Now is the time to put things in perspective and to decide what is most important to you. Hence the text says, "It is beneficial to have somewhere to go."

Scaling back and doing with less can strengthen your character. It will help you meet the challenges ahead. Do not be concerned if others have more than you do. The text says that "two small bowls" are sufficient to make the offering. This means that people who are devoted and down-to-earth will be accepted even if their worldly possessions are meager. What is in your heart is much more important than what is in your pockets. What matters is not what you have but who you are.

Don't put on airs or pretend to be something that you are not. It is completely unnecessary and may even be counterproductive. Act with sincerity and integrity, and the quality of your character will shine through to others. Be generous and helpful. Do not insist on taking the lead. Instead, be content to play your part. Be willing to give what you have to help others. Have faith: If you are decreased in the short run, you will surely be increased in the long run. As the text says, "decrease with sincerity brings about supreme good fortune."

THE IMAGE

At the foot of the mountain, a lake:
This is the image of Decrease.
Thus the superior person controls his anger
And restrains his desire.

Decrease is symbolized by a mountain above and a lake below. The mountain (Gen, Keeping Still) is a symbol of restraint. Decrease means eliminating what is excessive, both in your everyday behavior and in your emotional life. Self-indulgent behavior causes people to become hypersensitive and unrealistic in their expectations. As a result, they are unprepared for life's inevitable ups and downs. People who are excessive in their emotional life overreact. Hence they make bad judgments.

When things don't go your way, don't lose your temper or make a scene. Stop thinking of yourself as a victim. That is just another form of self-indulgence. Instead, restrain yourself. Control your emotions instead of letting them control you. If you step back for a bit, you will find that things are not as bad as they seem. If you can keep your emotional balance, you will be able to see the right course of action to take.

The text compares your circumstances to a lake at the foot of the mountain. The lake (Dui, Joy) symbolizes nourishment of others. It waters the ground, helping the plants to grow. The water in the lake evaporates and forms clouds, which produce rain that also nourishes the soil. Thus the lake decreases itself in order to serve and increase others. It does not worry about the decrease to itself; it simply acts naturally, and therefore benefits the whole. In the same way, consider how you can contribute to the situation without worrying about whether you will have something to gain thereby. If you act with devotion and sincerity, you need not worry about the outcome. People will naturally respond to your generosity; you will be replenished just as the lake is. Helping others will strengthen your abilities and develop your potential. This will benefit you in the long run.

THE LINES

The lines use the metaphor of decrease to describe proper behavior toward others: that is, how much we should "decrease" ourselves in order to "increase" others.

Initial Nine

When one has finished one's task, going quickly
Is without blame.
But one must consider how one diminishes others.

Be moderate and modest when you offer help to others. Before you extend aid, you must first live up to your existing responsibilities and carry through with your assigned duties. Then you can lend assistance to others. Moderation means respecting previous commitments and not biting off more than you can chew. Hence the text says that after finishing your work, "going quickly"—that is, going quickly to help others—is without blame. When you do so, however, be sure to exercise moderation here as well. You should not brag or make a show about the help you are giving. You should offer only so much assistance as is necessary to help people find their way and help themselves. You should neither interfere needlessly in their affairs or allow them to become dependent on you. The point of your assistance is to increase their autonomy and their sense of self-worth, not diminish them.

Nine in the Second Place

It is beneficial to persevere.
To set forth brings misfortune.
Without decreasing oneself,
One increases others.

If you want to help others, you must maintain your integrity and your dignity. Give only what feels right and appropriate. Do not act shamefully or weaken or demean yourself in order to cater to other people's unreasonable expectations. If you compromise your principles in order to help others, you decrease yourself but offer nothing of lasting value. This is the wrong sort of self-sacrifice. Hence the text says that to benefit others in the right way you must increase them without diminishing yourself.

Six in the Third Place (Constitutive Line)

When three people travel together,
Their number decreases by one.
When one person travels alone,
He finds a companion.

Two's company and three's a crowd. A close bond is possible now only between two people. The other person will have to depart. This is necessary, for jealousy and mistrust will inevitably arise in a group of three. If you try to become part of an established union or partnership because you are afraid of being by yourself, you will either find yourself playing second fiddle or you will cause disruption and unhappiness to the other parties. On the other hand, if you have the courage to go it alone for a time, you will eventually find new relationships and new opportunities. If you are willing and able to stand alone, you will not be lonely for very long.

Six in the Fourth Place

He decreases his affliction,
Diminishes his faults.
He acts quickly.
There will be joy.
No blame.

Negative attitudes feed on themselves and become self-fulfilling prophecies. Worse still, they tend to isolate you from others. If you are aggressive and angry, defeatist or insecure, people will not be attracted to you and they will not want to cooperate with you. But if you break the cycle of negative thoughts and strive to eliminate your faults, you will gain a fresh lease on life.

It is time to take a more positive approach. Resolve to discover your shortcomings and self-destructive behaviors and eradicate them. Stop blaming others for your misfortunes and start taking charge of your own destiny. The point is not to blame yourself for everything—for that is just another form of negative thinking—but to approach the world realistically, with a firm and confident belief that you can make things better. Abandon both your bitterness and your pride. Adopt a modest attitude. Be tolerant and generous and accept the current circumstances with equanimity. Then you will attract friends and helpers who will give your life much joy.

Six in the Fifth Place (**Ruling Line**)

Someone increases him.
Like ten pairs of tortoise shells.
It cannot be opposed.
Supreme good fortune.

Tortoise shells were a form of money and also a method of divination. The text suggests that you are marked by fate for good fortune and that nothing stands in the way of this. A basic theme of the *Book of Changes* is that our inner life and our experiences in the world are linked. Inner cultivation leads to happiness and achievement.

Take a positive attitude toward life and positive things will happen to you. Work to improve yourself and your situation will improve. Luck is the residue of design. The work you have done in the past to secure success will pay off in the future, even if it does so in unexpected ways. Self-cultivation and refinement of your abilities will lead you naturally into beneficial situations. You need fear nothing, because your luck is ordained by your previous actions. Efforts at self-improvement now will pay enormous dividends in the future. Good fortune.

Nine at the Top (Constitutive Line)

If one is increased without decreasing others,
There is no blame.
Perseverance brings good fortune.
It is beneficial to have somewhere to go.
One obtains servants
But no household.

To be increased without decreasing others means acting for the public good. You are increased because people support your worthy efforts and give you authority, but because you use your resources to help other people, they are not decreased. Similarly, "One obtains servants [b]ut no household" means that although people work under you, what you do is not for personal gain.

It is time to broaden your perspective and devote yourself to larger goals. You have talents you may not be aware of, and a great deal to give. If you devote yourself to helping others now, people will be happy to join in and assist you. The experience of pursuing something larger than yourself will give you a new lease on life. Your efforts may make you more prominent and give you new powers and responsibilities. They may even involve a new calling or a new lifestyle that suits you. Nevertheless, what you accomplish is not merely for yourself. It benefits everyone as a whole.

NOTES

41.0 "to have somewhere to go." Or, "to undertake something."

41.1 "When one has finished one's task," etc. Or, "Suspend one's own affairs. / Hurry forward, no fault. / Weigh how much one can decrease" (Alfred Huang).

41.1 "When one has finished one's task, " etc. Cf. Laozi, *Dao De Jing:* "When you have finished your work, retire."

41.2 "To set forth." I.e., to undertake something.

41.4 "decreases his affliction / Diminishes his faults." *sun qi ji:* decrease his illness (hatred). The translation attempts to convey two different meanings, illness and fault. Traditionally, one rejoiced at recovery from an illness. In this line we have the metaphor of rejoicing at eliminating an illness of the soul.

This is consistent with the Commentary on the Great Image: The superior person restrains (diminishes) his anger and controls his [base] desires. Cf. Wilhelm/Baynes: "If a man decreases his faults, / It makes the other hasten to come and rejoice. / No blame."

41.5 "Someone increases him." Or, "Someone does indeed increase him" (Wilhelm/Baynes). Cf. 42.2. *Huo* can mean "some" or "perhaps"; in this context it means "some."

41.5 "tortoise shells." *gui:* tortoise, tortoise shell. Cf. 27.1. The idea is that one is enriched by the tortoise shells, which were a form of currency, or that divinations using ten pairs of tortoise shells all concur that one's good fortune is assured. Cf. Wilhelm/Baynes: "Ten pairs of tortoises cannot oppose it."

41.6 "to have somewhere to go." I.e., to undertake something.

41.6 "no household" *(wu jia)*. That is, he no longer concerns himself with private, domestic affairs. *Chen,* "bondservant," can also mean a minister of the king. One might also translate the line as "Household matters cease." Cf. Wilhelm/Baynes: "One no longer has a separate home."

FORTY-TWO

Yi • Increase

Keywords:

Benefit
Harvest
Enrichment
Generosity
Sharing your bounty

Above: Xun • Wind (Wood)
Below: Zhen • Thunder

Yi is the natural counterpart of the previous hexagram, Sun (Decrease). As before, increase and decrease are interrelated. The theme of Yi is decreasing what is above in order to increase what is below. This is a net increase, because those above should serve those below. This idea is captured in the famous proverb that to rule is to serve.

The structure of the hexagram Yi symbolizes this relationship. It is a development of Hexagram 12, Pi (Standstill), in which three yang lines are above three yin lines. In Yi, one of the yang lines in the fourth place has descended to the first place, increasing the lower trigram, while one of the yin lines has replaced it, decreasing the upper trigram. Increase of what is lower comes from what is above, hence good fortune results.

THE JUDGMENT

Increase.
It is beneficial to have somewhere to go.
It is beneficial to cross the great river.

You are in the midst of a very fortunate time, one that offers excellent opportunities to resolve old problems and start new projects. You can now make progress on things that seemed too difficult before. Obstacles fall away. Your relationships with others bloom and grow. Everything flourishes.

There are two reasons why things are going so well. First, people are looking out for each other and helping each other. Their cooperation brings success. When those who are in more powerful and influential positions act to benefit those with less status and influence, everyone benefits. When people feel that those in charge have their interests at heart, they willingly cooperate in even the most ambitious projects, and even the most difficult tasks can be completed successfully.

Second, things are prospering because people pay attention to the fundamentals rather than to surface appearances. When a choice has to be made between making outward aspects of things more impressive or strengthening foundations, people choose the latter without hesitation, and they are right to do so.

These good times will not last forever. Therefore, it is up to you to capitalize on them. First you must decide what your priorities are. The text says that if you want to benefit from the time, you have to have somewhere you want to go. If you dither and hesitate between various projects, or try to do too many things at once, you will squander your opportunities.

Second, once you know what your goals are, you cannot hesitate; you need to take action. As the text says, you must cross the great river. When the time is propitious, you can afford to take calculated risks and embark on challenging endeavors. It is a matter of faith and commitment. Have the courage of your convictions.

Third, to make the most of the good times, you must comprehend the causes that produced them. That means paying attention to fundamentals rather than trivial matters. Spend more time on the foundations of the work and less time on impressing people or feathering your own nest. Always remember that the work is more important than you are.

Finally, you will succeed only if you do something that benefits people other than yourself. The secret to increase is reciprocity. If you work only for your own self-interest, or if you try to hog all the benefits for yourself, people will not join in, and you will not prosper. But if you are called to do something that serves a larger interest, and if you are willing to share the benefits with others, people will rally around you. Pass on your bounty to others, especially to the people who work with you. Your generosity will be rewarded in countless ways. When you focus on what you can contribute to the world rather than what you can take away from it, you help keep the good times going.

THE IMAGE

Wind and thunder:
This is the image of Increase.
Thus the superior person,
When he sees the good, imitates it;
When he has faults, corrects himself.

During the height of a storm, wind and thunder seem to reinforce each other and egg each other on. In the same way, during a period of increase, it is important to keep things moving forward. Be optimistic. Negative thinking weighs you down and drains your energies. A positive outlook is your most potent ally. If you believe you can succeed, you will greatly increase your chances of doing so.

Look to other people whom you admire. Find role models and imitate their good habits. Role models are important precisely because they offer worthy patterns of behavior that you can adopt. It is much easier to see the way forward when someone else has gone before you.

Conversely, consider what your bad habits are and strive to eliminate them. Work continuously to improve yourself and make yourself a better person. If you can maintain self-discipline and commitment over the long haul, you can accomplish a great deal.

THE LINES

The lines describe how to behave during a time of harvest or great benefit, emphasizing cooperation, generosity to others, and moderation. The only unfortunate line is line six, where these lessons have not been learned. Narrow-mindedness and selfishness lead to isolation from others and an end to the good times.

Initial Nine (Constitutive Line)

It is beneficial to begin a great undertaking.
Supreme good fortune. No blame.

You have the ability to do something great and ambitious, something that you normally would never have even considered or would have thought beyond your capacity. The most important thing is that your goal benefits others as well as yourself. If your motives are unselfish and your aspiration is truly worthwhile, there is no blame in attempting something so challenging. Fortune will be on your side because people will see that you bring good fortune to others.

Six in the Second Place (Ruling Line)

Someone increases him;
Like ten pairs of tortoise shells.
It cannot be opposed.
Constant perseverance brings good fortune.
The king makes an offering to the Supreme Deity.
Good fortune.

Tortoise shells were both a form of currency and a method of divination. The text explains that your good fortune stems from upright and proper conduct.

Good luck is the residue of good design. Increase comes because you set in place the conditions for success, so that you are able to maximize your advantages when opportunities arise and things break your way. Cultivate good habits of mind and behavior, choose worthwhile projects, and open yourself up to beneficial influences. Then good fortune will follow your endeavors as if success were foreordained. The same advice applies to your relationships with other people. Always remember to be modest and generous. This will attract others to you and help sustain your good fortune. Never forget that your success depends on serving the interests of others as well as yourself.

When things are going well, do not allow yourself to become reckless or overconfident. Rather you should maintain the behaviors and habits that have brought you success in the past. Keep centered and grounded in reality, and attend to the everyday details of your life. In this way you can preserve the momentum of this fortunate period. As the text says, "Constant perseverance brings good fortune."

Six in the Third Place

Enriched through unfortunate events.
No blame, if one is sincere,
And walks in the central path.
One reports with a jade tablet to the duke.

A jade tablet was used by messengers and officials; it is a mark of authority and symbolizes sincerity and trust. To walk "in the central path" means to behave with modesty and act in a principled fashion.

The situation seems unfortunate, but in fact things will actually turn out to your advantage. The most important thing now is to maintain your principles and be especially careful about doing the right thing. People will appreciate your steadfastness and integrity in difficult times. Your presence of mind will give you authority and influence that others will respect. And because your conduct is blameless, no one will reproach you when you succeed and others do not. By holding fast to what is right and riding through the difficult times, you will strengthen your character, develop new skills, and gain valuable experience for the future.

Six in the Fourth Place (Constitutive Line)

He walks in the central path
And reports to the duke,
Who follows his advice.
It is beneficial to use this
In order to move the capital city.

Moving the capital city was an especially difficult and important undertaking, which would only be entrusted to the most able and reliable persons. As in the previous line, to walk "in the central path" means to be principled and modest. But it also means being positioned between the authorities who plan and those who carry out the plan, i.e., to be an intermediary or go-between.

If you find yourself in the role of a mediator between two different sides, or between different groups of people within an organization, make sure that you are objective and fair to all concerned. Make clear to all sides how they can profit from cooperating, and work to ensure that everyone does in fact benefit. Emphasize to those in authority the importance of spreading benefits widely to those below, and emphasize to those below the importance of commitment to a common enterprise and cooperation with those in authority. If you are reasonable and fair-minded, people will trust and respect you and they will follow your advice. Your influence in the situation will be highly beneficial, for when people work together for the general good they can attempt even the most difficult undertakings with complete success.

Nine in the Fifth Place (Ruling Line)

If you are sincere, and have kindness in your heart,
You need not ask.
Supreme good fortune.
When there is sincerity, kindness is your power.

If you have a truly kind heart, you do not need to worry about whether you have done the right thing. Your generosity and your sincere concern for the welfare of others means that whatever you do will ultimately be for the best. People who are truly kind do not act in order to be rewarded for their good deeds. They are generous and kind because of the inner compulsion of their character. Nevertheless, others recognize their worth all the same and their influence spreads widely. Hence the text says that when you are sincere, "kindness is your power." What you do out of the goodness of your heart and without thought of gain will nevertheless bring you influence and recognition.

Nine at the Top

He increases no one.
Someone even strikes him.
He does not keep his heart and mind constant and steady.
Misfortune.

You have the ability to benefit others, but you fail to do so. Instead, you have allowed yourself to become isolated, indifferent, and selfish. Such behavior will cause hostility and resentment in others. You will lose your influence and respect, and no one will come to your aid when people attack you or try to undermine you.

The sixth line represents the end of a time of increase. Periods of great plenty end when people fail to cooperate and begin to become greedy and grasping. In this way they accelerate the forces of disorder. If you want to make your position secure, you must learn to be more generous and reliable. If you try to keep everything for yourself, people will not assist you when you need it most. If people find that you are not dependable, you will not be able to depend on them when the chips are down.

NOTES

42.0 "to have somewhere to go." To undertake something.

42.GI "imitates it." Or, "improves himself." *qian:* move, shift; hence, shifts to the good, follows, imitates. Cf. 42.4: "move the capital city."

42.GI "When he has faults, corrects himself." Or, "corrects them."

42.1 "begin a great undertaking." *yong wei da zuo:* take advantage of activating a great arousing. Or, "use this opportunity for a big project," "do great things," "undertake great things," "accomplish a great undertaking." The metaphor is to plant for a great harvest.

42.2 "Someone increases him." Or, "Someone does indeed increase him" (Wilhelm/Baynes). Cf. 41.5.

42.2 "tortoise shells." Cf. 41.5.

42.2 "the Supreme Deity." *Di:* Supreme Deity or Divine Ruler. Cf. 16.GI. Shangdi, or Di, was the principal Shang deity, associated with heaven itself.

42.3 A *gui,* or jade tablet, was used by messengers and officials. It is also a symbol of sincerity and trust. A duke *(gong)* is directly below the king; reporting to the duke signifies a position of some prominence, although not the same as reporting to the king himself.

42.4 "move the capital city." *qian:* move, shift. Cf. 42.GI. Moving the capital was a great and important undertaking. Hence the advice and the work are particularly worthy.

42.4 "duke." *gong*. Or, "prince." Cf. 14.3, 40.6, 42.3, 50.4, 62.5.

42.5 "kindness is your power." *hui wo de:* benevolence my power, i.e., benevolence is the source of one's good fortune. *De* can mean virtue, power, benefit, or ability. Cf. Wilhelm/Baynes: "Truly, kindness will be recognized as your virtue."

42.6 "heart and mind." *xin:* heart, but also refers to one's moral nature, desire, and will.Cf. 29.0.

FORTY-THREE

Guai • Resolution

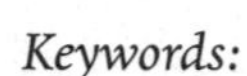

Keywords:

Resoluteness
Determination
Decisiveness
Speaking forthrightly
Elimination
Eradicating remaining evils
Parting
Cutting off
Breakthrough

Above: Dui • Lake
Below: Qian • Heaven

Guai originally meant separation or elimination. Later it was extended to eliminating hesitation, in other words, resolution. Hesitation and indecision cause tension. That tension is released when people eliminate indecision and finally make up their minds. Hence, Guai also means a breakthrough either in one's internal life or in the external world.

The theme of the hexagram is the elimination of evil or inferior elements. These elements are on the wane, but they may easily arise again. Therefore, it is necessary to resolve firmly to eradicate them once and for all.

If one puts hesitation aside and makes up one's mind to do so, there is a breakthrough. This is symbolized by the structure of the hexagram, which features five yang lines that are moving upward to eliminate the last yin line. The yin line is still above them and therefore still remains powerful. It is up to the yang lines to work together to eliminate it and push it away. The evil must be denounced firmly and publicly so that people of goodwill can rally together to eradicate it.

THE JUDGMENT

Resolution.
Declare it at the court of the king.
Proclaim it sincerely and truthfully.
There is danger.
Notify the city.
It is not beneficial to resort to arms.
It is beneficial to have somewhere to go.

Something is wrong and you must rectify it. Inferior elements still dominate the situation and you must eliminate them. If you do nothing, you will compromise yourself and make a bad situation worse. The problem may be external—people or institutions that undermine the good and prevent progress. Or it may be internal—your own bad habits and negative emotions that weigh you down. Either way, the obstacles are real. You must face up to them and surmount them.

You are not unaware of the problem. But you have hesitated, telling yourself that the problem is not so bad or that it will eventually take care of itself. But the time for hesitation and temporizing is past. If you do not act, nothing will get better. You must be absolutely convinced that change is necessary and you must be determined to play a part in that change.

When a problem is great, it requires cooperation to overcome it. If you attack the problem with insufficient resources, you will either be defeated or you will be forced to compromise. And you cannot compromise. The problem must be fully eliminated. Don't overreact and don't try to solve the problem by yourself overnight. You need help if you are to prevail.

The best way to gather public support is to state forthrightly what the problem is. If something bad has occurred, don't be afraid to say so honestly and candidly. Be courteous and evenhanded in dealing with others. You do not want to arouse unnecessary offense or opposition, and you do not want people to think that your emotions have gotten the better of you. But you cannot dissemble or sugarcoat what is wrong. You must speak the truth. You cannot rally people together if they do not understand the seriousness of the situation. Evils and injustices can never be eradicated until they are named and identified as what they are. To eliminate evil, you must first expose it in order to gain public support.

You must not use violent or underhanded methods to solve your problem. Force leads to more force, evil begets more evil. Do not get in the gutter with what you are trying to eliminate. If you allow yourself to get entangled in passion or hatred, you will become what you oppose.

The same principles apply if you are trying to eliminate bad habits in yourself. Be honest with yourself, but don't engage in self-loathing or self-defeating behavior. If you are trying to reform a relationship, you and your partner must have the courage to be sincere and candid with each other if you are to work through your problems. But you should not engage in backbiting, manipulation, and emotional assaults. That will only make the situation worse. You must discuss your problems openly and frankly, and try to recognize the causes of your present unhappiness. Strive to reach mutual understanding rather than mutual recrimination. Then put your previous struggles behind you and move on.

THE IMAGE

Water from the lake rises up to the heavens:
This is the image of Resolution.
Thus the superior person
Dispenses his riches to those below.
He abides in virtue by shunning evil.

Water evaporates from the lake and rises up to heaven, forming clouds that rain down below. If too much water accumulates without precipitation, the clouds build up until they burst. Too much rain too quickly floods the land, while a slow and steady rain nourishes the soil. Thus it is better that the clouds dispense their rain regularly rather than hold all the moisture until it must be surrendered in a cloudburst or a violent storm.

The same is true of human society. Evil flourishes when people try to hog everything for themselves. Eventually, they accumulate so much that their world collapses or things are taken from them by force. Such people fail to recognize the interdependence of all life and the interrelationship of their happiness with that of other people. As you accumulate the good things of life, be sure to share them with others. Distribute as you accumulate and you will be enriched in countless ways. By hoarding everything for yourself you will arouse envy and no one will want to cooperate with you when you need help. But by nourishing others like a gentle rain, you will foster goodwill and accumulate support for the challenges ahead.

The text says that enlightened people "abide[ ] in virtue by shunning evil." This does not mean closing yourself off from the world. Human beings cannot seal themselves off from life any more than a cloud can keep all the water it accumulates. Pressure builds until things must give way. You cannot shun evil by keeping the world at arm's length. Quite the contrary—what you must avoid above all is obstinacy and the conviction that you are completely and totally in the right. It is ironic but true that to shun evil we must be open to others and be willing to learn from them; it is when we close ourselves off to others that we open ourselves to evil.

Resolve to inquire into your own shortcomings. It is always easier to recognize moral compromise in others than in ourselves. The eradication of evil, like charity, begins at home, with an examination of your own behaviors and beliefs. While you must forthrightly reject and condemn misbehavior, you should also consider how you have contributed to the problems that you see in others.

Don't let self-criticism immobilize you. Everybody makes mistakes. Don't wallow in self-pity or self-abuse. The point of self-examination is not to beat yourself up. It is to work consistently, in small ways, to keep little problems in your life from becoming bigger ones. Self-examination should be an opportunity, not a punishment. Work on developing what you think is good about you rather than lacerating yourself for what you think is bad. Don't let the recognition of problems in your life keep you from going out into the world and experiencing it. Be open-minded and generous. You will eliminate your problems not by walling yourself off but from learning more about the world and about yourself.

THE LINES

The lines concern the virtues one must possess to overcome evil. In lines two and five—the central lines—one tempers one's determination with moderation and careful planning, and therefore succeeds.

Initial Nine

Powerful in his forward toes,
He goes forward, but is not able to overcome.
He incurs blame.

To be powerful in the forward toes means to be impatient—desiring to stride forward—and to allow base influences to dominate, because the toe is the lowest part of the body.

You are eager to press forward now, but you currently lack the ability to deal with the problems you face. You need to think carefully about what you can and cannot do in this situation. Stay within your limits for the moment. Discretion is the better part of valor. If you waste your resources on a rash advance, you will greatly jeopardize your chances of success later on.

Nine in the Second Place

Cries of alarm.
Arms at evening and at night.
Have no fear.

Battles were usually fought during the day, so to maintain arms "at evening and at night" means to be perpetually alert.

Resolution is not simply a matter of determination. It also requires preparation, caution, and readiness. Be on the lookout for signs of trouble brewing. Prepare for difficulties before they have a chance to sneak up on you. Keep your wits about you and do not lose your emotional balance. By developing inner strength, you can prepare yourself for any contingency. Remain focused and attentive to the circumstances around you, and you need have no fears.

Nine in the Third Place

Powerful in the cheekbones.
This brings misfortune.
The superior person is firmly resolved.
He travels alone,
And meets with rain.

He is soaked, angry.
No blame.

"Powerful in the cheekbones" means talking too much or talking at the wrong time. To meet with rain and become soaked means to suffer the indignity of misunderstanding and disapproval from others.

You face a difficulty that you must resolve by yourself. In dealing with the problem you may find that you have to use unorthodox methods. You may have to temporarily align with your adversaries or associate yourself with inferior people or elements. This means that you must keep your counsel to yourself. Others will inevitably misunderstand you, and they may criticize you. But if your reasons are correct and your motives are pure, you should not be dissuaded from doing the right thing. In dangerous times it is important to be true to yourself even if others misjudge you. If you persevere and maintain your integrity, you will remain without blame in the end.

Nine in the Fourth Place

There is no skin on his buttocks,
And walking is hard going.
If he were led like a sheep, regrets would disappear.
He hears the words, but does not trust them.

You suffer from restlessness and emotional upheaval. Faced with difficulties, you want to press forward at any cost and attain your goals. Yet you encounter one problem after another.

Your outer difficulties reflect an inner turmoil. You have become obstinate and continually try to impose your will on the world. You insist on doing things your own way, and your resolution has developed to such a degree that you have lost touch with reality and will not listen to reason. If you could only give up your stubbornness, your problems would vanish. If you could only follow good advice and let others take the lead, your difficulties would resolve themselves. But your emotional state prevents you from listening to others. Stop struggling. Rethink your goals. Calm down and try to gain some perspective before it is too late.

Nine in the Fifth Place (Ruling Line)

Eradicating the weeds
With firm resolution.
If one walks the middle path,
There is no blame.

When weeds are cut down, they often grow back, so diligence is necessary to eliminate them. The same is true with the problems you currently face. Powerful adversaries and circumstances oppose your progress. You need to summon great determination and persistence to deal with the situation. Unless you get to the roots of the problem, your difficulties will reemerge. Therefore, you must be tenacious. Do not allow yourself to be diverted from your goal. You must see things through to the end. Nevertheless, in dealing with the problem you must not stoop to unscrupulous methods. Always act with integrity, no matter how great the obstacles you face. As the text says, you must "walk the middle path," meaning that you must remain emotionally balanced and committed to proper principles. Then you will have no cause for regret.

Six at the Top (Constitutive Line)

He does not cry out.
In the end, misfortune.

The line describes a person who fails to recognize evils or waits too long to denounce them. As a result, they survive and grow strong, and misfortune results.

You may think that your problems are over and that you can relax and let down your guard. But this is an illusion. The seeds of disorder are still present in the situation even though they remain hidden to you. You must eradicate them now or they will grow back and become as strong as ever. What is true of the outside world is also true of yourself. There is no substitute for tenacity and circumspection in ridding yourself of bad habits and negative ways of thinking. If you become self-deluded, lazy, or conceited, you will make a wrong move at the wrong time. If you do not exercise thoroughness in eliminating harmful influences in your life, they will spring up again in a moment of weakness.

NOTES

43.GI "He abides in virtue by shunning evil." Literally, "He dwells in virtue by being aloof (averse)." *Ji:* avoid, shun. One interpretation, which is consistent with the theme of the hexagram, is that the superior person guards his virtue by decisively rejecting all evil as soon as he becomes aware of it. Thus, Wilhem/Baynes translates it as "refrains from resting on his virtue." That is, one must be resolute if one's virtue is to be lasting. A second interpretation is that the superior person is resolute in making strict prohibitions and judgments that keep him away from base influences.

43.1 "is not able to overcome." *sheng:* overcome, conquer, control, gain the upper hand. Or, "is not equal to the task."

43.1 "He incurs blame." Or, "He makes a mistake."

43.3 "firmly resolved." *guai guai:* literally, "resolute, resolute."

43.3 "He is soaked, angry." Another possible reading is "As if soaked [in the rain], there is anger." Because he travels alone, the superior person is misunderstood by others and they are angry at him. Thus, Wilhem/Baynes translates the line: "He is bespattered / And people murmur against him."

43.4 "There is no skin on his buttocks, / And walking is hard going." Cf. 44.3.

43.4. "If he were led like a sheep." *qian yang:* drag [with a rope] sheep. Or, "If [he] were to let himself be led like a sheep" (Wilhelm/Baynes); "Tie up a ram" (Alfred Huang).

43.5 "Eradicating the weeds / With firm resolution." *xian lu guai guai:* literally, "weeds, highlands, resolute, resolute." The doubled word intensifies the idea, hence "firm resolution." Cf. 43.3. Another version is "Eradicating the weeds from the highlands / With firm resolution." However, *xianlu* might refer to a kind of weed; hence, "eradicating the [highland] weeds with firm resolution." Cf. Wilhelm/Baynes: "In dealing with weeds, / Firm resolution is necessary." *Xian*, in turn, is sometimes read as *huan:* mountain goat; hence the line might be translated, "The mountain goat departs with resolution." In any case, the lesson of the line is contained in the second half: "If one walks the middle path, / There is no blame."

43.6 "He does not cry out." Or, "There is no cry." I.e., the time when it would have been appropriate for resolutely declaring the danger has come and gone.

FORTY-FOUR

Gou • Encounter

Keywords:

Temptation
Brief encounter
Coming to meet
Coupling of opposites
Two ships that pass in the night
Hidden dangers
The beginnings of corruption
Nip problems in the bud

Above: Qian • Heaven
Below: Xun • Wind (Wood)

Gou has a dual meaning. On the one hand, it refers to encounters between opposite elements that are temporary but potentially fruitful. These couplings are significant, but they are not designed to last. On the other hand, Gou also refers to elements of evil and inferiority that tempt us. If we allow them to enter the situation and remain there, they will eventually come to dominate and corrupt everything. The two themes are related because inappropriateness is often a source of evil and corruption. What was not meant to last long should not last long; for then it may become harmful.

The first theme of transitory encounter is reflected in the constituent trigrams: Wind blows under heaven, never staying long but always moving from one place to another. The second theme of danger and temptation is symbolized by the structure of the lines. One yin line enters from below, both tempting and threatening the five yang lines above it. An evil and inferior element has entered the situation and will grow over time if nothing is done to stop it.

Gou is the natural complement of Hexagram 43, Guai, which precedes it. In Guai one must put aside all hesitation and resolve to eliminate the last elements of evil in a situation before they have a chance to regroup. In Gou, by contrast, the first elements of corruption are just beginning to enter the picture, and one must be resolved to eliminate them before they have a chance to grow large. In Guai the evil is large but will prove vulnerable if something is done. In Gou the evil is small but will prove surprisingly powerful if nothing is done.

THE JUDGMENT

Encounter.
The woman is powerful.
Do not marry her.

The text analogizes temptation to a femme fatale who is young and seemingly harmless but who has powerful abilities to seduce others. She is represented by the single yin line, which seduces the five yang lines above it. Comparing temptation with a powerful woman seemed natural to the patriarchal society of ancient China; yin was traditionally associated not only with the feminine but also with the small, the dark, the evil, and the inferior. But we need not maintain these inegalitarian views to understand the point: There is no reason why the seducer could not be male and the victim female. In either case, the text advises not to marry the seducer. Marriage is a long-term commitment. In Gou there is a relationship that cannot and should not last. If one commits oneself to the temptation or allows it to become a permanent part of one's life, misfortune will result. The flirtation seems harmless at first—delightful and inviting. However, it gains its power from the fact that one comes to meet it and allows it to take over. Temptation advances on us because—whether we realize it or not—we meet it halfway.

You find yourself in a situation that seems outwardly pleasant and agreeable. But there are hidden dangers lurking behind an attractive façade. Troubles are brewing, although you don't yet realize it. It is possible that someone has a hidden agenda. Or the people you are dealing with are simply not right for you. In any case, be exceedingly careful about offers and promises that people make to you. It is not yet clear whom to trust. Watch what people do and not what they say. Try to get additional information about their uprightness and trustworthiness. You don't want to put yourself in a compromising position.

It is important not to let yourself be drawn into something that is beneath you or that you will later regret. Therefore, guard your independence and your integrity jealously. Don't allow others to manipulate you. Inferior people worm their way into your life only because you regard them as harmless and allow them entry. They get you to trust them and help them by making it appear that they need your help and your trust. They play on good tendencies of reciprocity and mutual sympathy to get their way. If you don't let yourself be duped in the first place, they will not gain influence over you. There is no need to be haughty or aggressive. You shouldn't overreact to the situation. But you need to make your own position clear so that you are not pushed around or misused. If you signal that you are committed to the right path and unlikely to be deceived, people who do not have your best interests at heart will move on to another target. Only those who are sincere will remain.

Temptation often seems small and harmless at first. But as soon as you indulge it and make it part of your life, it can grow in unexpected ways and gain more and more power over you. If you have embarked on something that is not worthy of you, turn back while it is still easy to avoid the situation and make amends. If you have started to develop bad habits, nip them in the bud before they have a chance to become fixed. If you have begun to be obsessed with doubts, worries, or negative thoughts, try to counteract them before they become a major part of your emotional life. Everything is easier to deal with when it is small. It is only when we neglect it that it has a chance to become large.

THE IMAGE

Under heaven there is wind:
This is the image of Encounter.
Thus, the prince disseminates his commands
And proclaims them to the four corners of the world.

Wind blows everywhere under heaven. It spreads its influence everywhere. It blows pollen from one plant to another, fertilizing the world. It blows ships from one harbor to another, bringing new goods and new ideas. All this is fitting and appropriate. It is only when the wind remains in one place that it becomes stagnant and dies.

Thus, Gou has a positive side—the benefits that come from temporary meetings between opposites. Encounters with others are beneficial when they stir you up and exercise your imagination. Creative synergies emerge when you encounter someone who is your natural opposite. When you are certain that another person has good intentions, be willing to meet them halfway. But if the meeting arises from dishonest motives, nothing good can come of it.

Heaven is far from earth but influences it through wind. In the same way governments may be far from their people but can stir up the people through just laws that give the proper incentives to beneficial action. Just laws are like a good and productive wind; unjust laws are like a harsh and stagnant wind. Good laws enrich human life. They provide a framework for human liberty. They encourage people to cooperate with each other; in this way they foster optimism and generosity. Bad laws make life stagnant. They turn people against each other and make them fearful and selfish. Just laws are like a pleasant breeze—they exercise a gentle and benign influence. Unjust laws are like a tornado or hurricane: they are aggressive, harsh, and destructive or they enable aggression and destruction by others.

THE LINES

The lines explain how to deal with temptation and with inferior influences. Most of the lines are difficult, or present a serious challenge; only line five is unambiguously positive.

Initial Six (Constitutive Line)

Fasten it with a metal brake.
Perseverance brings good fortune.
If one has somewhere to go, one experiences misfortune.
A raging pig is tied up; his hoof is damaged.

"A metal brake" prevents straying and halts movement in the wrong direction. Tying up a raging pig with a damaged hoof prevents the animal from thrashing around in pain and making its injuries greater. This gives the foot a chance to heal. Both figures symbolize prophylactic measures taken at the outset that prevent greater problems from developing.

An inferior element, or a destructive tendency, is beginning to enter the situation. You must take immediate steps to counteract it and prevent it from growing and becoming more powerful. Thus, the text says, it must be stopped "with a metal brake." If you do nothing, the problem will not go away. It will merely loom larger. The same thing is true of yourself. Harmful emotions and bad habits may start small but eventually become consuming. Nip destructive tendencies and negative thinking in the bud before they take over your life.

Nine in the Second Place (Ruling Line)

There is a fish in the wrapper.
No blame.
It is not beneficial to entertain guests.

The "fish in the wrapper" refers to the yin line at the bottom. It is covered by the yang line in the second place, which protects the lines above from the fish's eventual decay. The meaning is that one should keep a lid on corrupting elements in a situation, to prevent them from spreading more widely. Hence the text says, "It is not beneficial to entertain guests."

Keep inferior influences at bay, both for your own sake and for the sake of others. Temptation, despair, pessimism, hatred, fear, and all sorts of negative attitudes and behaviors are contagious. Given the opportunity, they can spread like a disease. For this reason it is best to contain them before they have a chance to do damage. Resist negative thinking, and don't allow yourself to be led astray or become discouraged by others. When you discover weaknesses or the beginnings of decay, control them with gentleness and do not let them affect other parts of your environment; otherwise they will infect the situation and cause you trouble.

Nine in the Third Place

There is no skin on his buttocks,
And walking is hard going.
Danger,
But no great blame.

Temptation beckons to you to get involved in something that is not right for you. You are seduced by an attractive possibility and you want to take it up. However, you are held back by circumstances. This causes you to vacillate, and you feel unhappy and frustrated. Count your blessings. It is good that you cannot follow your desire. You are in a dangerous position, although you may not yet realize it. Once you clear your mind and look more carefully into the situation, you will understand the right path to take and you will avoid making a mistake.

Nine in the Fourth Place

No fish in the wrapper.
This gives rise to misfortune.

This line is the converse of the second. The first yin line should correspond with the fourth yang line, but the second line intervenes. This symbolizes alienation and failure of communication.

Do not become haughty or aloof from people whom you regard as unimportant. You may need their help someday. Be courteous and tolerant of others even if you do not agree with them in all respects. If you alienate people now or remain standoffish, they will not support you later on. A person who systematically isolates himself from others meets with misfortune.

Nine in the Fifth Place (Ruling Line)

A melon wrapped in willow leaves.
Hidden beauty.
Then it falls down from the sky.

Like fish, a melon decays easily, and therefore symbolizes the potential for corruption. But if the melon is preserved properly, "wrapped in willow leaves," it is healthy and fragrant. In the same way, if a person takes the right steps and exercises patience, beneficial opportunities will fall to him like a ripe fruit from a tree.

Maintain your principles and quietly go about your business. Be modest and do not try to impress or manipulate others or attempt to impose your will on them. Instead, let the strength of your character and the quality of your efforts set an example. Simply do your best and act with integrity. Treat those who work under you with generosity and respect. Then the "hidden beauty" that lies within you will naturally influence others. Without any show or pretense, you will gain support and achieve your aims.

Nine at the Top

Coming to meet with one's horns.
Humiliation. No blame.

It is time to leave inferior elements and disagreeable people behind. If you state your intentions openly or make a decisive break, people will reproach you and you may experience some humiliation. Some may accuse you of being aloof or proud. On the other hand, if you try to withdraw from the situation quietly and unobtrusively, you may meet with less opposition, although people will still criticize you. Either way, don't be too concerned about what other people think. The important thing is to do what you feel is right. If you maintain your integrity and separate yourself from what is base and ignoble, you will be without blame.

NOTES

44.0 "Do not marry her." *wu yong qu nu:* Don't use this to take the maiden as a wife. Cf. Wilhelm/Baynes: "one should not marry such a maiden."

44.GI "prince." *hou:* prince, ruler, sovereign, feudatory.

44.1 "a metal brake." Or, "a brake of bronze." *jin:* metal, can refer to bronze or gold. In this context, "metal" seems to be most appropriate.

44.1 "A raging pig is tied up; his hoof is damaged." *lei shi fu zhi zhu:* literally "ruin (damaged, emaciated) pig captured hoof limping." The line is subject to many different interpretations. Among the various possibilities are "Even a lean pig has it in him to rage around" (Wilhelm/Baynes); "[I]t would be like a weak pig [sow] that but strives to romp around" (Lynn); and "Captives pacing like tethered pigs" (Whincup). The translation given above tries to be consistent with the lesson of the line; it is necessary to exercise restraint in order to avoid causing needless injury to oneself and others. This is like tying up a pig with an injured hoof, so that it cannot exacerbate its injuries.

44.2. *bao* translates as "wrapper." The same word appears in lines two, four, and five, but for lines two and four some gloss it as *pao* (slaughterhouse) or *paochu* (tank, kitchen). Thus, Wilhelm/Baynes translates the line as "There is a fish in the tank." Neither of these glosses makes particularly more sense than *bao.*

44.3 "There is no skin on his buttocks, / And walking is hard going." Cf. 43.4.

44.4 *bao:* wrapper. Or "tank." Cf. 44.2.

FORTY-FIVE

Cui • Gathering Together

Keywords:

Gathering
Massing
Joining others
Assembling
Having a common cause
Holding yourself together
Pitching in
Cooperation between leaders and followers

Above: Dui • Lake
Below: Kun • Earth

Cui is similar in structure to Hexagram 8, Bi, (Union). In Bi, water is over earth, in Cui it is lake over earth. In Bi one yang line in the fifth place—symbolizing the ruler—joins the other yin lines together. In Cui the fourth line—which represents the minister—assists the ruler in achieving unity. The special role of the deputy or underling in achieving unity is a theme of the hexagram. Another name for Cui is "massing together." It suggests that the group is especially large, so that the ruler needs assistance from trusted subordinates who put aside selfish considerations and devote themselves to the larger purposes of the group.

45 Cui • Gathering Together

THE JUDGMENT

Gathering Together. Success.
The king approaches his temple.
It is beneficial to see a great person.
Success. It is beneficial to persevere.
Bringing a great offering means good fortune.
It is beneficial to have somewhere to go.

Fostering unity takes skill and patience. In order to bring people together, whether in a community, a charitable organization, or a business, you must give them a shared sense of purpose. You must give the group direction; hence the text says, "It is beneficial to have somewhere to go." Common goals, shared symbols, and shared beliefs unite individuals and let them feel that they are working for something more than selfish interests or petty concerns. It is the duty of leaders to instill this sense of higher purpose. The text speaks of the king entering his temple. In ancient times rulers would lead their people by making a sacrifice to their ancestors. This sacrifice reminded people that they had common origins and that together they were keeping faith with something noble and valuable. Calling upon common ancestors and invoking shared traditions was a powerful symbol of community, which constituted them as a single people with a common history and destiny.

In the same way, if you are called to bring people together, you must instill in them a sense of shared history and purpose. You must give them something to believe in. You must bring "a great offering": something that performs the same function as the offering to the ancestors that the ancient kings made. You must find symbols that people can rally around and that express their joint commitment. You must create or invoke a common narrative through which people can connect themselves back to the past and ahead to the future. Thus gathering together means much more than simply assembling individuals at a single place and time. It means gathering them together with those who have gone before and with those who will be part of the group in the future. In this way, the group's members can see themselves as part of a continuing project or tradition.

In order to gather other people together, you must first gather yourself together. To do this you must be certain about your values and aims. If you are internally conflicted, you will be outwardly hesitant and you will not be able to inspire confidence. Clarity of moral vision is necessary to rally people together around a great cause. When that clarity is present, an association whose members are united around a common goal can do remarkable things.

Groups function best when their members willingly cooperate. If people become selfish, the group will not succeed and may even fall apart. Conflict is inevitable in any large organization because people have different interests and different points of view. But this is acceptable as long as the disagreements concern how best to realize shared values and goals rather than attempts by one faction to suppress and dominate another. If you are a member of a group, be willing to work with the leaders and help them succeed. Understand your place in the larger organization and give your best. If you are a leader, make sure that you act in the interests of everyone. Remember the Chinese proverb that to rule is to serve.

THE IMAGE

The lake rises above the earth:
This is the image of Gathering Together.
Thus the superior person repairs his weapons
In order to meet the unexpected.

Lakes flood when too much water gathers together and rises over the ground. Floods can be averted if people take precautions, like building dams and levees. In the same way, whenever you bring a large group of people together, you can expect that there will be disagreements and strife. But you can avert problems in the group if you take precautions in advance.

The *Book of Changes* teaches that change is inevitable; if you want to survive change, you have to be prepared for the bad times as well as the good. We do not know when the lake will flood, but we know that it will flood, and so we build levees and dams. In the same way, we do not know when problems will arise that will test the group, but we know that they will arise sooner or later. People simply have different interests and see things in different ways. Moreover, the group's cohesion is affected by life's inevitable ups and downs. Difficult times put stresses and strains on relationships. When things go badly, people begin to point fingers at each other and look for scapegoats. Some are tempted to abandon the group and to go their own way. Others simply become frightened and selfish.

Wise leaders lay firm foundations for the group so that it can remain solid and its members committed to each other even during difficult times. They instill a sense of common purpose. If you are in a position of leadership, keep informed and in touch. Try to meet people's concerns as they arise. Let people know that you care about them. Keep your eyes open for signs of trouble. Nip problems in the bud before they have a chance to grow. Think about the group's future and plan ahead.

When tensions rise, you must keep your head together even if other people in the group seem to be losing theirs. Maintain your emotional balance. Don't let external conflicts make you conflicted inside. Stick to your goals and remember your original vision. Believe in yourself and in the values that you hold dear. If other people see that you cannot be shaken, it will bolster their confidence. No matter what happens, devote yourself to doing the best you can for your group. In times of adversity people are likely to lose heart. Therefore, they look to their leaders for signals of continued commitment. If people understand that they can depend on you and that you will work for their interests even when times are difficult, they will have faith in you and support you. This will keep the group together.

THE LINES

As in Hexagram 13 (Tong Ren, Fellowship with People), the lines describe successive stages of uniting with others. Lines one, two, and three describe the problems of people who want to enter a group; lines four and five are concerned with issues of proper leadership. In line six, attempts to join in have been rebuffed, but the hope of eventual unification remains.

Initial Six

If one is sincere, but does not carry through to the end,
There will be confusion one moment and gathering the next.
But if one calls out,
With a single grasp of the hand
One makes laughter.
Do not worry.
Going is without blame.

You are hesitant to unite with others or to make a commitment. You vacillate, unsure about what to do. Your indecision keeps you from making progress. It causes you emotional upset and it confuses others. Do not be discouraged. Ask for help and you will receive it. If you are willing to join in, you will not regret it.

Six in the Second Place

Being drawn
Means good fortune and no blame.
If you are sincere and truthful,
It is beneficial to bring even a small offering.

The decision to join a group is not always conscious. Often hidden forces are at work that draw people together. If you feel drawn to a group of people or to a common endeavor, trust your best instincts. You will have no cause for regret. You may worry whether you will fit in. But if you sense a genuine empathy with others, you do not need to try to impress them. Just be yourself. Be open and sincere. They will accept you as you are.

Six in the Third Place

Gathering together with sighs.
There is nothing beneficial in this.
To go forward is without blame.
Slight humiliation.

You would like to join a group, but it seems closed to you. Do not try to force your way in. People will resent your pushiness and you will meet with a rebuff. Instead, seek out someone who is influential within the group. If you ally with them, they can introduce you or recommend you to others. Swallow your pride. Although there may be slight humiliation in proceeding this way, humility and patience constitute the best approach if you wish to join a group that has already formed without you.

Nine in the Fourth Place (Ruling Line)

Great good fortune. No blame.

Line four is the position of the loyal minister who works with and supports the leader. The text suggests that good fortune comes from accepting this role and performing it faithfully.

When you gather people together and work with them for the greater good, you need have no concerns: Your unselfish behavior will benefit everyone, including yourself. Help the leaders and be willing to do your part.

Putting the interests of the group above your own will bring both you and the group great success.

Nine in the Fifth Place (Ruling Line)

If in gathering together one has rank or position,
There is no blame.
If there is no sincerity and confidence,
Sublime and enduring perseverance is necessary.
Then regrets vanish.

Line five is the line of the ruler who must gather people of diverse attitudes and interests together.

If you are the leader of a group, some people may follow you simply because you have power and influence. They will attach themselves to you for selfish reasons, but you will not be able to depend on them. To be truly effective you must earn the trust of other people through the quality of your leadership and the strength of your character. Show your devotion to the group and its members. Be determined to persevere in what is right and honorable. If people sense that you have integrity and are committed to the interests of the group, they too will become committed to the enterprise and they will follow you unselfishly. Through gaining their confidence you will achieve your goals.

Six at the Top

Lamenting and sighing, floods of tears.
No blame.

You have tried to join in and make a contribution, but your efforts so far have not been appreciated. Do not blame yourself. People have misunderstood you. Reexamine your position and try to understand why you have failed to communicate your true motives. Express your regret and your sense of hurt openly but without rancor or accusation. Then people may change their opinion of you and it may be possible to join with them after all.

NOTES

45.0 "The king approaches his temple." Cf. 59.0. The metaphor of the king approaching also appears in 37.5 and 55.0.

45.GI "repairs." Or, "renews."

45.GI "the unexpected." Or, "the unforeseen."

45.2 "Being drawn." *yin:* draw out [like a bow], protract. Cf. 58.6, where the word is used in the sense of being seduced. Here it means that to be drawn into good company is without blame.

45.2 "a small offering." *yue.* A *yue* offering was brought in the spring when stores were low. Hence it means to sacrifice when one has limited resources. Cf. 46.2, 63.5.

45.5 "Sublime and enduring." *yuan yong:* fundamental everlasting.

45.6 "floods of tears." *ti yi:* literally, "tears and mucus," or "weeping and sniveling."

FORTY-SIX

Sheng • Ascending

☷
☴

Keywords:

Pushing upward
Rising
Climbing
Persistence and devotion
Progressing step by step
Making steady progress
The accumulation of small advantages

Above: Kun • Earth
Below: Xun • Wind (Wood)

Sheng consists of two yang lines that have just begun to move upward. The theme of the hexagram is slow and steady advance through exertion. One begins in relative obscurity and eventually reaches a position of influence. This theme is also suggested by the constituent trigrams. Xun (Wind, or, in this case, Wood) is beneath Kun (Earth). This suggests a plant that is pushing upward through the soil, attempting to reach the surface. The progress described in Sheng is not always rapid or easy as in Hexagram 35, Jin; nor is it necessarily aided by one's superiors as in Hexagram 19, Lin. Rather, it represents a slow, methodical ascent through persistent exercise of one's will.

THE JUDGMENT

Pushing upward. Supreme success.
See a great person.
Do not worry.
Setting out toward the south
Brings good fortune.

Step by step, you are making progress. Your upward movement meets with no resistance and therefore nothing holds you back. It is all a matter of time. You will not get where you want to go overnight, but devoted and persistent efforts will pay off handsomely in the long run. You need not worry about the ultimate result.

The secrets to your success are threefold. First, the time is right for your advance. Second, you have established the necessary groundwork. When the fundamentals are sound, every move forward brings cumulative benefits that bring you ever closer to your goal. Third, and most important, you succeed because you do not try to get everything at once. Instead, you move forward slowly but surely, inch by inch, never hesitating but always advancing in steady, deliberate steps.

If you want to reach your goal, all you have to do is maintain this successful strategy. Have faith in yourself. Proceed step by step. When you encounter obstacles, don't be discouraged. Don't lose your temper or try to force things. Instead, be modest and unassuming. Adapt to the situation and keep going. Imagine a young plant that is moving through the soil toward the light. When it encounters earth, it adapts and shifts directions until it finds the best possible space to push upward; then it simply continues its steady ascent. In the same fashion, you will find that if you put your mind to it you can easily move around whatever stands in your way.

Don't be afraid to ask people for help or advice. Because the time is right, they will be happy to give it to you. The important thing is to keep making steady progress. The text says that setting out toward the south brings good fortune, for the south represents activity. Be confident that if you work hard you will eventually get what you want. In the long run your continuous exertions will be rewarded with recognition and supreme success. Like a plant inching ever upward, you will reach the surface and feel the warm sunlight shining on you.

THE IMAGE

Within the earth, wood grows:
This is the image of Ascending.
Thus the superior person, with adaptable character,
Accumulates the small,
In order to achieve the great.

A young plant sprouts up out of the earth, finding its way through the gaps in the soil. It accommodates itself to the conditions it faces, makes use of whatever moisture and nutrients it meets along the way, and pushes ever upward in the direction of the sun. Unceasing in its movements, and yet without haste, it eventually grows into a great, flourishing plant. It accommodates itself to the soil because of its inner nature, not in spite of it. By adapting itself continuously, it realizes its nature in the context of its environment.

In a similar fashion, enlightened people accommodate themselves to the circumstances they face without compromising their inner natures. They continuously cultivate their virtues and accumulate resources. They keep their eyes fixed constantly on their ultimate goals. And, in the end, that is why they succeed. Because they never hesitate to accumulate small advantages, and because they work on improving themselves continually in small ways, they eventually become people of great character who achieve great things.

The same principles apply to any endeavor. Decide what you want, and who you want to become. Then commit yourself to making slow and steady progress. Do not attempt to do everything at once. Don't cut corners. Just try to achieve something positive, each and every day, no matter how insignificant it may seem in isolation. Make the slow, steady accretion of small improvements part of your everyday routine and the realization of your priorities part of your everyday life. The key to your success is persistence, constancy, and self-discipline. Over time, many small things heaped one on top of the other will become something very great indeed.

THE LINES

Each of the lines offers variations on the basic theme that progress does not come from dramatic gestures but from careful, thorough, step-by-step advance. The ascent begins at the bottom in line one and continues upward until line six, when the time of easy advance is over and we must be perpetually aware of the dangers that lie ahead.

Initial Six (Constitutive Line)

Ascending with confidence
Brings great good fortune.

The first line describes someone who is low in status or just beginning his or her ascent.

You can advance now through harmonious relationships with your superiors or other influential people. Work hard and do your best to earn their trust. Their confidence in you will help you achieve your goals.

Nine in the Second Place

If one is sincere,
It is beneficial to bring even a small offering.
No blame.

Although your resources are modest, you can still advance. You may be concerned that you have little to offer; perhaps you feel awkward and think that you don't fit into your social milieu. Do not worry. If you are sincere and genuinely wish to make a contribution, others will respond to you.

Nine in the Third Place

Ascending into an empty city.

Your advance seems effortless. You encounter no obstructions or resistance. Things seem altogether too easy. As a result, you may feel apprehensive, like a general whose troops have entered an empty and undefended city, who worries about whether an ambush is in the offing. Do not let your fears hinder your progress. Make the most of this propitious time, but do not compromise your integrity or lose your sense of perspective. The important thing now is to continue to act in a principled fashion. Maintain the good habits that brought you success in the past. Then you should have no guilt or unease about your advancement.

Six in the Fourth Place

The king makes an offering on Mount Qi.
Good fortune. No blame.

Mount Qi is in western China. It was the site of the temple dedicated to the ancestral lords of the Zhou. The line describes appropriate conduct at a moment when one's ambitions are about to be fulfilled. As the Zhou was ascending into power, the king offered a sacrifice in honor of his ancestors.

You are on the verge of achieving your goals. Everything is extremely favorable. Continue to act in a principled fashion. Remember those who have helped you along the way and maintain worthy habits and traditions. You are about to prevail; carry the best of the past with you into the future.

Six in the Fifth Place (Ruling Line)

Perseverance brings good fortune.
One ascends step by step.

Through calm, steady progress you will achieve your goals. You will not get what you want through an impetuous gesture, a dramatic coup, or a monumental effort at the finish. Rather, the best way to succeed is step by step. Pay attention to detail. Do not take shortcuts or slacken in your endeavors. Deal with each aspect of the problem as it comes without trying to skip any stages. Keep yourself grounded and do not get carried away by your success. Thoroughness and persistence will pay off in the long run. As the text says, "[p]erseverance brings good fortune."

Six at the Top

Pushing upward into darkness.
It is beneficial to be unremittingly persevering.

To push upward into darkness means to push forward blindly, unaware of the hazards that remain ahead.

The time of easy, unforced progress is coming to a close. Do not try to advance without constantly reevaluating your position and exercising the utmost care and discretion. Acting on blind impulse now will put you in danger. Try to gain intelligence about what lies ahead of you. Pause and consider whether you should proceed or wait for a more propitious time. Be consistent and principled in your efforts. The work may be exhausting (the next hexagram is 47, Oppression, or Exhaustion), but you should not give in to despair on the one hand or to recklessness and foolhardiness on the other. You must be exceedingly careful and conscientious now if you wish to avoid damaging your position or losing what you have gained.

NOTES

46.0 "south." In the Northern Hemisphere the sun appears in the south, and hence plants will tend to grow in that direction.

46.GI "with adaptable character." Or, "who follows virtue," "of yielding character," "with the virtues of yielding and conforming." The basic idea is that the superior person, like a young plant still buried underground, accommodates himself to the soil (i.e., his circumstances), follows the direction of the sun (i.e., virtue), and grows ever upward.

46.1 "Ascending with confidence." *yun:* true, honest, loyal, confident. Or, "sincere ascending," "ascending with trust." The idea is that one has trust and is trusted by others. Cf. Wilhelm/Baynes: "Pushing upward that meets with confidence."

46.2 "even a small offering." *yue:* the spring offering. Cf. 45.2, 63.5.

46.4 "The king makes an offering on Mount Qi." Cf. 17.6. Wilhelm/Baynes translates this, "The king offers him Mount Qi," meaning that he is especially favored by those above. Another reading is "The king extends his sway over Mount Qi."

46.4 "Mount Qi." Mount Qi, located in northwest China, was the site of the temple dedicated to the ancestral lords of Zhou.

46.6 "unremittingly persevering." Or, "unceasingly steadfast and upright."

FORTY-SEVEN

Kun • Oppression

Keywords:

Exhaustion
Being restricted
Hardship
Adversity
Inner affliction
Dried up
Impasse

Above: Dui • Lake
Below: Kan • Water

Kun means difficulty, hardship, and exhaustion. The theme of the hexagram is best symbolized by its constituent trigrams: Water is below the lake, symbolizing that the water has drained out of it. As a result, the lake is dried up and nothing living will grow in it. The theme of the hexagram is inner exhaustion and outer oppression. One's energies seem used up, and good people are restricted and persecuted by inferior forces.

Kun is indeed a difficult hexagram, but the law of change is always in operation. Periods of oppression and exhaustion contain the seeds of regeneration and renewal. At the very darkest moment the light is almost ready to shine again. Even so, it is not easy for people who are in the midst of oppression to understand and believe in this enduring truth. Dealing with oppression is a great test of a person's character.

THE JUDGMENT

Oppression.
Success.
With perseverance,
The great person brings about good fortune.
No blame.
What one says is not believed.

It seems as if the world is conspiring against you. You are faced with adversity everywhere you turn. Inside, you feel exhausted, tired, burned out. Life seems to have lost all its spark and attraction. Yet the text says that times of oppression hold the promise of success. How can this be?

The present situation is a test of your character. It takes a great soul to remain undaunted by adverse circumstances. Right now there is nothing you can do to make things better. You will simply have to wait out this very trying time. If you let your misfortunes get to you and crush your spirit, you will be utterly lost. But if you can maintain your equanimity and your patience, you will be able to endure, and you will become a stronger, better person in the process. If you do not allow them to defeat you, the difficulties you face will toughen your spirit and shape the conditions of your future success. That is why the text says that the great person brings about good fortune. People of truly sound and noble character bend in the face of adversity, but they are not broken. They emerge from the trial with renewed hope and the will to go forward and prevail. They succeed because they possess an inner strength that has been tempered and tested by fate.

For the time being, you will have little influence on the situation. The people who control your life do not listen to you and will not trust you. Anything you say to them will only fall on deaf ears. Because you cannot affect the outside world, you are thrown back on your own inner resources. Although you must bide your time, you must remain determined to succeed in spite of all obstacles. Now more than ever you must persevere, holding fast to your integrity and to your belief in yourself. When you face a world that you cannot control, your inner tranquility is the one thing that you do have a say about. No one can take this away from you unless you allow it. To prevail against the oppression you face from the outside world, you must face down and prevail against an inner oppression that consists of despair, self-abuse, and hopelessness. Emotions like these drain the life from you and rob you of the will to go on. To defeat them you must maintain your faith, your emotional balance, and your self-confidence. If you can win this inner victory, no outside foe can stand against you.

THE IMAGE

A lake without water:
This is the image of Oppression.
Thus the superior person
Realizes his destiny by following his will.

When water drains out of the lake, the lake dries up and becomes lifeless. This symbolizes the predicament of a person in difficult and desperate circumstances. Now you must summon up all of your courage. Recognize that both good and bad things happen to people even when they are not deserved. That is just the way life works. Accept the situation, but do not give up hope. You must ride out the bad times until things get better.

The text says that superior people realize their destiny by following their will. Your fate will ultimately be determined by how you deal with these difficult conditions. If you surrender to your negative emotions and allow yourself to wallow in self-pity and despair, you will do yourself great harm, and make it all but certain that you will lose. The world may oppress and exhaust you from without, but negative thinking oppresses and exhausts you from within. The only way to survive is to stay true to yourself and maintain an unswerving faith that things will in fact get better. A positive attitude is your greatest ally now. You must fight to maintain it. It is easy to be optimistic when things are going well. It is a true test of your character to remain full of faith and hope when everything seems to be falling apart. Yet this greatness of spirit will bring you through this difficult time and ensure your success in the long run.

THE LINES

The lines of this hexagram state a basic theme: Oppression comes from inner disquiet as much as outward circumstance. Each line presents a different crisis of the soul. In line six, oppression passes away, but we remain enslaved by the memory of bad times. We must free ourselves from the ghosts of the past and face life with renewed hope.

Initial Six

His buttocks oppressed at the stump of a tree.
He enters into a dark and gloomy valley.
For three years he sees no one.

One's buttocks are oppressed at the stump of a tree because one chooses to sit there rather than to move forward. To enter into a dark and gloomy valley means to descend into melancholy and the fears, doubts, and delusions that accompany it. The text does not offer a prognostication, but misfortune is certainly implied.

Faced with adverse circumstances, you see no way out of your present difficulties. Now is the time to strengthen yourself and avoid succumbing to negative emotions. You are indeed in danger, but not simply from outside circumstances. Rather, you are in danger of falling prey to a cycle of discouragement, gloom, and self-recrimination. If you give in to despair, you will only make matters worse for yourself. Fear, doubt, and bitterness will only build on themselves, sending you into a downward spiral. You will isolate yourself from others, and lacking emotional support, you will make defeat all the more certain. Your failure will be a self-fulfilling prophecy.

You cannot always control the outside world, but you do have some say about how you feel about it and how you feel about yourself. Stop treating yourself as a victim. Do not wallow in melancholy and self-pity. The secret to freeing yourself from outward oppression is to free yourself inwardly.

Nine in the Second Place (**Ruling Line**)

Oppressed at food and drink.
The man with the scarlet knee bands has just arrived.
It is beneficial to offer a sacrifice.
To set forth brings misfortune.
No blame.

Food and drink symbolize luxury and plenty. Hence to be "oppressed at food and drink" means to be oppressed inwardly, despite adequate resources. Scarlet knee bands were worn by princes or government officials. The arrival of the man with the scarlet knee bands symbolizes an offer to work for others or to participate in public service.

Outwardly, things seem to be going well for you. But inside you something is missing. You feel an emptiness or lack within. The problem may be boredom, depression, or self-indulgence. It may be a fear that you have compromised your principles to maintain your comfortable lifestyle, or a sense that things have come too easily and no longer satisfy you. As a result, your pursuits and your achievements seem banal and unrewarding. Life seems to have lost its meaning, and you in turn have lost your sense of direction. You can reenergize yourself through serving others. As the text says, "It is beneficial to offer a sacrifice." Stop focusing on your own advancement, and give yourself to a worthwhile endeavor that helps other people. This will give you a renewed sense of purpose and a renewed zest for living. Nevertheless, the text offers a warning: If you set forth without real devotion but with the secret hope of improving your status in the eyes of others, you will remain mired in the very approach that has brought you unhappiness to this point. Instead, you must learn to take joy in doing good work for its own sake. If you sincerely dedicate yourself to a valuable cause, you will be without blame.

Six in the Third Place

Oppressed by stone,
He leans on thorns and thistles.
He enters his house
But does not see his wife.
Misfortune.

To be "oppressed by stone" means that a person relies on things that harm him and acts in ways that lead to his oppression. He pushes against stone and complains of being oppressed, when anyone should know that stone is immovable. He leans on thorns and thistles when everyone knows that they are not stable and moreover that they are sharp and will cut him. Finally, he enters his house but shuts himself off from his loved ones. A person who acts this way can hardly avoid misfortune.

You are in great danger now, but the danger lies within yourself. Impatience, indecision, and bad judgment have prevented you from seeing things clearly. You have let yourself become oppressed by things that are not oppressive. Nevertheless, you react as if they were victimizing you, and so you become a victim. You rely on things that are not enduring, and you put your faith in things that are not trustworthy and cannot support you. Therefore, you set yourself up to be disappointed. Finally, you are unable to get your priorities straight and you cut yourself off from your friends and allies. Therefore, you alienate those who could help you. You must stop behaving this way and get a better perspective on events. Calm and center yourself now before it is too late.

Nine in the Fourth Place

He comes very slowly, oppressed in a golden carriage.
Humiliation,
But it will end.

A golden carriage is a sign of great affluence and high social position. To be "oppressed in a golden carriage" means to be held back from doing the right thing by one's social circumstances and connections, like a wealthy person whose ties to other rich and powerful people prevent him from helping the poor as he knows he should.

You would like to do the right thing, but your position in the situation holds you back, and you worry what other people will think. Temptations and doubts creep in. They divert you from the proper path, so that your progress is slow and halting. This is no doubt embarrassing. But if you look deep inside yourself and remember your values and what you stand for, you will correct your mistakes and achieve your goal.

Nine in the Fifth Place (Ruling Line)

His nose and feet are cut off.
Oppressed by the man with the crimson knee bands.
Joy comes slowly.
It is beneficial to make offerings and libations.

Crimson knee bands were worn by the public executioner; mutilation (i.e., cutting off body parts) was a method of criminal punishment. To have both one's nose and feet cut off means that one suffers oppression from both high and low places, that is, both from one's superiors and one's subordinates. To make offerings and libations means to cultivate an attitude of religious devotion and dedication to what is true and correct despite one's difficulties.

You have good intentions and you would like to do the right thing. But others frustrate your efforts. People mistake your motives and mistrust you.

You are opposed by those who should help you; you are tangled in a bureaucratic maze. Do not despair. Slowly but surely things will get better. Have patience and maintain your composure. Persevere in your devotion to the good and prepare yourself for the better times that are sure to come.

Six at the Top

Oppressed by creeping vines.
He is anxious and perplexed.
He says to himself, "If I move, I will greatly regret it."
Yet if he repents,
And sets out,
Good fortune comes.

Creeping vines symbolize bonds that appear strong but are easily broken.

The time of oppression is drawing to a close. Yet you hesitate. The memory of your previous condition is still clear in your mind and you despair of moving forward. You fear that if you try to change your situation you will meet new difficulties and experience more emotional anguish. Do not let the bad experiences of yesterday color your view of tomorrow. You can break free of your troubles now if you make the effort. Let go of the past and put your afflictions behind you. Nothing holds you back except your own attitude. View the future with generosity, optimism, and confidence, and you will succeed.

NOTES

47.GI "A lake without water." Or, "The water has drained out of the lake."

47.GI "Realizes his destiny by following his will." *zhi ming sui zhi:* bringing about fate (destiny, life, command) [by] following will (goals, purpose). Or, "Brings about his fate by pursuing his goals," "stakes his life / On following his will" (Wilhelm / Baynes).

47.1 "For three years he sees no one." Cf. 55.6, where the text is followed by the prognostication "misfortune." Cf. also 29.6, where the subject is bound up and achieves nothing for three years. In the *Book of Changes* three years symbolizes a considerable period of time that one is subjected to misfortune or through which one must wait patiently.

47.2 "The man with the scarlet knee bands." Scarlet knee bands were a ceremonial sign of high office. *Zhu* (scarlet, vermilion) is a brighter color than the *chi* (crimson, dark red) worn by the public executioner. Cf. 47.5.

47.3 "leans on." *Ju* means to grasp at, rest upon, lean on, or rely on, in the sense of relying on testimony. The idea is that this person relies on things that harm him and acts in ways that lead to his oppression. Thus, Wilhelm/Baynes translates the sentence as "He allows himself to be oppressed by stone."

47.4 "very slowly." *xu xu:* slow, slow. Wilhelm/Baynes translates this as "very quietly."

47.4 "golden carriage." *ji che.* A metal (golden) chariot would be a sign of affluence.

47.4 "But it will end." There will be a successful conclusion.

47.5 "slowly." *xu.* Or "softly" (Wilhelm/Baynes).

47.5 "libations." Or, "oblations."

47.6 "anxious and perplexed." *nie wu.* Or, "uneasy and unsteady."

FORTY-EIGHT

Jing • The Well

— —
———
— —
———
———
— —

Keywords:

Human potential
Human resources
Replenishing
Renewal
Nourishing others
Going deeply into things
Human nature
The unchanging

Above: Kan • Water
Below: Xun • Wind (Wood)

Jing is the converse of the previous hexagram, Kun (Oppression). In Kun everything dries up and is exhausted. In Jing everything is renewed and replenished. The well is an inexhaustible source of nourishment. The two yang lines below represent two wooden poles that were used to draw up a bucket of fresh, clear water. The bucket is raised to the edge of the well, symbolized by the yang line in the fifth place. The lid of the well is open so that the water can be drawn out; it is symbolized by the open sixth line.

The constituent trigrams feature Xun (here Wood) that is submerged beneath Kan (Water). This symbolizes not only wells but also plants, which use their cells to draw water upward for nourishment.

Jing teaches that people replenish themselves through replenishing others. They grow strong and happy not by trying to keep everything for themselves but through helping each other and growing together. This is a fundamental truth of human nature. The human need for love and mutual support is as basic as the drive for self-preservation. Thus, the text says that although one can change the "town," i.e., the conventions of society, one cannot change the "well"—what nourishes human beings and makes them flourish.

THE JUDGMENT

The Well.
One can change the town
But one cannot change the well.
It neither decreases nor increases.
They come and go, drawing from the well.
If the rope does not go all the way,
Or the jug breaks,
Misfortune.

The theme of Jing is the need to replenish yourself and others. A well that is properly tended is inexhaustible. When you draw water from it, there is still more water to draw on. But when you do not take care of the well, or the environment that surrounds it, the well becomes muddy or dries up. Then the well is of no use to anyone. To replenish other people you must support them and give them room to flourish. Accept people for what they are; do not try to force them into preconceived molds. Consider how you can be of help to others rather than how you can get everyone else to do your bidding. If you create conditions of trust and reciprocity in the world around you, your relationships with others will be like an inexhaustible well that you and everyone else can draw on. But if you act selfishly and high-handedly, people will not cooperate with you or with each other and the resources that mutuality produces will dry up.

The well is a model for how to live your life. Those who are like a well are dependable. They are unfailing in their abilities to nourish and benefit others. They are continually replenished by the cooperation that they receive and by the affection and esteem in which other people hold them.

Because they create an atmosphere of trust and mutual support, they are inexhaustible. The more that they give, the more they are enriched. If you have been neglecting your relationships, now is an excellent time to change things. Be generous and humane to other people, and they will respond naturally.

Similar considerations apply to the care and nourishment of yourself. Within you are the resources of your body, your mind, and your spirit. If you care for them properly, they are inexhaustible; but if you neglect them or abuse them, they will dry up. Your body needs proper nutrition and exercise. Your mind needs education and intellectual challenge. Your spirit needs something to believe in and to strive for.

Replenishing yourself means using your skills and talents rather than letting them waste away. It means challenging and stretching yourself so that you can continue to grow. Don't fritter your life away on meaningless and trivial things. Dedicate yourself to something you think is really valuable and pursue it. Focus on living up to your own potential rather than on whether you are sufficiently admired. Treat yourself with respect if you want others to respect you.

A key metaphor of this hexagram is depth. The text says that the rope must go down all the way into the well if you want to draw fresh water. If you want to achieve something worthwhile, you must not skate over the surface of things but go deeply into them. If you want to have healthy, lasting relationships with others, you must make genuine commitments rather than engage in superficial interactions. To succeed at life you must have depth in your character.

You may think that you do not have much to offer. But do not sell yourself short. Be willing to dig deep down inside yourself and realize your potential. Make the effort and the results will surprise you. You do not yet know all of the things that you are capable of.

To go deeply into things you also need devotion. Replenishing yourself and others takes time and attention. It is a continuous process. It requires commitment. If you are careless and neglect your talents and your relationships with others, you waste them and they will waste away. Then you are like the clumsy person who breaks the jug that the water is drawn from. The water is still there, but there is no way that you can get at it.

Your ability to replenish yourself is connected to how well you replenish others. If you are stubborn and difficult, or if you shut yourself off from other people, your mind, body, and spirit will eventually suffer. You are like a well that no one tends and no one visits; it is no surprise that such a well becomes muddy from lack of use. But if you engage with the world and cooperate with others in a spirit of reciprocity and goodwill, you will find that all aspects of your life will magically improve. Then you become like a well with clear, cold water that nourishes others and is continually replenished.

THE IMAGE

Water over wood:
This is the image of the Well.
Thus the superior person encourages the people at their work,
And urges them to help one another.

A healthy tree draws water upward through its wood cells. It distributes the water throughout, nourishing all parts of the organism. In the same way, make sure that you take care of and nourish all the parts of your life. Whatever you neglect will affect the other elements. In your relationships, recognize your interdependence. Do not be aloof or selfish. Work to renew others and you will end up renewing yourself. This is a deep truth of human nature.

The same principles apply in human society generally. The strength of the whole is dependent on the strength of the different parts and their mutual cooperation. When the poor or those on the margins of society are oppressed, it is like a tree that keeps all the water for the trunk and sends nothing out to the leaves. In the long run, such a tree cannot survive. All must work together for the benefit of the whole, and all must know that they will be nourished by the whole. The secret of a self-sustaining, self-replenishing social order is mutuality and reciprocity.

THE LINES

The theme of the lines is the use and misuse of human potential, symbolized through the metaphor of the well. The lines tell the story of gradual progress. A well that has been neglected (lines one and two) or underutilized (line three) is renovated (line four). As a result, in lines five and six, the clear, cold water of the well is a blessing to all.

Initial Six

The well is muddy. No one drinks from it.
It is an old well. No game.

A muddy well is not replenished or maintained and is left to decay. It symbolizes the misuse of human potential. "No game" means that the well is abandoned by all: Even animals will not drink from an old well like this one. The lesson is that human beings who do not take care of themselves and who let their mind and spirit atrophy are like a well that is never tended. Through neglect and desuetude its clear water gradually becomes muddy; eventually it becomes useless and no one visits it.

Do not neglect yourself or waste your talents. Take care of your body and your mind. Pay attention to your self-development and make the most of your potential. You may have much to offer, but if you squander your life on petty concerns and base pursuits, your life and your spirit will shrivel up and no one will have any use for you, including yourself. Throw yourself away and you will eventually be discarded by others. For if you regard your own life as an insignificant bauble, why should you expect other people to treat you any better?

Self-cultivation and self-development cannot be achieved alone. Exchanges with others replenish you like clear water replenishes a well. Open yourself to others and be willing to learn from them. If you become stubborn and opinionated, you cut yourself off from new experiences and new sources of enlightenment, and your talents and your life will waste away.

Nine in the Second Place

Shooting fishes at the bottom of the well.
The jug is broken and leaks.

"Shooting fishes at the bottom of the well" is not only a foolish way to catch fish; it is also the surest way to damage the well. The text thus symbolizes a person who misuses his potential.

You are not using your talents and abilities for worthwhile pursuits. You fritter your life away on trivial things and you waste your time with unworthy people. You do not challenge yourself sufficiently or give yourself the chance to grow. As a result, your abilities decay and your talents grow rusty, and so you cannot perform when it is really necessary. It is no wonder, then, that you feel you are not sufficiently noticed and admired. You cannot expect other people to take you seriously if you do not take your own life seriously. Turn your life around. Start living up to your potential if you want people to treat you with respect.

Nine in the Third Place

The well is dredged,
But no one drinks from it.
This is my heart's sorrow,
For it can be used to draw water.
If the king had clarity,
All would share in its blessings.

A well that has been dredged has been purified for use. Yet even though the well is now clear, the king's mind is not clear, so no use is made of this valuable resource.

You have talents and much to offer the world. Yet people do not recognize you or make use of your abilities. Perhaps you are overlooking an opportunity to put your potential to good use. This is unfortunate, not only for yourself but for others around you. If you could find a way to make a contribution, everyone would benefit.

Six in the Fourth Place

The well is being lined. No blame.

To line the well with stone means to take it out of service temporarily to fix it and renew it.

It is time to take stock and put your life in order. Rethink your strategies and reevaluate your priorities. Work on new skills and pay attention to your self-development. This will require you to pull back for a while and withdraw from the situation temporarily. You cannot achieve your goals at present and you cannot be so active in the lives of others. But working on your spiritual development and putting things in order now will make it easier for you to make a contribution in the long run. Such a renovation of body and soul, heart and mind, is therefore without blame.

Nine in the Fifth Place (Ruling Line)

In the well is a clear, cold spring.
Drink.

A well replenished by a spring symbolizes a person whose virtues benefit others. The clarity of the water symbolizes his wisdom. He is continually replenished through worthy activity just as a spring continually replenishes the well that surrounds it.

You have great potential to exercise leadership and to be a resource that others can draw on. People can benefit greatly from your insight, your wisdom, and your strength of character. But these potentialities will mean nothing unless they are realized in practice, just as clear water from a well does no good unless people bring it to the surface and drink it. You must ensure that your abilities are developed to their fullest and used for good.

Six at the Top

They draw from the well.
Do not cover it.
There is confidence.
Supreme good fortune.

A well in working order is available to everyone. Its water is clear and healthy. Continually fed by a spring, it is dependable and never runs dry, and everyone benefits from it. One should not cover up such a valuable resource or deny it to those in need. The well symbolizes a person of great character, whose goodness is an inexhaustible source of blessing to others. He is like a well perpetually replenished by a cold, clear spring, for the more he gives to others, the more he is enriched.

The text advises you to model yourself after the well. Be magnanimous and generous, humane and open-minded. You have clarity and wisdom to offer people; in you they will find a dependable source of strength and support. Do not hide your light or try to keep everything for yourself. If you give of yourself to others, they will have confidence in you and look up to you, and you will be rewarded countless times over. Make the virtues of humaneness and generosity your own, and they will bring you supreme good fortune.

NOTES

48.0 "They come and go, drawing from the well." *wang lai jing jing:* go come well well. Or, "Coming and going, drawing, drawing" (Alfred Huang); "People may come and go, but it remains the same Well, pure and still" (Lynn).

48.1 "No game." Cf. Wilhelm/Baynes: "No animals come to an old well."

48.2 "Shooting fishes," etc. *jing gu she fu weng bi lou:* literally, "well deep shoot fish jar ruin leak." Alternatively, "Shooting down the wellhole at fishes; the water jar has holes and leaks." The passage can be interpreted in many different ways. Edward Shaughnessy offers an elaborate discussion of the corresponding passage in the Mawangdui text, which he translates as "If the well is murky shoot the smelt; it is only the worn-out fish-trap."

48.3 "dredged." *xie.* An alternative reading is "The well seeps, and no one drinks from it."

48.3 "If the king," etc. Alternatively, "If the king possessed clarity, all would receive his blessings together."

48.6 "There is confidence." *you fu:* possessing sincerity (confidence, trust, dependability). Cf. 34.1. Cf. Wilhelm/Baynes: "It is dependable." Another possible translation is "Be sincere and truthful."

FORTY-NINE

Ge • Revolution

䷰

Keywords:

Molting
Shedding old skin
Metamorphosis
Transformation
Out with the old

Above: Dui • Lake
Below: Li • Fire

The original meaning of Ge was to molt or to shed one's skin. It was eventually extended to transformations generally and in particular to changes in government. Three yang lines ascend powerfully in the middle of the hexagram, while another yang line follows close behind. This symbolizes the successive waves of upheaval that attend transformation. Transformations do not come in a single stroke but in a series of disruptions to the established order, until that order surrenders or fades away.

The constituent trigrams are Dui (Lake) and Li (Fire). Lake and fire are opposites. In Hexagram 38, Kui (Opposition), the two trigrams are opposed but move away from each other. Fire, which is on the top, moves upward. Lake, which is on the bottom, moves downward. However, in Ge the order of the trigrams is reversed. Lake is on top; fire is on the bottom. As a result the two opposites are on a collision course. Each attempts to destroy the other: The fire tries to boil the water in the lake; the lake tries to drown out the fire. Their conflict symbolizes the struggle that accompanies a revolution.

THE JUDGMENT

Revolution.
On your own day
There is confidence.
Supreme success.
It is beneficial to persevere.
Regrets vanish.

Revolution means the abolition of an old order in preparation for a new one. Such drastic changes are appropriate only when there is no other alternative. If you are contemplating such a change, it is because you feel that things have gone as far as they can in their present form and something entirely new is called for.

When you realize that the time has come for revolution in your life, it is usually because you have already begun to experience a revolution in your heart. You may find yourself questioning long-held assumptions and beliefs. What once seemed so central and important to you now begins to seem irrelevant and beside the point. All of this means that your values and expectations are changing. You have begun to see things in different ways. It is dizzying and leaves you uncertain. But it is a necessary precondition to transformation of your life. The name of the hexagram, Ge, compares this process to the shedding of an old skin in preparation for a new one.

You should not be afraid of the changes that you want to make. Now more than ever you need to have courage and faith in yourself. But before you proceed, you must think things through carefully. Take the time to consider the ramifications of what you are about to do. Radical change that is well motivated and properly prepared invigorates your life. Change that is reckless and ill considered can be very destructive. Remember that you are not the only person who will be affected by the changes. You must take other people's feelings and interests into account. No one goes into a revolution alone; whether by choice or by circumstance one takes many others as well. You will need the support of others if you are to succeed in making a successful transformation. Discuss your change of heart with them and describe what you plan to accomplish. Talk openly about their fears and concerns as well as your own. If you show them that you are not being self-centered, capricious, and arbitrary but that this is what you really need to do, they will be more supportive than you expect. And they may offer helpful advice about how to achieve your goals.

When you have thoroughly considered the need for change and garnered the support of others, you are ready to act. Good timing is crucial to a successful transformation. Do not be afraid to make far-reaching changes in your lifestyle, your habits, or your environment. You must change your life in order to make it cohere with who you are now. As the text says, when your own day comes, there is confidence.

The same principles apply to political revolutions or to transformations in large organizations. Drastic change is a very serious matter. It should not be undertaken lightly, but only when there is nothing else to be done. A successful revolution requires a leader who is called to the task. You should not attempt radical change unless you feel a calling to lead and serve others, an inner compulsion that convinces you that a change must come and that you must play your part in it. A successful leader must act at the right time, and must gain the support of others. If you do not do this, your attempts will fail. Perhaps most important, you must make the changes not merely for your own sake but for the good of those who follow you. Revolution is justified when it helps the people and not merely their leaders. And you have a duty to guide the movement forward to something creative and positive, and to prevent events from spinning out of control and becoming excessive or destructive. If you can do all these things, you should have no regrets about making the necessary changes.

THE IMAGE

Fire in the lake:
This is the image of Revolution.
Thus the superior person
Sets the calendar in order
To illuminate in accordance with the times.

Fire and water attempt to destroy each other. The destruction of the old in preparation for the new is part of nature. The sun rises and then sets, only to rise again. The seasons of the year succeed each other, each one eliminating the last and replacing it. It would be unnatural if this did not happen. The law of change means that nothing lasts forever, and therefore revolution will come when the old order has reached its peak, declined, and is ready to exit the world. The challenge for you is to understand the needs of the time and to act on them. If you ally yourself properly with those needs, your transformation will be fruitful and dynamic. But if you stubbornly resist the transformation of events, or if you act recklessly and precipitously, the result will be disastrous not only for you but for others as well. Therefore, it is crucial that before you make major changes you deliberate thoroughly and determine whether you are in accord with the moment and are truly called to the task. Wise people read the signs of the times and adjust their actions appropriately. Then they travel with the flow of events rather than against them, and so even great and momentous changes go well.

THE LINES

The lines describe the steps that a person must undergo in order for radical change to succeed. At the beginning, we must wait until the time is right (lines one and two). Then we must gather support (line three). People will not follow us unless we act for a higher purpose than our own aggrandizement (line four). We must be firmly convinced that radical change is necessary if we want others to have confidence in our leadership (line five). Finally, after the changes have taken place, we must see to the details of practical reform in order to consolidate our new position (line six).

Initial Nine

Wrapped in the hide of a yellow cow.

Yellow is the color of the mean. A cow is a symbol of docility. Hence to be wrapped in the hide of a yellow cow means to restrain oneself through exercising moderation and patience.

Major changes should be undertaken only when they are necessary, and even then they require careful planning and preparation. You do not yet know whether it is proper to act and, even if so, when the right time for action would be. Exercise patience and weigh the situation thoroughly in your mind. You should act only when you have completely thought things through and are quite sure that there is no other alternative. If you go forward impulsively now, you may cause yourself trouble later on.

Six in the Second Place

When one's own day comes, one may create revolution.
Starting brings good fortune.
No blame.

"One's own day" is the moment in which all elements of the situation—including the self—are in proper alignment and thus the chances for success are maximized. This means inner resolve, meticulous preparation of the methods of attack, and the creation of public confidence for what you are about to do.

Revolutionary change is necessary when the status quo has become intolerable and lesser measures will simply not do. You have reached a point in your life when change is necessary. Do not be afraid to move forward. Decide what your goals are and what you want the outcome to be. Plan things thoroughly, work out a coherent strategy, and take all contingencies into account. Gather support from friends and associates. Prepare the people who need to know for the changes you are planning.

Above all, you must be firmly committed to success and the creation of a new order, not simply intellectually but emotionally and spiritually. Half-hearted measures will not succeed when revolutionary change is at stake. Imagine the new world that you wish to create. Visualize it in your mind, embrace it, and prepare yourself for its realization. When you have the right inner attitude and put all the pieces of the puzzle in place, your day has come. Starting out will bring you good fortune.

Nine in the Third Place

Starting brings misfortune.
Perseverance brings danger.
When talk of revolution has made the rounds three times,
There is confidence.

Effective change requires both courage and caution, both daring and careful preparation. Heart and mind must be disciplined toward success. Major change usually affects people beside yourself. If the support of others is necessary to success, as it often is, people must have confidence in what you are about to do. And for others to have confidence, you must have confidence in your own abilities and certainty in your own mind that your course of action is the right one.

For this reason, do not try to change things too hastily. Rash action without careful preparation will backfire. Reckless advance without the confidence of others will leave you vulnerable. Full and open discussion of the options is essential. Consider how the change will affect other people as well as yourself. You need to know whether conditions really are so bad that fundamental change is needed, and you need to know whether you will have the support you need if you begin to act. Hence the text says that "[w]hen talk of revolution has made the rounds three times"—i.e., when the issue has been fully contemplated and support for change is genuine—you may proceed with confidence.

Nine in the Fourth Place

Regrets vanish.
There is confidence.
Changing the order of government brings good fortune.

Radical change is possible now. Everything will go well if your goals are truly worthy and your motives correct. Make sure that your course of action is impelled by higher truths and ideals and that it will benefit others besides yourself. You should not pursue change merely for selfish reasons or out of base motivations. Other people will accept what you are doing only if they believe that it is fair, reasonable, and just and that you are truly committed to the good rather than simply your own aggrandizement. Then they will have confidence in you, and you will succeed.

This line offers advice both for leaders and individuals who seek to make changes. Successful revolutions require proper leadership and commitment to worthy aims. Leaders must inspire confidence that they are working for the greater good and are not simply motivated by a thirst for power, or else others will not follow them. In the long run, the ability to lead depends on the ability to influence people, and that influence exists because people have confidence in the character and inner strength of their leaders and in the values they stand for. The motives for change must also be admirable. Successful revolutions must pursue high ideals. People will give sustained support only to those movements and changes that they believe in their hearts to be just. To be sure, people are often moved to violent action by selfishness and hatred, bigotry and the need for retribution, but in the long run, nothing good can come from radical change based on these negative passions; for it will merely lead to even more selfishness, hatred, and violence. A revolution fed on bad motives and a lust for power will eventually consume itself.

What is true about a change of government is also true of the government of the self. Radical change in your lifestyle will succeed only if you are committed to something truly valuable and appropriate for you. You must be inspired by something higher and better that you wish to cultivate and realize within yourself. If your purposes are selfish or if you act from hatred, bitterness, or the desire for revenge, your actions will be poisoned by these emotions. You will not gain the support of others, and what you create will not last. But if your motives are worthwhile and you have prepared properly, you may proceed with complete confidence and you will meet with good fortune.

Nine in the Fifth Place (**Ruling Line**)

The great person changes like a tiger.
Even before he consults the oracle,
There is confidence.

The tiger is an animal of great energy and purpose. Its skin, with large black stripes on a yellow background, is distinctive and easily visible to others. The tiger symbolizes a great leader that inspires confidence and that others instinctively follow. He offers his position in clear, understandable terms—like the tiger's stripes—and the people believe him and follow him. Being trusted "[e]ven before [one] consults the oracle" means that you are sure in your heart that your cause is correct and that you have properly understood the nature of the times. Therefore, you do not need a sign that it is appropriate to proceed. Your confidence is its own spiritual power, which draws people to you as if by magic.

The time has come to act. Conditions are excellent to make a great and lasting change in the situation. Success is assured. You know exactly what to do. Trust your instincts. Your vigor and confidence will inspire others. They know where you stand. Because they believe that you are correct, they will trust you and you will gain their spontaneous support.

Six at the Top

The superior person changes like a leopard.
The countenance of the petty person is transformed.
Setting forth brings misfortune.
To remain persevering brings good fortune.

The leopard's coat has smaller marks than the wide stripes of the tiger. This symbolizes the period after a revolution, when the great principles that motivated the change must be articulated and applied in practical reforms and specific details. Petty people will see the handwriting on the wall and they will conform to the new order outwardly. Hence their faces are transformed, even though the change may be only skin-deep. For the moment, outward acquiescence is all that one can require. To press too far would destabilize the situation; now it is time to secure the new regime and guarantee that it will endure.

You have made significant changes in the situation and have achieved your major objectives. Take satisfaction in what you have accomplished and do not try to press for more. Like all changes, this one has been imperfect, and still bears some legacy of the past. But do not allow the best to become the enemy of the good. Instead, devote yourself to working out the details and consolidating your new position. Secure the advantages you have gained. A new order is forming. Make your reforms concrete and put your values to work in everyday practice. If you are determined to make the most of what you have achieved and to ensure that the changes are lasting, good fortune is assured.

NOTES

49.0 "There is confidence." Or, "You are trusted," "You are believed" (Wilhelm / Baynes).

49.GI "To illuminate in accordance with the times." Or, "In order to clarify the times (seasons)," "make the seasons clear."

49.3 "There is confidence." *you fu:* possessing sincerity (truth). Or, "People trust him," "People believe in him." Cf. 49.0, 49.4, 49.5.

49.4 "Changing the order of government." *gai ming:* change mandate (order, command). Hence, "Changing the mandate to rule."

49.6 "countenance." *mian.* Or, "face," "expression." Hence, "The petty person's face is transformed." Cf. Wilhelm/Baynes: "The inferior man molts in the face."

49.6 "To remain persevering." *ju zhen:* dwell [in] perseverance. Or, "To remain constant and steadfastly faithful." Cf. 17.3

FIFTY

Ding • The Caldron

Keywords:

Cultural renewal
In with the new
Establishing things
Formation of a new order
Devotion
Creation of new rituals
Polishing your talents
Seeking spiritual values
Being of service to others

Above: Li • Fire
Below: Xun • Wind (Wood)

A Ding is a sacred vessel, normally made of bronze, in which ritual foods were prepared and cooked during religious ceremonies. Because fire is applied to the Ding, it is sometimes called a caldron, but a Ding is a beautiful piece of art rather than merely a utilitarian device. The Ding is a symbol of civilization and of the benefits that flow from civilization and civilized behavior.

It is often said that the structure of the hexagram resembles the Ding. The lowest yin line resembles the legs on which the caldron sits. The three yang lines form the body. The next yin line represents the ears or rings, through which carrying rods (or handles) are placed. The yang line at the top represents the carrying rod.

The constituent trigrams are Xun (Wood) below and Li (Fire) above. This symbolizes the cooking of food. The theme of Ding is the creation of a cultural order that nourishes people spiritually just as food nourishes them bodily. Food is cooked to feed the body; culture is "cooked" to feed the soul. Thus this hexagram has something in common with Hexagram 27, Yi (Nourishment) and Hexagram 48, Jing (The Well). Indeed, The Well and The Caldron are the only two hexagrams that refer to man-made objects. The Well concerns how people replenish themselves through reciprocity; the Caldron concerns how people enlighten themselves through culture. Cooking is an apt symbol of this process. Through cooking, the raw elements of nature are transformed into cultural artifacts that nourish and assist people. Through culture, human beings become persons endowed with humanity. This is the meaning of the Ding.

THE JUDGMENT

The Caldron.
Supreme good fortune.
Success.

The Ding, or ritual caldron, formed part of a religious service in which sacrifices were made to a divinity. Through this ritual, people purified themselves and rededicated themselves to spiritual ends. The text urges you to model yourself after the Ding. It is time to purify your motives and devote yourself to worthy aims. The text promises success and supreme good fortune. But it is not necessarily worldly success. Indeed, it is time to abandon materialism and selfishness. You will make progress not from chasing after greater wealth or social status but from pursuing spiritual values such as kindness, generosity, and service to others.

Different ingredients were mixed in the ritual caldron and then cooked together to form a divine offering. In the same way, you must now gather the different ingredients of your world and combine them together to produce something worthwhile. Take the raw materials of your life and transform them into something new and wonderful.

These raw ingredients include your talents. Keep your skills in good repair by employing them in the service of others. Don't waste your abilities on things that are trivial or unworthy of you. The raw materials of life also include opportunities in your environment. Look around you. There are hidden possibilities everywhere for you to deploy and improve your skills.

You may fear that you lack the ability or the qualities of mind and heart necessary to succeed. Do not be concerned. You do have something to contribute to the situation, whether you know it or not. Within every person there lies a divine presence. It is up to you to discover it and develop it in your life.

Ding teaches that you can transform yourself and your world if you do so not for selfish ends but in pursuit of something truly valuable. Quietly support others and help them to succeed. Assist other people without any desire to take credit for their success. Conduct yourself with modesty and devotion. Like the ritual caldron, you can be a source of inspiration to others. People will draw strength from you and follow your example.

THE IMAGE

Above wood there is fire:
This is the image of the Caldron.
Thus the superior person consolidates his fate
By making his position correct.

Fire burns as long as it has fuel. Its fate is tied to the wood beneath it. If you want to know what your fate is likely to be, ask yourself what fuels your flame. People who act with righteousness and devotion, who take proper care of themselves and of others, who give and accept with generosity and mutuality, who choose worthy goals and bring them to completion, who understand the changing nature of the time and adjust to it with equanimity, humility, and good grace, put their future on a solid footing. They may not be guaranteed a happy life, but they have done everything they can to prepare for it. Thus the text says they secure their fate by making their position correct. It is often said that luck is the residue of design. If so, then good luck is the residue of good design.

THE LINES

The basic theme of the lines is the importance of devotion in the creation of something new and valuable. All of the lines except the fourth are essentially favorable, and the problem in the fourth is precisely that one lacks devotion and adequate preparation for the task. From line one—which promises that even the most lowly can make a contribution—to line six, which advises us to use our wisdom to support others—the message is one of hope and the promise of ultimate good fortune.

Initial Six

The caldron's legs are turned upside down.
It is beneficial to remove obstructions.
One takes a concubine for the sake of her son.
No blame.

To turn the caldron upside down is to remove refuse and stagnant elements in preparation for cleaning and renewal. This symbolizes self-purification and devotion. A concubine is a person at the bottom of the social order; her son represents hope for the future. Thus to take a concubine for the sake of her son means that no matter how lowly or imperfect people may appear, they have something to contribute and they should be accepted and recognized for this. The message of this line is therefore one of great optimism and hope: No matter how humble our origins, if we can purify ourselves, rid ourselves of that which is stagnant, and dedicate ourselves to worthy aims, we can make a difference in this world.

You would like to achieve something, but you feel inadequate to the task. You must rid yourself of old and outmoded habits. Eliminate the sources of your stagnation. Put aside any preconceptions about what you can and cannot accomplish. Be open-minded and ready to learn. To succeed, you may need to employ new and unorthodox methods. But you should have no concerns about this as long as your aims are worthy. Purify and renew yourself and you can succeed no matter how inexperienced you think you are.

Nine in the Second Place

The caldron is full.
My comrade is afflicted,
But it cannot reach me.
Good fortune.

You have all the resources you need to achieve something significant. Do not be deterred if others misunderstand you or resent you. Simply go about your business and do the best job you can. Work with devotion. No one can take your achievements away from you.

Nine in the Third Place

The ears of the caldron are removed.
Progress is blocked.
The fat of the pheasant is not eaten.
Rain falls everywhere, and regrets fade.
Good fortune comes in the end.

The ears of the caldron are holes through which a lifting rod or handle is inserted. If the ears are altered, the caldron cannot be lifted up and used, and people cannot enjoy the delicious food within it. The metaphors in the text symbolize a person who has something important to contribute but whose progress is blocked or is not recognized by others. The falling rain symbolizes the eventual release of tensions and the end of obstruction, which leads to good fortune.

You have much to offer, but others do not recognize it. This may be due to their mistakes or your own. As a result, your abilities remain hidden or underutilized. This is unfortunate and a waste of something quite valuable. But do not be disconcerted. Have faith in yourself. Take a more positive attitude. Eliminate any self-destructive tendencies that keep you from succeeding. Work on your talents and keep them in good shape. Your devotion and spiritual qualities will eventually bring forth a response from others. In time, things will change for the better and you will gain the recognition you deserve.

Nine in the Fourth Place

The legs of the caldron break off.
It overturns, spilling the duke's meal,
So that its body is soiled.
Misfortune.

When the legs of the caldron break off, it is because they were weak and unable to support its weight. The metaphor describes people who cannot bear the weight of responsibilities placed on them. "Spilling the duke's meal" means that they disappoint others through their incompetence. "Its body is soiled" means that they thereby bring disgrace upon themselves.

You need to be more realistic about your goals. Be careful that you do not bite off more than you can chew. You currently lack something that you need to succeed, whether it is energy, commitment, talent, ability, or support. Bad judgment or delusions of grandeur have led you to make promises you cannot keep. You may also be relying too much on untrustworthy or incompetent people to get you through. If you try to push forward without adequate preparation, you will let other people down and you will damage your reputation. Rid yourself of illusions and take a careful look at yourself. Reorder your priorities. Don't waste your talents on things that are wrong for you.

Six in the Fifth Place (**Ruling Line**)

The caldron has yellow ears and golden handles.
It is beneficial to persevere.

The ears of the caldron are rings through which carrying rods or handles are inserted. Yellow and gold are the color of the mean. Line five is the line of the ruler; hence the text symbolizes a leader whose modesty and devotion draw able helpers that enable him to succeed.

Approach the situation with a balanced attitude and a firm determination to see things through. If you exercise moderation and do not go to extremes, your chances of success are high. Act without pretension or haughtiness. These are often a sign of inner insecurity. A receptive attitude will allow you to learn from others and draw on their insights. Be friendly and accessible, and you will attract the support you need. If you can maintain these healthy habits and attitudes over time, and make them part of your character, you will not only succeed at your task but will grow in wisdom and enlightenment.

Nine at the Top (**Ruling Line**)

The caldron has jade handles.
Great good fortune.
There is nothing that is not beneficial.

Jade combines hardness with soft luster. It thus signifies a person who is outwardly mild and receptive but inwardly strong and determined. The combination of these qualities makes a person a natural leader but one who works behind the scenes, quietly supporting the ruler and ensuring his success. Line six is the position of the sage who has put worldly ambition behind him and devotes himself to helping others. Because of the sage's wisdom and unselfishness, all goes well.

Your motives are pure and your goals are worthy. You have much to offer others. You see the situation with clarity and you know how you can help. Give of yourself now and help others without any desire to take credit. Your insights and your assistance will ensure success and benefit everyone, including yourself. When people use their greatness for the common good and are accepted gratefully by others, "there is nothing that is not beneficial."

NOTES

50.GI "consolidates." *ning:* solidify; hence, makes secure and stable. I.e., he puts his future on a solid footing (secures his fate) by behaving with rectitude.

50.1 "obstructions." *pi:* the name of Hexagram 12; whatever is stale, stagnant, or evil. Hence another reading might be "It is beneficial to expel stagnant elements [from the situation]."

50.1 "son." *tzu:* son, posterity, sage, one who lives up to the ideals of one's ancestors. In this case, it symbolizes hope for the future.

50.2 "The caldron is full." I.e., of food. One has everything one needs, and more would be too much.

50. 2 "My comrade is afflicted, / But it cannot reach me." This line is subject to many different interpretations. *Chou* (comrade) can also mean rival, and *ji* (affliction) can also mean illness, anxiety, or hatred. Hence, Wilhelm/Baynes translates the line, "My comrades are envious, but they cannot harm me." Another reading would be "My enemies (or rivals) are envious, but they cannot harm me."

Ji usually means "illness" in the *Book of Changes* (cf. 25.5), but it might also mean an illness of the soul, like greed, vanity, or envy. It is translated as "affliction" to convey these multiple meanings. Because of this ambiguity, the line could read, "My comrade is ill, but it [the disease] cannot reach me," or "My comrade is anxious, but I cannot reach him [to reassure him]." The present translation seems to make the most sense, given the conclusion that there is good fortune.

50.3 "Progress." *xing:* movement, activity. Because the ears are removed, one cannot insert the lifting bars, so the caldron cannot be transported.

50.3 "fat." *gao:* fat meat, or gravy. A delicacy.

50.4 "break off." *zhe:* break off, sever, judge the true and the false. Hence symbolically the person was judged and found not up to the task.

50.4 "It overturns," etc. Another reading is "It overturns, and the stew spills on the duke, drenching him." Either way, the result is unfortunate.

50.5 "Yellow ears." *er,* "ears," are rings attached to the body of the caldron through which *juan* (carrying bars or handles) were inserted.

50.6 "jade handles." Jade handles lift the caldron up and support it. Jade is noted both for its hardness (symbolizing strength) and its soft luster (symbolizing mildness). Thus the line suggests that one in this position should be like jade: supporting the accomplishments of others through firmness that is modest and mild.

FIFTY-ONE

Zhen • Shock

䷲

Keywords:

Thunder
Shake
Quake
Upheaval
The arousing
Reassess your life
Shocking you out of your lethargy
Hidden potential in sudden change
Blessings in disguise
Taking action

Above: Zhen • Thunder
Below: Zhen • Thunder

Zhen originally meant shock or quake. One yang line pushes up against two yin lines repeatedly. Zhen concerns a sudden event that surprises and arouses a person. The theme of Zhen is not simply the shock itself but how one deals with it. The surprising event is a test of character. One who remains calm and at ease, and cautiously examines himself and his errors before going forward, will succeed.

Zhen is one of the eight hexagrams that consist of doubled trigrams.

The hexagram consists of the trigram Zhen (Thunder) doubled. Hence it symbolizes repeated shocks. Zhen is also associated with the eldest son, who seizes the initiative. Thus, another theme of the hexagram is taking action.

Zhen bears a certain similarity to Hexagram 24, Fu (Return), which also features Zhen (Thunder) in the lower trigram. Indeed, it resembles a truncated version of Fu that is placed on top of itself. One theme of Fu is the need to reassess your life and return to the right path. This is also a theme of Zhen. However, whereas Fu features earth in the upper trigram, suggesting the need for calm, gradual change, the upper trigram of Zhen is thunder. Here a sudden, shocking event forces you to rethink your priorities and gives you a chance to turn your life around.

THE JUDGMENT

Shock. Success.
Thunder comes—crack, crack!
Afterward there is laughter and talk—ha, ha!
The shock terrifies for a hundred miles,
But he does not let the sacrificial spoon and chalice fall.

Something unexpected has shaken you. You had not prepared for it. Suddenly, your life seems in upheaval. You experience fear and panic. But once your initial reactions subside, you will recognize that the sudden turn of events is for the best. You have been caught by surprise, but if you hold yourself properly, something positive can and will emerge from the shake-up.

The important thing now is to stay calm and keep your wits about you. Take a closer look at the situation. It is possible that you have simply taken on too much. The shocking event may be a blessing in disguise: it gives you an opportunity to reassess your priorities and lessen some of your burdens. Perhaps you have drifted into an unsatisfying and unrewarding routine. The shocking event can awaken you from your lethargy and force you to change your plans. The disruption of your everyday life can invigorate you and give you a fresh outlook on life. It is like being splashed with cold water. It is unpleasant at first, but it stimulates the senses. After the shake-up, you suddenly see new possibilities. Although the change may be disturbing in the beginning, maintain your poise and approach the new situation with an open mind. You will come out of this series of events stronger, better, and happier.

The *Book of Changes* compares the situation you now face to thunder pealing while a person is performing a sacred ritual. The shock comes just as the person is ladling out the sacramental wine. But he is so imbued with seriousness and a sense of purpose that he does not spill a drop. In the same way, you should consider the change as a test of your character. If you can maintain equanimity and composure in the face of outside upheaval, you are secure against whatever life can throw against you and you will always be able to spot the new potential in changed conditions. That is because the shock not only shakes you up; it also shakes up the world outside you. New possibilities are created out of the shards of the old. This is a key idea in the *Book of Changes:* Change—even sudden and startling change—is not only a hazard but an opportunity. People who let shocking events dictate their inner life will be disabled and mired in confusion. They are like people who are struck by lightning. But people who maintain balance in their inner life are quickly able to restore balance in their relations with the outside world. They can rise to the challenge and improve their lives in the process.

THE IMAGE

Repeated Thunder:
This is the image of Shock.
In fear and trembling,
The superior person examines himself
And sets his life in order.

Sudden change is like a wake-up call from God. It shocks you into considering whether you have been traveling down the wrong path, and it gives you a chance to change direction.

Many shocking events are simply out of your control; there is no way you could have foreseen them or prepared for them. But some shocks occur because you have been unwilling to face facts. Perhaps you have convinced yourself that something you don't want to happen could never happen, or perhaps you have been blindly pursuing an unwise or unhealthy way of life. Then one day the problems and fears you have neglected for so long suddenly catch up with you. You find that you have to confront them face-to-face. It is as if your unconscious self were giving you a not-so-gentle shove, forcing you to own up to your actions and asking you point-blank whether it isn't time to change your life. When this happens, it is partly accidental, but it is also partly a function of the road you have traveled up to this point, for that path made the accident happen in a particular way and it gave the events a particular meaning and force.

In any case, whatever the causes, when the upheaval arrives, it is up to you to make the most of the situation and learn from it. Search your soul and reconsider your attitudes. Have you been living your life the way it should be lived? Have you been treating other people the way you should? As the text says, when the thunder comes, it is time to examine yourself and put your life in order. Change has shaken things up. Think creatively. Open your mind and your heart. If you can take advantage of this opportunity, something very beneficial will come of it.

THE LINES

The lines concern how to deal with shocking events and sudden upheavals in life. The advice in all of the lines is to maintain composure and emotional balance in the face of changing circumstances. What appears at first to be a serious blow may turn out to be to one's ultimate advantage. On the whole, the lines are favorable except the fourth, in which the subject allows the shock to immobilize him. The larger lesson is that an enlightened person continually adjusts to change by preserving a balanced attitude; by changing with the change, he eventually masters it.

Initial Nine (Ruling Line)

Thunder comes—crack, crack!
Then there is laughter and talk—ha, ha!
Good fortune.

A shocking or unexpected event has thrown you for a loss. You are not sure what will happen next and you feel in grave danger. But the shock is only temporary, and the disturbance of your equanimity is actually a blessing in disguise. The surprise will pass, and you will feel relief. Your position will improve as a result, and what seemed shocking and harmful will turn out to bring you good fortune in the long run.

Six in the Second Place

Shock comes.
It brings danger.
One loses one's treasures,
and climbs the nine hills.

Do not pursue.
In seven days you will get them.

To climb the nine hills means to ascend to a high place away from danger.

A great upheaval threatens you with significant loss. You cannot stop forces and events that are already in motion. Resistance is futile. The best strategy is to accept the situation in the short run and remove yourself immediately from the source of the danger. Put yourself beyond the reach of harmful influences and wait out the difficulty. In the long run, you will recoup what you have lost.

Six in the Third Place

Shock comes.
It revives.
Shocked into moving.
No mistake.

A sudden upheaval tests your inner strength. Fate has struck you a grievous blow. Do not lose your head. Stay calm and collected. Maintain your composure. If you can keep your presence of mind, you will see a way out. Let the shock revive your ingenuity. Do not let the shocking event throw you, but instead allow it to spur your imagination. You will soon discover alternatives that can improve your situation.

Nine in the Fourth Place

Mired in shock.

A shocking event has completely thrown you off balance. As a result, you feel stuck, bewildered, unable to act. Get up off the floor. Shake yourself out of your confusion. Gather your wits about you. Try to figure out what the event means and what you can learn from it. If you allow yourself to become mired in shock, matters will only become worse. You cannot make progress until you start to think clearly again.

Six in the Fifth Place

Shock coming and going.
Danger.
But it does not mean loss.
There are things to do.

Life seems to be conspiring against you. You face one blow after another. Repeated shocks leave you breathless. But all is not lost. Stay calm. Maintain your emotional balance and your composure. Do not abandon your values. You will have to adjust to the new circumstances, but as long as you remain centered, you will be able to handle whatever life throws you. In the long run, your efforts will pay off and you will lose nothing. The lesson of this line is that those who lack emotional integrity will be thrown about like driftwood in a storm at sea, but those who keep their balance will roll with the tides and eventually come out on top.

Six at the Top

Shock comes. Trembling, trembling,
One looks about in terror.
Setting forth means misfortune.
If the shock has reached one's neighbor,
But not one's self,
There is no blame.
Yet even those joined in marriage will gossip.

Shocking events have caused widespread upheaval. Everyone about you is losing their head; it is essential that you keep yours. Do not let the fear and agitation of others cause you to act recklessly or imprudently. Stay above the fray and maintain your composure. You cannot stop the chaos by yourself, and others are too confused to help you. Therefore, it is best to retreat to safety. Some may criticize you for this, but they do not have your clarity of mind. Acting reasonably under these circumstances out of a desire for self-preservation is without blame.

NOTES

51.0 "crack, crack." *xi xi:* mimicking the sound of a thunderclap. An alternative reading is "startle, startle," or "fright, fright," i.e., very frightening.

51.0 "a hundred miles." Literally, a hundred *li,* a unit of distance in ancient China measuring approximately 1,800 feet.

51.0 "sacrificial spoon and chalice." Or, "ladle and libation of fragrant wine." The ladle was used to spoon out the wine for the libation.

51.GI "In fear and trembling." Or, "In fear and agitation."

51.2 "One loses one's treasures." Literally, "a hundred thousand cowrie shells." Cowrie shells were used not only for divination but as money.

51.2 "Do not pursue. / In seven days you will get them." Cf. 38.1, 63.2.

51.3 "revives." *su su:* revive, revive. The doubled word is for emphasis or intensification. Another reading is "threatening, frightening." Hence, "Shock comes and makes one distraught," or "Shock comes and makes one dispirited." Then the next line would read, "But if he goes forward shocked (in a shock-affected way, spurred to action), no mistake (or blunder)." In context, "revives" seems a better reading.

51.3 "Shocked into moving." Or, "Spurred into action," "Going forward like thunder."

51.3 "mistake." *sheng:* calamity or misfortune due to mistake or internal fault. One could translate the entire line in rhymed couplets as follows:

Shock arrives.
It revives.
Going forth like thunder.
No blunder.

51.4 "Mired in shock." *zhen sui ni:* thunder then mire. Hence, "Shock comes. He gets mired in it," or, "When shock comes, one is stuck in the mud."

51.5 "But it does not mean loss." *yi wu sang:* maybe (means) no loss.

51.6 "Trembling, trembling." *suo suo:* the sound of a thunderclap. The word *zhen* (shock, thunder) also means to quake or tremble. Hence, "Shock (tremble) makes people tremble, tremble." Another reading is "Anxious and distraught." Ritsema and Karcher read *suo suo* as *so so:* "twine, twine." The idea, apparently, is that things become unraveled, hence ruined. Similarly, Wilhelm/Baynes translates the line as "Shock brings ruin."

51.6 "If the shock has reached one's neighbor," etc. This reverses the order of the text, *bu yu qi gong yu qi lin,* which reads literally: "not go to one's body goes to one's neighbor." It conveys the idea that the lightning misses the subject and hits his neighbor instead.

51.6 "Yet even those joined in marriage will gossip." *hun gou you yan:* literally, "marriage alliance, there is talk." The present translation conveys the notion that in times of crisis even people who are close to one another may point fingers of accusation. Nevertheless, the line is subject to many different interpretations. It might also be translated as "There will be gossip about a marriage match," which does not seem in context. In his translation of the Mawangdui texts, Edward Shaughnessy uses the variant text *min gou,* or "confused slander." Thus, "In confused slander there is talk."

FIFTY-TWO

Gen • Keeping Still

Keywords:

Mountain
Restraint
Being quiet
Attaining inner peace
Enduring
Taking one day at a time

Above: Gen • Mountain
Below: Gen • Mountain

The hexagram Gen consists of the trigram Gen doubled. The original meaning of Gen is obscure. Some scholars think it originally meant "cleave." Eventually, it came to mean "keeping still," and the trigram Gen was associated with the mountains. It is the natural complement of the previous hexagram, Zhen. While Zhen rouses us out of our lethargy, Gen counsels us to keep still and find inner tranquility. Both hexagrams are concerned with self-examination, but in different ways.

The single yang line in the trigram Gen represents the mountain peak, and the yin lines beneath represent the sides of the mountain. The doubling of the trigram represents a chain of mountains or a mountain range. Mountains do not move. No matter what happens, they endure. Therefore the theme of Gen is restraint and the cultivation of equanimity and inner peace.

In the *Book of Changes* everything is connected to its opposite. Rest is merely an aspect of motion, and all motion from some perspective appears to be at rest. For example, the mountains seem to be motionless, but they are situated on a rotating globe that moves through the galaxy. Thus to be at rest often requires what from another perspective involves a certain type of motion. Hence it is not altogether surprising that the way to bring quiet to one's heart is to continue to move forward steadily, or as the saying goes, to take one day at a time.

THE JUDGMENT

Keeping Still.
He keeps his back still,
So that he no longer feels his body.
He goes into his courtyard,
And does not see his people.
No blame.

The *Book of Changes* teaches that you must make both your activity and your rest in harmony with the needs of the situation and the demands of the time. Success comes not only from moving forward at the right time but also from remaining still when it is appropriate to do so. The theme of Gen is recognizing that the time has come to be still so that you can regain your balance and find peace.

The text offers the metaphor of keeping the back still. The back represents the center of the body. Where the back goes the body goes, so if the back remains still, the body will be still. The back is also the location of the spine; hence to make one's back still means to calm one's nerves and thus one's mind. When your mind is calm and your thoughts are orderly, it is as if you no longer feel your body—that is, you no longer feel the pain of demands pressing on you from the outside and the urgency of desires pressing on you from the inside.

When you are angry and distressed, the world looks disordered and confused. But when you are perfectly calm, you see the world with greater clarity. Being still allows you to see beyond the surface turbulence of life and the petty struggles of the day and to look more deeply into the nature of things. Beyond the chaos and commotion lie deeper truths.

You have recently entered a difficult and trying period. The world seems disordered and confused. In part, that is because you have disorder and confusion within you. The most important thing for you to do right now is to restore your inner balance and find peace of mind. Do not let the chaos and the striving of the outside world distract you or upset you. There is nothing more that you can do in the present situation. You have done all that you can; any further exertions would only be counterproductive. Because struggling outwardly will do you no good, you should stop struggling inwardly as well.

Take a deep breath, collect your thoughts, and reflect. You will get nowhere if you obsess about your problems. That will only cause your anxiety to build and build until you feel that you absolutely must do something, and then you are likely to do precisely the wrong thing. If you make your decisions based on worry and apprehension, you are likely to misjudge and exaggerate things. But when your mind is still and your emotions are centered, you will make no mistakes. Calm yourself and you will be able to see more deeply into the situation. Then everything will appear in its proper perspective.

Being still does not mean abandoning your feelings. Quite the contrary, you will find that you will have a greater intuitive understanding of what is going on. The point is that you can best get in touch with those intuitions through stillness rather than through being in an emotional upheaval. And when you connect with those deeper parts of yourself, you will naturally select the right strategies and make the proper choices. You will instinctively know the right thing to do. In this way stillness becomes the necessary predicate for right action in the future.

THE IMAGE

A chain of mountains:
This is the image of Keeping Still.
Thus the superior person
Does not allow his thoughts
To go beyond his situation.

The mountain does not move. It does not change. The days pass; events occur and fade away; things come and go. But the mountain stays just where it is, and just as it is. Thus, it keeps still not only in space but also in time. That is why it endures.

The text advises you to model yourself after the mountain. To keep still you must remain anchored firmly in the here and now. The more you allow your thoughts to stray from the present, the more you will feel the pain of previous injustices and the pangs of unsatisfied desire and unfulfilled ambition.

Do not dwell on the past or obsess about the future. This will only make you unhappy and confused. Instead, focus your attention on what is before you. Try to take each day as it comes, responding to circumstances as they arise.

The mountain simply exists. It does not strive to be something other than it is. It is not wracked with resentment, longing, or ambition. It does not try to make itself bigger or grander. It is what it is, and that is why it is at peace. Every human being has inner resources of wisdom and discernment, although it is often difficult to gain access to them. When you are emotionally upset, it is especially difficult to do so. But if you can relax your body and quiet your mind, you can get in touch with the best and wisest parts of yourself. Then you will begin to understand who you are and who you are not, what you cannot do, and, equally important, what you can. From this stillness eventually comes acceptance of yourself, and from this acceptance comes inner peace. This acceptance is not despair or resignation but rather an appropriate regard for yourself. It is a source of genuine power. A mountain is at peace with itself, and there is nothing stronger or more mighty. Similarly, if you can learn to be still as the mountain is, you will become a happier, stronger, and more self-reliant person.

THE LINES

The lines discuss the virtue of emotional tranquility through the metaphor of keeping parts of the body still, from the feet in line one to the head in line five. Line six does not mention a body part. It may symbolize being above or beyond the body.

Initial Six

He keeps his toes still.
No blame.
It is beneficial to be continually persevering.

To keep the toes still means not to move. Before taking action it is best to assess the situation objectively and with a clear head. Once you begin, you may become invested in your current course of action, and then you will not be able to judge matters so dispassionately. Stop and deliberate when you are not yet committed and not yet entangled in self-serving desires and motivations. If you can approach things free from selfishness and self-delusion, you will find the right path.

Six in the Second Place

He keeps his calves still.
He cannot rescue the one he follows.
His heart is not glad.

The calves of the leg follow the motion of the body. If the legs are suddenly held back while the body moves forward, a person will fall. This symbolizes a person who is pulled in opposite directions, or one who is in the thrall of another and made unhappy by not being able to follow that person, even when the path is not the proper one.

You find yourself swept along by your emotions and by the forces you have set in motion. Events have spun out of control, and you no longer feel able to stop them, bringing you great unhappiness. You have lost your inner peace.

You may feel compelled out of a desire to follow another person or a group. But you are going in the wrong direction now because you lack clarity and balance. You are letting other people make choices for you and determine your destiny instead of making your own choices and thinking for yourself. This course of action will only bring you sorrow. You must calm and center yourself. The person or persons you desire are following the wrong path. You cannot stop them, but you do not have to follow them. You may be quite unhappy that you cannot pursue them now, but you would be even more unhappy if you did. The sadness you feel now is not due to your inability to throw yourself away but is caused by your own inner servitude. This is what you must free yourself from. Be true to your own values. That is the proper way to keep still in this situation.

Nine in the Third Place

He keeps his waist still.
Straining the spinal muscles.
This is dangerous.
The heart suffocates.

You are trying too hard to extinguish your inner turmoil. Faced with restlessness and emotional anxiety, you force yourself to be still. But you have not dealt with the source of the problem and have merely buried your conflicts temporarily. This is dangerous; for, as the text says, "[t]he heart suffocates." By stifling your emotions and not dealing with them honestly, you will create problems for yourself later on. Calmness is not something achieved through harsh or rigid methods. Rather, it is achieved through natural behavior and clearheadedness. You will achieve equanimity only if you face facts and accept yourself for what you are and the world around you for what it is. Take some time to relax, unburden yourself, and meditate about the proper course you should take.

The same advice applies to dealing with difficult situations. If you try to force matters to a conclusion, you will probably cause grave problems for yourself. Conflicts that you paper over now will surface later. Severe and unyielding responses to a problem will create hydraulic pressures that will build up over time. They will eventually produce cracks and fissures in the situation, and powerful and dangerous forces will be unleashed. The proper strategy to dealing with this sort of conflict is to let things play out and abate naturally. Be flexible and adaptable, and encourage others to do so as well. Set an example by acting with maturity and realism, and others will follow.

Six in the Fourth Place

He keeps his trunk still.
No blame.

To keep the trunk still means that the whole person is at rest. Hence it means that you keep your thoughts and desires at rest and in this way free yourself from egotism.

By maintaining your composure and not acting on impulse, you can bring peace to your life. Make decisions only when you are balanced and centered. Don't let your actions be driven by emotional neediness. Keep your ego firmly in check. Anxieties and fears will surely arise, but do not let them get to you. Simply let them go. Practicing meditation will help you maintain a healthy attitude.

Six in the Fifth Place

He keeps his jaws still.
His words have order.
Regrets vanish.

To keep the jaws still is to talk sparingly. To give words order is to consider carefully before you open your mouth. Harsh words and injudicious comments once spoken cannot be taken back; saying the wrong thing at the wrong time can cause much trouble later on. Thoughtless remarks usually result from not thinking.

How we feel affects how we communicate and vice versa. When people feel pressure or find themselves in a dangerous or awkward situation, they often express themselves badly and make unfortunate comments. If you are able to center yourself and maintain calm, you will be able to choose your words more carefully and avoid saying things you will later regret. Conversely, if you work consciously at picking your words with discrimination and care, you will be less likely to work yourself into an emotional state and become agitated or fearful. Learn to keep your mouth closed and speak only after you have put your thoughts in order, and you will be without blame.

Nine at the Top (Ruling Line)

Magnanimous. Keeping still.
Good fortune.

Emotional stability is the secret to success. Remain centered and nothing can cause you to lose your balance. The great lesson of this line is that peace comes to those who are at peace, while conflict seems ever to attach itself to those who are conflicted inside. The truth is revealed to those who are at rest and so are true within, while deception hounds those who have no rest and so deceive themselves. When your composure is so complete that it affects everything you say and do, your good fortune is assured. No matter what endeavor you pursue, your tranquility and self-possession will stand you in good stead.

NOTES

52.1 "to be continually persevering." *yong zhen*. Or, "to be constantly steadfast and upright." Cf. 2.7, 8.GI, 22.3, 42.2, 45.5, 62.4.

52.2 "calves." *fei*. Or "lower legs." Cf. 31.2.

52.3 "his waist." *xian:* waist. Also, "his hips."

52.3 "straining." *lie:* strains, splits, tears off.

52.3 "The heart suffocates." *xun xin:* literally, "smoke the heart;" thus another reading might be "The heart is heated up," or "The heart is enflamed."

52.4 "trunk." *shen:* body, one's person. The Mawangdui text reads *gong:* body, torso. The commentary on the small image for line four reads, "restraining the body" *(gong)*.

52.6 "Magnanimous." *dun:* greathearted, noblehearted, simple honesty and sincerity. Cf. 19.6, 24.5.

FIFTY-THREE

Jian • Developing Gradually

Keywords:

Gradual advance
Slow, steady development
Progress step by step
Faithfulness
Persistence

Above: Xun • Wind (Wood)
Below: Gen • Mountain

Jian consists of Gen (Mountain) below and Xun (Wind, or in this case Wood), above. It is symbolized by a tree growing slowly on a mountain. Gen stands for calmness and inner tranquility; Xun stands for gentle but insistent penetration. Slowly but surely, the trunk and branches of the tree penetrate upward into the sky, while its roots penetrate deep into the soil. The higher its branches spread, the more widely and deeply its roots reach. In this way the gradual development of the tree produces balance and stability. By contrast, a plant that grows too quickly is easily uprooted. A basic theme of Jian is that calmness, balanced growth, and gentle, slow persistence are characteristics necessary for successful gradual development.

Another symbol often associated with this hexagram is the wild goose.

Wild geese were thought to mate for life and hence were symbols of faithfulness, patience, and endurance in relationships. The need for such qualities is the hexagram's second major theme.

THE JUDGMENT

Gradual advance.
The maiden is given in marriage.
Good fortune.
It is beneficial to persevere.

There is the promise of future success, but you must allow the situation to develop gradually in order to realize it. The *Book of Changes* compares the situation to a long period of courtship, betrothal, and engagement. The parties must get to know each other and develop bonds of shared commitment and trust to accompany bonds of initial attraction. The couple's families must be brought together. Plans must be established. Ritual formalities must be observed. All of these things take time. What is true of marriage is true of all other forms of courtship and persuasion. If you are trying to get other people to make a major commitment, or to do something important, don't expect them to be convinced overnight. You must be considerate and allow them to move toward a decision gradually after they have obtained the requisite level of trust and confidence.

If you allow things to develop at their own pace, you will lay a firm foundation for your future success. Don't be anxious for quick results or greedy to get everything at once. You may well get some short-term benefits, but in the long term nothing good will come of it and what you have won in this fashion is unlikely to endure. Rash or reckless action will undermine the very features of the situation that are likely to produce the most good for the longest period of time. You must be patient and have faith that things will work out as they must, exactly in the right way.

Similarly, do not think that you can get immediate results through clever manipulation. This will also backfire. Rather, tried and true methods are the best way to obtain a positive outcome.

Although you must be patient, that does not mean that you should do nothing. To the contrary, you should continually focus on your long-term goal. Progress will often be slow. Hence you must persevere in order to ensure that things do not bog down. Be gentle. Do not try to force matters. As new problems arise—and they inevitably will—remain adaptable and flexible. Externally, maintain poise and calm. Internally, maintain your determination to succeed.

Similar concerns apply to the cultivation of your character. Perhaps you want to reform your life or make a change to a more rewarding lifestyle. It is entirely appropriate that you make some changes at once. But you cannot become a completely better, happier person overnight. You will need time to adjust to the new conditions.

THE IMAGE

On the mountain there is a tree:
This is the image of Developing Gradually.
Thus the superior person abides in worthiness and virtue
And so improves the lives and values of ordinary people.

A tree on a mountain grows slowly. But because it is high up, it has a commanding view of the countryside, and as it grows larger and larger, everyone below can see it. In time, it becomes a familiar and permanent part of the landscape. If you want to influence people in the right way, you must begin by developing yourself into the sort of person that people can trust and look up to. When they see that you are a person of substance, they will have confidence in what you say. Be gentle but firm. There is no need to put on airs or to try to trick people into agreeing with you. This sort of behavior will not have lasting influence, and it will probably backfire in any case. Be sincere. Do not be afraid to say what is in your heart. Let people see that what you believe is deeply connected to who you are. It is true that your influence will not be felt all at once. It is likely to be gradual. But over time, if you acquit yourself properly, your strength of character will shine through and you will win more and more people over to your side.

THE LINES

The lines describe the process of gradual development through the metaphor of wild geese traveling from the seashore to the highlands. The wild goose symbolizes marital fidelity, because the bird mates for life and does not take a new mate if the first dies. The gradual progress of the wild geese symbolizes the gradual progress of a commitment or joint enterprise that is worthy and lasting.

Initial Six

The wild goose gradually approaches the shore.
The small child is in danger.
There is talk. No blame.

The shore is the lowest place on land and the beginning of an ascent. "The small child is in danger" refers to one who has the status of a beginner. "There is talk" refers to the misunderstandings and calumnies of others.

You are at the very beginning of a long and slow process of gradual development. You do not yet know the best way to proceed and therefore you lack confidence in your abilities. The situation is difficult and you are basically alone. If you try to make progress, you will no doubt be subjected to criticism. But do not lose heart. The very difficulties you now must work through will strengthen you and help develop your skills. Now is the time to lay secure foundations for your later achievements. Move slowly and steadily, and you will eventually reach your goal.

Six in the Second Place (Ruling Line)

The wild goose gradually approaches the cliff.
Eating and drinking in joy and contentment.
Good fortune.

For a wild goose the cliff is safer than the shore. "Eating and drinking in joy and contentment" symbolizes generosity and concord as well as enjoyment, for the wild goose signals to others when it has found food.

After initial difficulties you have reached a more secure position. You now see the way forward and you realize that you can make steady progress. Thus you can afford to be more confident and relaxed. At this stage of your development you have reason to be optimistic. This is a time of peace and harmony in which you can share your good fortune with others. Doing so will increase your happiness.

Nine in the Third Place

The wild goose gradually approaches the plateau.
The husband sets out and does not return.
The wife conceives a child but does not give birth.

Misfortune.
It is beneficial to fend off bandits.

A high plateau is a position of danger for the wild goose because food is scarce and the bird is more open to attack. Thus to gradually approach the high plateau means to lose one's way. "The husband sets out and does not return" means to lose one's means of support, and "The wife conceives a child but does not give birth" symbolizes that one's plans do not come to fruition. Thus it is no wonder that misfortune follows. To "fend off bandits" means that one should take defensive action to protect one's position but not engage in aggressive methods in order to advance.

You have acted contrary to the principles of gradual progress and natural development and therefore have put your plans in jeopardy. If you provoke a conflict with others or try to make a bold advance without adequate preparation, you will endanger yourself and those you care about. Trying to get everything at once through an audacious maneuver or through open combat will cause you to overreach and to undermine your means of support. As a result, your plans will not bear fruit and all your striving will be for naught. Be patient. Exercise restraint. Do not let yourself be drawn into a fight. Secure what you have and be content to let things develop naturally and slowly. If you return to the path of gradual development that has brought you progress in the past, you will be safe for the future.

Six in the Fourth Place

The wild goose gradually approaches the tree.
Perhaps it will find a flat branch.
No blame.

A tree is not a natural or appropriate place for a goose but will do in a pinch. A flat branch can serve as a temporary resting place, allowing the bird to gather strength for its continued ascent. Thus resting on the flat branch of a tree symbolizes adaptability, cleverness and resourcefulness in the face of difficulty.

Despite your gradual development, temporary setbacks are inevitable. You must remain calm and flexible now. You need to adapt to present circumstances and avoid danger. You may feel that the situation is not right for you. But the condition is only temporary. Things will eventually change for the better, and you will be on your way again. Secure your position now so that you can be well situated for success later on. Take advantage of a safe harbor to gather your strength and prepare for your next advance.

Nine in the Fifth Place (Ruling Line)

The wild goose gradually approaches the top of the hill.
For three years the woman cannot conceive a child.
In the end, nothing can hinder her.
Good fortune.

The top of the hill is a comparatively high position where one is isolated from others and may thus become the object of envy and attack. Failure to conceive a child means that one's plans do not come to fruition.

The more you progress, the more people may envy you. Your elevated status may make others feel insecure. Some may disparage you and gossip behind your back. Misunderstandings between yourself and people that you care about or that you depend on may make you feel alone and particularly vulnerable. As a result of this isolation, you may make little progress for a time. Exercise patience. Temporary estrangements will eventually end, and you can begin to move forward again. Once you reestablish lines of communication, good fortune will follow.

Nine at the Top

The wild goose gradually approaches the high ground.
Its plumes can be used for the sacred dance.
Good fortune.

The high ground represents the fruition of all previous efforts. As the wild geese fly upward, their feathers fall to earth, and people use the feathers in ritual costumes. The imitation of the wild geese in the sacred dance is a metaphor for a person of great virtue who serves as a model for others to imitate.

Through gradual progress and steadfast devotion you have reached the top and achieved something truly worthwhile. You have become an example to others. People look up to you and emulate you. This is the highest form of praise. Reach out to others and use your position to help them make progress. This will mean good fortune for everyone.

NOTES

53.GI "abides in worthiness and virtue." *xian:* worthiness. Or, "abides in dignity and virtue" (Wilhelm/Baynes).

53.GI "the lives and values of ordinary people." *su:* literally, "the vulgar"; also, social mores, morals. Here it refers to the common people and the struggle of their everyday lives, as well as their values, social mores, and desires. Thus, the line might read, "And improves the morals and mores of his people."

53.1 "shore." *gan:* riverbank.

53.1 "small child." *xiao zi.* Or, "young son."

53.1 "There is talk." Or gossip, criticism. Cf. 6.1, 36.1, 51.6, 53.1.

53.2 "cliff." *pan:* large prominent stone or boulder, meaning something that is firm or stable

53.2 "in joy and contentment." *kan kan:* feast, feast, meaning to enjoy oneself, as at a feast. Doubling the word intensifies the quality.

53.3 "the plateau." The same word, *lu,* "highlands," is used in both this line and the sixth line. However, in the context of the entire hexagram the second usage should refer to a higher place. Hence in this line it is translated "plateau," and in the sixth line it is translated as "high ground," a metaphor for the sky.

53.3 "give birth." *yu:* to nurture or raise. Cf. 14.GI, 18.GI, 25.GI. Given the context of line five, it is translated here as bearing a child.

53.3 "fend off bandits." Or, "fight off robbers (outlaws)," "guard against harassment." Cf. 4.6.

53.6 "used for the sacred dance." *yishi:* ceremonial dress decoration, which is a gloss on the text's *yi,* meaning essentials, fundamentals, model, proper, decorum, or rites.

53.6 "high ground." *lu:* highland. See the discussion of line three. Some translators and interpreters gloss this as *kui,* "great thoroughfare," i.e., the sky, where birds fly.

FIFTY-FOUR

Gui Mei • The Marrying Maiden

☳
☱

Keywords:

The Maiden given in marriage
Playing a subordinate role
Subordination
Keeping in the background

Above: Zhen • Thunder
Below: Dui • Lake

Both Hexagrams 53 and 54 are concerned with marriage in different ways. Hexagram 53, Jian, describes the gradual achievement of a happy and prosperous marriage through courtship and ceremony. By contrast, Hexagram 54, Gui Mei, describes one who must subordinate herself and adjust to difficult conditions in a marriage she does not freely choose.

Hexagram 32, Heng (Enduring), is the primary hexagram associated with marriage. (It is the natural complement of Hexagram 31, Xian [Mutual Influence], which concerns initial attraction and courtship.) In Heng the eldest son, Zhen, takes as a wife the eldest daughter, Xun. In Gui Mei, the eldest son marries the youngest daughter, Dui. In ancient China, when an elder sister got married, a younger sister might be taken as a second wife. She was essentially a concubine; she had little or no authority in the household and had to take orders from the first wife. Often the situation was quite unhappy, and power struggles developed.

The metaphor of the marrying maiden made perfect sense to men as well as women in ancient China, for it described the counselor, statesman, or noble who was out of favor and had to subordinate his desires and take orders from someone else. Indeed, it was a metaphor for many different social situations in a strongly hierarchical society.

Subordination is often unjust, but this is not Hexagram 49, the hexagram of revolution. Rather, it deals with how to abide within a position of subordination that one must bear for the time being. Because China was so hierarchical, this was a common experience for the vast majority of the population. The advice given in this hexagram responds to that very common situation, which is still very much with us today, even in our more self-consciously egalitarian world.

THE JUDGMENT

The Marrying Maiden.
To set forth brings misfortune.
There is nothing for which this is beneficial.

Under the current circumstances you must play a subordinate role. Your contributions are not being fully recognized and your worth is not fully appreciated. However, for the moment there is nothing you can do about this. If you try to assert yourself, people will regard it as inappropriate. You will be either rebuffed or ignored. The text compares your situation to that of a secondary wife in a family in ancient China. The secondary wife had to behave with caution and circumspection. She could not shine too much lest she incur the wrath of the first wife. She had to be demure and self-sacrificing in order to preserve order and harmony in the family. Her position was very difficult and required the utmost tact and reserve; but if she behaved with suitable discretion, she could find a place of peace and dignity within the household.

The best strategy right now is to be flexible and adaptable. You are not going to receive very much recognition for your efforts, so you should be sensible. If your expectations are too unrealistic, then you will only make yourself unhappy. Don't be angry or resentful. Life is not always fair. Accept the situation for the time being. Stay out of the limelight and don't try to draw attention to yourself. Perform your assigned role without show or ceremony. Instead of bemoaning your fate, consider instead how you can be of service and make a contribution.

Relationships with others may be particularly difficult now. You cannot control the current situation. In particular, you cannot force other people to love you; you can only behave with love toward them. That means acting out of mercy and acceptance rather than out of anger and bitterness. Do not try to manipulate others and do not allow others to manipulate you. In the long run, what holds human relationships together are charity, tact, and discretion—not demanding everything that is yours but overlooking the inevitable slights and upsets of daily life.

Despite your subordinate position, it is still possible to act with honor and dignity. Hold yourself to the highest standards. Take pride in your work and in your good qualities. Believe in yourself even if others do not currently recognize you. By staying true to your own ideals and not allowing your self-worth to be determined by the opinion of others, you will gain inner strength and obtain inner freedom.

THE IMAGE

Above the lake there is thunder:
This is the image of the Maiden given in marriage.
Thus the superior person
Understands the imperfect and the transitory
In light of what endures in the end.

Thunder disturbs the tranquility of the lake. But the thunder eventually dies away and the tranquility is restored. All human relationships are subject to upsets and misunderstandings. But if a relationship is truly important to you, you should be able to see past them. Disagreements and tensions are inevitable in any relationship, especially those of long standing. If you are committed to make the relationship work, they will pass. Don't let jealousy and selfishness destroy something that is worthwhile. Keep your mind fixed on the long run and do not allow short-run disturbances to wreak havoc in your life and the lives of those closest to you. Relationships take work. Be kind and generous, and you will encourage others to behave in the same way with you.

The metaphor of thunder above the lake also refers to the situation of people who find themselves in a subordinate position or who must remain in the background unacknowledged. It is not pleasant to be subservient to others or to have your efforts unrecognized. But wise people understand that time is their best and strongest ally. In time, fads and fashions are forgotten, the enthusiasms of the moment subside. What remains is what we have made of our lives and of our relationships. Peace of mind comes from taking a longer view of things.

In the long run, the slights and upsets we suffer at the hands of others are as nothing compared to our own sense of ourselves. If we do not love and respect ourselves, the praise and recognition of others will not heal our inner wounds. Conversely, if we believe in and respect ourselves, it matters less what others think of us. Then the slights and indignities we suffer are like the momentary disturbances of a lake by a thunderstorm. The water on the surface is shaken about, but the deeper waters are undisturbed. The storm will eventually pass. The water endures.

THE LINES

The lines describe how to conduct ourselves when we must abide a secondary or subordinate position, and the different virtues appropriate to this situation. They are realism (line one), maintaining one's vision despite hardships (line two), patience (line four), humility (line five), and commitment (line six). Line three offers a different kind of advice. It points out starkly and dispassionately that subordination may require compromise with forces greater than our own, and that only we can decide what compromises we are willing to make with ourselves.

Initial Nine

The maiden is given in marriage as a secondary wife.
A lame person is able to walk.
To set forth brings good fortune.

Marrying as a secondary wife in ancient China meant that a woman entered a preexisting family structure subordinate to the primary wife as well as the husband. She could not hope for very much status, but if she knew how to play her role in the family, she might eventually gain the grudging acceptance of the elder wife, the love and protection of the husband, and have children by him. "A lame man is able to walk" suggests the same idea through a different metaphor: Although a lame man cannot run fast, he is nevertheless able to get by and move forward if he understands the nature of his situation and adjusts and compensates accordingly. Both of these metaphors had obvious analogies to the position of the courtier or minister, who was required to keep in the background but could nevertheless have an influence in affairs of state if he understood his subordinate role and acted with the utmost discernment.

Because of preexisting conditions over which you had no say, you have only very limited control in the current situation. Your status is comparatively humble. Putting yourself forward now or acting aggressively would be disastrous. Nevertheless, you can still make progress if you recognize your limitations and show a sincere desire to work within them for the good of others. Your kindness will attract the support of people who will protect you and help you advance. Then you will be able to have some influence as long as you are helpful and act with tact and discretion.

Nine in the Second Place

A one-eyed person is able to see.
The perseverance of a solitary person is beneficial.

A one-eyed person has been injured or blinded but is still able to carry on. "The perseverance of a solitary person" means sticking with your beliefs even if others have abandoned you.

Things have not turned out as you hoped they would. But it is important not to let disappointments undermine your ability to cope with life. Do not become bitter or angry at the world. Do not forsake your convictions. You must continue to have faith in yourself and in your original vision. Remain committed to what you believe is true and right. It is up to you now to carry on, even if you have to do so alone. Devotion to your principles will ultimately bring you success.

Six in the Third Place (Constitutive Line)

The maiden given in marriage waits.
She returns home and marries as a secondary wife.

This line tells the story of a woman who waits in vain for her Prince Charming to arrive. Eventually, she gives up and settles for life as a secondary wife. The text has no indication of good fortune or misfortune attached. It merely describes the situation without judging it, for sometimes compromising one's dreams is necessary while at other times it is a betrayal of one's deepest values.

To achieve your desires you will have to compromise yourself in some way. Are you sure this is what you want to do? Ask yourself whether it would not be better to exercise patience and wait for something more worthy and appropriate. Only you can decide this question.

Nine in the Fourth Place

The maiden given in marriage exceeds the allotted period.
She marries late, at the proper time.

"To extend the allotted period" means to delay past the end of the prescribed period of betrothal in a marriage agreement on the grounds that the time originally agreed to was not appropriate. It also means to delay marriage past the age when a woman would ordinarily be betrothed and therefore to risk becoming an old maid in a strongly patriarchal society. Obviously, this posed a real danger of poverty and perpetual dependence under the most unfortunate circumstances. Nevertheless, the story has a happy ending, because the woman marries the right person at a later time without compromising herself, and this means that she did marry at the right time after all.

If people offer you opportunities that you feel are not right for you, it is wise to refuse them. You may worry that you will be left behind and that the world will pass you by. You may fear that other people will think you are being foolish not to snap up an attractive possibility when it is offered. But do not let these opinions sway you. You alone must decide what is consistent with your beliefs and what would be an unacceptable compromise of your principles. Have faith. Ultimately, you will be rewarded for your perseverance and your unwillingness to betray your values. Hold on to your vision and keep focused on what endures. In the long run, you will be vindicated.

Six in the Fifth Place (Ruling Line)

The sovereign Yi gave his daughter in marriage.
The embroidered sleeves of the princess
Were not as fine
As those of the secondary wife.
The moon is nearly full.
Good fortune.

This line tells the story of an aristocratic woman who marries a man of lower rank and happily and gracefully adapts to her new circumstances. Even at her wedding she does not engage in ostentatious display; hence her garments are comparatively modest. "The moon is nearly full" means that matters have gone as far as they can without declining so that it is appropriate not to press any further.

Placing yourself at the service of others now will bring you good fortune. No matter how strong your position or how able you may be, this is a time to cooperate, subordinate yourself, and stay out of the spotlight. Overcome any pride and vanity you may have. Promoting your own interests now will only cause the situation to degenerate. Do not be competitive or aggressive, and do not try to take the lead or draw attention to yourself. Instead, carefully consider how you can be of assistance in the situation and do your best without any ostentation or any attempt to claim credit. Your selflessness and humility will bring happiness and harmony.

Six at the Top (Constitutive Line)

The woman holds out the basket, but it has no fruits.
The man stabs the sheep, but no blood flows.
There is nothing for which this is beneficial.

The line refers to rituals performed at a wedding. In this case, the couple merely make a pretense of form: the man stabs a sheep that has already been slaughtered; the woman brings a basket without harvest offerings. The lack of blood means lack of commitment; the empty basket of fruit means that there is no fertility and hence that things do not come to fruition.

Half measures and halfheartedness add up to a whole failure. If you wish to succeed at something, you must be sincerely committed to it.

Merely going through the motions will not lead to anything important or significant. If you are internally conflicted about what you are doing, you should come to terms with this immediately and decide what it is you really want. Life is not simply a matter of keeping your options open. You should not start at one thing with the hope that something better will come along. You must be devoted to what you are doing or you are simply wasting your time.

This advice also applies to the content of what you do as well as to your commitment in doing it. Do not be satisfied with empty rituals or mere formality. Pay attention to substance.

NOTES

54.0 "To set forth." Or, "Undertakings."

54.GI "the imperfect and the transitory." *pi:* cracked, broken, ruined, in tatters, unfit, unworthy.

54.GI "what endures in the end." *yong zhong:* perpetual complete. Or, "the lasting and enduring." Compare Wilhelm/Baynes: "Understands the transitory / In the light of the eternity of the end."

54.1 "secondary wife." *di.* Or, "younger sister." Wilhelm/Baynes translates *di* as "concubine."

54.1 "a lame person is able to walk." Cf. 10.3, where the lame person is not up to the demands of the situation.

54.1 "To set forth brings good fortune." Or, "Undertakings bring good fortune."

54.2 "a solitary person." *you:* dark, gloomy, secret, retired, lonely, subtle. Cf. 10.2.

54.3 "waits." *xu,* literally, "hair-growing"; i.e., waiting for one's hair to grow. Cf. 22.2. Another reading substitutes the word *jiu,* a lowly concubine or slave. Hence the line would read, "The marrying maiden as a slave; she returns home as a concubine" (Wilhelm/Baynes).

54.5 "The sovereign Yi gave his daughter in marriage." Cf. 11.5.

54.5 "gave his daughter in marriage." *Mei* means "daughter" or "younger sister." Thus the phrase could refer not only to his daughter but to any of his younger female relatives. The terms "brother" and "sister" were applied widely to different types of relations.

54.5 "sleeves." *mei:* sleeve, garment. Ornamentation of one's sleeves indicated one's rank and prominence. Richard John Lynn translates the line as "The sovereign's sleeves were not as fine," which also indicates modesty and virtue.

54.5 "The moon is nearly full." Or, "When the moon is nearly full." Cf. 9.6, 61.4.

54.6 "no blood flows." Or, "there is no blood." *wu xue.*

FIFTY-FIVE

Feng • Abundance

Keywords:

Zenith
Fullness
Splendor
Plenty
Being generous
Acting decisively
Living in the present
Making the most of the good times

Above: Zhen • Thunder
Below: Li • Fire

Feng concerns the moment of zenith or fullness which, according to the laws of change, will inevitably be followed by decline. The lower trigram is Li (Fire); the upper trigram is Zhen (Thunder). When thunder and lightning flash and light up the entire sky, the effect is brilliant but transitory. Nevertheless, when different energies (electricity, fire) culminate in a single great moment, one should surely take advantage of the situation. A basic theme of Feng is making the most of this abundant time. Li symbolizes clarity; Zhen symbolizes taking action. In moments of plenty your actions should be enlightened and generous, bestowing light on everyone. This is the hexagram's second theme.

55 Feng • Abundance

THE JUDGMENT

Abundance.
Success.
The king approaches.
Do not be sad.
Be like the sun at midday.

The sun at noon will surely descend just as it has ascended. But in the meantime it shines brightly, bestowing warmth and radiance on everything beneath it. In the same way, you now face a moment of rare brilliance and abundance. Everything is now possible. Relationships will flourish. Your ambitions can be achieved. Make the most of this time. Do not worry that things will not always be this perfect. That will only cause you to freeze up. If you mourn what has not yet happened, you will waste your opportunity to do good in the present. Therefore, the text advises you to be like the sun at midday—joyous, powerful, energetic, generous, and happy. Size up the problems before you. Weigh the circumstances objectively. Then go out and take care of business. Success is assured. It is your time to shine.

How can you make the good times last as long as possible? The answer, once again, is to take your cue from the sun. The sun is the very symbol of optimism and generosity: It does not try to keep its warmth and energy for itself. It spreads its light throughout the heavens, bringing clarity to everything beneath it. It does not worry that it will burn out someday. Rather, it gives freely, and then it gives some more, and in this way all life on earth is preserved and perpetuated. In the same way, it is time for you to be open, generous, and magnanimous. Like the sun, do what you can to illuminate the world and make your fellow creatures warm and happy.

If you want to perpetuate the good times, share your bounty with others. Do not worry about gain or loss, or about whether you will have enough in the future. If you try to hog all of the benefits for yourself, you will cut yourself off from others. People will envy you and refuse to cooperate with you. If you become fearful and obsessed that people are trying to take things from you, you will drain your energies and squander your opportunities. As a result, the good times will pass all the more quickly, and no one will be there to help you on your downward slide. On the other hand, if you share your good fortune with others, they will rejoice in your success and work with you to keep things moving forward. And you in turn will be renewed and stimulated by their goodwill and cooperation.

Be optimistic and you will feel better about yourself and your life. Be magnanimous and you will be enriched in countless ways through the gratitude, affection, and support of others. As paradoxical as it seems, the more you give to others, the more will be given to you in return. The less you worry about the transitoriness of the time of abundance, the longer it will remain with you and those you care for.

THE IMAGE

Thunder and lightning culminate as one:
This is the image of Abundance.
Thus the superior person judges cases
And carries out punishments.

Like Hexagram 21, Shih He (Biting Through), Feng contains both Zhen and Li—Thunder and Lightning. Shih He emphasizes the need for immediate reform; Feng concerns the need to take advantage of an especially propitious time. In both cases swift action should always be premised on clarity of judgment (Li symbolizes enlightenment) and knowledge of all the relevant facts. If you have wanted to achieve something valuable and important, now is the time to move forward with courage and hope. Conditions like these do not come often, and they will not last forever. The best way to ensure future success is to lay the proper foundations now.

Like the sun at midday, you are at center stage. People will be influenced by what you do and they will look to you for approval before they act. Therefore, you should be upbeat and optimistic. Devote yourself to something truly worthy and let nothing undermine your confidence. By maintaining a positive attitude, you will inspire others and redouble your strength. Live in the present and be determined to take full advantage of it. Don't mourn your lack of advantages in the past. Yesterday is gone and will not return. Don't worry about whether things will be as good tomorrow. Tomorrow has not yet arrived. If you act appropriately and decisively now, you will be in a much better position to handle whatever the future brings.

THE LINES

Although the theme of the hexagram judgment is abundance, in lines two, three, and four abundance is blocked (or, in the alternative, what is abundant is the screen that covers the sun). The lines emphasize the values of forbearance, openness, receptivity, generosity, and cooperation. Indeed, the central idea of the lines is that true abundance is always the result of appropriate relations with other people.

Initial Nine

When one meets his lord and counterpart,
They can be together ten days,
And there is no blame.
Going forward beings esteem.

Allying yourself with someone who has goals and values similar to yours will create a beneficial synergy. Together you can achieve something neither of you could do alone. It is not a mistake to work closely together for a specific purpose until you have achieved your goals.

Six in the Second Place

Abundance is screened so completely
That one can see the polestars at noon.
If one sets forth, he meets with enmity and distrust.
But if one has sincerity that shoots forth like an arrow,
Good fortune comes.

When one's abundance is screened, it means that one's gifts and abilities are hindered or are not properly recognized. Because of intense opposition, one's light is hidden.

Although you have great potential and much to offer, you are unable to make progress now. Obstacles obstruct your advance. Circumstances that you did not cause stand in your way. Other people mistrust and disparage you. If you try to push forward or force the issue, you will only bring more enmity and suspicion on yourself. Therefore, you must be patient. Maintain faith in yourself and your ideals. Do not forsake your ultimate goals. If you are sincere and trustworthy, you will eventually win over others through the strength of your character and the goodness of your intentions. Then the right people will recognize your value and they will support you. Eventually, your influence will spread.

Nine in the Third Place

Abundance is shaded so completely
That one can see the dimmest stars at noon.
He breaks his right arm.
No blame.

The line describes a total eclipse of the sun, which blots out its light and energy. This symbolizes a temporary eclipse of one's influence and authority. The small stars represent petty people who rise in importance and power when capable and worthy people are hindered by circumstances. To break one's right arm means that one has lost the ability to accomplish things.

Despite your abilities and talents, you cannot achieve anything at present. Less able people capitalize on the situation and are able to advance. However, circumstances beyond your control keep you from taking any sort of effective action. This is not your fault. Be patient. Matters will eventually improve.

Nine in the Fourth Place

Abundance is screened so completely
That one can see the polestars at noon.
He meets a lord who is his equal.
Good fortune.

Your ability to advance has been blocked for some time now. Now at last you encounter the elements that you need to succeed. You are able to unite with people with similar aims who can help you make progress. Work with them. You may find that you have complementary talents: great drive and enthusiasm on the one hand, shrewdness and sound judgment on the other. If you can combine enthusiasm with wisdom and energy with prudence, together you will achieve great things.

Six in the Fifth Place (Ruling Line)

Beauty and brilliance come forward.
Blessing and fame draw near.
Good fortune.

"Beauty and brilliance" refers to people of brilliance and abundant talents who come forward to aid the sovereign. Line five, the line of the ruler, is a yin, or yielding, line, meaning that the king accepts their contributions gladly, without envy or hesitation. He honors them, and all benefit.

Be open and receptive. You have much to learn from other people. Do not be afraid to accept help when it is offered. Take full advantage of the talents and wisdom of people who can advise you about the best course of action. If you recognize their contributions appropriately, they will be only too happy to help you. Modesty and a cooperative attitude will bring great success that will benefit everyone.

Six at the Top

Abundance in his house.
He screens off his family.
He peers through the door,
Lonely, abandoned.
For three years he sees no one.
Misfortune.

In line six, the season of abundance has ended. The lesson is that times of plenty are destroyed when people become selfish and uncooperative. In their shortsightedness they destroy the very conditions through which good fortune can be reproduced and sustained.

Your desire for power and success has cut you off from other people. You have become arrogant and obstinate and obsessed with control. As a result, you have failed to share your blessings with others. Remember those who helped you in the past and be generous to those who are striving upward as you have strived before. If you insist on keeping everything for yourself, you will become completely isolated and will lose touch with other human beings. This will rob you of the most precious of all possessions.

NOTES

55.1 "lord and counterpart." *pei zhu.* The counterpart of line one is line four. Both are yang lines, hence the concern that their union might be a mistake.

55.1 "there is no blame." Or, "it is not a mistake" (Wilhelm/Baynes).

55.1 "esteem." *shang.* Or, "reward," "honor," "recognition."

55.2 "Abundance is screened so completely." *feng qi bu.* Lines two, three, and four employ a similar metaphor. In lines two and four it is a screen or curtain; in line three it is a veil or underbrush. This can be translated in two ways: first, that an abundant (i.e., vast) screen blocks everything, or second, that one's abundance (which is analogized to the sun at midday) is screened and blocked. Both readings are plausible. I choose the latter because it fits better with the hexagram's theme, the gradual emergence of abundance.

55.4 "a lord who is his equal." *yi zhu:* literally, "hidden lord," but *yi* can also mean to make equal or level by lowering. In this case, lines one and four refer to each other. Each is the other's lord. Both are yang lines, hence the better translation is "equal," or "of a similar kind."

55.5 "Beauty and brilliance." *zhang:* brilliance, beautiful creation. Cf. 2.3 and 44.5. Here it refers to people of brilliance and great ability who come forward to assist the ruler and are happily accepted and recognized by him.

FIFTY-SIX

Lü • The Wanderer

䷷

Keywords:

Traveling
Unsettled
Tentative
Uncertain
In transition
Exploring
Trying new experiences

Above: Li • Fire
Below: Gen • Mountain

Lü (The Wanderer) is the converse of Feng (Abundance). In Feng our moment has come and we are encouraged to act decisively. In Lü we are in a period of transition in which things are not yet clear; therefore, our actions should be tentative and circumspect. Feng holds that we should try to make the good times last as long as possible; Lü holds that another cycle has already begun and we must set out in search of something new. The lower trigram of Lü is Gen (Mountain), which moves downward or keeps still; the upper trigram is Li (Fire), which moves upward and away. The two trigrams cannot stay together long; hence they symbolize traveling and separation. Similarly, fire on the mountain is blown about by the wind. It cannot remain in one place or else it will be extinguished. Hence it symbolizes wandering.

THE JUDGMENT

The Wanderer.
In small matters, success.
Perseverance brings good fortune
To the wanderer.

You are in a period of transition. Things are not yet certain, and it is not yet clear how you fit into them or what your identity is supposed to be. The text compares your situation to that of a wanderer who is traveling through a strange land. The wanderer is a sojourner—he does not expect to stay long, but he is not quite sure where he is going next. He knows very few people. He is not exactly sure what the local customs are or whom he can trust. He does not completely understand what is expected of him. Because his situation is uncertain, he is circumspect and cautious. He does not call attention to himself nor does he get involved in matters that do not concern him. He associates only with reliable and trustworthy people and does not get involved in anything underhanded or unscrupulous, much less anything that would get him in trouble with the local authorities. Instead, he tries to learn as much as he can from his new surroundings, and in this way he learns something about himself.

Apply these principles to your own life. You are on a journey whose destination is not yet determined. This is not a time to make definite commitments. Instead, it is a time to explore. You need to gather new information, gain new perspectives, experiment with new ways of living, and meet new people. Don't be afraid to try something different. You won't know what the right path is until you try a number of different possibilities. Be flexible and adaptable and willing to learn.

However, precisely because you don't yet know where you are going, you must also be politic and discreet. When you find yourself in new situations with new people, be respectful but also reserved. It will take time to know whom you can really trust. Try to associate with good people and make friends with those you respect. This will help keep you out of harm's way and ensure that you get the most out of your new experiences.

Relish the uncertainty of this time. You have a wonderful opportunity now to expand your horizons and make important connections. You may well encounter new people and new experiences that will change your life. But don't do anything that is beneath you and don't compromise your integrity just to fit in or to get others to like you. Instead, just be yourself. If you behave with courtesy and discretion, you will attract the right sort of people. A sincere and friendly approach will meet with a natural and positive response, no matter where you are. When people go out of their way to help you, make sure that you let them know that you appreciate their generosity; and then do your best to help them in return. In this way you will begin to form bonds of reciprocity that will help you through this period of transition.

THE IMAGE

Fire on the mountain:
This is the image of the Wanderer.
Thus the superior person
Is clear-minded and cautious
In imposing penalties,
And protracts no lawsuits.

A fire burning on the top of a mountain is subject to heavy gusts of wind. It is easily blown out and is likely to spread from place to place. Therefore, it is not stable or secure. It does not have the resources necessary to stay where it is for long; it must either move or be extinguished. In the same way, people who are in a period of transition lack the resources to engage in a protracted struggle with others. Therefore, they do not get themselves enmeshed in controversies and commitments that will exhaust their energies.

Periods of transition are both dangerous and exciting. You are trying out new ideas and experiences, and questioning long-held assumptions. You may well emerge from this period a different person. But because you are sailing in uncharted waters, you must be circumspect and not get into situations from which you cannot easily extricate yourself. Don't make yourself a target for exploitation by others. If you are not careful, your journey will indeed come to a conclusion, but not in a place of your own choosing and not in a way that you will particularly like.

Journeys in the world are often only an outward manifestation of journeys of the soul. There are some parts of this journey that you will simply have to make alone. There is no one else who can prepare you for the changes. Therefore, you will have to learn to rely on yourself. You must develop the resources to adapt to the new and adjust to the unfamiliar, both in the world and in yourself. Do not become anxious or fearful. Just keep your balance, no matter what comes your way. And be prepared to learn. As you move forward, you will discover to your surprise that you have developed the inner strength to handle each new situation. And eventually, you will discover which path is the right one for you.

THE LINES

The lines explain how to deal with new and transitional situations through a series of stories about a wanderer, who travels to a foreign country in line one and eventually wins acceptance and a place in the regime in line five. Line four describes the emotional state of the wanderer, who despite his many years in a foreign country and his many achievements realizes that he still feels like an outsider.

Initial Six

If the wanderer dwells on trivial things,
He brings calamity upon himself.

Do not try to win the approval of other people by demeaning yourself or playing the role of a buffoon. You may think that people will like you better if you seem harmless and inoffensive, but in fact you will only bring contempt and ridicule on yourself. Instead, when you are in an uncertain situation, you should act with reserve and dignity. People will respect you only if you behave as if you are worthy of respect.

What is true about interpersonal relations is also true of your goals. Don't waste your time on trivial or base pursuits in the hope that they will make you popular or help you fit in. Life is too short to waste it on trivialities. If you devote your energies to what is irrelevant, you will make your life an irrelevancy.

Six in the Second Place

The wanderer comes to an inn.
He carries his belongings with him.

He obtains a young servant.
He should persevere.

The text is an elaborate metaphor for how to behave in a new environment. A wanderer should always keep "his belongings" with him. These are the things that properly belong to him—his values, his principles, his integrity, and his self-possession. When he does so, he gains something else—the support of "a young servant," a metaphor for the friendship and assistance of others.

When you find yourself in a strange or unusual setting, be modest and maintain your self-possession. You do not yet know the lay of the land or whom you can trust. For this reason it is better to be too reserved than too raucous. Your gravitas and your quiet self-confidence will shine through to others. They will be attracted by your integrity and give you support.

Nine in the Third Place

The wanderer's inn burns down.
He loses his young servant.
Perseverance brings danger.

The burning of the inn symbolizes powerful negative emotions, arguments, and even violence. It also symbolizes loss of one's place and one's self-possession. Losing the young servant means that the wanderer loses the support of others because of his arrogance and rash behavior.

You should not interfere in matters that do not concern you. You may lose what security you have and alienate the people who support you. Don't be arrogant or aloof. Avoid losing your temper and picking fights with others. If you are careless and offensive to people, they will withdraw and you will be left isolated and vulnerable. Then you will lose everything you have worked for.

Nine in the Fourth Place

The wanderer rests in a shelter.
He obtains his property and an ax.
My heart is not glad.

A shelter is a temporary resting place, not a final destination. The ax is a symbol of office, hence a symbol of significant achievement, but it also suggests the wanderer's need to protect himself. His heart is not glad because he remains a stranger in a strange land. Despite all of his wanderings and his achievements, he still does not know who he is, how he fits in, or, ultimately, where he is headed. The text is an apt metaphor for a person in the middle of his life's journey.

You have accomplished much, but you have not achieved everything you want. Your final goal still remains ahead of you. Despite all your efforts, you feel that you have not yet arrived. You would like to maintain what you have achieved so far, and yet when you look back on what you have done, you don't feel fulfilled. You sense that something is missing, although you are not sure what it is. As a result, you feel lost, uneasy, and unsure about what to do.

Your unease is due to the fact that you are at a crossroads, a temporary resting place where you must stop and plan the next steps of your journey. Proceed slowly and cautiously now. A change is necessary if you are to move forward. That change will either have to come from outside circumstances, or, equally likely, from a change within yourself. But do not act precipitously, because you do not yet know what the nature of that change will be. Look deep into yourself and you will eventually find the right path.

Six in the Fifth Place (Ruling Line)

He shoots a pheasant.
He kills it with one arrow.
In the end, this brings him praise and office.

This line tells the story of a wanderer who introduces himself in a new land through a feat of great skill, which gains him an introduction to the prince and eventually high office. Shooting a pheasant and presenting it as a gift demonstrates both accomplishment and liberality.

If you know how to use your abilities to best advantage, you can find a satisfactory place in any new situation. Act with generosity and magnanimity. Demonstrate through your words and actions that you are comfortable with yourself and know your own worth without being arrogant or immodest. Then people will accept you and introduce you into their circle. You will have great success in your new environment.

Nine at the Top

The bird's nest burns up.
The wanderer laughs at first,
But later he weeps and wails.
He loses a cow in the field.
Misfortune.

"The bird's nest burns up" symbolizes the loss of home and security. The wanderer has become careless and arrogant. Because he forgets the constraints of his position as a wanderer, he "laughs at first," but later "weeps and wails." The cow is the symbol of docility, modesty, and adaptability. By forsaking these qualities, which are necessary for survival in a strange land, the wanderer brings misfortune upon himself.

You have become careless and are in danger of losing something very important to you. Value what you have by taking proper care of it. This may be your body, your property, your health, your abilities, your values, or your relationships with other people. You may think that you are on top of the situation and can afford to be carefree. But if you become arrogant and inflexible and forget how to adapt to new situations, you will become isolated and vulnerable.

More generally, this line serves as a reminder of your position as a wanderer. You misunderstand your relationship to your surroundings and the transitory nature of your involvement in the situation. You have become caught up in affairs that do not concern you and that are unrelated to your personal development and your personal goals. As a result, you have forgotten what is peripheral and transitory and what is central and enduring in your life. If you do not reform, you will lose your way and misfortune will inevitably result.

NOTES

56.GI "Is clear-minded and cautious," etc. Or, "Is enlightened and careful both in using punishment and in not delaying (drawing out) litigation."

56.1 "dwells on trivial things." *suo suo si qi suo:* literally, "fragment fragment chop one's dwelling." *Suo suo* means "tiny things, trivalities." Hence one might translate the line as "occupies himself with trivial matters," "lets himself be occupied with trivialities," or "wastes his time on trivial things."

56.2 "carries . . . with him." *huai:* carry on one's person, cherish.

56.2 "belongings." *zi:* wealth, property, goods, capital.

56.2 "He should persevere." *zhen:* determination, perseverance. Another interpretation is "And stays" (Whincup). Ordinarily, the word *zhen* would be followed by another mantic text, such as "beneficial" or "good fortune." Here only the word *zhen* appears. Wilhelm / Baynes translates the line as "He wins the steadfastness of a young servant."

56.5 "office." *ming:* authority, command, mandate, to issue orders with authority.

56.6 "weeps and wails." Or, "laments and weeps." *hao tao:* crying out [and] sobbing.

56.6 "He loses a cow in the field." Here again the word *yi* is translated as "field," and the reference is to the story of the legendary culture hero Wang Hai. Cf. 34.5. The standard reading of *yi,* however, is "easy" or "change." The word is the same as appears in the name *Yijing,* meaning either the classic *(jing)* of changes *(yi),* or the classic of "easy" divination, i.e., easier than using tortoise shells or other forms of animal divination. Under the traditional interpretation, *yi* might refer to a change in fortunes, or it might mean "easily" or "in a time of ease," hence "careless" or "lax." Thus the line might be translated, "Through a change in circumstances he loses his cow," or "Through carelessness he loses his cow" (Wilhelm / Baynes).

FIFTY-SEVEN

Xun • Gentle Influence

Keywords:

Compliance
Humility
Gentleness
Penetrating
Wind
Persistence

Above: Xun • Wind (Wood)
Below: Xun • Wind (Wood)

Xun is composed of the trigram Xun (Wind, Wood) doubled. The trigram Xun is associated with the eldest daughter. The theme of the hexagram Xun is gentleness and penetration. Wind is gentle, yet penetrates everywhere. Wood penetrates the earth through slow yet persistent exertion.

Xun has a double meaning. On the one hand, it means compliance or submission. On the other hand, it means to influence and penetrate through gentle means. This duality is the key theme of the hexagram. It means that a person gains influence and the ability to penetrate an institution by being willing to submit to it and to comply with its leadership. People who assist their leaders become indispensable and hence exert enormous influence over time, although they often exert that influence in small ways and behind the scenes. Thus it is through compliance that one exerts influence; it is through humbleness that one penetrates through resistance and exerts power.

THE JUDGMENT

Gentle Influence.
Success in small matters.
It is beneficial to have somewhere to go.
It is beneficial to see a great person.

The best way to affect the situation right now is through gentle, persistent action and subtle forms of influence. The text compares the right way of proceeding to that of wind. A mild breeze seems inconspicuous. But it can penetrate everywhere. Its effects are gradual but are considerable over time. It is delightful and unassuming. Therefore, it is not feared or resisted but is gladly and gratefully accepted. And because it is accepted, it has influence.

The key is to be both gentle and persistent. A violent or forceful approach will be counterproductive and meet with a rebuff. But a gentle approach will be more readily received and, if you are persistent, will eventually have the right effect.

Because you can only influence the situation in subtle ways, clarity and singlemindedness of purpose are essential. If you are uncertain about what you want or if you waste your time pursuing multiple and conflicting ends, your message will be dissipated and you will have no influence at all. Therefore, you must be absolutely clear in your mind what your goals are. Define your objectives and stick to them. The wind is most powerful when it blows in only one direction.

You will not change the situation all at once, but only through steady and persistent influence. Things will proceed slowly, but if you have patience, over time you can have a significant effect. Restrain any impulsive tendencies. Be patient and flexible. Adjust to changing circumstances rather than fighting them, and continually look for opportunities to persuade and win people over to your side. Under no circumstances should you act aggressively or try to dominate the situation. That will surely backfire. Instead, let others take the lead. Stay in the background and serve them. You will make the most progress by subordinating yourself and making your presence felt in small but significant ways.

THE IMAGE

Winds follow one another:
This is the image of Gentle Influence.
Thus the superior person
Spreads his commands widely,
Motivates activity and influences events.

Wind is powerful even when it is barely felt because it is unremitting and persistent. In this way what is most gentle can also be most powerful. To influence people you must penetrate their hearts and minds. The best way to do this is gradually, through modest and considerate behavior. Trust and credibility are among the most important factors in persuading others. But trust and credibility only come with time. Just as wind disperses dark clouds and stagnant odors, your kind and persistent efforts can improve the situation. The quality of your character is your greatest asset in persuading and influencing others.

The elements of successful influence are not difficult to discover. They are simply difficult to put into practice unless you have the proper attitude. They do not require great strength or aggressiveness. They simply require devotion and relentlessness commitment, expressed in the most delicate ways.

First, you need clarity of purpose. Second, you need complete and sincere belief in yourself and in your cause. Third, you need total determination to succeed. Fourth, you must continually channel your resources and efforts toward achieving your aim. Fifth, you need strength of character in order to follow through consistently and adapt naturally to changing circumstances. If you can do all of these things, you will succeed. It is as simple as that. Opportunities will present themselves, seemingly without any special effort on your part. In fact, they will appear because you have prepared the way for them through your persistence and devotion. Then your single-minded commitment will give you the tools to take advantage of those opportunities when they arise.

THE LINES

The basic theme of the lines is gentle persistence and perseverance toward clear goals. In lines three and six indecision and hesitation lead to misfortune.

Initial Six (Constitutive Line)

Advancing and retreating.
It is beneficial to persevere like a warrior.

Indecisiveness and vacillation will achieve nothing now. You must approach matters with a more disciplined attitude. Don't let yourself be controlled by your doubts and fears. Decide what the right course of action is and see it through. Adopt the military virtues of courage, determination, and self-discipline if you want to succeed.

Nine in the Second Place

Penetration under the bed.
Using priests and shamans in great numbers.
Good fortune. No blame.

"Penetration under the bed" means that hidden influences or prejudices are at work. You must discover what these bad influences are and how they have infiltrated the situation. Hence the text says to use "priests and shamans in great numbers," because traditionally priests and shamans were thought to be able to reveal what is hidden or immanent. The problem may be that people have lost confidence in you and are conspiring against you, or it may be a weakness or self-destructive tendency in yourself. Try to figure out what people's motives are. Look for hidden agendas. Be brutally honest with yourself and consider whether you are unconsciously holding yourself back. Whatever the problem, once you expose it and place it out in the open, its ability to harm you will be greatly reduced, and you can begin to make progress.

Nine in the Third Place

Repeated and insistent penetration. Humiliation.

You are trying too hard to weigh all the pros and cons of the situation. It is good to plan things in advance, but you risk becoming neurotically obsessed with figuring out every possibility. No one can know in advance all of the consequences of their actions or exactly how things will turn out. You must make up your mind, form a plan, and act on it. Instead, you are overthinking things and consuming yourself with needless worries. Too much deliberation will confuse you as you imagine more and more possible things that could go wrong. This will cause you to become indecisive and lose the initiative. Then your worries will become a self-fulfilling prophecy. You will prevent yourself from making a successful start, and this will inevitably lead to failure and humiliation.

Six in the Fourth Place (Constitutive Line)

Regrets vanish.
During the hunt
Three kinds of game are caught.

"Regrets vanish" means that one should have no concerns or doubts about going forward. To capture three kinds of game in a single outing means that the hunt was especially successful.

It is time to take the initiative. Acting energetically and decisively will produce great success. You have prepared well and accumulated the necessary ability and experience. Put it to good use now. Follow through on what you start, and enlist all your efforts at doing the best job you can. Be modest and steadfast in your efforts. If you confront your adversaries with industry and determination, you need have no concerns. You will get everything you need.

Nine in the Fifth Place (Ruling Line)

Perseverance brings good fortune.
Regrets vanish.
There is nothing that is not beneficial.
There is no beginning, but there is an end.
Before the change, three days.
After the change, three days.
Good fortune.

It is now possible to change the entire situation for the better. To do this you will have to consider thoroughly what you need to do and then carefully prepare a plan of action. Although things may not have gone your way recently, with steadfastness and perseverance you can turn the situation to your advantage and the result will be highly successful.

Nevertheless, you must keep a close eye on how things develop and be sure to reevaluate the situation and make necessary corrections and adjustments as you move forward. Take your cue from the theme of the hexagram—the gentle but constant influence of the wind. The problem you face can be reformed only through persistent and continuous effort. This means that you must be thorough and attentive both before you make the changes and after you begin. Be patient. It will take some time for results to appear. But when your strategy begins to produce good effects, you will know that you are on the right path.

Nine at the Top

Penetration under the bed.
He loses his property and his ax.
Perseverance brings misfortune.

You have become obsessed with uncovering every nook and cranny of the situation, and you have allowed yourself to be distracted by irrelevancies and harmful influences. Inner conflict has diverted you in an unhealthy way. Your preparations have become so elaborate that you are wasting the energy you need to succeed. It is time to stop investigating and start acting. You must come to a decision and begin to move forward. If you don't set your life in order soon, you will lose something very precious indeed.

NOTES

57.0 "Success in small matters." Or, "Success through what is small."

57.GI "Motivates activity and influences events." *xing shi:* literally, "moves affairs."

57.1 "retreating." *tui:* retreat, withdraw. Cf. 20.3, 34.6.

57.3 "repeated and insistent." *pin:* pressing, urgent. One might translate the line as "urgent penetration" or "pressing penetration with too much insistence."

57.5 "Before the change," etc. Cf 18.0. *geng:* to husk; hence, to alter. Another interpretation is that *geng* refers to one of the ten heavenly stems, i.e., a date in the Chinese calendar.

57.6 "his property and his ax." Cf. 56.4.

FIFTY-EIGHT

Dui • Joy

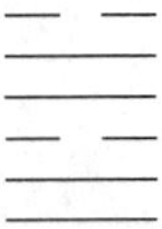

Keywords:

The lake
Giving and receiving
Communication
Sharing
Integrity
Inner stability
Inner peace

Above: Dui • Lake
Below: Dui • Lake

Dui originally meant an open mouth, hence talking. Later it came to mean exchange. Dui concerns the joy that comes from harmonious interaction and communication with others.

The hexagram Dui consists of the trigram Dui doubled. The trigram Dui is associated with the youngest daughter and with a marsh, lake, or swamp. It features a yin (or open) line on the surface and two yang lines below it. The yin line symbolizes openness, receptivity, and gentleness toward the outside world. The yang lines symbolize strength and stability within. The basic theme of Dui is that joy comes from integrity and balance within the self and tolerance and acceptance toward the outside world. People who lack peace will not find joy in the pursuit of pleasure or esteem. People who are obstinate and stubborn shut themselves off from shared experiences that replenish the soul.

THE JUDGMENT

Joy. Success.
It is beneficial to persevere.

Joy comes from inner peace and inner balance. It requires integrity and strength within and gentleness and acceptance without. Put differently, joy is a matter of character on the one hand and communication on the other. People lack joy because they lack inner stability. Then they chase after pleasures that cannot fill the emptiness inside them. People lack joy because they cannot freely communicate with others. Then they are cut off from the pleasures of shared experience.

In the *Book of Changes,* joy is symbolized by two lakes that are joined together. Their waters flow freely into each other and thus replenish each other. Yet although the two lakes freely share with each other, each retains its individual integrity.

Joy emerges naturally from freely communicating and sharing experiences with others. It is infectious. If you are cheerful and happy, you will make others feel cheerful and happy as well. And when people are optimistic and outgoing, they share their thoughts and experiences more easily. Reach out to other people in a spirit of goodwill. Let people know that you are interested in what they have to say. Work to create a positive, accepting atmosphere. If you are warm and friendly, people will respond naturally and positively. They will be willing to help you and give you the benefit of their perspective. If you try to make people joyous through devious means, or through manipulating them, you may have temporary success. But without the creation of trust and mutual respect, joy cannot last.

When people take joy in each other's company, they are willing to make sacrifices for each other. Difficulties seem to melt away. Troubles seem smaller and less threatening than before. When people feel supported and encouraged, they are willing to take on even the most difficult tasks. Thus, joy has enormous power. It brings people together, moves them to do great things and bestows success on their efforts.

Joy is not the same thing as pleasure. The pursuit of pleasure comes from an inward lack; the experience of joy stems from an inner plenitude.

Pleasure soon fades and demands repeated stimulation to be re-created and sustained. Joy requires nothing outside itself. Indeed, it gives freely to others, and in this way continually renews itself.

Try to run after joy and you will not get it. Joy must come from within. It is the product of inner peace and emotional stability. A person who is not balanced inwardly will not find that balance externally. You cannot depend on other people to make you happy, or rely on things to fulfill you. That is simply a recipe for frustration. Whenever your happiness depends on the accumulation of things or the approval of other people, you have no real security. You are at the mercy of forces beyond your control. You will continually be anxious and fearful that what you have will be taken away from you or that you will never get what you think you need to be complete.

Instead, take a different approach. If you want to take joy in the outside world, you must first learn to find some joy in your own heart. Make peace with yourself. Stop chasing after things in order to prove that you are worthy of love. Instead, devote yourself to something that nourishes and replenishes you. Stop looking outside yourself for the key to your happiness or for the confirmation of your self-worth. You have everything within yourself that you need in order to be happy. Accept life for what it is and accept yourself for who you are. Have a little faith in yourself and your abilities. Learn to share with other people and have fun doing so. Then you won't have to look outside yourself for joy. You will find that it is already within you.

THE IMAGE

Lakes attached to each other:
This is the image of Joy.
Thus the superior person joins with friends
For discussion and practice.

When two lakes are joined together, they replenish each other and this prevents the water in them from drying up. In the same way, communicating with others will renew you and bring you fresh ideas and experiences.

Encourage people to express their views sincerely and forthrightly. If you let people know that they will be accepted, they will be more willing to participate spontaneously. Then conversation flows freely and happily and life becomes fun, enjoyable, and stimulating. People learn from each other and enrich each other. But here too it is important to be inwardly strong and outwardly gentle and accepting. You must have inner stability and firmness of conviction without being obstinate or stubborn. When you possess emotional balance, you can share your views with others without anyone feeling threatened. When you have a healthy sense of yourself, you can accept the ideas of others and learn from them without surrendering your integrity or your principles. Joy in communication thus rests on sincerity and inner truth; it must flow freely from a heart that is open to others and at peace with itself.

THE LINES

Only the first two lines of this hexagram are favorable; the last four serve as warnings. When joy comes from inner stability, and strength of character (lines one and two), the result is beneficial. But when people lack a stable center and make their happiness depend on things outside themselves, the result is unfavorable.

Initial Nine

Harmonious joy. Good fortune.

"Harmonious joy" means joy that comes from within. Such joy results from having a balanced and proper attitude toward life. A harmonious self provides an inner security that can stand against outward misfortune. People with this sort of equanimity are sufficient unto themselves. That is why they can take such joy in others. They are freed from the slavery of egotism. Their hearts are fortified against the vicissitudes of this world.

Apply these principles to your own life. Allow yourself to be happy just as you are. Let go of selfish desires and you will attain real freedom. You do not need the external world to make you happy, and it will not guarantee your happiness in any case. If you look deep inside yourself, you will discover that the true source of contentment is already within you.

Nine in the Second Place (Ruling Line)

Sincere joy. Good fortune.
Regrets vanish.

You may be tempted to engage in activities or seek pleasures that are unworthy of you because you want to fit in or be accepted by others. But that sort of joy is ultimately unfulfilling. Maintain your integrity and your principles and you will have no cause for regret.

Sincere joy comes from pursuing what is meaningful to you and replenishes you. If you spend your time and attention on things that are unworthy, you will waste your resources and have nothing to show for it. The time you spend on such pursuits is lost forever. But if you devote yourself to things that have true value and meaning for you, then the time and effort are not wasted, and you should have no regrets. That is what your time and your resources are for. The joy that comes from doing work for which you are suited and engaging in activities that truly nourish you will reward you over and over again. This is good fortune.

Six in the Third Place (Constitutive Line)

Chasing after joy. Misfortune.

Chasing after joy means to pursue outside pleasures and diversions because one has no joy within. The emptiness within the soul can only be filled momentarily. Then the lack soon reappears and must be fed again. As a result, the self is lost in the pursuit of what can never nourish it. Misfortune is the inevitable result.

Joy that is true and lasting must come from within you. Because of a hurt or lack inside, you are tempted to throw yourself headlong into the pursuit of pleasures in the outside world. These diversions are precisely that—diversions from the more difficult task of balancing yourself and finding value in yourself. You may try to paper over the emptiness within you through the pursuit of anesthetizing pleasure or through a never-ending quest for power, esteem, or status. But the result is the same in either case: The more you chase your self-respect in the outside world, the more it will elude you. Do not demean yourself in this way. If you want to avoid misfortune, you must turn yourself around and return to the right path.

Nine in the Fourth Place

Deliberating over joy, not yet at peace.
Get rid of affliction and there will be rejoicing.

You are uneasy and indecisive because you do not know what course of action to pursue. You are faced with a choice between higher and lower pleasures or between one set of values and another. Picking the right values means treating yourself as a person worthy of respect and your life as something of genuine value; picking the wrong ones means losing yourself and reducing your life to the mere avoidance of inner pain through the accumulation of pleasure in the outside world.

As long as you allow yourself to be tempted by baser pleasures and activities that are not really right for you, you will not be at peace with yourself. You have a choice. Pick the path of lasting benefit. Don't confuse temporary pleasure with lasting fulfillment, mere gratification with genuine happiness, or emotional denial with inner tranquility. Forsake what is inappropriate and self-destructive and strive for what is higher and worthy of you. Choose activities and values that are consistent with self-respect. As soon as you do this, you will find joy and peace, and you will rid yourself of the inner conflict that has tormented you.

Nine in the Fifth Place (Ruling Line)

Placing confidence in what is deteriorating is dangerous.

When an institution begins to deteriorate, the first victims are usually honesty, reciprocity, and mutual confidence. Conventions that benefited everyone begin to break down as people begin to act selfishly and can no longer be relied on—as a result, the situation deteriorates even further. The text advises against investing yourself in such institutions or situations.

If you put your trust in unscrupulous or dishonest people, or if you allow yourself to become involved in a dubious situation or underhanded methods, you will regret it. You will become ensnared in difficulties. Bad influences may corrupt or compromise you. But if you can recognize such a situation early on, you can protect yourself from the danger and remain unaffected.

Generosity and sincerity are among the most valuable social virtues. But they should not be expended on those who will take advantage of them. Trust is a matter of reciprocity, and where reciprocity is lacking, trust must be earned. You should not put your faith in people who are unreliable and are unable to conduct themselves properly. If you find yourself in such a situation, be exceedingly cautious. Keep your eyes wide open. Make sure that you are not being exploited or put in a compromising situation.

Finally, the text warns you to shun pleasures and pursuits that waste your resources and undermine your self-respect. Such pleasures and pursuits are "deterioriating," because in small and unnoticed ways they gradually eat away at you. If you throw yourself into activities that are unworthy of you,

you will contribute to the deterioration of your self, your life, and your relationships with others. If you pursue something that is corrupt, it will corrupt you as well. Do not start down a path whose ultimate end is misfortune.

Six at the Top (Constitutive Line)

Seductive joy.

For a person to deal with change in the outer world he must have a stable core of beliefs and values within. This core of beliefs and values is the true source of his freedom. If a person offers no moral resistance to the world beyond him, but merely chases after its pleasures, he is blown about like a leaf in the wind or pushed aside like debris on a riverbank. As a result, the text offers no statement of good fortune or bad, for such a person has abandoned his life and any such warning would be irrelevant. One who allows himself to be cast about like so much garbage should not be surprised if he comes to feel like garbage and if others treat him in much the same way.

You have let yourself be totally taken over by your response to the outside world. You have allowed external events to become the sole support of your happiness and your sense of self. This stems from a lack of stability and integrity within. As a result, you are swept along by circumstances and have lost your freedom. You have ceded the direction of your life to chance and to the whims of others, and are thrown upon their mercy.

Stop trying to gain the approval of other people. Give up your vanity and your thirst for status and esteem. Your life means much more than the evaluations and opinions of other people. Your self will only be worthy if you develop a sense of self-worth. If you rely on others for joy and happiness, you will never be secure. Try to remember what your own values are and act on them. Begin now to rebalance your life and regain your integrity. Only then can you begin to experience the sort of joy that is worth having.

NOTES

58.GI "attached." Or, "connected, linked."

58.GI "practice." Or, "study."

58.1 "harmonious." *he.* Or, "contented."

58.3 "Chasing after." *lai:* come.

58.4 "affliction." *ji:* illness. Cf. 16.5., 41.4, 50.2. Here it means an illness of the soul.

58.5 "Placing confidence in what is deteriorating." Or, "Putting one's trust in what deteriorates," "Sincerity toward the deteriorating."

58.6 "seductive." *yin:* drawn out, protracted. Cf. 45.2.

FIFTY-NINE

Huan • Dispersion

Keywords:

Dispersion
Dissolution
Getting rid of egotism
Bringing people together
Finding a common purpose
Clearing up blockages
Melting the ice
Eliminating obstacles within yourself

Above: Xun • Wind (Wood)
Below: Kan • Water

Huan means "dispersing" or "dissolving." The upper trigram is Xun (Wind); the lower trigram is Kan (Water). Wind blowing over ice dissolves it; wind blowing over water causes it to evaporate or turn into mist and foam. Kan stands for danger, heart, and emotion; here it represents danger from a blockage of one's emotional life. Feelings of resentment and anger have been dammed up. Xun represents humility and kindness. Through gentleness and devotion one melts the blockage and frees the soul.

The text of the judgment for Huan (Dispersion) is quite similar to that of Hexagram 45, Cui (Gathering Together). These seem to be opposite ideas, but in fact they are not. Cui encourages people to find a single great idea to rally around; Huan seeks the discovery of a single great idea to eliminate selfishness and mistrust and thus bring people together. In Cui one gathers others together by gathering one's self togther. In Huan one dispels egotism and hatred in others by dispelling them in one's self. This shows the deep connection between dispersion and gathering together.

THE JUDGMENT

Dispersion. Success.
The king approaches his temple.
It is beneficial to cross the great river.
It is beneficial to persevere.

You can now make progress by bringing people together. To do this you must dissolve the things that keep them apart. Egotism, selfishness, and insecurity have pitted people against each other. They are unable or afraid to communicate with each other openly and sincerely. Hence they pursue their narrow self-interest in a shortsighted way. You have the power to change all that. Strive to clear up misunderstandings and doubts. Work to reconcile people and break up factions and cliques. Progress will come only when you eliminate mutual suspicion and antagonism and restore harmony and cooperation. The same principles apply with special force to yourself. It is time to break through the barriers that separate you from others. You must dissolve the selfishness and egotism within you. This is the path to happiness and success.

To eliminate egotism and dispel misunderstanding, you must exercise gentleness, flexibility, and tact. If you try to force people to come together, they will resist. If you try to dominate people, you will simply drive them further apart. The text compares the best strategy to wind blowing gently over floes of ice that separate people. Over time, the ice melts and the barriers that once divided people are gradually removed. In the same way, you need to open channels of communication slowly and give people a sense of comfort with each other. Gradually, they will begin to come together. The melting of ice starts slowly at first and then proceeds more quickly; the same is true of trust. Trust begins in little things and then, once it is established, the forces of solidarity and reconciliation build on each other more rapidly.

What is the best way to dissolve faction and bring people together? The text offers two solutions—the first is a great symbol or idea; the second is a great project.

The text says, "The king approaches his temple." In ancient China, religious ceremonies brought people together both physically and spiritually and called on their common commitments and beliefs. Rituals and sacred music inspired them and bound them together emotionally. Invoking tradition through symbols and religious ceremony gave people a sense that they were one people with a long history and a common destiny. If you want to dissolve the barriers that separate people, you should appeal to their shared beliefs and practices. Remind people of the many things they have in common. It may be a common history, a common set of values, a common tradition, or an everyday activity common to all. Invoke a great idea or cause that everyone can believe in and rally around. Draw on symbols of shared history and community. When people feel that they are keeping faith with something noble and valuable that is greater than themselves, their estrangement and selfishness will dissolve and they will rally together.

Similarly, the text says that "it is beneficial to cross the great river." If you want to remedy alienation, you must give people a shared sense of purpose. Call them together to a great undertaking. Set a high and noble goal. When people work together on a single task, the barriers between them begin to dissolve. If you cannot get people to work on something big, start with something small. Laboring together—even on something minor—has an important symbolic effect. Cooperating on joint projects allows people to find what they have in common. It humanizes others and lets the participants see each other as allies rather than adversaries. Instead of worrying about whether others will grab something that is theirs, people instead focus on whether they will be able to reach a common goal. And when they achieve that goal together, they will celebrate as one.

THE IMAGE

The wind moves across the water:
This is the image of Dispersion.
Thus the ancient kings made offerings to the Supreme Deity
And established temples.

Wind blows over water and melts the ice. Ice is hard and brittle, like a selfish and insecure heart. People are separated from others because they fear and mistrust them. Then they grow rigid and inflexible. You must melt the hardness in others as well as in yourself through gentleness, tolerance, and accommodation. You must rise above existing divisions and offer people something higher than themselves that they can believe in and rally around.

The text says that the ancient kings made offerings and established temples of worship. They did so not only for the sake of their subjects but also for their own sake. They knew they could not inspire others to acts of selflessness and generosity unless they were themselves inspired. The same principles apply to you. If you want to dissolve the obstructions in the world, you must dissolve the obstructions within you. To eliminate selfishness and egotism in others, you must first eliminate them in yourself. For what may really be blocking your progress is not something in your external environment but something in your mind and heart that you have not yet come to terms with.

If something has been keeping you from communicating with people or working with others, it is time to face the problem squarely and dissolve the misunderstanding. You must break down all the emotional barriers that isolate you from other people. Perhaps you are jealous of others or harbor hidden resentments. Perhaps you are insecure and fear that other people will abuse or manipulate you. Or perhaps you are too ambitious and fear that other people will get more than you or will advance more quickly. Confront your fears and anxieties. Get rid of these negative emotions. They are holding you back. Be tolerant and forgiving and let go of your anger. Take a wider perspective and let go of your selfishness. Believe in yourself and let go of your insecurity. Stop torturing yourself for failing to live up to unrealistic expectations.

In the end, your destiny is enmeshed with the destiny of others. What you do affects others; what others do affects you. The great lesson of this hexagram is that to succeed in life you must dissolve yourself—the limited vision of who you are that holds you back and prevents you from uniting with others. Reach outward with compassion and understanding. Only through joining with others freely and cooperatively will you be able to find your proper path.

THE LINES

Each of the lines (except the first) uses the metaphor of dissolving or dispersion. In lines two, three, four, and five, dissolving means eliminating anger, egotism, parochialism, and discord (respectively) in order to create unity. In line six, unity may no longer be possible and dissolving primarily means avoiding danger.

Initial Six

Rescuing with the aid of a strong horse.
Good fortune.

"A strong horse" is a symbol of spirit. Hence to rescue with the aid of a strong horse means to save others through inspiring them with a sense of common purpose.

Conflicts and discord are starting to arise. Don't let things progress any further. Act now to reconcile differences and resolve misunderstandings. Be decisive. Remind people of what they have in common and move quickly to restore trust and unity. It is much easier to keep people together when disagreements are still minor than to reunite them after they have broken things off entirely.

Nine in the Second Place (Constitutive Line)

He dissolves by fleeing to what supports him.
Regrets vanish.

This line tells the story of a person who dissolves anger and conflict by remembering what supports him: his values, his commitments, and his relationships with friends and family.

You have begun to feel alienated and estranged from other people. This is the result of negative thinking and unhealthy attitudes. Don't let the problem progress any further or you will cause serious damage to yourself and to others that you really do care about. You must try to regain your balance and your sense of humor. A little goodwill toward others now will help you feel better about yourself. Try to put yourself in other peoples' shoes and think of them with more tolerance and charity. Nourish yourself emotionally by reaching out to other people and helping them. If you do this, the storm clouds will soon disperse and you will gain a new lease on life. Hence the text says, "Regrets vanish."

Six in the Third Place

He dissolves himself.
Regrets vanish.

To dissolve one's self means to surrender egotism and selfishness.

You face a difficult task that you cannot achieve by yourself. To accomplish it you will need to change your attitude. Stop thinking in terms of your own self-interest. Break down the barriers that separate you from other people. You will gain a sense of fulfilment through working with others and devoting yourself to a worthy shared goal that benefits everybody. This will strengthen your character and you will be able to achieve great things.

Six in the Fourth Place (Constitutive Line)

He dissolves his group.
Supreme good fortune.
Dispersion leads to the summit.
This is something that ordinary people do not think of.

To dissolve one's group is to foreswear parochialism and partisan self-interest and make outside alliances in order to work for something that is in the interest of all.

You can achieve something very significant now if you can put aside your personal interests and those of your party or group and work for the general good. Through a sincere commitment to larger values and ideals, you can end disharmony and bring peace among people and groups that have previously been opposed. In this way you can dissolve tensions and forge a greater unity. To do this will take considerable courage and vision. The task ahead may lead you to new experiences and new alliances with people outside your circle. This in turn will shake you out of accustomed ways of thinking. But if you are truly devoted to something that transcends narrow partisan interests you will meet with supreme good fortune.

Nine in the Fifth Place (Ruling Line)

He disperses his sweat, crying out in great shouts:
"Dissolve!"
The king abides without blame.

Sweat is a symbol of struggle and exertion, so to disperse one's sweat widely means not only that one makes a great effort but also that one is able to get others to join in the struggle. To cry out "Dissolve!" means to urge others to let go of their partisanship and self-interest. "The king abides without blame" means to exercise leadership or take control of the situation. It also means that one provides a rallying point for unity and common efforts.

Things have come to a standstill. People are not cooperating with each other. Discord and disunity abound. It is up to you to take the initiative now to make things better for yourself and for everyone else involved. First, you must completely rethink the situation. Look for a solution that can bring people together rather than drive them further apart. Ask yourself how everyone can benefit.

Second, you must let people know about your project and persuade them to join with you. A great idea in a time of stagnation can rouse people's spirits and inspire them to unite again. Consider what key idea, concept, or symbol people can agree with, identify with, and rally around. Progress will come when people can find a reason to work together. Employing an easy-to-understand symbol of this common goal or ideal may be helpful in order to persuade people to unite for a higher purpose.

Third, you must be completely committed to your course of action and willing to see it through. This will take great effort on your part. But if you show that you are committed and put your money (or your resources) where your mouth is, others will see that you are serious and they will join in. People will rally around you and your new idea and together you will be able to succeed.

Nine at the Top

He dissolves his blood.
He departs and stays far away from things.
No blame.

Blood is a symbol of strife, anger, danger, violence, and warfare. Hence to dissolve one's blood is to defuse the situation so that danger is eliminated and violence is unnecessary. To disperse one's blood also means to send one's relations (or one's dependents) away from the source of strife.

You are in the midst of a crisis. The situation is perilous. You must exercise the utmost care to protect yourself and those who rely on you or who are close to you. Do whatever is necessary to escape the danger, even if this means withdrawing from the situation altogether. Because you act not only for yourself but for others, there is no blame in this.

NOTES

59.0 "The king approaches his temple." Cf. 45.0.

59.GI "Supreme Deity." *Di.* Cf. 16.0, 42.2.

59.1 "a strong horse." Cf. 36.2.

59.2 "He dissolves by fleeing to what supports him." Or, "Dissolution. Fleeing to one's support."

59.3 "He dissolves himself." Or, "He dissolves his self" (i.e, his person). *gong:* body, self. Cf. 4.3, 39.2, 51.6.

59.4 "Dispersion leads to the summit." *qiu:* hill, hilltop. Cf. 22.5, 27.2 Another reading is "dispersion leads in turn to accumulation" (Wilhelm/Baynes), the idea being that one will heap up new riches (or gain new friends).

59.4 "This is something," etc. *fei yi suo si:* in-no-way ordinary (hidden, level) place reflect. Or, "One cannot think about it in the normal way."

59.5 "He disperses," etc. Or, "His loud cries are as dissolving as sweat" (Wilhelm/Baynes).

59.5 "Dissolve!" Or, "Disperse!"

59.5 "The king abides without blame." Or, "The king abides (dwells, remains). No blame." Another possibility is to combine this phrase with the previous word *huan* (dissolve, disperse), thus: "Dispersing the king's residence. No blame" (Shaughnessy).

59.6 "He departs and stays far away from things." Or, "Departing, keeping at a distance, going out, / Is without blame" (Wilhelm/Baynes).

SIXTY

Jie • Limitation

Keywords:

Control
Restriction
Limitation
Articulation
Separate and distinguish
Setting boundaries
Constraint
Self-control

Above: Kan • Water
Below: Dui • Lake

Jie originally meant a joint on a bamboo stalk. Because the joints divide the bamboo into parts, the word came to mean to delimit or set the boundaries of something. Later it meant restraint or economy and eventually took on the moral connotations of self-control and principled behavior. Moral people set boundaries on what they will do and not do based on their values and principles.

The structure of the hexagram reflects the theme of limitation. The upper trigram is Kan (Water); the lower trigram is Dui (Lake). A lake contains water and therefore limits it. Water must be limited and contained if it is not to overflow. When water increases without limits, it runs wild and floods the land.

Jie is the inverse of the previous hexagram, Huan (Dispersion). Huan says that one succeeds by dissipating anger and egotism and dissolving the boundaries between the self and others. In Jie one succeeds by limiting one's desires and restraining the self. Although these are opposite strategies, they also complement each other, because self-restraint also helps us avoid selfishness and enables us to live harmoniously with others.

THE JUDGMENT

Limitation. Success.
One should not engage in bitter limitation.

Limitation is a necessary element of a happy life. Limiting expenditures is necessary to remain solvent; limiting passions is necessary for maturity and sound judgment. The best limitations are those we choose for ourselves. They strengthen our character and make life easier to bear.

You are facing a situation in which limitation is necessary. Perhaps you have taken on too much, or perhaps you have become self-indulgent or carried things to extremes. Whatever the problem, it is up to you to rectify matters by enforcing boundaries and reining things in a bit. Moderation is the key here. You have to strike a new balance in your life. To do that you will need to exercise some self-restraint. If you work at self-discipline, it will eventually come naturally to you. Adopt good habits and doing the right thing will become easy rather than a burden. The same principles apply to your finances. Keep an eye on your expenditures, and avoid anything that is too extravagant. Be prudent without being stingy.

Limitation means setting priorities. Decide what your responsibilities are and be prepared to live up to them. You may have to make some tradeoffs. Short-term sacrifices may be necessary. But in the long run, it will be worth it. You cannot have everything in life. You need to decide what is most important to you. That is how to achieve peace of mind.

You may be facing limitations in your everyday environment. If so, be realistic. Don't bite off more than you can chew. Accommodate yourself to present conditions with optimism and good humor. Accept the restrictions with grace and without rancor. You can do more now if you remain adaptable and flexible. Don't give up hope; instead, make the most out of what you have. Be content to make progress in smaller steps, taking one thing at a time. Don't try to do more than present circumstances allow.

Limitation is good when it strengthens people, increases their self-control, and makes them more self-reliant. It is bad when it is punitive and counterproductive. You will gain nothing by being too hard on yourself. Your goal should be balance and moderation, not asceticism or self-abuse. Similarly, if you are too hard on others, your attempts at discipline will do you and them no good. People will either lose confidence in you or they will rebel at your attempts to control them. Thus the text says that you should avoid bitter limitation, because that is going too far. You need to exercise restraint in all things, including the exercise of restraint itself.

THE IMAGE

Above the lake is water:
This is the image of Limitation.
Thus the superior person
Establishes measures and limits,
And deliberates about the nature of virtuous conduct.

Water will flow everywhere if it is not contained. Hence it is contained by the lake, which limits it. The power of water is increased by limitation, as in the case of hydraulic pressure. In the same way, limitations on your actions are necessary if you want to achieve anything in the world.

People often think of themselves as limited by external circumstances. But the most important limitations in your life are those you choose for yourself. If you limit yourself in the wrong way, you cripple yourself and make yourself unhappy. If you limit yourself in the right way, you make yourself free and strong.

Principled behavior means knowing when cases should be treated as similar and when they should be distinguished from each other. Morality means deciding what you may do and what you may not. You make sense of your life by discriminating between things and setting limits. You become free by setting limitations on yourself voluntarily and sticking to them. Then you are in control of yourself rather than being at the beck and call of internal desire and external forces.

The task before you is to put your priorities in order. If you flit about from project to project, you will waste time and resources and never dig very deeply into anything. If you try to do too many things, you will do them badly, or end up doing nothing at all. You probably would like to do many different things. But each of them will take time and effort if you want to do them really well. Therefore, you have to decide what is most important to you. You must make a commitment to something and stick with it. Look inside yourself and decide where your priorities really lie. Learn to restrain the desires and fancies that distract you. They keep you from making genuine progress. It is like traveling on a road. If you try to travel in every direction at once, you will go nowhere. Or else you will become lost. In order to give your life direction, you must choose a direction and follow it.

Limitation means being realistic not only about your goals but also your abilities. You have to decide what you can do and what you cannot. If your expectations are out of line, you will only make yourself unhappy. You will waste your resources and undermine your self-confidence. Be honest with yourself about your capabilities and how much you are willing to give up in order to get what you want. Focus on practical, achievable goals that make sense for you. Then you will discover that you can actually do a great deal, and you will improve your abilities in the process. You can take pleasure in doing things well and you will bolster your self-confidence. In short, by focusing your energies in the right way, you can take on increasingly ambitious tasks. This is the secret power of limitation. Wisely employed, restraint can actually expand your horizons and take you past the limits of what you thought you could do. Practice limitation correctly and you will learn and grow as an individual.

THE LINES

Lines one and two concern proper timing; they point in opposite directions. The theme of lines three, four, and five is developing habits of self-control. In line six, discipline has gone too far and is counterproductive.

Initial Nine

Not going out of the door into the courtyard.
No blame.

The courtyard surrounds the house and separates it from the street. Hence not to even go out the door into the courtyard symbolizes special restraint.

You would like to push ahead, but there are too many obstacles at present. The best way to succeed in the long run is to exercise restraint and discretion now. Be realistic. Quietly gather your resources and bide your time. This is not a mistake. If you know how to maintain silence and self-control, you will be able to act with great effectiveness when the time is right.

Nine in the Second Place

Not going out of the gate of the courtyard.
Misfortune.

The gate of the courtyard separates the street from the house. Not going out of the gate means failing to enter into the public world. This line is the converse of the first. Whereas the first points out that limitation means knowing when to hold back until the time is propitious for success, this line points out that limitation also means knowing when to move forward, because the times for appropriate action are also limited.

The point of making preparations is to be ready for action. Get yourself set to move forward when the moment is right. Keep your eyes and ears open. When the time comes, don't hesitate or have doubts. If you have taken the necessary measures, there is no cause for anxiety. You must seize the opportunity when it arrives. If you vacillate, you will miss your chance and your bad timing will bring you misfortune.

Six in the Third Place

No limitation,
Then lamentation.
No blame.

Limitation means self-control and moderation. It means knowing when to act and when to hold back, when to indulge innocent pleasures and when to avoid excess. Self-limitation is not only a product of good character; it also builds character. Over time, self-restraint makes achievement easier and the pleasure of achievement sweeter. If you work at being modest and maintain a balanced attitude toward life, you will have fewer problems exercising self-control when you really need to, and so you will be without blame. On the other hand, if you give into temptation and don't learn to control yourself, you will be unable to stop yourself from going too far.

Lack of self-control is a major source of human unhappiness. Inability to set priorities will exhaust your energies and keep you from accomplishing anything of value. Extravagant behavior and self-indulgence will get you into endless trouble. If you cannot control your anger, you will get into unnecessary fights; if you cannot control your desires, you will engage in self-destructive behavior. Then you will have no one but yourself to blame.

Six in the Fourth Place

Serene limitation. Success.

Serene limitation is self-restraint that has become easy because it derives from the cultivation of character.

Work at developing self-discipline and it will come naturally to you. Let moderation, balance, and restraint become part of your everyday life. Then you will find that doing the right thing and avoiding the wrong thing becomes easy. You will be able to apply your energies to the task at hand without distraction, and this will help ensure your success. If you don't adopt good habits, then life becomes much more difficult. You will be able to exercise self-control and finish what you start only though an enormous exertion of will and effort.

Realism is an important part of this equation. Look at the situation with a clear head and be willing to adapt where necessary. Accommodating yourself to present conditions does not mean giving up your principles or surrendering your ultimate goals. Rather, it means not fighting battles that will simply exhaust your resources and make it more difficult for you to succeed later on. Deal with one thing at a time and don't try to do more than the present situation permits. Take the longer view. Remember that persistent effort and preparation over time will allow you to achieve things that you could not achieve all at once.

Nine in the Fifth Place (**Ruling Line**)

Sweet limitation brings good fortune.
Going forward brings esteem.

If you want to influence other people, you must lead by example. Accept the limitations and restrictions of the current situation with grace and tact. Do the best you can with the resources you have. If circumstances require that people restrain themselves or make do with less, take these restrictions upon yourself first before you ask anyone else to do so. By exercising self-restraint, you will demonstrate that your motives are beneficent and that you are worthy of trust and emulation. Moreover, you will prove that it is possible to succeed with modest means. When other people see that you have accepted and handled the situation with dignity and skill, you will win their praise and respect and they will happily follow your lead.

Six at the Top

Bitter limitation.
Perseverance brings misfortune.
Regrets vanish.

A bitter limitation is one that is too harsh and is therefore ineffective or counterproductive. Persevering in such measures leads to misfortune.

Immoderate restriction can sometimes be as bad as lack of moderation itself. If you are too hard on yourself, you will become disheartened and give up. Severe self-discipline may be necessary to get through a particularly difficult period, to make an important change in your life, or to do appropriate penance. But it will not work if carried on too long. Everything must be in appropriate proportion, including discipline. But if you strike the proper balance, you need have no regrets.

The same principles apply when you are setting limitations for others. If you impose restrictions that are too harsh, people will resent you and they will rebel. The best limitations are those that promote self-development and self-reliance. They give people security and confidence and increase their freedom in the long run.

NOTES

60.0 "bitter limitation." Or, "galling limitation," "bitter constraints."

60.GI "Establishes measures and limits." *yi ji shu du:* literally, carves up (pares) reckons measures.

60.GI "And deliberates about the nature of virtuous conduct." *yi de xing:* deliberate (consider) virtue action. Or, "discusses a moral code for social conduct" (Alfred Huang), "evaluates moral conduct" (Lynn).

60.1 "door into the courtyard." Or, "door of the courtyard." The door *(hu)* separates the inside of the house from the courtyard *(ting)*. Hence "out of the house and into the courtyard."

60.2 "gate of the courtyard." Cf. 60.1. While the door *(hu)* separates the inside of the house from the courtyard *(ting)*; the gate *(men)* separates the courtyard from the street. Hence "out of the courtyard and into the street." Cf. Wilhelm/Baynes: "Not going out of the gate and the courtyard / Brings misfortune."

60.3 "No limitation, / Then lamentation." Or, "One who has no limitation / Will have cause for lamentation."

60.3 "No blame." *wu jiu*. The commentaries gloss this as "There is no one else to blame."

60.4 "Serene." *an:* peaceful, contented, easy.

60.5 "Sweet." *gan:* sweet, agreeable, happy. Cf. 19.3, where the sweetness is insincere; in this case, it is sincere and good fortune results.

60.6 "Bitter." *ku*. Or, "Galling" (Wilhelm/Baynes).

SIXTY-ONE

Zhong Fu • Inner Truth

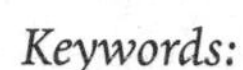

Keywords:

Inner sincerity
Inner faithfulness
Confidence
Trustworthiness
Conformity between what is outside and what is inside

Above: Xun • Wind (Wood)
Below: Dui • Lake

Zhong means central, core, or middle. Fu originally meant captive, but later came to mean sincere and trustworthy, and hence true and confident. Thus, Zhong Fu means being sincere and truthful at one's core. The structure of the hexagram symbolizes this in various ways: It consists of two yin lines surrounded by four yang lines, two above and two below. The two yin lines at the center of the hexagram represent the heart, which is open, gentle, accepting, and receptive to the truth. At the center of each trigram there is a yang line—in the second and fifth positions—so there is also strength of character.

The upper trigram is the eldest daughter, Xun (Wind or Wood). The lower trigram is the youngest daughter Dui (Lake). The first represents gentleness; the second represents joy. There is love and trust between the two sisters; hence their relations are harmonious.

The great theme of Zhong Fu is being true to oneself. This is the right way to influence others and the right way to lead one's life.

THE JUDGMENT

Inner Truth. Pigs and fishes.
Good fortune.
It is beneficial to cross the great river.
It is beneficial to persevere.

The *Book of Changes* regards truth as one of the most powerful forces in the universe. If you want to influence other people, there is no better way than through the truth that lies within you. Possessing inner truth means that you are sincere. You are on the inside what you appear to be on the outside. You are honest and genuine both in your words and your deeds. You say what you mean and you mean what you say. Such a person naturally inspires trust and confidence in others.

Even the most difficult and contentious people will respond to someone whom they recognize is sincere and aboveboard. The most powerful advocates are those who genuinely believe in the rightness of their cause. Many speakers try to win influence by manipulating or flattering others. They may confuse and even impress momentarily, but their audiences do not really trust them. On the other hand, when people are completely sincere, their character shines through to others with the most powerful effect. Indeed, the text says that even pigs and fishes respond to the power of inner truth.

To influence others, you must approach them in the proper manner. If you want them to be receptive to you, then you must also be receptive to them. Listen to what other people have to say. Try to see things from their point of view. Open your heart and your mind, and assume that you have as much to learn from them as they have to learn from you. When you do this, you will be able to see the truth in their way of thinking, and they, in turn, will be able to see the truth in yours. Once you understand what is important to them, you will be able to express yourself in the right way.

Nevertheless, inner truth is not simply a device for persuading others. It is a way of living your life. The word for truth *(fu)* is also the word for confidence, trust, and reliability. If you want to have these things in your dealings with the outside world, you must possess each of them within.

First, to possess inner truth you must know yourself. Then you can trust your instincts in any situation.

Second, to possess inner truth means that you have personal integrity, a stable center, and a core of beliefs and principles to which you remain true. If you lack these things, your life will be shallow and unfulfilling. You cannot compensate for them by relying on other people and things to give yourself stability or fill an inner emptiness.

Third, inner truth means inner confidence. To possess inner truth means that you are self-reliant and have faith in yourself. If you are conflicted and uncertain, this will be reflected in your behavior and in your dealings with others. As a result, people will lose confidence in you. You must believe in yourself if you want others to believe in you. Indeed, you will find that the power of inner truth is contagious. A person with supreme confidence inspires others and gives them confidence as well.

Fourth, to possess inner truth means that you must be honest with yourself. Self-deception will inevitably affect your choices and your relationships. People who hide things from themselves cannot help hiding things from others. That is why inner truth is crucial to behaving with rectitude toward the outside world. You cannot be true to others if you are not true to yourself.

THE IMAGE

Wind over lake:
This is the image of Inner Truth.
Thus the superior person discusses criminal cases carefully
And postpones executions.

Wind symbolizes gentleness; the lake symbolizes joy. When people approach each other with gentleness and joy, they put aside their differences and try to see each other's point of view. Hence the text says that enlightened people do not rush to judge others but instead show mercy and understanding. It is often said that to understand all is to pardon all. This is the power of inner truth.

The secret to changing the world is creating trust and reciprocity among human beings. The *Book of Changes* holds that sincerity and inner truth are among the most basic of human virtues because they are the basis for trust and reciprocity, and hence for cooperation, from which all great achievements flow. When these virtues are present, the foundations of society can be secured.

THE LINES

The lines feature three basic themes of inner truth: Lines two and five teach that sincerity draws a natural response from others; lines three and four emphasize that inner truth requires you to stand up for your own values. Lines one and six warn that if you are not honest with yourself and with others, misfortune will result.

Initial Nine

Being prepared brings good fortune.
If there is something else, no peace.

"Being prepared" refers to cultivation of character. "Something else" refers to ulterior motivations.

By developing and maintaining emotional balance and inner strength, you can best handle whatever life throws at you. This sort of equanimity comes easier for some people than others, but in every case it is only achieved over time. Hence the text says that you must prepare yourself by working on your inner virtue.

First, be sincere and upright in your dealings with other people. Avoid secret deals and do not approach people with ulterior motives. Do not be tempted to engage in any enterprise that seems shady or compromised. Inner truth means being true to yourself and to the values that you hold most dear.

Second, get to know yourself better. If you understand your inner conflicts and the sorts of things that disturb you, you will be much better prepared to handle crises and upsets when they occur. Self-understanding will increase your autonomy and help you become the person you would like to be. You cannot be honest with others unless you are able to be honest with yourself. Outer truth in the form of trustworthiness depends on the inner truth that comes from self-examination.

Third, learn to be more self-reliant. Self-reliance presupposes inner truth: If you want to be independent, you must know who you are. Conversely, if you possess inner truth, you are able to trust yourself and your instincts in any situation. If you rely on other people to give you stability and to compensate for weaknesses in your character, you will be at the mercy of events that are beyond your control. You will be thrown about by changing circumstances and will know no peace. But if you remain true to yourself and to your values, you will develop an inner strength that will see you through changes in fashion and fortune.

Nine in the Second Place

A crane calling in the shade.
Its young answers it.
I have a fine goblet.
I will share it with you.

A crane calling in the shade is heard by its young even though it is hidden. In the same way, a person's sincerity and generosity of spirit speak to others no matter how humble his status. What a person says and does from inner truth has the power to extend its influence, starting with a narrow circle, and then expanding to a wider and wider domain. Like a bell that rings true, its vibrations spread progressively outward, influencing all who hear it.

Be genuine and sincere in your words and deeds. If what you say and do comes from the heart, it will resonate with other people no matter how lowly or isolated you may think you are. True sincerity is more influential than any shallow form of display. It reaches to hearts and minds near and far. It calls forth a natural response in others that extends over time. It brings forth generosity that enriches both the one who gives and the one who receives.

If your relationships with others spring from genuineness and sincerity, they will be rewarding and long-lasting. Because you have a good heart, your wisdom and influence will grow steadily, and your actions will meet with a favorable response. The power of your inner truth will bring happiness to many, including yourself.

Six in the Third Place (Constitutive Line)

He finds a rival.
Now he beats the drum, now he stops.
Now he sobs, now he sings.

If you rely on other people to make you happy, or to give you a sense of strength and self-confidence, you will become dependent on their opinion of you, and your happiness will turn on whatever their moods and sentiments happen to be at any time. As a result, you may feel on top of the world one day and in the depths of despair the next. It is perfectly appropriate for people to feel happy or sad depending on the opinions and support of those they love and admire. But a healthy attitude toward life requires that you develop your own sources of self-worth. If you know who you are and are able to be true to yourself, your relation to others will have a sounder and more solid basis. You cannot have truly rewarding relationships with others unless you have a stable self to draw upon.

The same principles apply if your life is given meaning only through your comparative status with competitors and rivals. Your life will be taken over by this struggle: their victories become your defeats, and your emotional state becomes pegged to the rise and fall of their fortunes. This is not autonomy. Indeed, it is a form of servitude. If you have no emotional center within yourself, you cannot maintain your balance in life. The text offers no statement of good fortune or bad, for a person who has surrendered control of his life to others cannot be guided.

Six in the Fourth Place (**Constitutive Line**)

The moon is nearly full.
A paired team of horses. One abandons its mate.
No blame.

"The moon is nearly full" means that things have progressed as far as they can without change. The horse that abandons its mate symbolizes a person who goes his own way.

It is time to put self-interest aside and do the right thing. Things cannot remain as they were before. Higher ideals and nobler goals call to you. You must adhere to your own values and do what you genuinely feel to be true and just, even if this means leaving others behind. This is not a mistake. The power of inner truth is the source of your freedom. Do not abandon it. If you find yourself uncertain about what to do, it is entirely appropriate to seek advice from wise and experienced people whom you respect and trust. But ultimately, you must be guided by your own light and follow your own path.

Nine in the Fifth Place (Ruling Line)

Possessing sincerity that binds like a tether.
No blame.

Sincerity that binds like a tether is a metaphor for true leadership. A great leader binds people together through the strength of his convictions and the force of his personality. The power of inner truth is contagious: A person with supreme confidence inspires confidence in others, giving them hope, a coherent vision of the future, and faith in their ultimate success. In this way inner truth emanates outward, bringing people together in pursuit of a great and noble cause. In this way the power of truth transforms the world.

If you are fully convinced of the rightness of your principles and the justness of your cause, you will attract others to you. Your sincerity and devotion will motivate other people, and together you can make real changes that will improve the situation. The results will be fortunate for everyone concerned.

Nine at the Top

A soaring sound rises into the sky.
Perseverance brings misfortune.

The soaring sound refers to empty words expressed in lofty rhetoric. Mere words are not the same thing as inner truth. They cannot inspire others in the same way that genuine commitment does. And even if they do attract some followers, because the leader is not properly motivated, the results cannot be sustained. They will either degenerate into failure or into something base and ignoble. Thus one who lacks inner truth should not persevere.

Be careful what you say. Don't make promises that you cannot keep. Don't enter into enterprises that you are not fully committed to. If you have ambition that is not backed up by devotion, you will only cause problems for yourself and others. You need to find what is truly in your heart and commit yourself only to what your heart is truly in.

NOTES

61.0 "Pigs and fishes." Or, "Inner Truth can influence even pigs and fishes."

61.1 "If there is something else." *you ta:* literally, "there is this." Cf. 28.4. The passage is subject to many different interpretations. It might mean *ta,* "unanticipated harm," i.e., "if there is an accident, there will be no peace." This makes sense of the line, but has little to do with the theme of inner sincerity. Or *ta* might mean "else" in the sense of "more" or "another." The idea is that one is secretly devoted to another person or enterprise and so cannot be truly sincere. Wilhelm/Baynes translates the line as "If there are secret designs, it is disquieting."

61.2 "in the shade." *yin.* This is the yin of yin and yang, and it originally meant the shaded side of a northern slope. It can also mean "shadows," or "darkness." Given the context, "shade" seems most appropriate.

61.2 "share it with you." Literally, "empty it with you."

61.3 "rival." *di:* equal. It also means "rival" or "enemy."

61.3 "sobs." Or, "weeps."

61.4 "The moon is nearly full." Cf. 9.6, 54.5.

61.4 "A paired team," etc. Or, "A horse abandons its mate."

61.5 "binds like a tether." *luan ru:* tie together-like, like a tying. Or, "He has sincerity that connects together"; "He possesses truth, which links together" (Wilhelm/Baynes).

61.6 "soaring." *han:* soar, firebird, fowl, golden pheasant. Or, "The sound of the golden pheasant ascends into the heavens." Some translate *han* as "cockerel"; hence, "A cock's crow ascends into the heavens."

SIXTY-TWO

Xiao Guo • Exceeding Smallness

䷽

Keywords:

Preponderance of the small
Smallness in excess
Conscientiousness
Keeping a low profile
Reining in your ambitions
Maintaining your dignity in everyday life
Paying attention to detail
The little bird flies close to the ground

Above: Zhen • Thunder
Below: Gen • Mountain

Xiao Guo features two yang lines in the center surrounded by four yin lines. It is related to Hexagram 28, Da Guo (Greatness in Excess), which also features yang in the center and yin on the outside. In Da Guo, however, the four yang lines in the center predominate, while in Xiao Guo the two yang lines are outnumbered by the four yin lines on the outside. In addition, unlike the previous hexagram, Zhong Fu (Inner Truth), there is a weak line in the center of each trigram in the second and fifth places. Therefore, this is a time when the weak and the small preponderate over the strong and the great. Under these conditions exceptional modesty and forbearance is necessary.

When the small preponderates, a person must pay special attention to the little things in life and not attempt anything grand or lofty. One who tries to fly too high will only end up crashing to earth. But one who stays close to the ground will be saved from harm.

THE JUDGMENT

Exceeding Smallness. Success.
It is beneficial to persevere.
Small things may be done; great things should not be done.
The flying bird leaves behind its song:
"One should not go up; one should go down."
Great good fortune.

This is not a time to undertake something big or difficult. Conditions are not in your favor for significant accomplishment. You lack the strength and resources to achieve what you would like. Therefore, you need to understand the demands of the time and scale back your expectations. You should not expect great success, but that does not mean that there is nothing you can do.

The text compares your situation to a small bird. If the little bird attempts to fly too high, it will get into trouble. But if it stays low, it will be safe and find its nest. In the same way, your best strategy right now is to maintain a low profile and attend to everyday matters. Stick to your ordinary routine. Success will come from scrupulous dedication to the minutiae of everyday life. Be especially conscientious and pay careful attention to detail. If you resolve to undertake only small things but to do them well, you will get through this difficult period in good shape.

Just as a small bird should not fly too high, you should not bite off more than you can chew. This is not a time for risk taking. Play it safe for the time being. Recognize your limitations and don't take on more than you are able. Don't try to show off or call attention to yourself. Be simple and unpretentious and keep your feet firmly planted on the ground. If you are too big for your britches, people will resent you and your projects will fail. But if you are modest and dignified and simply attend to your business, you will earn respect.

THE IMAGE

Above the mountain there is thunder:
This is the image of Exceeding Smallness.
Thus the superior person
In his conduct is exceedingly respectful,
In his mourning is exceedingly sorrowful,
In his expenditures is exceedingly temperate.

Thunder on the mountain seems closer because the mountain is higher up. It does not have the advantage of a large flat plain against which to resonate. As a result, it makes a smaller, less impressive sound when heard from a distance. In the same way, you cannot make a big noise right now. You must rein in your ambitions. The present situation is a test of your character and your patience. When you are blocked from engaging in lofty or important activities, you must content yourself with more minor details. The important thing is not to become lazy or dispirited. Resist the temptation to become angry about your lowly state or frustrated by your lack of progress. You must accept the current limitations on what you can do with composure and good grace. This is no time to get angry or resentful. Be modest and unassuming. Do not complain or draw attention to yourself. If you act out, you will not get a positive response and you will probably only make things worse for yourself. Instead, persevere. Carry on with your daily life. Approach every task before you with conscientiousness and devotion. Regard none of the parts of your daily life as beneath you. Simply do your job and do it well.

The challenge of this time is to keep your pride and ambition in check while maintaining your dignity and equanimity. Be courteous and unpretentious in your dealings with other people. Be simple in your habits and take joy in everyday experiences. With the proper attitude, you can make it through this period in an excellent position and you will be able to shine again.

THE LINES

Although the hexagram name concerns "surpassing" smallness, the lines employ the metaphor of "passing by." In any case, the theme in both the hexagram judgment and the lines is the importance of lowering expectations and not trying to go too far. All of the lines except the second and fifth are unfortunate, and even these are only mildly positive.

Initial Six:

A flying bird meets with misfortune.

The text refers to a bird that tries to leave the nest before it is ready and therefore meets with misfortune.

You are not yet strong enough and experienced enough to launch out on a bold new endeavor. For the time being, stick to established patterns and tried-and-true methods of dealing with the situation. The traditional path is the way to success. Once you have gained more experience and greater resources, you can begin to move forward. But if you try to do anything out of the ordinary now, you will only tax your abilities and endanger yourself.

Six in the Second Place (Ruling Line)

Passing by his ancestor,
He meets his ancestress.
He does not reach his prince,
He meets his minister.
No blame.

One looks to ancestors for inspiration and support. In the ideology of ancient China, the female is more receptive than the male, and the minister is to the prince as the woman is to the man. Thus the ancestress is easier to approach than the ancestor, the minister is easier to approach than the prince. The text thus suggests that you should scale back your ambitions and do what is most likely to succeed at first.

The situation restricts what you can accomplish, and your resources are limited. Do not try to bite off more than you can chew. Stay within your capabilities and understand the demands of the time. Stick with traditional methods, keep a low profile, and don't try to get everything at once. Use your connections to secure your position. It is less important to forge alliances with the most important or influential people at the outset than to connect yourself with trustworthy people that you can relate to. They in turn can help you make connections with others.

Nine in the Third Place

If he is not exceedingly careful
Someone may come up from behind and strike him.
Misfortune.

You are in grave danger of becoming overconfident. Just because things have gone well in the past gives you no excuse to be careless. This is a critical juncture and you cannot afford to be lax. Be particularly modest, diligent, and cautious. You must pay careful attention to details and guard against things going wrong. If you don't take precautions now, you may be caught unawares later on.

Nine in the Fourth Place

No blame.
He does not pass him.
He meets him.
Going means danger.
One must be cautious.
Do not act.
Be constantly persevering.

The text describes a position of danger in which great caution becomes necessary. Do not attempt to do any more than the situation permits. Discretion is the better part of valor now. Be inwardly strong and outwardly compliant. Remain committed to your ultimate goal, but do not take any steps to realize it now. If you try to force matters, you will be rebuffed and cause great problems for yourself. Be patient. The situation will change in time. Until then you must sit tight. Persevere.

Six in the Fifth Place (Ruling Line)

Dense clouds,
No rain from the outskirts of our western region.
The prince shoots and hits one in the cave.

"Dense clouds, no rain" describes a process of accumulation and means that things cannot yet be brought to fruition. Hitting one in the cave means that the prince draws someone out of seclusion.

You have the ability and the desire to achieve your goals but find you cannot do it alone. Without some help, your plans will not come to fruition. You will need to seek out people with the necessary experience and ability. However, the right people will not come running simply because you call them. You must approach them the right way. Treat them with respect. Be modest and appreciative, and you will be able to persuade them to assist you.

Six at the Top

He does not meet him.
He passes by him.
The flying bird is caught in the net.
Misfortune.
This means blunder and disaster.

"Pass[ing] by" means missing a goal by overshooting it. The flying bird is caught in the net because it tries to fly too high and is not sufficiently attentive to its surroundings. Hence the result is "blunder and disaster," which means not only bad luck but also errors in judgment that exacerbate the misfortune.

You have great ambitions and dreams of grandeur. But they will do you no good if conditions are not appropriate and you are not up to the task. Understand your limitations and recognize the constraints of the situation. You will gain nothing by vanity or braggadocio. Indeed, pride goes before a fall. If you are reckless or aggressive and try to push beyond what is possible, the result will be disaster. Wise people know when to call things to a halt. In this way they are able to accumulate small advantages over time without endangering their position.

NOTES

62. GI "In his conduct is exceedingly," etc. In each of these three phrases the idea is that the superior person errs on the side of showing too much of a particular characteristic or virtue rather than too little. Cf. Wilhelm/Baynes: "gives preponderance to."

62.GI "In his conduct is exceedingly respectful." Or, "In his actions is exceedingly reverent."

62.GI "In his mourning is exceedingly sorrowful." Or, "In his bereavement is exceedingly full of grief."

62.GI "In his expenditures is exceedingly temperate." Or, "In his business is exceedingly thrifty."

62.2 "Passing by." *guo*. The word *guo*—"exceeding, preponderance"—which forms part of the name of the hexagram, is given a slightly different meaning in most of the the lines. Here it means "passing by" or "transgressing."

62.2 "prince." *jun:* ruler, sovereign, chief. Cf. 7.6, 10.3, 19.5, 24.6, 54.5.

62.2 "minister." *chen:* official, servant.

62.3 "If he is not exceedingly careful." *fu guo fang zhi:* not exceed guard it (them). Or, "Go not too far / Guard against this" (Alfred Huang).

62.3. "come up from behind and strike him." Or, "follow behind and injure (assault, kill) him."

62.4 "One must be cautious." *bi jie:* must (necessary) cautious (alert). Cf. Wilhelm/Baynes: "One must be on guard."

62.5 "Dense clouds," etc. Cf. 9.0.

62.5 "The prince shoots and hits one in the cave." Or, "The prince shoots an arrow and hits the other (another) living in the cave." The other refers to a person in comparative seclusion whose assistance is important.

62.6 "The flying bird is caught in the net." *li:* clinging, fasten. Li is also the name of Hexagram 30, so it might be translated it as "radiates outward," i.e., flies away, "leaves him" (Wilhelm/Baynes). In the Mawangdui text the word is *luo,* net; thus Edward Shaughnessy translates the line, "The flying bird is netted."

62.6 "blunder and disaster." *zai sheng:* disaster from without combined with inner fault, blunder, or mistake. Or, "calamity and disaster from without and within." Cf. 24.6.

SIXTY-THREE

Ji Ji • After Completion

Keywords:

Ferrying complete
Mission accomplished
Everything in its place
After fording the stream
After fulfillment
Consolidating gains
Maintaining equilibrium
Nipping problems in the bud
Preventing deterioration
Watching carefully
Minding the kettle

Above: Kan • Water
Below: Li • Fire

Ji Ji means "already across the stream," or "already forded." Because crossing a river was considered a very arduous endeavor, the expression eventually took the more general meaning of having successfully completed a task or undertaking.

The structure of the hexagram symbolizes that everything has been put in proper order. Traditionally, it has been understood as a further development of Hexagram 11, Tai (Peace). In Tai there are three yang lines below three yin lines. This arrangement is auspicious but not completely perfect, because there is a yang line in the second place (a weak, or yin position) and a yin line in the fifth place (a strong, or yang position). In Ji Ji two of the yang lines have moved upward to occupy the third and fifth positions (or, in the alternative, the lines in second and fifth positions have been switched). This produces a structure of absolute balance and harmony. There are yang lines in all of the odd-numbered places; there are yin lines in all of the even-numbered places. In addition, the first and fourth, second and fifth, and third and sixth lines correspond—that is, a yang line in one position complements a yin line in the other.

However, the problem with the situation is its very state of perfection. If any line moves or changes from yin to yang, the order is ruined. If (for example) all three yang lines were to continue to move upward, this would produce Hexagram 12, Pi (Standstill). Hence special efforts have to be made to keep the situation from deteriorating.

The delicacy and danger of the situation is also symbolized by the two constituent trigrams: Li (Fire) is below; Kan (Water) is above. Fire and water are mutually antagonistic. They are in perfect balance now, but any change could disturb the equilibrium. The theme of Ji Ji is how to maintain harmony, order, and good fortune after the victory has been won. Nothing lasts forever. In the long run, there will be change, and hence disintegration. The trick is to keep things working well as long as possible.

THE JUDGMENT

After Completion. Success in small matters.
It is beneficial to persevere.
In the beginning, good fortune.
In the end, disorder.

The situation has reached completion. You have achieved what you wanted. Details remain to be worked out, but the essential features have been achieved. It is perfectly all right to celebrate your accomplishments. But now the next phase of your efforts must begin. The final elements must be hammered into place. Promises and commitments must be fulfilled. And after all of this is done, you must maintain your new position and consolidate your good fortune.

The key is not to let success go to your head. You may be tempted to relax and let things move along on their own momentum. But that would be a mistake. Keeping things running smoothly will take effort. The law of change holds that as soon as things have reached perfection, they will begin to disintegrate. And as soon as a person achieves success, problems begin to emerge. Those problems will become more serious unless you deal with them at the outset. Therefore, your task is to maintain the fruits of your victory and to eliminate difficulties and obstacles before they have a chance to grow large. Don't regard any part of the task as beneath you. Pay careful attention to detail. Keep alert to any signs of possible decay in the situation. Do not take your previous successes for granted. Instead, continue to nurture the situation and strive to keep things healthy and vital. Now is definitely not the time to slack off.

If you don't make the effort to consolidate your gains, you will lose them. But if you pay attention to the little things, you can keep the situation in good order and enjoy the benefits of your hard-won success. The key is devotion and perseverance. The lesson of this hexagram is that when things have reached completion, your work has only begun.

THE IMAGE

Water over fire:
This is the image of things After Completion.
Thus the superior person
Contemplates difficulties
And guards against them in advance.

Fire and water are natural opposites. When opposites are harnessed together properly, the result can be beneficial—water boiling in a kettle can cook food; water in a steam engine can generate electricity. But precisely because fire and water are antagonists, they must be tended carefully. If a steam engine gets too hot, it may explode. If you do not watch a boiling kettle, the water may boil over and extinguish the fire, or the water will evaporate away. Thus water and fire have to be kept in proper equilibrium in order to avoid trouble. And this requires constant surveillance and care. It is often said that a watched pot never boils, but once the water starts to boil, it needs to be watched.

The task before you is to keep your particular pot boiling, whether it is an enterprise, an achievement, or a relationship with another person. This means that you must keep your eyes open and watch out for the first signs of trouble. Nip problems in the bud before they have a chance to get out of hand. Consider where future difficulties may arise and immediately take steps to forestall them. Keep things balanced and maintain harmony between opposing forces. You may have achieved a great deal, but there is still work to be done in consolidating your achievements and preserving things in proper working order. It is not always glamorous work, but it is necessary. If you are lazy or careless, you will find that things can deteriorate very quickly. But if you are conscientious and pay attention to the situation, you can keep things running smoothly for a long time to come.

THE LINES

The lines for this hexagram are unusually diverse and lack a common metaphor. Lines three, four, and six are closest to the theme of the hexagram as a whole; they call for caution and perseverance in the face of growing dangers (line three) and possible decay or deterioration (lines four and six). Line two advises patience when things do not go well, while line one counsels the exercise of self-control. Line five offers a different theme altogether, arguing that sincerity is more important than ostentation.

Initial Nine:

Dragging his wheels,
His tail gets wet.
No blame.

To drag one's wheels means to slow down to avoid losing control. To get one's tail wet means a setback or minor inconvenience. In this case it is unpleasant but hardly fatal.

You are making progress, but it would be wise not to press too hard or try to advance too rapidly. Steady, step-by-step progress is the best approach. Remain grounded and maintain a realistic, balanced attitude. This will help guard against errors and carelessness caused by overenthusiasm. And it will also keep you safe from the anxieties and doubts that inevitably arise when you start to feel the pressure and the expectations created by your previous success. There is no need to become worried or disheartened. Now is not the time to back down, just as now is not the time to become reckless or imprudent. Instead, you must finish what you have started and carry your work through to the end. What you have begun will doubtless challenge you, and you may suffer some temporary embarrassments and setbacks. But if you keep moving forward, it will not matter much in the end, and you will be without blame.

Six in the Second Place (Ruling Line)

The wife loses her veil.
Do not pursue.
In seven days you will get it.

To lose one's veil means that one is exposed. Seven days represents a complete cycle of time. Hence the advice is to wait until events have played themselves out and a new cycle begins.

You face a temporary setback. It is not serious. Don't try to force matters. Have patience and wait for things to adjust themselves. You will get what you want in due time.

Another interpretation of the text is that you may be exposed or put in a compromising position either through carelessness or through circumstances for which you are not to blame. As a result, you may be weakened and people may withdraw their support from you. Do not worry. Don't try to stonewall or cover up. Accept the situation and the change in your circumstances with grace. Maintain your principles and act with integrity. Behaving appropriately in a difficult situation will demonstrate your true character. Eventually, confidence in you will be restored.

Nine in the Third Place

The Exalted Ancestor
Attacks the Demon Territory.
After three years he conquers it.
Inferior people should not be employed.

The Exalted Ancestor is King Wu Ding of the Shang. The Demon Territory was northwest of the Shang state and inhabited by a people whom the Shang regarded as barbarians. The idea is that great undertakings require commensurate effort. Moreover, once a new political order has been established, a wise ruler installs capable people to oversee it.

You would like to achieve something very ambitious. If you work hard and devote yourself to the attainment of your goal, you will ultimately prevail. When you do so, however, you must not squander what you have achieved. Do not employ people who are unskilled, untrustworthy, or unreliable. Take particular care to establish firm foundations for the new situation. Above all, do not cut corners or let things slide simply because you have enjoyed an initial success. Securing your victory is as important as obtaining it in the first place.

Six in the Fourth Place

The finest clothes turn into rags.
Be careful all day long.

Fine clothes are a symbol of culture and refinement. "The finest clothes turn into rags" means that even at the height of civilization the seeds of deterioration are present and will prevail if they are not properly cabined and neutralized.

Even though things are going well, do not be fooled. The situation already contains elements of decay and disorder. It is important to be on the lookout for problems hidden just beneath the surface of things. Remedy emerging difficulties before they have had a chance to grow larger. Be disciplined and do not let the people you work with become careless or lazy. Only if you exercise prudence and caution can you keep things sailing smoothly.

Nine in the Fifth Place

The neighbor in the east who slaughters an ox
Does not compare with the neighbor in the west
And his small offering.
For this truly receives blessings.

The "small offering" is the *yue* sacrifice. It was the most meager of sacrifices, brought during the spring when resources were low. It was small in absolute terms but significant in proportion to the time. Hence it symbolizes the genuine devotion that lies behind a modest exterior.

Be sincere and genuine in your words and deeds. You do not have to show off in order to impress people. Avoid extravagant gestures and ostentatious displays. They will exhaust your resources. Live your life simply and take comfort in simple things. Do not throw your weight around or try to overpower people. It is better to act modestly and unpretentiously but with devotion and true feeling. Then you will influence people in exactly the right way. In the long run, doing the little things well and for the right reasons will bring you happiness and good fortune. Heaping up small advantages consistently over time will achieve more than a massive effort performed in a single try.

Six at the Top

He gets his head wet. Danger.

The text concerns fording a great stream. One gets one's head wet when one acts imprudently and waits too long to finish the crossing. Delaying allows the tide to rise and the currents to sweep forward. As a result, one gets in over one's head.

Do not rest on your laurels. Once you start something, make sure that you carry it through to the end. Don't assume that things will naturally take care of themselves. If you fail to follow through at the right time, you will endanger everything you have worked for. When you begin a course of action, you necessarily take on responsibilities. Don't shirk them or you will be in trouble. You must keep moving forward until your success is secured.

NOTES

63.GI "Contemplates difficulties," etc. Cf. Wilhelm/Baynes: "Takes thought of misfortune / And arms himself against it in advance."

63.1 "Dragging." Or, "He breaks." Cf. 64.2.

63.1 "His tail gets wet." Or, "He gets his tail in the water" (Wilhelm/Baynes).

63.2 "veil." *fu:* head ornament, wig, curtain, veil.

63.2 "Do not pursue," etc. Or, "Do not run after it." Cf. 38.1, 51.2.

63.3 "The Exalted Ancestor." *gao zong:* high ancestor. Or, "Illustrious Ancestor." This refers to the Shang king Wu Ding, who ruled about two hundred years before the Zhou conquered the Shang. His reign is traditionally assigned the dates 1324–1266 B.C.

63.3 "Attacked." Or, "Disciplined."

63.3 "Demon Territory." Or, "Devil's Country." *gui fang:* land of the Gui, a northwestern tribe bordering on the Shang territory, who were generally regarded as barbarians.

63.3 "Inferior people should not be employed." Cf. 7.6.

63.4 "The finest clothes turn into rags." *ru you yi ru:* literally, "the jacket has clothes in tatters." The line can be translated in several different ways. For *ru* (fine clothes), some read *ru* (wet), i.e., "For wetness one has rags," or "Use rags to deal with leaks [in a boat that ferries one across]."

63.4 "Be careful all day long." *ri jie:* day cautious.

63.5 "does not compare with," etc. Cf. 54.5.

63.5 "small offering." *yue:* sacrifice. Cf. 45.2, 46.2.

63.5 "truly receives blessings." Or, "really receives the blessing." Cf. Wilhelm/Baynes: "The neighbor in the east who slaughters an ox / Does not attain as much real happiness / As the neighbor in the west."

SIXTY-FOUR

Wei Ji • Before Completion

☲
☵

Keywords:

Not yet across
Before the end
Nearly home and dry
Bringing order out of confusion
Exercising caution and circumspection

Above: Li • Fire
Below: Kan • Water

Wei Ji means "not yet across the stream," or "not yet forded." It is the opposite of Hexagram 63, Ji Ji (After Completion). Ji Ji is concerned with maintaining order and avoiding the onset of decay. It represents the end of an old cycle that has culminated in perfect harmony and has now begun to decline. By contrast, Wei Ji involves a new cycle that begins in chaos and strives toward concord. It represents a difficult period of confusion that nevertheless has all of the elements necessary for eventual success. It is all a matter of putting everything in the right place. Thus the theme of Wei Ji is how to bring matters from disharmony to harmony and from chaos to order.

This theme is reflected in the structure of the hexagram. All of the yang lines are in even-numbered places, and all of the yin lines are in odd-numbered places. This is the exact opposite of how things should be. However, things are not completely disordered. The first and fourth, second and fifth, and third and sixth lines correspond, that is, a yin line in one position complements a yang line in the other. So even though the lines are placed incorrectly, the beginnings of harmony are still present.

Wei Ji can be understood as a further development of Hexagram 12, Pi (Standstill). In Pi three yang lines sit above three yin lines. Heaven and earth move in different directions; this means disharmony. However, in Wei Ji two of the yang lines have descended to mix with the yin lines (or, in the alternative, the second and fifth lines have switched places). So Wei Ji is more auspicious. The situation is not perfect, but there is greater balance and there is significant potential for future success. However, much work is necessary to move to Hexagram 11, Tai (Peace), in which three yang lines are at the bottom and heaven and earth are in complete accord.

The uncertainty of the situation is also symbolized by the two constituent trigrams: Kan (Water) is below and sinks downward; Li (Fire) is above and shoots upward. Water and fire are mutually antagonistic and are moving in opposite directions. If they could cooperate, they could produce great energy (think of a steam engine). The theme of Wei Ji is to take these disparate elements and put them in their proper places so that they can work together for good.

Wei Ji, and not Ji Ji, is the final hexagram in the *Book of Changes* because the processes of change never cease. The completion of a cycle (as in Ji Ji) is not the end but is only the beginning of a new cycle. Such is the nature of the universe, and such is the nature of human life. Wei Ji reminds us that we are always in the middle of things, between the past and the future, partly in harmony and partly in confusion, but always with the promise of ultimate success. With this message of optimism and hope the *Book of Changes* draws to a close.

THE JUDGMENT

Before Completion. Success.
But if the little fox,
Almost across the river,
Gets its tail wet,
There is nothing for which this is beneficial.

You face a difficult situation. The elements for successful change are there, but everything seems confused and unsettled. It is up to you to bring order out of chaos. It is a great responsibility. The problem is, you don't yet know what to do. There are contradictory indications and contradictory forces at work in the situation. You feel tugged at from all sides. Yet you must make a decision.

The text compares your situation to that of an old fox that is trying to cross a frozen river. It does not know where the ice is too thin. Therefore, it proceeds slowly and cautiously, listening carefully for the first sounds of a crack in the surface. No matter how far across it is, it does not lose its balance or its caution. By contrast, a young fox lacks this prudence and circumspection; if it rushes ahead boldly when it is nearly across the river, it may fall into the icy waters.

In the same way, when you are trying to bring order to a confusing situation, you must begin slowly and methodically. First of all, decide what your goals truly are. There is no sense starting out if you don't know where you want to go. Clarifying what you want the outcome to be will go a long way toward formulating the right strategy. Second, don't rush matters. Rome wasn't built in a day. Take things one step at a time. Don't try to resolve everything at once. Third, be wary. Take the time to gather information and intelligence. Deliberate thoroughly about the best way to proceed. Be on the lookout for any signs that your strategy is counterproductive. In sum, be like an old fox navigating the ice—cautious, alert, flexible, surefooted, and willing to change directions at a moment's notice. If you can keep your wits about you, you will get across.

THE IMAGE

Fire over water:
This is the image of things Before Completion.
Thus the superior person
Carefully distinguishes things
So that everything is in its place.

Fire is above, water below. Fire shoots upward; water sinks downward to find its own level. These two opposites are working at cross purposes rather than synergistically.

Creating order out of chaos means bringing opposites together in a harmonious relationship. To do that you have to understand the elements of the situation and all the forces at your disposal. You have to get people working together rather than against each other, and you have to get all of your resources working together in sync rather than randomly and haphazardly. Bringing order means recognizing the different natures of different things and assigning each to its proper place in a larger scheme.

What is true of the world outside you is also true of yourself. The confusing situation has probably left you a bit confused as well. And, in any case, the world just seems more disorganized and befuddling when your mind is in upheaval. If you want to succeed, you will have to bring order to your thoughts and your actions. That means setting priorities and clarifying your values. You must sort out your feelings and put your emotions in their proper place. Then you will know what steps to take.

This is a crucial time. The decisions you make now could determine whether you will ultimately succeed or fail. For this reason, take the time to balance and center yourself. Think things through carefully before you proceed. You shouldn't expect a resolution of the situation immediately. Straightening things out will take time, and you will not know for a while whether your efforts have paid off. Having to wait in uncertainty may make you anxious and insecure. But if you rush matters, you may spoil all the hard work you have done so far. Therefore, it is essential to be patient and methodical. If you are willing to proceed slowly, one step at a time, you will have the best chance of reaching a successful conclusion. The same principles apply to your inner self. You are trying to bring order to your own life. You will not do this in a single day. There is no point in holding yourself to unrealistic standards. You may be uncertain whether you are up to the task. But you need not worry. Have faith in yourself. You have every reason to be hopeful.

THE LINES

The lines tell the story of a struggle that is ultimately victorious. The first three lines concern preparations for the struggle. In line four the battle is on, and one must summon all one's determination to prevail, but in line five the result is ultimately victorious. The victors then celebrate, but line six warns that abandoning moderation risks losing what has been gained.

Initial Six

He gets his tail wet.
Humiliation.

A fox who tries to cross the water too quickly gets his tail wet. The text symbolizes a setback that could have been avoided through prudent conduct.

You would like to press forward and settle everything. You want to bring order out of chaos and complete your mission. Don't get carried away by your enthusiasm. You don't understand all of the elements of the situation. Things are more complicated than they appear. If you act too hastily, you will simply make everything worse. Events must take their natural course, and you will not be able to complete things until the time is right. Therefore, you must restrain yourself for now. Acting precipitously will only exacerbate a delicate situation and ultimately bring you humiliation.

Nine in the Second Place

He drags his wheels.
Perseverance brings good fortune.

To drag one's wheels means to slow down in order to avoid moving too precipitously and losing control. One applies the brakes now in order to develop strength for later action.

Although you should prepare yourself for action, the time is not yet right to move forward. Hold back, plan carefully, and accumulate your resources. Keep your goal firmly in mind. Gather your strength and maintain your determination to act promptly and decisively when the right opportunity presents itself. Do not be discouraged. Patience now will pay dividends later on. As the text says, "Perseverance brings good fortune."

Six in the Third Place

Before completion, attack brings misfortune.
It is beneficial to cross the great river.

You cannot handle this situation by yourself. You have not planned correctly and you lack sufficient resources. The problem is that circumstances are not properly aligned for a successful result. If you move forward on your own, you will be defeated. Then you will squander what resources you have and endanger others as well as yourself. Hence you must retreat and start over again. You must create a new environment that is more propitious for success. Gather support from friends and allies. Get the help you need. The endeavor you propose is a great one. If you plan carefully and create the right conditions for action, you will ultimately succeed.

Nine in the Fourth Place

Perseverance brings good fortune.
Regrets vanish.
Like thunder he attacks the Demon Territory.
In three years, great realms are awarded.

The Devil's Country was a barbarian state northwest of the Shang empire. It represents not only danger but also barbarism and decadence, whether within oneself or in others. The text suggests that strong, decisive action is necessary and will take considerable time—symbolized by a period of three years—but that it will pay off in the end. The great realms awarded by the victorious Shang king symbolize the rewards of a valiant battle against evil and chaos.

You face a difficult and prolonged contest. It may be a struggle between you and another person, or it may be a struggle within yourself. In either case, important principles and values are at stake. You must marshal all of your courage and determination to win, for once you begin the battle, you must fight it out until the end without doubts or misgivings. As the text says, one should have no regrets if the cause is a just one. It may take all of your resources to triumph, but you can prevail, and in the end your perseverance will be richly rewarded.

Six in the Fifth Place (Ruling Line)

Perseverance brings good fortune.
No remorse.
The brilliance of the superior person shines forth.
He possesses truth and sincerity.
Good fortune.

Because of your patience, devotion, and unflagging determination, you have achieved a great victory. A new era dawns. If you have maintained your integrity and kept faith with your principles, the strength of your personality will naturally draw others toward you. You will win their support and confidence, and together you can achieve great things. Your leadership and steadfast uprightness will bring good fortune to you and to everyone concerned.

Nine at the Top

He possesses truth and sincerity.
He drinks wine and celebrates.
No blame.
But if he gets his head wet,
The one who has truth and sincerity
Loses it.

To get one's head wet is to become intoxicated and to engage in excessive, reckless, or arrogant behavior. As a result, one loses the confidence of others.

The struggle is over and you are about to emerge victorious. It is appropriate to celebrate and enjoy your good fortune. There is no blame in looking forward to the promise of good times ahead. But it is important not to get carried away, or to succumb to haughtiness, arrogance, or carelessness. Do not be self-indulgent or go to extremes. Even in the midst of celebration the wise person must remember the virtues of moderation and modesty. If you do something imprudent or foolish now, people will lose confidence in you. By losing their trust, you will lose one of your most valuable assets and you will undermine all you have labored for. As you go forward into the future, remember the vision and the ideals that brought you to this point, and maintain the habits of perseverance and determination that helped secure your victory. Only in this way can you remain without blame.

NOTES

64.0 "Almost across the river." *qi ji:* at the point of crossing over the stream. Or, "After nearly completing the crossing."

64.GI "Carefully distinguishes things." Or, "Considers the differing nature of things," "Carefully discriminates the nature of things."

64.GI "So that everything is in its place." Or, "So that each finds its place," "And so keeps each in its proper position," "And situates them in their correct places" (Lynn).

64.2 "drags." Or, "brakes." Cf. 63.1.

64.3 "attack." *zhong:* chastise, attack. This is often translated elsewhere in the *Book of Changes* as "to set forth," or "to undertake." An attack is a metaphor for an undertaking. However, given the context, "attack" seems most appropriate, i.e., that one should not attack until one is fully prepared. Another reading might be "to undertake something new," or "to set forth on another project," meaning that one should finish what one has started before launching a new enterprise.

64.4 "Demon Territory." *gui fang:* land of the Gui. Cf. 63.3.

64.5 "The brilliance of the superior person shines forth." *jun zi zhi guang*. Or, "The superior person is radiant (brilliant, glorious)." Cf. 20.4. Another possible translation is "The superior person shines forth with truth and sincerity." Cf. Wilhelm / Baynes: "The light of the superior man is true."

64.6 "He drinks wine and celebrates." *yu yin jiu:* at drinking wine.

64.6 "The one who has truth and sincerity / Loses it." *you fu shi shi:* possessing truth loses this. *Fu* might refer to inner truth, sincerity, trustworthiness, the subject's self-confidence, the subject's ability to trust others, or the confidence and trust they repose in the subject. Thus the line could be translated in many different ways: "Having [too much] confidence, he acts incorrectly," or, "He loses the confidence (trust) he has."

Appendix:

The Sequences of the Trigrams and Hexagrams

Over the centuries scholars have devoted enormous study to the order of the trigrams and hexagrams. The order of the trigrams is important mostly for mystical studies like geomancy *(feng shui)* and Chinese astrology. The received order of the hexagrams has symbolic importance and its origins have long been a topic of debate. Moreover, because the trigrams and hexagrams can be represented both as geometrical figures and as binary numbers, the sequences of the trigrams and hexagrams have produced endless fascination for scholars with a mathematical cast of mind. This appendix offers some of the basics of a very complicated subject.

The Earlier Heaven and Later Heaven Arrangements of the Trigrams

If we take the sequence of the trigrams generated from the Great Ultimate (Tai Ji):

Tai Ji
(The Great Ultimate)

Yin				Yang			
Greater Yin (Winter)		Lesser Yang (Autumn)		Lesser Yin (Spring)		Greater Yang (Summer)	
Kun Earth	Gen Mountain	Kan Water	Xun Wind	Zhen Thunder	Li Fire	Dui Lake	Qian Heaven

Generation of the Trigrams
from the Tai Ji (Great Ultimate)

and arrange them in a circle, we get a famous arrangement called the earlier heaven arrangement (*xian tian,* "preceding heaven"). The earlier heaven arrangement identifies the trigrams with the points of a compass. Note that in Chinese maps the south is traditionally placed at the top and the north is placed at the bottom:

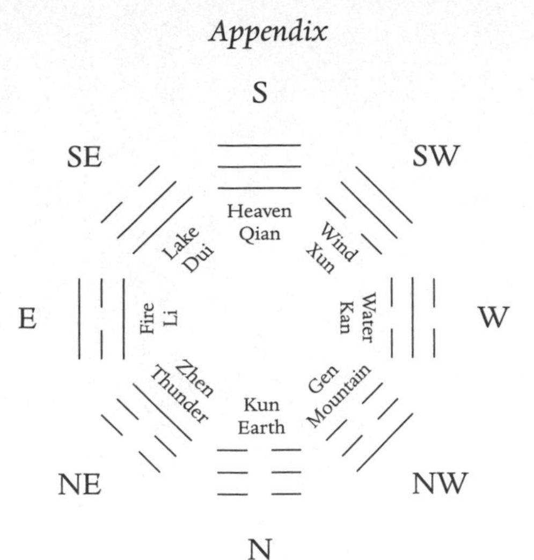

The Earlier Heaven Arrangement

Qian (Heaven, pure yang) is placed at the south, the sunny side (when one is located in the Northern Hemisphere). Kun (Earth, pure yin) is placed at the north, the shady side. The other hexagrams are placed counterclockwise from these two poles. Qian is followed by Dui, Li, and Zhen, while Kun is followed by Gen, Kan, and Xun. Note that the earlier heaven arrangement is symmetrical. Trigrams that are opposite each other in the circle are complementary: each has yin lines where the other has yang lines, and vice versa.

The earlier heaven arrangement is also sometimes called the Outer World, or Fu Xi, arrangement. Fu Xi was the legendary emperor who is supposed to have invented the trigrams. There is no evidence that Fu Xi actually existed, much less that he created this particular arrangement. In fact, it may have been devised as late as the eleventh century A.D.

There is, however, another famous arrangement of the trigrams, which assigns the trigrams to compass points differently. It is called the later heaven arrangement (*hou tian,* "following heaven"):

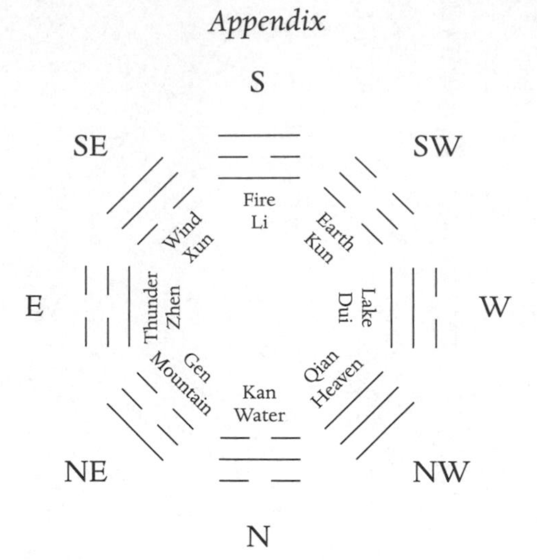

The Later Heaven Arrangement

The later heaven arrangement is sometimes called the Inner World, or King Wen, arrangement. King Wen was the founder of the Zhou Dynasty, who according to legend first created the hexagrams by doubling the trigrams and who also wrote the hexagram judgments. Unlike the earlier heaven arrangement, the later heaven arrangement is not symmetrical. Rather, it follows a clockwise cycle that is derived from a passage in the Eighth of the Ten Wings:

> God comes forth in the sign of the Arousing [Zhen];
> He brings all things to completion in the sign of the Gentle [Xun];
> He causes creatures to perceive one another in the sign of the Clinging [Li];
> He causes them to serve one another in the sign of the Receptive [Kun].
> He gives them joy in the sign of the Joyous [Dui];
> He battles in the sign of the Creative [Qian];
> He toils in the sign of the Abysmal [Kan];
> He brings them to perfection in the sign of Keeping Still [Gen].[1]

The first sign, Zhen, symbolizing spring and the beginnings of life, is placed in the east, where the sun rises. All of the other trigrams follow in clockwise order.

The later heaven arrangement associates Kun (Earth) with the south-

1. Willhelm/Baynes, Eighth Wing (*Shogua*), in *I Ching*, p. 268.

west. The southwest (or "the south and the west") are mentioned in the hexagram judgments 2.0 and 40.0. The commentaries state that this refers to the characteristics associated with earth—receptiveness, acquiescence, and docility. The passage quoted above from the Ten Wings suggests that the later heaven arrangement was known by the Han Dynasty. If so, this suggests that despite its name, the so-called "later" heaven arrangement is actually earlier than the so-called "earlier" heaven arrangement.

In fact, the terms "earlier than heaven" *(xian tian)* and "later than heaven" *(hou tian)* are never used to describe trigrams or hexagrams in the *Book of Changes* itself. They were applied by later commentators, possibly as late as the Song Dynasty. The expressions are taken from a passage in the Seventh of the Ten Wings, the *Wenyan,* or Words of the Text: "When [the superior person] precedes heaven, heaven is not contrary to him, and when he follows heaven, he obeys the timing of its moments."[2] They were confusingly called "earlier heaven" and "later heaven" and used to describe different sequences of trigrams and hexagrams.

The earlier heaven and later heaven arrangements are important because they associate the trigrams with directions. For this reason they became crucial to the development of geomancy *(feng shui),* which tries to determine how buildings should be harmonized with their surrounding landscape.

The two arrangements are also associated with two famous diagrams,[3] called the Luo Shu (writing from the River Luo) and the He Tu (Yellow River Map). Each consists of a series of numbers represented by black and white dots—black dots for the even (yin) numbers, white dots for the odd (yang) numbers.

2. Commentary on the Words of the Text *(Wenyen),* quoted in Lynn, ***The Classic of Changes,*** p. 138.
3. See The Great Treatise, I, xi, 8 (Lynn trans., p.66).

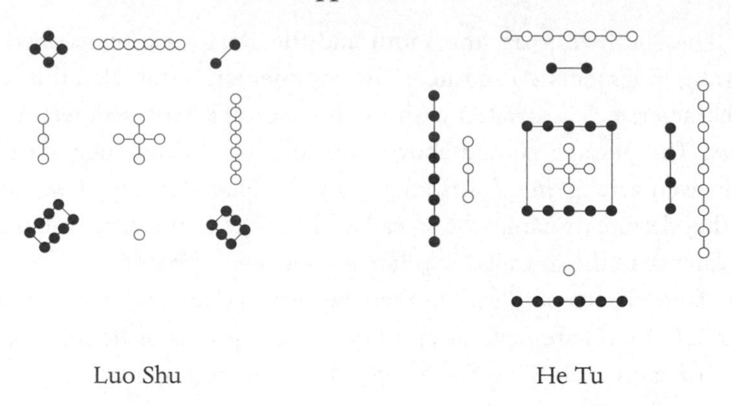

Luo Shu He Tu

The later heaven sequence is often associated with the Luo Shu; the earlier heaven sequence is associated with the He Tu. A number of ingenious numerological theories have been offered to explain these associations; they are beyond the scope of this book.

The King Wen Sequence of the Hexagrams

Today we know the hexagrams in a numerical sequence from 1 to 64. This sequence is sometimes called the King Wen, or later heaven, sequence. (There is no obvious connection between the later heaven sequence of hexagrams and the later heaven sequence of the trigrams mentioned above.) The King Wen sequence of hexagrams is divided into two halves. Hexagrams 1–30 are called the Upper Canon; Hexagrams 31–64 are called the Lower Canon. The Upper Canon begins with Qian (pure yang) and Kun (pure yin) and ends with Kan (Water, or The Abyss) and Li (Fire, or Radiance). The Lower Canon begins with Xian (Mutual Influence) and Heng (Enduring), and ends with Ji Ji (After Completion) and Wei Ji (Before Completion).

According to the traditional explanation, the Upper Canon is supposed to be concerned with metaphysical questions, because it begins with Heaven and Earth and ends with Water and Fire. The Lower Canon is supposed to be concerned with human affairs, because it begins with Influence (symbolizing courtship) and Enduring (symbolizing marriage), which are basic human relations. However, many of the hexagrams in the Upper Canon concern human society, including 6 (Conflict), 7 (The Army), 8 (Union), 13 (Fellowship with People), and 17 (Following).

The King Wen sequence consists of thirty-two pairs, each consisting of a hexagram and its inversion. (The inversion of a hexagram is the hexagram turned upside down.) The only exceptions are the eight hexagrams that are identical to their inversions: 1, 2, 27, 28, 29, 30, 61, and 62. When these eight are turned upside down, they do not change. Therefore, in the King Wen sequence each of these eight hexagrams is paired with its complement. The complement of a hexagram is produced when every yang line is turned into a yin line and vice versa. Thus, Qian (six yang lines) is the complement of Kun (six yin lines). There is no clear principle that explains which hexagram in the pair of complements comes first and which comes second.

111111 The Dynamic (1)	000000 The Receptive (2)	100010 Difficulty in the Beginning (3)	010001 Youthful Inexperience (4)	111010 Waiting (5)	010111 Conflict (6)	010000 The Army (7)	000010 Union (8)
111011 Small Accumulation (9)	110111 Treading (10)	111000 Peace (11)	000111 Standstill (12)	101111 Fellowship with People (13)	111101 Great Possession (14)	001000 Modesty (15)	000100 Enthusiasm (16)
100110 Following (17)	011001 Remedying (18)	110000 Overseeing (19)	000011 Viewing (20)	100101 Biting Through (21)	101001 Adornment (22)	000001 Splitting Apart (23)	100000 Return (24)
100111 Innocence (25)	111001 Great Accumulation (26)	100001 Nourishment (27)	011110 Greatness in Excess (28)	010010 The Abyss (29)	101101 Radiance (30)	001110 Mutual Influence (31)	011100 Enduring (32)

001111 Retreat (33)	111100 Great Power (34)	000101 Progress (35)	101000 Darkening of the Light (36)	101011 The Family (37)	110101 Opposition (38)	001010 Obstruction (39)	010100 Deliverance (40)
110001 Decrease (41)	100011 Increase (42)	111110 Resolution (43)	011111 Encounter (44)	000110 Gathering Together (45)	011000 Ascending (46)	010110 Oppression (47)	011010 The Well (48)
101110 Revolution (49)	011101 The Caldron (50)	100100 Shock (51)	001001 Keeping Still (52)	001011 Developing Gradually (53)	110100 The Marrying Maiden (54)	101100 Abundance (55)	001101 The Wanderer (56)
011011 Gentle Influence (57)	110110 Joy (58)	010011 Dispersion (59)	110010 Limitation (60)	110011 Inner Truth (61)	001100 Exceeding Smallness (62)	101010 After Completion (63)	010101 Before Completion (64)

The King Wen Sequence of the Hexagrams with Binary Equivalents

Countless theories have been offered trying to show the basis of the King Wen sequence. Many commentators have speculated that the sequence is actually determined by the meaning of the hexagrams, which progress from the basic principles of yin and yang and end with the principles of completion and incompletion. The last hexagram, Wei Ji (Before Completion), signifies that the process of change never stops, so that the cycle must begin again with Qian and Kun. Even so, it is difficult to figure out how the principles of the different hexagrams flow into each other. The Ninth Wing, called the Sequence of the Hexagrams *(Xugua),* tries to offer a theory of how one hexagram follows another. It is often quite strained and unconvincing.[4] In his book *Rediscovering the I Ching,* Gregory Whincup has offered the theory that the sequence of hexagrams tells the story of the rise of a nobleman in Zhou times who overthrows his leader and assumes command.

Other commentators have tried to show that the sequence can be explained by some geometrical or mathematical pattern in the structure of the successive pairs of hexagrams. None of these theories is particularly persuasive. In fact, it is likely that if there was a pattern to the sequence, it was disrupted or disturbed at some point in history. The best evidence of this is that although the ancient Chinese were quite fond of symmetry, the Upper Canon and the Lower Canon are asymmetrical. One has thirty hexagrams and the other has thirty-four.

That asymmetry, along with a few other peculiarities in the King Wen sequence, may give us some clue as to what the original order might have been. For example, as noted above, eight hexagrams are their own inversions and are therefore paired with their complements. But they are not distributed evenly throughout the sequence. They appear at Numbers 1, 2, 27, 28, 29, 30, 61, and 62. Three of these pairs of hexagrams fall in the Upper Canon, and one falls in the Lower Canon. In addition, eight other hexagrams have the property that their inversion is also their complement: 11, 12, 17,18, 53, 54, 63, 64. Of these eight hexagrams, Numbers 11, 12, 53, and 54 are symmetrically placed—11 and 12 are ten hexagrams from the beginning, 53 and 54 are ten hexagrams from the end—but the others are not. All of this suggests that if there was an earlier symmetrical ordering based on the structure of the hexagrams, it was disrupted at some point.

4. Here is an example, trying to explain how one goes from Viewing [Hexagram 20] to Biting Through [Hexagram 21]: "Only after something can be viewed is there the possibility to one come together with it. This is why *Guan* [Viewing, Hexagram 20] is followed by *Shihe* [Bite Together]. The *he* [in *Shihe*] means *he* [unite, i.e., join the jaws together]." Lynn, p. 267.

A more logical and symmetrical ordering would have two Canons of thirty-two hexagrams each. Each Canon would begin with a pair of complementary hexagrams and end with another pair. That would mean that the first pair of the Upper Canon would have been Numbers 1 and 2 (Qian, Heaven, and Kun, Earth) and the last would have been what are now Numbers 27 and 28 (Yi, Nourishment, and Da Guo, Greatness in Excess). The Lower Canon would then have begun with what are now Numbers 29 (Xi Kan, the Abyss, or Water) and 30 (Li, Radiance, or Fire) and ended with what are now Numbers 61 (Zhong Fu, Inner Truth) and 62 (Xiao Guo, Exceeding Smallness).

However, at some point, the editors of the *Book of Changes* may have decided to emphasize the theme that the cycle of change is never-ending. Therefore, the hexagrams that are now numbered 63 (Ji Ji, After Completion) and 64 (Wei Ji, Before Completion) were moved to their present positions at the end of the sequence. Note that these two hexagrams have the additional characteristic of being inversions as well as complements of each other. Finally, one other pair was probably moved from the Upper Canon to the Lower Canon to produce the asymmetry we now see. The most likely candidates are Hexagrams 43 (Guai, Resolution) and 44 (Guo, Encounter). The reason is that each has five yang lines and one yin line. All other hexagrams of this type are located in the Upper Canon.

The King Wen sequence is not the only one that has been used to organize the book. The Mawangdui manuscript, which has been dated to 168 B.C., arranges the hexagrams based on the structure of their constituent trigrams. It does not divide the material into an Upper and Lower Canon. The structure of the first four of the Ten Wings is based on the King Wen sequence and its division into Upper and Lower Canons. Therefore, the sequence was probably well known by the time of the composition of the first four of the Ten Wings—the last part of the third century or the beginning of the second century B.C. Another possibility is that the people who wrote the first four wings also established the King Wen sequence. However, the existence of the Mawangdui manuscript suggests that the King Wen ordering may not have become canonical until much later.

The Fu Xi Sequence and Binary Arithmetic

In the eleventh century, the Song Dynasty philosopher Shao Yong (1011–1077) produced a different sequence of hexagrams based on binary arithmetic. He began with the generation of the trigrams by successively adding yin and yang lines from the top.

Tai Ji
(The Great Ultimate)

Yin	Yang

Greater Yin (Winter)	Lesser Yang (Autumn)	Lesser Yin (Spring)	Greater Yang (Summer)

Kun Earth	Gen Mountain	Kan Water	Xun Wind	Zhen Thunder	Li Fire	Dui Lake	Qian Heaven

Generation of the Trigrams

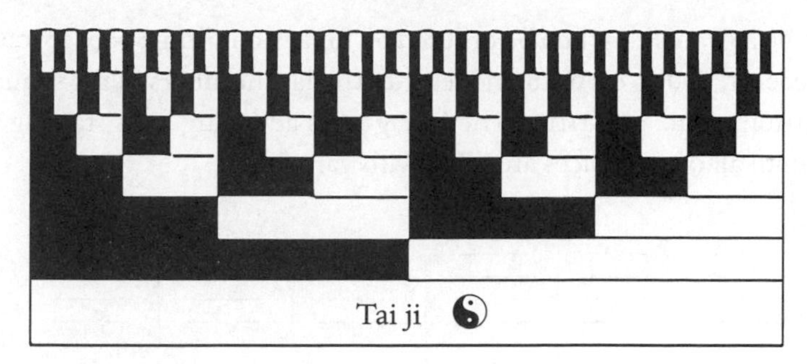

Shao Yong's diagram

Then he added three more layers, creating a set of 2^6 or 64 combinations.

In this diagram the shaded elements are yin and the bright elements are yang. Reading the columns from left to right produces all sixty-four hexagrams.

Shao Yong's diagram showed that the sixty-four hexagrams could be arranged in a simple mathematical sequence, which we know today as binary counting. He called the sequence the Fu Xi sequence, or the earlier heaven *(xian tian)* sequence of hexagrams, to distinguish it from the King Wen order, which is sometimes called the later heaven *(hou tian)* sequence.

In 1701 a young French Jesuit priest named Joachim Bouvet, who had been doing missionary work in China, sent the German philosopher Wilhelm Leibniz a copy of Shao Yong's diagram. Leibniz, who had outlined the principles of binary mathematics in 1679, was astounded to learn that the Chinese had anticipated his discovery by centuries.

The Fu Xi sequence can be described mathematically as follows: Any hexagram can be represented as a series of zeros (for broken or yin lines) and ones (for solid or yang lines).

Using the convention that the top line represents the smallest or rightmost digit, every hexagram can be described as a binary number from 0 to 63, or in binary terms, from 000000 to 111111. Here are three examples:

———	1	— —	0	— —	0
———	2	— —	0	———	2
— —	0	———	4	— —	0
— —	0	———	8	———	8
— —	0	———	16	— —	0
— —	0	— —	0	———	32
Guan Viewing	3 (000011)	Heng Enduring	28 (011100)	Ji Ji After Completion	42 (101010)

Binary Equivalents

The hexagrams can then be ordered by binary counting: 000000, 000001, 000010, 000011, and so on until one reaches the last numbers in the sequence, 111100, 111101, 111110, and 111111. The hexagrams add yang lines starting from the top until all of the places are filled with yang lines:

<table>
<tr><td>000000
The
Receptive
(2)</td><td>000001
Splitting
Apart
(23)</td><td>000010
Union
(8)</td><td>000011
Viewing
(20)</td><td>000100
Enthusiasm
(16)</td><td>000101
Progress
(35)</td><td>000110
Gathering
Together
(45)</td><td>000111
Standstill
(12)</td></tr>
<tr><td>001000
Modesty
(15)</td><td>001001
Keeping
Still
(52)</td><td>001010
Obstruction
(39)</td><td>001011
Developing
Gradually
(53)</td><td>001100
Exceeding
Smallness
(62)</td><td>001101
The
Wanderer
(56)</td><td>001110
Mutual
Influence
(31)</td><td>001111
Retreat
(33)</td></tr>
<tr><td>010000
The
Army
(7)</td><td>010001
Youthful
Inexperience
(4)</td><td>010010
The
Abyss
(29)</td><td>010011
Dispersion
(59)</td><td>010100
Deliverance
(40)</td><td>010101
Before
Completion
(64)</td><td>010110
Oppression
(47)</td><td>010111
Conflict
(6)</td></tr>
<tr><td>011000
Ascending
(46)</td><td>011001
Remedying
(18)</td><td>011010
The
Well
(48)</td><td>011011
Gentle
Influence
(57)</td><td>011100
Enduring
(32)</td><td>011101
The
Caldron
(50)</td><td>011110
Greatness
in Excess
(28)</td><td>011111
Encounter
(44)</td></tr>
</table>

Appendix

100000 Return (24)	100001 Nourishment (27)	100010 Difficulty in the Beginning (3)	100011 Increase (42)	100100 Shock (51)	100101 Biting Through (21)	100110 Following (17)	100111 Innocence (25)
101000 Darkening of the Light (36)	101001 Adornment (22)	101010 After Completion (63)	101011 The Family (37)	101100 Abundance (55)	101101 Radiance (30)	101110 Revolution (49)	101111 Fellowship with People (13)
110000 Overseeing (19)	110001 Decrease (41)	110010 Limitation (60)	110011 Inner Truth (61)	110100 The Marrying Maiden (54)	110101 Opposition (38)	110110 Joy (58)	110111 Treading (10)
111000 Peace (11)	111001 Great Accumulation (26)	111010 Waiting (5)	111011 Small Accumulation (9)	111100 Great Power (34)	111101 Great Possession (14)	111110 Resolution (43)	111111 The Dynamic (1)

Binary Construction of the Hexagrams in the Fu Xi Sequence.
(Equivalents in the King Wen sequence
are noted in parentheses.)

The Fu Xi sequence can also be constructed in the opposite direction, using the convention that the bottom line represents the smallest or rightmost digit. Then the yang lines are added starting from the bottom of the hexagram and move upward. In this sequence the first hexagram would be The Receptive (000000), followed by Return (000001), The Army (000010), Overseeing (000011), Darkening of the Light (000101), Peace (000111), and so on. The sequence continues until it reaches The Dynamic (111111). I call this the reverse Fu Xi sequence. Starting from the bottom instead of the top produces a different set of equivalents. For example, in the traditional Fu Xi representation, the binary number 000011 is equivalent to Hexagram 20 (Viewing) in the King Wen sequence. In the reverse Fu Xi representation, the binary number 000011 is equivalent to its inversion, Hexagram 19 (Overseeing).

Bibliographical Essay

The following essay describes the sources I used in preparing this book, which can also serve as a guide to further reading. I have divided the sources into five basic categories: (1) the Chinese text, (2) translations, (3) commentaries, (4) discussions of divination practices, (5) the history and development of the *Book of Changes,* and (6) general background materials on Chinese history and philosophy.

The Text

The standard Chinese text of the *Zhouyi* is available in many places. Liu Dajun and Lin Zhongjun, *The I Ching: Text and Annotated Translation* (Jinan, China: Shandong Friendship Publishing House, 1995), translated into English by Fu Youde and Frank Lauran, contains the received text plus commentaries written by two modern Chinese scholars. Chan Chiu Ming, *Book of Changes: An Interpretation for the Modern Age* (Singapore: Asiapac, 1997), contains the Chinese text for both the *Zhouyi* and the Commentary on the Great Images (which forms part of the Third and Fourth Wings). Both of these translations draw on modern historical studies. The text of the *Zhouyi* is also available online at the I Ching Lexicon (http://home.attbi.com/~cpolish/default.htm). The standard dictionary of Classical Chinese used in preparing the translation is R. H. Mathews, *Mathews' Chinese-English Dictionary* (Cambridge: Harvard University Press, rev. American ed., 1943).

Richard Alan Kunst, "The Original *'Yijing'*: A Text, Phonetic Transcription, Translation, and Indexes, with Sample Glosses (Ph.D. dissertation, 1985) (Ann Arbor: University Microfilms International, 1985), offers not only the standard text of the *Zhouyi* but also a character-by-character translation, as does Wu Jing-Nuan, *Yi Jing* (Washington, D.C., Taoist Study Series, distributed by Honolulu: University of Hawaii Press, 1991). Kunst's unpublished Ph.D. dissertation has been very influential in suggesting how the work might have been understood in the Bronze Age. Wu Jing-Nuan's translation, which also draws on historical scholarship, likewise attempts to strip away neo-Confucian elements. However, he seeks to produce a Daoist interpretation of the text. He translates both the *Zhouyi* and all Ten Wings.

The study of the early history of the *Book of Changes* has been greatly advanced by the discovery of silk manuscripts at Mawangdui dating from 168 B.C. These differ in important respects from the received text of the *Zhouyi*. The order of the hexagrams is different and the text employs different names for several of the hexagrams. Edward Shaughnessy's *I Ching: The Classic of Changes* (New York: Ballantine Books, 1996) contains both the received text and the Mawangdui text for the *Zhouyi*. It also includes versions of those parts of the Ten Wings and additional essays that appear in the Mawangdui manuscripts. Shaughnessy translates the Mawangdui text, using the received text only where the manuscript characters are not legible.

Translations

There are a number of excellent translations of the *Zhouyi* and the Ten Wings in addition to those noted above. They reflect different assumptions and have different emphases, so the choice between them depends on what one is looking for.

The first great translation into English was James Legge, *I Ching: The Book of Changes* (New York: Dover Publishers, 2nd ed., 1975), originally published in 1882. Legge translated all of the Ten Wings as well as the *Zhouyi*. His translation, a significant achievement in its time, is also a piece of Victoriana that is too complicated for most contemporary readers. Legge added additional explanatory materials in brackets to explain the terse language of the original. As a result, many readers find his version confusing. However, the translation is actually quite serviceable once one gets used to his style. The translation is now in the public domain, and Raymond van Over produced a modernized edition, *I Ching* (New York: New American Library, 1971).

The standard English translation of the *Book of Changes* is actually a translation of a translation: Richard Wilhelm's 1924 translation into German, which was rendered into English by Cary Fink Baynes in 1950. Richard Wilhelm, *I Ching: The Book of Changes,* trans. Cary F. Baynes (Princeton: Princeton University Press, 1950; 3d ed., 1967). The Wilhelm/Baynes translation, as it is usually known, is characterized by its beautiful, quasi-biblical style. Wilhelm translated all Ten Wings in addition to the *Zhouyi*. However, he adopted neither of the traditional methods of presenting the material. He placed the *Zhouyi* plus the Commentary on the Great Images together with his own commentaries in Part I; the other Wings appear in the remainder of the book. The result is repetitious but not as confusing as many critics have suggested. John Blofeld, *I Ching: The Book of Change* (New York: Penguin Books, 1965), is a more homespun version that, over the years, has been quite popular as an alternative to Wilhelm/Baynes.

Legge's, Wilhelm's and Blofeld's versions were made in ignorance of the archeological discoveries of the twentieth century, which have greatly changed our understanding of the book and its evolution. As a result, there have been several new scholarly translations of the *I Ching* in the past fifteen years. Several of them—like Kunst's noted above—aim to reconstruct the meaning of the earliest sections of the book to people who lived during the Bronze Age when the core text was originally composed. A few others—like Shaughnessy's translation of the Mawangdui manuscripts—try to reconstruct the meaning of the book during the Han Dynasty (206 B.C.–220 A.D.).

Alfred Huang, *The Complete I Ching: The Definitive Translation by the Taoist Master Alfred Huang* (Rochester, Vt.: Inner Traditions, 1998), is perhaps the finest traditional translation that has appeared since Wilhelm/Baynes. Huang's approach is to provide the simplest possible rendering of the text that does not sacrifice readability. He translates all of the *Book of Changes* except the Great Treatise and the Eighth Wing.

The team of Kerson and Rosemary Huang, by contrast, have attempted to remove all traditional Confucian glosses from their translation: Kerson Huang and Rosemary Huang, *I Ching* (New York: Workman Publishing Co., 1987). They translate only the *Zhouyi*. They also include a brief but excellent historical introduction.

Richard Rutt, *The Book of Changes (Zhouyi): A Bronze Age Document* (Richmond, U.K.: Curzon Press, 1996), also discussed below in the section on history, contains a complete translation of the *Zhouyi* and the Ten Wings. The *Zhouyi* is translated in rhymed couplets as it would have been understood in the Bronze Age; the Ten Wings are translated as separate documents.

Gregory Whincup, *Rediscovering the I Ching* (New York: St. Martin's Press, 1986), reimagines the work as the story of a Bronze Age nobleman who rises from obscurity to power. It translates only the *Zhouyi*.

Richard John Lynn, *The Classic of Changes: A New Translation of the I Ching as Interpreted by Wang Bi* (New York: Columbia University Press, 1994), is invaluable for scholars. It provides the full text of the *Book of Changes* interspersed with Wang Bi's commentary. Lynn's aim is to present the book as it would have been understood at the end of the Han Dynasty.

One of the most unusual translations in recent years—and one of the most useful for a translator—is Rudolf Ritsema and Stephen Karcher, *I Ching: The Classic Chinese Oracle of Change, The First Complete Translation with Concordance* (Rockport, Mass.: Element Books, 1994). Ritsema and Karcher present a word-by-word transliterated text of everything in the *Book of Changes* except the Great Treatise and the Eighth Wing. Each Chinese word is then followed by a list of all of the most common English equivalents. In addition, there is an elaborate concordance showing where each Chinese word appears in the text.

Commentaries

Every commentary on the *Book of Changes* builds on previous commentators, and mine is no exception. It is therefore particularly important to note the sources used and to give credit where credit is due.

Traditional commentaries on the *Book of Changes* discuss the relative placement of lines within a hexagram and offer explanations for why they are auspicious or inauspicious. They also attempt to explain the metaphors in the text in relation to the line placements and the constituent and nuclear trigrams. In these traditional commentaries the ethical meaning of the lines is often described very tersely and often must be inferred from context. Good examples of this form of commentary can be found in Lynn's translation of Wang Bi's commentary, as well as Alfred Huang and Book III of Wilhelm. By contrast, modern commentaries on the *Book of Changes* tend to dispense with discussions of line placement and turn directly to the ethical significance of the text. This is the practice followed in the present book.

In my opinion the best, clearest, and most straightforward set of modern commentaries for the average person is Sarah Dening, *The Everyday I Ching* (New York: St. Martin's Press, 1995), which despite its title is anything but workaday or ordinary. Dening is a Jungian psychotherapist and she brings an analyst's skill to her interpretations. She consistently offers practical, sensible advice that brings the modern reader into the heart of the book, and I have drawn repeatedly on her insights. Dening's book, in turn, is clearly influenced by the excellent commentaries of R. L. Wing, which appear in R. L. Wing, *The Illustrated I Ching* (New York: Doubleday, 1982), and especially R. L. Wing, *The I Ching Workbook* (New York: Doubleday, 1979). I have also learned a great deal from Wing's approach. Wilhelm's commentaries—especially those in Book I of his translation—are also splendid, and are particularly helpful for understanding the text's imagery, although they are pitched at a more abstract level than Dening's or Wing's. Wilhelm summarized the Neo-Confucian tradition of Song Dynasty commentaries as interpreted in the Qing Dynasty.

Sam Riefler's *I Ching: A New Interpretation for Modern Times* (New York: Bantam Books, 1974) interprets the book in light of Hindu and Buddhist concepts. Also helpful are Christopher Market, *I Ching: Ancient Wisdom for Modern Decision-Making* (New York: Weatherhill, 1998); Elizabeth Moran and Master Joseph Yu, *The Complete Idiot's Guide to the I Ching* (Indianapolis: Alpha Books, 2002); and Roderic Sorrell and Amy Max Sorrell, *The I Ching Made Easy* (New York: HarperCollins Publishers, 1994), which introduces the idea of keywords for each hexagram that is also employed in the present book. Quite apart from its occult subject matter, W. K. Chu and W. A. Sherrill's *The Astrology of I Ching* (London: Routledge & Kegan Paul, 1976; New York: Penguin Books, 1993) contains helpful discussions of the personality characteristics, strengths, and weaknesses associated with each hexagram and line position. Alfred Huang's *The Complete I Ching*, discussed above under translations, offers a good discussion of the origins of the meaning of each hexagram. Thomas Cleary has translated the Song Dynasty philosopher Cheng Yi's commentary under the title *I Ching: The Tao of Organization* (Boston and London: Shambhala, 1988). Last, but certainly not least, I have regularly consulted Wang Bi's commentary, translated into English by Richard John Lynn (see under translations). Lynn's notes helpfully explain when the Song commentators Cheng Yi and Zhu Xi interpreted the book differently from Wang Bi.

Readers who are interested in Western philosophical reinterpretations of the *Book of Changes* might look at Carol Anthony, *The Philosophy of the I Ching* (Stow, Mass.: Anthony Publishing Co., 2nd. ed., 1998), and Carol Anthony, *A Guide to the I Ching* (Stow, Mass.: Anthony Publishing Co., 3rd ed., 1988). Hellmut Wilhelm and Richard Wilhelm, *Understanding the I Ching: The Wilhelm Lectures on the Book of Changes* (Princeton: Princeton University Press, 1995), contains two sets of lectures by a father and son: Hellmut Wilhelm's *Change: Eight Lectures on the I Ching,* and his father Richard Wilhelm's *Lectures on the I Ching: Constancy and Change.*

Divination Practices

A good selection of divination practices can be found in W. A. Sherrill and W. K. Chu, *An Anthology of I Ching* (London: Routledge & Kegan Paul, 1977); and Edward A. Hacker, *The I Ching Handbook: A Practical Guide to Personal and Logical Perspectives from the Ancient Chinese Book of Changes* (Brookline, Mass.: Paradigm Publications, 1993). Zhu Xi's twelfth-century treatise on *Yijing* divination, *Introduction to the Study of the Classic of Changes (yi xue qi meng),* is available on the Internet in a translation by Joseph Adler at http://www2.kenyon.edu/depts/religion/fac/Adler/Writings/Chimeng.htm. Larry Schoenholtz, *New Directions in the I Ching* (Secaucus, N.J.: Carol Publishing Group, 1975), describes the method of sixteen; Kerson and Rosemary Huang, discussed above under translations, offer a streamlined version of the yarrow-stalk method.

A good discussion of the Plum Blossom method appears in Jou Tsung Hwa, *The Tao of I Ching: Way to Divination* (Piscataway, N.J.: Dai Ji Foundation, 1984). Thomas Cleary, *I Ching: The Book of Change* (Boston and London: Shambhala, 1992), pp. xiv–xv, gives a shortened version of the Plum Blossom method. Astrological methods of consulting the *Book of Changes* are found in Chu and Sherrill, *The Astrology of I Ching,* described above in the section on commentaries. Hua-Ching Ni, *I Ching: The Book of Changes and the Unchanging Truth* (Santa Monica, Calif.: SevenStar Communications Group, 2nd ed., 1999), contains elaborate commentaries and a discussion of Taoist astrology. Alfred Huang, *The Numerology of the I Ching: A Sourcebook of Symbols, Structures, and Traditional Wisdom* (Rochester, Vt.: Inner Traditions, 2000), is a companion volume to his excellent translation. It offers a discussion of Taoist numerology.

On the mathematical basis of divination, see, in addition to Hacker, A. G. Clarke, "Probability Theory Applied to the I Ching," *Journal of Chinese Philosophy* 14 (1987), pp. 65–72; Martin Gardner, "The Combinatorial Basis of the I Ching," *Scientific American,* January 1974, pp. 108–13; and Shih-chuan Chen, "How to Form a Hexagram and Consult the I Ching," *Journal of the American Oriental Society* 92, no. 2 (1972), pp. 237–49.

On the history of Chinese divination practices, see R. J. Smith, *Fortune-Tellers and Philosophers: Divination in Traditional Chinese Society* (Boulder,

Colo.: Westview Press, 1991); and Michael Loewe and Carmen Blacker, eds., *Oracles and Divination* (Boston and London: Shambhala, 1981).

The History and Development of the Book of Changes

Richard Rutt, *The Book of Changes (Zhouyi): A Bronze Age Document* (Richmond, U.K.: Curzon Press, 1996), offers the most complete discussion of the history of the book from its origins in the Bronze Age to the present day.

On the composition of the *Book of Changes,* see Edward Shaughnessy, "I Ching," in *Early Chinese Texts: A Bibliographical Guide,* ed. Michael Loewe (Berkeley: Society for the Study of Early China and the Institute of East Asian Studies, University of California, 1993), pp. 218–223.

On the early history of the *Zhouyi* and its composition, see Richard Alan Kunst, "The Original 'Yijing': A Text, Phonetic Transcription, Translation, and Indexes, with Sample Glosses (Ph.D dissertation 1985) (Ann Arbor: University Microfilms International, 1985), discussed above in the section on translations; Edward Shaughnessy, "The Composition of the Zhouyi" (Ph.D. dissertation, 1983) (Ann Arbor: University Microfilms International, 1983); F. M. Doeringer, "Oracle and Symbol in the Redaction of the I Ching," *Philosophy East and West,* 30, no. 2 (Hawaii, April 1980), pp. 195–209; Iulian K. Shchutskii, *Researches on the I Ching,* trans. William L. McDonald and Tsuyoshi Hasegawa, with Hellmut Wilhelm (Princeton: Princeton University Press, 1979); and Arthur Waley, "The Book of Changes," *Bulletin of the Museum of Far Eastern Antiquities* 5 (Stockholm, 1933), pp. 121-42. S. J. Marshall, *The Mandate of Heaven: Hidden History in the I Ching* (New York: Columbia University Press, 2001), argues that the text of the *Zhouyi* actually describes the history of the rise of the Zhou Dynasty.

Michael Nylan, *The Five "Confucian" Classics* (New Haven: Yale University Press, 2001), pp. 202–52, contains a useful chapter on the history and philosophy of both the *Zhouyi* and the Ten Wings.

On the Great Treatise's theory of change see Willard J. Peterson, "Making Connections: Commentary on the Attached Verbalizations of the Book of Changes," *Harvard Journal of Asiatic Studies* 42, no. 1 (June 1982), pp. 67–116; and Gerald Swanson, "The Concept of Change in the Great Treatise," in Henry Rosemont, Jr., ed., *Explorations in Chinese Cosmology,* JAAR Thematic Studies, 50/2 (Chico, Calif.: Scholars Press, 1984), pp. 67–93. On the correlative cosmology of Han Confucianism, see Steve Moore, *The Trigrams of Han: Inner Structures of the I Ching* (Wellingborough, U.K: Aquarian Press, 1989).

Good discussions of Zhu Xi and of the the Song Dynasty Neo-Confucian philosophers can be found in Kidder Smith, Jr., et al., *Sung Dynasty Uses of the I Ching* (Princeton: Princeton University Press, 1990).

General Sources on Chinese History and Chinese Philosophy

General histories of China and Chinese thought that discuss the *Book of Changes* include A. C. Graham, *Disputers of the Tao: Philosophical Argument in Ancient China* (LaSalle, Ill.: Open Court, 1989); Benjamin Isadore Schwartz, *The World of Thought in Ancient China* (Cambridge: Harvard University Press, 1985); and Joseph Needham, *Science and Civilization in China*, vol. 2 (Cambridge: Cambridge University Press, 1956).

On the history of the Shang and early Zhou dynasties, see David N. Keightley, *Sources of Shang History: The Oracle Bone Inscriptions of Bronze Age China* (Berkeley: University of California Press, 1978); Edward L. Shaughnessy, *Sources of Western Zhou History: Inscribed Bronze Vessels* (Berkeley: University of California Press, 1991); and Edward L. Shaughnessy, *Before Confucius: Studies in the Creation of the Chinese Classics* (Albany, N.Y.: State University of New York Press, 1997).

Good treatments of Chinese philosophy can be found in Feng Yu-Lan, *A Short History of Chinese Philosophy* (New York: Free Press, 1948); and *A Source Book in Chinese Philosophy*, trans. and ed. Wing-Tsit Chan (Princeton: Princeton University Press, 1963). Quotations from Confucius's *Analects* are taken from Confucius, *The Analects*, trans. D. C. Lau (Harmondsworth, Middlesex, U.K.: Penguin Books, 1979).

Index

Hexagram Chart

Trigrams upper ➤ lower ▼	☰ Qian Heaven	☳ Zhen Thunder	☵ Kan Water	☶ Gen Mountain	☷ Kun Earth	☴ Xun Wind	☲ Li Fire	☱ Dui Lake
☰ Qian Heaven	1	34	5	26	11	9	14	43
☳ Zhen Thunder	25	51	3	27	24	42	21	17
☵ Kan Water	6	40	29	4	7	59	64	47
☶ Gen Mountain	33	62	39	52	15	53	56	31
☷ Kun Earth	12	16	8	23	2	20	35	45
☴ Xun Wind	44	32	48	18	46	57	50	28
☲ Li Fire	13	55	63	22	36	37	30	49
☱ Dui Lake	10	54	60	41	19	61	38	58

About the Author

Jack M. Balkin is Knight Professor of Constitutional Law and the First Amendment at Yale Law School. He is the founder and director of Yale's Information Society Project, an interdisciplinary center that studies law and the new information technologies. A prominent legal theorist and constitutional scholar, his writings range over many different fields, from philosophy to politics, from cultural evolution to legal and musical interpretation. His books include *Cultural Software: A Theory of Ideology, Processes of Constitutional Decisionmaking* (with Brest, Levinson, and Amar), and *What Brown v. Board of Education Should Have Said.* He lives in Branford, Connecticut.